Exploring the Modern

Exploring the Modern

Patterns of Western Culture and Civilization

John Jervis

Blackwell
Publishing

350 Main Street, Malden, MA 02148-5020, USA
108 Cowley Road, Oxford OX4 1JF, UK
550 Swanston Street, Carlton, Victoria 3053, Australia

First published 1998 by Blackwell Publishing Ltd
Reprinted 2004 , 2005

Library of Congress Cataloging-in-Publication Data

Jervis, John.
   Exploring the modern: patterns of western culture and civilization / John Jervis.
      p. cm.
   Includes bibliographical references and index.
   ISBN 0-631-19621-8 (alk. paper). — ISBN 0-631-19622-6 (alk. paper)
   1. Civilization, Western – 20th century. 2. Civilization, Western – 19th century.
3. Civilization, Modern -- 20th century. 4. Civilization, Modern – 19th century.
5. Social change. 6. Modernism (Art) 7. Modernism (Literature) 8. Modernism
(Aesthetics) I. Title.
CB245.J47   1999
909'.0982108—dc21   98-7114
                                                                              CIP

A catalogue record for this title is available from the British Library.

Set in 10½ on 12½ pt Ehrhardt
by Best-set Typesetter Ltd, Hong Kong
Printed and bound in Great Britain by
Marston Book Services Limited, Oxford

For further information on
Blackwell Publishing, visit our website:
http://www.blackwellpublishing.com

Contents

List of Plates   vi
Acknowledgements   vii

Introduction   1

Part I: The Modern Self
 1 The Theatrical Self: Social Drama and Personal Identity   15
 2 Subjects and Citizens: The Politics of Everyday Life   42
 3 Street People: The City as Experience, Dream and Nightmare   65
 4 The Consolations of Consumerism   91
 5 'We Are Born Naked – Everything Else Is Drag': Clothing the
    Body, Fashioning the Self   117
 6 The Seduction of Romance: Fictions of Love, Narratives of Selfhood   147

Part II: The Modern Age
 7 Sacred, Secular, Sublime: Modernity Performs the Death of God   177
 8 Machines and Skyscrapers: Technology as Experience, Hope
    and Fear   202
 9 From Enlightenment to Holocaust: Modernity and the End
    of Morality   227
10 Modernism, Art and Culture   250
11 The Image, the Spectral and the Spectacle: Technologies of
    the Visual   280
12 Postmodern Times?   310

Key Terms   342
Biographical Notes   345
Guide to Further Reading   347
Index   349

Plates

1 Passage Choiseul, Paris, 1825–7 (The Architectural Association Photo Library)
2 Lucky Strike cigarette advertisement (*American Magazine*, September 1930)
3 Stiletto heel (photo by Chris Bell, from Skin Two, *Retro I: The First Six Issues*, Tim Woodward Publishing Ltd, 1991)
4 John Galliano, Fallen Angels fashion collection, 1985–6
5 *The Modern Woman*: *Vogue* fashion plate, 1927 (Victoria and Albert Museum Picture Library)
6 G. Scott: *The Passenger* (from *L'Aviation*, 1923)
7 Mies van der Rohe: Seagram Building, New York, 1958 (The Architectural Association Photo Library)
8 Henri Matisse: *The Red Room*, or *Dessert: Harmony in Red*, 1908 (The Bridgeman Art Library, © Succession H. Matisse/DACS 1998)

Acknowledgements

As an academic who has survived for several decades in university life without ever having published anything, despite the unremitting pressure to do so – an achievement of which I am quite proud – I have naturally accumulated some debts. In some cases, these were incurred long ago, but have not been forgotten. I therefore want to thank John Ferguson, Trevor Pateman, Derek Sayer, John Parker, Chris Harris, Paul Hammersley, David Morgan, Louise Tythacott and Chris Ramsden, for intellectual stimulus at various times over the years. Specifically in connection with this book, I am grateful for assistance and encouragement from many sources, but must single out Nicola Kerry, whose good humour and support have been as indispensable as her extremely efficient word processing; Mary Evans, for her constant interest and her invariably shrewd, helpful advice; and, above all, Claire Norris, who has read and commented on every chapter, unflinchingly and insightfully, and has saved me from many errors. Her contribution has been invaluable. And I would like to thank Naoko, for her words of wisdom at times of particular stress, and for her endless patience in coping with the intrusive presence of The Book during our lives together. Finally – and most of all – I wish to thank the generations of students who have endured my teaching and invigorated my thinking, and whose existence makes life in these bizarre institutions bearable. This book is for them.

Introduction

General Approach and Aims

What is 'modern' in 'modernity'? This book seeks to uncover patterns that under-lie the shifting 'images of modernity' through which we attempt to grasp the cultural and social processes of the 'modern age'. As such, it is a synoptic, wide-ranging work, attempting to draw together the research on the socio-cultural dimension of modernity in the West that has been generated over the last couple of decades in the areas of sociology, cultural studies and gender studies. The book seeks to uncover the peculiarities of the modern experience in a historically informed way, but it is not a historical work; it presents modernity as a 'form of life' rather than a 'period of history'. The emphasis is always on the past as source of the present, the roots of contemporary experience. And the concern is exclu-sively with the modern West; there is no discussion of the impact on non-Western societies, or the fusion of imported and indigenous cultures in these societies. This is a crucial area, but would need a separate book.

The book seeks to complement the usual emphasis on the conventional – and characteristically male-oriented – pieties of the 'rational' technological orientation of modernity with a discussion of other aspects of modern life and culture, including aspects that have frequently been disparaged or regarded as less central. In the light of this, the book traces the adventures of the modern self through the pressures and possibilities of gender identity, fashion, consumerism and city life, along with the influence of the images and fictions of popular culture and the media, and explores the general significance of 'modernism' in culture and the arts. A picture emerges of modernity as a drama in which tension and conflict, exuberance and excess, fantasy, fiction and the forbidden, artifice and theatrical-ity, both coexist with, parody and subvert the orthodox self-image of rationality and control.

I have tried to write in a lively and approachable way, drawing on material from a variety of sources – literature, fashion, art – but the book does not shirk difficult theoretical issues. Hopefully, it may have some appeal to the adventurous, inquisitive general reader who wants to gain a sense of the connections between what can appear to be confusingly disparate aspects of modern cultural and social life. This is not a textbook, though doubtless its range means that it could in some ways serve as one. It is thematic rather than comprehensive; each chapter is not so much intended to give a thorough survey of its subject matter, as to highlight certain issues and themes that are particularly central. In my view, these are not areas where there is any agreed consensus that can simply be summarized, and the obvious alternative – to present the debates between authors with differing views – can easily take us too far from the substantive issues, and risks becoming arcane and scholastic. I would rather offer the reader a direct – if at times controversial – contribution to understanding the issues themselves, one that draws on the valuable work of other authors in the field but doesn't generally engage in academic debate with them. If the book is found to be stimulating and thought-provoking, it will have achieved its aims.

For the benefit of the general reader or student, I would add that each chapter contains sections of varying degrees of difficulty; one or two sections, usually later ones, are quite theoretical, and if necessary these could be skimmed or skipped while still gaining some insight into the issues. It is probably also true that a few chapters, such as some of those in the last part of the book, are more difficult than others. In general, one can read chapters in isolation, and treat the book as a series of semi-autonomous essays; nevertheless, inevitably something would be lost in doing this. Later chapters do, to some extent, presuppose earlier ones; and those who like to treat a book as an unfolding story will find that, broadly speaking, there is some chronological development through the book, even though ultimately the themes are defined and related to one another structurally, rather than historically. I try to keep technical terms to a minimum; nevertheless, some relatively ordinary terms are given a theoretical slant that might be puzzling to non-specialists, so I include a glossary (and a brief guide to the main theorists whose work I draw on).

The general reader may, in one respect, have an advantage over the specialist. Most academics operate within reasonably clear boundaries: sociology, cultural studies, history, and so on. This book refuses these distinctions; it grows out of developments in social, cultural and gender theory that challenge the conventional division between 'social sciences' and 'humanities' and the boundaries between the 'disciplines' – revealing word – within them. After all, to operate narrowly *within* one of the traditional disciplines would amount to a reliance on the division of labour – the mastery of the world through specialization – that is *itself* an aspect of the 'modernity' that I am attempting to bring into focus, an attempt that necessarily involves the display of underlying patterns that transgress these categories. There is, of course, a danger of eclecticism; but this risk is worth taking in order to illuminate the key issues that so often lie across, or between, the boundaries. For me, boundaries and limits are things to work with, not within.

This comes out in other ways, too. I hope the book offers evidence of rational thought, albeit intermittently; but I also think it important to harness the imagination. Without this fusion, real insight is impossible. The book makes an argument, but also paints a picture. Again, it is always reasonable to ask where an author is writing *from*, how he or she is situated relative to the text. It is an implication of the concluding chapter that writing a book *about* modernity is a paradoxical enterprise. One is left betwixt and between: it seems a very 'modern' thing to do, yet one is implicitly elsewhere to do it; already postmodern, perhaps? An uncomfortable, but perhaps productive, place to be.

The book could be seen as a study in applied cultural theory: its subject matter is social life as culture, as cultural practices. It is an essay on 'modernity in its cultural aspect' rather than 'modernity as product of socio-economic change'. The aim is not to make empirical generalizations, or causal claims, or to write narrative history; rather, it is to explore the range of possibilities opened up by the modern imagination, the patterns that constitute the framework of experience and culture in the modern West. If sociology is about social institutions, this book is not sociology; instead, it seeks the fabric of meaning out of which such institutions are woven and in which they are embedded. In order to do this, I try to find a level between the empiricism that restricts itself to describing actions and institutions, and the abstraction of grand theory, by presenting a limited number of cases in theoretical terms, thereby rescuing them from being mere examples of generalizations or laws and enabling them to stand as exemplars of patterns. Hopefully, this will show something of the usefulness of theory by 'putting it to work' rather than merely discussing and assessing it from outside.

However, it is also important to point out that the book is not about ideas, values and representations in themselves, in their self-sufficiency; it is not intended as an 'idealist' reaction to 'materialism'. It considers such values and representations through their embeddedness in cultural practices. If the book eschews the traditional social science emphasis on causal analysis, whereby those phenomena are seen as explicable in terms of something external but 'deeper' (e.g. the economy), it breaks with the traditional humanities perspective too, in that the latter tends to seek 'depth' in the internal features of the work or works concerned (painting, novel; genre, school), as refracted in the consciousness of the viewer or reader. The interest in patterns, after all, means that these distinctions themselves (internal/external, surface/depth) become topics for analysis.

There is another implication. 'Patterns' are not just matters of conventional or 'official' stereotypes: what we should do, how we should think. As hinted at above, the tabooed and the unstated are as significant as the approved and explicit, the prohibited as much as the prescribed. Hence, in practice, these patterns can be manifested in different ways in our institutions and actions. Indeed, the untypical, the obscure, or the extreme can be just as illuminating as the ordinary, since it is here that the latent possibilities of the everyday world become manifest, thus clarifying the 'normal'. It is as though the normal ultimately becomes a subset of the abnormal, and continuous with it. And we find that, in practice, the patterns can have contradictory implications, manifest in strains and tensions.

Abnormalities, extremes, contradictions, tensions: there is indeed a sense in which I want to rescue these, bring them into the open, since not only are they important and significant, but they tend to subvert the rather smug complacency of the 'official' ideologies of modernity, the narratives of progress and rationality. From this point of view, the ordinary and the everyday also need rescuing, dismissed, as they often are, as inherently trivial, shallow, steeped in mystification. There is also a crucial gender dimension to this: the dismissal of issues as 'trivial' often reflects an unwittingly masculinist bias, as, conversely, the same bias is reflected in the selection of issues as 'significant'. Certainly this book would not have been possible without the explosion of feminist scholarship in recent years. The aim, then, is to redress the balance, point to these 'other' strands. From this point of view, authors in the dissenting tradition of social and cultural theory, from Rousseau and Sade, through Nietzsche, to Bataille and Foucault, authors who take their distance from the Enlightenment tradition and the optimistic evaluation of Western culture and civilization, do at least offer a refreshing contrast.

It is important to mention here that the book was originally a third as long again, presenting problems for the publisher. On reflection, it seemed best to use what had been the first part of the book as the basis for a second volume, to be published shortly after this one, under the title *Transgressing the Modern: Explorations in the Western Experience of Otherness* (Blackwell, 1999). As the title implies, the aim is to mount a more detailed exploration of modernity's 'other side', what is distorted, repressed, or tabooed, while yet retaining a powerful fascination for the modern imagination. After a discussion of the role of the 'civilizing process' in the formation of modernity, including its contribution to the destruction of Carnival, the book will systematically explore these 'other' dimensions, notably the construction of 'other cultures' as primitive and exotic, along with modern orientations to madness, nature, sexuality, aspects of the feminine, and so on. While each book is intended to be relatively self-sufficient, it is inevitably the case that there will be times when further comprehension of the subject would be aided by consulting the other volume.

Central Themes

'To be absolutely modern', Milan Kundera informs us, 'means to be the ally of one's gravediggers.'[1] Baudelaire adds that 'We are each of us celebrating some funeral':[2] doubtless our own? To be modern is to know that one's fate is to become outdated, that one's doings will pass on into obscurity; yet it is also, in a sense, to embrace this, to eschew the illusory charms of otherworldly hopes.

The implication is that modernity is served by renunciation, of that which is familiar, that which we love, in order to live in the unfolding of an uncertain future. Not surprisingly, this precipitates a deep ambivalence, characteristic of the modern attitude since Baudelaire, Marx, and their contemporaries, if not before. Modernity offers hope of progress, civilization and emancipation; but it has also been inseparable from nostalgia, rootlessness, fragmentation and uncertainty. The consolation of goals achieved can turn readily into dust; and, perhaps even worse, they can be revealed as empty, grandiose, absurd. This duality of response, corresponding to real tensions in modernity itself, makes ambivalence a feature not just *of* modernity but of attitudes *to* it. There is a reflexive dimension here: to be modern is, among other things, to see oneself in these terms, to be aware of oneself *as* modern. And the sources of this ambivalence and reflexivity must be sought deep in the modern experience.

But we must start further back. What do we mean by 'modern', a word we use often enough, and take for granted? There seem to be two key uses of the term. At one extreme, historians may describe anything that has happened since the Renaissance as 'modern' history; at the other, we often use the term to mean 'contemporary', here and now, what is currently fashionable. Fashion, indeed, reinforces this sense of context-dependence: relative to the history of fashion, a Chanel suit is doubtless 'modern', but for this month's magazines, the term would be applied to the current season's 'look'. But this example suggests another complexity. Some would argue, after all, that the Chanel suit is somehow *quintessentially* modern, that in its elegant simplicity it represents the 'modern style' to perfection, and hence in being both the founding instance and the ultimate embodiment of this style, it becomes timeless, achieving an iconic status as a signifier of the modern. Again, we typically regard certain cultural or technological products as inherently 'modern', such as film, air travel, or skyscrapers, which in turn means that suitable examples can achieve instantly recognizable status both as embodiments of modernity and as representations of it, suggesting that modernity is as much a culture of representation as it is a form of experience or a period of history.

This can serve to remind us of Baudelaire's claim that the modern painter should 'distil the eternal from the transitory'; although modernity may be 'the transient, the fleeting, the contingent',[3] *representing* modernity has to go beyond this. Modernity *is* change, but it is not *only* change; we have to try to grasp this deeper dimension, whatever it may be. And perhaps what has made Baudelaire a key figure in discussions of the modern is the sense that, implicit in his work, is a challenge to the 'modern age', to those who live *as* moderns, who are conscious of their modernity: how do we represent this modernity, how can we make sense of it, how can we *live* it? For if modernity is an aesthetic problem, it is also an existential and a moral one. Can there be moral or aesthetic codes, guiding criteria, in a world which we experience as ever-changing, in which situations never recur exactly, in which everything is irredeemably particular? Baudelaire gives at best an unclear, ambiguous response to the challenge implicit in his own perspective here; but, as we shall see, it is not apparent that anyone else has been that much more successful.

Let us return to the sense of the modern as the contemporary, the present, the here and now. This is close to what the Latin *modernus*, derived from *modo*, actually meant, and that already suggests puzzles. Modernity is not necessarily so modern, it would seem; or, conversely, everything that happens is modern for those who experience it. It is certainly true that the term 'modern' has occurred at times in the West before one reaches the 'modern age', whatever one may take its boundaries to be. The fact remains that not all cultures have the concept, or anything like it, and these earlier uses in the Western tradition cannot conceal differences in the meaning and significance of the term. We now live in a culture in which the kind of consciousness implied in the use of a term like 'modern', along with the experience on which it is based, testify to a powerful dynamic of world-transformation. Perhaps this is what 'modernity' means: the experience of the world as constantly changing, constantly engendering a past out of the death of the here and now, and constantly reproducing that 'here and now' as the present, the contemporary, the fashionable. In this perspective, the past is inert and the future unreal; what is real is the momentary experience of the 'now', as it moves from an unrealized future into a lifeless, shadowy past. The 'eternal in the transient' is perhaps the eternal recurrence of the transient itself.

Even so, the other sense of modernity is at least as central, though again remains vague and relative until one specifies the substantive attributes that count as being 'modern' and that define the central orientations of the culture and society that have developed in the West in recent centuries. One can start by observing that what historians call 'Early Modern' – from the end of the Middle Ages till about the seventeenth century – is important formatively, but the period to concentrate on is surely that from around the mid-eighteenth century – when modern notions of selfhood became well established – and on into the nineteenth century, with the explosive implications of the technological, industrial and political transformation of the world. And here, it is important to remember that while a historical analysis of the origins and development of modernity might well identify phenomena like the Industrial Revolution or capitalism as suspects for the role of 'prime cause', these are not necessarily so appropriate if one is carrying out a cultural analysis which must simultaneously 'deconstruct' modernity while seeking thematic links that in effect reconstitute it in different terms. From this point of view, a concept like 'project of modernity' can serve as a suitable key to open up the issues, since it can be made specific enough to carry meaningful content while yet remaining open-ended, available for interpretation in (and of) specific contexts.

Let us say, then, that a 'modern' society is one in which 'project' – an orientation to rational purposive control of the environment (both natural and social), thereby both understanding and transforming it – becomes the central dynamic of the society, one in which humans are reconstructed as appropriate subjects that can 'carry' this process through becoming 'civilized' and 'Enlightened'. It is of course at once apparent that those latter terms are inherently loaded: they are not just neutral descriptions of a process, they are implicitly evaluative, part of the framework of assumptions that has served to legitimize such a culture. It is also apparent that this construction of the unified, coherent modern subject involves a difficult process of controlling or expelling aspects of selfhood that fail to fit in the mould. This will be a focus of the accompanying volume,[4] but one aspect is important here: the way issues of cultural and personal identity are not just about values, ideas and imagery, but about bodies; more precisely, about *embodiment*, the way the body is itself a potent resource for cultural symbolism and manipulation. The body is a cultural signifier and is, as such, subject to social regulation, and modernity has been accompanied by a distinctive regime of body management.

Furthermore, since the body is necessarily a sexed body, gender relations and gender symbolism are necessarily at the core of the analysis.

The civilizing process, like other aspects of modernity, has always been controversial. In its emphasis on public forms and appearances, defining 'civic virtue' through manners and refinement, it has been criticized on the one hand by Romanticism and associated movements, for allegedly ignoring 'deeper' questions of moral integrity and personal transfiguration through art and culture, and, on the other, by proponents of the rationalist and utilitarian project-centred model of human conduct, who distrust its theatricality. And these are not just intellectual debates; they reflect real tensions that are constitutive of the very possibilities of social interaction and self-identity in the modern period.

One can usefully situate the Enlightenment itself against the backdrop of these tensions and debates. In effect, Enlightenment transforms 'civilizing' into a project; it becomes incorporated as an increasingly explicit aim of policy among intellectuals, and thereby comes to have a political dimension, influencing state policy. In theory, it tries to resolve the tensions by calling for the production of 'better citizens' through a fundamental process of political and educational reform; in practice, as will be seen, it never really succeeds, and produces extra problems of its own, in the form of ideological conflicts over the interpretation of the goals, and the embeddedness of Enlightenment programmes in the political dynamics of state and class power. Thus Bauman points to the fateful link between rationalism and imperialism here: if I am enlightened, it is my *duty* to enlighten you; Enlightenment becomes a mission, necessarily intolerant of otherness.[5] The ambition of these programmes – even their grandeur – is captured by Kumar, who writes of the way Enlightenment thinkers 'converted millennial beliefs into a secular idea of progress' whereby 'The millennium became scientific and rational, the dawn of an era of unending human progress on earth.'[6]

We thus return to the theme of change; for clearly modernity has been inseparable from the idea of *history*, time as linear, developing out of the past and towards the future in a process of constant change that is nevertheless rationally intelligible, and is generally seen as subsumed under the notion of 'progress'. The opposite possibility – decline – is also present as a cultural resource, however, and is frequently realized in the coupling of progress and nostalgia, paradise in the future yet also paradise lost. This notion of change is problematical, however, as it necessarily implies its opposite: if there is change, there is also something that is (relatively) static, or what is it that changes? The Enlightenment inheritance polarizes this: the powerful endorsement of change, harnessed to realization of a better future, goes hand in hand with the construction of a notion of 'human nature' as timeless and absolute. In this sense, the Enlightenment claims 'simply to render visible a latent nature that was always there', as Docherty puts it, suggesting that this is also characteristically true of another product of the period, the novel.[7] Revolution becomes a form of conservatism: clear away the debris of obsolete and oppressive social forms, and what stands revealed is what was already there; and we *know* it to be there because it has been uncovered by Reason, its equally timeless double. Furedi can therefore complain that

Enlightenment rationality had a one-sided limited character. It posed reason as a transcendental force which was destined to be realised through history. This abstraction of reason into a transcendental idea minimised the significance of reasoning human beings. . . . In this form, reason itself becomes a constant, violating the fundamentals of historical thinking.[8]

And while the novel may have its roots in Enlightenment assumptions, it is in some ways the novel that also provides a more open-ended, fluid sense of time, resulting from a sensitivity to the presence of repetitive patterns that are nonetheless transformed in specific contexts and situations.

Nature itself tends to be the focus of these tensions. In the modern period, nature is seen as constantly subject to transformation, yet also a bedrock, a final court of appeal. This comes out most vividly, perhaps, in the distinctive gender politics of modernity. For much of the period, 'natural' differences between the sexes have been taken for granted, and it is *men* who have been seen as carriers of culture. Yet this has been coupled with an uneasy awareness that 'gender' may not be simply an outgrowth of nature; that if 'culture' has to supplement 'nature', then there is potential for something different, an area of freeplay, a possibility that can provoke a passionate advocacy of change, or an equally passionate horror at the very thought. The implications of all this for gender roles and gender identities are outlined by Rita Felski, who points to the way

spatial categories of private and public were mapped onto temporal distinctions between past and present. By being positioned outside the dehumanizing structures of the capitalist economy as well as the rigorous demands of public life, women became a symbol of nonalienated, and hence nonmodern, identity. A proliferating body of scientific, literary, and philosophical texts sought to prove that women were less differentiated and less self-conscious than men and more rooted in an elemental unity.[9]

In short, women have been seen as less historical than men, less important as agents of change. When these attributes are solidified into gender stereotypes, they can produce intriguing results. Women are 'closer to nature' yet have a key cultural role as 'moral exemplars' for their children and husbands; men can more readily transcend nature yet their virility, a 'natural' attribute, is a key signifier of their masculinity, and muscularity can become an element of the masculine ideal.

Recapitulating, it can be said that by the nineteenth century a project of modernity had come to occupy the heart of Western culture – often as the subject of intense debate and controversy. This project involved rational–purposive strategies of organization and control in order to appropriate the world, ostensibly for human benefit, in the process drawing on the disparate strands of the civilizing process and the Enlightenment inheritance, and it was manifested powerfully in the ramifications of the industrial and technological revolutions. And it is important to point out that from early on many of the critics regarded the remorseless dynamic of the process as being in tension with its alleged ends, suggesting that the operations of the market and bureaucratic organization can have decidedly un-Enlightened consequences. In *this* sense, there may be a tension between Enlightenment ideals and the project of modernity.

How are these two senses of modernity – as the contemporary and as project – to be related? They would certainly seem to point in opposite directions. The 'here and now', the experience of change and its manifestations, in fashion, for example, correspond to the non-rational; project entails the idea of planning, purposive rationality. One emphasizes ruptures and discontinuities; the other, controlled, manageable change. One is responsive, accepting the unpredictable openness of experience; the other is proactive, oriented to *harnessing* experience, *using* the world, turning it to our purposes.

In effect, these contrasts remind us that we do not experience the world *as* project, even though the world we experience is fundamentally marked *by* project. There is modernity as experience, as well as modernity as project. This can include experience of the unintended and unexpected consequences of project, experience of the otherness that is distorted or repressed by project, and the experience of the 'trivia' of everyday life that are disparaged by project. Above all, we experience the world as multiple and recalcitrant, and this can be a challenge, something to overcome, or an opportunity to celebrate it in its diversity and complexity. From this point of view, modernity gives us the world as a rich tapestry of transient impressions, bright lights and advertising hoardings, the pleasures and dangers of city life, the instant temptations of consumer excess, and the fashions and foibles of 'street culture'. And in the texture of our lives, modernity as experience is as central as the project dimension.

This, too, has implications for the forms of self-identity and social interaction. Theatricality becomes a key mode of existence for the self in such a world of experience. It is a means whereby one can try on the mask of otherness, experience the world as other, while actively participating in it; and respond to the novelty of situations, in a context of endless flux and change, by drawing on a repertoire of rules and conventions. Through this, the passivity of experience can be fused with the active rehearsal and transformation of images and roles. Thus can the self learn to be multidimensional, adaptable, open to the variety of experiences made possible by modernity. This does not, however, sit easily with the self of project, in its emphasis on rational self-control and an instrumental attitude towards the world, and these tensions will need to be explored.

In the light of this, we can return to the ambivalence noted at the beginning; for it could be said that the effect of experience and project as orientations, pulling in different directions, is to produce a distinctive 'modern attitude'; one of simultaneous involvement and detachment, immersion and distancing, fascination and repulsion. This is one source of the way in which modernity can be said to involve a degree of alienation or 'homelessness', a sense in which we all become strangers both to ourselves and to others. This 'modern attitude' is seen as having its strong points, encouraging adaptability and awareness, but it also presents problems – of commitment, belief and consistency – and is difficult to reconcile with a sense of community. It is, in short, a critical stance: ironic, even subversive, yet embedded in what it would subvert; unable to transform the world because of a rejection of, or unease at, the idea of project, at the politics of 'progress', yet able to move quite effectively within this instrumental world, partly because of this very ability to distance the self from it, and get a grasp of it as an observer.

This stance is *reflexive*: self-aware, self-conscious. Part of being modern is the ability to reflect on one's practices and experiences, learn from them, and this is as true of institutions as it is of individuals. From the point of view of project, lack of control is experienced as unacceptable constraint, as unfreedom, so the striving to improve self-understanding – along with understanding of the environment of action – is essential to expanding the arena of freedom. However, since part of what one learns is that the world, whether of self or other, defies such appropriation, to inhabit this reflexive mode is, again, to be fractured, to live the tension between project and experience, gaining partial resolution through a heightened self-awareness, but at a cost that can include a pervasive sense of exile, unreality or fragmentation.

Returning to the 'modern attitude' itself, it has often seemed as if it is the artist who best exemplifies it. From at least the early nineteenth century there has been a marked tendency for artists to be hostile to the project of modernity, rejecting what they see as its philistine utilitarianism, its lack of interest in the aesthetic, the tendency to reduce life to a one-dimensional pursuit of instrumental self-interested goals. Artists have characteristically seen it as their task to recreate the unity and harmony of the world through the creative imagination, hence being in a crucial sense *detached* from the world. This can easily trap them in a creative paradox, since they have to immerse themselves *in* the world in order to acquire the stimulus on which their imagination can work. Baudelaire is again the classic instance here. The artist must find his halo in the gutter, immerse himself in the variety of modern experiences, the squalid as well as the salubrious, the excluded and the transient as well as the approved and the established, and then transmit this to the reader or spectator through the transfiguring power of the creative imagination.[10] Perhaps, indeed, the artist has ultimately to strive to represent the unrepresentable, what challenges our canons of representation; and with this move, the artist shifts decisively towards modernism.

The term 'modernism' itself is decidedly ambiguous: it can be used both in a general sense, to refer to 'modern attitudes' and the modern consciousness – including a readiness for change, an interest in the fashionable and the contemporary, and a broadly secular, materialist outlook – and in a more specific sense, referring to the series of radical movements in the arts that culminated in the early decades of this century. Either way, however, modernism reminds us of the fact that the experience of modernity poses distinctive challenges to our potential for representing it, for grasping it in consciousness and picturing or describing it through imagery or language. How can we 'read' the modern world in all its confusing multiplicity? How can our experiences of it be rendered meaningful without being betrayed by bias, distortion or oversimplification? How can the fleeting, the transient, be captured in the solidity of paint or text? Signs and images become central to our modes of negotiating the modern world and our identities within it. And while imagery itself is concrete and specific, it also embodies imagination, and, as has been implied above, the role of the imagination in structuring perception, cognition and desire seems to undergo a significant shift in the modern period. It is reconstructed as an 'inner faculty', the powerful source of fantasy, which in turn becomes a constitutive aspect of self-identity, with wider cultural as well as individual dimensions. Fantasy is an important channel through which those possibilities that are 'excluded' or devalued in the modern project nevertheless remain important as sources of meaning and experience.

As time goes on, modernity seems to consist increasingly of this weight of representations – billboards, fashion shows, television images, video games – so that modernity seems to become endlessly representational and reflexive, always referring back to itself. Ads recycle former ads and draw on images and sounds that are already representations; pictures picture other pictures, and are infinitely reproducible; films refer to other films and to images of a world that already consists of images. Some have even argued that experience and project themselves become increasingly dependent on this power of representation: our experiences of love repeat and recycle Hollywood clichés, our capacity to plan and organize our lives becomes a simulation of rationality rather than its reality. But this takes us into the world of late or post- modernity. . . .

To conclude: this book will deploy the distinctions between project, experience and representation to clarify the characteristic features of the modern world, including what is challenged or made problematical by the modern outlook. In particular, it will attempt to show that 'modernity as project' has always been in tension both with our actual experience and consciousness of the modern world, and with the theatrical dimension of modern identity, the exploration of culture as contingent, arbitrary, 'excessive', irreducible to project. Furthermore, these tensions increasingly result in a shift towards a 'reflexive' grasp of the world and our place in it, at both the individual and the institutional level; and this occurs both through a heightened concern with self-consciousness and self-monitoring, and with problems of image and representation that become central, in the media age, without resolving the underlying problems.

Notes

1 M. Kundera, *Immortality* (Faber, 1992), p. 159.
2 C. Baudelaire, 'On the Heroism of Modern Life', in *The Mirror of Art: Critical Studies by Charles Baudelaire* (Phaidon, 1955), p. 127.
3 C. Baudelaire, 'The Painter of Modern Life', in his *Selected Writings on Art and Artists* (Cambridge University Press, 1981), pp. 402, 403.
4 See especially chs 2, 7.
5 Z. Bauman, *Intimations of Postmodernity* (Routledge, 1992), pp. xiv, xvi.
6 K. Kumar, *From Post-Industrial to Post-Modern Society* (Blackwell, 1996), p. 79.

7　T. Docherty, 'Postmodern Characterization: the Ethics of Alterity', in E. J. Smyth (ed.) *Postmodernism and Contemporary Fiction* (Batsford, 1991), pp. 171–2.

8　F. Furedi, *Mythical Past, Elusive Future* (Pluto, 1992), p. 195.

9　R. Felski, *The Gender of Modernity* (Harvard University Press, 1995), p. 18. See also my *Transgressing the Modern* (Blackwell, 1999), ch. 5.

10　M. Berman, *All That Is Solid Melts into Air: The Experience of Modernity* (Verso, 1983), ch. III. And see the Introduction, for the challenges of modernism generally.

Part I
The Modern Self

1 The Theatrical Self:

Social Drama and Personal Identity

On 25 May 1895, Oscar Wilde, playwright, critic, man of letters, public figure, was found guilty of 'acts of gross indecency' with men. He was imprisoned in Reading Gaol; his plays in the West End were instantly taken off; friends and acquaintances disowned him. 'Everyone knew that Oscar was a forgery, a fake', writes Neil Bartlett. 'He was not what he had appeared to be.' The apparently respectable father, husband and moralist was shown to have modelled himself on the liars, comedians and critics, 'anyone who had signed no contract with truth; the embroiderers and inventors of the truth, the prostitutes'.[1] But Oscar Wilde was also the great exponent of the theatricality of the modern self; to be human is necessarily to be 'unnatural', and to embrace diversity, fashion, the superficial, the endless play of roles, none of them any more 'natural', authentic or sincere than any other. If, therefore, he was exposed as a fake, was it not the fake that he had always claimed to be? 'If one tells the truth', writes Oscar, 'one is sure, sooner or later, to be found out';[2] and he had indeed been 'found out', hiding in the light, his own truth the inauthenticity he had long preached.

Oscar Wilde defended the arts, and culture generally, precisely because of what he saw as their inherent theatricality. This he linked with individualism, and the latter, he claimed, was 'a disturbing and disintegrating force. Therein lies its immense value. For what it seeks to disturb is monotony of type, slavery of custom, tyranny of habit.' Individualism is not selfishness; *that* comes not from living as one wants to live, but from imposing one's will on others, through cultural and political policing. Individualism celebrates diversity, and opposes that 'immoral ideal of uniformity of type and conformity to rule which is so prevalent everywhere, and is perhaps most obnoxious in England'. These quotations are from *The Soul of Man under Socialism*, and show that, for Wilde, socialism is not the antithesis of individualism, but its true fulfilment. He adds that 'the only thing that one really knows about human nature is that it changes',[3] that it is fluid, shifting, that it cannot be anchored to any underlying essence, any 'true nature'; the 'truth' of role-playing, the exploration of deceitful appearances, changing fashions, playful transgressions, should subvert the conventional truth of fixed social and moral identities. In a theatrical world, in which appearances deceive, values reverse themselves; and the artist, in exploring this, should not run away from artifice, lying, insincerity and inauthenticity. The artist becomes 'the cultured and fascinating liar', who knows 'the secret that Truth is entirely and absolutely a matter of style'.[4]

All this clearly rests on a particular view of the self: that 'insincerity, inauthenticity, and unnaturalness become the liberating attributes of decentred identity and desire', so that 'a non-centred or vagrant desire is both the impetus for a subversive inversion, and what is released by it', as Dollimore suggests.[5] In *The Picture of Dorian Gray*, Wilde has his hero speculate: 'Is insincerity such a terrible thing? I think not. It is merely a method by which we can multiply our personalities', and he used to wonder at 'the shallow psychology of those who conceived the Ego in man as a thing simple, permanent, reliable, and of one essence. To him man was a being with myriad lives and myriad sensations, a complex, multiform creature.' He draws the conclusion: 'It is only shallow people who do not judge by appearances. The true mystery of the world is the visible, not the invisible.'[6] It is a world of surfaces, rather than depths; one lives in the performance of the moment, and life is the set of one's performances, a stage one can never quit.

There is a revealing tension here. If we say theatricality involves 'artifice', then this term has two dimensions: 'artificial', and therefore in a sense unreal, spurious, fake, 'unnatural'; and 'artefact', cultural product, therefore 'added' to nature, but without any implication of fakery. If theatricality celebrates the 'artifice' of culture, it does so by swinging between both poles, thus subverting the timeless, 'natural' pretensions of culture, and creating it anew. And when Wilde claims that 'The first duty in life is to be as artificial as possible',[7] the comment is poised with delicate ambiguity over *both* dimensions. Suggesting that Wilde had 'never claimed to be other than both forger and forgery', Bartlett points out that this same dualism is present here, too: 'to forge' can be to imitate fraudulently, or to create something. In the first sense, 'To forge is to make a copy, a fake which, when detected, alarmingly reveals that a fake has just as much life, as much validity as the real thing – until detected. It is then revealed as something that has no right to exist.' It questions authenticity. Thus, Wilde was married and a gentleman; yet he slept with working-class men, even in his own home, thus subverting terms like 'marriage' and 'gentleman', demeaning them: 'The scandal of his existence was not simply that he had lied, but that he had effectively debased the very values which he had appeared to endorse.' But he also, in the second sense, 'made' identities, forged them: 'He was always on the make, making things up, wearing make-up.' After his release from prison, he lived his few remaining years on the Continent, as 'Mr Sebastian Melmoth', 'the most brilliant forgery yet'.[8]

This 'forgery' also subverts claims to originality; Wilde's works, like his clothes, involve fragments copied and borrowed from elsewhere, as though the second sense of 'forge' slides easily into the first and may not be ultimately distinguishable from it. When he writes that 'Most people are other people. Their thoughts are someone else's opinions, their lives a mimicry, their passions a quotation', he could hardly exempt himself.[9] And his interest in fashion reminds us that theatricality can, in certain respects, trivialize the 'individuality' it purports to serve: 'His life was *fashionable*, if fashion is the art and industry of making an imitation look like a novelty', as Bartlett puts it. Nor is theatricality necessarily present in Wilde as a blessing; it may be perverse and joyless, even, as with Dorian Gray, a curse. Wilde's own sexuality gives his role-play a *driven* quality. Nevertheless, in claiming Wilde for the gay experience, Bartlett also points to the features that give his life its more general emblematic quality, its capacity to make statements about modern identity:

> There is no 'real' us, we can only ever have an unnatural identity, which is why we are all forgers. We create a life, not out of lies, but out of more or less conscious choices; adaptations, imitations and plain theft of styles, names, social and sexual roles, bodies. . . .
> We are all fakes, all inventions. We are making this all up as we go along.[10]

But *can* we 'make it all up as we go along'? What is the 'it' and who are the 'we'? When Nietzsche tells us that 'Every profound spirit needs a mask',[11] and Wilde, similarly, that 'Man is least himself when he talks in his own person. Give him a mask and he will tell you the truth',[12] we can wonder whether this is because the self *needs* to hide, or whether there is a sense in which it is only the mask that can 'realize' selfhood; that without it, there may be nothing there. For the modern self has been constructed as resting on something fixed, *needing* something fixed, an identity, *the* identity, self-as-identity, even while this emphasis has to coexist with the realities of change, the problems of appearance and recognition, that make theatricality possible in the first place, and engender the risks of misrecognition and inauthenticity. Nina Auerbach points out that it may have been this that most deeply scandalized Wilde's contemporaries: if, as she suggests, the Victorians 'had nothing left to believe in but their lives', nevertheless 'lives could be dangerously like masks'.[13]

It is as though, for Wilde, 'self' disappears into 'personality', rather than being grounded on 'underlying character', a sense of continuous self-identity. As the eighteenth-century idea of 'natural character' had come to seem too undifferentiated and static, so increasingly, for the spokesmen of cultural orthodoxy, this had to be complemented by a notion of selfhood as based on a clearly constructed and coherent 'life project', a future-oriented sense of rational development. This would be distinctive to each individual, while still unfolding according to the 'natural givens' of gender and sex, increasingly constructed by science and medicine as the underlying bedrock. Hence the way Victorians 'cast their life cycles into inspirational allegories'. Through self-help and self-control, this culture of the unified self could convince itself of the integrity of life, the possibility of a life purposively fulfilled; and the great Victorian biographies, like John Forster's *Life of Charles Dickens* (1872–4), are monuments to this ideal, as much as to their purported subjects. 'Biography' becomes the cure for theatricality, as it were. Selfhood required sincerity, what Auerbach calls 'communion with invisible forces', and hence 'the hidden connection of the self to powers that authenticate it'; the artist is therefore in contact with a deep well, rather than a superficial mask. 'Reverent Victorians shunned theatricality as the ultimate, deceitful mobility', writes Auerbach. It 'connotes not only lies, but a fluidity of character that decomposes the uniform integrity of the self'. Always at the heart is the fear that the self may turn out to be 'a carrier of theatrical disorder',[14] that the rational progress of one's life might be threatened by theatrical excess; that life, in short, might collapse into drama rather than unfold according to project.

But along with the further refinement of this orthodox view went a cultural fascination with its opposite. If the nineteenth century was the age of the novel and the biography, it was also the age of melodrama. Considering the extensive appeal of the latter to working-class audiences, and, frequently, to the 'respectable' also, Judith Walkowitz claims that 'Melodrama was the most important theatrical and literary form of the nineteenth century.' Melodrama was a theatre of extremes, a battle of good and evil: character was subordinated to type ('villain', 'helpless victim'), spectacle took precedence over psychological development, plots were wildly improbable, and only at the end, and largely by chance, did virtue triumph.

Increasingly, the language of melodrama spread on to the public stage. Stead's famous article in the *Pall Mall Gazette* of July 1885, the 'Maiden Tribute of Modern Babylon', widely taken to be the first big mud-raking exposé of the emerging age of the popular press, purported to reveal the truth about a 'white slave trade', and did so in classic melodramatic guise, with wicked, corrupt upper-class villains enslaving innocent young girls and selling them to brothels abroad. Josephine Butler, agitating – successfully – for the repeal of the notorious Contagious Diseases Acts, which victimized prostitutes, cast herself as a melodramatic heroine, identifying with the 'fallen woman', and presenting women as innocent victims of male pollution and lust. Walkowitz comments that Butler and Stead were both masters of imposture and disguise, 'crossing over the stable boundaries of class through their respective identification with working-class victims and upper-class villains'.[15]

So when Oscar Wilde was called on to play his most dramatic role, in 1895, the ground had been well prepared. The advocate of the theatrical self was to be the star in his own melodrama. The respectable married man was to be exposed as the upper-class villain, rotten to the core, thoroughly 'unnatural', a corrupter of youth and virtue. His fall was to be swift and absolute. Through an improbable plot – involving a letter that goes astray, blackmail, impersonation, duplicity – and largely by chance, virtue would triumph, the right order would be reaffirmed, punishment meted out. . . .

Consequently, we can say that if it has often been felt, during the modern period, that it was possible to gain insight into the social world through the metaphor of the world as a stage, or society as a theatrical experience, then this metaphor is not accidental, free-floating; it is an attempt to grasp, and shape, real – and historically novel – dimensions of experience. There may be a sense in which society has indeed presented itself *as* theatrical; that the theatre itself, and its influence, draw on those same strands of experience that lead us to describe society and the activities of the self as 'theatrical'. Thus Raymond Williams suggests that dramatic conventions are 'profoundly worked and re-worked in our actual living relationships', since 'They are our ways of seeing and knowing, which every day we put into practice.'[16] And although there may perhaps be some level of analysis at which social life can be analysed as 'theatrical' in some transhistorical sense,[17] it is also clear that if all the world's a stage, it is not always so in the same way, nor is it necessarily seen and experienced in these terms. 'Melodrama', for example, as a concept and a form of theatre, only dates from the end of the eighteenth century, and its first use in English dates from around 1809. It is therefore necessary to be sensitive to the distinctively modern aspects of theatricality, and to the different modes of theatricality during the modern period.

The Theatre and the Street

By the eighteenth century, Sennett suggests that when people spoke of the world as a theatre they began to imagine a new audience for their 'posturing' – each other – the sense of an audience willing to enjoy, perhaps somewhat cynically, 'the playacting and pretenses of everyday life'.[18] What, then, had changed from the older notion of the world as a theatre?

The medieval and Renaissance image of the *theatrum mundi* portrayed individuals as puppets of God, embodiments of abstract virtues and vices: to see the world as a theatre was to see through the vanity of human achievements to the spiritual reality behind. The world becomes a morality play, in which the inconsequentiality of the stage teaches us the pre-eminence of Death and the life hereafter. The world was *merely* a stage; indeed, a physical stage might well be absent, reinforcing the lack of clear distinction between actors and audience. With Renaissance court masques, a similar allegorical relationship to power was maintained, but now it was the power of the monarch that was celebrated; hence, theatricality became 'one of power's essential modes', as Greenblatt puts it.[19] But by now, theatricality in its more modern sense was clearly emerging. Elizabeth Burns characterizes this change as a shift from personification to impersonation:

> Personification referred always to man in his relationship with the unseen, inferred world of spiritual reality or to universals or to spiritual beings, impersonation to the known social world. . . . Characters were presented as impersonations of possible human beings rather than personifications of predetermining virtues, vices, or passions.[20]

Thus Agnew suggests that by the sixteenth century, actors had increasingly taken on these recognizable 'characters' to impersonate, and were increasingly free to 'appeal to the social idiosyncrasies of their audience, indeed to create and manipulate their audience through the power of illusion'.

What can be suggested is that 'theatricality' emerged in a context where traditional social positions, conventions and rituals no longer conveyed a clear meaning, and where, in the new social conditions of rapid change and the emergence of the market, a degree of flexibility and adaptability became part of the very constitution of the self. Agnew points to the political and social context of eighteenth-century Britain, where public life assumed 'an extraordinarily theatrical style' as classes, factions and individuals manoeuvred on a cultural terrain that had been rendered increasingly unfamiliar by violent upheaval and slow economic change.[21]

In his book *Worlds Apart*, Agnew argues that although 'market' and 'theatre' may appear unconnected, in fact one illuminates the other; he tries to explore how 'the market was made meaningful at the very moment that meaning itself was becoming marketable'. The theatre provided a language and imagery that helped make sense of the world of commodities and market relationships, just as the latter provided the themes and challenges that the theatre thrived on. Examining the 'character' books of the early modern period, Agnew finds that they revealed widespread anxiety about the conditions and conduct of public life in general and of business life, market exchange, in particular. Given the decay of the guilds and the old certainties of status, how should the self present itself in public? Could one trust appearances any more? Given the absence of any clear legal and moral framework, how unscrupulous could one be in everyday transactions? Accountability, honourable intentions, creditworthiness: how could these be 'represented', recognized? Hence what Agnew refers to as the 'crisis of representation',[22] and Sennett calls the 'problem of audience', or how to arouse belief in one's appearance, and what it represents, in a world of strangers, the emergent towns and cities of modernity.[23]

This 'problem of audience' is essentially the same as that faced by actors in a theatre. Only if there are clear conventions governing how one behaves, talks, gestures and dresses can one satisfactorily 'perform' the roles one claims, whether in public life in general or the theatre in particular. And the problems and dangers of appearance, reliability and duplicity were precisely problems that constituted central themes of the drama of the period. The themes of mistaken identity, misplaced trust and misdirected suspicion were to be found everywhere. Watching plays did not give reassurance – a change of clothes on stage might signify not a new role but an intention to deceive – but crystallized these themes, presented them as inescapable in modern life, and suggested ways of handling them. Catherine Belsey suggests that the theatrical soliloquy both mirrored and reproduced the emerging sense of the interiority of the subject, the foundation of the 'imaginary unity' underlying the diversity of roles.[24] Above all, then, a new image of the self was embedded in this drama, a self that evolves, plays roles, manipulates appearances. To watch a play, writes Agnew, was 'to confront the possibility that the self was a contingent, arbitrary and instrumental affair, not a natural or supernatural calling', and the new drama showed 'how precarious social identity was, how vulnerable to unexpected disruptions and disclosures it was, and therefore how deeply theatrical it was'.[25]

Nor are we far from the language of economics here. Role-playing was an 'asset', an essential stratagem for the self; the individual could be said to 'invest' in his or her performance. A seventeenth-century observer claimed that 'man in business is but a Theatricall person, and in a manner but personates himself';[26] customs and roles are like costumes, to be put on and off at will, hence the idea of the 'self-made' man, who could 'act' for himself, and thereby 'make' himself. By the time of Hobbes, in the mid-seventeenth century, the idea that to be a person was to be an actor had become widely accepted. And 'actor' had two aspects: an actor both 'impersonated' or 'acted as', and also 'represented' or 'acted for'. Thus Hobbes can claim that 'person' and 'actor' are coextensive, since 'to personate, is to act, or *represent* himself, or another'.[27] Representation thus becomes bound up with agency in the public world of politics and business, carrying with it this fusion of theatricality and market.

In short, becoming a self could be said to involve a 'rehearsal' of identity, a taking-on and casting-off of roles, which are tried on, worn, almost like clothes: the self becomes a series of such identities, never really assimilated to them, yet clearly marked by them. These roles constitute the public, interpersonal structure of selfhood; indeed, they constitute 'the public' as a set of interacting role-playing selves. Using the theatrical analogy, we can say the self is both actor, and audience or spectator; actor and spectator become part of the structure of self-identity.

According to the stimulating account in Sennett's *The Fall of Public Man*, by the eighteenth century theatricality had come to serve as a bridge that linked the theatre and the street. Public life, whether in politics, business or culture, was theatrical in its very essence. In 1749, the novelist Fielding spoke of London as having become a society in which stage and street were 'literally' intermixed; the world as a theatre was no longer 'only a metaphor', as he put it.[28] With this, writes Sennett, 'it is possible to believe in the reality both of unknown people and of imaginary characters as in a single realm'.[29] Certainly theatricality is important in the emergence of the modern novel; Castle, remarking on the significance of the carnivalesque interludes in novels of the period, suggests that the novelists 'reenacted a larger collective flight into theatricality'.[30] The eighteenth-century theatre was a microcosm of the conventions of dress and manner found in the street and the coffee house, and shared conventions of public performance facilitated sociability. We can begin to see how this solves the problem of belief in imaginary characters on the stage, and in unknown strangers encountered on the street; it is not necessary to know a person's history, background or individual characteristics, since the presentation of self occurred through standard social forms.

There are several aspects to this. The body was treated as a mannequin, that is to say clothes were a matter of convention and social contrivance, not a statement about one's individuality. At home, loose-fitting garments were worn by all; but on the street, clothes were sharply differentiated by class and status. In public, one wore clothes whose purpose was to make it possible for other people to act as if they knew who you were. In this sense, 'clothes had a meaning independent of the wearer'. In effect, clothing was costume, as in the theatre; and the costume was more significant than the individuality of person or body; the role you were playing was what mattered. Hence the intense artificiality of the costumes; for artifice celebrates clothes as a social code, a cultural creation independent of nature and need.

Then again, behaviour, including speech, was treated as a matter of signs rather than symbols. If we tend to see behaviour as symbolic or expressive, of our 'individuality', that implication is not there in this earlier period; the behaviour carries its own meaning in itself. In Sennett's words, social expression was conceived '*as presentation* to other people of feelings which signify in and of themselves, *rather than as representation* to other people of feeling present and real to each self'.[31] If, at the theatre, the tragic hero 'dies', you weep copiously, because to fall on to the stage in a particular way *is* to die, and to weep is the appropriate reaction to that being a 'real event'. One is aroused to appropriate responses at appropriate moments, whether in the theatre or on the street; what matters is the conventional response, not your private feelings.

This could also be seen in love itself, which was portrayed as a matter of convention or artifice. 'Falling in love' was highly theatrical; the object of one's affections served as an excuse to invest emotion in the convention. Emotion was to be trained, shaped, given a public form, at some distance from the self. Love was not about abandoning oneself to passion, but about dramatizing it in the 'correct' form. Apparently the absolute in spontaneity, it actually involved being most imitative. Since the self was not 'exposed' through emotion, it could invest in it fully, hold nothing back. It was the form, the role, that counted. Hence Sennett can claim that the very capacity for public emotional display actually rests on this apparent paradox of *distance* from the self.

If it was quite usual to find, in the 1750s, that members of the audience were seated on the stage, or even that people wandered across the stage when the mood took them, this testifies to the sense of continuity between theatre and 'real life'. 'A play did not "symbolize" reality; it created reality through its conventions.' Actor and spectator were very much participants in the same world: 'Playacting in the form of manners, conventions and ritual gestures is the very stuff out of which public relations are formed', and from which they derive their 'emotional meaning'. For this reason, Sennett concludes that the eighteenth century was the great age of public life because it was the age of civility, the latter seen as the production of a public world through the institutionalized theatricality of daily interaction:

> Civility is treating others as though they were strangers and forging a social bond upon that social distance . . . it is the activity that protects them from each other and yet allows them to enjoy each other's company. Wearing a mask is the essence of

civility. Masks permit pure sociability, detached from the circumstances of power, malaise, and private feeling of those who wear them.[32]

The Spectacle of Theatre

As an institution, the theatre rests on distinctions and separations which both permit, and limit, its 'theatricality'. There is a distinction between the theatre and the world outside: the theatre reconstitutes persons as actors and audience, spectacle and spectators in a specific, anomalous space and time which are not those of the everyday. The participants – especially the actors – are allowed 'disguise', a remnant or inheritance of carnivalesque 'misrule', a permitted 'will to deception'.[33] The world outside is temporarily suspended, rendered 'unreal'. Nevertheless, in the end the world outside is rejoined, and the theatre itself is what has become problematic: simultaneously 'real' as experience, yet 'unreal' relative to the outside.

This ontological insecurity of the theatre, so troublesome in some ways, was also significant for establishing its role in the modern world. With the assault by both scientists and church reformers – Catholic and Protestant – on pre-modern beliefs in the efficacy of 'unlicensed' spiritual powers, and those of the devil, in everyday life, the theatre became acceptable as a counterpoint, precisely because it was candidly anti-ritual, *mere* representation, 'commercial entertainment based upon the cunning manipulation of illusion', as Greenblatt puts it. Referring to official condemnations of practices such as exorcism, and beliefs in the powers of witchcraft, Greenblatt argues that

> the public theater depends for its force upon the availability of social energies detached from their ritual origins and marked out as legitimate objects of histrionic representation. . . . The official church dismantles and cedes to the players the powerful mechanisms of an unwanted and dangerous charisma; in return, the players confirm the charge that those mechanisms are theatrical and hence illusory.[34]

Yet this very 'illusory' quality is, as will be seen, basic to the critique of the theatre offered by other writers, and this is hardly surprising; for it is difficult to corral illusion within the walls of the theatre, nor is it so clear that illusion is ever *simply* illusion. It refers, after all, to the workings of the imagination, and with the imagination being increasingly separated from the 'outside' world – no longer a channel through which 'influences' could flow – and being increasingly reconstructed as a faculty of self, so it emerges as a potent but troublesome force, an actor on the stage of modernity that is potentially as unruly as those it replaces.[35] For in a world of selves, imagination takes on the form of theatricality, and theatricality becomes the very texture of social life. The very idea of 'role-playing', as it develops out of the collapse of the old pre-modern *theatrum mundi*, cannot, by definition, be restricted to the theatre itself, and raises crucial questions about the nature of social life in a society in which 'role-playing' comes to be seen as basic to self-definition and social interaction.

When Sennett writes that 'the creation of theatrical illusion is simply the realization of a certain power of expression in . . . "real life" ',[36] one can therefore remark that the 'simply' is not necessarily so simple. The source of the controversies over the theatre has always rested on the fact that the theatre is never *only* the theatre; it may or may not be a 'mirror of life', but it certainly has implications for the audience who watch it, and is itself a product of a particular kind of society. The significance of the theatre is that it draws on, and influences, a form of social life that is already theatrical. . . . And if it *is* a mirror, Montrose points out just how disturbing this can be: 'If the world is a theatre and the theatre is an image of the world, then by reflecting upon its own artifice, the drama is holding the mirror up to nature.'[37]

If the theatre implies a problematic separation between itself and the wider world, it also rests on key internal distinctions: script and performance, stage and audience, actor and role. And these, too, prove troublesome, forever being interrogated and subverted within the theatre, and raising issues about the theatricality of the world outside the theatre's doors, pointing to areas of tension and ambiguity.

If we play a part, who writes the script? This raises the issue of *authorship*; and the very idea of a play having an 'author', rather than being the product of an anonymous tradition, arises from early modern attempts to contain and control problems posed by the emergence of ideas of the 'creative individual', or to use *this* idea to mitigate the dangers of theatricality itself. The author of a play had to be both permitted and compelled to keep tight control of its performance and interpretation, lest the freedom of actors to influence this be turned against the authorities themselves, through satire, irony or interpolation. If the author is seen as legally responsible, this will operate as a constraint on him, a form of subtle self-censorship. And the actor would be the direct 'representative' of the author, having to 'act for' him, just as the audience would be mere passive recipients of authorial intentions. Bristol concludes that 'This individualization of artistic production is the basis for the legitimation of the theater', since in this allocation of functions there would be no one left to say 'forbidden things', and the dangers of 'an ambiguously allocated or dispersed authority' would be contained.[38]

In practice, the theatre has generally been subjected to direct censorship: until 1843, performances of plays in the UK had to be licensed, and even after this, the Lord Chamberlain's Office wielded powers over new plays, powers only repealed in 1968. And in practice, again, this censorship has always proved, in varying degrees, to be ineffective. Audiences, and indeed actors, have always been adept at subverting both authorial intentions and the intentions of the censorship. One is reminded of the fate of Václav Havel's plays in pre-revolutionary Czechoslovakia: mutilated, apparently emasculated by the censor, totally innocuous on the written page, they could nevertheless prove dynamite in front of an audience. There is, after all, a sense in which the author is 'merely' a channel for the anonymous social and cultural influences that 'write' the script, with the actors therefore rehearsing and performing *social* roles, which are thereby crystallized and recirculated, creatively, within society itself. Perhaps, as suggested above, it is really society that rehearses its ever-changing identity, the theatre being essentially a vehicle for this; in which case, the censorship, even in advance, is always too late. . . .

This also raises the question of whether there is necessarily a clear distinction between audience and performers: are 'audiences' and 'performer' totally separate roles, or are they reversible? As has been seen, the issue was by no means clear-cut in the eighteenth century, when today's taken-for-granted distinction between stage and audience was not so well marked. What matters here is the possible political significance of audience and actors being 'role makers', of actor–audience reversibility. After all, keeping the applauding audience firmly separate from the actors on the *political* stage effectively traps the audience in a passive role, mere admirers of a political spectacle they cannot influence. The possibility that the audience might actually become actors on the political stage is a clue to the deep passions aroused by the French Revolution, when the spectre of 'The People' first threatened the spectacle laid on for their political edification and entertainment.

The final relationship to ask about is that of actor and role, the person and the part played. It is sometimes said that the great actor 'becomes' the role; that without some role or another, there is 'nothing there'. (This was frequently said of Laurence Olivier.) Or is it that the relation is purely external, so that the role is just a prop, manipulated from 'behind the scenes' by the self? Do we escape into roles, hide behind them, or – as has often been suggested in an age when 'authenticity' has become a central value – escape from them? It is worth remarking that the word 'person' originally meant 'mask', in the sense of 'social role'; for the Romans, your 'persona' was your public status. Writing in the seventeenth century, Hobbes observed that 'Persona in latine signifies the disguise, or outwarde appearance of a man, counterfeited on the Stage',[39] showing again the disturbing implications of these notions.

In the next century, Diderot summarized what he called the 'paradox of acting' by asking what people meant by calling someone a great actor, and replying that 'They do not mean by that that he feels, but that he excels in simulating, though he feels nothing.'[40] Appearances mislead; the greater the actor, the greater the deception. As Bristol suggests, an actor is not just 'someone whose speech is "dissembling": the deeper problem is that he is most valued for his ability to dissemble convincingly'.[41] And if, in the eighteenth century, that could be experienced – by some – as a liberation, an escape into sociality, it has more often been seen, since, as threatening, inauthentic, a surrender to conformity and social control, as with Goffman's 'solitary player' who has to play the role but tries to escape it through 'role distance', even though that is merely another role. . . .[42]

It is hardly surprising, then, that there has been a long tradition of Western distrust of the theatre. Greenblatt points to the 'powerful tendency to identify the stage with unreality, debased imitation, and outright counterfeiting'.[43] In the seventeenth century, writes Dollimore, we find a 'general cultural disturbance generated by the theatrical emphasis on artifice, disguise and role-playing'; in particular, the theatre subverted 'metaphysical fixity',[44] the idea of a well-defined, stable identity, keeping categories of rank, age and gender clearly distinct. The theatre, after all, suggests that social positions might be arbitrary and contingent, rather than necessary and natural: a pauper can play a king, a boy can be a girl. . . . During the period of Puritan supremacy in mid-century, theatres were closed down altogether; and in the following century, masquerade was widely denounced for its mixing of categories, its 'excess' of theatricality that revealed the inherent vices of the latter. Barish feels able to make the following generalization about anti-theatrical currents, suggesting they belong to

> a conservative ethical emphasis in which the key terms are those of order, stability, constancy, and integrity, as against a more existentialist emphasis that prizes growth, process, exploration, flexibility, variety and versatility of response. In one case we seem to have an ideal of stasis, in the other an ideal of movement, in one case an ideal of rectitude, in the other an ideal of plenitude.[45]

And even today, a writer on the theatre can claim that 'Theatre is worthwhile because it is antagonistic to official views of reality.'[46]

It is Rousseau, above all, who takes up and generalizes the critique of the theatre that this makes possible. The theatre is inherently counterfeit; pretence comes to dominate truth, imagination overwhelms reason. And given the theatricality of the social world, this becomes, in Rousseau's hands, a devastating critique of modernity. He complains that 'the heart is more readily touched by feigned ills than real ones',[47] because each of us has become an actor, 'expert in the art of counterfeiting, of putting on another character than his own, of appearing different than he is'.[48] Hence 'The man of the world is entirely in his mask', and 'Almost never in himself, he is always a stranger there.'[49] Barber concludes that for Rousseau, the theatre

> nourishes a silent conspiracy in imaginative self-deception, joined in by audience, actor and dramatist. A titillating fiction is created, and the common illusions it generates permit all the participants to live out sterile fantasies without substance, to feel passions without consequence, to take risks with nothing at stake, to enjoy vicarious emotions without suffering, and to revel in sentiments without commitment or obligation.[50]

We become alienated from our inner truth, and dependent on the approval of the audience of other actors: artifice and hypocrisy become social virtues, and real virtue becomes impossible. We trade reputations, not just commodities, and become subject to fashion, dependent on the whims of the fickle audience. In the end, suggests Turner, 'reality becomes entirely representational', since social success 'hinges crucially on the presentation of an acceptable image'.[51] Sennett summarizes Rousseau's critique in these terms:

The great city is a theater. Its scenario is principally the search for reputations. All city men become artists of a particular kind: actors. In acting out a public life, they lose contact with natural virtue. The artist and the great city are in harmony, and the result is a moral disaster.[52]

Rousseau's question is, essentially: how can the self be real in a world of others? The implication of the question is that self-knowledge and self-identity may be bound up with the theatrical incorporation of the other through imagination, just as this, in turn, makes possible the only knowledge of the other that is consistent with this emergent world of social appearances and market relations between actors on the social stage. And if Rousseau's own analysis is distinctive and extreme – standing at the origin of powerful strands of social criticism in the otherwise divergent French and German traditions of social theory – the assumptions he draws on are widely shared, suggested as they are by the experience of social life under the conditions of developing modernity. Much the same assumptions can be found in Adam Smith, hardly a theorist who would generally be regarded as similar in orientation.

Central to all these accounts is the presentation of social life as enshrining a separation between self and image, self and other, a separation that both permits, and rests on, the role of the imagination in constructing a grasp of both self and other through theatricality. The self becomes both spectator at, and actor in, its own performance, and this constitutes the fantasy structure of interpersonal experience and communication in the world of modernity.

How is self-identity possible? The self is constituted through recognition. But how is it to know, recognize, what it has not yet become? We have here a process of projection and dramatization; the self makes itself what it will then be able to recognize itself as (or in). This occurs through the appropriation of such images or roles as happen to be available; through appropriating, rehearsing and thereby projecting such images, through 'trying them out' (or 'on'), the self comes to know itself as the sort of self it has been privileged to become. Hence theatricality, as this mode of imaginative appropriation and construction, is the process whereby the self can become a fluid, changing, yet continuous creation, carrying the multiple burdens of modernity. Through theatricality, the representation of self could become the construction and content of self; whether it becomes the construction of *selfhood*, the integrated, narrative self of project, is another matter. For Rousseau, indeed, the theatrical self made the unified self forever impossible; and even for Adam Smith, much more in tune with this world, the worry remains present.

In *The Theory of Moral Sentiments*, 1759, Adam Smith explores the role of that characteristic eighteenth-century concept, 'sympathy', in a world of spectators and spectacles, a world of representation and theatrical distance. Through the theatrical imagination, we can approach the other 'sympathetically'; but our understanding of the other's feelings can only come through our own. 'Through a representation of our own feelings, we can represent to ourselves the feelings of the person we witness', suggests Marshall.[53] Such sympathy, adds Agnew, 'required the spectator to impersonate the sufferer within the theater of his own mind', hence 'To be a spectator in this sense was to be an actor, and to be an actor in this sense was to risk the loss of the self whose sympathy was at stake.'[54] But this is also how we come to 'see' ourselves. For Adam Smith, writes Marshall, we know ourselves by internalizing the gaze of the spectator, hence 'we are both actors and spectators of our characters'. He adds: 'Imagining ourselves as a spectacle, we look at ourselves in exactly the same way that we look at others', and we thus attempt 'to sympathize with ourselves, to enter into our own feelings and persons'.[55]

Since the roles of actor and spectator can never be simultaneously identical, there is a sense in which this self-identity is itself undermined by the very theatricality that constitutes it, and the self's reflexivity, its self-monitoring, can never really resolve this. In the taken-for-granted round of everyday existence, this need not matter; nevertheless, this is always potentially a questing, dissatisfied self, formed through the interaction with others so that it becomes 'other' to itself, with an 'outsider' consciousness, never fully able to 'belong'. We can at least see why Barber can suggest that

> In Rousseau's ambivalence about imagination and about a theater in which imagination was the chief moving force is revealed the principal dilemma of modernity: the fragmentation of the modern self, alienated both from the world and from its own nature, into pieces apparently beyond the integrating ministrations of educators, lawgivers or artists.[56]

And for Adam Smith also, sympathy was 'a mark of the immense distance that separated individual minds rather than a sign of their commonality',[57] with spectatorship being a kind of substitute for an impossible 'emotional communion'. Modern civilization essentially *is* this exchange of sympathy, based on an exchange of fantasy identifications through the theatrical imagination. Modernity requires us to become actors and spectators, thereby making spectacles of ourselves.

And finally, the term 'spectacle' itself could do with further consideration. Huet defines a spectacle as 'that organization in which the activity and the actor . . . requires a spectator and excludes his participation'.[58] As has been seen, this can be mapped on to social interaction and the structure of the self, and, taken together with the idea that images are central to the content of these representations of self and other, we find that 'spectacle' has become an influential concept in cultural analysis in our own time. In his discussion of contemporary culture, Chaney claims that identity itself becomes 'a repertoire of selves we can see enacted as spectacle in drama and adapt and borrow for our selves'. More generally, he writes that since 'we can use features of the way we dramatise ourselves to delineate the main characterisation of modernity', we find that 'forms of public drama' in effect constitute 'reflexive accounts of collective experience'.[59] These 'forms of public drama', and their links with developing notions of 'personality', can now be explored in this more recent period.

Starring the Person

In tracing the later dynamics of theatricality, in the nineteenth and twentieth centuries, we need to examine three phenomena that are not obviously linked: personality, stardom and melodrama. A central problem is raised by all of them, that of authenticity, and they draw on, and exist in, a specific context: that of a post-religious world in which moral dilemmas and the significance of the stresses and strains of everyday life are articulated through the language and imagery of the increasingly 'spectacular' forms of modern 'entertainment', including cinema and television, as they develop out of, and to some extent supplant, theatre and novel.

Let us start with 'personality'. The eighteenth-century idea of theatricality as a mask that permitted impersonal role-playing, thereby 'liberating' the self in the public arena, had coexisted uneasily with developments that led to our later sense of 'personality' as entailing a distinctively 'individual' touch to everything we do or say, and how we appear, with the implication that the self has to be careful in public because it can be 'read', so it is easy to 'give oneself away'. Anything – details of clothes and manners – can be said to display one's personality. The term 'personality' itself, used in this sense, seems to be a product of the nineteenth century. If the problem for the earlier period was 'virtue' – whether the self was sincere in the roles it played, whether the mask was being manipulated – the problem later was one of 'authenticity', whether one's public stance was 'true' to one's 'real' self, whether one was truly showing one's feelings.

Authenticity, one might say, is not about public roles, but about consistency between 'personality' and 'character'. In the eighteenth century, theatricality was acceptable in the public sphere because the 'intimate self' of the private sphere was unimportant; now, this self has become important enough for its possible *lack* of fit with the public self to become a problem, and the basis for a critique of theatricality, in the language of authenticity. The early modern self was homogeneous, undifferentiated, through its very exile from the public sphere. But as the public self and the private one become equally important, so individuality acquires the potential to develop, through 'personality', which becomes the 'sign' of individuality in the public sphere. In the nineteenth century, this resulted in a certain caution about the display of feelings, precisely because 'being authentic' might render one socially vulnerable.

Later in the twentieth century, however, an increasing cult of authenticity made it seem desirable to be 'truly oneself' in the public sphere, so that manifesting aspects of one's individual personality would *increase* the likelihood of being taken seriously as a person. Trilling suggests that an 'unmediated exhibition' of the self, with the intention of being 'true' to it, implies that truth to self has become a self-sufficient goal, no longer tied to public roles; we are more bothered by self-deception than feigning or dissimulation in role-playing.[60] And Berger adds that 'roles no longer actualize the self, but serve as a "veil of *maya*" hiding the self', so that identity is increasingly defined '*against* the institutional roles through which the individual expresses himself in society'.[61] It is through individualizing roles that we show selfhood.

But for all that, we cannot conclude that 'personality' loses touch with the theatrical. It is rather that 'personality' and a new mode of theatricality come into being together. And in exploring this, we have to ask what is meant by 'personality', and make a shift towards melodrama.

'Personality' is that which has to be expressed, yet never really can be, for what is it that can mark 'individuality' without at the same time having typological, emblematic features, features that are in principle just as available to others to mark *their* 'individuality'? The novelist Balzac suggested that personality is immanent in appearance, but is also 'a secret which will not itself speak';[62] hence it requires symbolization, typification. Representations (expressions) of personality are always simultaneously inadequate and excessive: inadequate, for they necessarily fail, yet excessive, as they strain for the significance that eludes them, through exaggeration and reduplication. The self, straining for authenticity, is constantly threatened by self-parody, as it takes on the melodramatic qualities that purport to indicate the presence of the self as the guarantee of both the individuality and the authenticity of appearance, of what shows on the surface. Personality is always excessive in its representations, because those representations always fail to guarantee what they point to, the deeper truth of individual authenticity. Personality is the charisma of the individual: to carry off what is involved in 'having a personality', every individual has to be a star.

Personality entered the public realm through an emphasis on individual talent and expressiveness, in the performing arts, and through a focus on the histrionic and presentational skills of politicians in contexts of public debate; this meant that such figures could be seen as 'charismatic performers', not just role players. By 1810, the violin virtuoso Paganini had become, suggests Sennett, 'the first musician to be a popular hero'.[63] Indeed, the very concept of a 'virtuoso' conveys the idea that the performer – and the performance itself – are as important as the music (as written by the composer); and great virtuosi (from Paganini to Heifetz) have often been distrusted by 'purists' for precisely this reason. By the 1830s and 1840s, the craze for melodrama, combined with this new emphasis on expressiveness, was producing actor–stars who exemplified this congruence between personality and melodrama; for melodrama involved playing a role to the limit and beyond. The extremes of plot and action positively invited theatrical excess and a display of the foibles and ingenuities of personality. Actors *used* the standard categories of melodrama, the stock roles (heroine, villain) as resources for putting across their personalities.

Of course, the 'star', as the 'larger than life' personality, only exists when accepted as such by others: the star of the spectacle is also its subject, its victim. The star only exists through the public, who share the emerging interest in public personality and display; the star's 'charisma' rests on the fantasy identifications of the public, and Suzanne Moore refers to 'the ability that all great stars have of asking us to make it happen for them, of asking us to fill up their emptiness'.[64]

Conversely, the forces which pushed personality into the public sphere 'robbed most of those who lived in public of the conviction that they possessed "real" personality', so they went in search of the few who did, 'a search to be concluded only by acts of fantasy'.[65] In effect, we see by mid-century the emergence of a rudimentary 'star system', long before Hollywood; long queues would build up for tickets for public readings by authors like Dickens.[66]

If we turn to politics, we find that the same forces were at work. 'Politicians began to be judged as believable by whether or not they aroused the same belief in their personalities which actors did when on stage', claims Sennett; a politician succeeded by conveying a sense of himself as having his own impulses, his own distinctive traits, yet by being in control of himself, manifesting a 'controlled spontaneity' that made him seem believable, real. One celebrated example, from a later period, was that of the 'Chequers Speech' by the then vice-president Nixon, future villain of the Watergate drama. Already plagued by allegations of financial impropriety, he turned the tables on his critics by appearing on television with his dog, Chequers, and making an emotional but calculated appeal to the viewing public. His breaking down in tears showed he was 'real'; it did not matter that the spectacle was banal, for the focus on 'spontaneous trivia' helped carry off the act, diverting attention from the alleged misdeeds to the 'real-life', emotional person on the screen.[67]

If we move on to contemporary stardom, as it has developed out of the Hollywood film industry since the 1930s, we find essentially similar features. Christine Gledhill asserts that 'stars function as signs in a rhetorical system which works as melodrama'. Expanding on this, she suggests links between everyday life, stardom, and the issue of authenticity:

> If the excessive moment in melodrama infuses ordinary characters and relationships with excitement and significance, stars represent ordinary people whose ordinary joys and sorrows become extraordinary in the intensity stardom imparts to them . . . the melodramatic demand for clearly defined identity has shifted from fictional to star personae who offer the advantage of authenticating the moral drama in reference to a real person outside the fiction.[68]

Hence the 'persona' of the star 'forms the private life into a public and emblematic shape, drawing on general social types and film roles', while deriving authenticity from 'the unpredictability of the real person'.

These 'general social types' and distinctive genres are clearly important here. 'The Western' at once conjures up characteristic images and themes, embodied in the persona of the melodramatic figure, the hero or villain who 'carries' the underlying moral and existential themes. Yet a John Wayne western is markedly different from a Clint Eastwood one: the former occupies the more traditional melodramatic space of moral and gender absolutes, while the latter is more interested in exploring the tensions and paradoxes of the 'macho' role taken to extremes, often to the point of parody (as in Sergio Leone's 'Spaghetti' westerns). And as stars, they come to embody type and individual, genre and personality, in a distinctive way: person and persona play off one another, reinforce one another. Gledhill suggests that 'Internalisation of the social is accompanied by a process of exteriorisation in which emotional states or moral conditions are expressed as the actions of melodramatic types.'[69] Social currents and pressures become personalized, while at the same time they are projected outwards; psychological depth, the exploration of the 'interior world', is not a feature of melodrama. It is the 'types' that provide the pegs on which the personality of the star hangs, that govern the action and realization of the themes; hence the 'personalization' is melodramatic rather than novelistic (as with Nixon's tears). Brooks suggests that in this way, 'psychology has been externalized, made accessible and immediate through a full realization of its melodramatic possibilities'.[70] These moral and psychological dimensions are projected through gesture, action and dress and 'character' is explored less as an interior quality than as subordinate to the externals of personality, storyline and 'special effects'.

This sense that 'person' and 'persona' can be mutually reinforcing is important when considering the issue of authenticity. Dyer argues that this 'aura', this authentic 'star quality', depends in general on 'the degree to which stars are accepted as truly being what they appear to be';[71] performance has to be carried off as 'true' to the performer, and the performer has to be carried off as the person who is indeed capable of being 'there' in the performance. The off-screen person is as crucial as the on-screen persona. There is a 'rhetoric' of authenticity, whereby the essential continuity between person and persona – the combination that constitutes 'personality' – can be produced.

This can be illustrated by examining the construction of Judy Garland's image and role in the film *A Star is Born*, as analysed by Dyer. The film is intriguing in that at one level it makes it clear that stars *are* manufactured, mere media products, yet all the time it wants to argue that there are *real*, authentic stars, and that Garland is certainly one of them. So how is her 'aura', her 'star quality', constructed? In one example in the film, she is shown informally, with a jazz band, performing in a way that seems improvised, unrehearsed, as though they do not know they are being observed, that they are 'on'; the camera just 'happens' to be there, unnoticed, as it were, like 'fly-on-the-wall' television. Hence the gestures can count as 'authentic', as do Garland's facial and behavioural mannerisms, presented as 'unpremeditated', natural; redundant and excessive to the mere requirements of singing a song, hence genuine. Thus her 'star quality' is presented as being real, grounded in her essential self; it is not mere media hype, manipulation.

Lying behind all this is always the puzzle about modern selfhood: how *can* we be sure whether the person is 'real', or a constructed product of social pressures, media manipulation? Are we all puppets? In an era that emphasizes individuality and authenticity, yet suggests plenty of ways in which these might be thought to constitute ideals, demands, or pressures, rather than actualities, a 'rhetoric' of authenticity becomes fundamental to the presentation of self in everyday life, to strategies of coping. It is through the melodramatic mechanisms of excess and redundancy that we learn to 'carry off' the authentication of self, become stars in our own shows, while simultaneously persuaded that the media existence of the 'real' stars highlights our own, individual, mundane realities as *not* being a world of hype and spectacle. Media stars may be the 'real' stars, but at the same time they are 'only' stars, and the media 'inauthenticity' of stars *as stars* sharpens our own sense of our own authenticity, the validity of our self-identity. Similarly, the critical use of terms like 'theatrical' and 'melodramatic', applied to the gestures and actions of others, helps to reinforce our sense of ourselves as 'normal', sensible, genuine. . . .

The Melodrama of Everyday Life

Implicit in the above account is the suggestion that 'melodrama' is not simply a genre of entertainment, that there is a sense in which everyday life *is* melodramatic, or at least that our experiences of life can be said to unfold in parallel with the structure of the melodramatic scenario, so that it is easy to move between the two registers; they are mutually consistent. Thus Smith suggests that 'we see most of the serious conflicts and crises of our everyday lives in melodramatic, rather than tragic terms' and that melodrama is hence 'the dramatic form which expresses the reality of the human condition as we all experience it most of the time'.[72] Jackie Byars agrees that melodrama is 'the modern mode for constructing moral identity', developing its myths 'at the level of the individual and the personal, drawing its material from the everyday'.[73]

The theoretical understanding of these issues is explored most thoroughly by Brooks. He presents melodrama as 'the principal mode for uncovering, demonstrating, and making operative the essential moral universe in a post-sacred era', arguing that it represents 'both the urge toward resacrilization and the impossibility of conceiving sacrilization other than in personal terms'. Melodrama finds the ghosts of the sacred still prowling around in – and behind – the trivia of everyday life, which thereby become 'charged with meaning'. The world exhibits what he calls the 'moral occult', or the domain of 'operative spiritual values which is both indicated within and masked by the surfaces of reality', and this is articulated through the melodramatic highs and lows of daily moral traumas and resolutions. Hence 'Ordinary life can be made "interesting" through heightened dramatic utterance and gesture that reveal the true stakes', the conflict of good and evil in the world.[74] A complementary point is made in Ang's suggestion that 'The melodramatic imagination is therefore the expression of a refusal, or inability, to accept insignificant everyday life as banal and meaningless.'

This sense of the 'moral occult', the 'depth' behind – or in – appearances, is nevertheless difficult to express, and necessarily so. There is no clear code for translating or representing this 'other' dimension. In Ang's words, 'it is as though the melodramatic imagination must impress itself so emphatically because what it wants to express is so uncertain, so difficult to grasp, and therefore too so difficult to justify'.[75] Melodrama makes what Brooks calls 'large but unsubstantiable claims on meaning'; everything has to be drawn into the maelstrom, rendered significant;

nothing can be left unsaid. Melodrama hence tries persistently, frenetically, to express the inexpressible, aware of the threat that 'its plenitude may be a void', as Brooks puts it, since there can be no clear 'evidence' for the moral occult, this residue of the sacred in a scientific age.[76] Byars argues that

> Realism depends on the assumption that the social world can be adequately explained, through social-scientific methods, and that adequate representation is possible. Melodrama has no such confidence; irrational forces exist in the world, and our representational systems are incapable of adequately and directly representing them.[77]

Melodrama derives a framework for rendering intelligible the desires and frustrations, the conflicts and dilemmas of life, from those very forces themselves, through dramatizing them; questions about commitment, justification and ultimate significance are resolved through representing, through drama, the very traumas that produce them in the first place. Meaning is resolved through melodramatic excess; the morality of the ordinary is transfigured through the extraordinary. Some novelists, like Balzac, Dickens, James, Dostoevsky and Conrad, are adept at presenting the melodrama of the mundane, the dualisms of moral conflict.

We can also see wider social and political dimensions to this. In the hands of Marx and Darwin, suggests Sypher, 'the world becomes a theatre of tensions between abstractions. Melodrama has become social, if not cosmic.'[78] The drama is worked out through the great forces that shape human destiny, often impenetrable to the actors who struggle to grasp them, as they are buffeted by the conflicts that result from them. For Brooks, the French Revolution itself – contemporary with the birth of melodrama on the stage – in turn became melodrama, 'incessant struggle against enemies, without and within, branded as villains, suborners of morality, who must be confronted and expunged, over and over', to ensure the triumph of virtue.[79] Sennett suggests that the 'logic of collective personality is the purge'. There are no half-measures, no grey areas; for the Jacobin, Saint-Just, 'Republican government has virtue as its principle; or if not, terror'.[80] Brooks adds that modern politics more generally, a politics of personality, produces a rhetoric of melodramatic struggle, where virtue and evil are constantly personalized: 'the modern political leader is obliged to point continuous battle with an enemy'.[81]

While the utterances of politicians, and the plots of melodramatic theatre or cinema, *may* offer the hopes of resolution, the victory of virtue and progress, the logic of melodrama itself seems to point towards a profound scepticism about progress. The melodramatic imagination of the world encompasses the triumph of good, but it is a transient triumph, for humans are ultimately at the mercy of uncontrollable and incomprehensible forces. There is a sense of the passivity of experience, an openness to the daily contingencies of life, good or bad, almost a celebration of this passivity. Ang argues that

feelings of masochism and powerlessness, which are the core of the melodramatic imagination, are an implicit recognition, in their surrender to some power
outside the subject, of the fact that one can never have everything under control
all the time, and that consequently identity is not a question of free and conscious choice but always acquires its shape under circumstances not of one's own
making.[82]

In this light, one could say melodramatic struggle always represents the struggle
between reality and desire, just as it represents the always inadequate effort to
represent this struggle.

And spectacle? In the theatre, 'melodrama was spectacular from its birth',
claims Booth, 'spectacular' here having connotations of both 'dramatic' and 'pictorial'. In The *Streets of London* (1864), a real fire engine crashed on to the stage,
with bells ringing, as a house went up in flames; volcanic eruptions, storms at sea,
and battles, were all well within the capacity of Victorian set designers and theatre
managers. The spectacular, then, represented an intensification of the spectacle as
a relationship between audience and stage; the audience, enthroned as spectators,
were presented with a world that was 'saturated with pictures' as they enjoyed
the 'essentially passive act of viewing'.[83] And Chaney suggests that as 'the form
of performance became characterised by an attempt to combine spectacular
artifice with pictorial naturalism',[84] so we can see how this could lead easily into
cinema.

In the cinema, this 'logic' incorporated the complex use of the total available
resources, including music and costume, to elaborate and intensify the impact of
the narrative, strategies for engendering the elements of 'suspense' basic to the
plot, and careful attention lavished on the scenic backdrop. The pictorialism is
significant in that it can give a naturalistic, realistic background to the display of
unfolding events and emotions that embody the 'moral occult' in its most spectacular mode, thereby reinforcing the 'authentic' portrayal of the world as a site
where the unexpected, the romantic, the wicked, the catastrophic and the blissful
can all be possible dimensions of experience. Even so, the 'backdrop' is always in
principle available as a further melodramatic resource, and can itself become
centrally implicated as an actor in the film, another of the 'modes of excess' that
make up the total impact.[85]

Taken together, these developments enhance a sense of experience as passive
and as involving distance; the imagination has become spectacular and visual,
rather than interactive. This both results from, and reinforces, the experience of
the world as spectacle, and makes possible the presentation of that world as a
world of entertainment, a world that can be *enjoyed* as spectacle, precisely because
of the sense of simultaneous participation and distance that makes this world *safe*.
This visual world becomes a panorama that induces a variety of pleasures; it
becomes *vicarious*, simultaneously involving and uninvolving, real and unreal.
Through its separation from the rest of life, it can engage the imagination all the
more vividly; while at the same time this separation is itself problematical, since it

is the product of a world that is itself 'spectacular'; in this sense, a true heir to the earlier theatre and its problematical relationship to its world.

Yet in the age of television it is soap opera, in its various forms, that seems to carry the inheritance of melodrama most clearly, while infusing distinctive elements of its own. The melodramatic elements are not far to seek: sensationalism and emotional drama characterize the plots, with affairs, marriages, divorces, murders, illnesses, legal battles, endless triumphs and disasters, passing by with great rapidity; and psychological 'depth' is subordinated to the functioning of characters in dramatic situations, with inner conflicts always given immediate external realization. There are of course differences: the undivided moral protagonists of nineteenth-century melodrama, who are not only heroes or villains but *know* themselves to be such, have found it difficult to survive, and we do not find the clear-cut resolution, the decisive triumph of good over evil. As Tania Modleski suggests, it would be impossible to resolve the contradiction between 'the imperatives of melodrama – the good must be rewarded and the wicked punished – and the latent message of soap operas – everyone cannot be happy at the same time'. Like the family, its core subject matter, the soap never ends: 'Tune in tomorrow, not in order to find out the answers, but to see what further complications will defer the resolutions and introduce new questions.'[86] Anticipation becomes an end in itself, successes and failures are never conclusive, problems recur endlessly. Somehow, the family, like the soap, survives, yet plagued by breakdowns, walkouts, infidelities, crises of every kind, including (frequently) the activities of the family villain or villainess.

In place of clear-cut moral absolutes, the moral structure of everyday life is conveyed through emotionally ambiguous situations and conflicts; moral imperatives have become emotional dilemmas. Morality exists latently, through these emotional pressures, frequently requiring choices in difficult situations; but it is not a matter of rules so much as of relationships, rights and wrongs that involve balancing obligations rather than applying absolutes. And this reminds us that the very notion of 'morality' is not gender-neutral: what we find here is a more feminine approach, and this may help account for the appeal of soaps to women. When Carol Gilligan writes that, for women, moral problems arise from 'competing responsibilities rather than from competing rights', and require thinking that is 'contextual and narrative' rather than 'formal and abstract',[87] this is entirely consistent with the moral ethos of soaps. Christine Geraghty develops this into a more general depiction of soap opera as presenting a 'woman-centred' perspective:

> Soaps rehearse to their female audience the process of handling personal relationships – the balancing of each individual's needs, the attention paid to every word and gesture so as to understand its emotional meaning, the recognition of competing demands for attention. . . . In soaps, competence in the personal sphere is valued and women are able to handle difficult situations because of it.

Hence male characters in soaps can be left in a position of 'baffled impotence' as they attempt, incompetently, to navigate in this world. Citing Brunsdon's work, she also suggests a sense in which soaps 'colonise the public sphere and claim it for the personal', revealed in the tendency 'both to bring personal relationships into the work arena and to deal with relationships at work as if they were personal'.[88] Gledhill traces these gender dimensions back through the Hollywood tradition, claiming that realism came to be associated with the 'masculine sphere of action' while 'the woman's film was identified with melodrama'. She adds that since melodrama's 'over-investment' in the symbol – what Geraghty calls the 'excess of meaning over motivation'[89] – produces a 'complex, highly ambivalent field for women', so reading its political significance is not straightforward: 'Melodramatic pathos could be turned to assertion', it could be empowering rather than paralysing, a validation of women's perspectives rather than a furtherance of their dependence.[90]

Certainly we encounter the identification-distancing dynamic again; the audience is drawn in, but also pushed back. Recognition of, and sympathy with, emotional traumas, can help identification, but criticism of shortcomings, and an awareness of the narrative line, a knowledge not given to the participants, helps distancing. There are always 'secrets' known to some characters – and the viewer – but not to others. As Laura Mulvey puts it, 'Characters caught in the world of melodrama are not allowed transcendent awareness or knowledge',[91] and tend to be unreflective; but the viewer is aware of the structure in which they are embedded. In her study of the appeal of romantic melodrama, Kirsten Drotner concludes that the binary structure of romantic melodrama, with its 'textual oscillation between linear narration (suspense) and spectacular intensity (pathos)', facilitates 'an oscillation for the recipients between intellectual distanciation and emotional immersion'.[92] In the end, then, soap opera feeds off the problematic possibilities through which we construct and live our lives, investing them with layers of meaning, so that the pleasures and frustrations offered by viewing it become, as Ang claims, 'not a *compensation* for the presumed drabness of daily life, nor a *flight* from it, but a *dimension* of it'.[93]

Over recent centuries, then, there have clearly been changes both in the modes of theatricality, and in its social context. Agnew points out that as late as 1870, an actor could still be denied Christian burial in New York; a century later, and one would be elected president.[94] Taking the modern period overall, we can say that theatricality involves a play of difference, in which fluidity, adaptability, and role-playing have both entered into the construction of selfhood and have rendered its unity and integrity problematical. When one is struggling to construct a coherent sense of self, the theatricality of the social world is a problem, threatening to dissolve unity in excess and artifice; but when one is trying to subvert or deconstruct it, this theatricality becomes the central resource. Through theatricality, the self encounters the otherness that is crucial to its own identity.

Melodrama, in turn, could be described as the dominant mode of theatricality in the age of personality; the theatricality of the 'integrated' self, presenting a heroic fantasy of the self in its dealings, for good or evil, with the unpredictable conundrums of life. 'Personality' may be little more than a rhetoric of identity, an excess that covers a lack, a plenitude masking a nothingness; though it may, of course – as we saw with Oscar Wilde – revel in the plenitude of this very absence. And if theatricality raises problems about what self-identity is, melodrama questions how to develop or preserve it in a world that has become an arena of forces and events that can never be reduced to control through project, since 'self' and 'world' alike come to be constructed rhetorically, given a phantom unity through melodrama. It is as though the ontological insecurity of the seventeenth-century theatre, poised uneasily between reality and unreality, has spread to affect both self and world. We are thus presented with a world in which meaning is everywhere, but always undecidable, always in excess of our capacity for understanding; and a self which cannot be grasped reflexively, but only 'played at', through role and image. It suggests that the precarious attainment of selfhood is only ever a fantasied success, and brings costs in the vulnerability of this self to the world it purports to control.

But this issue of 'control' reminds us that if the French Revolution seems to have carried with it the seeds of the melodramatic struggles of selfhood and the social, it also has another legacy; and to this we now turn.

Notes

1   N. Bartlett, *Who Was That Man? A Present for Mr Oscar Wilde* (Penguin, 1993), p. 163.
2   Cited in ibid., p. 162.
3   O. Wilde, 'The Soul of Man Under Socialism', in his *The Artist as Critic* (W. H. Allen, 1970), pp. 272, 286, 284.
4   Cited in J. Dollimore, *Sexual Dissidence* (Oxford University Press, 1991), p. 11.
5   Dollimore, *Sexual Dissidence*, p. 14.
6   O. Wilde, *The Picture of Dorian Gray* (Penguin, 1949), pp. 158–9, 29.
7   Cited in Bartlett, *Who Was That Man?*, p. 163.
8   Bartlett, *Who Was That Man?*, pp. 163, 169, 166, 166, 169.
9   Cited in ibid., p. 190.
10   Bartlett, *Who Was That Man?*, pp. 201, 169, 171.
11   F. Nietzsche, *Beyond Good and Evil* (Vintage, 1966), p. 51.
12   Cited in N. Auerbach, *Private Theatricals: The Lives of the Victorians* (Harvard University Press, 1990), p. 38.
13   Auerbach, *Private Theatricals*, pp. 3, 4.
14   Ibid., pp. 58, 6, 4, 118. On contemporary implications for gender identity and gender politics, see A. Sinfield, *The Wilde Century* (Cassell, 1994).
15   J. Walkowitz, *City of Dreadful Delight: Narratives of Sexual Danger in Late-Victorian London* (Virago, 1992), pp. 86, 120, and ch. 3, passim. See also R. Maltby, 'The Social Evil, the Moral Order and the Melodramatic Imagination, 1890–1915', in J. Bratton et al., *Melodrama* (British Film Institute, 1994).
16   R. Williams, 'Drama in a Dramatized Society', in his *Writing in Society* (Verso, 1991), p. 18.
17   There are hints of this in the work of E. Goffman, e.g. *The Presentation of Self in*

Everyday Life (Anchor, 1959) and V. W. Turner, *From Ritual to Theatre* (Performing Arts Journal Publications, 1982).

18 R. Sennett, *The Fall of Public Man* (Faber, 1986), p. 35.
19 S. Greenblatt, 'Invisible Bullets: Renaissance Authority and its Subversion', *Glyph* (1981), 8, p. 56.
20 E. Burns, *Theatricality* (Longman, 1972), pp. 163, 165.
21 J.-C. Agnew, *Worlds Apart: The Market and the Theater in Anglo-American Thought, 1550–1750* (Cambridge University Press, 1988), pp. 106, 188.
22 Ibid., pp. 12, 60.
23 Sennett, *Fall*, p. 38.
24 C. Belsey, *The Subject of Tragedy: Identity and Difference in Renaissance Drama* (Methuen, 1985), p. 23.
25 Agnew, *Worlds Apart*, pp. 113, 112.
26 John Hall, cited in ibid., p. 97.
27 Hobbes, cited in ibid., p. 99.
28 Cited in Sennett, *Fall*, p. 64.
29 Sennett, *Fall*, p. 40.
30 T. Castle, 'The Carnivalization of 18th Century Narrative', *Proceedings of the Modern Languages Association* (1984), 99:5.
31 Sennett, *Fall*, pp. 68, 39; and see pp. 64–5.
32 Ibid., pp. 79, 29, 264.
33 M. Bristol, *Carnival and Theater* (Routledge, 1989), p. 113.
34 S. Greenblatt, 'Loudon and London', *Critical Inquiry* (1986), 12, p. 341.
35 This is important for the later role of the cult of the imagination in the arts (ch. 10).
36 Sennett, *Fall*, p. 80.
37 L. Montrose, 'The Purpose of Playing: Reflections on a Shakespearean Anthropology', *Helios* (1980), 7, p. 57.
38 Bristol, *Carnival*, p. 121.
39 Cited in ibid., p. 120.
40 Cited in Sennett, *Fall*, p. 110.
41 Bristol, *Carnival*, p. 113.
42 Goffman, *Presentation*, p. 235 and passim.
43 Greenblatt, 'Loudon', p. 328.
44 Dollimore, *Sexual Dissidence*, p. 290. See also J. E. Howard, *The Stage and Social Struggle in Early Modern England* (Routledge, 1994).
45 J. Barish, *The Antitheatrical Prejudice* (California University Press, 1981), p. 117. On gender aspects, see also L. Ferris, *Crossing the Stage* (Routledge, 1993).
46 A. Read, *The Theatre and Everyday Life* (Routledge, 1993), p. 1.
47 J.-J. Rousseau, *Letter to M. D'Alembert on the Theatre* (Cornell University Press, 1968), p. 25.
48 Cited in B. Barber, 'Rousseau and the Paradoxes of the Dramatic Imagination', *Daedalus* (1978), 107:3, p. 85.
49 Cited in Barber, 'Rousseau', p. 87.
50 Barber, 'Rousseau', p. 85.
51 B. Turner, *The Body and Society* (Blackwell, 1984), p. 111.
52 Sennett, *Fall*, p. 119.
53 D. Marshall, *The Figure of Theater* (Columbia University Press, 1986), p. 170.
54 Agnew, *Worlds Apart*, p. 183.
55 Marshall, *Figure*, pp. 175, 174.

56   Barber, 'Rousseau', p. 79.

57   Agnew, *Worlds Apart*, p. 178.

58   M.-H. Huet, *Rehearsing the Revolution; The Staging of Marat's Death, 1793–7* (California University Press, 1982), pp. 68–9.

59   D. Chaney, *Fictions of Contemporary Life: Public Drama in Late Modern Culture* (Routledge, 1993), pp. 41, 2, 18, 10.

60   L. Trilling, *Sincerity and Authenticity* (Oxford University Press, 1972), pp. 4, 16.

61   P. Berger, *The Homeless Mind* (Penguin, 1974), pp. 87, 86.

62   Cited in Sennett, *Fall*, p. 157.

63   Sennett, *Fall*, p. 200. See also pp. 203–4.

64   S. Moore, *Guardian* (22 November 1995).

65   Sennett, *Fall*, p. 212.

66   S. Ewen, *All Consuming Images: The Politics of Style in Contemporary Culture* (Basic Books, 1988), p. 92.

67   Sennett, *Fall*, pp. 196, 270, 280.

68   C. Gledhill, 'Signs of Melodrama', in C. Gledhill (ed.) *Stardom: Industry of Desire* (Routledge, 1991), pp. 207, 213, 218.

69   Ibid., p. 210.

70   P. Brooks, *The Melodramatic Imagination* (Yale University Press, 1976), p. 204.

71   R. Dyer, '*A Star is Born* and the Construction of Authenticity', in Gledhill, *Stardom*, p. 132.

72   J. L. Smith, *Melodrama* (Methuen, 1973), p. 8.

73   J. Byars, *All That Hollywood Allows: Re-Reading Gender in 1950s Melodrama* (North Carolina University Press, 1991), p. 11.

74   Brooks, *Melodramatic Imagination*, pp. 15, 16, 22, 5, 14.

75   I. Ang, *Watching Dallas: Soap Opera and the Melodramatic Imagination* (Methuen, 1985), pp. 79, 80.

76   Brooks, *Melodramatic Imagination*, pp. 199, 200.

77   Byars, *Hollywood*, p. 13.

78   W. Sypher, 'Aesthetics of Revolution: The Marxist Melodrama', in R. Corrigan (ed.) *Tragedy: Vision and Form* (New York University Press, 1965), p. 262. See also Bratton, *Melodrama*, Part 4.

79   Brooks, *Melodramatic Imagination*, p. 15.

80   Sennett, *Fall*, p. 223.

81   Brooks, *Melodramatic Imagination*, p. 203.

82   I. Ang, 'Melodramatic Identifications: Television Fiction and Women's Fantasy', in M. E. Brown (ed.) *Television and Women's Culture* (Sage, 1990), p. 86.

83   M. Booth, *Victorian Spectacular Theatre, 1850–1910* (Routledge, 1981), pp. 60, 8.

84   Chaney, *Fictions*, p. 7.

85   On costume, see J. Gaines, 'Costume and Narrative: How Dress Tells the Woman's Story', in J. Gaines and C. Herzog (eds.) *Fabrications: Costume and the Female Body* (Routledge, 1990).

86   T. Modleski, *Loving with a Vengeance* (Routledge, 1988), pp. 90, 88.

87   C. Gilligan, *In a Different Voice* (Harvard University Press, 1982), p. 19.

88   C. Geraghty, *Women and Soap Opera* (Polity, 1991), pp. 43, 47, 51, 53, 54. And see C. Brunsdon, 'Crossroads: Notes on Soap Opera', in E. A. Kaplan (ed.) *Regarding Television* (University Publications of America, 1983), p. 70.

89   Geraghty, *Women and Soap*, p. 31.

90   C. Gledhill, 'The Melodramatic Field: An Investigation', in C. Gledhill (ed.) *Home Is*

Where the Heart Is: Studies in Melodrama and the Woman's Film (British Film Institute, 1987), p. 35.

91   L. Mulvey, 'Notes on Sirk and Melodrama', in Gledhill (ed.) *Home*, p. 77.
92   K. Drotner, 'Intensities of Feeling: Modernity, Melodrama and Adolescence', *Theory, Culture and Society* (1991), 8, p. 81.
93   Ang, *Watching Dallas*, p. 83.
94   Agnew, *Worlds Apart*, p. xiii.

2 Subjects and Citizens:

The Politics of Everyday Life

The Theatre of Revolution and the Politics of Virtue

The French Revolution – conventionally taken to inaugurate the politics of modernity – has, as a central theme, the conflict of theatricality and 'virtue', and, through tracing this, we will encounter a new 'politics of the everyday' that is central to the constitution of modern selfhood.

There was no doubt, at the time, that the drama of the Revolution was indeed a *drama*, being enacted on the public stage. According to Outram, it was widely agreed that 'political figures *were* actors in a theatre, not only playing to an audience, but actually creating that audience through the existence of their drama', and she adds that 'Role-playing was the essence of the struggle for political authority.'[1] In effect, the audience were created as the spectators of the revolutionary drama; they could, suggests Parker, thereby '"perform" their role as members of the new public'.[2]

But if a politician was an actor on the stage, could he be trusted? Did he truly 'represent' the people, as politicians increasingly claimed to do? After all, Rousseau would have none of it: 'The moment a people allows itself to be represented, it is no longer free.'[3] If, as seen in the previous chapter, it is possible to present acting as being inherently corrupt, how can 'the people' be represented on the political stage at all? But the problem is even deeper than this: if we are *all* actors, the web of corruption spreads everywhere. 'The people', then, can hardly be just the sum of all these corrupt individuals, lacking virtue. In this sense, 'the people' does not yet exist; it must be created; or rather, it must in a sense create itself. The people creates itself through virtue, and thereby transcends the artifice, the theatricality of the social world.

What this meant in practice was that people had to *become* revolutionaries or be *led* by them. Political leaders had to be men of virtue: autonomy and inner authenticity. If they played a part on the public stage, it could no longer be a role but an *identity*. As a bearer of republican virtue, the true leader could be a true representative of the people; his own interests are now identical with the general will. Those who perform the role of virtue must not seem to play a role, indeed must not do so; their 'theatricality' should be self-cancelling, so they can expose the theatricality of others.

Thus, theatricality has become inauthenticity, posing serious problems for the politics of representation: if the public world is a world of masks and appearances, in which the self only appears as other, appears to and for the audience of other selves, who come similarly attired, then political life is corrupt at its core, and representation always problematical. The act of representation, through which one or more members of the community have to be recognized as its agents, able to act for it, therefore always becomes a potential betrayal, leaving endless scope for fantasy identifications and political manipulation. Hence the idea that the political representative – through whom the community recognizes itself in action – has to reflect some ideal, abstract 'citizen', the essence that underlies the masks, the 'social individual' as universal; and hence also the tension between this dimension and the inevitable particularity of the representative, who remains trapped within the world of appearances where he, too, may not be as he seems. . . . The result is a constant crisis of legitimacy between government and political subject, wherein the strains inherent in both political and symbolic 'representation' produce the dialectic of abstraction and particularity, freedom and subjection, that are central to the politics of modernity.

How is the Revolution to represent itself to itself? How can the virtuous be recognized, in the public sphere? Whatever the answers, Butwin is surely right that 'Republican representation was profoundly and consciously theatrical in its conduct and in its principles',[4] even if it purported to distrust this very theatricality. Iversen points to 'a tension between an ideal of transparency in the sphere of representation and a need for persuasive symbolization in the political sphere':[5] true virtue meant the coincidence of appearance and essence, representation and reality, so the separate existence of 'representation' implied their non-coincidence, the sense in which virtue had to be stimulated, even created, by 'persuasive' symbols. As for the hero on the public stage, Hunt suggests that radicals 'linked oratorical eloquence with purity and virtue of the heart', since this would manifest the hero's essential transparency, his integrity. He, at least, would be able to fuse symbolism and persuasion without losing virtue.

Inevitably, then, any symbol of the Revolution itself would not be *just* a symbol, but an instrument of education as well, helping to crystallize public identification with the Revolution as *its* Revolution; but for precisely that reason, *any* choice of symbol was problematical, since it raised the issue of legitimacy again. Should such a symbol not be instantly understandable by 'the people', if it was truly *theirs*? In practice, of course, this was not so easy. David, the painter of the Revolution, tried to promote the figure of Hercules in this role, but as Hunt points out, Hercules reveals 'the ambiguity involved in the effort to represent the people to themselves'. When he appeared at a festival in August 1793, the president of the Convention had to 'explain' him to the people: it was, he said, 'to show the people their own image', but as Hunt says, clearly 'their recognition of its import depended on speeches provided by their representatives'.[6] Thus did the festivals reinstate images and representations even as they were denounced.

These revolutionary festivals were in effect a direct attempt to institute or manifest the required 'transparency' between citizens and between citizens and government. The Rousseauan ideal, writes Starobinski, was that these festivals would manifest equality, reciprocity, immediacy, genuine community; everyone would be 'simultaneously audience and actors'; so 'The spectacle would be everywhere and nowhere', since 'When the festival is present in men's hearts, theaters are redundant.'[7] And Foucault, too, refers to this Rousseauan dream that motivated many of the revolutionaries: 'the dream of a transparent society, visible and legible in each of its parts, the dream of there no longer existing any zones of darkness'.[8]

In practice, of course, the 'heroes' turned out to be far from the ideal, as did 'the people'. Many had to be 'unmasked', as hypocrites and counter-revolutionaries. When Robespierre proclaimed that 'The most magnificent of all spectacles is that of a great people assembled', since 'Under the eyes of so many witnesses neither corruption, intrigue nor perfidy would dare show itself',[9] it is clear that this has to be an *enlightened* people. Constant vigilance was called for; the Revolution is menaced by the enemy within, those who *merely* play a role, for their own corrupt motives. And here the hypocrite becomes a crucial actor on the modern revolutionary stage. The hypocrite, who pretends to virtue, plays a role and identifies wholly with it; a victim of his own mendacity, he has eliminated his incorruptible self. His crime, suggests Hannah Arendt, is that he bears false witness against himself; he represents the 'vice of vices', since integrity can exist under the cover of all other vices save this: 'only the hypocrite is really rotten to the core'. Hence

> the unmasking of the hypocrite would leave nothing behind the mask, because the hypocrite is the actor himself in so far as he wears no mask. He pretends to *be* the assumed role, and when he enters the game of society it is without any play-acting whatsoever. In other words, what made the hypocrite so odious was that he claimed not only sincerity but naturalness, and what made him so dangerous . . . was that he instinctively could help himself to every 'mask' in the political theatre . . . as a contraption for deception.

So, in the end, how could one be sure of telling the hero from the hypocrite, when *both* abstain from play-acting? Ultimately undecidable, the pursuit of the hypocrite becomes potentially unending. Distrust and corruption are spread everywhere, and Arendt concludes that 'every effort to make goodness manifest in public ends with the appearance of crime and criminality on the public scene'.[10] And along with this, we find the probing of motives: if there can be no 'external' proof of hypocrisy, then pursuit of the hypocrite stands in need of validation by the hypocrite himself. Motives must be explored, interrogated, ultimately 'confessed'. . . . Motives become political factors, and the probing of motives part of the everyday politics of selfhood.

And Robespierre himself? On this logic, his life may have been a fraud anyway. Perhaps, as Trilling suggests, 'this most militantly sincere and single-minded of honest souls' was indeed, or became, a hypocrite, 'an actor, the leading player in a comedy of principle, perfidy, and blood'.[11] After all, he had himself admitted that he would prefer an illusion that united the people over a truth that failed to do so. . . .[12]

The long-term legacy of the Revolution is implicit in this idea that 'the people' cannot be taken for granted, that there is a sense in which they are yet to be created. The people had to be re-formed in the image of republican virtue. Here the Enlightenment project moves, via education, into the politicization of everyday life. The education of the public was, therefore, also a project of control. Hunt writes that 'By politicizing the everyday, the Revolution enormously increased the points from which power could be exercised, and multiplied the tactics and strategies for wielding that power.'[13] Thus it contributed to the growth of a class of politicians and intellectuals who would seek to reform the people, govern them on enlightened principles, and thereby exercise power *over* them.

This can be vividly instanced by the education law that was passed by the Convention in July 1793. Introducing it, Robespierre demanded the provision of schools for all children, at which attendance would be obligatory. The aim of this compulsory education would be the 'physical and moral formation of human beings'. In effect, these schools would be what are sometimes called 'total institutions': children would be confined there for the whole of their school years. In these schools, explained Robespierre, the children would be

> continually under the eye and in the hands of an active supervisor, with each hour being duly marked for sleep, eating, work, exercise, or rest; the whole regime of life will be invariably regulated . . . a wholesome and uniform regulation will affect every detail, and a constant and easy execution of the rules will guarantee good results.

The result would be a 'new race', who would be 'work-loving, orderly, disciplined, separated by an impenetrable wall from all polluting contacts with the prejudices of our old species'.[14] In short, a detailed supervision of young lives is fundamental to the production of citizens, and this in turn requires a massive programme of social intervention. We can see how Fehér can claim that the Jacobins created the 'social question' as the main problem for the revolution and the ensuing new social order.[15] And, remembering Robespierre's all-seeing eye, Foucault in turn claims that the Revolution 'establishes the unimpeded empire of the gaze',[16] with ramifications throughout the social system.

Constructing the Social Subject

Education is itself an arena in which these new strategies of power become most apparent. A factory inspector wrote, in 1837:

> To put the necessity of properly educating the children of the working class on its
> lowest footing, it is loudly called for as a matter of police, to prevent a multitude of
> immoral and vicious beings, the offspring of ignorance, from growing up around us,
> to be a pest and a nuisance to society; it is necessary in order to render the great body
> of the working class governable by reason.

Donald adds that for both right and left on the political spectrum, 'the provision
of welfare went hand in hand with the extension of surveillance and the gathering
of information – the strategy of policing families'.[17]

Clearly the term 'police' is crucial here. Rose suggests that it refers to 'policing
in the sense of a science, a knowledge and technique for producing and maintaining the good order of the population and of every person within it'.[18] This notion
of 'policing' emerges in the sixteenth and seventeenth centuries as an aspect of
good government; gradually, the 'theory of police' came to be a theory of the
objects on which state power should bear, the regulation of individuals and
populations through the promotion of health, efficiency and discipline.
Delamare's *Traité de la police*, 1705, included chapters on religion, morals, health
and roads;[19] and in the early nineteenth century, the reformer Jeremy Bentham
advocated the establishment of eight police departments, for the prevention of
offences, calamities and epidemics and for commerce, health, the poor, charity
and the collection of statistics.[20]

The government of populations and the government of the self were to go hand
in hand. 'Discipline' is the key notion here; Miller suggests that the term refers to
the way the modern West has sought 'to produce a knowledge which was also to
provide the basis for an ethics of personal conduct'.[21] Through 'normalisation',
discipline both subjects individuals to norms and makes them 'normal'. Generalizing over the period since the seventeenth century, Rose suggests that

> Discipline not only consists in a way of organising social life according to
> rational thought, exactitude and supervision, it also embraces a mode of personal
> existence within such practices. It entails a training in the minute arts of self-
> scrutiny, self-evaluation and self-regulation ranging from the control of the body,
> speech and movement in school, through the mental drill inculcated in school and
> university, to the Puritan practices of self-inspection and obedience to divine
> reason.[22]

Through discipline comes *self*-discipline, self-control, the heightened ability to
work purposively and diligently, the ability to become a *subject* through the
mastery and control of the self. Hence the significance of Foucault's claim that
power becomes *productive*: it is no longer primarily a matter of violence or prohibition, but about the constitution of the self as an active subject. Power is no longer
just external, it is internal too. In Foucault's words, 'The individual which power
has constituted is at the same time its vehicle.'[23] 'Policing' becomes both constitutive (of the self as subject) and regulatory (of the self as other, and the otherness
within): in the former sense, it becomes invisible, part of the dynamics of everyday

life; in the latter sense, it gains institutional embodiment in *the* police and in other, indirect organs of state power, such as psychiatry. Of the former dimension, Miller writes:

> In obtrusively supplying the place of the police in places where the police cannot be, the mechanisms of discipline seem to entail a relative *relaxation* of policing power. No doubt this manner of passing off the regulation of everyday life is the best manner of passing it on.

Suggesting that both dimensions can be seen operating in the novel, Miller points out that Fagin, the villain in *Oliver Twist*, reads the *Police Gazette*, and regularly betrays gang members to the police; delinquents, criminals and police live in an enclosed, self-reproducing world, separate from that of 'respectable' everyday life. And in the latter arena, it is the benevolent Mr Brownlow, needing a 'full account' of Oliver's activities, who is the manifestation of disciplinary power.[24] It is as though 'police' and 'policing' have become yoked together in a relation of mutual exclusion: 'police' can patrol the frontier because 'policing' has entered the very structure of the everyday.

When Foucault suggests a distinction between two modes of power – a binary mode, operating through exclusion, and a disciplinary mode – we can therefore see that they operate together in the modern world, although it is the second that has become more significant. He contrasts the medieval treatment of leprosy with the later strategies for coping with plague and cholera as follows:

> If it is true that the leper gave rise to rituals of exclusion . . . then the plague gave rise to disciplinary projects. Rather than the massive, binary division between one set of people and another, it called for . . . an organization in depth of surveillance and control, an intensification and a ramification of power . . . Underlying disciplinary projects the image of the plague stands for all forms of confusion and disorder; just as the image of the leper, cut off from all human contact, underlies projects of exclusion.[25]

These new disease-control strategies of central and local government involved the extension of the legal, political and economic regulation of life, through the definition and implementation of policies of quarantine, promotion of hygiene, supervision of burial, and systematic information-gathering, via police reports and social surveys. This involves not exclusion, but the elaboration of categories and distinctions, linked to the detailed supervision of particular areas, activities and groups. Developing this in the context of 'mental illness', Armstrong asserts that the old binary distinctions and exclusions (sanity/insanity, etc.) become mediated and modified by the development of the 'neuroses', which 'celebrated the ideal of a disciplined society in which all were analysed and distributed'.[26] We are *all* neurotic, in our various ways, after all; so an emphasis on 'neurosis' gives a slippery, evasive quality to 'mental disorders', simultaneously rendering them potentially widespread and making possible the further expansion of therapeutic intervention. Thus, concludes Rose, 'Selves who find choice meaningless and their identity constantly fading under inner and outer fragmentation are to be restored, through therapy, to unity and personal purpose.'[27]

This increasing awareness of 'the social' as an issue, a problem, can be seen in the way the sciences that evolved to constitute and study it were inherently interventionist, from the very beginning. They were intended to be contributions to public policy, instruments for the *shaping* of 'the social' as much as for its discovery. 'Discipline' and 'disciplines' are closely linked; both imply the intimate relation of knowledge and power. Medicine becomes an instrument of public policy as the promotion of 'health' becomes as important as the cure of disease; Comte and Durkheim saw sociology itself as contributing to the scientific betterment of society. Both of the major variants of the social politics of modernity – the emphasis on individual responsibility and the emphasis on social provision – rest on this underlying project, the construction of 'social health' as the central aim of policy; a 'regulation of bodies' in the interests of 'an abstract conception of health as a component of citizenship', in Turner's words.[28] And Hewitt points to the role of social policy in forming 'the social': 'It promotes and organises knowledge, norms and social practices to regulate the quality of life of the population – its health, security and stability', and gives birth to the central concerns of modern welfare, through notions of 'needs' and 'rights'.[29] With the nineteenth century, then, we find the first large-scale social surveys, a multiplication of hospitals, clinics and schools, growing government intervention in the regulation of private life and the beginnings of a welfare state, all geared to the anticipation of problems, the management of dissidence and the production of a tolerated social order; the combination of 'control' and 'caring' that characterizes what Donzelot calls the 'tutelary complex',[30] the family/education/social-work nexus.

The key element here is the family. Using the plague metaphor from Foucault, Armstrong writes that the 'enclosure and purification of the house produces a new household free from the taint of any unregulated intercourse with the world', and from 'the indiscriminate mingling of bodies'; hence 'households serve as magical spaces where people go to die in order that they may be reborn as modern individuals – enclosed and self-regulating'.[31] This concern with the family is revealed in medical activities: the development of inoculation and vaccination, stimulating medical interest in childhood generally; the theorization of sexuality and sex differences, particularly in reproduction; and the role of the medical profession as an influence on childcare and family life generally. Through medicine, claims Foucault, 'The family is assigned a linking role between general objectives regarding the good health of the social body and individuals' desire or need for care.'[32]

The family is important because it is constituted as the point of intersection between two major concerns: hygiene and reproduction. 'Hygiene' here means the positive promotion of health through physical and moral purity, the two not being clearly distinguished (as is still evident in contemporary reactions to AIDS). Through reproduction, sexuality emerged as intimately bound up with the politics of population control, via the nineteenth-century fascination with the need to produce a 'healthy' population by influencing fertility and class differences in reproduction rates, often spilling over into a concern with eugenics and 'racial purity'. Medicine could play an important role here because its emphasis on the confidentiality of the doctor–patient relationship permitted it to penetrate the 'private' world of family domesticity; even the secrets of the bedroom could be exposed to its gaze, and it played a crucial role in elaborating notions of sexual normality and deviance. Foucault shows how this 'discourse of sexuality' itself produces the 'problems' it claims to uncover.[33] That favourite nineteenth-century obsession, the 'masturbating child', for example, becomes a circular, self-validating model, to which actual children can be assimilated, thereby being both produced and reproduced as the subjects of the discourse, subjected to the practices associated with it. After all, if masturbation produces illness, the unwell child who denies masturbating does not thereby refute the model; it is well known that masturbation renders the child feckless and dishonest, so the 'refutation' becomes further evidence for the truth of the discourse. . . .

Discussing the politics of family intervention in the UK and France respectively, Rose and Donzelot bring out some of the gender and class aspects. Donzelot observes that the strategy of intervening in family life, since the later years of the nineteenth century, has rested mainly on the women, with mothers, in particular, being subjected to a barrage of literature and medical advice, and given new skills and powers.[34] Lynda Nead also points out that philanthropy developed as a mediation between family and state, giving a significant role to middle-class women, and thereby being a means of social control for the many and emancipation for some: 'one woman's emancipation can be another woman's subordination'.[35] The poor or 'problem' family becomes a missionary field; the working-class family must be regulated, through various forms of intervention and control, lest it contaminate society through 'bad hygiene' and general irresponsibility. Overall, concludes Turner, 'The family became the site where individuals are formed and trained' and where 'decentralized political power is to be located for the reform of populations'.[36]

That these concerns with reproduction and population are still with us, and central to the politics of medicalization, is apparent in this passage from a standard text, *Williams Obstetrics*, (1980 edition):

> The concept of the right of every child to be physically, mentally, emotionally 'well-born' is fundamental to human dignity. If obstetrics is to play a role in its realization, the speciality must maintain and even extend its role in the control of population. . . . This concept of obstetrics as a social as well as a biologic science impels us to accept a responsibility unprecedented in American medicine.[37]

Exploring the implications of this in more detail will enable us to clarify the links between disciplinary strategies and the construction of subjecthood as they have developed in one specific area, along with the controversies engendered.

In the 1860s, confinement in hospital seems to have been six times more dangerous than confinement at home, and these rates were only equalized by the

1920s. By the 1930s it was becoming fashionable in middle-class circles to have one's confinement in hospital, just as it would later become fashionable in those same circles to have it – or want to have it – at home. The hospital rapidly became the 'normal' place for childbirth: in the US the proportion of births occurring in hospital rose from a third in the 1930s to 99 per cent by 1977, and UK figures were similar. By the 1950s, medical control in this area had become all-powerful, and childbirth had increasingly been transformed into a technological drama in which the mother was the passive object of medical manipulation and surgical intervention. By the 1960s and 1970s this had engendered controversy even within medicine itself, with widespread questioning of the extensive use of Caesarean sections, and many women had become alienated from it and attracted to ideas of 'natural childbirth'.

This history conceals a significant shift that dates from around the mid-1940s: what Shorter calls 'the discovery of the foetus'.[38] From this period, greater knowledge about the unborn foetus could be used to rationalize greater medical control over women's bodies; the technology of 'foetal monitoring' makes it possible to survey the whole period of pregnancy, and thereby influence its whole course, through influencing the mother, rather than just intervening in childbirth itself. As Arney suggests, 'Every aspect of every woman's life is subject to the obstetrical gaze because every aspect of every individual is potentially important.' The battery of tests and monitors reinforces the sense that the boundary between the normal and abnormal is unclear, that all sorts of things can potentially go wrong, and that one can anyway maximize the prospects of success, for both mother and unborn child, through submission to this intensification of the 'clinical gaze'. The concept of 'foetal distress', which entered obstetrics in the 1940s, as the justification for medical intervention, had by the 1970s become totally obscure, but it no longer mattered, since the thorough surveillance of *all* pregnancies was now accepted practice.[39] And this surveillance was extended after birth, too. In the French case, Castel points out that by the 1970s a system was developed for the routine testing and screening of all infants in their first two years of life, and that this included the collection of extensive data on the mother. The occurrence of sufficient 'risk factors' would automatically lead to a visit from the relevant 'expert' (e.g. a social worker), even if there appeared to be nothing wrong with mother or infant.

This emphasis on 'risk factors' is significant; indeed, Castel suggests that it is 'factors', rather than individuals, that constitute the raw material of this 'systematic predetection'. There no longer have to be any obvious 'symptoms', it is enough to display 'whatever characteristics the specialists responsible for the definition of preventative policy have constituted as risk factors'.[40] Arney claims that

> After the 'normal' trajectory of a process is known and probability distributions of deviations from the 'norm' are constructed, each individual must be monitored, subjected to surveillance, and located precisely in terms of deviations on those probabilistic normalizing distributions. . . . Treatment schemes become lighter,

more individualized, more precise, more rapid, one might even say 'more humane', but management schemes become infinitely more effective means of control as well.[41]

This is consistent with the swing towards 'managing health', rather than just reacting to ill-health; and in this sense, *everyone* is in need of a 'management policy'. Castel spells out the implications:

> Instead of segregating and eliminating undesirable elements from the social body, or reintegrating them more or less forcibly through corrective or therapeutic interventions, the emerging tendency is to assign different social destinies to individuals in line with their varying capacity to live up to the requirements of competitiveness and profitability.

'Discipline' becomes more a matter of efficient performance than of conformity, of subjection to specialization and differentiation rather than similarity and uniformity.[42]

Within medicine itself – and the management of childbirth – this seems to point in two directions simultaneously. On the one hand, increasingly sophisticated and automated diagnostic testing seems to suggest the possible elimination of the doctor–patient relationship altogether; but on the other, the emphasis on the individual as necessarily involved, in an active way, in the management of health, would seem to permit the transformation of patient into 'experiencing subject' in a more thorough way than hitherto, as Arney and Bergen suggest:

> Medicine has been undergoing a transition in the structure of its discourse that not only allows the patient to speak as an experiencing person, but *needs, demands,* and *incites* him to speak. . . .
>   . . . both doctor and patient are compelled to speak with one another in a common language around which a field of power forms to govern them both. . . . By reformulating its field of power to be incorporative, medicine multiplies its paths for the expression of power, makes them finer, more penetrating, and farther reaching. . . .
>   Technologies of control and domination compel silence; technologies of monitoring and surveillance incite discourse.[43]

Hence, Arney can argue that 'natural childbirth' and the rejection of crude medical dominance is not inconsistent with this ongoing shift in medicine itself, and he points out that, in the US, obstetrics has been moving in this direction with 'surprising quickness'. The technology of monitoring is perfectly consistent with involvement by the woman as a partner in the childbirth process, with greater sensitivity to her wishes; but while this is an escape from the brutality of the old regime, it represents in some ways a further deepening of subjection, as her own desires, hopes and fears are articulated through this new, more sophisticated medical discourse.[44] But this whole idea of the role of 'discourse' in the subjectification of the self now needs further discussion.

Confessing the Self

Medieval spiritual management incorporated a role for individual conscience, the techniques for the application of moral rules, through casuistry, and the pastoral correction of error and confusion through the 'cure of souls'. These came together in the institution of confession. It was *sins* that had to be confessed, and sins were acts, externals of behaviour that contradicted the law (biblical or secular). Sins were the misdeeds of the flesh.

Gradually, however, the priests in the confessionals began to ask not just about the act as such, but about motives, intentions. One might say that increasingly sin became a matter of *talk*: it is through talk that one probes murky motives. We find the emergence of the idea that motives are deep and obscure, as are the roots of the sexuality that is so often involved in sinfulness. And while the 'cure of souls' is formally rejected by Protestantism, the fascination with the idea of the self as a maelstrom of complex, interior drives and motives is, if anything, increased. Motives become central to the construction of self-identity; it might be said that the modern self emerges as something that has to be 'confessed'. And the decline of the religious confessional itself nevertheless goes hand in hand with the spread of the confessional mode of self-construction into other areas. 'Western man has become a confessing animal', claims Foucault, who has been mainly responsible for developing this analysis: 'The confession is a ritual of discourse in which the speaking subject is also the subject of the statement; it is also a ritual which unfolds within a power relationship.'[45] In confessing, one is subjectified by another, while simultaneously constituting oneself, so that, in Rose's words, confession is 'the diagram of a certain form of subjectification that binds us to others at the very moment we affirm our identity'.[46]

By the eighteenth century, we encounter the emergence of the modern self as an object of self-examination, at the same time being exposed to public scrutiny, the gaze of the other; and, also, the further development of the confessional mode of creating the self, through writing it. Rousseau's own *Confessions* provide interesting evidence both of this project and of the paradoxes to which it leads.

Rousseau asserts his wish 'to reveal myself absolutely to the public'; in doing this, 'Nothing about me must remain hidden or obscure. I must remain incessantly beneath its gaze.'[47] But this is not, it transpires, a straightforward venture. The act of writing both creates and affirms the self it purports to describe. 'Rousseau confesses in order to justify his existence', claims Gutman. 'He would constitute a self, in writing, as he feels his self to be.'[48] Yet Rousseau is himself aware of these threats to the integrity of his project. He writes: 'No one can write the life of a man but himself, but in writing it he disguises it . . . he shows himself as he wants to be seen.'[49] The self rationalizes itself in its very inability to grasp itself reflexively, imposing an order as it struggles to recognize itself as the self it wants to be. The rational ideal of the project of the self is summarized thus by Rose:

The self is not merely enabled to choose, but obliged to construe a life in terms of its choices, its powers, and its values. Individuals are expected to construe the course of their life as the outcome of such choices, and to account for their lives in terms of the reasons for those choices . . . the norm of autonomy secretes, as its inevitable accompaniment, a constant and intense self-scrutiny, a continual evaluation of our personal experiences, emotions, and feelings in relation to images of satisfaction, the necessity to narrativize our lives in a vocabulary of interiority. The self that is liberated is obliged to live its life tied to the project of its own identity.[50]

Rousseau's significance is that he presents us with the modern, questing, dissatisfied self which, in its relentless pursuit of self-identity, becomes a product of fashion, fantasy and desire, and which, in trying to emancipate itself through self-consciousness, at best succeeds in imposing an artificial and improbable unity on the otherness within, a recognition of its 'self' that can only ever be a fantasy construct. The self can only ever grasp itself through images, wishes and memories that conceal as much as they reveal. And hence the notorious paradox of Rousseau's own personal odyssey, the obsessive search for an honesty that never escapes transparent dishonesty and special pleading. And this fate always threatens one who seeks 'To Be That Self Which One Truly Is', to quote the aim of the 'client-centred therapy' of Carl Rogers, one of the 'alternative' therapies so fashionable since the 1960s.[51]

Constituting the self through confessing it, narrating it, therefore encounters problems of reflexivity. Revealing the self, representing it through writing, also masks it, threatens its self-identity through theatricality. Rousseau's writing, suggests Marshall, 'always puts him in the paradoxical position of revealing and concealing himself; he must write and hide himself simultaneously'. Indeed, 'writing in which meaning is hidden offers the only language of revelation or confession', since 'The self reproduced in autobiography must be both imaged and imagined: seen at several removes.'[52] Ultimately, the threat of theatricality must be countered by self-discipline. Hence this detour through the self has brought us back to the self as subject, for 'confessing the self' is always to subject the self to the gaze of the other, indeed makes it other; and constituting the self as a fantasized unity, imposing a coherence on it, also makes it a product of discipline. After all, as we have seen, the self has to meet standards. Armstrong suggests that disciplinary power makes us afraid of ourselves: 'Believing in the presence of a self that is essentially subversive, we keep watch over ourselves – in mirrors, on clocks, on scales'.[53]

The idea of the self as intractable to its own self-analysis, together with the imperative to self-revelation through confession, provides the ground within which psychoanalysis can flourish. For Foucault, it is above all psychoanalysts who replace priests, who develop the theory and practice of selfhood as necessitating endless probing through discourse, entailing a 'talking cure' that, whether or not it ever actually cures anybody of anything, certainly fits in with the modern idea that the self is something that must be talked about, indeed perhaps only exists through being talked about. In probing dreams and fantasies, psychoanalysis disciplines them, constitutes them as aspects of the lives of subjects, again showing a fusion of understanding and control, knowledge and power. Weeks suggests that psychoanalysis is 'both the discoverer of the mechanism of desire and the organiser of its control';[54] though perhaps one might say that the constitution of sexuality as an object of theory and therapy is *already* an exercise in its control.

In confessional mode, sexuality itself is reconstructed. It becomes a matter of mind as much as body; the scope of the sexual increases to include thoughts, fantasies and dreams and includes them even if they are not ostensibly 'sexual' at all. The mysterious interiority of the modern self is comprehensively sexualized and further spatialized through the language of drives, repressions and the unconscious: as Foucault suggests, '"sexuality" is far more of a positive product of power than power was ever repression of sexuality'.[55] The 'repression' or 'prohibition' of sexuality is simply one mode of its production as a key, even *the* key, to modern identity. He concludes:

> It is at the junction of these two ideas – that we must not deceive ourselves concerning our sex, and that our sex harbours what is most true in ourselves – that psychoanalysis has rooted its cultural vigour. It promises us at the same time our sex, our true sex, and that whole truth about ourselves which secretly keeps vigil in it.[56]

Hutton accurately remarks that, for Foucault, 'Theories of the self are a kind of currency through which power over the mind is defined and extended.' And ultimately, there can be no final point, no secure ground, in the search for self-identity. The search is endless, if endlessly fascinating, for the goal is a chimera. As Hutton concludes:

> The quest for self-understanding is a journey without end. Even in the deepest recesses of our psyches there are no experiences which, if evoked, will reveal our true identities . . . we are condemned to a quest for meaning whose meaning is that our human nature is continually being reconstituted by the forms that we create along the way.[57]

The Panoptic Gaze

Disciplinary power produces the active involvement of subjects in their own subjectification, through the subordination of life to project, through the narrative structure of selfhood, and through the normative imperatives of the confessional. But there is another strand in this, implicit at times in the above discussion: the idea of *surveillance*, of the visibility of the subject, of subjection through the gaze, of a surveillance that is internalized as an important element in self-monitoring. Sennett comments on the development of 'silent observation as a principle of public order' in the nineteenth century,[58] an age which saw the emergence of the mass public, the 'disciplined crowd'; and these links between visibility and self-regulation need further investigation.[59]

Foucault presents the rise of the prison, in the nineteenth century, as important in contributing to the rise of modern forms of power – incorporating surveillance – in social institutions more generally, but also as a metaphor for modern power itself, in its diffuse omnipresence. Foucault begins his major work on this theme, *Discipline and Punish*, with a lengthy and gruesome eye-witness account of the prolonged torture, mutilation and death of Damiens, who had attempted to assassinate the French king, in 1756. The major point is that punishment was made into a spectacle; power *existed* through spectacle. The hideous death of Damiens was witnessed by an immense public, and that was fundamental to it. Power existed through its public exhibition; the spectacle organized the glorification of the monarch through the sacrificial degradation of the victim. Sovereign power was organized round the visibility of the monarch; here, it is the centre that is illuminated, while the periphery is in darkness, or only picked out in the light reflected from the centre. Power is public, and its source alone is fully visible. And if, within just a few decades, the fate of Damiens will come to be seen as barbaric, that is to a considerable extent because the prison, as the new form of punishment, is also a carrier of the new principle of disciplinary power, incorporating a new form of surveillance.

Punishment is not now displayed in public; it is hidden away, in the institution. But although the prisoners are invisible to the wider society, they are ever-visible to the controlling authorities in the prison. It is *they*, the prisoners, who are illuminated now, not those who have power over them. And through this surveillance, discipline can be inculcated, along with self-discipline; in this sense, the prison regime becomes another aspect of the workings of disciplinary power, as outlined here by Foucault:

> He who is subjected to a field of visibility, and who knows it, assumes responsibility for the constraints of power; he makes them play spontaneously upon himself; he inscribes in himself the power relation in which he simultaneously plays both roles; he becomes the principle of his own subjection.[60]

And this is what Foucault refers to as panopticism.

The panopticon itself was a prison design put forward by the utilitarian philosopher Bentham. It featured a circular building around a central control tower. This central tower would command a view of every prison cell, for the cells would be arranged, in tiers, in the circular building around the tower, each cell being entirely open to observation from the tower itself. In theory it would be possible for one person in the tower to observe every prisoner in the building. Bentham did not intend to restrict panopticism to prisons; he saw it as a useful principle for the organization of workshops, barracks, schools and hospitals. In Bentham's own words, the principle was that of '*seeing without being seen*', so that at every instant the inmate, 'seeing reason to believe as much, and not being able to satisfy himself to the contrary, he should *conceive* himself "to be under inspection" '.[61] In short:

There was of course no way of knowing whether you were being watched at any given moment. How often, or on what system, the Thought Police plugged in on any individual wire was guesswork. It was even conceivable that they watched everybody all the time. But at any rate they could plug in your wire whenever they wanted to. You had to live – did live, from habit that became instinct – in the assumption that every sound you made was overheard, and . . . every movement scrutinized.

This passage is actually from George Orwell's *Nineteen Eighty-Four*,[62] but it seems to encapsulate the spirit of Bentham's panopticism quite vividly. As does this:

The Eye: that horrible growing sense of a hostile will that strove with great power to pierce all shadows of cloud, and earth, and flesh, and to see you: to pin you under its deadly gaze, naked, immovable. . . .
  And suddenly he felt the Eye. . . . It leaped towards him. . . . Very soon it would nail him down, know just exactly where he was. . . .

After all, the evil Sauron, of *Lord of the Rings*,[63] whose all-seeing Eye this is, surveys his cowed kingdom from inside the top of a tall tower-like fortress. . . . But this obviously raises a problem. Whatever the status of panopticism as a utopian or nightmare project of the future, is it helpful as a metaphor of the present? Does it capture an aspect of the subjection of the self in the daily processes of life? Or is it rather a form of paranoia, not uncommon either in everyday conversation or in some stands of left-wing politics – the idea that 'they' are always watching?

At this everyday level, there are clearly good grounds for thinking that we live in a 'society of surveillance'. Military surveillance technology is now in use on the street; car-park and city-centre surveillance becomes ever more widespread and sophisticated. The American Sonitrol bugging system is now in use in over two hundred schools in the UK, and a system for domestic use is available. Cars and people can be electronically tagged. Companies set up elaborate databases on target populations, and charge cards enable supermarkets to build up detailed 'consumer profiles' on specific customers. Even if Foucault is paranoid, it doesn't follow that they aren't watching us. . . . But there is another side to this; the 'power' involved is by no means homogeneous. For under £10, a device can be bought that enables you to listen in on a whispered conversation at up to a hundred feet away. So 'you' and 'I' can be part of the 'they'. We can all be watchers and watched. After all, two-way baby monitors, very useful for detecting a baby's cries in another room, are basically just bugs; when bugging enters everyday life, it can have many uses, not all of them dependent on the power structure. It can also, indeed, have anti-establishment political uses. 'Scanners', who eavesdrop on radio and telephone conversations, have intercepted White House calls, and have revealed data the authorities wanted covered up, like the 1984 episode when a Russian submarine went down off Bermuda. In this sense, a 'society of surveillance' need not imply an all-seeing 'Big Brother'.[64]

Being both watchers and watched: this also suggests a kind of democracy of panopticism in everyday life, turning it against itself. After all, 'looking' and 'being looked at' have considerable resonance in our culture. Hebdige observes that subculture 'forms up in the space between surveillance and the evasion of surveillance, it translates the fact of being under scrutiny into the pleasure of being watched. It is a hiding in the light.'[65] While this will be further explored later, particularly in connection with fashion, it nevertheless implies that being 'open to the gaze' can transform panopticism into a kind of reflexive playfulness, rather than a sense of onerous subjection; theatricality as an appropriation of vision and visibility, a revenge of life on the disciplinary project.

Another point is implied by Martin Jay, in his claim that the object of power is 'everywhere penetrated by the benevolently sadistic gaze of a diffuse and anonymous power, whose actual existence soon becomes superfluous to the process of discipline'. It is really the subject's self-subjection that is crucial here: 'the psychological dependence of the ideological "I" on the totalizing gaze of the "eye"', as Jay adds.[66] Donald therefore suggests that '*Self*-monitoring is the key to Foucault's conception of panopticism.'[67] It is the 'inner eye' that is crucial; self-control through reflexive self-observation. For Ewald, visibility 'has no source other than those whom it makes visible, thus visible to themselves'.[68] If the 'panoptic gaze' is useful for understanding the construction of modern selfhood, it is because it ultimately subverts the necessity for the actual existence of the all-seeing power that is its alleged source; the panopticon becomes Foucault's 'myth of origin'.

We thereby return to paranoia, in a position to present it as an appropriate and significant product of the modern experience of selfhood. Through self-surveillance, we attempt a panoptic grasp of self that can only succeed through the self becoming other to itself; surveillance is always by and of the other. Through reflexive self-awareness, we project self into other as all-seeing observer; and the result can be a paradoxical world, paranoid yet solipsistic, with the simultaneous inflation and diminution of the self as centre of experience, menaced by 'the gaze' it has itself projected. The other is no longer there as a presence but is omnipresent as fear, a principle of surveillance. One cannot relate to otherness, only submit to it, be subject to it – but it cannot be known to be there, save as a presupposition of one's own subjecthood. The panopticon itself is the imagination of panopticism: a nightmare product of the paranoid imagination of modernity, implicit in the construction of selfhood through the 'reflexive gaze'. And like all good nightmares, one cannot be sure it isn't real. . . .

Power, Domination and Citizenship

The notion of 'power' that has been developed in this discussion is clearly not a narrowly political one. Power is a feature of everyday life, of the ongoing constitution of subjects, and Foucault can claim that 'Power is everywhere; not because it embraces everything, but because it comes from everywhere.'[69] Hence, modern power

> categorizes the individual, marks him by his own individuality, attaches him to his own identity. . . . It is a form of power which makes individuals subjects. There are two meanings of the word *subject*: subject to someone else by control and dependence, and tied to his own identity by a conscience or self-knowledge. Both meanings suggest a form of power which subjugates and makes subject to.

This power to 'make' individuals operates through discipline, whereby individuals become both objects and vehicles of power. And as we have seen, modern 'pastoral power' cannot be exercised without knowing 'the inside of people's minds, without exploring their souls, without making them reveal their innermost secrets'; it has a confessional dimension.[70]

And can these subjects be citizens, active participants in the social and political order? Can freedom be consistent with subjecthood? After all, a citizen is supposed to have rights and freedoms, yet the emphasis on 'producing' or 'constructing' citizens seems to imply being passive, controlled, shaped to a specification. And as we know, if the French Revolution inaugurated the politics of modernity, it did so in a thoroughly ambiguous way; its legacy seems as much to do with totalitarianism as with democracy. This dual heritage seems to have been implicit from the start, and becomes explicit in Robespierre: only the virtuous can be citizens, and although human virtue should stand revealed once old forms are swept away, in practice this requires intensive education, even indoctrination. Other desirable features, such as freedom of speech, clearly become subordinate to the production of the citizen, as embodiment of republican virtue. One is reminded of the famous utterance of Rousseau, that mankind has to be 'forced to be free'. And at times the forcing may be more apparent than the freedom.

From Robespierre to Bentham seems a short step; the vision of the panopticon appears to be inherent in this, the totalitarian version of the project. There is one shift of emphasis: from 'virtue' to 'happiness', as the policy goal. The idealized, utilitarian version of this is spelt out by Bauman:

> With a modicum of effort one can read the *Panopticon* as a parable for *the society at large* – a viable society, an orderly society, a society without crime and with non-cooperation easily spotted and dealt with, a society which seeks actively the highest benefit and greatest happiness of its members.

Such a society 'carefully classifies its members into categories', thus offering them 'differing measures of freedom and unfreedom' so as to suit 'the smooth working of the whole, and hence everybody's happiness'.[71] And it is a commonplace of the contemporary political situation in the West that the progressive rhetoric of this model is seen as inherently illusory, a cover for totalitarianism, and is rejected as the complete antithesis of the liberal tradition of free citizenship and political democracy.

It is therefore tempting to ask whether the collapse of monolithic communism in Eastern Europe in 1989 finally resolves the question of the 'two legacies'; whether liberal – democratic capitalism indeed represents the conclusive victory of the 'freedom' alternative. The claim that this is so has indeed been implicit in the triumphalist rhetoric of Western politicians in the years since then. And Bronislaw Geremek, one of the leading activists of the Solidarity movement in Poland, claimed in 1990 that we are indeed witnessing a process in which 'subjects' are transformed into 'citizens', implying a sharp distinction between totalitarianism, with its 'subjects', and democracy with its 'citizens'.

These are big issues, and it would be absurd to attempt to resolve them here. But in the light of the above discussion, it can be suggested that the rigid duality of 'totalitarianism' and 'democracy' is in certain respects naive, and that the ambiguous legacy of the French Revolution cannot be dispelled so easily. The dualistic model sets up a timeless notion of 'totalitarianism' which can be contrasted with the 'democracy' that is the real essence of modernity; but there are clearly grounds for revising this. In particular, it can be suggested that modern totalitarianism is not simply an instance of some ahistorical, universal potential for 'dictatorship'; that this modern totalitarianism is continuous with democracy, while yet distinct from it; and that the central feature they share is a mode of constructing the political individual as both subject *and* citizen. The two categories – 'subject' and 'citizen' – are not, therefore, mutually exclusive.

Some ideas of Václav Havel – who was himself heavily involved in the dramatic events in Eastern Europe – are useful for approaching this.[72] He distinguishes between 'dictatorship' or 'totalitarianism' on the one hand, and what he calls 'post-totalitarianism' on the other. The first refers essentially to a regime that is based on force, and need not give much attention to questions of its own legitimacy. This seems to be close to what Foucault calls 'domination', which occurs when relations of power 'find themselves firmly set and congealed'; such a state of domination is incompatible with freedom.[73] And Havel's point is that while there were, of course, elements of this in the communist regimes of the East – rather more than elements, one might think, in the case of Ceausescu's Romania – those regimes cannot usefully be subsumed under that model. Rather, they were forms of 'post-' or 'modern' totalitarianism. While clearly not democratic, they rested on a degree of passive consent, or at least acquiescence, partly because of their emphasis on the 'welfare provision' aspects of citizenship.

These regimes are not best seen as having been dictatorships by one group (or individual) over others. They were not really 'run' by anybody; the bureaucrats *operated* them, but were under as many constraints as everyone else. The system served people, but only to the extent necessary to ensure that they served it. Crucial is Havel's observation that 'everyone in his or her own way is both a victim and a supporter of the system . . . it draws everyone into the sphere of power'. The fault-line ran *within* the individual, as it were; each individual was part of the system and perpetuated it, but also suffered from it, and this could come out in ambiguous or contradictory political attitudes, or a blasé indifference. If a green-grocer put the conventional 'Workers of the world, unite!' slogan in the window, among the vegetables, he was probably hardly aware that he did it, and his customers would hardly notice its presence.

Havel suggests that this is not so different from what happens in the West. He writes: 'the automatism of the post-totalitarian system is merely an extreme version of the global automatism of technological civilization'. While it is true that, in the West, 'people are manipulated in ways that are infinitely more subtle and refined', these ways are not *fundamentally* different.[74] Furthermore, if 'domination' occurs to some extent in any regime, the West would be no exception, as anyone who has experienced the tyrannies of petty bureaucrats or police will testify; nor can power and domination be completely distinct anyway, in practice. In short, Havel – along with Foucault – seems to suggest that freedom and subjection are not incompatible.

Exploring this further reveals that there are tensions within the notion of citizenship itself. On the one hand, it involves the development of both individuality and of 'individualism' as an ideology; but there is also 'social' citizenship, which grows out of the idea of equality of rights of citizens, including rights to welfare provision, and which entails bureaucratic intervention. Turner argues that 'in order to provide services on a universalistic basis, the state intervenes in society and the result is a bureaucratic individuation of the individual'. This 'individuation' uses standardized, formal criteria to subject individuals to bureaucratic registration, categorization and examination, and hence it can be seen as a danger to privacy and freedom. One might say that it is this individuation that makes possible the 'personalized letter', sent – by business or government – 'uniquely' to you. Yet, this very example shows how such individuation can at the same time permit the full flowering of 'individuality', through providing opportunities otherwise denied. Turner usefully summarizes the implications of this:

> At least we should recognize the paradox of individuation. First, it makes the social and political surveillance of large numbers of people possible; it is thus obviously a threat to individual autonomy. This is the Orwellian version of individuation as the obliteration of personal difference. Secondly, individuation provides a uniform basis for individual development and contributes to the creativity and individuality of the person. . . . The paradox is that capitalism develops individualism while also requiring individuation; individualism is an oppositional critique of public surveillance, while individuation is the necessary basis for the surveillance of subjects as citizens.[75]

Thus, citizenship both promotes the freedom of individualism and the subjection of individuation, and this is an important aspect of what Foucault means in his claim that 'Power is exercised only over free subjects, and only insofar as they are free.'[76]

Freedom entails both self-discipline and self-empowerment, and these do not coexist comfortably, for one implies 'freedom through constraint' and the other, 'freedom from constraint'. The first always raises the problem of how freedom is to be known and experienced as such, for how can I be sure that the constraints are necessary to my goals, and that my goals are indeed *mine*? So it becomes tempting to 'test' freedom through asserting dissent; hence Pizzorno's claim that freedom exists when 'contestation, unruliness, indocility, intractability are not yet abolished, when the recalcitrant is not transformed into the dutiful',[77] and Foucault's suggestion that power always entails the possibility of resistance.[78]

Yet the commonplace alternative to which we have been driven, freedom as freedom from constraint, is no less paradoxical. Firstly, lack of constraint merely becomes another imperative, another pressure, hence another constraint; critiques of permissiveness and 'sexual liberation' point out that whatever the advantages, there is a sense in which the new doctrines are as much exercises in discipline as the old. And secondly, there is the myth of the individual as charismatic creator of its own world, 'naturally' able to choose its own, uniquely appropriate goals, recognized and known as such. In practice, of course, these 'freely chosen' goals tend to be those of the fashions of the time. And the 'unbounded' individual, free of constraints, desperately seeks the experience of those very constraints, the sense of limits, without which identity is inconceivable anyway.

The modern sense of the possibilities of freedom thus rests on a distinctive set of assumptions about selfhood, rationality and project, which in turn suggest the inseparability of freedom and subjection. Essential here is the notion of project itself, implying rationally selected means to chosen goals, within given constraints. And in practice, it is situations where this very notion of 'project' can be questioned, attacked, played with, transformed through drama, that permit experiences of 'freedom' that partially, at least, break through this structure of assumptions. . . .

It is tempting to end by going forward 200 years from the French Revolution, and changing cities: Paris, 1789 to Prague, 1989. Here we encounter popular politics as theatre: a powerful totalitarian regime that nevertheless turns out to be make-believe, and can be swept away in a make-believe revolution in which no one bears arms and no one gets killed; a revolution in which actors play the leading roles, for it was the closure of the Prague theatres, in protest at the regime, that brought the crowds on to the streets, and the actors helped mobilize public opinion, fanning out from the capital into the towns and villages; and a revolution in which it turns out that the leading actor in the drama, Havel, was a playwright.[79] The demonstrating crowds carried bells and jangling keys, to 'ring out the clowns', ridiculing the power structure, and affirming their belief in the make-believe. An actor carried a placard reading 'Would you sell your soul by not acting now?'; and another claimed that 'from the first day of our revolution it appeared on a stage, the platform of real life', suggesting that popular politics can only exist through a fusion of life and theatre. If the 'Velvet Revolution' was an affirmation of freedom, it was through this delayed repudiation of Robespierre's politics of virtue, a revenge of theatricality on project. . . .

Notes

1   D. Outram, *The Body and the French Revolution* (Yale University Press, 1989), pp. 79–80, 100.
2   N. Parker, *Portrayals of Revolution* (Harvester, 1990), p. 50.
3   Cited in B. Barber, 'Rousseau and Brecht: Political Virtue and the Tragic Imagination', in B. Barber and M. McGrath (eds.) *The Artist and Political Vision* (Transaction Books, 1982), p. 9.
4   J. Butwin, 'The French Revolution as *Theatrum Mundi*', *Research Studies* (1975), 43: 3, p. 144.
5   M. Iversen, 'Imagining the Republic: The Sign and Sexual Politics in France', in P. Hulme and L. Jordanova (eds.) *The Enlightenment and Its Shadows* (Routledge, 1990), p. 122.
6   L. Hunt, *Politics, Culture and Class in the French Revolution* (California University Press, 1984), pp. 45, 107, 107.
7   J. Starobinski, *The Invention of Liberty* (Rizzoli, 1987), p. 101.
8   M. Foucault, 'The Eye of Power', in his *Power/Knowledge: Selected Interviews and Other Writings* (Pantheon, 1980), p. 152.
9   Butwin, 'French Revolution', pp. 143, 145.
10 H. Arendt, *On Revolution* (Penguin, 1973), pp. 103, 107–8, 98.
11 L. Trilling, *Sincerity and Authenticity* (Oxford University Press, 1972), p. 69.
12 Parker, *Portrayals*, p. 29.
13 Hunt, *Politics, Culture and Class*, p. 56.
14 Cited in Z. Bauman, 'On the Origins of Civilisation', in *Theory, Culture and Society* (1985), 2:3, p. 11.
15 F. Fehér, *The Frozen Revolution: An Essay on Jacobinism* (Cambridge University Press, 1987), p. 134.
16 M. Foucault, *The Birth of the Clinic* (Tavistock, 1973), p. 39.
17 J. Donald, *Sentimental Education* (Verso, 1992), pp. 22–3, 28.
18 N. Rose, *Governing the Soul: The Shaping of the Private Self* (Routledge, 1989), p. 221.
19 See M. Foucault, 'The Political Technology of Individuals', in L. Martin et al., *Technologies of the Self* (Massachusetts University Press, 1988), pp. 162, 153.
20 M. Hewitt, 'Bio-Politics and Social Policy: Foucault's Account of Welfare', in M. Featherstone et al., *The Body* (Sage, 1991), p. 238.
21 P. Miller, *Domination and Power* (Routledge, 1987), p. 200.
22 Rose, *Governing the Soul*, p. 222.
23 M. Foucault, 'Two Lectures', in *Power/Knowledge*, p. 98.
24 D. Miller, 'The Novel and the Police', *Glyph* (1981), p. 137 and passim.
25 M. Foucault, *Discipline and Punish* (Peregrine, 1979), pp. 198–9.
26 D. Armstrong, *Political Anatomy of the Body* (Cambridge University Press, 1983), p. 22.
27 Rose, *Governing the Soul*, p. 228.
28 B. Turner, *Medical Power and Social Knowledge* (Sage, 1987), p. 225.
29 Hewitt, 'Bio-Politics', pp. 225, 229.
30 J. Donzelot, *The Policing of Families* (Hutchinson, 1980), ch. 4.

31 N. Armstrong, 'Some Call it Fiction: On the Politics of Domesticity', in J. F. MacCannell (ed.) *The Other Perspective in Gender and Culture* (Columbia University Press, 1990), pp. 65, 67, 66.

32 M. Foucault, 'The Politics of Health', in P. Rabinow (ed.) *The Foucault Reader* (Peregrine, 1986), p. 281.

33 M. Foucault, *The History of Sexuality, Vol. I: Introduction* (Penguin, 1979).

34 Donzelot, *Policing*, p. 40.

35 L. Nead, *Myths of Sexuality* (Blackwell, 1988), p. 197.

36 B. Turner, *The Body and Society* (Blackwell, 1984), p. 162.

37 Cited in W. R. Arney, *Power and the Profession of Obstetrics* (Chicago University Press, 1982), p. xi.

38 E. Shorter, *A History of Women's Bodies* (Penguin, 1984), p. 39 and passim; and Arney, *Power*.

39 Arney, *Power*, pp. 153, 85, 139.

40 R. Castel, 'From Dangerousness to Risk', in G. Burchell et al., *The Foucault Effect* (Harvester, 1991), p. 288.

41 Arney, *Power*, p. 89.

42 Castel, 'From Dangerousness to Risk', pp. 294, 295.

43 W. R. Arney and B. J. Bergen, *Medicine and the Management of Living* (Chicago University Press, 1984), pp. 46, 169, 170.

44 Arney, *Power*, pp. 216, 230, 236.

45 Foucault, *History of Sexuality*, pp. 59, 61.

46 Rose, *Governing the Soul*, p. 240.

47 J.-J. Rousseau, *Confessions* (Penguin, 1975), p. 65.

48 H. Gutman, 'Rousseau's *Confessions*: A Technology of the Self', in Martin, *Technologies*, p. 105.

49 Rousseau, *Confessions* (French edition), cited by D. Marshall in 'Rousseau and the State of Theater', *Representations* (1986), 13, p. 105.

50 Rose, *Governing the Soul*, pp. 227, 254.

51 C. Rogers, *On Being a Person* (Constable, 1961), ch. 8.

52 Marshall, 'Rousseau', pp. 107, 107, 109.

53 Armstrong, *Political Anatomy*, p. 69.

54 J. Weeks, *Sexuality and its Discontents* (Routledge, 1985).

55 Foucault, 'Two Lectures', p. 120.

56 M. Foucault, Introduction to *Herculine Barbin* (Harvester, 1980), p. xi.

57 P. Hutton, 'Foucault, Freud and the Technologies of the Self', in Martin, *Technologies*, pp. 135, 140.

58 R. Sennett, *The Fall of Public Man* (Faber, 1986), p. 126.

59 See T. Bennett, 'The Exhibitionary Complex', *New Formations* (1988), 4.

60 Foucault, *Discipline*, pp. 202–3.

61 Cited in Z. Bauman, *Freedom* (Open University Press, 1988), pp. 14, 15.

62 G. Orwell, *Nineteen Eighty-Four* (Penguin, 1954), p. 6.

63 J. R. Tolkien, *Lord of the Rings* (Unwin, 1983), pp. 656, 421.

64 J. McClellan, 'Who's Bugging Who?', *i-D* (December 1990), p. 87.

65 D. Hebdige, *Hiding in the Light* (Routledge, 1988), p. 35.

66 M. Jay, 'In the Empire of the Gaze: The Denigration of Vision in 20th Century French Thought', in L. Appignanesi (ed.) *Postmodernism* (Free Association Books, 1989), pp. 68–9, 52.

67   Donald, *Sentimental Education*, p. 19.

68   F. Ewald, 'A Power Without an Exterior', in *Michel Foucault: Philosopher* (Harvester, 1992), p. 172.

69   Foucault, *History of Sexuality*, p. 93.

70   M. Foucault, 'Subject and Power', Afterword to H. Dreyfus and P. Rabinow, *Michel Foucault: Beyond Structuralism and Hermeneutics* (Harvester, 1982), pp. 212, 214.

71   Bauman, *Freedom*, pp. 19, 20.

72   V. Havel, *Living in Truth* (Faber, 1987).

73   M. Foucault, 'The Ethic of Care for the Self as a Practice of Freedom', in J. Bernauer and D. Rasmussen (eds.) *The Final Foucault* (MIT Press, 1988), p. 3.

74   Havel, *Living*, pp. 53, 52, 115, 116.

75   B. Turner, *Citizenship and Capitalism* (Allen and Unwin, 1986), pp. 132, 122, 132–3.

76   Foucault, 'Subject and Power', p. 221.

77   A. Pizzorno, 'Foucault and the liberal view of the individual', in Ewald, *Michel Foucault: Philosopher*, p. 207.

78   Foucault, 'Ethic of care', p. 12.

79   See J. Sweeney, 'Fairytales in Prague', *The Face* (February 1990), p. 17.

3 Street People:

The City as Experience, Dream and Nightmare

The city is where modernity happens; it is also where modernism happens. In the city, modernity imposes itself as project, but the city is also where the experience and consciousness of modernity coexist uneasily with this, collide with it, challenging our ability to 'represent' this modernity that we are immersed in. Separate aspects of the city both coalesce and pull apart: the city is rational project, and the excess of theatricality; it is pleasure and danger, a site of moral conflict; fragmented, yet interconnected, monolithic, yet heterogeneous; masculine and feminine. It is a place of fluidity and diversity, rather than rootedness and community, yet simultaneously reproduces communities within itself.

In order to survey the implications of the urban experience, the very essence of the modern project must be suspended, so that the city can be explored in its richness, through creative appropriation and passive absorption; this cannot be done by a one-dimensional imposition of 'rational sense'. The city diffuses everywhere, its focus is nowhere; a book on modernity is implicitly about the city, in every chapter, yet there can hardly not be a chapter on the city, so what is left to write about? Yet 'writing the city' has been one of the main arenas for the exercise of the modern imagination; indeed, the experience of the city, grasped or transformed in the writing, has been formative of this imagination. The city furnishes us with the imaginative framework of the modern experience: it is a modern exercise of the 'savage mind', operating through the dualisms that both capture that experience and constitute it *as* experience; it is a condition of the modern experience that can hardly be grasped *in* experience, yet forces one to make the attempt. This imagination works through the use of space and time to synthesize the transient, the impressions of passing life; yet space and time are part of this passage, a framework that can never be stable.

But we must start further back. What *is* the modern city, and why does it pose these challenges? 'The city' is not, after all, necessarily modern. Some ancient cities were, indeed, very large. But they were relatively isolated; they were political and trading centres in the middle of peasant societies, and had little impact on their surrounding areas. The modern city, on the other hand, has been an engine of change and a channel for the transformation of social life. The extent of urban growth has indeed been staggering. By 1851, Britain had become the first country in the world with an urban population that had reached the 50 per cent mark; France and Germany were still a long way behind. In the UK, the proportion of the population in big cities went from 8 per cent to 40 per cent during the century; the population of London rose from one million to nearly seven million, Paris from half a million to nearly three million, Berlin from under 200,000 to two million, and New York from 60,000 to over four and a half million.[1] And the process has continued throughout the world: at the beginning of this century, only a dozen cities had populations of a million or more, London being easily the largest; by the year 2000 there may be 500, some with populations of over 20 million.[2]

Whatever else can be said about it, modernity has clearly been a civilization of the urban – a formulation that points in several directions, reminding us as it does that 'civilization', 'civility' and 'city' have the same root etymologically.[3] And if what Raban calls the 'hard city' of buildings and statistics already shows much variation, then the 'soft city' of experience and imagination, of 'illusion, myth, aspiration, nightmare', makes the problem of how to convey the diversity, without sacrificing underlying patterns, even greater.[4] The Paris of Baudelaire and Balzac, Dumas *père* and Victor Hugo, of the 1840s to the 1860s, was not the same as the Paris of Louis Aragon and the surrealists, in the 1920s; nor was the latter the same as the contemporary London of Virginia Woolf, or Walter Benjamin's Berlin. But these contrasts suggest a method: the cultural significance of the city can be probed through the exploration of certain specific cities already constructed as emblematic, key sites through which we can reconstruct and re-experience the modern. And Paris, at least, has to be on the list; for it is in the Paris of Baudelaire that the term 'modern' first comes into widespread use, particularly in his own poetry and criticism.

For Baudelaire and other writers of his time, what was new was the sense of novelty itself, and the difficulty, the challenge, of pinning it down. Novelty is repetitive, but each time the content changes; as Berman puts it, 'The fact that you can't step into the same modernity twice makes modern life especially elusive and hard to grasp.' Hence modern life presents itself as 'a great fashion show, a system of dazzling appearances, brilliant façades'.[5] The modern city is the fashionable, the contemporary, the here and now; time is the present, there is no sense of beginnings and endings, only points of rest in the stream of experience. And hence modernism in the arts, as the strenuous search for an adequate means to express and convey this immersion of the senses, through novel language or imagery.

Accompanying this is the multiplicity of city experiences. In this respect, a city has to be large enough to be varied; it possesses ethnic, social and cultural diversity, contributing to a sense of restlessness and colour, a sense that there is always something happening, and something *else* happening, somewhere, day or night. Sennett defines a city as a settlement 'in which strangers are likely to meet'; it is where one finds the cosmopolitan, who 'moves comfortably in diversity'.[6] All cities grow essentially through immigration; and writing of the experiences of immigrants in American cities, Ewen claims that

> As one navigated this vast new world of strangers, one quickly learned that to the eyes of countless others one becomes a 'stranger' oneself. Anonymity was not only the characteristic of others; it was also becoming a component of subjectivity, part of the way one came to understand oneself. Part of surviving this strange new world was the ability to make quick judgements based, largely, on immediate visual evidence. The city was a place where surfaces took on a new power of expression. The very terms of everyday experience required, as part of the rules of survival and exchange, a sense of *self as alien*, as an object of scrutiny and judgement.

New immigrants would buy the 'correct' clothes at once, since impressions counted for everything; and the skill of 'reading' appearances would have to be acquired quickly, as a vital survival strategy.[7]

Increasingly, this 'city experience' came to seem all-pervasive: 'there seemed little reality in any other mode of life', writes Raymond Williams; 'all sources of perception seemed to begin and end in the city, and if there was anything beyond it, it was also beyond life'.[8] And contrary reactions were produced by this. If Wordsworth could stand on Westminster Bridge and proclaim that 'Earth has not anything to show more fair/. . ./This city now doth, like a garment, wear/The beauty of the morning . . .',[9] it was that same London that precipitated Blake's awareness of the 'mind-forg'd manacles' of the modern world, and it was in London's streets that he heard how 'the youthful Harlot's curse/Blasts the new born Infant's tear/And blights with plagues the Marriage hearse'.[10] And if Raban can observe that 'Not knowing one's neighbours may be a privilege, not a dreadful fate',[11] there are many who feel differently, so that, for them, 'Struggle, indifference, loss of purpose, loss of meaning . . . have found, in the City, a habitation and a name.'[12] The city of dreams can also be the city of alienation, the 'lonely crowd', the urban community that isn't really a community; and Stallybrass and White can claim that this sense of exclusion from the crowd is at 'the very root of bourgeois sensibility'.[13]

But above all, it is in the city that the tensions around project, theatricality and experience come to a head. Conventionally, the modern city, with its sleek buildings, its streamlined streets, can be presented as a hymn to rationality, a key exemplar of the project of modernity. The modernization of the city has been an attempt to impose a rational form on an inchoate mass, and thereby produce a city that would be intelligible, legible. Yet modern city planning, suggests Raban, entails a rationality that is, despite itself, geared to melodrama. In this city of planners, we can see

> the moral extremes, the melodrama, which has so afflicted modern town-planning. A city is a very bad place which one might convert into a very good place, a dangerous place to be made safe. . . . The city, [planners] sense is the province of rogues and angels . . . a place where individuals are so little known that they can be conveniently transmuted into moral ciphers.

And 'The city itself becomes an allegorical backdrop, painted with symbols of the very good and the very evil.'[14] In the city, everyday life becomes a highly-coloured moral drama; the city, in its gaudy theatricality, tends to polarities, extremes, excess and caricature, which become not just modes of existence but modes of recognition, ways of perpetuating and asserting the precarious sense of personality that 'carries' identity in the maelstrom of urban life. And these presentational forms can also be captured in media and literary images of the city; the distortion and exaggeration of identity in the city becomes a central resource in Dickens, for example. Negotiating all this, in everyday life, is what Baudelaire long ago called 'the heroism of the modern'.

In this sense, 'modernity' becomes existential, a matter of how to live, of involvement, of choice, without guidelines from the past. And this 'heroism' cannot be morally censored, either; it cannot exclude the refuse of the streets. Hence Baudelaire's celebrated demand that the poet pick up his halo from the gutter, and his contribution to what Elizabeth Wilson has called an 'aesthetic of the ugly', whereby poets and novelists have found in 'the very ugliness and squalor of those cities a melancholy, perverse beauty and eroticism'.[15] In doing this, the artist can avoid being trapped in the deadening utilitarianism of project, the bourgeois subordination of everyday life to material goal, of experience to purpose, and can reclaim the sense that life is 'rich in poetic and marvellous subjects. The marvellous envelops and soaks us like an atmosphere, but we don't see it.'[16]

If the 'rationality' of the city can so easily be compromised in theatricality, it is also compromised in other ways. There is, after all, a tension between the purported smoothly-functioning rationality of city life and our everyday experience of what life in the city really entails. The city of project and consumerism is a city in which fragmentation, change and disorder are as apparent as their opposites, providing the dynamism that makes city life so challenging. 'Reading' this city is not so straightforward, and Raban suggests that

> people often have to live by reading the signs and surfaces of their environment and interpreting them in terms of private, near-magical codes. . . .
>
> When reason is lost, magic is there to take its place; when people can no longer relate themselves to the overall scheme of things, to civic life as a programme and consensus, then they take to private attic-superstitions, charms, tokens, spells to win their personal fortune from the mysterious, florid abundance of the city.[17]

And this city can become strange indeed. Daydreaming in a Paris café, in the 1920s, Louis Aragon wrote of how 'Reverie imposes its presence, unaided. Here, surrealism resumes all its rights', in a place where there were 'Images, images everywhere. On the ceiling. In the armchairs' wickerwork. In the glasses' drinking straws. In the telephone switchboard. In the sparkling air. . . .' If, as he claimed, 'Lucidity came to me when I at last succumbed to the vertigo of the modern', then it is an opaque, baroque lucidity, of image and aphorism; a language of the city and its own imaginings. He adds:

Wherever the living pursue particularly ambiguous activities, the inanimate may sometimes assume the reflection of their most secret motives: and thus our cities are peopled with unrecognized sphinxes which will never stop the passing dreamer and ask him mortal questions unless he first projects his meditation, his absence of mind, towards them. But if this wise man has the power to guess their secret, and interrogates them in his turn, all that these faceless monsters will grant is that he shall once again plumb his own depths. Henceforth, it is the modern light radiating from the unusual that will rivet his attention.[18]

All very mysterious: who are these sphinxes? Elizabeth Wilson provides some clues; she points to crucial ways in which the experience of the city is gendered, and suggests that women have in a sense been 'an irruption in the city, a symptom of disorder, and a problem: the Sphinx in the city'. The city presents a tension between 'intervention and mastery' and 'appreciation and immersion':

> The city is 'masculine' in its triumphal scale, its towers and vistas and arid industrial regions; it is 'feminine' in its enclosing embrace, in its indeterminacy and labyrinthine uncentredness. We might even go so far as to claim that urban life is actually based on this perpetual struggle between rigid, routinised order and pleasurable anarchy, the male–female dichotomy.[19]

Whether we go so far or not, it is clear that the dynamic of project and experience has gender as a key dimension, and that powerful gender stereotypes are involved here.

But all this remains rather abstract. It is time to get to particulars. Let us go for a walk in the city.

A Stroll in London

Virginia Woolf writes of 'moments when we are set upon having an object, an excuse for walking half across London between tea and dinner'; and thus it happened, one day, desiring to go 'street rambling', she chose 'buying a pencil' as the pretext, thus giving herself permission to enjoy this slightly illicit pleasure. And on the walk, coming across a boot shop, she again finds herself making 'some little excuse, which has nothing to do with the real reason', and enters it. Always we have to fabricate excuses, invent necessities: 'One must, one always must, do something or other; it is not allowed one simply to enjoy oneself.' The pleasures of experience must be subordinated to the tyranny of purpose, of project; yet project itself, through that tyranny, reveals a slide from rationality into rationalization. Reasons are exposed as ruses, ploys, under this glare of self-awareness enforced by immersion in the nuances, delights and challenges of city life. And when the mind 'cringes to the accustomed tyrant', the feminine experience of immersion is being subordinated to masculine control, the discipline of project. Experience itself is a threat to this domination, in its purposeless 'being', its inherent passivity; Woolf can accommodate herself to this relatively readily, but the same is not necessarily so true of the male stroller in the city, as we will see. And this essay, 'Street Haunting', is, in large part, an essay in the gendered imagination of the city.[20]

These inhabitants of the city carry this irreducibility of experience to project in their very amorphousness, their collective separateness: 'The fascination of the London street is that no two people are ever alike; each seems bound on some private affair of his own.'[21] The whole bustle of city life provides images of complexity: 'Buses, vans, cars, barrows stream past like the fragments of a picture puzzle', but 'The puzzle never fits itself together, however long we look', she writes in another essay, 'Oxford Street Tide'.[22] If the city makes sense it is not a sense we can make of it, impose on it; we can at best respond to it, 'read' the fragments. There is a sense in which the city as experience returns to nature; to immerse oneself in this complexity is 'to leave the straight lines of personality' and 'to deviate into those footpaths that lead beneath brambles and thick tree trunks into the heart of the forest where live those wild beasts, our fellow men'. This seems little different in tone, after all, from her description of a London square with grass and trees, where 'one hears those little cracklings and stirrings of leaf and twig'.[23] Wandering in London therefore leads her to experiences that parallel those of her contemporary Walter Benjamin in Paris:

> Not to find one's way in a city may well be uninteresting and banal. It requires ignorance – nothing more. But to lose oneself in a city – as one loses oneself in a forest – that calls for quite a different schooling. Then, signboards and street names, passers-by, roofs, kiosks or bars must speak to the wanderer like a cracking twig under his feet in the forest, like the startling call of a bittern in the distance, like the sudden stillness of a clearing with a lily erect at its centre. Paris taught me this art of straying.[24]

If the modern city is a manifestation – and a manifesto – of culture against nature, it nevertheless ends up posing the same challenges as nature, and is just as recalcitrant and perplexing. As Steven Marcus suggests, '"The city" repels nature and yet becomes a "second" nature as well.'[25] But this formulation takes us too far from Woolf; perhaps she would be more likely to say, as does Wilson, that 'instead of setting nature against the city', women may be more likely to 'find nature *in* the city'.[26]

Further aspects of this gendered experience of city-as-nature come out strongly elsewhere in Woolf, notably in the all-pervasive metaphor of street life as river-like, conveying a sense of dynamism and creative flow that is essentially organic. Sometimes, in a lull in the traffic, she suggests, one becomes aware of 'a force in things which one had overlooked. It seemed to point to a river, which flowed past, invisibly, round the corner, down the street, and took people and eddied them along'; a young man and woman get into a cab, and it 'glided off as if it were swept on by the current elsewhere'.[27] The city is a 'river of turning wheels', and Oxford Street is 'washed by a bright stream', where everything 'glitters and twinkles', and where barrows of flowers are 'frail vessels' that 'eddy vaguely' in the traffic. Thus do London's 'vessels' weave their way everywhere in the city, spreading a spring-like fecundity and abundance even in the heart of technology.[28] But this all comes out most vividly in the following remarkable passage from *Orlando*, describing a scene by the Thames as Orlando, having returned to London, gives birth to a child:

> Behold, meanwhile, the factory chimneys and their smoke; behold the city clerks flashing by in their outrigger. . . . Hail! natural desire! Hail! happiness! divine happiness! and pleasure of all sorts, flowers and wine, though one fades and the other intoxicates; and half-crown tickets out of London on Sundays, and singing in a dark chapel hymns about death and anything, anything that interrupts and confounds the tapping of typewriters and filing of letters and forging of links and chains, binding the Empire together. . . . Hail, happiness! kingfisher flashing from bank to bank, and all fulfilment of natural desire, whether it is what the male novelist says it is. . . . Blue, like a match struck right in the ball of the innermost eye, he flys, burns, bursts the seal of sleep; the kingfisher; so that now floods back refluent like a tide, the red, thick stream of life.[29]

Here is an exuberant, life-affirming, yet also defiant, hymn of praise to a creativity mapped simultaneously as organic and feminine: here, in the masculine heart of the city, with the factory chimneys and the 'links and chains' that bind the Empire, we encounter an organic flow that sweeps all before it in its joyous fecundity, its procreative surge, silencing the tapping typewriters of male politicians and novelists alike. It is a distinctive means of appropriating the city, uncovering a dynamic sense of order existing in the very drama of surface fragments; this vision celebrates origin and connectedness, against the pessimism of the male modernist novelists and poets of the 1920s, with their sense of impotence and lack of control in the modern city. Thus a similar aura of exuberant fantasy occurs in her portrayal of the commuters who, having left their offices, are caught up in 'some narcotic dream', and become 'great cricketers, famous actresses', as, 'Dreaming, gesticulating . . . they sweep over the Strand and across Waterloo Bridge.'[30] How different from T. S. Eliot's nightmare vision of the commuters that 'flowed over London Bridge, so many,/I had not thought death had undone so many', from whom 'Sighs, short and infrequent, were exhaled,/And each man fixed his eyes before his feet.'[31]

The buildings, too, can be incorporated into the imagery of a cycle of life, fecundity and reproduction:

> The charm of London is that it is not built to last; it is built to pass. Its glassiness, its transparency, its surging waves of coloured plaster give a different pleasure and achieve a different end from that which was desired and attempted by the old builders. . . . We knock down and rebuild as we expect to be knocked down and rebuilt. It is an impulse that makes for creation and fertility.[32]

Fecundity requires death; but this is a kind of 'organic' death, part of a 'natural cycle' of life, death and rebirth.

In the end, though, the dynamism of the city, its reproductive, creative power, requires an incorporation of the masculine element, not a defiant rejection of it. That there *is* a sense in which the city is masculine is clear from this account in 'The Docks of London':

> As we come closer to the Tower Bridge the authority of the city begins to assert itself. The buildings thicken and heap themselves higher. . . . One hears the roar and the resonance of London itself. . . . Here growls and grumbles that rough city song that has called the ships from the sea and brought them to lie captive beneath its warehouses.

It is as though the masculine presence is granted sullenly; no exuberant creative flow here. And the imagery becomes intriguing. The 'captive' ships have to be opened up, violated: 'Indefatigable cranes are now at work, dipping and swinging, swinging and dipping. . . . Rhythmically, dexterously, with an order that has some aesthetic delight in it, barrel is laid by barrel, case by case.' Is this rhythm sexual or procreative? Is this rape or childbirth? It could almost be a well-ordered hospital delivery: 'not only is each package of this vast and varied merchandise picked up and set down accurately, but each is weighed and opened, sampled and recorded, and again stitched up and laid in its place'. But even here, the richness of the creative, liquid flow is still celebrated, even if it is now the wine in barrels, rather than the waters of the Thames: 'side by side the objects of our worship lie swollen with sweet liquor, spouting red wine if tapped', so that 'A winy sweetness fills the vaults like incense.'[33]

If London in some of its central aspects, its 'authority' and assertiveness, is unquestionably masculine, we can be more specific again: London is the 'master', the upper-class man, and the rest of the population become assimilated, by contrast, to working-class housemaids. Woolf comments on the dismal 'blight and squalor that surrounds us' in dockland; behind the factories and offices lie 'the meanest streets in London'. This filth and wretchedness is caused by the master, and she identifies with the garbage barges that labour to create cleanliness and order: 'Here is London's scullery, its washing up place, its kitchen offices.'[34] In her essay 'Great Men's Houses', she discusses Thomas and Jane Carlyle, and associates the latter with the maid, since both occupy the lower physical spaces in the house, and labour to maintain the house while the 'great man' writes in his study at the top.[35] In short, here we have Woolf's equivalent to Baudelaire's insistence that the artist must pick up his halo in the grubby, crowded street; for Woolf, as Jane Marcus suggests, the metaphor is 'the artist as charwoman to the world', down on her knees with dustpan and broom, with the housemaids.[36] So if the artist – especially, by implication, the female one – can draw on the 'organic' creativity of the city, so there is also a 'social' creativity to draw on, in the role of women in the city: vital, central, yet marginalized, even hidden. A social aspect of reproductive power, to complement the organic one.

In effect, this feminist reading of the city decentres it, rearranges it, emphasizing what is often shifted to one side. And the net spreads, to encompass all that is 'off-centre'. On her walk across London, in the boot shop, she had encountered a dwarf: and she writes that the dwarf 'had called into being an atmosphere which, as we followed her out into the street, seemed actually to create the humped, the twisted, the deformed'. Thus, a couple of blind men now appeared in the street. 'Indeed, the dwarf had started a hobbling grotesque dance to which everybody in the street had now conformed.' It is not just that we meet strangers in the city; it is that the city makes us all strange. She passed 'the humped body of an old woman flung abandoned on the step of a public building with a cloak over her like a hasty covering thrown over a dead horse'; and she adds that 'Often enough these derelicts choose to lie not a stone's-throw from theatres', and 'close to those shop-windows where commerce offers to a world of old women laid on doorsteps, of blind men, of hobbling dwarfs, sofas which are supported by the gilt necks of proud swans'.[37] They 'choose' their sites; they are not, suggests Rachel Bowlby, just a reprimand to the consuming gaze, they are also an exercise of it, 'connoisseurs of the pleasures of spectacle for its own sake'. Woolf is not just drawing a contrast, but making an identification. The normal becomes strange, and this spreads to encompass us all: 'everyone is grotesque, just as all the seeming poor can turn out from one point of view to be equivalent to affluent consumers'.[38]

Returning home, Woolf recounts these stories, and concludes that 'Into each of these lives one could penetrate a little way, far enough to give oneself the illusion that one is not tethered to a single mind, but can put on briefly for a few minutes the bodies and minds of others.'[39] In the light of this, one can understand Susan Squier's disappointment, in that the stroll 'leaves her neither morally, spiritually, nor politically changed, but merely entertained'.[40] Yet perhaps Woolf's stance is precisely what makes possible the imaginative appropriation and transformation of experience into a fascinating documentation of the city; and perhaps it is the city itself that anaesthetizes the moral sense, while stimulating the aesthetic, thereby breeding a kind of amoral survivalism. Woolf herself points out that there are, in moral terms, some 'queer, incongruous voices', and she lets them have their say, passing no judgement:

> I am a thief, says a woman of that persuasion, and a lady of easy virtue into the bargain. But it takes a good deal of pluck to snatch a bag from a counter when a customer is not looking; and it may contain only spectacles and old bus tickets after all. So here goes![41]

What is it, then, about the city, that has these consequences? When we go out, she suggests, we become 'an enormous eye', and hence 'are only gliding smoothly on the surface'; the eye does not dig for buried treasure, it 'floats us smoothly down a stream', and the brain 'sleeps perhaps as it looks'.[42] The eye does not theorize or moralize; it is keyed to the visual imagination. This, perhaps, is why Raban can suggest that 'The city as a form is uniquely prone to erode that boundary between the province of the imagination and the province of fact.'[43] Woolf suggests that it is the night that is particularly powerful here: it is the evening hour that gives us 'the irresponsibility which darkness and lamplight bestow. We are no longer quite ourselves', and 'become part of that vast republican army of anonymous trampers',[44] a suggestion echoed in Berman's claim that the city at night has a magical aura, becoming 'at once more real and more unreal'.[45]

Ultimately, these experiences provoke tension within the very sense of self, questioning the whole notion of self-identity. For a moment, on the point of finally buying the pencil, Woolf defies 'the accustomed tyrant', the 'rod of duty', in order to go in search of a fragment of her past self, a memory. Her street-haunting compels her to ask: 'Am I here, or am I there? Or is the true self neither this nor that, neither here nor there, but something so varied and wandering that it is only when we give the rein to its wishes and let it take its way unimpeded that we are indeed ourselves?' But the attractions of the conventional roles may prove too strong. 'Circumstances compel unity', and the 'good citizen' who opens his door in the evening must be 'banker, golfer, husband, father'. When returning home, 'it is comforting to feel the old possessions, the old prejudices, fold us round'.[46] A last twist, then, another decentred perspective: for this domestic sphere, convention-ally coded as feminine, is revealed as having an essentially masculine dimension. Possessions cement identity, the public status of firm roles, the solidity of the home, the prejudices of self-interest. In this sense, 'returning home' is returning to the self as project: 'Once safe in the private home, the self is monolithic, male and moneyed', as Squier puts it.[47]

Clearly the tensions are unresolved. And Woolf makes the revealing comment that if one is a woman 'one is often surprised by a sudden splitting off of con-sciousness, say in walking down Whitehall, when from being the natural inheritor of that civilization, she becomes, on the contrary, outside of it, alien and critical'. But this is not presented as tragic; it may be a key to women's experience of the city, and hence a spur to creativity, through a sensitivity to the ordinary, often unremarked aspects of city life, and an insight into all the 'infinitely obscure lives' that 'remain to be recorded'.[48] She writes that 'one catches a word in passing and from a chance phrase fabricates a lifetime',[49] and 'fabricates' is clearly decisive: both making, and making up. This exploration – part fiction, part fact – is presented as literary in its very essence, a continuation of a tradition that Raymond Williams describes in these terms: 'The experience of the city is the fictional method; or the fictional method is the experience of the city.'[50]

Thus does Woolf struggle towards an aesthetic that would convey a sense of women's experiences of the city, the possibilities as well as the restrictions, the pleasures as well as the fears. She seeks to do so not because she would thereby be representing the inherently or exclusively feminine, but because she would thereby do justice to aspects of consciousness and experience that are all too often marginalized. Woolf is struggling towards a conception of identity involving not unity, but coexisting differences and possibilities that cannot really be captured in rigid distinctions, whether male/female or nature/culture. What she writes of artistic creativity would, after all, apply also to the creativity and dynamism of the city: 'Some collaboration has to take place in the mind between the woman and the man before the act of creation can be accomplished.'[51]

Virginia Woolf, then, was a female *flâneur*, a city stroller; as such, her very existence questions some of the taken-for-granted assumptions about the latter, who is conventionally presented as a masculine hero of the city. But to explore this, we must change time and place, and visit Paris.

A Stroll in Paris

If Paris was indeed the capital of the nineteenth century this was surely because, as Sennett remarks, it was where all the 'fears and fantasies' of the bourgeoisie were concentrated;[52] it was in its arcades and boulevards that the arrival of the new social world of the modern consumer spectacle was most decisively dramatized. Already by 1828, according to Richard's guidebook, there were 137 'protected ways', arcades, 29 of these being shopping arcades,[53] lit from above and glazed with the new cheap plate-glass that made possible the window displays of the novel luxury goods and textiles that characterized the early age of mass production (plate 1). These arcades, suggests Benjamin, were 'the original temple of commodity capitalism', and 'they beamed out into the Paris of the second Empire like fairy grottoes'.[54] But by then, in the 1850s and 1860s, medieval Paris was being swept away ᴀs Baron Haussmann, Louis Napoleon's Prefect of Paris, drove the new, straight boulevards through the decaying quarters of the old city. Decisive breakthroughs in modernizing the city, Berman indeed claims that they were the most spectacular urban innovation of the century.[55] Ostensibly justified by the need for sanitation – in the form of sewers – and ease of communication, the fact that the boulevards were also difficult to obstruct with barricades was also commented on at the time. This exercise in the project of modernity, linking social improvement with greater surveillance and control, changed Paris for ever: 'on the whole', claims Olsen, 'Paris is either as Haussmann left it or as he intended it to be.'[56]

Once again, though, the experiences opened up by these changes cannot be seen purely in these terms. With the wide pavements, the trees, the cafés on every corner, the Paris of spectacle and dazzle, of promenading, strolling and window shopping, was further encouraged. Everywhere, Paris was being described as dream, mirage, masquerade, the dazzling manifestation of the new consumer culture. Paris had become, suggests Green, 'a sequence of spectacles to be grasped in the pleasure of a gaze that structured the flow between promenade, theatre, café, and arcade';[57] a gaze 'both covetous and erotic', adds Pollock.[58] And it is these arcades and boulevards that were the haunt of the *flâneur*, the 'stroller'. Wilson points to a pamphlet of 1806 that contains the term, apparently referring to a man of limited independent means, enjoying the streets and restaurants, and the capacity of the ever-changing urban landscape to stimulate the curious observer, challenging him to learn to 'read' the signs and work out their associations;[59] but it is later, in Balzac's work, that the word is popularized, having taken on something of the connotations of the bohemianism of the 1820s and 1830s. Thus the narrator at the beginning of his story *Facino Cane*:

I walked the streets to observe the manners and ways of the neighbourhood, to study its inhabitants and learn their characters. . . . I mingled in their groups, watched their bargains, heard their disputes, at the hour when their day's work ended. The faculty of observation had become intuitive with me; I could enter the souls of others, while still conscious of their bodies – or rather, I grasped external details so thoroughly that my mind instantly passed beyond them; I possessed, in short, the faculty of living the life of the individual on whom I exercised my observation, and of substituting myself for him.[60]

Like the cafés and arcades he inhabits, the *flâneur* is both inside and outside; he is a marginal figure, on the edge of the city as also of the bourgeois class, at home in neither. 'He sought his asylum in the crowd', suggests Benjamin, in a nicely ambiguous turn of phrase.[61] Yet the 'crowd', as a 'community of strangers', is not really something one can 'belong' in. And this is the emblematic role of the *flâneur*, his capacity to encapsulate the city experience: in the city, no one need be an outsider, yet no one is an insider, either. Very much of his time and place, he also embodies elements of the universality of the modern city.

So, to be lost in the city is to be lost in the crowd, and this is the fate he thrives on. What, then, is the attraction? The pleasure is in a vicarious sense of adventure, linked with a satisfaction gained through decoding, 'reading', the signs of the city. This, after all, is the era when the individualization of the self has proceeded to the point where the categories of social identity – class, status, gender – have become 'personalized'. Since appearances are crucial to this, offering the possibility, and the risks, of self-revelation, so the finer distinctions of clothing and deportment become of great concern. For Balzac, personality is immanent yet mysterious, a melodrama of selfhood in which small details can carry a heavy symbolic load; for him, suggests Sennett, 'personality has become the fundamental social category of the city'.[62]

Yet perhaps it is Edgar Allan Poe's story 'The Man of the Crowd', from 1840, that brings out what this entails most clearly. The author sits in a coffee house, observing his fellows, and the passers-by outside. Class distinctions can all be read in small details; businessmen, junior clerks and senior clerks can all be distinguished. There were 'individuals of dashing appearance', who 'obviously' belonged to 'the race of swell pick-pockets, with which all great cities are infested'. It was difficult to see how they could really be mistaken for gentlemen: 'Their voluminousness of wristband, with an air of excessive frankness, should betray them at once.' Gamblers could be distinguished by 'a certain sodden swarthiness of complexion, a filmy dimness of eye, and pallor and compression of lip', along with 'a more than ordinary extension of the thumb in a direction at right angles with the fingers'.

But then, the horror and the challenge: a man is seen, hurrying, who defies the categories, who cannot be 'read', even after being pursued for hours round the city. Interestingly, it is *he* who is described by Poe as 'the man of the crowd',[63] which in effect reveals an insecurity, moral and epistemological, about the whole interpretive venture of 'reading the city'. As Dana Brand suggests, 'the old man's unintelligibility has opened up the possibility that no man or woman of the crowd can be read as the narrator has presumed to read them'. He represents a zero point, 'personality in itself', an ideal of absolute unrepresentability. Taking up Poe's suggestion that this man is 'the type and genius of deep crime', Brand adds that it is as though 'illegibility is itself a form of crime'.[64] And there is always the challenge of imposture. Discussing Ronnie Kray, one of the brothers who dominated London's gangland in the 1960s, Raban points to his success in fooling large numbers of people, thriving on mobility, effortlessly changing roles for separate audiences; in the city, 'appearances are easy to come by, and very hard to test for authenticity'.[65]

There is a sense, then, in which making sense of street life makes us all detectives, and the *flâneur* is well advanced on this road. A world in which everything can depend on the angle between thumb and finger is clearly a world in which the detective can feel at home. The detective, writes Raymond Williams, is 'the man who can find his way through the fog, who can penetrate the intricacies of the streets',[66] in pursuit of the small clues that will expose guilty secrets. Moretti argues that in this world, 'Innocence is conformity; individuality, guilt', and that it is always 'something irreducibly personal that betrays the individual: traces, signs that only he could have left behind',[67] and this follows Benjamin's suggestion that detective fiction is a kind of antidote to the individual's ability to hide among the masses, an erasure of individualism that is nevertheless only possible because of it.[68] And Catherine Belsey adds that if the project of the Sherlock Holmes stories is 'to dispel magic and mystery, to make everything explicit, accountable', this ultimately fails before the imponderables of gender and politics, presented as mysterious and shadowy, Conan Doyle's equivalent of 'the man of the crowd'.[69] In the end, the detective's quest is never-ending; the city always defies ultimate resolution, presenting further puzzles to solve. The detective's determination to subordinate everything to project, to capture it without remainder, is constantly subverted by contingencies that break out elsewhere even as they are 'mastered' here.

All this time, the assumption has been made that the *flâneur* – and the detective, for that matter – is generally male. Is Griselda Pollock right, backed up by Janet Wolff, that the *flâneur* is 'an exclusively masculine type', since whereas the man could be said to find himself by losing himself, in the crowded streets, the woman finds herself in the home, and risks losing herself, and her virtue, when outside?[70] The experiences of Virginia Woolf might already make us wonder about this, and Wilson indeed suggests that the city could be 'a place of liberation for women',[71] a point backed up by Judith Walkowitz's argument that 'expanded opportunities for shopping, philanthropy, civic participation, and an "independent" life in the 1890s generated a new urban style of "being at home" in the city', a style that 'women had to diligently cultivate against male harassment'.[72] To some extent, this last quotation provides the clue; it seems highly likely that there *was* a greater scope for unattended women to explore the city by the last decade or two of the century, in comparison with the classic 'age of the *flâneur*' in earlier decades. Nevertheless, this issue of the gendered aspects of the role requires further investigation.

Walter Benjamin, who himself adopted the role of the *flâneur* in the 1920s, tells us that 'The city is the realization of humanity's ancient dream of the labyrinth. Without knowing it, the *flâneur* goes in search of this reality.'[73] A labyrinth is confusing, interminable, leading hither and thither, nowhere and everywhere, an exploration without limit, without fulfilment, a neurotic deferral of resolution or satisfaction; and there is always the risk – or temptation? – of encountering a minotaur, embodying 'death-dealing forces'. He adds: 'The labyrinth is the home of the hesitant. The path of someone shy of arrival at a goal easily takes the form of a labyrinth.'[74] Here is an anxious, melancholic view of the city, one with ramifications in Benjamin's own intimate experiences; thus he describes his middle years in Berlin as 'a period of impotence before the city'.[75] The *flâneur* is here revealed as a rather neurotic, precarious, marginal individual, hardly a model of purposeful masculinity; 'the gaze' is nervous, passive, rather than assertive, dominating. In the end, the *flâneur* is as much a deconstruction of masculine identity, as an exemplification of it. In him, the 'heroism of the modern' encounters the tensions between active project and passive experience, rational control and theatrical display, masculine and feminine, and becomes broken-backed, impotent. In Wilson's insightful words:

> The *flâneur* represented not the triumph of masculine power, but its attenuation . . . masculinity as unstable, caught up in the violent dislocations that characterized urbanization. . . .
>
> In the labyrinth the *flâneur* effaces himself, becomes passive, feminine. In the writing of fragmentary pieces, he makes of himself a blank page upon which the city writes itself. . . . The Minotaur of some horrible love object – a decayed prostitute, an androgyne – still waits around every corner.[76]

But if melancholia is found here, so is a kind of frenetic hyperactivity, as we saw with the 'man of the crowd', forever unsettled, frantically off in pursuit of new experiences, lest ennui and emptiness overtake him. If we leave the argument here, however, with this picture of the *flâneur* as inherently neurotic, we may unintentionally reify the gender stereotypes of modernity by making it seem as though the gender ambiguity of the role must necessarily be crippling. One of the earliest of the *flâneurs*, Baudelaire himself, is a useful corrective:

> For the perfect *flâneur*, for the passionate spectator, it is an immense joy to set up house in the heart of the multitude, amid the ebb and flow of movement, in the midst of the fugitive and the infinite. To be away from home and yet to feel oneself everywhere at home; to see the world, to be at the centre of the world, and yet to remain hidden from the world. . . . The spectator is a *prince* who everywhere rejoices in his incognito.[77]

To enjoy this, one has to be filled with 'love of disguise and of the mask, with hatred of the home and a passion for voyaging'; that same passion, no doubt, that sent other intellectuals and artists to the Orient. And there is a quasi-sexual dimension that hardly comes out as melancholic:

That man who can easily wed the crowd knows a feverish enjoyment which will be eternally denied to the egoist, shut up like a trunk, and to the lazy man, imprisoned like a mollusc. . . . What men call love is very meagre, very restricted and very feeble, compared to this ineffable orgy, to this holy prostitution of the soul that abandons itself entirely . . . to the unexpected arrival, to the passing stranger.[78]

In its exuberant excess, this passage invites comparison with Virginia Woolf's paean of praise to the creativity of the city and of the artist in the city, particularly when we recall that Baudelaire's theme is the necessity of the creative artist to draw inspiration from the role of *flâneur*. . . .

So, if the public spaces of the city can produce melancholia and agoraphobia, they can also be experienced in terms of freedom and creativity. Wilson sums up appropriately:

The heroism – for both sexes – is in surviving the disorientating space, both labyrinthine and agoraphobic, of the metropolis. It lies in the ability to discern among the massed ranks of anonymity the outline of forms of beauty and individuality appropriate to urban life. The act of creating meaning, seemingly so arbitrary, becomes heroic in itself.[79]

In the end, then, the *flâneur* is the very embodiment of ambiguity, whether crippling or creative: endlessly caught between doing and being,[80] involvement and detachment, margin and centre, insider and outsider. As we all must be, in the city?

Fear and Danger, Temptation and Pleasure

The 'crowd', so prevalent in these accounts of the city, requires further examination. The crowd, itself innocent, could easily slide into the 'mass', and then there are definitely hints of trouble. Benjamin suggests that 'the "crowd" is the veil that hides the "mass" from the *flâneur*',[81] and this veil could always be rent. The mass is amorphous, an aggregate in which individuality is lost, unpredictable, always potentially dangerous. 'The masses' could always emerge on the political stage, manipulated by subversives, agitators. We would then have that central component of bourgeois fear, 'the mob', captured in dictionary definitions as a 'tumultuous crowd bent on lawlessness', a 'promiscuous assemblage', disorderly, a rabble, anarchic and dangerous. Something of the fear this engendered is captured by Lynda Nead in her comment that the city was seen as 'the breeding-ground of revolution, disease and moral corruption', and the public streets were 'the domain of the fallen, the promiscuous, the diseased and the immoral'.[82]

Mobs are always 'lower-class'. Indeed, class is the hidden term in all of this, though it becomes increasingly explicit as the nineteenth century wears on; it was essential for the attractions of the crowd, for the *flâneur*, that it should be a mixture of classes, or at least not too uniformly working-class. In the first half of the century, industry and class are not central to novelistic portrayals of the city, but as towns like Manchester forced themselves increasingly into the bourgeois imagination of the city, class became a more overt theme. With writers like George Gissing, in the 1880s and 1890s, a strong sense of class uniformities is transmitted; there are descriptions of crowds of workers streaming out of the factories at the end of their shifts, the buildings described as 'barracks . . . housing for the army of industrialism'.[83] And certainly there was fuel for middle-class fear: in February 1886, a 'mob' of unemployed dock and building workers threw stones at the Carlton Club, and looted Piccadilly and Oxford Street; and on 'Bloody Sunday', in November 1887, troops beat back working-class marchers attempting to enter Trafalgar Square.[84]

But it is not only class that is involved in these fears; there is also gender. Wilson claims that the crowd was increasingly invested with feminine attributes, while retaining its negative associations. The 'threatening masses' were described as 'hysterical', or, 'in images of feminine instability and sexuality, as a flood or swamp. Like women, crowds were liable to rush to extremes of emotion.'[85] And Huyssen, too, argues that this fear of the masses is also 'a fear of woman, a fear of nature out of control, a fear of the unconscious, of sexuality, of the loss of identity and stable ego boundaries in the mass'; thus 'the male fear of woman and the bourgeois fear of the masses become indistinguishable'.[86] The sociologist Le Bon, writing in 1895, indeed claimed that 'crowds are everywhere distinguished by feminine characteristics'.[87] However, if gender is indeed so central, one cannot presuppose that the masculine and feminine perspectives on this aspect of city life are necessarily identical; and in order to pursue this, it is worth looking at Elizabeth Gaskell's novel *North and South*, written in the mid-1850s, and based, like the celebrated work by Engels a decade earlier, on Manchester, and the class disputes that had become dramatically evident between mill owners and millhands in the cotton industry.

Moving to the northern town, away from London and the South, the heroine, Margaret, quickly becomes aware of the ramifications of class and the pervasive antagonism between the two major classes. She also encounters the working-class mass. Two or three times a day, out of the mills, 'poured streams of men and women', who came 'rushing along', with 'bold, fearless faces, and loud laughs and jests':

> The tones of their unrestrained voices, and their carelessness of all common rules of street politeness, frightened Margaret a little at first. The girls, with their rough, but not unfriendly freedom, would comment on her dress, even touch her sleeve or gown to ascertain the exact material. . . . She did not mind meeting any number of girls, loud spoken and boisterous though they might be. But she alternately dreaded and fired up against the workmen, who commented not on her dress, but on her looks, in the same open, fearless manner. . . . But the very outspokenness marked their innocence of any intention to hurt her delicacy, as she would have perceived if she had been less frightened by the disorderly tumult.[88]

These working-class masses, in their 'disorderly tumult', and their rough, direct manners, inspire both fear and fascination; and this fascination continues even when the danger appears much more real, when she encounters the marching strikers.

At the mill, she could hear their distant approach. She felt there was 'a thunderous atmosphere, morally as well as physically, around her'; she heard 'the first long far-off roll of the tempest; saw the first slow-surging wave of the dark crowd come, with its threatening crest'. When they saw the owner, they yelled, like 'some terrible wild beast'; they were 'gaunt as wolves, and mad for prey'. She sensed that 'in another instant the stormy passions would have passed their bounds, and swept away all barriers of reason'. This is a crowd possessing an elemental, 'natural' fury, like a storm or an angry sea; and it sweeps on, in an unstoppable, orgasmic surge.[89] It is clearly coded as masculine, with sex, class and nature powerfully superimposed. Furthermore, it is almost a feminine equivalent of the masculine initiation rites in 'darkest Africa'; for the confrontation with the northern city is fundamental to the process of Margaret's developing maturity, establishing as it does some distance, both physical and moral, from the more effete, genteel culture of London and the South. An encounter that can be dangerous, polluting, corrupting, can nevertheless be both tempting and, in a sense, desirable.

More generally, this combination of fear, disgust and fascination reveals the way the city is a place where the categories can mix, where the streets can be 'promiscuous'; where, in short, 'dirt' can be encountered. 'Transgressing the boundaries through which the bourgeois reformers separated dirt from cleanliness', write Stallybrass and White, 'the poor were interpreted as also transgressing the boundaries of the "civilized" body and the boundaries which separated the human from the animal.'[90] Hence the fascination with the sewers, seen as a dark underworld of unspeakable horrors, where the unacceptable products of the body mix amorphously and threaten to pollute the clean, carefully divided world above.[91]

But it is above all in the figure of the prostitute that these dimensions of class and gender, individual and mass, purity and pollution, become most vividly superimposed. The prostitute, suggests Nead, was 'the link between slum and suburb, dirt and cleanliness, ignorance and civilization, profligacy and morality'; hence she made it impossible to keep these categories apart.[92] On the one hand, she was clearly a threat, simultaneously immoral and seditious. A commentator in 1859 wrote that anyone walking certain streets at night would notice at once 'what a multitudinous amazonian army the devil keeps in constant field service. . . . The stones seem alive with lust, and the very atmosphere is tainted.'[93] But we also encounter the image of the prostitute as victim, an object of bourgeois guilt, 'a suffering and tragic figure – the passive victim of a cruel and relentless society', in Nead's words.[94] And either way, conventional representations tended to portray the 'career' of prostitute as an inevitable downward spiral, resulting in death. Of course, such stereotypes can be seriously misleading; Judith Walkowitz points out that 'The stereotyped sequence of girls seduced, pregnant, and abandoned to the streets fitted only a small minority of women who ultimately moved into prostitution', and her own research suggests that prostitution could in many ways be a rational choice for working women trying to maintain some degree of independence.[95]

Crucial here is the fact that 'prostitution' is in no way a homogeneous category. In a Parisian context, the prostitutes of the streets and brothels have to be distinguished, in turn, from the *lorettes*, operating from their own apartments and maintaining a façade of respectability. Such women of the *demi-monde*, the 'twilight world', shaded into the higher-status courtesans, whose lovers were from the aristocracy and the moneyed classes. Those indefatigable commentators on Second-Empire Paris, the Goncourt brothers, tell of a visit to the *Opéra* in March 1862:

> A dazzling audience. . . . The balcony was resplendent with *demi-mondaines* and the corridors were crowded with those handsome men wearing foreign decorations who fill the corridors of the *Opéra* on ball nights. In the boxes there was quite a pretty array of prostitutes. It is wonderful what a centre of debauchery the theatre is . . . presenting an overall picture of Pleasure, Orgy and Intrigue. . . . It is like a Stock Exchange dealing in women's nights.[96]

Indeed, not only were courtesans objects of conspicuous consumption, but they themselves were often active in the orgy of financial speculation that characterized the period; Napoleon III's rise to power was partly financed by the English courtesans Cora Pearl and Miss Howard, for example. And these 'brilliant professionals of desire' were leaders of fashion; with them, the body became an elaborate spectacle, 'artfully constructed according to the codes defining modern desirability . . . in a play of intriguing signs and changing masks', as Bernheimer puts it.[97] And Clark adds that 'The category *courtisane* was what could be *represented* of prostitution'; in this sense, too, she was definitely not the prostitute of the streets.

These issues of representation and recognition go to the heart of the cultural significance of prostitution. The courtesan's game, argues Clark, 'was to play at being an honest woman; and she played very skilfully, though not so well as to deceive her clients; that would have spoilt the whole thing'. She tried on, and discarded, roles and identities at will, 'declaring them false like the rest of her poses. And falsity was what made her modern.'[98] Given that young women were increasingly engaging in the pleasures of display made possible by the changes of fashion, so that they might *be* respectable but *look* the opposite, it was as though the codes of femininity were breaking down, becoming hopelessly unclear, and threatening the moral integrity of the bourgeois ethos. Maxime du Camp complained, at the end of the 1860s, that 'One does not know nowadays if it's honest women who are dressed as whores or whores who are dressed like honest women.'[99] Anyone could dress as anything, provided they had the money. Hence a sense that the prostitute's lie, her deceptive appearance, represented the truth of the modern city, with her influence spreading insidiously everywhere. Clark suggests that it was rapidly becoming a cultural commonplace that these women 'had more and more usurped the centre of things and seemed to be making the city over in their image'.[100] Indeed, 'We are on our way to universal prostitution', proclaimed Dumas in 1867.[101] Just as for Virginia Woolf, the city made us all strange, deformed, so for Baudelaire the city made us all prostitutes; the *flâneur*, too, becomes a street-walker, selling his poetry to any paper or journal that would buy it, just as surely as the prostitute sells her body.

This 'inflation' of prostitution clearly rests on the increasing significance of the market economy. Mass production is also production of the masses, in which labour power is alienated for money; a 'generalized prostitution' could be said to result. Thus Benjamin argues that prostitution is where 'the commodity attempts to look itself in the face. It celebrates its becoming human in the whore', and hence 'In the prostitution of the metropolis the woman herself becomes an article that is mass-produced.'[102] Something of this is captured in a recent statement in a collection of writings by prostitutes: 'Prostitution isn't like anything else. Rather everything else is like prostitution because it is the model for women's condition.'[103] Money is clearly basic here: the prostitute, suggests Wilson, takes 'the cash nexus into the very heart of intimacy'.[104] Her body is alienated, sold, to her client, then reclaimed and sold again; even the most private zone thereby enters the sphere of commodity exchange.

Yet here again the categories blur, for it is never *only* a material transaction: there is always a sense in which the client buys what she *represents*, some dream of bliss and release, for in modern sexuality, sex is never only a bodily act. The client seeks the absolute experience, in which the prostitute is a mere cipher, fulfilment of his desires, exorcism of his devils; but always her very existence defies this appropriation. She withholds as much as she gives, even plays reflexively, fulfils but subverts 'his' scene; if he wants her, he only gets 'her', the appearance, the theatre of the feminine, 'faked by disguise and make-up'.[105] Perhaps it is only the surrealist imagination that can hint at the complexities of this particular labyrinth; here is Aragon, writing of his experience of Parisian brothels, encountering 'my melodious mistress, my appealing shadow', with her hair of 'knives and stars', but a mistress who also has other hues:

> Mirage or mirror, a great enchantment glows in this darkness and leans against the doorjamb of ravages in the classic pose assumed by death immediately after shedding her shroud. O my image of bone, here I am: let everything finally decompose in the place of illusions and silence. The woman espouses my wishes submissively, and anticipates them, and depersonalizing my instincts suddenly, reaches out perfectly naturally for my tool and demands of me perfectly naturally what *she* loves.[106]

Knives and shrouds, stars and decomposition; there is danger in this encounter. We find that if the prostitute represents the masculine imagination of the city, an imagination that is also an appropriation, then this is fraught with risk; for the prostitute is also the other that defies, takes, and escapes, laughing and grimacing; the prostitute is also, once again, masculine impotence. If the client seeks confirmation, through fulfilment of his fantasy, in this gaze of the other who can never really be a projection of his own desires, yet has to be, then despair – and the possibility of violence – can never be far beneath the surface.

Despair, and horror: for the commodity can never really 'look itself in the face'. It fractures itself, in the impossibility of the reflexive gaze. As the self projects itself on to the other, attempts to grasp itself in the other, so both self and other threaten to fragment, to decompose into frightening death and destruction. This is the unstated term in the transaction, the price that the client cannot avoid paying. Thus, Benjamin's claim that, in Baudelaire, women, particularly prostitutes, 'the most precious spoils', bring 'Life, which means Death. . . . It is the only thing which one may not bargain for and for Baudelaire, it is the only thing that counts.'[107] And in this sense, he concludes, 'the whores in the doorways of tenement blocks' are like the 'household goddesses' of a 'cult of nothingness'.[108]

In this perspective, the prostitute becomes a mannequin, a 'gaily decked-out corpse';[109] fashionable display cannot conceal, indeed can emphasize, the fetishistic fragmentation and decomposition of the body, the dialectic of desire and death. This is brought out graphically in the Goncourt brothers' horrified description of the celebrated courtesan La Paiva: underneath the glitter was a figure 'one hundred years old', who 'takes on at times the undefinable terror of a painted corpse'.[110] And Bernheimer points out that we are not far from the appropriation and florid disfigurement of the prostitute's body by modernism;[111] one of the celebrated founding paintings of twentieth-century art, Picasso's *Les Demoiselles d'Avignon* (1907), is after all a painting of prostitutes, and who is to say whether their static, fractured poses, their grotesque masks, are an invitation to the dance of life, or of death?

The City of Death and Transfiguration

Clearly this city of pleasure is also a city of death, and Benjamin's 'goddesses of nothingness' can also be ghosts; a city can be full of 'places and moments when it bears witness to the dead, shows itself full of dead'.[112] Here is Hessel, describing Berlin's *Kaisergalerie* – modelled on the Parisian arcades – in 1929:

> The whole center of the arcade is empty. I rush quickly to the exit; I feel ghostly, hidden crowds of people from days gone by, who hug the walls with lustful glances at the tawdry jewellery, the clothing, the pictures. . . . At the exit . . . I breathe more freely; the street, freedom, the present.[113]

If the gaze of modernity is still 'covetous and erotic', it is now also morbid and nostalgic. By the early years of this century, the original arcades had failed financially, destroyed by the department stores; the other side of the modern city's cult of the new is its constant creation of 'dead matter', no longer viable or fashionable. Aragon, as always, gives a more idiomatic epitaph for the arcades:

> Although the life that originally quickened them has drained away, they deserve, nevertheless, to be regarded as the secret repositories of several modern myths: it is

only today, when the pickaxe menaces them, that they have at last become the true sanctuaries of a cult of the ephemeral, the ghostly landscape of damnable pleasures and professions. Places that were incomprehensible yesterday, and that tomorrow will never know.[114]

'Incomprehensible yesterday' because dreamlike, a transient, mythic world of images in which one is immersed; and when they return, as childhood memories, 'as evanescent and as alluringly tormenting as half-forgotten dreams',[115] they are just as inscrutable. For Baudelaire, this is a city where one finds oneself 'Stumbling over words like cobblestones/colliding at times with lines dreamt of long ago'.[116] Only now, suggests Susan Buck-Morss, when 'these decaying structures no longer hold sway over the collective imagination', is it possible to recognize them as 'the illusory dream images they always were'.[117]

In what Aragon wrote, there is a suggestion that meaning only flashes up as the past disappears into a future that as yet does not exist. And yet, the past is also repetition. The modern city returns endlessly, repeats itself endlessly; the new and the transient are celebrated even in their constant recurrence. The city constantly anticipates its own patterns of return. Baudelaire can only write of the arcades and the *flâneur* when they are already past; yet they are no further in the past in the 1920s, when Benjamin writes of them: 'the great writers perform their combinations in a world that comes after them, just as the Paris streets of Baudelaire's poems . . . only existed after 1900'.[118] In the city, the ghosts are there in advance; the future exists in the past, gives it momentary meaning, through making it present.

For Benjamin, as for Virginia Woolf, cities are part of the cycle of life and death. But the visions are in marked contrast. For Woolf, the city can retain a powerful sense of organic fecundity, the living process of renewal, and something of this can be drawn on in the writer's art. Renewal implies death and dying, but this is all part of the cycle, a cycle in which culture is an aspect of nature; indeed, 'culture' and 'nature' cannot be distinguished and opposed in the standard way. For Benjamin, on the other hand, 'The high point of a technical arrangement of the world lies in the liquidation of fecundity',[119] so the modern city cannot 'die', in an organic sense; it can only 'petrify', like a medusa's head, turned to stone. This is ruination, not organic renewal. The city's 'death' is as artificial as its 'life': if culture sets itself against nature, the 'death' of cultural products is both a defiance of nature, and nature's revenge; it becomes a parody of death, a grotesque play of death. Death becomes 'unnatural', a product of technological change and the vagaries of fashion. The city becomes a place of ghosts and empty forms, an allegory of the death of nature, rather than a symbol of its resilience; a testament to the ultimate futility of project confronted with its own evanescent products. And if these two visions testify to the gendered experiences of female and male modernist writers of the 1920s, they also both point forward to later attempts to capture the experience of the city, with Woolf as a harbinger of certain strands of postmodern optimism, and Benjamin the authentic voice of *fin-de-siècle* pessimism.

And today? Another cycle of novelty and repetition has been worked through, in the twentieth-century city; and perhaps, by the late 1980s, the pessimistic vision was particularly conspicuous. 'These futurist cities have become the urban nightmare of the 1980s', writes Wilson: 'the gouged out twilight zones, the tower block wastelands, and the motorways carving through the picturesque old city quarters . . . creating blitzed zones of despair.'[120] This language remains, after all, very close to the language the critics of Haussmann used in the 1850s, and doubtless ignores the recuperative powers of the city, and our experiences of it. Analysing a string of distinctive ads from 1988, Judith Williamson claims that they can be seen as

> briefly illuminating dark city streets with images of private survival. . . . Many of these, again, use black and white to emphasise the grimness of urban dereliction before cash floods pavements and shop windows with light and colour. At the insertion of your plastic, the city comes alive; yet there is an almost necrophiliac quality to the relationship between cash-card carrier and these cities raised from the dead. . . . There is no pleasure anywhere here; money is like a weapon, cards are pulled from pockets like knives or guns, in gestures of *defence*. . . . Against what? Everywhere in these ads is the sense that the city is a threat (until it becomes a shopping precinct) and that people are not merely alone, but aggressively alone. . . . Without cash, bleakness is everywhere.[121]

And even with cash, bleakness is at best held at bay.

Death and transfiguration still haunt the city, as modern debates with postmodern. And with this, the contours of the city become ever less clear. When urbanism spreads everywhere, the city's boundaries lose any clarity, and its inhabitants lose their distinctiveness. Thus Buck-Morss suggests that if the *flâneur* becomes extinct, it is only by 'exploding into a myriad of forms', shoppers, tourists, consumers of mass culture: 'This is the "truth" of the *flâneur*, more visible in his afterlife than in his flourishing.' And then, the arcades: 'The restored Paris arcades still function as dreamworlds, but now instead of celebrating urban modernity, they provide fantasies of escape from it',[122] like English tea shops, antique shops, old bookshops, and travel agencies. The city returns, this time as heritage centre. But overall, the diffusion of urbanism can lead to a lack of focus, a waning sense of place, an inability to say what the city might mean; Sharpe and Wallock point to the 'delocalized city' of current fiction, with residence and workplace featuring merely as unreal, uninteresting background to the socializing of the protagonists.[123] But again, this only repeats the challenge of the modern city, its excess of significance as the everywhere and nowhere of modernity itself.

Notes

1   A. Lees, *Cities Perceived: Urban Society in European and American Thought, 1820–1940* (Columbia University Press, 1985), pp. 2–5.
2   D. Harvey, 'Cities of Dreams', *Guardian* (15 October 1993).

3 R. Williams, *Keywords* (Fontana, 1976), pp. 46, 48.
4 J. Raban, *Soft City* (Collins Harvill, 1988), p. 10.
5 M. Berman, *All That Is Solid Melts into Air: The Experience of Modernity* (Verso, 1983), pp. 143, 136.
6 R. Sennett, *The Fall of Public Man* (Faber, 1986), pp. 39, 17.
7 S. Ewen, *All Consuming Images* (Basic Books, 1988), p. 72.
8 R. Williams, *The Country and the City* (Hogarth, 1985), p. 235.
9 W. Wordsworth, 'Composed upon Westminster Bridge, September 3, 1800', cited in Williams, *Country and City*, p. 5.
10 W. Blake, 'London', from 'Songs of Experience', in his *Complete Writings* (Oxford University Press, 1969), p. 216.
11 Raban, *Soft City*, p. 155.
12 Williams, *Country and City*, p. 239.
13 P. Stallybrass and A. White, *The Politics and Poetics of Transgression* (Methuen, 1986), p. 187.
14 Raban, *Soft City*, pp. 28, 34.
15 E. Wilson, *Adorned in Dreams* (Virago, 1985), pp. 130, 127.
16 C. Baudelaire, cited in Berman, *All That Is Solid*, p. 144.
17 Raban, *Soft City*, pp. 160, 165.
18 L. Aragon, *Paris Peasant* (Picador, 1987; originally 1926), pp. 94, 129, 28.
19 E. Wilson, *The Sphinx in the City* (Virago, 1991), pp. 9, 25, 7–8.
20 V. Woolf, 'Street Haunting, A London Adventure', in *Collected Essays*, Vol. 4 (Hogarth, 1967), pp. 155, 157, 164.
21 V. Woolf, *A Room of One's Own* (Grafton Books, 1977), p. 91.
22 V. Woolf, 'Oxford Street Tide', in *The London Scene: Five Essays by Virginia Woolf* (Hogarth, 1982), p. 18.
23 Woolf, 'Street Haunting', pp. 165, 156.
24 W. Benjamin, 'Berlin Chronicle', in his *Reflections* (Schocken, 1986), pp. 8–9.
25 S. Marcus, 'Reading the Illegible: Some Modern Representations of Urban Experience', in W. Sharpe and L. Wallock (eds.) *Visions of the Modern City* (Johns Hopkins University Press, 1987), p. 235.
26 Wilson, *Sphinx*, p. 8.
27 Woolf, *Room*, p. 92.
28 Woolf, 'Oxford Street', pp. 18, 16–17.
29 V. Woolf, *Orlando* (Grafton Books, 1977), pp. 183–5.
30 Woolf, 'Street Haunting', p. 163.
31 T. S. Eliot, 'The Waste Land' (1922), in *Collected Poems* (Faber, 1963), p. 65.
32 Woolf, 'Oxford Street', pp. 19–20.
33 V. Woolf, 'The Docks of London', in *London Scene*, pp. 10, 10–11, 11, 13.
34 Cited in S. Squier, *Virginia Woolf and London: The Sexual Politics of the City* (North Carolina University Press, 1985), pp. 53, 56.
35 V. Woolf, 'Great Men's Houses', in *London Scene*.
36 Cited in S. Squier, 'Virginia Woolf's London and the Feminist Revision of Modernism', in M. A. Caws (ed.) *City Images* (Gordon and Breach, 1991), p. 110.
37 Woolf, 'Street Haunting', pp. 158, 159, 159.
38 R. Bowlby, 'Walking, Women and Writing: Virginia Woolf as *Flâneuse*', in I. Armstrong (ed.) *New Feminist Discourses* (Routledge, 1992), pp. 41, 43.
39 Woolf, 'Street Haunting', p. 165.
40 Squier, *Virginia Woolf*, p. 47.

41   Woolf, 'Oxford Street', p. 21.
42   Woolf, 'Street Haunting', p. 156.
43   Raban, *Soft City*, p. 70.
44   Woolf, 'Street Haunting', p. 155.
45   Berman, *All That Is Solid*, p. 198.
46   Woolf, 'Street Haunting', pp. 161, 161, 166.
47   Squier, *Virginia Woolf*, p. 51.
48   Woolf, *Room*, pp. 93, 85–6.
49   Woolf, 'Street Haunting', p. 163.
50   Williams, *Country and City*, p. 154.
51   Woolf, *Room*, p. 99. See also the introduction to T. Moi, *Sexual/Textual Politics* (Methuen, 1988).
52   Sennett, *Fall*, p. 129.
53   D. J. Olsen, *The City as a Work of Art: London, Paris, Vienna* (Yale University Press, 1986), pp. 225, 325.
54   Cited in S. Buck-Morss, *The Dialectics of Seeing: Walter Benjamin and the Arcades Project* (MIT Press, 1991), p. 83.
55   Berman, *All That Is Solid*, p. 150.
56   Olsen, *City*, p. 54.
57   N. Green, *The Spectacle of Nature: Landscape and Bourgeois Culture in Nineteenth-Century France* (Manchester University Press, 1990), p. 25.
58   G. Pollock, 'Modernity and the Spaces of Femininity', in her *Vision and Difference* (Routledge, 1988), p. 67.
59   E. Wilson, 'The Invisible *Flâneur*', *New Left Review* (1992), 191, p. 94.
60   Written 1836; cited in J. Rignall, 'Benjamin's *Flâneur* and the Problem of Realism', in A. Benjamin (ed.) *The Problems of Modernity: Adorno and Benjamin* (Routledge, 1989), p. 115.
61   W. Benjamin, *Charles Baudelaire: A Lyric Poet in the Era of High Capitalism* (Verso, 1983), p. 170.
62   Sennett, *Fall*, p. 156.
63   E. A. Poe, 'The Man of the Crowd', in *Tales of Mystery and Imagination* (Everyman, 1984), pp. 109, 110, 110, 116.
64   D. Brand, 'From the *Flâneur* to the Detective: Interpreting the City of Poe', in T. Bennett (ed.) *Popular Fiction* (Routledge, 1990), pp. 225, 224.
65   Raban, *Soft City*, p. 75.
66   Williams, *Country and City*, p. 227.
67   F. Moretti, 'Clues', in Bennett, *Popular Fiction*, p. 238.
68   Benjamin, *Baudelaire*, pp. 40, 43.
69   C. Belsey, 'Deconstructing the Text: Sherlock Holmes', in Bennett, *Popular Fiction*, p. 279.
70   Pollock, 'Modernity', pp. 67, 69, and J. Wolff, 'The Invisible *Flâneuse*: Women and the Literature of Modernity', *Theory, Culture and Society* (1985), 2:3. See also P. P. Ferguson, 'The *Flâneur* On and Off the Streets of Paris', in K. Tester (ed.) *The Flâneur* (Routledge, 1994).
71   Wilson, *Sphinx*, p. 7.
72   J. Walkowitz, *City of Dreadful Delights: Narratives of Sexual Danger in Late-Victorian London* (Virago, 1992), p. 46.
73   W. Benjamin, cited in D. Frisby, *Fragments of Modernity* (Polity, 1988), p. 229.
74   W. Benjamin, 'Central Park', in *New German Critique* (1985), 34, p. 40.

75 Benjamin, 'Berlin Chronicle', p. 4.
76 Wilson, 'Invisible *Flâneur*', pp. 109, 110.
77 C. Baudelaire, 'The Painter of Modern Life', in his *The Painter of Modern Life and Other Essays* (Phaidon, 1964), p. 9.
78 C. Baudelaire, 'Crowds', in *Twenty Prose Poems* (City Lights Books, 1988), p. 27.
79 Wilson, 'Invisible *Flâneur*', p. 110.
80 See K. Tester, Introduction to Tester, *The Flâneur*, for further discussion of 'doing' and 'being'.
81 Cited in Frisby, *Fragments*, p. 250.
82 L. Nead, *Myths of Sexuality: Representations of Women in Victorian Britain* (Blackwell, 1988), p. 117.
83 G. Gissing, quoted in Williams, *Country and City*, p. 223.
84 G. Stedman Jones, *Outcast London* (Clarendon, 1971), pp. 291–7.
85 Wilson, *Sphinx*, p. 7.
86 A. Huyssen, *After the Great Divide: Modernism, Mass Culture, Postmodernism* (Macmillan, 1986), p. 52.
87 Cited in ibid., p. 52.
88 E. Gaskell, *North and South* (Penguin, 1970), p. 110.
89 Ibid., pp. 226, 232–3.
90 Stallybrass and White, *Politics and Poetics*, p. 132.
91 C. Herbert, 'Rat Worship and Taboo in Mayhew's London', *Representations* (1988), p. 23.
92 Nead, *Myths*, p. 121.
93 J. Miller, cited in ibid., p. 117.
94 Nead, *Myths*, p. 106.
95 J. Walkowitz, *Prostitution and Victorian Society* (Cambridge University Press, 1980), p. 18; and see pp. 9, 200, 211–12.
96 R. Baldick (ed.) *Pages from the Goncourt Journals* (Penguin, 1984), p. 68.
97 C. Bernheimer, *Figures of Ill Repute: Representing Prostitution in Nineteenth-Century France* (Harvard University Press, 1989), pp. 92–3, 96.
98 T. J. Clark, *The Painting of Modern Life: Paris in the Art of Manet and His Followers* (Thames and Hudson, 1990), pp. 109, 111, 111.
99 Cited in Bernheimer, *Figures*, p. 92.
100 Clark, *Painting*, p. 79.
101 Cited in ibid., p. 104.
102 Benjamin, 'Central Park', pp. 42, 40.
103 F. Delacoste and P. Alexander (eds.) *Sex Work: Writings by Women in the Sex Industry* (Virago, 1988), back cover.
104 Wilson, *Adorned in Dreams*, p. 143.
105 A. Rauch, 'The *Trauerspiel* of the Prostituted Body, or Woman as Allegory of Modernity', *Cultural Critique* (1988), 10, p. 87.
106 Aragon, *Paris Peasant*, pp. 122, 119.
107 Benjamin, 'Central Park', p. 39.
108 Benjamin, 'Berlin Chronicle', p. 11.
109 W. Benjamin, cited in Buck-Morss, *Dialectics of Seeing*, p. 101.
110 Cited in Bernheimer, *Figures*, p. 102.
111 Bernheimer, *Figures*, p. 266.
112 Benjamin, 'Berlin Chronicle', p. 28.
113 Cited in Buck-Morss, *Dialectics of Seeing*, p. 38.

114 Aragon, *Paris Peasant*, pp. 28–9.
115 Benjamin, 'Berlin Chronicle', p. 28.
116 C. Baudelaire, '*Le Soleil*', from *Les Fleurs du Mal*, my translation.
117 Buck-Morss, *Dialectics of Seeing*, p. 159.
118 W. Benjamin, 'One-Way Street', in his *Reflections*, p. 64.
119 W. Benjamin, cited in Buck-Morss, *Dialectics of Seeing*, p. 99.
120 Wilson, *Adorned in Dreams*, p. 141.
121 J. Williamson, 'Beauty and the Adman', *Guardian* (9 December 1988).
122 Buck-Morss, *Dialectics of Seeing*, pp. 346, 342.
123 W. Sharpe and L. Wallock, 'From "Great Town" to "Nonplace Urban Realm": Reading the Modern City', in their *Visions of the Modern City*, p. 26.

4 The Consolations of Consumerism

The tone of the advertisement shown in plate 2 conveys a subtle mix of reassurance and pressure. Reassurance, in that it preaches moderation in all things, even the smoking it is attempting to sell, and calls on comforting, taken-for-granted, folk notions ('heat purifies'), powerfully reinforced by the medical endorsement ('20,679 physicians'); and pressure, with the woman riding hard to keep ahead of the double-chinned nightmare behind her, the bloated, unhealthy shadow of her own future self.

A strong image is conveyed: the get-ahead, 'modern' woman must keep her 'ever-youthful figure', thereby simultaneously attaining the social power now being opened up to her, while maintaining her femininity, her 'pretty curves'. Indeed, these come together in the configuration of woman and horse, curves and surging potency. This, after all, is the era of the 'New Woman'; the ad comes from American Tobacco's highly successful campaign of 1929–30, attempting to open up the market for women's cigarettes. And the vaunted 'moderation' of the consumer is not, of course, moderation for the producer: large numbers of women smoking 'moderately' are vastly better than hardly any smoking at all.

Already, then, the cigarette is well on its way to its status as an icon of modernity. It embodies messages of democracy, availability, standardization, convenience, and progress. Easy to light up, hold, and extinguish (unlike pipes or cigars), quick to consume, yet also not consumed, hence not fattening (unlike sweets and snack bars), the cigarette became, as Schudson remarks, 'the preferred smoke for people aiming for a streamlined, cultural modernity, involved in the fast pace of city life'.[1] When time matters, when it is conceived as something that can be 'spent', convenience becomes a central virtue; but convenience also has other social connotations, for cigarettes are 'mild', inoffensive (relative to pipes, cigars), hence sociable. And while 'democratic', cigarettes carry a certain hint of luxury, a reminder that consumerism is not about necessities so much as a celebration of excess, an indulgence in waste; consumerism is destructive in its very essence. For Klein, cigarettes themselves should be celebrated, and not for their utility, but their futility, the 'sublimely, darkly beautiful pleasure' they bring.[2]

The cigarette, then, also carries a darker message, hinted at in the ad's reference to doctors, a message that has been there from very early on: a message about modernity and ill health. In the 1930s, Camel cigarettes took up this theme in their ads: cigarettes were sold for 'soothing nerves', protecting against the stresses of 'the modern', all-purpose cures for the pressures of contemporary life.[3] And over time, while retaining this image of health-giving relaxation, relief from tension, cigarettes have of course come to acquire the darker hue themselves; not only do they become as addictive as the consumer pressures from which they promise relief, but the shadow in the ad becomes, in the end, the shadow cast before it by the cigarette itself, the shadow of death, the shadow of the X-ray of the lung. And by 1991, Death cigarettes, the brand that 'tells the truth about smoking', were becoming a cult in California, with Dark Lights, the low tar and nicotine version – marketed as a 'slower death' – spreading later to the UK.

The gender theme, too, has been central from the start. Initially developed in the 1880s, the cigarette made only slow progress; in 1900, it was banned in the US Navy as a 'debasement of manhood', whereas the cigar and the pipe were perfectly acceptable. It only really took off among men in the First World War, when British and American soldiers were issued with tobacco rations, and the greater convenience of the cigarette began to tell, so that what had hitherto been seen as a rather precious, 'feminizing', product began to have an association with masculinity, through war; by 1935, 65 per cent of American men under 40 were smoking cigarettes.[4] The qualities that had previously been unacceptable now made the cigarette seem refined, sophisticated, and by the late 1920s, women were smoking more; for younger women, the cigarette symbolized freedom, equality, cosmopolitanism and a rejection of convention. The femme fatale of 1940s and 1950s films, from Joan Crawford to Lauren Bacall, made smoking appear glamorous; and by the late 1950s, cigarette smoking among women had reached its highest point, at 44 per cent of British women and 33 per cent of American.

Throughout the period, there are essential continuities in the sales pitch to women; as Jacobson suggests, cigarettes are presented to women as a route to 'sexual success, sophistication and slimness'.[5] Analyses of 1970s and 1980s ads suggest that the dual appeal of the Lucky Strike ad remains in place, a combination of the traditional 'feminine' and the contemporary 'feminist'.[6] Kellner suggests that the 1980s 'Virginia Slims woman' is exhibiting 'modernity, thinness, or female power when she lights up her Slim', along with 'individuality, sexuality, fashion, and style'; while simultaneously the Marlboro Lights ads are selling low-tar cigarettes, originally targeted at women, to men, by showing the Marlboro cowboy in wholesome, 'natural', hence 'healthy' environments.[7]

And the effect of advertising? It is often assumed that ads produce smokers; but Schudson argues that 'major consumer changes are rarely wrought by advertising', and that advertising 'followed rather than led the spread of cigarette usage'. Tens of thousands of women were smoking before any ads were directed at them; ads responded to changes, rather than causing or leading them.[8] Of course, a particular campaign that caught the trend could be quite successful, as with the Lucky Strike campaign,[9] or Virginia Slims in the 1980s. Jacobson concludes that research tends to confirm the assumption that 'smoking parents, friends and teachers tend to produce smoking children', and that this is more important than ads as such. And while her claim that 'men depend on women and women depend on cigarettes'[10] puts a rather different emphasis from Barbara Ehrenreich's claim that 'boys smoked to be tough and girls smoked to intimidate boys, if not to challenge the whole concept of gender',[11] both are referring to underlying patterns and tensions in gender relations that are more fundamental than the ads in themselves.

Ultimately, the cigarette derives its iconic power and social significance not from the manipulation of advertisers and producers, but from the culture of consumerism itself. And it is this culture that demands further exploration.

The Shopping Trip

Consumption is universal; so, doubtless, is pleasure-seeking as a motive of human conduct. Consumerism, however, is modern, and clearly involves a distinctive way of linking these. At this stage, it is sufficient to say that consumerism entails a market-oriented quest to articulate and satisfy desires, and desires are as much to do with identity as with material goods; so the fact that the resulting acquisitions are never *merely* acquisitions, but also statements of self-image and aspiration, ensures that the quest is liable, for any particular individual, to be never-ending; the pleasures, like those of smoking, are precarious, restless, yet addictive. A culture of consumerism therefore both presupposes and implies the experience of the world as a consumer spectacle, whereby the marketability of the commodity interpenetrates that of the self, constituting a language and imagery through which self-identity is presented and represented. Whether we go as far as Miller, in his claim that 'consumption is now at the vanguard of history',[12] or Davidson, who suggests that consumption is now 'how we appropriate the world around us',[13] it is at least clear that consumerism has become a crucial aspect of modern social and cultural life.

Until the last century or two the quantity and variety of consumer goods available to most people has generally been very limited. In contrast with this, however, we encounter, in the early modern period, the lifestyle of the elite, referred to by Rosalind Williams as the 'closed world' of 'courtly consumption'. The mode of behaviour found in European courts in this period coupled an increasing emphasis on civility and manners with great ostentation in matters of material culture; courts were modes of display as much as centres of political intrigue, and the two were connected. Writing of Louis XIV, Williams claims that the sumptuous style of life was not geared to pleasure; rather, the 'ceremonies of consumption' served to enhance political authority, as the king 'transformed consumption into a method of rule'.[14] These patterns clearly influenced the bourgeois lifestyle of the eighteenth century, following the mechanisms of diffusion associated with the 'civilizing process'; and though in practice this lifestyle was not so display-oriented, less ostentatious, it was all the more steadily permeated by the objects and images that 'were now emerging as a form of social currency in an increasingly mobile commercial world', as Ewen puts it.[15]

By the middle of the century, the debate between Voltaire and Rousseau on the merits – or otherwise – of luxury consumption and its relationship to the 'civilizing process' was already defining the parameters of later debates on consumerism. Whatever the merits of the argument, Williams suggests that there is indeed a sense in which the civilizing process, with its regulation of behaviour and restraint of emotional display, makes the use of material acquisitions all the more appropriate as a language for expressing needs and aspirations.[16] And by 1790, a Dr Adair could make the very modern-sounding claim that 'as societies advance in civilization, the active mind of man, not contented with the means of satisfying our natural wants, is anxiously employed in creating artificial wants, and inventing the means of their gratification', resulting in the 'empire of fashion'.[17]

By this period, it is clear that middle-class consumption patterns had developed to the point where historians can refer to this period as one of 'consumer revolution'; McKendrick, indeed, refers to an 'orgy of spending'.[18] This recent historical scholarship has tended to push back the origins of consumerism into ever-earlier decades, and this certainly tends to confirm the view that consumerism pre-dates the Industrial Revolution, and support Braudel's contention that it was changes in consumer demand that 'started the engine' of capitalism, with luxury goods, rather than necessities or capital goods, playing the key role. It has even been argued that there were twice as many shops per capita in 1750 as in 1950.[19] As will be seen, this period is indeed decisive for the development of the 'consuming self'; nevertheless, the age of *mass* consumer culture comes later. And if we want a focus for this, it is useful to take the department store, since it is with this institution that 'shopping' in its modern sense developed.

The term itself seems to have been coming into use in the mid-eighteenth century, though Elizabeth Wilson points out that it was generally still necessary to haggle over prices, so that 'the process of purchase remained a lengthy and anxious one'.[20] In effect, modern shopping involves an exchange of rights: the right to browse, to inspect the goods, is gained, and the right to negotiate the price is given up. This was already apparent in the fixed prices on the goods, and the 'window shopping', in Nash's fashionable Regent Street, and the adjoining shopping streets, in London in the 1820s. This was then given a revolutionary impetus by the department stores that were developing in Paris, London, Manchester, Newcastle and New York between the 1830s and the 1860s.[21] At these stores, prices were fixed and clearly marked; profits were made through high volume of sales rather than high mark-ups on individual items; and social skills of impersonal civility came to structure the new relationship between buyer and seller.[22] These stores, like the celebrated Bon Marché in Paris, and its successor as the world's largest store, Macy's of New York, along with John Lewis and Harrods, in London, became central to consumerist expansion in the decades to follow; and Barth, writing of the American experience, is right to claim that 'shopping as a new social art and the department store as a new social institution rose simultaneously, complementing one another',[23] just as Miller, in his study of the Bon

Marché, can add that the department store 'gave shape and definition to the very meaning of the concept of a bourgeois way of life'.[24]

By the 1920s and 1930s, it was increasingly the chain stores that were leading the next wave of expansion, incorporating the working-class market ever more comprehensively into the consumer spectacle; in the British context, Michael Marks, a pedlar in the 1890s, was, by the 1920s, a partner in one of the most successful of these, Marks and Spencer. Cross argued that it was in this period that it became increasingly apparent that 'growth meant endless expansion of consumption but not a parallel extension of free time'. Thus holidays, too, became exercises in consumerism. By 1937, seven million people visited Blackpool for their holidays; on arrival, many headed at once for the 'World's Greatest Woolworths' store, opposite the station, and it was in Blackpool that England had its first cinema. In this democratic consumerist utopia, one could explore the exotic in the 'Indian sharma', childhood in the Punch and Judy show, the novelties of technology in the 'Telepathic Robot', the past in the wax museum, and the famous lights, the 'Illuminations', at night.[25] And so, via the spread of suburbanization and home ownership, to the superstores, shopping malls, out-of-town shopping centres and catalogue shopping of recent decades: Thurrock Lakeside, in the early 1990s, could offer a one million-square-foot glass-domed palace with over 200 shops, 12,000 free car-parking spaces, and a 20-acre lake in which eager health-conscious consumers could try scuba-diving.

This all illustrates one feature of consumer culture that was apparent from early on: the way it straddles public and private space. 'In the ambiguous boundaries of the shopping town, there is space for fantasy, for inversions, for pleasure', suggests Ferrier.[26] This is particularly significant in the area of gender; shopping evolved in the nineteenth century as an arena in which women could have a legitimate presence, the shop itself being an intermediate zone, neither properly private nor unambiguously public. Indeed, Barth suggests that 'shopping appeared as the most widely visible sign of female emancipation in the modern city'.[27] By the 1890s, it was clear that women constituted the great majority of shoppers, and spent over three times as much as men.[28] The store that Selfridge opened in London in 1909, in a blaze of advertising and publicity that heralded the more aggressive sales techniques of the new century, was quite clearly designed with women in view, and in later years he indeed claimed that he had helped emancipate women: 'They came to the store and realised some of their dreams.'[29]

Dream, fantasy: these terms recur endlessly in discussions of the consumer spectacle. By 1900, writes Williams, in her account of the great world fairs and expositions, a 'dream world of the consumer'[30] was emerging. In these expositions and department stores, the commodities seemed to revel in their own theatricality; their mode of display became part of their being, image and object fused in a 'phantasmagoria', a world simultaneously real and fantastical, so that 'a study of the barest facts of commodity culture always turns out to be an exploration of a fantastic realm in which things act, speak, rise, fall, fly, evolve', as Richards puts it in his own account of Victorian consumer culture. This is a world described not only by Marx but by novelists like Dickens, in whose stories 'furniture, textiles, watches, handkerchiefs, seem to live and breathe'.[31] But it is Zola's novel *Au Bonheur des Dames*, where the department store in question is based on the Bon Marché, that brings this out most clearly. For Zola, 'The merchandise in the windows breathes, emits a suggestive tremor; throbbing warmly, it hints at, yet hides, the treasure within', and in the store itself, 'the atmosphere is, if anything, more caressing, more seductive still'.[32] And Zola writes of a showcase where 'slumbered the heavy fabrics, the special weaves, the damasks, the brocades, the beaded and lamé silks, amidst a deep bed of velvet', where 'women, pale with desire, leaned over as if to see themselves'.[33]

Commodities, 'throbbing warmly', tempting women, 'pale with desire': clearly there is an erotics of consumerism. Shopping is not, perhaps, so innocent a pleasure; it implies delicious, vicarious transgression. Lady Jeune wrote in 1896 of the 'overwhelming temptations' in the department store, so that women may well 'succumb before leaving'.[34] Boucicaut himself, owner of the Bon Marché, claimed that it was desirable to get the customers 'lost' in the store, so they would then 'succumb at the sight of things which grab them on the way'; and Zola's store owner wanted 'to conquer woman . . . he had built her this temple to hold her at his mercy there'.[35] Any respectable married man would clearly have to think twice before exposing his susceptible wife to such seductive experiences; and a woman would have to be aware of the dangers, as well as the pleasures, of the consuming embrace.

Zola's women, leaning over 'as if to see themselves', also remind us that, as Mary Ann Doane claims, 'all consumerism involves the idea of self-image',[36] and hence elements of narcissism. Rachel Bowlby expands on this as follows:

> Seducer and seduced, possessor and possessed of one another, women and com-
> modities flaunt their images at one another in an amorous regard. . . . Consumer
> culture transforms the narcissistic mirror into a shop window, the *glass* which
> reflects an idealized image of the woman (or man) who stands before it, in the form
> of the model she could buy or become. Through the glass, the woman sees what she
> wants and what she wants to be. . . .
>   The window smashes the illusion that there is a meaningful distinction in mod-
> ern society between illusion and reality, fact and fantasy, fake and genuine images of
> self.[37]

Women, then, are constructed as archetypal consumers, but there is paradox here: their consumerism both reinforces gender stereotypes through their passive role as 'the seduced', but also implicitly grants an active, more transgressive role, a capacity to act independently in the public sphere; women 'spend', and this has, after all, been a metaphor for sexuality, usually *male* sexuality. Similarly, *men* as consumers are subject to this ambiguity, being appealed to in ads *as men* yet implicitly 'feminized' in the act of consuming. The pleasures and pitfalls of shopping are gender-coded.

Ad Culture

During 1984–86 a series of anti-heroin ads appeared in newspapers, London Underground hoardings, and the media generally, sponsored by the government. They contained bleak, haunting pictures of wasted, ravaged junkies under such straplines as 'Heroin screws you up', 'Skin care by heroin'. But it was found that some people were using the posters as pin-ups; in some areas, they became a cult. In his discussion of this, Davidson points out that the ads were unintentionally presenting a seductive image; particularly for those left out of the mid-1980s boom, the 'self-indulgent melancholy' of the junkie could be attractive. Laurie suggests that if taking heroin is a kind of delayed suicide, the addict has 'the pleasure of being around to see the effect of finality. He hugs the catastrophic image of the junkie'. There is, after all, a long tradition of romantically-tinged images of drug use, going back to opium in the last century. In effect, the ad agency had unwittingly branded heroin; far from countering the reasons people have for trying drugs, suggests Davidson, the campaign actually 'mined and reinforced them'.[38] Ads are necessarily about consuming, even when ostensibly about non-consuming; and, in tapping the 'dark side' of consumerism, the complexity of 'pleasure', these particular ads remind us that the 'effectiveness' of advertising depends on its ability to mine deep layers of cultural meaning that frequently have contradictory aspects.

Of course, 'effectiveness' is an odd word to use here, when the ads seem to have had the opposite effect to that intended. But this is not so rare; if we think of advertising in terms of its professed aim, to shift more product, then Schudson makes a good case for concluding that, as we have seen with cigarettes, advertising may be less powerful than its critics – and some of its advocates – suggest, and that when it *does* work, it may not be for the most obvious reasons. Advertising is part of business culture; it 'must' be effective, because everyone else does it, and anyway it is necessary for the company's prestige. Ads help convince the investors by fitting in with their expectations of good business practice, and keep the sales force and the retailers committed to the product; indirectly, then, ads can 'affect the *goods available to consumers* even if they do not persuade consumers which goods to buy', and hence advertising may help sell goods 'even if it never persuades a *consumer* of anything'.[39] And advertisers themselves see it as a very hit-and-miss affair, with half a dozen failed campaigns to every clear success.

Conversely, it became clear in the 1980s that ads could be 'consumed', enjoyed, *in themselves*, as an art form or branch of entertainment, without reference to any interest in purchasing the commodity. Interesting accounts of how ads 'work' – in terms of how they are constructed, how form and content are related, and so on – do not amount to proof of how, or whether, they 'work' in terms of 'making consumers consume'; what these analyses do, however, is to reveal clues to the underlying patterns out of which *both* advertisers *and* consumers go about the daily task of coding and decoding the images and messages that are encountered all around. If, as Goldman claims, advertising has become a form of 'internal cultural colonialism',[40] then it must be one where the colonialist and the colonized are present simultaneously in each of us. Hence it may be more appropriate to read the content of ads for what they tell us about patterns of meaning in consumer culture, and to see advertising, as such, as a revealing form of conspicuous waste, than to see either dimension as manifesting a rational strategy for the effective manipulation and exploitation of gullible consumers.

In the eighteenth century, 'advertising' merely referred to basic information about where products could be bought; attempts to *sell* products, by singing their praises, were examples of 'puffery'. By the middle of the next century, 'advertising', both the word and the phenomenon, had acquired their modern sense, in which it could be said that it is the 'puffery' that has won out. And 'puffery' was a disparaging term; its incorporation in advertising has always gone hand in hand with widespread distrust of the latter, particularly by the cultural elite. Advertising, after all, can be seen as a modern form of rhetoric, an art of persuasion appealing to the emotions and prejudices of its audience, tapping the non-rational, bypassing the conscious mind; necessarily manipulative, then, and a corruption of norms of rational argument. Yet it is also troublesome in that it implicitly questions the narrowness of that notion of rationality; it taps the reality of everyday life, in which emotions and feelings, traditions and aspirations, enter into the fabric of our experience and our choices; its persuasive skills are only those we *all* acquire, in surviving in the modern consumer jungle. And if ads can carry messages that influence us, as consumers, in ways we are not necessarily fully aware of, this is also true of those who produce the ads in the first place. If ads are about selling things, they are not *only* about selling things; their images can carry symbolic meanings, transmit messages, and create moods, in ways that cannot be reduced to the conscious intentions of their creators, and cannot be wholly controllable and predictable in their effects.

The increasing importance of ads has gone hand in hand with an increasing significance attached to questions of design and style. Before the nineteenth century 'design' referred to the preliminary planning stage, as in many contexts it still does; but Ewen suggests that by the 1830s, the term was assuming its modern meaning, 'describing the superficial application of decoration to the form and surface of a product'.[41] 'Style', too, testifies to the significance of questions of form and expression, appearance and presentation, the mode by which a product is displayed, with connotations of fashion. By the early decades of this century, large companies were increasingly incorporating styling divisions in their organization, and matters of style and design were being pushed to the forefront in advertising. This seems to correspond to an increasing awareness that commodities indeed address fantasies as well as material needs, and that matters of form and presentation are critical in enabling the potential consumer to make the identification with the product that would clinch a sale; the buyer did not just want utility. In the 1920s, the first wireless sets were certainly not 'wire-less'; they were crude assemblies of wires, valves and resistors, with no attempt at concealment. Very quickly, these were transformed into what in essence remains the modern radio, encased in a cabinet that could be designed according to the basic tenets of design that had existed since Wedgwood in the eighteenth century: either 'traditional', reassuringly nostalgic in form, like furniture cabinets, or more aggressively 'modern', futuristic, streamlined and simplified.[42] And by the end of the decade, style had become a concern of the mass media, particularly noticeable in magazines aimed at a mass market. Increasingly, claims Ewen, style has become 'the official idiom of the marketplace', so that whether in advertising, packaging, product design or corporate identity, 'the power of provocative surfaces speaks to the eye's mind, over-shadowing matters of quality or substance'; it has become inseparable from 'the evolution and sensibility of modernity'. And by the 1980s, the so-called 'designer decade', even politics could increasingly be seen in these terms: 'democracy itself becomes style',[43] participation becomes consumption.

Writing of the American experience, Marchand suggests that designers of ads in the 1920s and 1930s saw themselves as 'missionaries of modernity', and that 'in their efforts to promote the mystique of modernity in styles and technology, while simultaneously assuaging the anxieties of consumers about losses of community and individual control', they reflected a 'cultural dilemma' of the modern period. And in this period of developing mass-media advertising, we find that the audience was characteristically seen as female; trade journals commonly attributed 85 per cent of all consumer spending to women. Mass-circulation women's magazines, like *Good Housekeeping*, *Woman's Own* and *Woman*, date from this period. And it was above all in the newly constructed woman's sphere of housework that women were seen as most open to influence; 'labour-saving devices' could replace the by now fast-disappearing servant class. Here, women could be 'modern' in both senses – efficient, yet also interested in fashion – and this combination was ideal for both the designers and the advertisers of domestic technology.[44] Together, they could use the imagery of science to convey 'a vision of a future free from discomfort and anxiety', and promote what Forty refers to as the 'absurd and impossible' idea that 'machines could turn housework from laborious drudgery to a few minutes' pleasure', with spotless electric cookers miraculously producing hot meals under the admiring gaze of the awestruck housewife.[45] These ads were still central by the 1950s, even though the evidence is that hours spent on housework had actually increased over the period, and would continue to do so until at least the 1970s.[46] Over this whole period, from the 1920s to the present, one can indeed detect two main shifts in the general content of ads: from a focus on the product (as seen in these 'housework' ads) to a focus on the consumer and the consumer's lifestyle; and from images of social conformity to images of self-fulfilment, escapism and fantasy.[47] Both these trends culminate in a decade of which it could be written: 'If you wanted to know what was really happening in the 1980s, you watched the ads.'

If, in the 1980s, ads were celebrated as a 'non-stop carnival of images which didn't just sell, but also crystallised contemporary aspirations, fantasies, moods and fears',[48] this reminds us that ads appeal through tapping a variety of ideas, feelings and emotions. As was seen with cigarettes – and heroin – ads can testify to complexities and a deep ambivalence in consumerism. At a general level, this is what Williams is getting at when she writes that while the 'unprecedented expansion' of goods has obvious benefits, 'it has also brought a weight of remorse and guilt, craving and envy, anxiety, and, above all, uneasy conscience, as we sense that we have too much, yet keep wanting more'.[49] But this guilt can, in turn, become a source of pleasure. Davidson analyses a Smirnoff ad from 1987, a 'vignette of scandal laughed off', purporting to be an incriminating photo of a yuppie couple meeting illicitly in a nightclub: if a 'lifestyle of pleasure' means there is inevitably something to feel guilty about, so 'there is also immunity to be had in exultantly riding that guilt . . . in guilt, precisely in guilt, lies pleasure'.[50]

But it isn't just having too much that is at issue, but fear of loss, of having too little; if consumerism is about pleasure-seeking, it can also reveal worries about its transience, its impermanence. Judith Williamson analyses Volkswagen's 'Changes' ad, which won the UK industry award in 1988: it showed an angry, well-dressed woman, walking out on a relationship, slamming the door in a fury, discarding the fur coat on a convenient parking meter, and slinging her pearls into a dustbin. She writes:

> The image of the pearls in the dustbin perfectly encapsulates a sense of the closeness of riches and destitution. . . . Images frequently speak of their opposites, and throwing away also involves a concern about keeping. Throwing things away is, in a sense, a way of pre-empting things being taken away . . . a kind of anticipatory survivalism.

And she concludes that the appearance of this 'throwing-out and nightmare imagery' in an advertising world purportedly about consumer pleasure testifies to deep anxieties in this culture of consumerism.[51]

To pursue this further, it is useful to draw on Davidson's account of the significance of the brand in advertising. The ad transforms product into brand:

> All brands are products, but not all products are brands, and the difference is advertising. That extra is called *added value*. Not just mints, but the elegance and sophistication of *After Eights*; not just a hamburger, but the fun and optimism of *McDonalds*; not just a cube of artificial flavourings, but the quintessence of *Oxo* family life. . . . The mechanisms of pleasure, fantasy, our different selves, our social worlds, and social status all colour and texture the larger sense that turns products into brands.[52]

So a brand is a label on a package of possible experiences: holiday ads offer locations elsewhere, fun, 'broadened horizons . . . a new you; living history; spiritual tranquillity; exoticism; personal challenges'. And ultimately 'it is in the brand that consumerism and culture meet', so that 'culture is the society we build into our brands', and advertising is about 'what it is for something to be cultural'.[53]

More specifically, a branded product is 'a hybrid between art and junk'. It is disposable, yet 'laced with associations and powers' normally attributed to art, i.e.

'endowed with enduring qualities, and expressive of the world around it'. Its disposability is not, after all, a 'natural' feature of it; rather it depends on fashion, and whim; it has a capacity to attract and repel, and this too is only associated with its 'natural' qualities insofar as these have been transformed by the cultural imagination. A branded object is an appropriation of nature via consumerism, and advertising is the 'way of seeing' that is an essential aspect of this, a 'way of seeing'[54] that necessarily adds to what is seen, appropriating it in ways that render it meaningful; hence Chaney's claim that 'the project of advertising is the dramatisation of mundane experience'.[55]

This 'appropriation' of nature, simultaneously literal and imaginative, is essentially *excessive*; it goes beyond 'natural needs' and 'naturalistic representation'. Hence it is simultaneously creative and destructive, since to appropriate 'excessively' is to be wasteful, and the power of the branded object to influence us represents precisely the power of this wasteful excess that *is* the culture of modernity in its consuming mode. Waste is appropriation under the sign of excess. In the light of this, Davidson claims that 'Works of art embody ways of seeing that are metamorphically in excess of the literal, while bits of junk are literally in excess of what we need, and therefore discardable', and this grounds his suggestion that the brand possesses attributes of both, giving it 'pride of place at the heart of culture',[56] a culture in which the objects of excess, the detritus of consumer culture, become more meaningful as art itself declines in significance. In the end, style, design and the ad come together, as mutually reinforcing aspects of the language and imagery of consumer excess.

'Getting and Spending, We Lay Waste Our Powers': Consuming Desires, Health and the Body

Wordsworth's implicit suggestion that consumerism entails 'waste', not just in the sense of 'excess' but as a diminution of human well-being, can further illuminate the problematic role it plays in modern culture. The central significance of waste in the former sense is apparent most particularly, perhaps, in the areas of fashion obsolescence, media spectacle and the very existence of advertising itself. If, in the nineteenth century, 'the mode of excess became a mode of producing the *material world*', as Richards suggests,[57] citing the spectacular display of commodities at the great world fairs, then this has clearly continued and intensified. For most people, writes Ewen, 'waste is seen as an inherent part of the process by which they obtain replenishment and pleasure', and he adds:

> From a marketing point of view, disposability is the golden goose. It conflates the act of *using* with that of *using up*, and promotes markets that are continually hungry for more. . . . It is in the representation and aestheticization of waste that the modern phenomenon of style plays its most ubiquitous and persistent role. In the market, the underlying invocation of nearly all contemporary style is to consume, use up, and consume again.[58]

This equation of 'using' and 'using up' takes us into the heart of the notion of 'consumption', what Williams calls 'its mingled nature as achievement and destruction'. In English, the terms 'consume' and 'consummate' have interlinked histories, and in the French *consommation* the intermingling of the terms is near-complete. In effect, there are two aspects to these terms. One means 'use up', devour; and in English, 'consumption' was the traditional popular name for tuberculosis, which was seen as 'consuming' its victim. In this sense, 'consumption is considered equivalent to destruction, waste, decay – in short, to a death-directed process'.[59] The second aspect means 'sum up', carry to completion, as a positive process in life (and which can, indeed, have sexual connotations). Hence, putting them together, we can say that in 'using up', destroying, we further life, but we thereby also move closer to 'summing up' our life, in death.

This duality seems to have been present in both the discourse and the experience of modern consumerism from quite early on. Porter suggests consumption was seen to raise 'broader moral and cosmic questions of order, harmony, balance, teleology, and health in its widest sense'; it posed a challenge, 'suggesting both an enlargement through incorporation, and a withering away, both enrichment and impoverishment'. Both literally and metaphorically, consumption could be a 'disease of waste'; yet economists pointed out that 'under-consumption' could also be dangerous.[60] As for the disease itself, 'consumptions' were seen as a serious scourge by the early years of the eighteenth century, and by the end of the century one in four deaths in London were listed as being due to pulmonary consumption; medical discourse itself oscillated between seeing the disease as due to a deficit, or an excess, of 'consumption', a deficit that signified an excess of delicacy and refinement, or an excess that signified a grossness, a deficit of those qualities.[61]

Such excesses and deficits, mirroring those of consumerism itself, were also seen to be implicated in the epidemic of 'nervous disorders' that characterized the nineteenth century. These links could seem very plausible: after all, many of the key items of soaring consumption were drugs, or addictive substances more generally, like tea, coffee, alcohol, tobacco, opium and patent medicines, and the extent to which these either 'cause' or, alternatively, 'relieve' symptoms has been, and remains, much discussed.[62] Richards has argued that the advertising and sale of patent medicines was crucial in the growth of modern consumerism: 'the quacks constituted the human body as a new kind of commodity spectacle'. These 'medicines' were, in effect, placebo drugs; and since the placebo is 'the ultimate commodity: it has no intrinsic value', it, like the cigarette, can also serve as an 'icon of consumer capitalism'.[63] And, like the cigarette, the dangers were there, too: in popular literature, there was no clear medicine/drug distinction, and patent medicines, cocaine and opium could be sold indiscriminately. These themes have continued: by the 1920s, the links between health, consumerism and medicine are being further consolidated in the ads, and products like Listerine are being promoted to cure medical-sounding conditions like 'halitosis' (bad breath) or 'acidosis' (indigestion).[64] And discussing the use of heroin in the 1980s, Davidson suggests that drugs in effect exaggerate normal consumerism: 'they transform the ordinary into the extraordinary, otherworldly bliss of fantasy and pleasure and express a whole lifestyle in so doing, all to the tune of complete price inelasticity'; hence 'Addiction is the ideology of advertising taken to its logical conclusion.'[65]

It is in the body itself that many of the paradoxes and tensions of consumerism are concentrated. The 'civilized' body is subject to control, self-discipline; and increasingly, this has coincided with the slim, 'fashionable' body. Yet the 'consuming' body is necessarily tempted by excess, encouraged to view health as abundance, hedonism, relaxation, *release* from control. Jackson Lears points out that from early this century, a set of values favouring leisure, spending and a morality of individual fulfilment has become ever more widely shared, entailing the links between ideals of 'personal growth', health and consumption that he calls a 'therapeutic ethos'.[66] And Crawford points to how this ideal of 'release' exists in tension with that of 'control':

> The releasing motif suggests pleasure-seeking rather than ascetic self-denials, the satisfaction of desire instead of the repression of desire. . . . Instead of a language of will-power and regulation, there exists a language of well-being, contentment and enjoyment. . . .
>
> The culture of consumption demands a model personality contrary to the personality required for production. The mandate for discipline clashes with the mandate for pleasure.[67]

Susan Bordo adds that 'conditioned to lose control at the very sight of desirable products, we can only master our desires through rigid defences against them'.[68]

Consuming, swallowing, eating: it is hardly surprising that the bodily incarnations of consumerism have become so tension-laden. Problems with swallowing, choking, became key signifiers of hysteria in the late nineteenth century; and Richards points to ads produced by sellers of patent medicines in which 'swallowing remedies becomes a figure for constituting the self. . . . You are what you swallow, and what you swallow determines who you are and what you can become.'[69] And eating, itself: for the anorexic, this becomes 'a shameful and disgusting act', writes Brumberg, and the anorexic thereby 'makes nonconsumption the perverse centrepiece of her identity'.[70] Pointing out that refusal to eat in an era of relative plenty is a deeply symbolic act, Turner argues that anorexia is a 'disorder of abundance', hence 'an anxiety directed at the surface of the body in a system organized around narcissistic consumption'.[71]

It is indeed bulimia and anorexia that exemplify these dilemmas most vividly, though they do so in slightly different ways. If eating induces guilt, and non-eating induces desire, then the binge becomes a perfect, circular resolution, an act of consumption that simultaneously cancels itself, that 'consumes' itself so totally that further consumption is needed, and the cycle can continue: the apotheosis of the shopping trip. It is bulimia, then, that reflects the control/release dialectic most acutely. Anorexia and obesity, on the other hand, emerge as attempted resolutions in opposite directions.[72] For the anorexic, the 'grotesque body' of Carnival never really went away; but now, it is not a figure of celebration but of threat, of fear, representing unrestrained impulse, uncontained desire, the neediness and craving that threatens autonomy.

And it is, of course, particularly women who have recourse to these ultimately paradoxical, self-destructive coping strategies; it is women whose desires have been taken to be particularly problematical, particularly embedded in 'bodily' drives, particularly in need of strong control. We can recall Dijkstra's discussion of the threat of all-devouring, all-consuming women in late nineteenth-century representations of sphinxes and other horrors, grotesque embodiments of power-ful yet censored desire.[73] Kim Chernin writes: 'A woman obsessed with the size of her appetite, wishing to control her hungers and urges, may be expressing the fact that she has been taught to regard her emotional life, her passions and "appetites" as dangerous.'[74] Desire is everywhere, fulfilment nowhere, so the anorexic is 'fed up and hungry'.[75] From this angle, anorexia is only the extreme point of a con-tinuum: a 1984 magazine survey in the US of 33,000 women showed that 75 per cent believed they were fat, although only 25 per cent were actually overweight; and weight loss was chosen ahead of success at work or in interpersonal relations as a source of satisfaction.[76] In this way, the language of inarticulate desire is expressed through the very body that has to be the source of its repression; weight loss becomes powerfully meaningful, a mark of autonomy, an achievement that, in the case of anorexia, 'at once exemplifies the feminine stereotype of perfect slimness and repudiates it by making a mockery of it', as Marilyn Lawrence puts it.[77] Thus is independence asserted in the teeth of fashionable slimness; but, when, by the 1990s, 'anorexia' had become appropriated by fashion, with a Kate Moss or an Emma Balfour as cultural icons, what would the future hold for anorexia itself?

Daydreams, Desires and the Consuming Self

Writing at an early stage in the development of modern consumerism, Kant was aware that his own philosophical analysis of desire, as the ability to convert impulses into rationally justifiable goals that would encourage social harmony, was not a guide to the nature of desire as it was emerging in the world around him. 'Reason has this peculiarity that, aided by the imagination, it can create artificial desires which are not only unsupported by natural instinct but actually contrary to it', he writes; and these desires 'gradually generate a whole host of unnecessary and indeed unnatural inclinations called luxuriousness'.[78] This is a very prescient summary, even down to the disapproving tone, which would be echoed by com-mentators on consumerism in our own time; and it brings out both the irreducibil-ity of desires to 'natural' needs, and the insatiable, apparently limitless character of these desires. Campbell develops this by arguing that while needs can bring satisfaction, desires can bring pleasure, albeit transient, and that 'while only reality can provide satisfaction, both illusions and delusions can supply pleasure'.[79]

Modern consumer behaviour thus entails 'a distinctive form of hedonism, one in which the enjoyment of emotions as summoned through imagery or illusory images is central'.[80] In tracing the sources of this, Campbell's own work suggests that the aspirations and longings of the emergent modern self could be translated into the language of desire for commodities, as material embodiments of these fantasies and longings; and implicitly points out that the tension already referred to, between 'release' and 'control', with its gender dimensions, has a long history in consumer culture, and bears the imprint of Romanticism and Puritanism in this history.

Crucial to this process is the way the development of the modern self entailed the construction of an 'inner realm' in which the imagination and the emotions could play on each other, for this would prove to have momentous consequences. It can be argued that[81] the interiority of the self meant a strong sense of boundary, a clear separation between subject and object. Campbell claims that 'only in modern times have emotions come to be located "within" individuals as opposed to "in" the world'; terms like 'awe', for example, hitherto regarded as an attribute of God, and 'fear', referring to a quality of unexpected events, now become internalized, as feelings and emotions of the self. Along with this, the imagination is increasingly reconstructed as an internal faculty of the self, its creativity channelled into the subjective, so that Campbell can suggest that there is a sense in which 'the disenchantment of the external world required as a parallel process some "enchantment" of the psychic inner world'. By the eighteenth century, we increasingly find the imagination being used to shape the emotions; the imagination can conjure up images which stimulate the emotions, pictures of situations that would produce pleasurable emotion.[82] Emotions are thus amenable to a degree of *control*; they can be *cultivated*. Hence the eighteenth-century 'cult' of feeling known as 'sensibility'. Traditional hedonism, the search for pleasurable sensations dependent on external stimuli, can give way to modern hedonism, the controlled use of images and fantasy to shape the emotions; 'pleasures' can give way to 'pleasure'.

Romanticism, influential in the arts and culture in the decades around the beginning of the nineteenth century, is significant here in several ways. For the Romantics, wedded to the creative role of the imagination in the exploration of beauty, the exercise of the imagination was inherently pleasurable, and this could be intensified through strong emotion.[83] While the Romantics were strongly anti-utilitarian, and contemptuous of bourgeois ideals of comfort, this non-materialist ethos nevertheless entailed what Gouldner suggests was an attempt to endow 'the ordinary, everyday world with the pathos of the extraordinary', since 'the insignificance of things was born of a failure of imagination'.[84] Indeed, they were not only interested in nature, but in books, paintings, clothes, china – the sort of 'expressive' goods that had led the surge in consumerism in the preceding period.

In his account of the development of the modern self, Taylor argues that this whole era manifested something of an 'expressive revolution'. Just as the external world required 'representation' by and for a self now clearly seen as separate from it, so the self, too, as a mysterious inner entity, could only be manifested through externals: language, clothes, objects, can become 'our way of manifesting through expression what we are, and our place within things'; we become 'expressive beings'.[85] Each person thereby finds an inner voice, and this becomes an exercise in self-constitution, a basis for individual identity. And increasingly, in the world of the commodity, objects come to define and carry the message of self-identity, our 'place within things', and consumption is basic to this: 'The "self" which exists potentially within us . . . becomes actual through the process of consumption', as Ferguson suggests.[86]

The relationship between imagination, pleasure and consumerism is structured within the self through longing, through desire. Campbell argues that

> individuals employ their imaginative and creative powers to construct mental images which they consume for the intrinsic pleasure they provide, a practice best described as day-dreaming or fantasizing. . . . This is the distinctively modern faculty, the ability to create an illusion which is known to be false but felt to be true.[87]

Hence the nebulous daydreams and longings, the 'dream worlds' referred to by Williams in her book on the consumer spectacle.[88] Let us trace out some consequences of this development. Where daydreaming intervenes, *anticipation* is possible, and anticipation *itself* becomes pleasurable. One might almost say that the wanting rather than the having becomes central to pleasure; we refer to pleasure-*seeking*, after all. *Deferring* gratification, through anticipation, is part of the pleasure. Indeed, being seduced by the product in the imagination can be more rewarding than the reality; the consummation of the consuming act can be something of an anti-climax. Consumption falls short of its own anticipation; its pleasures are real enough, but in turn engender a restless dissatisfaction, though this, too, can have enjoyable elements. Meanings are both realizable – and realized, in part – and also in a sense inaccessible, displaced, ideal. If they were just the former, they would be reducible to objective qualities of the object, satisfying some limited and specific need; and if they were just the latter, they could not be 'carried' by objects at all. It is these meanings that attract, yet they can never be fully realized in the object.[89]

Longing, daydreams, are more diffuse, unfocused, than desire, more a matter of moods than of goals. These indefinite longings can be transformed into desires, with more specific ends in view, as the self becomes the subject of consumption. Desire both presupposes and constitutes the self, in its acquisitive orientation to the world, and guarantees that self-consciousness will take the form of a consciousness of self as project. Desire becomes an imposition of project on longing, yet the imposition can never be complete, since there is a sense in which fantasy, anticipation and aspiration cannot be fully realized in achievement, goal and acquisition. Desire, like longing, testifies to the centrality of ever-renewed deferral in the self, the gap that constitutes the self in relation to the otherness it wishes to incorporate yet strives also to maintain in its otherness, so as to enjoy the pleasures of the craving and yearning the gap makes possible. Desire requires and creates distance; hence the appeal of the exotic. Yet in being brought closer, and consumed, it loses its appeal, seems to be 'other', even as it comes to 'realize', express, the identity of the self that consumes it.

Daydreams themselves can be characterized as vaguely formulated aspirations, unsettled longings, imaged in hazy, shifting visions of exotic holidays, slightly displaced scenarios of everyday life, a new home. These can be produced relatively autonomously, through the unpredictable workings of our imagination, but this imagination necessarily derives its content, directly or indirectly, from our experiences of everyday life and the images we see around us. And sometimes, the imagination can be stimulated in a direct, immediate way, responding to a visit to a friend's new house, a striking ad on television, or a Christmas present; daydreams can change focus, evolve, as they incorporate the plethora of new goods and situations opened up by consumerism.

A clue to some of the processes involved here is given by McCracken's discussion of an article written by the eighteenth-century philosopher Diderot, entitled 'Regrets on Parting with my Old Dressing Gown'.[90] A friend had given him a new dressing gown, obviously thinking that the old, tatty one he slouched around in left something to be desired. This smart new gown, worn by Diderot in his study, had unexpected effects; it turned out to be 'imperious', he writes, and 'forced everything else to conform with its own elegant tone'. The curtains now looked unacceptably scruffy, and the desk looked old and worn: 'Now the harmony is destroyed. Now there is no more consistency, no more unity, and no more beauty.'[91] Several shopping sprees later, the situation has been rectified. McCracken summarizes the outcome, as Diderot sits, bemused and a little melancholic, in his study: 'It was once crowded, humble, chaotic, and happy. It is now elegant, organized, beautifully appointed, and a little grim.'[92] One might add, though, that this is not so unusual; nothing that couldn't be cured by a little more shopping, a further exercise in retail therapy.

In this allegory of consumerism, it is the gift that triggers what McCracken calls the 'Diderot effect', the drive to consistency between possessions, and between possessions and self-image; and this effect can only occur in a society in which there is already a range of social meanings that are attached to goods, in a fluid way, together with an imperative towards the realization of choice and individual aspiration by the potential consumer. Things are seen as 'going together'; they share cultural categories, and a place in the ads and fashions that reproduce these. And the 'redundancy' of the goods reinforces and clarifies the message of the categories, through their very excess. This 'Diderot effect' can be conservative, reinforcing an existing image, or, as in Diderot's own case, it can enforce change, as with so-called 'impulse' purchases generally; and the two dimensions can be closely connected, producing a never-ending cycle of consumption. What we find here could be called 'lifestyle unities', and as such they become ever more central to consumerism. Mort suggests that 1980s advertising policies reveal increased emphasis on market segmentation and a diversity of lifestyle profiles, supplanting the older, broader target categories ('working-class youth', 'middle-class housewife');[93] and Faurschou instances Ralph Lauren taking over a floor of Bloomingdale's to market a self-contained universe, a 'total home environment', geared to a specific aspirational lifestyle, where you can purchase matching Ralph Lauren wallpaper, glass, sheets, rugs, slippers and, yes, a dressing gown.[94]

These longings manifest not just aspirations to possession, but fantasies of identification, so that possessions themselves serve as images, badges of identity and ambition. Consumption thereby carries messages of style and status, speaking not just of who one is, but of who one wants to be. And there is no end to this, no fixed point. Trends and fashions speak to longings and fantasies, undermining and shifting the patterns of self-identity; thus are identities subverted, altered and restabilized. The pleasures and frustrations in consumerism are inseparably part of its internal dynamism, in a world in which commodities have become signifiers of identity and realizations of dreams. Thus we can understand both of the following, apparently contradictory claims: that of Campbell, who asserts that 'the spirit of modern consumerism is anything but materialistic',[95] and Williams, who writes that 'reveries . . . become the alluring handmaidens of commerce', and a dream becomes a sales pitch in disguise.[96]

The 'Accursed Share': Consumption, Production and Excess

As already indicated, controversy has dogged consumerism since at least as early as Rousseau. The most influential critical tradition in recent decades has been what Featherstone calls the 'production of consumption' approach,[97] a fusion of Rousseauan and Marxist strands. This approach postulates that consumerism entails the production of passive consumers ready to buy the commodities produced by capitalism; consumers are endlessly bamboozled into buying what they don't need, through the inculcation of 'false needs' by the machinations of the advertising industry. In practice, however, it is held that some suffer this fate to a greater extent than others. If consumerism produces the passive, indoctrinated 'masses', it has traditionally been thought that immunity, even resistance, is more likely among the cultural elite, the bearers of 'high' culture. Mica Nava attacks the condescension towards ordinary people implicit here: 'Their pursuit of commodities and their enjoyment of disdained cultural forms is cited as evidence of their irrationality and gullibility.'[98] Recent tendencies in cultural analysis, however, have in effect tended to generalize this model of resistance, so that oppositional aspects in everyday life have become widely apparent; 'mass' culture can exist with elements of 'popular' culture, subordination can be supplemented by resistance, and consumer purchasing power can incorporate quite effective boycotts of particular goods and companies.

This tension – between conformity and resistance – runs through the literature. If Bauman can write that 'The modern project of individual autonomy has been subordinated and subsumed by the market-defined and market-oriented freedom of consumer choice',[99] and Shields can remind us that 'Leisure and legitimation have the same Latin root, *lex*, law', so that leisure spaces can be seen as 'zones of permitted, *legitimated* pleasure',[100] Fiske can reply that 'consumption is a tactical raid upon the system',[101] and McRobbie can argue that for the crowds of shoppers and strollers in streetmarkets, 'the atmosphere is almost festive . . . the tempo symbolises time rescued from that of labour, and the market seems to celebrate its own pleasures'.[102]

These apparently rival interpretations are both ultimately undecidable and, in a sense, are two sides of the same coin, testifying to the ambiguities of subjecthood discussed in a previous chapter in connection with Foucault's work. This comes out clearly in Fiske's suggestion that wearing torn jeans shows how 'what is to be resisted is necessarily present in the resistance to it', since 'torn jeans signify both a set of dominant American values and a degree of resistance to them'.[103] And Nava adds that while young people are of course influenced by ads, they too are sophisticated consumers who 'play an active part through the creation of their own street styles in what is manufactured and marketed'.[104]

The deep hostility to consumerism evidenced in many accounts is itself significant, and requires further exploration. We can approach this by noting Campbell's remark that consumerism is linked to 'fashion, romantic love, taste and the reading of fiction'.[105] These links will be explored later; for now, it suffices to point out that fashion can be seen as the mechanism whereby the importance of novelty can be transmitted to consumers, and the reading of fiction can be seen as the transmission of aspirations and longings that cannot be satisfied and which, again, are translated into restless consumer behaviour. If we connect these points to a central strand in the conventional critique of consumerism – that of the *passivity* of consumers – we are led to an inevitable conclusion: that the alleged victims of consumerism are, first and foremost, *women*, and that, in this sense, as has been implied earlier, consumerism could be seen as both feminine and *feminizing*. And one can suspect that this has contributed to the devaluation of consumerism among analysts of it, an unwitting bias present in the tendency to disparage consumers as gullible victims. The 1960s generation of feminists tended to endorse this critique – thus Betty Friedan, for example, wrote of American women as 'victims' of their power at the point of purchase[106] – but more recently there has been a revaluation. Rosemary Pringle points to why consumerism is 'troublesome':

> Consumption stands for destructiveness, waste, extravagance, triviality and instability – in fact for all the things that men traditionally hate or fear about women. It is only safe to talk about it in appropriately negative or *passive* terms. Accordingly it must be subjected to production, as women are to men, and reduced to a role in 'reproducing' labour power.[107]

And Angela McRobbie protests at the way women have been presented as 'slaves to consumerism', and the prevalence of the idea that 'to enjoy shopping is to be passively feminine and incorporated into a system of false needs'.[108]

The other side of the coin has been a tendency to overvalue utilitarian rationality. Campbell points to the assumption that 'the only genuine gratification which consumers can obtain from products and services is that provided by their intrin-sic utility';[109] if consumers buy for other reasons (e.g. being swayed by the prod-uct's 'image') then they are being 'irrational', and are not acting 'sensibly'. Indeed, if emotion or fantasy enter into purchases, rather than rational calculation, then 'manipulation' or 'exploitation' *must* be involved. In short, consumption ought to be simply the obverse of production, but it is distorted by 'irrational' factors: production is seen as active, rational, utility-oriented, masculine; consumption is passive, irrational, impulsive, image-oriented, feminine. Overall, then, this approach distracts us from analysing consumerism as *culture*, a distinctive dimen-sion of the experience of modernity that raises important questions about the place of imagery, fantasy and desire in social life. Thus Nava argues that 'consumerism does not simply mirror production', as it is 'far more than just economic activity: it is also about dreams and consolation, communication and confrontation, image and identity'.[110] Of course, issues of manipulation and exploitation *are* raised here, but the significance of consumerism cannot be captured wholly in terms of the dialectic of conformity and resistance; nor can the darker side of consumerism discussed in this chapter, the sense in which we *can* become 'victims', consumer junkies needing our fix, be reduced to this. This model does not help us to an adequate grasp of the sense in which 'commerce and consumerism have helped to release a profane explosion of everyday symbolic life and activity', as Willis puts it in his account of youth culture.[111] Ultimately, through its over-valuation of ration-ality and its assimilation of the irrational and the feminine, it is more a *continuation* of the project of modernity than an *analysis* of it.

Indeed, questions could be asked about production itself. Baudrillard goes so far as to argue that the idea of 'production' as a separate, let alone determinant, sphere of activity is becoming obsolete: 'The entire sphere of production, labour and the forces of production must be conceived as collapsing into the sphere of "consumption"', where the latter is conceived as 'a coded exchange of signs, a general lifestyle'.[112] And in his analysis of the sign system of American consumerism, Sahlins attacks the misleading self-image of capitalism, 'leaving the impression that production is merely the precipitate of an enlightened rationality'.[113]

The contrast between 'production' and 'consumption' is worth developing further. 'Production' is implicitly seen as goal-directed, associated with self-restraint, sobriety, work. It involves struggle, yet also the promise of 'progress': it occurs in conditions of scarcity, but through struggle the needs of life can be met, and there is the promise of a better world. 'Implicit here was the faith that labor is the genuinely creative source of value, capable of overcoming nature in any contest', writes Birken.[114] Gradually, labour harnessed to technology can ensure progress towards abundance. Production can be planned, is subject to rational control, at either the level of the firm (capitalism) or the society (socialism). It subordinates everything to the one standard, that of usefulness (utility), rational appropriation. In short, it is an exercise in the project of modernity, and postulates a seamless homology between individual rationality and the exigencies of the wider economy.

Consumption, however, seems to march to a different tune; it seems to point to a dimension that was always present alongside, though has perhaps become more apparent with, the full flowering of capitalism in the twentieth century. If we take the whole derogatory language of 'irrationality' that is frequently applied to it, and re-cast it instead as 'non-rationality', a recognition of 'something else', something other *than*, or *in*, 'rationality', we can perhaps gain further insight. After all, if we unpack this language, we encounter certain terms used recurrently in descriptions of consumerism, whatever the values of the author: excess, waste, luxury, superfluity, destruction, abundance. It is associated with self-indulgence and pleasure, even when, as has been seen, these can include the apparently paradoxical pleasures of self-destruction. Limits on desire are there to be broken; excess, limitless extravagance, is of the essence. It all points to no purpose beyond itself; unlike production, which in being subordinated to control can easily be subordinated to morality also, consumption is fundamentally amoral. Swayed by fashion, it is nevertheless individualistic; it cannot be readily 'socialized', rendered consistent with social goals; nor indeed, with ecological ones. It is an experience of the non-rational as the embodiment of symbolic excess, of a 'meaning' forever irreducible to function. Hence, in a sense, the subordination/resistance dualism is right, but as a surface reflection of this deeper tension in the culture, between rational appropriation and symbolic excess. Like the sun, consumption gives out its energy, and receives nothing back; it celebrates its own expenditure of energy; the pleasure lies in the destruction itself.

If it is indeed through consumerism, and its 'carnival of images', that we appropriate the world around us, then this marks a distinctive mode of transforming nature into culture, one that cannot be grasped simply as an aspect of the purposive exploitation of nature associated with modernity, one that challenges the understanding of this appropriation in 'rational' terms. Indeed, in some ways it mimics nature itself, in its teeming abundance and destructiveness, its endless cycles. If it points to the arbitrary, the meaningless in human culture, it also suggests that, at a deeper level, this has a certain continuity with nature itself. And just as women have been seen as presiding over the natural cycle, representing and embodying a principle of fecundity that is both distrusted, and subjected to control by, 'masculine' modernity, so it is through consumerism that women represent and embody this ambivalent appropriation of nature, subject as it is to attempts at control which can never be really successful.

But this language – of the sun (the 'solar principle'), of expenditure, fecundity, waste – testifies to the significance of the work of Georges Bataille, and his exploration of the idea that true 'sovereignty' entails the pursuit of excess and extravagance, in emancipation from the shackles of utilitarian production. Excess, as waste and destruction, is not a perversion of consumption, but its very essence. Generalizing across cultures, he argues that activities like 'luxury, mourning, war, cults, the construction of sumptuary movements, games, spectacles, arts, perverse sexual activity' – and, he adds elsewhere, sacrifice and carnival – all represent forms of 'unproductive expenditure', and 'at least in primitive circumstances, have no end beyond themselves'.[115] Hence, immoderate consumption is a social statement: 'Consumption is the way in which *separate* beings communicate.' It represents a shared emancipation from the constraints of work, utility, indeed from the constraints of constraint itself. This 'excess' over need, an excess through which culture both transcends and, as we have seen, rejoins nature, is the *part maudite*, the 'accursed share', the 'heterogeneity' through which culture challenges the 'homogeneity' of one-dimensional utilitarianism.[116]

When applied to modernity itself, this perspective implies that if there is indeed a 'carnival of consumerism', then its mode is not necessarily exuberant; indeed, as we have seen, it can be celebratory or fearful, enjoyable or guilt-ridden. The exploration of pleasure, excess and 'sovereignty' entails constant struggle with the unity and rationality of project, its pull towards homogeneity. Attempts to subordinate and control the *part maudite*, in the name of reason, purpose or need, along with the attendant emphasis on the 'disciplined' self, necessarily lead to tension with the dynamics of release, extravagance and excess. The symbolism of consumerism can indeed be 'used' by individuals and groups to make statements about status affiliation and aspiration; Bataillean 'expenditure' can be subordinated to mere 'acquisition' or 'use' of objects, for practical need or as status-markers, hence becoming 'functional', subject to utility. Bataille claims that in *this* sense 'The hatred of expenditure is the raison d'être of and justification for the bourgeoisie.'[117] All this testifies to the profound interpenetration of production and consumption in modern culture, and the way consumerism itself is inscribed with the resulting tensions.

Ultimately, then, it can be suggested that the vocabulary of utility, purpose and function necessarily proves inadequate. If the purposive appropriation of the world under the aegis of utility is one aspect of the construction of identity, nevertheless identity cannot be reducible to this; 'desire' is not a product of a pre-existing, fixed or integrated self, but a manifestation of a self in transition, never fully able to grasp itself reflexively, never fully open to self-understanding, always more than it can ever know. Consumption reconstitutes identity, challenges it, develops it, so can never wholly be controlled by it. Campbell's work can therefore be seen as complementing that of Bataille; and a synthesis of these strands can help illuminate the promises and paradoxes at the heart of the consumer dream.

Notes

1   M. Schudson, *Advertising, the Uneasy Persuasion* (Routledge, 1993), p. 199.
2   R. Klein, *Cigarettes are Sublime* (Picador, 1995), p. 17.
3   R. Marchand, *Advertising the American Dream: Making Way for Modernity, 1920–1940* (California University Press, 1985), p. 341.
4   Schudson, *Advertising*, pp. 184, 187, 203.
5   B. Jacobson, *Beating the Ladykillers: Women and Smoking* (Pluto, 1986), pp. 45, 40.
6   A. Wernick, *Promotional Culture: Advertising, Ideology and Symbolic Expression* (Sage, 1991), p. 39, and ch. 2; and see Jacobson, *Ladykillers*, pp. 55–6.

7   D. Kellner, 'Popular Culture and the Construction of Postmodern Identities', in S. Lash and J. Friedman (eds.), *Modernity and Identity* (Blackwell, 1992), pp. 167, 162.

8   Schudson, *Advertising*, pp. 179, 183.

9   Marchand, *Advertising*, p. 102.

10 Jacobson, *Ladykillers*, pp. 66, 113.

11 *Guardian* (19 March 1994).

12 D. Miller, *Material Culture and Mass Consumption* (Blackwell, 1991), p. 213.

13 M. Davidson, *The Consumerist Manifesto: Advertising in Postmodern Times* (Routledge, 1992), p. 203.

14 R. Williams, *Dream Worlds: Mass Consumption in Late 19th Century France* (California University Press, 1982), p. 28 and ch. 2.

15 S. Ewen, *All Consuming Images* (Basic Books, 1988), p. 29.

16 Williams, *Dream Worlds*, p. 24; and, for the Voltaire–Rousseau debate, and the civilizing process generally, see ch. 2 of my *Transgressing the Modern* (Blackwell, 1999).

17 Cited in R. Porter, 'Baudrillard: History, Hysteria and Consumption', in C. Rojek and B. Turner (eds.), *Forget Baudrillard* (Routledge, 1993), p. 12.

18 N. McKendrick et al., *The Birth of a Consumer Society: The Commercialization of Eighteenth-century England* (Indiana University Press, 1982), p. 10.

19 Ibid., and see H. and L. H. Mui, *Shops and Shopping in Eighteenth-Century England* (Queen's University Press, 1989); C. Shammas, *The Pre-Industrial Consumer in England and America* (Clarendon Press, 1990); F. Braudel, *The Wheels of Commerce* (Harper and Row, 1982); and J.-C. Agnew, 'Coming Up for Air: Consumer Culture in Historical Perspective', in J. Brewer and R. Porter (eds.) *Consumption and the World of Goods* (Routledge, 1993).

20 E. Wilson, *Adorned in Dreams* (Virago, 1985), p. 144.

21 A. Adburgham, *Shops and Shopping 1800–1914* (Allen and Unwin, 1981).

22 R. Sennett, *The Fall of Public Man* (Faber, 1986), p. 144; and D. Chaney, 'The Department Store as a Cultural Form', *Theory, Culture and Society* (1983), 1:3.

23 G. Barth, *City People: The Rise of Modern City Culture in Nineteenth-Century America* (Oxford University Press, 1980), p. 136.

24 M. Miller, *The Bon Marché: Bourgeois Culture and the Department Store, 1869–1920* (Princeton University Press, 1981), p. 182. See also W. Lancaster, *The Department Store* (Leicester University Press, 1995).

25 G. Cross, *Time and Money: The Making of Consumer Culture* (Routledge, 1993), pp. 10, 177–81.

26 Cited in J. Fiske, *Reading the Popular* (Unwin Hyman, 1989), p. 24.

27 Barth, *City People*, p. 137.

28 J. Craik, *The Face of Fashion* (Routledge, 1993), p. 71.

29 Cited in Chaney, 'Department Store', p. 24.

30 Williams, *Dream Worlds*, p. 66.

31 T. Richards, *The Commodity Culture of Victorian England: Advertising and Spectacle, 1851–1914* (Verso, 1991), pp. 11, 2.

32 P. Gay, *The Bourgeois Experience, Vol. II: The Tender Passion* (Oxford University Press, 1986), p. 318.

33 Cited in R. Bowlby, *Just Looking: Consumer Culture in Dreiser, Gissing and Zola* (Methuen, 1985), p. 72.

34 J. Walkowitz, *City of Dreadful Delight: Narratives of Sexual Danger in Late-Victorian London* (Virago, 1992), p. 49.

35   Bowlby, *Just Looking*, p. 75; and cited in ibid., p. 74.

36   M. A. Doane, 'The Economy of Desire: The Commodity Form in/of the Cinema', *Quarterly Review of Film and Video* (1989), 11:1, p. 30.

37   Bowlby, *Just Looking*, pp. 32, 34. See also G. Reekie, *Temptations: Sex, Selling and the Department Store* (Allen and Unwin, 1993).

38   Cited in Davidson, *Consumerist Manifesto*, p. 158.

39   Schudson, *Advertising*, pp. xiii, xiv, xv. See also M. Nava, *Changing Cultures: Feminism, Youth and Consumerism* (Sage, 1992), p. 179.

40   R. Goldman, *Reading Ads Socially* (Routledge, 1992), p. 8.

41   Ewen, *All Consuming Images*, p. 33.

42   A. Forty, *Objects of Desire: Design and Society 1750–1950* (Thames and Hudson, 1986), pp. 10–12.

43   Ewen, *All Consuming Images*, pp. 22, 22, 23, 268.

44   Marchand, *Advertising*, pp. xxi, 66, 168.

45   Forty, *Objects*, pp. 207, 208.

46   A. Oakley, *Housewife* (Penguin, 1976), p. 7; and R. Pringle, 'Women and Consumer Capitalism', in C. Baldock and B. Cass (eds.) *Women, Social Welfare and the State* (George Allen, 1983), p. 92.

47   S. Jhally, *The Codes of Advertising: Fetishism and the Political Economy of Meaning in the Consumer Society* (Routledge, 1990), pp. 128, 201–2.

48   *A Decade of i-Deas: The Encyclopaedia of the '80s* (Penguin, 1990), p. 12.

49   Williams, *Dream Worlds*, p. 4.

50   Davidson, *Consumerist Manifesto*, p. 68.

51   J. Williamson, 'Beauty and the Adman', *Guardian* (9 December 1988).

52   Davidson, *Consumerist Manifesto*, pp. 23, 26.

53   Ibid., pp. 29, 26, 124.

54   Ibid., pp. 125, 125, 125, 139.

55   D. Chaney, *Fictions of Collective Life: Public Drama in Late Modern Culture* (Routledge, 1993), p. 184.

56   Davidson, *Consumerist Manifesto*, pp. 125, 138.

57   Richards, *Commodity Culture*, p. 55.

58   Ewen, *All Consuming Images*, pp. 236, 234, 239.

59   Williams, *Dream Worlds*, pp. 7, 6.

60   Porter, 'Baudrillard', pp. 6, 7, 7.

61   Porter, 'Consumption: Disease of the Consumer Society?', in Brewer and Porter, *Consumption*, p. 66.

62   Porter, 'Baudrillard', p. 9.

63   Richards, *Commodity Culture*, p. 196.

64   Marchand, *Advertising*, pp. 18–20.

65   Davidson, *Consumerist Manifesto*, p. 159.

66   T. J. Jackson Lears, 'From Salvation to Self-Realization: Advertising and the Therapeutic Roots of the Consumer Culture, 1880–1930', in R. F. Fox and T. J. Jackson Lears (eds.) *The Culture of Consumption* (Pantheon, 1983), pp. 3, 4.

67   R. Crawford, 'A Cultural Account of "Health": Control, Release, and the Social Body, in J. B. McKinlay (ed.) *Issues in the Political Economy of Health Care* (Tavistock, 1984), pp. 81, 92, and see also p. 93.

68   S. Bordo, 'Reading the Slender Body', in M. Jacobus et al., *Body/Politics: Women and the Discourses of Science* (Routledge, 1990), p. 97. This is also in S. Bordo,

Unbearable Weight: Feminism, Western Culture and the Body (California University Press, 1993), along with other material.

69   Richards, *Commodity Culture*, p. 201.
70   J. Brumberg, *Fasting Girls: The Emergence of Anorexia Nervosa as a Modern Disease* (Harvard University Press, 1988), pp. 266, 271.
71   B. Turner, *The Body and Society* (Blackwell, 1984), p. 93.
72   Bordo, 'Reading', pp. 97–9.
73   B. Dijkstra, *Idols of Perversity* (Oxford University Press, 1986), p. 29. And for the 'grotesque body' of Carnival, see my *Trangressing the Modern*, ch. 1.
74   K. Chernin, *Womansize* (Women's Press, 1983), p. 2.
75   M. Lawrence (ed.) *Fed Up and Hungry* (Women's Press, 1987).
76   Brumberg, *Fasting Girls*, p. 32. For further discussion, see L. Gamman and M. Makinen, *Female Fetishism* (Lawrence and Wishart, 1994), chs. 4, 5.
77   M. Lawrence, 'Education and Identity: The Social Origins of Anorexia', in Lawrence, *Fed Up*, p. 220.
78   I. Kant, *On History* (Bobbs-Merrill, 1963), pp. 55–6.
79   C. Campbell, *The Romantic Ethic and the Spirit of Modern Consumerism* (Blackwell, 1989), p. 61.
80   C. Campbell, 'Understanding Traditional and Modern Patterns of Consumption in Eighteenth-century England: A Character-action Approach', in Brewer and Porter, *Consumption*, p. 48.
81   See my *Transgressing the Modern*, ch. 2.
82   Campbell, *Romantic Ethic*, pp. 72, 73, 76.
83   Campbell, 'Understanding Traditional and Modern', p. 53; and *Romantic Ethic*, passim.
84   A. Gouldner, *For Sociology* (Penguin, 1975), p. 331.
85   C. Taylor, *Sources of the Self* (Cambridge University Press, 1992), p. 198.
86   H. Ferguson, 'Watching the World Go Round: Atrium Culture and the Psychology of Shopping', in R. Shields (ed.) *Lifestyle Shopping: The Subject of Consumption* (Routledge, 1992), p. 27.
87   Campbell, *Romantic Ethic*, pp. 77, 78.
88   Williams, *Dream Worlds*.
89   Campbell, *Romantic Ethic*, pp. 86–8.
90   G. McCracken, *Culture and Consumption* (Indiana University Press, 1990), ch. 8.
91   D. Diderot, *Rameau's Nephew and Other Works* (Bobbs-Merrill, 1964), p. 311.
92   McCracken, *Culture*, p. 118.
93   F. Mort, 'The Politics of Consumption', in S. Hall and M. Jacques (eds.) *New Times* (Lawrence and Wishart, 1989).
94   G. Faurschou, 'Obsolescence and Desire: Fashion and the Commodity Form', in H. Silverman (ed.) *Postmodernism – Philosophy and the Arts* (Routledge, 1990), pp. 244–7.
95   Campbell, *Romantic Ethic*, p. 89.
96   Williams, *Dream Worlds*, p. 65.
97   M. Featherstone, *Consumer Culture and Postmodernism* (Sage, 1991), ch. 2.
98   Nava, *Changing Cultures*, p. 190.
99   Z. Bauman, *Legislators and Interpreters* (Polity, 1987), p. 189.
100 R. Shields, 'Spaces for the Subject of Consumption', in Shields, *Lifestyle Shopping*, p. 8.

101   J. Fiske, *Understanding Popular Culture* (Unwin Hyman, 1989), p. 35.
102   A. McRobbie, 'Second-Hand Dresses and the Role of the Ragmarket', in her *Zoot Suits and Second-Hand Dresses* (Macmillan, 1989), p. 32.
103   Fiske, *Understanding Popular Culture*, p. 4.
104   Nava, *Changing Cultures*, p. 194.
105   Campbell, *Romantic Ethic*, p. 7.
106   Cited in Nava, *Changing Cultures*, p. 128.
107   Pringle, 'Women and Consumer Capitalism', p. 86.
108   McRobbie, *Zoot Suits*, p. 25; see also Nava, *Changing Cultures*, p. 166, and P. Willis, *Common Culture* (Open University Press, 1990), p. 85.
109   Campbell, *Romantic Ethic*, p. 48.
110   Nava, *Changing Cultures*, p. 167.
111   Willis, *Common Culture*, p. 27.
112   J. Baudrillard, *Symbolic Exchange and Death* (Sage, 1993), p. 14.
113   M. Sahlins, *Culture and Practical Reason* (University of Chicago Press, 1976), pp. 166–7.
114   L. Birken, *Consuming Desire: Sexual Science and the Emergence of a Culture of Abundance, 1871–1914* (Cornell University Press, 1988), p. 27.
115   G. Bataille, 'The Notion of Expenditure', in his *Visions of Excess: Selected Writings, 1927–1939* (Minnesota University Press, 1985), p. 118.
116   G. Bataille, *The Accursed Share*, Vol. I (Zone Books, 1988), p. 58, and passim.
117   Bataille, 'Notion', p. 124.

5 'We Are Born Naked – Everything Else Is Drag':

Clothing the Body, Fashioning the Self

It stands sleek, stylish, graceful, yet bold, resplendent, self-confident: a stiletto heel, an immediately recognizable product of modern fashion (plate 3). A 'mere' article of clothing, one might say; yet it is replete with signification, available for various scenarios of the imagination, an object of fantasy as well as reality. How is it to be 'read'?

Throughout the modern era, fashion has always been contentious, under frequent attack for the impracticality, irrationality, extravagance and exploitation it has been alleged to embody. In recent decades, it has frequently been feminists who have led the attack. And what easier target than the stiletto? It has been seen to symbolize the subordination of women, their reduction to decorative fetish objects, a sort of modern-day equivalent of Chinese foot-binding. An examination of this interpretation, using Lee Wright's account of the history of the stiletto,[1] can serve to introduce many of the key issues raised by clothes and fashion, and elaborate the truth of Jennifer Craik's claim that 'Through clothes, we wear our bodies and fabricate our selves.'[2]

Although the high heel, as such, had become established as an element of feminine footwear during the nineteenth century, the stiletto itself was an invention of the 1950s. Stylistically, it developed out of Dior's 'New Look' of the late 1940s, as a reaction against the 'Utility' style of the war years. Feminine difference was to be celebrated again, rather than the ungendered practicality and restraint of wartime. The stiletto appeared in 1953, though it was not until 1957 that the technology was perfected, with the metal pin inside plastic coating that ensured relative unbreakability. By 1959, it was sweeping all before it. Though intended for evening wear, its phenomenal success meant it was worn more widely, even to work. Sales increased until 1962, by which time a reaction had set in. Not for the first time, fashion had become news: a growing volume of complaints filled the newspapers, and there were even claims that the heels were destroying road surfaces; doctors weighed in with warnings that the pressure on the feet, and the 'unnatural' body position, were leading to a variety of health problems.

Consumption of the stiletto was consumer-led from early on, its success surprising the industry. By the late 1950s, the stiletto, in the form of the 'winkle-picker', had been adopted as an icon of youthful glamour and rebellion, representing the 'modern', independent young woman; and it is particularly ironic, in view of the later criticism that it rendered women immobile and passive, that it signified social mobility and independent sexuality. Wright adds that this stiletto therefore 'symbolised *liberation* rather than subordination, despite the fact that high heels of any form were part of a stereotyped framework of what women wore'.[3] And she concludes by pointing to the paradox that the rejection of 'feminine' items like the stiletto, by later feminists, has often gone hand in hand with the adoption of what are conventionally 'masculine' items, such as flat-heeled shoes. She might well agree with Elizabeth Wilson, writing as part of the 1980s revaluation of fashion, that 'the most important thing about fashion is *not* that it oppresses women';[4] while remaining embedded in the complex effects of the dynamics of power in everyday life, explored in a previous chapter, fashion can just as easily provide a language within which women's desires and fantasies can be articulated.

And the stiletto today? It is still very much with us; but its cultural significance has shifted again. As it declined – in relative terms – as a conventionally fashionable item for women, so its overt history as a classic fetish object began, its life as an ambiguous signifier of transgressive sexuality. In the world of fashionable fetish fashion, it plays a key role; the models and party-goers portrayed in *Skin Two* frequently sport it as an essential accessory, and its gender-coding is endlessly uncertain. The assertive woman of the late 1950s can become the dominatrix or the victim, and the six-inch high-heeled black boot an essential accoutrement in unusual sex scenarios, with both sexes claiming to find it erotic. And this, too, raises questions about the relationship between 'normal' clothing and fetishism: are these scenarios simply a continuation, a more extreme version, of a fetishism inherent in modern attitudes to clothes and fashion? Clothes as a 'second skin' could perhaps take on the fetishistic allure of body parts, testifying to the immersion of selfhood in the objects and vestments that may do more than just provide cover for it, but may enter into its constitution, becoming part of the web of fantasy and desire central to the modern self in its problematical relation to the body.

Furthermore, we have been here before. Fashion entails novelty, but novelty turns out, frequently, to be a recapitulation. In this sense, the history of the stiletto is a reprise of the history of an older garment, the corset. It has generally been assumed, in the period since the corset ceased to be a major fashion item, in the late nineteenth century, that corsets were physically cruel and symbolized women's oppression; but Valerie Steele's re-examination of these issues revises this estimation.[5] She points to the fallacy of the assumption that the size of corset is a reliable guide to the narrowness of the resulting waist, in that the lacing was not intended to 'close' the corset, so waist sizes were in practice likely to have been greater than critics have assumed. On the one hand, the corset was respectable; being 'straight-laced' was not just a sartorial style, but a moral state, since 'The loose lady reflects loose morals', as Turner puts it.[6] Yet the corset also carried the opposite significance; prostitutes made extensive use of it, and upwardly mobile young women adopted it as a symbol of independence. In an age that emphasized the maternal role, the corset could carry an anti-maternal message; the slender waist was hardly the maternal waist, after all. Hence Gamman and Makinen conclude that 'it would be inappropriate for feminists to simply dismiss such clothing as a metaphor of patriarchal oppression'.[7] And, of course, as with the stiletto, fetishism is never far away. 'Tight-lacing', after all, has bondage connotations; and the bizarre correspondence in *The Englishwoman's Domestic Magazine* in the 1860s, analysed in the almost equally bizarre tight-lacing debate of the early 1980s,[8] suggests that 'tight-lacing' has been as much fantasy as fact from very early on.

Nor has the corset ever really gone away completely; and the 1980s saw its reappearance in several fashion collections, stimulated by Vivienne Westwood's use of it in her 'punk' collections of the late 1970s. After all, Madonna took up the corset in the mid-1980s, and it became part of her show of sartorial defiance and self-display, a self-display that is as much self-construction as self-expression, a parody of gender rather than a mere exemplification of it. Above all, Madonna's clothes suggest that 'images are not mimetic of a natural world prior to representation', as Kim Sawchuk puts it;[9] they are not 'expressions' of some given, 'natural' identity, that exists in complete independence of them. Fashion may have a logic, but it is a logic that both rests on, and reproduces, a relation to the world that depends more on its own internal relationships than on any ability to 'represent' or 'express' the world it so seductively embraces. Hence Barthes can argue that 'Fashion's reality is essentially the arbitrariness that establishes it', that it 'luxuriantly elaborates' meaning, hence 'maintaining meaning without ever fixing it'.[10] It is inherently excessive to the world it clothes, representing a play of meaning that always exceeds the possibility of its own definitive interpretation. As we have seen, the stiletto and the corset are not lacking in 'meaning': but meaning *for whom*, and *in what respect*? Even when we distinguish between conscious individual intentions, unconscious motives, and wider cultural significance, and even when we go on to distinguish, in the latter case, between overt cultural values and perceptions, and covert meanings that require 'decoding', we are left, in the end, with a pattern of possibilities that defies final closure.

The relationship between fashion and the body, through clothes, is of course crucial. In clothes, nature and culture meet through tension and contrast, a tension that is exacerbated by the insistence of fashion on the transience and changeability of clothes. Hence the problematic status of fashion in modernity, its defiance of the imperative to 'express' a fixed, stable 'inner nature' of identity. Evans and Thornton suggest that dressing up allows the possibility of 'fantasy and exploration, not in any sense of finding a "true self": but, rather, of exploring the shifting relation between being and appearance, seeing and being seen';[11] but this can also be regarded as dangerous, threatening. If the body thereby becomes in part a work of culture, it necessarily possesses elements of artifice in the clothes and cosmetics that dress it, 'artifice' in turn signifying possibilities of 'corruption' through artificiality, superfluity, irrationality. Castle summarizes the fears and challenges this can entail:

> The massive instability of sartorial signs, and their susceptibility to exploitation, may account for that deep contempt in which clothing has been held in Western culture. Clothing has always been a primary trope for the deceitfulness of the material world – a mutable, shimmering tissue that everywhere veils the truth from human eyes. Inherently superficial, feminine in its capacity to enthrall and mislead, it is a paradigmatic emblem of changeability.[12]

Saying It With Clothes: Self, Identity and Status

If the 'modern way with clothes' presents challenges of interpretation, it remains true that there is stability as well as change, uniformity as well as difference. Crucial to this is the way taken-for-granted notions of 'taste', 'fashion' and 'style' come together in the late eighteenth century, as a mutually constitutive set of terms that reveal the key elements of the modern clothing system in its relation to self and society.

For Kant, 'good taste' – the sense of what is appropriate, harmonious or beautiful – was an acquisition, associated with the civilizing process; it required emancipation from the tyranny of the body and the seductions of the senses, aesthetic contemplation rather than sensual indulgence. Bourdieu has pointed out that this distinction has a long subsequent history, and was implicated in class relations right from the start.[13] In effect, the Kantian notion is a projection of the values of the educated middle class; 'taste' has therefore carried connotations of status, through this implication of aesthetic discernment (or lack of it). Taste, then, is a mode of experience appropriate to the age of the status-conscious individual, found in a culture where individualism, as a value, intersects the dynamics of status and class. A 'person of taste' would reveal it through his or her dress, in an ability to embody this 'taste' in a 'personal style' that would exhibit a harmonious sartorial sense, and, therefore, aesthetic appreciation. 'Style' thereby emerges as the mode of self-presentation appropriate to a world in which judging by appearance becomes critical, embodying 'taste' and revealing one to be a 'person of quality'. If 'taste' could therefore be a mark of status, the possibility is also opened up that taste could reveal status aspiration. In revealing 'dress sense', clothes can be aesthetically, morally and socially 'uplifting'.

From the start, though, these comforting assumptions proved highly indeterminate in practice. Campbell points out that the late eighteenth century saw the definitive collapse of the received classical ideals of aesthetics. In the absence of clear, uncontroversial criteria, 'good taste' became a battleground; for who could judge it? He argues that taste is crucial in linking 'imaginative hedonism' with the institution of modern fashion, in that the search for pleasure through novelty and daydreaming – discussed previously in connection with consumerism – joined up with the desire to manifest personal quality through 'taste', resulting in the sensitivity to change in the arena of appearance that we see as central to modern fashion. Beauty became implicated in consumerism, a function of pleasure achieved through novelty.[14] Ironically then, the Kantian programme was, in effect, turned on its head. 'Good taste' was supposed to be the foundation of fashion, insofar as the latter can be seen as a principle of gradual, rationally justifiable change in dress; in fact, fashion burst its bounds, and, as an aspect of consumerism, came to dictate what counted as 'good taste'. Fashion became the mediating term between taste and status; a person's aspirations to social acceptability would depend crucially on their fashion sense, as revealed through their taste in clothes.

Through the nineteenth century we find what Sennett calls the development of 'personality as a social category', whereby a person's social position can be 'read' in their dress and manner, their 'personal style'. Clothes were widely seen as 'expressive' of personal identity, hence there should be continuity between 'inner' and 'outer': clothes were the 'form' through which identity would be revealed. Taken with the increasing emphasis on personality management and self-improvement, this reveals an increasing tension between clothes seen as revealing, often involuntarily, an already constituted self, and clothes as constructing and perfecting the self. Either way, personality becomes a matter of appearance, carefully controlled. Central to individuality, then, was display, through clothes and behaviour, but it has to be self-conscious, cautious; there is a lot at stake. If every detail matters, it was not necessary to be *too* different; to dress in a cosmopolitan, sophisticated way was to dress to be unremarkable. Hence 'people wanted to protect themselves by blending into the crowd', suggests Sennett, and the new mass-produced clothes gave them the means to do so.[15]

Clues to how this works can be seen, in another context, in an interesting account of Hollywood costume policy given by Jane Gaines. According to this Hollywood aesthetic, as it developed in the 1920s and 1930s, film costume – an exaggeration of everyday clothing that thereby illuminates the logic of the latter – had to 'bring forth' character traits, via typification. This was based on the idea of an equivalence between the clothing system and the character system, so that one could be 'read' through the other: wool tweed signified a serious person, or mood; black satin was wicked or decadent; tulle, light-hearted. Ideally, these equivalences came to be taken for granted, so that neither actor nor spectator would be aware of them; the more perfect the fit between the two systems, the more 'natural' it would seem and the less the costume would be seen as costume; 'at some point, we will see a character as merely wearing clothes', and will know automatically what sort of person we are seeing. But always, costume is potentially dangerous; it has 'the potential to distract the viewer from the narrative, which could result in breaking the illusion and the spell of realism'.[16] The extravagance of dress, and the temptations of lingering with fashion, present a danger of seduction, a risk of immersion in display and indulgence, an all-consuming theatricality.

These images of fashion, then, provide fantasy identification, ways to 'fix' identity, make it coherent, but also explore it, experiment with it; identities, like clothes, can be tried on. And personality becomes this public shaping of the self, in the light of self-image and aspiration.

In the modern period, dress has had to balance social conformity and individuality, and this has led to tension in the arena of fashion. Wilson states the problem clearly: 'To dress fashionably is both to stand out and to merge with the crowd, to lay claim to the exclusive and to follow the herd.'[17] Fiske replies that, in practice, 'The desire to be oneself does not mean the desire to be fundamentally different from everyone else, but rather to situate individual differences within communal allegiance.'[18] Fashions are inherently social, after all; a fashion only exists if recognized as such. The fashion-conscious may therefore assert a sense of taste and style *through* group solidarity.

Here is Daisy, already, at seventeen, an accomplished style warrior:

> Clothes are a major signal of who you are. I select friends by the clothes they wear and if someone's wearing something that doesn't look as though they understand the rules, I probably wouldn't want to know them. Clothes are like a shorthand for the kind of person you are, and they display your ideas on style and music. If someone came in wearing all black and Doc Martens, or if their shoes were all wrong, I just know we wouldn't have anything to talk about.[19]

At this end of the continuum, the whole point is that the fashion, as signifier of group identity, is to be followed slavishly. It is a universe in which everything can depend on whether your trainers are Nike or Reebok. Everything: even your life; by 1991 around 100 Chicago teenagers had been killed for their sportswear. Yet there may, in many cases, be no difference at all in the items, *except* for the labels, the ultimate arbitrary signifier to give the identity that is craved; something to kill for, or, alternatively, something to fake, for the fake may be enough. What matters is the acquisition, the seizure of a sign that is to be made into a symbol, part of you. And for the style warrior, this 'you' depends on group affiliation.

Whatever the vagaries of 'taste', then, it has in practice operated as a marker of group membership and status aspirations. In her account of how this might work, Angela Partington argues that class differences are characteristically re-articulated through fashion, rather than being concealed as one class 'copies' another. Taking the post-war New Look as an example, she argues that it was adopted by both working-class and middle-class women, but in different ways. 'Simultaneous adoption, therefore, does not mean identical adoption.' Whereas the New Look was assimilated in moderate and 'tasteful' ways by middle-class consumers, working-class women tended to adopt New Look clothes in hybrid ('incompatible') combinations with the more conventional 'utility' styles; hence, styles were 'sampled and mixed together by the consumer to create fashions which depended on class-specific consumer skills for their meaning'. The frivolous and impractical were mixed with the comfortable and serviceable, so that working-class women 'collectively simulate class differences' by 'incorporating elements from styles which designers assumed would take their meaning from the clear distinctions between them'.[20] This fits in with Fiske's claim that 'self-display is, for those denied social power, a performance of their ability to be different, of their power to construct their meanings from the resources of the system'.[21] And ironically, the consequence is that it was middle-class women, who might well despise this eclecticism, who ended up rather more as 'fashion victims' than their working-class counterparts.

When thinking of the links between fashion and status, it is of course *haute couture* that springs most readily to mind; its exclusivity is, after all, central to its appeal. By the 1850s, the social elite was beginning to differentiate itself by raising the status of its own designers and insisting on the exclusiveness of individually designed clothes. From the start, however, the manifest social conservatism of *haute couture* in some respects has not stopped it having an association with the sexually and socially *risqué*. In 1860s Paris, the fashion leaders were generally women of the *demi-monde*, courtesans; and *couture*, especially in the first half of the twentieth century, was a channel for women's advancement, the only creative profession offering possibilities for material and critical success.[22]

Haute couture has always been slow to adopt mass-production techniques; however, this has in some ways benefited it, enabling it to maintain its exclusive image of hand-sewn and hand-finished garments while moving into the mass made-to-measure market. From the 1920s, some designers, like Chanel, showed an interest in opening up the market; and it was Chanel, along with Dior and, later, Yves Saint-Laurent, who spearheaded the post-war drive for the new mass ready-to-wear market. Nowadays, it is mainly ready-to-wear collections that constitute the catwalk shows covered by journalists; even at the top end of the market, *haute couture* has largely given way to expensive, ready-to-wear designer labels. The top Paris houses have only some 700 regular private customers among them;[23] hardly surprising when these original designs can easily cost from £5,000 to £40,000 per item, and when outfits would need to be changed at least twice a year.

Indeed, *haute couture* as such has fallen on hard times. If it could be said that the 1950s and 1960s marked the age of 'mass fashion', when *couture* was able to retain a degree of social exclusivity while extending its market and social influence, the decline since then has been marked, with the rise of 'street culture' and greater resistance to fashion imperatives from above. The fashion houses themselves have been in crisis: the intricate framework of regulations have proved increasingly archaic and uneconomic. Nowadays, the *haute couture* names generate three-quarters of their income from cosmetics and scents; hence the paradox that the relative decline of *haute couture* has nonetheless left the houses as tempting targets for big business, with Yves Saint-Laurent itself suffering the indignity of being taken over by an oil company. Whether this all amounts to the 'end of fashion' is another matter; it is worth remembering that the overall importance of *couture* in the history of fashion, implicit in identifying its fate with that of fashion itself, has frequently been exaggerated.

The Moment of Fashion: Change, Challenge and the Eternal Present

In the late stages of the French Revolution, *Directoire* fashions involved a conscious return to what was seen as the classical style of the Greeks and Romans; a vivid example of Marx's dictum that revolutions are made in the borrowed clothes of the past. For the women, gossamer-thin, near-transparent muslin dresses, frequently sprinkled with water, so as to cling to the body, revealed its outlines quite clearly, even the nipples; nothing must be allowed to 'spoil the contours of nature', as a contemporary put it.[24] This could, then, be seen as an attempt to bring nature into the public realm, allowing a transparency of the 'natural' self, and of sexuality, revealing the wearer to be an honest, revolutionary citizen, without mask.[25] Thus could a springlike rite of fashion celebrate a rebirth of society, simultaneously revolutionary, yet also a purified repetition of a past, unsullied, 'natural' state. And this return to the ancients was itself to return. John Galliano's Fallen Angels collection of 1985–6 (plate 4) was carefully researched *Directoire* dress, even down to the hints of blood on one or two of the models, harking back to one of the more surreal facets of *Directoire* fashions, the *bal des pendus*. In these balls, simultaneously a celebration of the end of the Terror and a memorial to those who had fallen, hair would be cut short, in the style of those about to be guillotined, and a red gash across the neck would carry an all-too obvious meaning.[26]

The past returns, then, but frequently shorn of its original associations, as it is re-created and reappropriated to celebrate the now; not so much a memory of the past, as the distinctively modern mode of its oblivion. And it is through fashion that this past is shattered and incorporated into the eternal present of the now, the moment of fashion itself. Roland Barthes writes that 'Fashion's *today* is pure, it destroys everything around it, disavows the past with violence, censures the future'; it is always 'an amnesiac substitution of the present for the past'. And if 'every new Fashion is a refusal to inherit, a subversion against the oppression of the preceding Fashion', asserting the right of the present over the past, it 'nevertheless lives in a world it wants to be, and sees as, ideally stable, completely penetrated by conformist glances', a present that is never-changing.[27] It thereby implicitly disavows its own inevitable transience.

If fashion therefore simultaneously expresses and denies the ever-present change that has been a central feature of the consciousness of modernity, then fashion may also embody irony, an element of self-parody. Each changing fashion has simultaneously to claim its own timeless perfection, its own importance as the touchstone of style in the here and now, while inevitably carrying within it the sense of its own mortality, an awareness of the inescapable 'pathos and absurdity of time',[28] whereby the here and now becomes the dead and gone. There is nothing more dead than yesterday's fashion, after all. This does *not*, however, necessarily apply to the day before yesterday's fashion; as we have seen, the ostensible novelty of fashion does not prevent the return of the more distant past. If, as Benjamin suggests, 'Fashion is the eternal recurrence of the new',[29] then this has a paradoxical quality; where everything is novelty, nothing seems to be really new. Hence fashion as self-parody, since it 'subtly undercuts its own assertion that the latest thing is somehow the final solution to the problem of how to look', as Wilson puts it.[30]

Of course, fashions vary in the extent to which they embody a self-conscious, self-subverting awareness of their own transience, or a deliberate use of historical reference in a self-cancelling way, to assert novelty. At one extreme, *haute couture* has generally taken itself very seriously, and has presented a model of measured, controlled change, instilling conservatism within the very framework of novelty that makes fashion possible in the first place. Ironically, Chanel's own once-revolutionary suit became, in this sense, conservative, an icon of style that alters slowly and defies the ravages of fashion. 'Fashions change; only style survives', she remarked. Style, one could say, aspires to the sacred, to timelessness, emancipated from the vagaries of fashion. Here we encounter what Polhemus and Proctor have called 'anti-fashion', which is concerned with 'time in the form of continuity and the maintenance of the status quo'.[31] Something of this can be seen in 'preppie' fashions among Ivy League graduates in the US, but also in the work of influential UK designers who aspire to a 'timeless' style, such as Jean Muir.[32]

At the other extreme, we have the work of Vivienne Westwood, the most influential British designer of the 1980s. Distancing herself from what she saw as Chanel's pared-down, masculine-oriented modernism, and commenting that 'I've never thought it powerful to be like a second-rate man',[33] she argues that fashion should rather celebrate difference, revitalize dress through plundering history and other cultures. For her, suggest Evans and Thornton, fashion is 'a discourse that works through excess, eccentricity and paradox',[34] and a happy acceptance of flux and change. Her work exemplifies the more subversive, street-centred approach of those who accept the creative but transient aspects of fashion, and she uses historical references to make the past defiantly present and thereby demystify both its pretensions and those of the here and now. One way she does this is through juxtaposing polarities: 'Art is parody', she argues, 'it uses what went before; it simplifies, but it also synthesises something else with it, that's what makes it interesting.'[35] For example: the hooped crinoline was a feature of Victorian fashion, conventionally taken to symbolize decorative uselessness and conformity, and sexual prudery, while the mini-skirt, conversely, was taken as an icon of 1960s 'liberation'. So Westwood's mini-crini of the mid-1980s juxtaposed them, implicitly raising questions about the originals, in the very act of 'remembering' them. Are freedom and sexuality about covering or uncovering the body? Was the crinoline necessarily so anti-sexual? Hiding sexuality is, after all, notoriously a means of revealing it, displaying it.[36] Westwood concludes: 'I do things in a little adventure world really, so they have their own little space, not really present, not really past; that's what makes them modern.'[37] The modern moment is that of the past annihilated by the future, experienced through the imaginative reappropriation of memory.

Westwood herself initially came to prominence as one of the most influential originators of punk, with her boutiques, Sex and Seditionaries, being a crucial focus for the movement in the mid- to late 1970s. She indeed described punk as 'confrontation dressing', and later claimed of her own contribution that 'sex is the thing that bugs English people more than anything else so that's where I attack'.[38] Sexual imagery was certainly conspicuous, but this was just one of the displacements: there were fishnet stockings, spike heels and bondage gear, but also bin bags, white school shirts splattered with fake blood, and unusual uses for safety pins and lavatory chains.[39] Punk questioned every notion of good taste, and transgressed the boundaries between life and art, reality and pretence, pornography and respectability. In some ways, there are similarities with the surrealists in the attempt to make the normal 'strange', to look at the everyday world in a new way, in the process trashing conventional aesthetic canons.[40]

Unusually, among street subcultures, punk seemed to appeal to women as much as to men. Women asserted their right to a presence on the street, and a *collective* presence, but also manifested the traditional signifiers of the 'bad girl' in the process. Their dress and behaviour articulated the contradictions in traditional feminine stereotypes, particularly 'whore' and 'virgin'. Hebdige points out that punk girls were 'parodying the conventional iconography of fallen womanhood – the vamp, the tart, the slut, the waif, the sadistic *maitresse*, the victim-in-bondage'; and 'They skirt around the voyeurism issue, flirt with masculine curiosity but refuse to submit to the masterful gaze.'[41]

In juxtaposing and jumbling categories, punk questioned everyday assumptions about the 'meaning' of the items that were so disturbingly reappropriated and rearranged. Mort suggests that punk thereby 'upset realist commonsense which said that one thing equalled another: that swastikas meant you were a Nazi or bondage gear meant you were a pervert'.[42] Again we find that meaning is not necessarily 'expressive' of some deep underlying identity; meaning could be constituted by the very juxtapositions themselves. The ensembles of punk, argues Hebdige, 'did not so much magically resolve experienced contradictions as *re-present* the experience of contradiction itself in the form of visual puns', like the ripped T-shirt; hence punk 'experienced itself through rupture'.[43] And punk itself occupied a paradoxical position: deeply opposed to conventional fashion, its transposing of garments from symbols into signs makes it fashion of the purest kind. In this sense, argue Evans and Thornton, it was never 'betrayed' by subsequently being pillaged for ideas and themes by 'high' fashion, as it manifested the central dynamic of fashion in its very origin. However, it developed a certain continuity *as* a tribal costume, hence stabilizing into anti-fashion as the clothes became symbolic of the 'punk tradition', representations of its lifestyle.[44] Once again, we see that immersion in the now of fashion promises oblivion; either the inevitable replacement by a new fashion, or its continuation, but no longer as fashion, rather as the uniform or costume of a group that aspires to an identity 'out of time'.

Modern fashion, then, moves between these two poles: a paradoxical conservatism that implicitly denies the change that makes it possible, and self-cancelling parody, celebrating the fact of its own transience. And neither can escape the sense that if fashion is novelty, then novelty is also illusion, the recurrence of the same.

If, for T. S. Eliot, 'history is a pattern/Of timeless moments',[45] then fashion is the kaleidoscope in which these timeless moments endlessly reappear; the juxtapositions that constitute a perpetual but ever-shifting present. The time of fashion is not the time of project, with a clear sense of space, time and direction, rather it is the time of the experience that project disavows, yet may contribute to making possible; the time of immediacy, grasped as fragmentation, repetition and excess. So it is not the time of organic growth and decay either, of natural cycles. As Faurschou writes, 'In fashion, the representation of the "new" erases the record of growth, maturation and decay that history inscribes on material objects and bodies',[46] or what Benjamin has called their 'testament' to a 'history that has been lived through'. Hence Benjamin can add that fashions 'compensate for the fateful effects of forgetting, on a collective scale'.[47]

It is in the figure of the 'fashion victim' that these tensions and possibilities are most vividly manifested. While the style warrior aspires to an idealized group identity emancipated from the ravages of time, the fashion victim seeks immersion in the moment of fashion in itself, the experience of fashion as the absolute here and now, the signifier of the presence of the present. The fashion victim has no choice but to live frenetically. To 'set' a fashion is then to follow it, like everyone else; one then needs to escape it, re-establish one's identity as creative source and pure victim, rolled into one. Once caught up with, the latest fashion is already *passé*. The fashion victim is always too late. One wants to be seen, one wants to be recognized, represented, as 'fashion in itself'; yet to be 'captured' in a caption or picture, even the glance of the other, is to risk losing one's 'fashionableness', find it copied, find oneself frozen into history, the photo or image becoming an epitaph. For the fashion victim, representation is death, the point at which one's pretensions are betrayed, at which one becomes yesterday. No sooner does punk exist, than it is transfixed in the images of magazines, embalmed on record sleeves, stereotyped on fashion plates, killed even as it is born. Thus is representation fatal to its object; as Hebdige writes, 'once "developed" as a photographic image, and as a sociological and marketing concept, each group fades out of the now (i.e. ceases to exist).' If the moment of fashion is the moment of the absolute present, to be named or represented is to be exiled from the now.[48] Hence fashion is a war on death, yet can only win via death itself, since only instant death and transfiguration can keep the death of representation at bay. 'Fashion exercises the rights of the corpse over the living', observes Benjamin,[49] adding that a fashion victim mimics a mannequin, becomes a parody of a 'gaily decked-out corpse'.[50] The death of the past in the present becomes the death of the present: the present never happens once, and fashion is the mode of its recurrence. It – and we – have always been here before, but can have the illusion of not knowing it.

Men, Women and the History of Modern Fashion

Pre-modern dress codes emphasized class differences, rather than gender ones; with modern fashion, this is reversed. If one takes this in conjunction with two other factors – the role of clothes as a key signifier of identity, the 'outward show' of the 'inner self', and fashion as a key aspect of consumerism – then these can together be taken to be the distinguishing features of what has come to be called the 'Western European fashion pattern',[51] or modern Western fashion.

While fashion itself can be identified in court circles as early as the Renaissance, if not earlier, and while distinct male and female dress codes had emerged by the Tudor period, it was really in the second half of the eighteenth century that these came together in the revolution that inaugurated modern fashion. Crucial here was the emergence of a simpler style of male clothing. The connotations of this are important: Steele claims that 'As early as the 1760s, plainer male dress had begun to be associated in England with liberty, patriotism, virtue, enterprise, and manliness.'[52] Rouse adds that this 'new sobriety', this relatively 'drab and austere image', carried a message of 'discipline, reliability and honesty . . . restraint, not flamboyance'.[53] With the 'Empire' style (*circa* 1795–1815), male dress shifted permanently towards this greater simplicity, with jacket, trousers and cravat or tie already apparent as the constituents of what was in effect to become the modern male uniform.

The ideological implications of this, for our understanding of male clothing, are spelt out clearly by Jennifer Craik:

> Accordingly, the rhetoric of men's fashion takes the form of a set of denials that include the following propositions: that there is no men's fashion; that men dress for fit and comfort, rather than for style; that women dress men and buy clothes for men; that men who dress up are peculiar (one way or another); that men do not notice clothes; and that most men have not been duped into the endless pursuit of seasonal fads.[54]

Men, in short, are held to be 'manly', which entails restrained, respectable, 'sensible', practical clothes and a relative independence of the irrationality and excess of consumerism; indeed, 'menswear', as a branch of fashion, has really only existed since the 1950s.[55] This powerful ideological conjunction has, historically, been influenced both by the Protestant work ethic, and by the civilizing process, both of which have emphasized moderation, self-discipline and self-control as virtues that are pre-eminently those of middle-class masculinity. By the 1840s, these attributes were being symbolized by the drab colours of masculine dress – brown, black, dark blue or grey – and by the enforcement of a strong consistency between middle-class male clothes at work and in the public arena outside. Changes in men's fashions therefore have to be presented as motivated by notions of 'rational improvement', and hence milder and less frequent than changes in women's fashions.

When men *are* influenced by fashion, therefore, they must not *appear* to be so, and this has influenced sales techniques, which have to be careful and discreet, implying a subtle eliding of masculinity into the taken-for-granted, the 'normal', rather than through directly addressing men *as* men. Doing the latter, suggests Mort, 'targets men in gendered terms rather than the norm which defines everything else. Masculinity's best-kept secret is broken open.'[56] 'Masculinity' is the

benchmark, the embodiment of the sensible and rational; femininity is its difference, the irrational excess that fluctuates around the straight, undeviating line of
masculine progress. And as femininity is marked, defined and imaged, even in its
difference, it can be appealed to, *as* fashion, and through advertising, *in* this very
difference. Some implications of this will be explored later, but some of the
perhaps contradictory aspects of this are captured in Kaja Silverman's claim
that

> The endless transformations within female clothing construct female sexuality
> and subjectivity in ways that are at least potentially disruptive, both of gender
> and of the symbolic order, which is predicated upon continuity and coherence.
> However, by freezing the male body into phallic rigidity, the uniform of orthodox
> male dress makes it a rock against which the waves of female fashion crash in
> vain.[57]

And this leads Steele to conclude that, as a result, 'western women have much
greater leeway than men to choose the clothing they feel happiest in'.[58]

Yet this unselfconscious male fashion that isn't fashion, this style of clothing
that isn't a style but is simply, and invisibly, 'clothing', this 'natural' assertion of
a masculinity that implies a claim to cultural superiority, rests on a deep irony of
history, as can be seen if we explore the case of the dandy, in the early nineteenth
century.

'Without sacrificing elegance or grace', writes Moers, the dandy 'invented a
costume that was indubitably masculine';[59] in short, he embodied the so-called
'great masculine renunciation',[60] the rejection of elaborate eighteenth-century
wigs and cosmetics in favour of an unadorned style, with an emphasis on well-
fitting clothes, especially trousers. The apparent straightforwardness of the dress
was deceptive, however; for a start, it could take lengthy and careful preparation
to get it right; further, it concealed the fact that the dandy characteristically had
far from elevated social origins. The dandy lived the life of a leisured gentleman,
preferably on borrowed money; Beau Brummell has generally been taken as the
typical exemplar, though Lord Byron and Baudelaire fit the general stereotype as
well. Refinement was the core of the dandy ideal, and a cultivated detachment
from social obligations; the true dandy should neither work nor raise a family. For
Baudelaire, this refinement manifested an 'aristocratic superiority of mind';[61]
dandyism becomes, in effect, a mode of aristocracy, surviving as style in the
transition to a democratic age. For the dandy, then, aristocracy became its own
performance; always on show, equally polite to all, a matter of form and appearance, a perpetual incognito; 'an unmistakable yet understated disguise: the possibility of not being what you seem',[62] or perhaps the possibility of disappearing *into*
what you seem, the appearance *becoming* the substance. This figure, such a
powerful stimulus to bourgeois male fashion, was hence anti-bourgeois in his
whole stance. Yet he could not escape immersion in the bourgeois world so
easily. Aristocratic chic was 'inherently tainted by commercialism', suggests
Rosalind Williams; the dandy 'expressed himself as a consumer'.[63] Here again we

encounter Campbell's fusion of the 'romantic ethic' and the 'spirit of modern consumerism'.

Above all, the dandy was *cool*. 'The role of the dandy implied an intense preoccupation with self and self presentation', writes Wilson; 'image was everything'. Hence the dandy was the very type of the 'new urban man who came from nowhere and for whom appearance *was* reality'.[64] At the Battle of Waterloo, it was noted that Wellington's dandy officers seemed to show more concern with keeping their handsome uniforms immaculate than with anything as tedious as fighting the enemy.

As a model for masculinity, then, the dandy is somewhat paradoxical. On the one hand, he was clearly *male* – there were no female dandies – and arguably, Beau Brummell had more influence on male dress for the next century and a half than anyone else. On the other hand, the dandy combines social marginality and rebellion with social impotence; his clothes, his whole orientation, represent a triumph of style over substance, an aesthetic orientation *to* the world rather than an active involvement *in* it. Furthermore, as Evans and Thornton put it, 'dandyism flirts with the conventionally feminine areas of narcissism, artificiality and fashion'.[65] And this can become quite openly controversial and subversive of gender assumptions; Oscar Wilde, after all, was a classic dandy. Masculinity disappears into style, becoming a matter of display rather than drive, of contrivance and appearance. As Bracewell observes, 'The gap between effeminacy and elegance has always been slender.'[66] In this sense, dandyism has been a perennial tendency within modern male fashion; the Mods of the 1960s also dressed for one another's admiration and cultivated the cool.[67] So if, as Angela Carter suggests, 'the dandy is always a rebel',[68] it is because he embodies paradox in his very being, he embodies the unanswerable questions about the social realities of class, gender and identity, the suggestion that clothes are both more and less than they seem to be. This 'first modern man' is a very ambiguous role model, and seems to interrogate the very assumptions of modernity and masculinity: aristocratic, yet also bourgeois; masculine, yet also effeminate; actively passive; fashionable, yet an icon of anti-fashion; modern, yet pointing to the postmodern.

If we turn to women's fashions, it can be said that the contrast with the premodern was less marked – the stays, crinolines, farthingales, panniers and bustles of earlier centuries were still prevalent in the nineteenth – but the subsequent swings in fashion were rather more noticeable than in the case of men. In terms of the mapping of gender differences on to fashion, it is of course the Victorian period which is seen as the era of maximum divergence between the sexes. Corsets, bustles, extravagant gowns and dresses, huge skirts and shawls that could reach eight feet across, all reproduced on the body the dualism of the 'separate spheres' of gendered social life.[69] Veblen long ago interpreted the dress of Victorian women as the modern style of 'conspicuous consumption', adding that it symbolized their dependent social status, so that 'the performance of conspicuous leisure and consumption came to be part of the services required of them'.[70] As we have already seen, however, these interpretive issues are not so clear-cut, and Steele concludes that 'the clothing of the Victorian woman reflected not only the cultural prescriptive ideal of femininity, but also her own aspirations and fantasies'.[71]

The fact remains that the reaction was dramatic. Already, by the 1890s, in the US, the 'Gibson Girl' was showing the simpler style that foreshadowed the revolution to come; in the late 1900s, corsets, bustles, crinolines and the paraphernalia of Victorian excess were swept away; and, through the 1920s, the rejection of Victorianism became a rejection not just of the clothes, but of the values and lifestyle as well. If the dandy could be said to represent the modernization of masculine fashion, the 'New Woman'[72] of the 1910s and 1920s performed the same role for women's fashion. Clothes became simpler, the cut straighter, the appearance more severe; no hint of the decorative or ostentatious here. Women took increasingly to plain skirts, jackets and suits (plate 5). And over it all presided the figure of Gabrielle 'Coco' Chanel, the most influential figure in the history of modern fashion.

Demi-mondaine in origin, set up in business originally by her lover, Chanel, in spirit, a true dandy, celebrated disguise as the central principle of her own life. Her biographer, Charles-Roux, points to 'the enigma she contrived to present to everyone who came near her . . . in her attempts to mask her origins'; in short, 'the art she lavished upon rendering herself *unintelligible*'.[73] Both her origins and her image fused to make her the key icon of the modern woman, her whole style carrying a message of democratic opportunity; copying Chanel made you modern. Her 'poor look', with sweaters, jersey dresses, flannel and lock-knit suits, subverted fashion as display, celebrating 'mobility' in both the practical and the social senses. With her 'less is more' modernism, the rich could look like street girls and shop assistants, paying a lot for clothes that made them anonymous, yet through her interest in selling to the mass market – she proclaimed that 'Fashion does not exist unless it goes down into the streets'[74] – street girls could also look rich. She did not invent the 'little black dress', trousers for women, or the other specific innovations she is often credited with; yet she was always in the right place at the right time, a consummate publicist, modern also in her ability to market herself and her clothes as one.[75] By the 1930s – and again with the 'Chanel suit', the vehicle for her comeback in the 1950s – her designs were influencing the American mass market, showing a broad appeal to emancipated women who saw themselves as active, involved, public figures in a way not possible for their Victorian forebears.

It was not just a matter of clothes: the 'New Woman' was also the slim woman; Connor refers to the 'modernist body', celebrating functionality and mobility, rather than fertility.[76] One should remember, then, that the new stripped-down female body, freed of its stifling adornments, remained a *disciplined* body, even if this was now the self-discipline of diet and exercise, rather than corsets and crinolines. Ewen adds that 'The external, *social* ideal of thinness is a by-product of modernity. Whatever flesh remains is *too much*; image must be freed from the liabilities of substance.'[77] When fashion emphasizes a feminine 'will to power', the maternal takes a back seat.[78] But this in turn results in paradox: the model of femininity offered here seems to be decidedly *masculine*. It is as though in order to become independent, become a person in her own right, a woman must become a man; indeed, Chanel herself is alleged to have said that she 'always dressed like the strong independent male she had dreamed of being'.[79] Just as the dandy represents masculinity with a feminine hue, so the New Woman is the masculine face of femininity. But this whole issue of gender images and identities clearly requires further investigation.

The Mirror, the Look and the Gaze

Soap opera stars are not born; they have to be made: '*Dynasty*'s Linda Evans turned herself from a Plain Jane into a beautiful star . . . by massaging her face with honey every day and trying to stick her tongue up her nose. . . . "But I reckon most women could do what I did", she said.'[80] 'Putting on one's face' is clearly hard work; but the rewards are manifest. Beauty is there, for a woman prepared to strive for it; and success too, since, as a study of women's magazines found, all this remains embedded in the 'discourse of improvement' whereby '"improvement" in appearance leads to self-improvement in other areas of life'.[81] Thus do fashion and beauty, mutually defining, serve to structure women's relationships to images of themselves. It is the ambiguous construction of femininity whereby woman becomes both subject and object, discussed in my *Transgressing the Modern* (ch. 5), that comes into play here. And as object to her own self-examination, she is simultaneously object to the examination of others, and able to compare herself with others. This tension of subject and object, self and other, is mediated through the image. Berger argues that 'A woman must continually watch herself. She is almost continually accompanied by her own image of herself', and so 'she comes to consider the *surveyor* and the *surveyed* within her as the two constituent yet always distinct elements of her identity as a woman'.[82] It is through the image that woman becomes object to herself.

Here we have a clue to the obsession with mirrors in Western narratives and portrayals of femininity. Simone de Beauvoir suggests that woman, 'knowing and making herself object, believes she really sees *herself* in the glass'; a woman in a mirror is caught in a 'motionless, silvered trap'.[83] Dijkstra discusses late nineteenth-century explorations of this theme, and suggests that woman, mirror and moon were frequently assimilated: the moon, after all, only shines with a reflected light, that of the sun, just as woman needs man's light; but, at an everyday level, moon and sun *seem* mutually exclusive, since the moon apparently only exists in the absence of the sun, shining with a pale, steady, uniform light, enclosed in its circular self-sufficiency. There were several versions of this possibility that woman's imitation and reflection could be self-sufficient, independent of men, all of them equally alarming: perhaps it was the wildness of nature that she reflects; or the emptiness of endlessly reflecting images of nothing but the reflecting itself; or, worst of all, the spectre of the other-as-same, the Medusa of lesbianism, becoming by the early twentieth century an obsessive fear and focus of masculine culture. Either way, she *needs* her mirror: 'To see herself was her only hold on reality.'[84]

There is a sense, then, in which the 'normal' woman – in relationship with a man – must 'break' her mirror, and thereby 'die' as an independent presence in the world; she must become moon to the man's sun. She needs her mirror, but she also needs to break it; and the only way out is to live in her self-image as she sees it, but a self-image that is necessarily also an image of herself as desired by a man. Outside this framework lie madness and death. In escaping the living death of a world of shadows, seen only through a mirror, in taking independent action by asserting the right to the power of her own gaze, in looking down to 'tower'd Camelot', the Lady of Shalott knew, in that very instant, as 'The mirror crack'd from side to side', that she was doomed.[85]

In these accounts, then, the mirror emerges as a focus for concerns about danger and control, the potential for feminine 'unruliness'. There is an implicit awareness that the mirror can play a creative role; it is indeed 'merely' reflective, but in reflecting one's self-image, it can encourage the creation of new elements of self-identity. It can reflect truth, or reflect the creation of fiction, or reflect the truth of fictional creation. Hence the self in the mirror can be 'the self confirming itself as a created image', as Anne Hollander puts it.[86] It is not so easy to 'police' the mirror, as it were. Simone de Beauvoir claims that 'It is impossible to be *for one's self* actually an *other* and to recognize oneself consciously as object',[87] and for Lacan this implies a 'splitting' that is constitutive of selfhood, the incorporation of an otherness that means the self can never be self-identical:[88] the object in the mirror is both self and other, and self-image is both reflection and creative appropriation.

Berger's claim that 'Men look at women', while 'Women watch themselves being looked at',[89] so that women exist in a self-image that seems to be defined entirely through the male gaze, does not therefore capture the whole complexity of the issue. That 'the look' *is* gendered is incontestable. Men look at women in crowd situations, where the woman tends to lower her eyes; women look more at men in one-to-one conversations, where the man's tendency to look away more frequently could serve as an index of dominance or at least independence, non-reciprocity. The expressions, gestures and eye direction of male and female models in fashion photos are markedly different: male models look up, or away; and when looking towards the viewer, they tend to look at or through, asserting control rather than availability.[90] But this only establishes that *the way* the look functions is gendered, not that it is in some sense inherently *masculine*, that the look has to be a penetrating, possessive *gaze*.

Perhaps it might therefore be useful to draw a tentative distinction between 'the gaze' and 'the look'. The gaze is active, acquisitive, voyeuristic, dominating, with a hint of aggression. The look, on the other hand, can refer to a state as well as an action, with elements of passivity and narcissism, as in 'the look' referring to a fashion. The grammar brings out this distinction: 'How do I look?' makes sense in this way (whereas 'How do I gaze?' makes no sense at all). 'The look' has elements of both masculine and feminine, active and passive; voyeurism, but narcissism, too. If, following Lacan, one can argue that the subject always experiences itself as seen, necessarily incorporating the look of the other, then this must be true of the male subject as well as the female.[91] 'The gaze' has elements of male hysteria as much as of male power; men may disavow exhibitionism and narcissism, but they cannot escape them. The 'male gaze' is not what it seems; it can be found to incorporate auto-eroticism, homoeroticism and fetishism, as seen in Hollywood westerns,[92] or masochism, as in Gaylyn Studlar's account of Sternberg's films with Marlene Dietrich.[93] 'The gaze' cannot elude the ambiguities of 'the look', however desperate the attempt.

The history of Western fashion, argues Kaja Silverman, therefore 'poses a serious challenge both to the automatic equation of spectacular display with female subjectivity, and to the assumption that exhibitionism always implies woman's subjugation to a controlling male gaze'.[94] The possibilities for an 'active female gaze' have been discussed;[95] Jackie Stacey has explored the fascination of women for other women's images, analysing it as an interplay of both identification and desire, narcissism and voyeurism;[96] and Evans and Thornton have speculated on the 'indeterminate or bisexual desire' that women seem to manifest when looking at fashion photographs, suggesting that such photos may 'at the same time prescribe women's fantasies or desires *and* permit a free space in which women map for themselves'.[97] Fantasy identifications can alter self-image, and need not just mirror orthodox gender stereotypes.

All this reinforces the sense that while there clearly are respects in which the 'masculine gaze' has indeed been an important element of the modern construction of gender relations, it is also true that – corresponding to the ambiguous status of woman as subject and object – 'looking' and 'the look' run through modernity as key elements of the construction of subjecthood itself, linked with surveillance and display in the context of the market economy and panopticism. And this sense of the self as consumer and spectator, looking and being looked at in ways that emphasize fashion, appearance and personal style, is related to the idea that late modernity has become increasingly narcissistic. Lasch and Sennett have suggested that images and revelations of self have become ever-more basic to self-identity, and it is increasingly as though the world becomes a mirror of personality.[98] 'All of us, actors and spectators alike, live surrounded by mirrors', as Lasch puts it;[99] and, he might have added, men as well as women.

Dresses for the Boys

In the early 1980s, the London club scene was host to an extravaganza of male costume excess, in which cross-dressing was central; and although this so-called 'Blitz culture' – linked to pop, the British fashion revival, and the prominence of the gay scene – itself went out of fashion, a series of clubs like Kinky Gerlinky continued the pattern into the 1990s. In America, meanwhile, several decades of Harlem drag balls culminated in 'vogueing', itself becoming a hit in the wider culture. Nor, of course, was any of this wholly new: cross-dressing has been a perennial temptation in male dress in the modern period, even though generally sanctioned.

Traditionally, feminists have cast a rather sceptical eye over all this; flirting with transvestism is a means whereby men can vicariously 'try on' femininity without really risking anything. And undoubtedly there is much truth in this.[100] The film *Tootsie*, featuring Dustin Hoffman in drag, is often seen in these terms; Hoffman as 'Dorothy' can get the best of both worlds, while remaining a man. But Marjorie Garber questions this interpretation, arguing that transvestism in the film is an 'enabling fantasy', not a joke on women; the power of 'Dorothy' comes from the transvestite role itself, the 'blurred gender', not from either of the two gender identities in themselves.[101] Indeed, criticisms of transvestism do tend to rest on orthodox assumptions about 'masculinity' and 'femininity', and their allegedly mutually exclusive, 'natural' basis, yet these assumptions may turn out to be precisely what is at issue. Something of this is hinted at by RuPaul Charles, entertainer and fashion model, when he says: 'The truth is that I'm a man. The illusion is I look like a woman. But the illusion is truer.'[102] And Annie Lennox's assertion that she cross-dressed because 'I wanted to reinvent myself'[103] again implies that there can be a liberating potential in 'mere' clothes. Nor is there any reason, then, on this approach, why women cannot be drag queens as well as men. Marcus claims that

> glamour, drag and power are intimately related. Drag, like camp, recognises the element of purposeful self-presentation in fashion and parodies it. Drag no longer refers just to men dressing as women but to anyone who consciously borrows the costume of another. Women can access drag and they do.[104]

Drag therefore emerges not as a minor deviation from conventional stereotypes, but as a joker in the pack that is also the ace, the card that can reveal the parochial, ideological and arbitrary nature of the orthodox gender dualism. Both because it represents a confusion of categories, and because it can be taken as an ambiguous signifier of homosexuality, drag has been distrusted and quarantined in the modern West, clouding as it does the clarity of gender recognition. And it is this problematical link with 'homosexuality', in its social identity, that can enable us to go deeper into these issues.

'Homosexuality' in its modern sense – referring to a 'type of person', rather than just a category of sex act – emerged alongside the model of the 'two sexes', the fusion of sex, gender and sexuality that constitutes the basis of modern identity. How this 'type' is to be conceptualized in terms of sex and gender characteristics was – and is – obscure and controversial, and the issue of recognition has always been crucial.[105] In practice, there has always tended to be an assimilation of homosexuality and effeminacy. In late eighteenth-century London, before the emergence of the modern homosexual, the 'molly' was already seen as passive, effeminate, with transvestite tendencies, and attracted to other men, and it was the appearance that was troublesome, rather than sexuality as such.[106] Later, as 'homosexuality' developed, and sexuality was seen as central to it, the implicit paradox comes to the fore: if men who seek sex with other men are homosexual, then this must include both active and passive dimensions, and there is no reason why an 'active' partner, in particular, should necessarily look effeminate. Hence the potential for 'moral panics' and witch hunts, and the twentieth-century idea that macho masculinity is not necessarily what it seems. Thus Rock Hudson fell victim to what was still being described in some quarters as the 'gay plague', though he was the quintessential 'macho' Hollywood star.

The development of an intimate relationship between personal identity, sexuality and gender seems fundamental here, since it is only this conjunction that serves to stake out 'homosexuality' as a major potential arena of taboo and transgression. Indeed, there is a sense in which the 'homosexual person' becomes a necessary founding fiction, a figure of confusion, fear and travesty, hence able to mark the distance from heterosexuality as norm, the 'natural' form of gender identity. 'Heterosexuality here presupposes homosexuality', as Judith Butler puts it.[107] And the unclarity over the gender-coding of homosexuality, in terms of appearance, identity and role, spawned a variety of theories ('third sex', 'invert'), reinforcing the idea that effeminacy or transvestism was bound to be present as a key indicator somewhere; the attractions of 'otherness', even within the context of 'the same', will mean that one partner or the other will be bound to manifest elements of the feminine. Hence, except on certain highly specific and ritualized occasions, transvestism has served as a signifier of sexual and gender deviance to the wider community, and, often, to gays themselves, even though it is clear that 'transvestite' and 'gay' are, in principle, independent identity choices, and neither need necessarily compromise a man's sense of his own 'masculinity'.

The effect of all these ambiguously gendered performances is therefore to raise questions about orthodox gender categories themselves; indeed, 'gender identity' stands revealed as a site of uncertainty and confusion, once sundered from its conventionally presupposed biological foundations. And Butler suggests that heterosexual styles in gay subcultures are not a mere persistence of oppressive stereotypes, rather they bring into relief 'the utterly constructed status of the so-called heterosexual original', whereby 'gay is to straight *not* as copy to original, but, rather, as copy is to copy', since heterosexuality is a learned role, not simply a reflection of 'nature'. In short, masculinity and femininity, and the heterosexuality that is conventionally linked to them, *seem* clear enough, when embedded in the taken-for-granted roles of everyday life, and marked by differences of dress; but the certainties evaporate when the boundaries are crossed, for then it is no longer clear what the 'boundaries' *really* serve to separate, what is actually *there*. What, other than the obvious *biological* difference, is really 'under', or beyond, the clothes, to constitute the difference of gender? Or is it that the clothes, and the other signifiers, are not *expressive* of essential difference, but are *all that there is*?

Developing the implications of the latter possibility, Butler argues that gender attributes are not expressive but performative, in that they 'effectively constitute the identity they are said to express or reveal'. There is no deeper 'essence' being revealed on the surface; in effect, the surface performance, the display of body and clothes, becomes repetitive, a learned pattern whereby 'gender' emerges as 'the repeated stylization of the body', giving, over time, the appearance of stability and naturalness. Gender performance produces gendered identity as a fantasized unity of interior self and 'natural difference'. This approach seems to connect with the work of Elias, Foucault and Taylor on the significance of the interiority of selfhood in the modern relationship between body and person, while clarifying the sense in which this interiority is the *effect* of 'the public regulation of fantasy through the surface politics of the body'.[108] And it is important to remember that the 'theatricality' of gender is not wholly reducible to conscious self-display or self-creation; what is 'displayed' is also a disavowal of what remains opaque, latent, unacceptable.[109] And it is this that drag draws on for its creative energies.

'This is the scandal of transvestism', proclaims Garber; that it 'tells the truth about gender'.[110] The significance of drag is that it suggests a distinction between gender identity and gender performance, between 'reality' and 'appearance', but then subverts these very distinctions. Drag *imitates* gender, thereby suggesting that gender itself may be no more than its own imitation, a performance that can only ever provide the illusion of its own adequate grounding. A drag act, concludes Butler, suggests that 'gender is a kind of persistent impersonation that passes as the real'.[111] Identity becomes not essence but rehearsal, the self as a theatrical construct; you're only yourself when you're another. So Mark Simpson playfully inverts the devaluation of drag, portraying it as a

> glorious, glamorous celebration of surface over substance, artifice over nature, pretence over authenticity; the carnival of drag overturns the fear of woman-as-nature and replaces it with woman-as-artifice; appearance is held up for approval and essence mocked.[112]

The novelist Angela Carter observed that 'For transvestites, the appearance of femininity is its essence. As I grow older, I do begin to believe this might be so.'[113] So woman, too, is a female impersonator?

The Feminine Masquerade

The apparent 'masculinity' of the dress style of the 1920s flapper or 'New Woman' requires further interpretation. Examining the lives and works of women literary figures like Djuna Barnes and Virginia Woolf, Carroll Smith-Rosenberg suggests that these feminist modernists 'turned to dress and to body imagery to repudiate gender and to assert a new order'. She elaborates the argument as follows:

> Feminist modernists, by rejecting the 'naturalness' of gender, insisted that society's most fundamental organizational category – gender – was artificial, hence 'unnatural', as changeable as dress. From this first principle, it then followed that nothing social or political was 'natural'. Institutional structures, values, behaviour, all were artifact, all relative, all reflective not of nature but of power.[114]

It is more a matter of gender reflecting dress than dress reflecting gender; what we wear is what we become. If gender is really just costume, then gender stereotypes are oppressive in inhibiting the possibilities of self-creation and exploration.

Virginia Woolf's fantasy novel *Orlando* is a key text here. Gender and sex are assimilated, and both are presented as results rather than causes of shifts in self-identity; it is as though sex and gender identity can be changed as readily as dress. And the choice of sex becomes in a sense arbitrary. 'Different though the sexes are, they intermix', writes the author; 'In every human being a vacillation from one sex to the other takes place.'[115] This seems consistent with Woolf's own view, expressed elsewhere, that 'It is fatal to be a man or woman pure and simple; one must be woman-manly or man-womanly.'[116] Of Orlando, Woolf concludes that there was 'this mixture in her of man and woman, one being uppermost and then the other. . . . Whether, then, Orlando was most man or woman, it is difficult to say and cannot now be decided.'[117] And it is implied that it does not much matter. This all seems to connect with aspects of the 'lesbianism' found in some 'New Woman' circles; for such relationships, in private, frequently manifested a fluidity of role-play and a compatibility with heterosexual relations as well. Thus Katrina Rolley, in her study of these relationships, argues that 'lesbian' roles were 'fugitive rather than fixed', and that the lesbian's ability to 'change her gender through manipulation of her self-presentation' had the effect of 'exposing the artificiality of society's masculine and feminine ideals'.[118]

This, however, reminds us of the 'power' dimension, mentioned by Smith-Rosenberg. For male modernist authors, like Joyce, Eliot and Lawrence, challenges to gender orthodoxy, and the irreducibility of biological sex distinctions, had to be fought off, and distinctions in clothing are necessary, not arbitrary. Sandra Gilbert writes: 'For the male modernist . . . gender is most often an ultimate reality, while for the female modernist an ultimate reality exists only if one journeys beyond gender.'[119] And the 1920s were indeed a decisive decade in the construction of 'lesbianism' as a stereotypical deviant identity, a direct instrument of social control, even through prosecution in the courts, reminding us of Butler's dictum that 'identity categories tend to be instruments of regulatory regimes'.[120]

The 1920s was also the time when Joan Rivière was elaborating her theory of the feminine masquerade. She, too, asks if femininity is a construct, or an underlying bedrock. Noticing the behaviour of women who were successful in the public sphere of work – thereby taking on implicitly 'masculine' roles – she observed that they combined this with the opposite pattern of behaviour, playing up, in clothes and manner, to ideas of femininity as submissiveness, adornment and flirtatiousness. The latter, she argued, could be seen as a defensive reaction, or compromise, for fear of men's hostile reaction to the appropriation of masculinity implicit in the former. This would seem to imply that 'femininity' might be a mask that covers a real underlying femininity that cannot gain expression. But this is *not* what she means. She writes: 'The reader may now ask how I define womanliness and the "masquerade". My suggestion is not, however, that there is any such difference; whether radical or superficial, they are the same thing.'[121] Heath elaborates: 'In the masquerade the woman mimics an authentic – feminine –

womanliness but then an authentic womanliness *is* such a mimicry, *is* the masquerade'; so 'to be a woman is to dissimulate a fundamental masculinity, femininity is that dissimulation'.[122] The woman disappears into the mask, the essence into the appearance; masquerade represents femininity, but femininity is representation anyway.

And the content of masquerade? This involves above all the images of femininity embodied in the clothes of the time, so that fashion itself becomes its primary site. Here, narcissism and voyeurism – together with fetishism – come together as subject and object dimensions of the 'gaze' that constitutes femininity in its very mix of active appropriation and passive display. So, as Partington suggests,

> 'Masquerade' implies an acting out of the images of femininity, for which is required an active gaze to decode, utilise and identify with those images, while at the same time constructing a self-image which is dependent on the gaze of the other. In this sense, womanliness, or femininity, is a 'simulation', a demonstration of the representations of women in a 'masquerade', acted out by the female viewer.[123]

This neatly encapsulates the undecidability at the core of the masquerade: is this subjection to patriarchy and the male gaze, or an evasion of it? Does masquerade block any escape, or does the woman escape into it?

One possibility can be seen in the way a leading figure of 1930s fashion, Schiaparelli, appropriated the spirit of masquerade in her clothes. Influenced by surrealism, she espoused excess and folly in fashion, seeing clothes as play and illusion. Wearing her clothes, suggest Evans and Thornton, a woman 'creates herself as spectacle; but the moment she displays herself she also disguises herself'.[124] She gives herself room to manoeuvre. This approach is also present in Westwood, but is most graphically captured in the photography of Cindy Sherman. Her endless series of self-portraits always capture herself, but herself playing a role, herself *as* . . . hooker, girl next door, Renaissance scholar, bathing beauty, doll, medieval queen, corpse. And if one asks, which is the *real* Cindy Sherman, or is there one, the answer implied in the photos is that she has always already moved on, exists as and in the differences between the pictures, a chain of signifiers that point to a non-identity at the heart of identity, an interplay of revelation and concealment that challenges the masculine desire to identify and define. Hence Laura Mulvey claims that she 'performs femininity as an appearance', and that 'There is no stable subject position in her work, no resting point that does not quickly shift into something else.'[125] And Judith Williamson points to the fusion of witty parody, vulnerability, anxiety and eroticism in the pictures, all mixed up 'as are the imagery and experience of femininity for all of us'.[126] It is as though the self that disappears into the photos also exists as a gaze, at a distance from them, with these tensions between immersion and distance being worked out through disguise, which is congruent with Luce Irigaray's idea that a woman plays with her image, and in putting it on signifies that it is a 'put-on' and can always be taken off; a woman is always 'elsewhere',[127] even if that 'elsewhere' is another image.

This all casts an interesting light on Chanel's modernism. Appropriating characteristically 'modernist' axioms of the time – 'less is more', functionality, antipathy to adornment – Chanel's clothes could serve as a costume in which women could enter traditionally masculine spheres. This could be seen as a symbolic capitulation to masculinity in order to achieve a share of its power, or else as a transvestite strategy whereby women parody the masculine, comment on it, show it to be *itself* 'masquerade'. There is a sense, then, in which masculinity cannot escape the masquerade either, whatever its pretensions. If New Women can dress in suits, take on the 'trappings of authority', this makes a statement about the ultimate reducibility of the authority to the trappings. Men haven't got the phallus either, really. The New Woman 'returns masculinity to them as equally unreal, another act, a charade of power', as Heath puts it.[128] And since disguise and display are coded as feminine, adds Lacan, the feminine mask has the 'curious consequence of making *virile* display in the human being itself seem feminine.'[129] It follows that masculinity can only be itself by resorting to strategies that reveal the feminine other as actually constitutive of itself.

To imply a complete symmetry between 'masculinity' and 'femininity' would, however, be misleading; it would not pay sufficient attention to the way the culturally constructed nature/culture distinction is mapped on to gender. And 'dress' is important here partly through the significance of its opposite, 'undress'. There is a sense in which a man becomes a man through culture, through clothing; a woman, however, is always a 'woman', clothed or unclothed. Angela Carter suggests that a woman 'can accede to a symbolic power as soon as her clothes are off, whereas a man's symbolic power resides in his clothes, indicators of his status'; in this sense, 'The female nude's nakedness is in itself a form of dress.'[130] Perhaps this is why, as Barthes suggests, conventional female striptease is re-veiling rather than revealing; the gloves, fans and G-strings make the strip a pretence, prevent the final revelation of the castrating nothingness underneath.[131] So that insightful old misogynist Nietzsche can claim, appropriately, that women ' "put on something" even when they take off everything'; that perhaps they '*have* to be first of all and above all actresses'.[132] Showalter adds that 'Female self-unveiling can be a shocking act, for female unveiling substitutes power for castration';[133] whereas with the man, one might say, it is the other way round. A penis is . . . merely a penis. So a male stripper, writes Simpson, 'can never be naked enough, never *stripped* enough, because the phallus can never be shown – instead we are palmed off with a paltry penis', and 'the climactic finale of the strip is . . . an anticlimax'.[134] To bear its cultural weight, the penis must be veiled; only then can penis become phallus, the signifier of male status.

It is as though femininity refuses a rigid nature/culture distinction, so that clothes no longer have to mark this boundary; and if, in this sense, clothes do not matter, they can become, in principle, infinitely variable, constrained only by choice and fashion. Hence women's clothes can even be inclusive of men's (as in jeans and trousers). The man, on the other hand, embodying 'culture' and disavowing 'nature', marks his distance from the latter by embodying a standard, a uniform. Now, clothes *do* matter, in a sense they are *all* that matters, both displaying and concealing the precarious self-sufficiency of masculine identity, and doing so by circumscribing their cultural potential for difference and variation, so as to draw attention not to themselves, but to the wearer. (Men *must* wear trousers, which are therefore only really noticeable in their absence.) For men, clothes represent functionality, rationality, uniformity; for women, they can include these dimensions, but also become 'adornment', display, a celebration of excess, added to and continuous with nature, rather than opposed to it. Culture is but nature in a different dress, a different 'guise', so women can exemplify both nature and artifice.[135]

And what is adornment, after all? To see it as 'mere' decoration is to belittle it; and this could *seem* to be implied by Nietzsche's suggestion that 'women would not have their genius for adornment if they did not have the instinct for playing a *secondary* role'.[136] Yet there is a sting to this, for he also claims that 'Women have known how to secure for themselves by their subordination the greatest advantage, in fact the upper hand.'[137] From this point of view, femininity as adornment or passivity need not be that which is defined or controlled, but that which resists such power, that which masks, encompasses, transcends it. Femininity performs both the absence of power, and its subversion. Baudrillard has tried to develop aspects of this in his theory of seduction, whereby 'it is the feminine as appearance that thwarts masculine depth', or rather the feminine emerges as 'indistinctness of surface and depth'; femininity embodies seduction as a kind of obverse of power, embodying artifice.[138]

Yet this all remains within the rigidity of gender dualism itself, what Derrida calls the 'essentializing fetishes'[139] of gender. If Nietzsche is right to claim, of woman, that 'Her great art is the lie',[140] this can, in the end, only be because it is the feminine that has most dramatically represented the site of 'trouble' in the modern dualism of gender itself, pointing to the sense in which this dualism, in its closure and fixedness, is necessarily a fiction.

In their different ways, the dandy, the New Woman, and the punk, can all be taken as examples of 'modernism' in fashion. All implicitly proclaim that fashion has its own autonomy, its own creativity; it is not reducible to a mere manifestation of the 'real' self or an underlying 'essence' of gender. Modernist fashion celebrates the artifice of culture, suggesting that gender is a fantasy identification enacted through the body and its modes of display, decoration and concealment. Fashion can be conservative, transgressive or playful, but above all it suggests that identity is a performance, a construct. If modernity as project has tried to rest gender distinctions on underlying 'natural' differences, modernism in fashion questions this project, plays with it, even ridicules it, presenting gender as a role, something one 'plays at'. Codes of representation are not reducible to what is represented; culture is a continuation of nature by other means. Indeed, fashion suggests a meaninglessness at the heart of culture; its very 'triviality', its pointlessness, is precisely the 'serious' point, the point at which culture parodies itself in an exercise of carnivalesque theatricality, albeit disavowed and constantly subject to rationalist and functionalist discipline. Fashion involves status and manipulation, but is not to be identified wholly with this; for it also involves fantasy and daydreams, embodying them in the here and now, as a source of pleasure, as well as anxiety, with the potential for creativity, as well as conformity; always, in principle, an aspect of popular culture.

Notes

1   L. Wright, 'Objectifying Gender: The Stiletto Heel', in J. Attfield and P. Kirkham (eds.), *A View from the Interior: Feminism, Women and Design* (Women's Press, 1989).

2   J. Craik, *The Face of Fashion* (Routledge, 1994), p. 16.

3   Wright, 'Objectifying Gender', p. 14.

4   E. Wilson, *Adorned in Dreams* (Virago, 1985), p. 13.

5   V. Steele, *Fashion and Eroticism: Ideals of Feminine Beauty from the Victorian Era to the Jazz Age* (Oxford University Press, 1985), chs. 5, 9.

6   B. Turner, *The Body and Society* (Blackwell, 1984), p. 197.

7   L. Gamman and M. Makinen, *Female Fetishism: A New Look* (Lawrence and Wishart, 1994), p. 60, and see pp. 201–6.

8   See Steele, *Fashion and Eroticism*, and D. Kunzle, 'Dress Reform as Antifeminism', *Signs* (1977), 2–3, pp. 570–9.

9   K. Sawchuk, 'A Tale of Inscription/Fashion Statements', in A. and M. Kroker (eds.), *Body Invaders: Sexuality and the Postmodern Condition* (Macmillan, 1988).

10   R. Barthes, *The Fashion System* (Cape, 1985), pp. 272, 287 (emphasised in the original), 288.

11   C. Evans and M. Thornton, *Women and Fashion: A New Look* (Quartet Books, 1989), p. 42.

12   T. Castle, *Masquerade and Civilization: The Carnivalesque in Eighteenth-Century English Culture and Fiction* (Methuen, 1986), p. 56.

13   P. Bourdieu, *Distinction: A Social Critique of the Judgement of Taste* (Routledge, 1984), p. 53 and passim.

14   C. Campbell, *The Romantic Ethic and the Spirit of Modern Consumerism* (Blackwell, 1989), pp. 94, 158.

15   R. Sennett, *The Fall of Public Man* (Faber, 1986), pp. 157, 164, and ch. 8.

16   J. Gaines, 'Costume and Narrative: How Dress Tells the Woman's Story', in J. Gaines and C. Herzog (eds.), *Fabrications* (Routledge, 1990), pp. 187, 192, 193.

17   Wilson, *Adorned in Dreams*, p. 6.

18   J. Fiske, *Understanding Popular Culture* (Unwin Hyman, 1989), p. 3.

19   Quoted in the *Guardian* (6 January 1992).

20   A. Partington, 'Popular Fashion and Working-Class Affluence', in J. Ash and E. Wilson (eds.), *Chic Thrills: A Fashion Reader* (Pandora, 1992), pp. 152, 157, 157, 159.

21   J. Fiske, *Reading the Popular* (Unwin Hyman, 1989), p. 29.

22   Evans and Thornton, *Women and Fashion*, p. 110.

23   Craik, *Face*, p. 58.

24   A. Ribeiro, *Fashion in the French Revolution* (Batsford, 1988), p. 124.

25   Sennett, *Fall*, p. 186.

26   Ribeiro, *Fashion*, pp. 124–6; Evans and Thornton, *Women*, p. 70.

27   Barthes, *Fashion*, pp. 289, 289, 273, 273.

28   S. Sontag, cited in Craik, *Face*, p. 93.

29 W. Benjamin, 'Central Park', in *New German Critique* (1985), 34, p. 46.

30 Wilson, *Adorned in Dreams*, p. 9.

31 T. Polhemus and L. Proctor, *Fashion and Anti-Fashion* (Thames and Hudson, 1978), p. 9.

32 T. Polhemus, *Body Styles* (Lennard, 1988), p. 138.

33 Interview in *i-D* (March 1987), p. 42.

34 Evans and Thornton, *Women and Fashion*, p. 150.

35 Quoted in J. Ash, 'Philosophy on the Catwalk: The Making and Wearing of Vivienne Westwood's Clothes', in Ash and Wilson, *Chic Thrills*, p. 172.

36 Evans and Thornton, *Women and Fashion*, p. 148.

37 Interview on *The South Bank Show* (8 April 1990).

38 Evans and Thornton, *Women and Fashion*, p. 24.

39 D. Hebdige, *Subculture; The Meaning of Style* (Routledge, 1988), p. 107.

40 Wilson, *Adorned in Dreams*, p. 196.

41 D. Hebdige, *Hiding in the Light* (Routledge, 1988), p. 28.

42 F. Mort, 'Boy's Own? Masculinity, Style and Popular Culture', in R. Chapman and J. Rutherford (eds.), *Male Order* (Lawrence and Wishart, 1988), p. 205.

43 Hebdige, *Subculture*, pp. 121, 122.

44 Evans and Thornton, *Women and Fashion*, pp. 30–1.

45 T. S. Eliot, 'Little Gidding', in *Collected Poems* (Faber, 1974), p. 222.

46 G. Faurschou, 'Obsolescence and Desire: Fashion and the Commodity Form', in H. Silverman (ed.), *Postmodernism – Philosophy and the Arts* (Routledge, 1990), p. 254.

47 Cited in S. Buck-Morss, *The Dialectics of Seeing* (MIT Press, 1991), p. 98.

48 Hebdige, *Hiding*, p. 170.

49 Cited in A. Rauch, 'The *Trauerspiel* of the Prostituted Body, or Woman as Allegory of Modernity', *Cultural Critique* (1988), 10, p. 84.

50 Cited in Faurschou, 'Obsolescence', p. 101.

51 N. McKendrick et al., *The Birth of a Consumer Society* (Indiana University Press, 1982), p. 21.

52 Steele, *Fashion and Eroticism*, p. 52.

53 A. Rouse, *Understanding Fashion* (Blackwell, 1989), pp. 109, 111.

54 Craik, *Face*, p. 176.

55 J. Ash, 'Tarting Up Men: Menswear and Gender Dynamics', in J. Attfield and P. Kirkham (eds.), *A View from the Interior: Feminism, Women and Design* (Women's Press, 1989).

56 Mort, 'Boy's Own?', p. 212.

57 K. Silverman, 'Fragments of a Fashionable Discourse', in T. Modleski (ed.), *Studies in Entertainment: Critical Approaches to Mass Culture* (Indiana University Press, 1986), p. 148.

58 Steele, *Fashion and Eroticism*, p. 246.

59 E. Moers, *The Dandy: From Brummell to Beerbohm* (Nebraska University Press, 1960), p. 36.

60 J. C. Flugel, *The Psychology of Clothes* (Hogarth, 1930), pp. 117–19.

61 Cited in V. Steele, 'Chanel in Context', in Ash and Wilson, *Chic Thrills*, p. 119.

62 Evans and Thornton, *Women and Fashion*, p. 124.

63 R. Williams, *Dream Worlds* (California University Press, 1982), p. 120.

64 Wilson, *Adorned in Dreams*, p. 180.

65 Evans and Thornton, *Women and Fashion*, p. 123.

66 M. Bracewell, *Guardian* (25 September 1993).

67 Wilson, *Adorned in Dreams*, p. 191.
68 A. Carter, *Nothing Sacred* (Virago, 1982), p. 88.
69 Rouse, *Understanding Fashion*, p. 118.
70 T. Veblen, *The Theory of the Leisure Class* (Unwin, 1970; originally 1899), p. 126.
71 Steele, *Fashion and Eroticism*, p. 100.
72 For the term itself, originally used for the generation coming to maturity in the 1880s and 1890s, and extended to this 'second generation', see C. Smith-Rosenberg, *Disorderly Conduct* (Oxford University Press, 1986), pp. 176–7.
73 E. Charles-Roux, *Chanel* (Cape, 1976), p. xviii.
74 Cited in Evans and Thornton, *Women and Fashion*, p. 128.
75 Steele, 'Chanel in Context'.
76 S. Connor, *Postmodernist Culture* (Blackwell, 1989), p. 190.
77 S. Ewen, *All Consuming Images* (Basic Books, 1988), p. 183.
78 Evans and Thornton, *Women and Fashion*, p. 95.
79 Cited in Steele, 'Chanel in Context', p. 119.
80 J. Craik, ' "I Must Put My Face On": Marking Up the Body and Marking Out the Feminine', *Cultural Studies* (1989), 3:1, p. 1.
81 R. Ballaster et al., *Women's Worlds: Ideology, Femininity and the Women's Magazine* (Macmillan, 1991), p. 151.
82 J. Berger, *Ways of Seeing* (Penguin, 1992), p. 46.
83 S. de Beauvoir, *The Second Sex* (Cape, 1972), pp. 599, 598.
84 B. Dijkstra, *Idols of Perversity* (Oxford University Press, 1987), p. 132, and see pp. 125–33.
85 A. Tennyson, *The Lady of Shalott*.
86 A. Hollander, *Seeing Through Clothes* (Viking, 1978), p. 397.
87 de Beauvoir, *Second Sex*, p. 598.
88 J. Lacan, 'The Mirror-phase as Formative of the Function of the I', *New Left Review* (1968), p. 51.
89 Berger, *Ways of Seeing*, p. 47.
90 R. Dyer, 'Don't Look Now', in A. McRobbie (ed.), *Zoot Suits and Second-Hand Dresses* (Macmillan, 1989).
91 Silverman, 'Fragments', p. 143.
92 See, for example, S. Neale, 'Masculinity as Spectacle', in S. Cohen and I. R. Hark (eds.), *Screening the Male* (Routledge, 1993).
93 G. Studlar, 'Masochism, Masquerade and the Erotic Metamorphosis of Marlene Dietrich', in Gaines and Herzog, *Fabrications*, pp. 229–49.
94 Silverman, 'Fragments', p. 139.
95 S. Moore, 'Here's Looking at You, Kid!', in L. Gamman and M. Marshment (eds.), *The Female Gaze* (Women's Press, 1988), p. 45.
96 J. Stacey, 'Desperately Seeking Difference', in Gamman and Marshment, *Female Gaze*, p. 115.
97 Evans and Thornton, *Women and Fashion*, p. 83.
98 R. Sennett, 'Destructive *Gemeinschaft*', in A. Soble (ed.), *The Philosophy of Sex* (Rowman and Littlefield, 1980), and see Sennett, *Fall*, chs. 1, 14.
99 C. Lasch, *The Culture of Narcissism* (Warner Books, 1979), p. 167.
100 Evans and Thornton, *Women and Fashion*, pp. 45–6, and ch. 3.
101 M. Garber, *Vested Interests: Cross-Dressing and Cultural Anxiety* (Penguin, 1993), p. 6.
102 Cited in *Elle* (March 1992), p. 33.

103 Cited in Evans and Thornton, *Women and Fashion*, p. 35.

104 T. Marcus, 'What is Glamour?', *i-D* (1992), p. 104.

105 J. Weeks, *Sex, Gender and Society* (Longman, 1981), ch. 6. See also J. Marshall, 'Pansies, Perverts and Macho Men: Changing Conceptions of Male Homosexuality', in K. Plummer (ed.), *The Making of the Modern Homosexual* (Hutchinson, 1981).

106 R. Trumbach, 'London's Sodomites: Homosexual Behaviour and Western Culture in the 18th Century', *Journal of Social History* (1977), 11:1; R. Trumbach, 'London's Sapphists: From Three Sexes to Four Genders in the Making of Modern Culture', in J. Epstein and K. Straub (eds.), *Body Guards: The Cultural Politics of Gender Ambiguity* (Routledge, 1991); and A. Sinfield, *The Wilde Century* (Cassell, 1994), ch. 2.

107 J. Butler, 'Imitation and Gender Insubordination', in D. Fuss (ed.), *Inside/Out: Lesbian Theories, Gay Theories* (Routledge, 1991), p. 32.

108 J. Butler, *Gender Trouble: Feminism and the Subversion of Identity* (Routledge, 1990), pp. 31, 141, 136.

109 J. Butler, *Bodies That Matter* (Routledge, 1993), pp. 232, 234.

110 Garber, *Vested Interests*, p. 250.

111 Butler, *Gender Trouble*, p. x.

112 M. Simpson, *Male Impersonators* (Cassell, 1994), p. 186.

113 Carter, *Nothing Sacred*, p. 98.

114 C. Smith-Rosenberg, 'The New Woman as Androgyne: Social Disorder and Gender Crisis 1870–1936', in *Disorderly Conduct*, pp. 288, 289.

115 V. Woolf, *Orlando* (Grafton, 1977), p. 118.

116 V. Woolf, *A Room of One's Own* (Grafton, 1977), p. 99.

117 Woolf, *Orlando*, p. 118.

118 K. Rolley, 'Love, Desire and the Pursuit of the Whole: Dress and the Lesbian Couple', in Ash and Wilson, *Chic Thrills*, pp. 36, 38, 38.

119 S. Gilbert, 'Costumes of the Mind: Transvestism as Metaphor in Modern Literature', *Critical Inquiry* (1980), 7, p. 196; and see S. Gilbert and S. Gubar, *No Man's Land, Vol. 2: Sexchanges* (Yale University Press, 1984), pp. 215, 359.

120 Butler, 'Imitation', p. 13.

121 J. Rivière, 'Womanliness as a Masquerade', in V. Burgin et al., *Formations of Fantasy* (Methuen, 1986), p. 38.

122 S. Heath, 'Joan Rivière and the Masquerade', in Burgin, *Formations*, p. 49.

123 Partington, 'Popular Fashion', p. 156.

124 Evans and Thornton, *Women and Fashion*, p. 141.

125 L. Mulvey, 'A Phantasmagoria of the Female Body: The Work of Cindy Sherman', *New Left Review* (1991), 188, p. 142.

126 J. Williamson, *Consuming Passions* (Marion Boyars, 1986), p. 112.

127 L. Irigaray, *This Sex Which Is Not One* (Cornell UP, 1985), p. 76.

128 Heath, 'Joan Rivière', p. 56.

129 J. Lacan, 'The Signification of the Phallus', in his *Ecrits: A Selection* (Norton, 1977), p. 291.

130 Carter, *Nothing Sacred*, pp. 104, 103.

131 R. Barthes, *Mythologies* (Paladin, 1973), p. 84.

132 F. Nietzsche, *The Gay Science* (Vintage, 1974), p. 317.

133 E. Showalter, *Sexual Anarchy* (Virago, 1992), p. 156.

134 Simpson, *Male Impersonators*, p. 187.

135 Evans and Thornton, *Women and Fashion*, p. 113.

136   F. Nietzsche, *Beyond Good and Evil* (Gateway, 1955), section 145.
137   Cited in J. Derrida, *Spurs: Nietzsche's Styles* (Chicago University Press, 1979), p. 111.
138   J. Baudrillard, *Seduction* (Macmillan, 1990), pp. 10, 2.
139   Derrida, *Spurs*, p. 55.
140   Nietzsche, *Beyond Good and Evil*, section 232.

6 The Seduction of Romance:

Fictions of Love, Narratives of Selfhood

When his mouth finally left hers, her whole body throbbed, and had it not been for his arms around her she might have fallen. . . .

Instinctively she had guessed that it would be like this; some primitive wisdom had warned her that this man was unique. Somehow she had recognised in her soul that his body lodged a force that would assail and shock, leaving her trembling and troubled and unsure, exactly as she was now. But she had never dreamed that there could be so much magic in a mere kiss.

But this is 1990, so for Fay and Craig the appropriate consummation cannot be too far off:

and when he came to her and she felt the touch of his flesh she turned to him in a wild, strong surrender that cleansed her of all inhibitions. . . . She gave herself joyfully to a million sensations of arousal as he found the tender secret roots of sexual pleasure. . . . Craig groaned suddenly then moved, his hands under her hips, lifting her to receive him in a rhythm as old and deep as time. Inside her, heat grew, swelling and spreading to suffuse her body, bearing her to a sudden, amazing triumph.[1]

Clearly not Jane Austen; yet not necessarily *so* far, as will be seen. This relatively explicit eroticism is no doubt the most obviously apparent difference, yet even in the above excerpts the sexuality is clothed in the circumlocution of metaphor and cliché, relatively unspecific, and this is true also of the eroticism in the 'classic' novels.

The novel in question is *Wild Champagne*, by 'Kate Kingston'.[2] It is a Mills and Boon romance that I plucked at random from several shelves full of them in a local bookshop, as part of the research for this topic. At least, that's my story; and it seems that a man in possession of a Mills and Boon must indeed be in need of a good cover story. In several years of teaching this topic, I have only found one male student who has confessed to reading any – and that was immediately rationalized by saying that they were his sister's, and had just been lying around, so he picked them up. . . . But 'confession' seems to be the order of the day for women, too, as though one has to 'own up' to a secret vice, and face the public shame. Thus Angela Miles entitles her article on the appeal of Mills and Boon/ Harlequin novels 'Confessions of a Harlequin Reader'.[3] No doubt we have all absorbed the message that these novels are somehow unacceptable, trashy, not 'real' novels, unlike the long, heavy, nineteenth-century 'classics', and this reflects the division between 'elite' and 'mass' culture that will be returned to in a later chapter; but this particular genre is also strongly gender-linked, so it is even more unacceptable for a man to read it. Indeed, while there has been a mass of 'cultural studies' scholarship on these novels over the last decade or so, there is still a frequent air of condescension about it, as though the repetitive reading of romances by women is somehow intrinsically more in need of explanation and justification than equally repetitive male rituals (watching football, say, or going to the pub). Part of the seductiveness of romance, clearly, is that the 'cover stories', stratagems, confessions, deceits and pleasures of the protagonists are reflected in those of the readers.

The first Harlequin romance was published in 1958; by 1971 the company had merged with its predecessor and earlier supplier, Mills and Boon. These novels were not, of course, the first popular fiction geared to the women's market – there is a line going back to the now almost-forgotten women's 'sensation novel' of the 1860s, and beyond – nor are they alone, having been accompanied by the 'historicals', from Barbara Cartland to Catherine Cookson, and the assorted best-selling 1970s and 1980s 'blockbusters', 'bonkbusters' and 'bodice-rippers'.[4] But the extent of their collective success does make them remarkable. By the early 1980s, they were coming out at the rate of twelve titles a month, and by 1987 some 220 million were being sold annually round the world. In 1992, some 15 million were being sold in the UK, about half the total number of romances of all categories. They are made to a very strict format, even in detail. Authors are told the books should be 'approximately 188 pages', and so they are, time after time. There have of course been some shifts over the years: it is apparently no longer necessary for the heroine to be a virgin – though Fay certainly was – and she may well have economic independence, in the form of a job that she will not give up. Nevertheless, the basic story remains constant: the heroine always gets her man, but only after a long series of misunderstandings and miscalculations, and only in the last few pages.[5]

Already, this suggests a recurrence of patterns deeply embedded within the tradition of romantic fiction, and a comparison with Jane Austen's *Pride and Prejudice* and Charlotte Brontë's *Jane Eyre* will help to draw this out. The initial frosty encounter, for example. Craig immediately strikes Fay as 'unbelievably conceited', and later, too, she finds him 'utterly insufferable'. But from very early on, there is also the other side. 'He's all the "A's", she thought – arrogant, autocratic, and totally antipathetic. And devastatingly attractive? a tiny voice inside her head suggested.'[6] The initial impact of Darcy in *Pride and Prejudice* is similar: Elizabeth and her family found him 'the proudest, most disagreeable man in the world, and everybody hoped that he would never come there again'. While it takes longer for the attraction to manifest itself, by page 68 she is exclaiming '*That* would be the greatest misfortune of all! – To find a man agreeable whom one is determined to hate!'[7] And Jane Eyre initially finds Rochester 'grim' and 'rather sarcastic'; indeed, so far is he from the conventionally handsome hero that she says that most people might actually regard him as ugly. But soon, for her, he is not ugly at all; his face became 'the object I best liked to see'.[8]

These initial dislikes and misunderstandings are seen by Tania Modleski as reflecting two central thematic problems in these novels, both associated with problems of representation and recognition. Firstly, the initial hostility or indifference of the hero, and its role in the plot, convey a complex message: that men both are, and aren't, callous, instrumental and brutish. Men are thus, because that's just how men are; on the other hand, underneath, *some* men are not really – or wholly – like that; but how can these be distinguished from the others? After all, men are supposed to be dominating, assertive and autonomous, and this can easily be seen as sliding into insensitivity or even brutality. Men may be scornful or bullying, but it is men – *some* of them – who provide excitement, romance, even fulfilment. And this parallels what she sees as the other central problem, how is the man to ensure that she is a 'good' woman, not just a 'scheming little adventuress', since as a man goes about his daily business he is, it would seem, constantly at risk from such adventuresses, out to steal his hard-earned money, his posh country house, and his virtue too. As Modleski puts it,

> While the novels are always about a poor girl finally marrying a rich man . . . they must be careful to show that the girl never sets out to get him and his goods. This is of course a simple reflection of the double bind imposed upon women in real life: their most important achievement is supposed to be finding a husband; their greatest fault is attempting to do so. . . .
>
> How to get your heroine from loneliness and penury to romance and riches, without making her appear to have helped herself along or even to have thought about the matter, is an old problem for novelists.

She has to attain the necessary goal without consciously seeking it, so to speak, and this is a difficult act to carry off. The woman's dislike of the hero is useful here, as it 'at once absolves her of mercenary motives and becomes the very means by which she obtains the hero's love, and, consequently, his fortune'.[9] The woman is only 'poor' relative to the hero, it should be emphasized. Darcy may bemoan the 'inferiority' of Elizabeth Bennet's 'connections', but she is of the minor gentry, after all; hardly a peasant. Nevertheless, the gap is big enough, and Jane Austen employs her skill in sailing quite close to the wind in the way she presents Elizabeth's attitude here. When she initially sees Pemberley, Darcy's country seat, with its magnificent grounds extending as far as the eye can see, and beyond, we are told that 'at that moment she felt, that to be mistress of Pemberley might be something!' Later, when her sister asks when she knew she had fallen in love, she replies: 'I believe I must date it from my first seeing his beautiful grounds at Pemberley.' She is at once chided for 'joking', and indeed such gentle – though often pointed – irony and facetiousness are features of Elizabeth's character. But even so. . . . As for Jane Eyre, the problem over her motivation is resolved by the fact that she is all the more interested in Rochester *after* Thornfield is burnt down and he is blinded. The same basic situation obtains with Fay and Craig, but with an interesting twist – it is *she* who owns Brantye, not he, so it is her doubts about what Craig is after that have to be resolved, as they are when it becomes clear that he is prepared to buy it from her even if she does not want him, and, moreover, is rich enough to buy it 'three times over'.

One should not, in other words, marry for money; particularly, one should not delude oneself about one's own motives, and those of others. 'Do anything rather than marry without affection', says Elizabeth's sister, anxiously, as yet unsure of Elizabeth's motivation for accepting Darcy.[10] Austen's novels carry examples of marriages made for financial calculation, and through empty-headed notions of 'romance' distorted by sexual passion, and although these marriages are neither necessarily condemned nor doomed, it is clear that they really serve as models of how not to do it. Mary Evans suggests that Austen constructs a model of individualism in which both acquisitive capitalism and its opposite, a 'romantic indifference' to material concerns, are rejected. As for the latter possibility, she develops 'a sustained and coherent attack upon fantasies of romance' as a viable basis for relationships between men and women; notions like 'love' and 'passion' have to be questioned.[11] Polhemus adds that *Pride and Prejudice* implicitly distinguishes between 'a rational blend of affection and desire for a person, and an involuntary, often blind, power of emotion that seizes one'.[12] And in a subtle way all this may also be true of much 'romantic' fiction subsequently. Neither money nor passion are adequate on their own; although in *Wild Champagne* we encounter the full-blown rhetoric of romantic love, it seems to coexist quite nicely, in practice, with a degree of 'realism' in the choice of a mate, and Fay ends up with the financial security necessary to pursue her aspirations as an independent fashion designer. After all, as Tanner observes, marriage is *the* central subject for the bourgeois novel, and is presented as the means by which passion and property can be brought into 'harmonious alignment', attempting to unify the natural, the familial and the social.[13]

The issue of motivation – love and money – is a pointer to another dynamic in these novels: the whole question of the 'moral quality' of a relationship, the extent to which a meaningful relationship must actually necessitate a real sense of equality between the partners. It is as though these novels have to struggle with the social context that actually makes marriage systematically unequal in so many ways, while trying to articulate a rival ethic of sharing and mutuality. Most interesting in this respect is *Jane Eyre*. Charlotte Brontë seems to have set out from the most extreme contrast, and then works through to resolve it. After all, Rochester is pure patriarch: two decades older than Jane, affluent owner of a landed estate and a separate, smaller house (Ferndean) nearby. And Jane is an orphan, educated in a charity institution. The process of equalizing the situation occurs under all three possible headings, the economic, the physical and the moral. Under the first, Thornfield is burnt down, and Jane comes into a modest inheritance that secures her financial independence; then, in the fire, Rochester is blinded and loses an arm, thereby becoming physically dependent. Morally, of course, the major way he is brought down is by the revelation of his deceitfulness over the little matter of the mad wife in the attic; but this happens in another way, too. He has to admit to Jane that his flirting with the well-connected Miss Ingram was merely an attempt to make her, Jane, jealous. Jane pounces, gleefully: 'Excellent! Now you are small – not one whit better than the end of my little finger. It was a burning shame, and a scandalous disgrace to act in that way.' And, at the end, she tells him that she loves him better, now, than in his previous state of 'proud independence, when you disdained every part but that of the giver and protector'.[14]

But conversation itself can also be an equalizer. The liveliness of the heroine falls into place both as an indicator that the man is looking for a relationship with a person, not a cipher, and as a means whereby the woman can assert and maintain a degree of independence. Darcy is, despite himself, attracted from the start by Elizabeth's 'easy playfulness', and, at the end, comparing herself with others, Elizabeth states: 'The fact is, you were sick of civility, of deference, of officious attention. . . . I roused and interested you, because I was so unlike *them.*'[15] And she makes it quite clear that she intends to continue in that vein, just as Jane will continue to use her 'needle of repartee'[16] when the occasion demands. Indeed, conversation in these novels emerges not just as a surface phenomenon but as the very stuff of relationships themselves, and is certainly crucial to the emerging reciprocity of attraction. As Evans remarks, 'Access to the person, the self, through conversation, was, as Jane Austen well knew, the most deeply erotic form of everyday exchange between the sexes.'[17]

The key moment in the equalization process is when the hero has to recognize his need for the heroine, a need manifested through the threat of losing her. He has to acknowledge his love, and its implications; and this entails a cost, since his autonomy is henceforth compromised. Nevertheless, this does not make him 'weak'; his is not the need of a dependent man, rather a further testimony to his maturity. And the heroine is generally portrayed as able to detect this moment of vulnerability, argues Ann Rosalind Jones: 'The heroine lets loose her passion for the hero deliberately, at the moment when she perceives that his desire for her makes him as dependent on her as she is on him.'[18]

But in these novels, love must, in the end, contain a residue of irreducible mystery; for love is always person-specific, geared to the unique individuality of lover and beloved. Polhemus suggests that 'the idea of the distinctive, unique *personality* is to erotic faith what the concept of the individual soul is to Christian faith'. Hence a novel like *Pride and Prejudice* 'expresses the passion of modern individualism: the need to be noticed and loved for your own distinctive self'.[19] Here we encounter the 'individualisation of desire' that Nancy Armstrong detects in the Victorian period, the idea that 'no two women could be right for the same man, nor any two men for the same woman'.[20] And *Jane Eyre* is interesting here. In order to avoid all risk that the protagonists might fall in love with the other as a social category, as it were, rather than as the specific, unique person, we find love being defined *against* social pressures and social conformity. The very fact that Jane is 'poor and obscure' means that Rochester's love for her must indeed be for *her*, not for her money or status. Individualism is giving rise to the notion of an individual desire that can be wayward, asocial, even anti-social, finding powerful expression in Romanticism as a cultural movement. With Emily Brontë's *Wuthering Heights* this reaches its logical culmination in the desire that seeks absolute purity and perfection in an impossible union with the unique other, with the love of Heathcliff and Catherine that can be consummated only in death.

In these novels, then, the seductive rhetoric of romance can coexist with a more implicitly rational approach to the love relationship, while there is always the potential for them to be read in more transgressive ways. The rhetoric of romance itself, in relation to modern love, now needs further investigation.

Aspects of Love

That there is a distinctively modern 'way of love' has been widely assumed, but capturing this sense in a historically valid way has proved contentious. Claims that pre-modern marriage was largely devoid of love seem exaggerated, and have, as an unfortunate corollary, a tendency to take modern love at its own face value, downplaying the pressures and tensions that coexist with the opportunities for self-expression and fulfilment. What does seem true, though, is that marriage was more a matter of political and economic links between families, rather than a psychological link between unique individuals. Love was not, therefore, seen as a sufficient, or even necessary, basis for marriage; it was of secondary importance.[21]

Already, with Puritanism, this is changing; we find a growing emphasis on the spiritual value of the marriage relationship as such, and of the love involved in it.[22] Although conventionally associated with restraint and repression, Puritanism sanctified sex within marriage, and this became an accepted aspect of love, part of love's sacrament. By the eighteenth century, love is becoming 'civilized', a sign of emotional refinement: 'Romantic love is not only a mark of freedom but an assertion of finer feeling and superior social status', as Jacqueline Sarsby puts it.[23] What Taylor calls the 'companionate marriage',[24] with an emphasis on the emotional tie between husband and wife rather than with wider kin networks, becomes a new ordering of obligations and responsibilities. By the late eighteenth century, then, love has become an accepted basis for marriage, indeed comes to be seen as essential: 'Now for the first time ... love, and love alone, was the sovereign consideration in the choice of partners', argues Campbell, adding that the ideology itself was in large part a result of the secularization of religious passion that had been occurring since the previous century.[25]

This emergent private sphere is not, however, just the sphere of the personal and the domestic; it is the sphere of interiority, the feelings, to be cultivated and moralized, thereby rendering intimacy possible, the public shaping of these feelings through communication in the private realm.[26] And as we know from discussion elsewhere, it is women who preside over this sphere; it is women who become charged, *de facto*, with 'managing the transformation of intimacy which modernity set in train', as Giddens puts it. They become, indeed, 'specialists of the heart'.[27] Indeed, it can be argued that not only does love come to play a rather different part in men's and women's lives, but that even the concept and experience of love may differ. For a man, love can become a possible threat, involving fear of entrapment, a loss of autonomy; in this area, argues Stevi Jackson, 'It is through the idiom of sexual bravado and conquest, not the language of romance, that masculinity is asserted.'[28] Francesca Cancian also suggests that 'The dominant definition of love in our culture is feminized', in that 'we identify love with emotional expression and talking about feelings, aspects of love that women prefer and in which women tend to be more skilled than men', thus excluding the more practical and physical aspects of relationships from the purview of 'love'.[29]

If the core of the modern way of love is the attempt to institutionalize this orientation of individualized romantic love, thus using it as the necessary basis of marriage, then we can already see how it is constantly threatened by the differing expectations men and women bring into the relationship. But the whole premise that romantic and conjugal love can be easily rendered consistent, producing a seamless unity, is open to doubt anyway, when the ideology of romantic love is given closer examination.

We can distinguish two dimensions, both of which reveal the structure shared with its religious origins. First, there is love as cleansing, redemptive, sacrificial, something that takes you out of yourself, and involves subordination to the other. As a consequence of this, love is directed at a specific person, but that person is idealized. Rousseau writes that 'Love, as I see it, as I have felt it, grows ardent before the illusory image of the beloved's perfection.'[30] This points insightfully to the element of idealization that both transfigures the loved one, yet also ensures the ultimate failure of romantic love to consummate its object: the loved person and the idealization can never fully coincide. Second, then, there is love as longing, yearning, involving a sense of lack, of a gap between desire and fulfilment. In a sense, love becomes necessarily unsatisfiable; it reveals a tension between lover and loved, with the loved one always liable to disappoint. Love carries with it the potential for frustration and dissatisfaction, yet the ideal remains; indeed, the dissatisfaction and the ideal feed off one another, reinforce one another. To put it another way, Juliet Mitchell suggests that if romantic love *does* in some sense attain its object, then it ceases to be romantic love; it becomes either disillusion, or is transformed into affection.[31] In the latter case, the relationship can purchase longevity, but at a price many are clearly not prepared to pay.

One point that comes out clearly from studies of modern attitudes to love is that girls and women think more about love and romance than do boys and men, more readily read and construct narratives about it, and handle the emotional complexities in a more confident, interested and knowledgeable way. Jackson indeed suggests that for women love is a kind of script, or narrative, that is learnt through adolescence: the Western literary tradition 'supplies us with narrative forms with which we begin to be familiarised in childhood and through which we learn what love is', and these narratives of love thereby become 'very much a part of everyday cultural competences'.[32] The suggestion here is that if life and literature can illuminate each other, it is through this sense that both partake of an underlying narrative structure, that both can be seen as 'stories'. 'I was well versed in the tender passion, thanks to novels', writes Elizabeth Gaskell;[33] novels helped instruct her in the ways of love, and she drew both on these novels, and her own experiences, in writing her own novels. Stories matter in our lives in part because our lives can be conceived as stories; our selves are constituted *reflexively*, through the very stories we tell ourselves about ourselves. And one way of extending this analysis of love and its relation to narrative and reflexivity is to remember the tensions and paradoxes of civility and theatricality in relation to the self.

How genuine is the other person's show of feelings? How reliably can one decode the signs, get beneath the appearances? One has to trust one's own feelings when one cannot even be sure how to recognize them, and the other's true feelings can be all the more opaque. And if there is a lot at stake, this is particularly so for the woman; a bad choice, and she may not only encounter the misery of an unsatisfactory relationship but may, in a culture where 'double standards' have been deeply ingrained, stand to lose her 'reputation' too. Hence the importance of reflexive awareness to both parties, but especially the woman. And hence, also, the part played by narrative, for one can say that love-as-narrative becomes an attempted resolution to these problems of recognition, genuineness, the mask of civility, and flirtatiousness. Through constructing a plausible ongoing narrative of identity, for both self and other, and a narrative that incorporates feeling and emotion as important clues to the 'quality' of the person, through 'testing' love, one develops integrated, reflexive stories that permit the emotional complexities of life to be charted and negotiated. Hence Giddens can argue that 'The rise of romantic love more or less coincided with the emergence of the novel: the connexion was one of newly discovered narrative form.'[34] The novel, suggests Peter Conrad, 'owes its power to its discretion in seeing through people who congratulate themselves on their impenetrability, in making the obtuse aware of their own shifty motives'; it is effective because it is 'circumspect, stealthy and externally innocuous'.[35] The novel constructs 'character' as having continuity and depth, and can convey a sense of this as an imperative for the modern self in its dealings with the world of others. Thus love, gender, reflexivity and narrative are linked in highly significant ways.

Fictional Worlds: the Novel and its Others

As the imagination is increasingly cultivated as a faculty of the self, and turns to explore the 'inner world' of feelings and emotions, examining how these both result in, and are influenced by, the 'personal relations' of love and marriage, so the novel is produced; and this both reflects these developments, and becomes complicit in them, itself becoming an agent in the production of modern selfhood.[36] And in doing so, the novel can also be seen to construct its own identity as distinct from, and in varying degrees opposed to, other cultural products like drama, melodrama, and traditional 'romance', seen as repositories not only of unacceptable or inadequate aesthetic forms, but as carriers of unacceptable, even transgressive models of selfhood and social relations.

The imagination plays a powerful role here, and that makes it both something to celebrate, and a source of danger. While Austen distrusts it, the Brontës are fascinated by it, and seek to explore it. So do their heroines. Jane Eyre tells us that she liked most of all 'to open my inward ear to a tale that was never ended – a tale my imagination created, and narrated continuously; quickened with all of incident, life, fire, feeling, that I desired and had not in my actual existence.' Here we encounter the idea that the imagination can serve both to compensate for the deficiencies of life, and yet could thereby also be troublesome, pointing to disruptive new possibilities. Jane's thoughts and feelings are described later as 'straying through imagination's boundless and trackless waste', and as having to be called to order, submitted to 'wholesome discipline'.[37]

In effect, we are tracing out the implications of the seventeenth- and eighteenth-century construction of the 'inner self', with the imagination firmly established as a subjective faculty of mind, hence available to become a creator of fictions; and these invariably have elements of fantasy, or may indeed *be* fantasies. Not only this, but with the clear delineation of the imaginary and the real as distinct categories, 'imaginary' increasingly takes on the implication of 'falsity', and from childhood we pick up this sense that the products of the imagination, while perhaps admirable in themselves, are to be distrusted, a distrust or disparagement that is particularly strong in the case of fantasy. In Greek, 'fantasy' meant 'making visible', related to 'showing', and this sense continued in Old English, where it referred to 'appearance' as a process of perception, a link between mind and world. Now, however, it is all too often the reverse, mind's withdrawal from the world into delusion, 'wishful thinking'.

Nevertheless, a fictional world is not, primarily, a mystification of the real world, a mechanical reflection of it, or an escape from it, though it *can* perfectly well be any of these: it is, first and foremost, a congruent world that acts as a perspective *on* the world, a place from which the world appears as other in itself, transfigured. It is *because* it is thus, that it can be available for these other specific and varied functions and pleasures. If it contrasts with the 'real' world, this is the contrast of imaginative transfiguration, not that of inferiority or inadequacy. It is only in the light of fiction that the world is constituted as 'real', yet simultaneously only one possibility among others, dependent on an outside for its 'sense', never self-sufficient. Thus Armstrong can suggest that fiction comes 'to constitute a mode of representation that is neither fantastic nor real in any conventional sense'; it explores the 'inner world' it contributes to constructing.[38] If fiction is an illusion, the whole point is that it is not thereby a deceitful veil, distorting our understanding of 'real' life, but rather a parallel mode of experiencing and appropriating life that constitutes it *as* 'real', and in the modern world we have to navigate this dimension as surely as we do the other; indeed, if we do not, our capacity to navigate the 'real' world is impoverished.

In making the world real *for us*, fiction incorporates fantasy, the transforming presence of the imagination in the world of individual consciousness, thus conveying a sense of the world as a place fit for the subject to inhabit, a place for it to feel 'at home'. Through structuring desire, fantasy is crucial to the process whereby subjectivity is formed out of the dramas of separation and otherness, repression and taboo. Thus Ien Ang can suggest that fantasy is 'an imagined scene in which the fantasising subject is the protagonist, and in which alternative scenarios for the subject's real life are evoked'.[39] When Rochester calls to Jane, across the miles, he hails the reader too: 'His call has the catalyzing appeal of fiction itself: when we hear it, we, like Jane, recall ourselves', in Nina Auerbach's words.[40]

An epistemological revolution, 'to discriminate the "factual" from the "fictional" in a way that is recognizably "modern"', as McKeon puts it,[41] hence has to occur if the novel is to be constituted as a clear-cut category, but of course this only occurs gradually. After all, a 'fiction' is something that has been shaped or fashioned to become other than it was; only by the eighteenth century has this come to take on a particularly *literary* emphasis. Nor was the novelist clearly distinguished from the historian or newsmonger; indeed, prose fictions were often referred to as 'histories'. By the early nineteenth century, 'novel' and 'fiction' had acquired their modern, near-identity of sense:[42] a novel has become a work of fiction, a story of the adventures of the self in a world of others, in which its 'novel' experiences are captured and reproduced, in a structured way, through the assumption of the continuity of a narrative itself seen as continuous with the selfhood it deploys and exhibits. It is in this context that we can interpret Ian Watt's claim that the novel is characterized by 'formal realism', namely the premise or convention that it is 'a full and authentic report of human experience', exhibiting plots that are plausible in the light of this, with characters who are individual persons (rather than the medieval Everyman, or character types), situated in conventional space and time whereby the past is causally related to the present.[43] And this literary form had become a major cultural phenomenon, with a wide and increasing readership, particularly through the new public libraries; and the new profession of author had been decisively established.

Nevertheless, the novel never really overcomes the challenges that constitute it in the first place; it is always criss-crossed by the tensions that result from its own rejections, evasions, and aspirations to self-consistent narrative purity. Tanner suggests that the novel, in its origin, 'might almost be said to be a transgressive mode, inasmuch as it seemed to break, or mix, or adulterate the existing genre-expectations of the time'. This may have been true of both form and content. Adultery, the ultimate crime against the bourgeois order in personal relations, is a central theme in many of the great novels, introducing an 'agonizing and irresolvable category-confusion into the individual and thence into society itself', the 'unfaithful wife' marking the place of an impossible and indefensible contradiction;[44] nor is the portrayal of this 'unthinkable' possibility necessarily such as to render it lacking in temptation. But really, it is the whole mix of formal and substantive issues – epistemology, style and content – that constantly reproduce the insoluble dilemmas that have traversed the novel's history.

Let us take the novel and its relation to 'romance', for instance. A medieval 'romance' was a verse tale of adventure, chivalry or love.[45] By the seventeenth century, these were increasingly becoming prose stories, and often much longer; and they were also being increasingly criticized as exercises in imaginative extravagance and excess, generally with few realistic pretensions. In short, they were becoming 'romantic' in a sense that is closer to twentieth-century usage, when 'romance' came to refer to an idealized, extravagant, yet stereotyped story of heterosexual love, generally regarded with disdain by 'serious' novelists. Hence, the antagonism between novel and romantic fiction has a history as long as that of the novel itself. Laurie Langbauer's work suggests that seventeenth-century romance fiction represented a principle of undisciplined chaos and energy that had to be channelled or repressed before the novel as a representational genre could exist; and the novel, in turn 'scapegoats' romance, defining it as other to itself, as whatever it hopes it is not. Langbauer thus claims that

> The utility of romance consisted precisely in its vagueness; it was the chaotic negative space outside the novel that determined the outlines of the novel's form. To novelists and, they hoped, to their readers, the novel was unified, probable, truly representational because romance was none of these. The contrast between them gave the novel its meaning . . . romance is excessive fiction, so excessive that it is nonsensical, ultimately mad.

Yet it is not so easy for the novel to escape what is also a lure and a temptation. Analysing Charlotte Lennox's novel of 1752, *The Female Quixote; or, the Adventures of Arabella*, intriguing in that it takes the dangerous attractions of romance as its explicit theme, Langbauer suggests that Lennox tacitly acknowledges that 'the problems of romance are the problems of fiction, and of the novel as well'. The novelist tries to cast out exactly the power she envies and wishes to usurp; ridiculing romance exposes its attractions, and its hold over the reader. Thus Arabella's sickness from grief at her father's death is presented as acceptable, yet seems indistinguishable from romantic extravagance exposed elsewhere: 'To repudiate romance may be to subject oneself to its essential disorder.' After all, the implication of juxtaposing Jane Austen and a Mills and Boon in the first section of this chapter is precisely to suggest that the novel isn't necessarily so lacking in 'romance', nor is romance so lacking in features of the novel.

Gender is of course important here. 'The novel's very definition of romance echoes the way patriarchy defines women: they are both seen as marginal, the negative of the defining agents', argues Langbauer, so the novel 'associates the dangers of romance with the sins of women'.[46] Romance, like woman herself, is capricious, irrational, licentious, excessive. And this judgement has often been reflected in the views of later novelists and critics, including some feminists, who have seen romance as reflecting a masculine idea of the 'irrational feminine'.[47] But of course it is also true that many women readers, and some writers and critics, have defended romance as an opportunity for women to tell stories with their own distinctive slant, which may well diverge from the orthodox or expected.

Stalking through the pages of romantic fiction – and of other 'deviant' forms, like Gothic, and the 'sensation' novel – we find what Lyn Pykett calls the 'improper feminine',[48] the avenging, irrational or excessive other both of the novel and of the culture it both symbolizes and promotes; and this figure brings together these two dimensions in that she manifests a fundamental theatricality that is deeply troublesome to both. We thus encounter a deep tension between the narrative principle of the novel, and the theatricality – particularly in the form of melodrama – that constantly threatens it, evades it, and yet insinuates itself into it. And often, elements of Gothic, romance and melodrama disrupt and fracture the unitary text as encountered in the canonical works themselves, those of the Brontës, Dickens, George Eliot, Mrs Gaskell, James and Conrad. In one of her letters, Charlotte Brontë acknowledges that *Jane Eyre* is steeped in romance and melodrama;[49] and in Mrs Gaskell's *Mary Barton*, the basically realist frame nevertheless encloses a melodramatic plot, with characteristic protagonists such as the 'fallen woman', and episodes of violence, unreason and dream. And among the great novelists, Dostoevsky comes closest to an explicit endorsement of this vision: 'what other people call fantastic', he wrote, 'I hold to be the inmost essence of truth'.[50]

Jane Austen herself is clearly fascinated by the temptations of theatricality; the famous theatricality chapters in *Mansfield Park* show her awareness of its temptations, as well as her determination to show its inferiority to the morality of novelistic narrative. Fanny's refusal to act in the play that is to be performed while Sir Thomas is away reveals, writes Peter Conrad, 'the fortitude of novelistic character', and contrasts with 'specious dramatic character, forever revamping itself to please an audience'.[51] In this sense, adds Tanner, 'you must be true to your best self', whereas 'the theatre is a place where you can explore and experiment with other selves'.[52] The Crawfords, from London, are only really alive when playing a role; they are brilliant mimics, because deeply insincere, without real feelings. When Henry Crawford tries to 'play' sincerity, Fanny sees right through him; and if, as Trilling suggests, we find in Mary Crawford 'the first brilliant example of a distinctively modern type, the person who cultivates the *style* of sensitivity, virtue and intelligence',[53] we are not at all surprised to find that both the Crawfords are heavily implicated in the moral disasters later in the book, when theatrical disorder becomes its real-life equivalent.

What is at stake in this conflict is the nature of selfhood and self-knowledge. 'The drama conspires to frustrate self-knowledge, allowing character to beguilingly transform itself by dressing up', argues Conrad, whereas 'The novel, on the contrary, is the province of self-knowledge, because it can penetrate the minds and hearts of characters.' Novels can exhibit 'absence, delay and silence, three conditions of interior, novelistic reality which drama cannot contain';[54] Fanny, sensitive to this, can develop a self-consciousness and self-knowledge which can then guide her through the maze of uncertainties, the moral quandaries, of everyday life.

Yet, in the end, can Jane Austen so easily escape this theatricality herself? Gilbert and Gubar suggest that, in her novels,

> women who are refused the means of self-definition are shown to be fatally drawn to the dangerous delights of impersonation and pretense. But Austen's profession depends on just these disguises. What else, if not impersonation, is characterization? What is plot, if not pretense? . . . she can reprove as indecent in a heroine what is necessary to an author. Authorship for Austen is an escape from the very restraints she imposes on her female characters.[55]

The novel itself calls on the skills of drama, even as it postulates a rival moral and aesthetic order. And this order is itself clearly involved in the world of the Enlightenment project. Docherty points out that in the novel, 'characters are also the site of the dramatization of "enlightenment"; as such, they become models of a particular manifestation of what the age and ideology consider as "reasonable"'.[56] The novel, like the Enlightenment, claimed to be uncovering the nature of human nature; it makes visible the reality, and the potential, underlying the encrustation of tradition, the potential for self-awareness and self-development. And in doing this, it becomes an agent in what it purports to describe. Armstrong argues that in many ways the novel is a means of continuing the project of the 'civilizing process' as embodied in the conduct books, and that the production of these began to decline in the eighteenth century as the novel became more widely read. By Austen's time, the rules of the conduct books could be taken for granted: 'her readers had identified these rules not only with common sense, if not always with nature, but also with the form of the novel itself'. The fulfilment of individual desire through socially appropriate goals became the key subject matter of domestic fiction as a continuation of the conduct books.[57]

But the links with the Enlightenment are subtle, for domestic fiction sought to disentangle the personal from the political, celebrate a realm of human freedom in 'civil society' that could be independent of political pressures and conflicts. Conrad suggests that this hostility towards man in his public and official capacity is 'a constant assumption of the novel as a literary form'.[58] For Madame de Staël, writing in 1800, 'modern man' considers liberty not as the chance to be politically active but as 'guarantee of his invulnerable privacy', and 'the literary form which coincides with this introversion is the novel'.[59] Thus did fiction, avowedly non-political, play its part in what could be seen as a new kind of 'politics', extending the moral influence of narrative form into the domestic sphere itself; but it could not do so in an uncontentious or unitary way, since, as we have seen, it was contentious in itself, frequently flirting with the theatrical and the transgressive. Above all, it raised difficult issues about reading, writing and gender. Terry Lovell observes that those who criticized the novel, whether as poor literature or for its moral dangers, were influenced by 'the belief that the novel was in some sense a feminine form, one particularly adapted to women's interests both as writers and as readers',[60] a point that now requires more detailed examination.

The Pleasures and Perils of Writing and Reading

In her pioneering feminist essay of 1928, *A Room of One's Own*, Virginia Woolf remarked that the point at which the middle-class woman began to write, in the late eighteenth century, was more important than the Crusades or the Wars of the Roses.[61] Certainly there is no doubt about the extent of the ensuing explosion of women's writing. By the 1870s and 1880s, 40 per cent of the authors at large English publishing houses were women, and in the US three-quarters of the novels published in the period were by women.[62]

Going back to the eighteenth-century origins of this, Watt tells us that the Georgian house frequently incorporated a closet or private apartment adjoining the bedroom, with a writing-desk and books; a 'room of one's own' that was indeed frequently female, a 'new forcing-house of the feminine sensibility' where letters could be written and diaries kept. And this is reflected in the novel: Richardson's heroines inhabit houses where 'each room has its feverish and complicated inner life', and 'Their drama unrolls in a flow of letters from one lonely closet to another.'[63] Writing a letter is invariably a significant event in a novel, as is reading one; in *Pride and Prejudice*, Elizabeth's developing capacity for reflexivity and self-understanding is stimulated by the privacy and quietness of letter-reading. Diaries, too, seem to have become a pervasive feature of middle-class women's lives in the nineteenth century, flourishing in the world of the public/private distinction. A diary was a kind of social relationship in the private sphere, someone to talk to, a trusted confidant; we often encounter what the historian Peter Gay has described as 'an active emotional investment in these sympathetic and silent friends to whom one could entrust pent-up feelings and unrealized wishes'.[64] A diary was orderly, but encompassed emotion; it was a practice for life itself, indeed a continuation of the story of one's life by other means, encouraging the reflexive self-consciousness so necessary in a literate and literary culture. It was half-way between history and fiction, its reflexivity contributing to the construction of a self that could be both self-aware and self-deluding.

It has become increasingly apparent, in recent historical research, that we are here in the presence of a middle-class women's culture, in which diaries and letter-writing provide key activities through which the self and its relationships become the subject of a narrative in which gender is fundamental.[65] In her sensitive exploration of this 'female world of love and ritual', Carroll Smith-Rosenberg uncovers 'a very private world of emotional realities central both to women's lives and to the middle-class family in nineteenth-century America'. Letter-writing was a central friendship ritual, and these letters continued the free intimacy that was a feature of the relationships between these women, operating in complete independence of the men to whom they were, normally, married.[66] This culture of women's writing and reading is important for understanding debates about the significance of 'writing' in gender relations, casting an interesting light on some of the assumptions made in such debates.

How, then, should we interpret the significance of these writing women? Do their texts, their letters, and more especially, their novels, give us unproblematical access to a 'woman's view'? There were, after all, major obstacles in their path. Virginia Woolf points to the subtle biases induced by male priorities, claiming that

> it is obvious that the values of women differ very often from the values which have been made by the other sex; naturally, this is so. Yet it is the masculine values that prevail. . . . This is an important book, the critic assumes, because it deals with war. This is an insignificant book because it deals with the feelings of women in a drawing-room. A scene in a battle-field is more important than a scene in a shop – everywhere and much more subtly the difference of value persists.[67]

For this reason, among others, the texts can be awkward, constrained, taking on a voice that is only partly their own, as though having to make implicit concessions to a masculine view of the world.

Sandra Gilbert and Susan Gubar have argued that literary creativity has been presented in patriarchal ideology as a fundamentally masculine quality. The writer 'fathers' his text; he becomes Author, the sole source of its meaning, imposing a decisive form on the recalcitrant material.[68] Elaine Showalter's discussion of the 'male quest romance' of the late nineteenth century fits this well; authors like Rider Haggard and Kipling were attempting to reclaim novelistic creativity for men, and adventure stories of the time frequently embodied myths of self-fathering and self-creation in which women could be effectively sidelined.[69] And Susan Morgan adds that both then and later there has been a prevalent masculine belief that women novelists 'describe or mimic their worlds rather than invent them . . . women lack the creative fire to be like Yeats' golden smithies, forging art out of the unpurged images of life'.[70] And if women could not be true artists, and could only write according to formulae, neither could they be genuine professionals; as Pykett puts it, 'they could not be truly professional because their womanly duties must always come first, and they could not have a writer's vocation because being a woman was in itself a woman's true vocation'.[71]

It would hardly be surprising, then, if women authors were indeed to manifest what Gilbert and Gubar call an 'anxiety of authorship', due to an 'inappropriate' deployment of a creative power coded as masculine.[72] As Woolf observed, the resulting double bind leaves a woman writer to choose between admitting she was 'only a woman' or protesting that she was 'as good as a man'. Women have therefore disguised themselves in their texts; the surface of the work conceals less socially acceptable levels of meaning.

Clearly there is a lot of truth in this; but there is another side to the coin. Woolf's argument that it had been very difficult hitherto to write 'as a woman' was not, after all, intended to make this seem necessarily impossible; indeed, she cites Jane Austen as a writer who manages it successfully.[73] Nor should we forget the 'women's world' referred to above, a supportive network that in effect constitutes a whole 'alternative culture'; so one cannot presuppose that writing will necessarily be so 'anxiety-inducing'.

Indeed, 'culture' (as 'the arts'), conventionally kept distinct from the masculine sphere of work, can all too easily be assimilated to femininity. In this sense, as Rachel Bowlby suggests, 'being an artist might not sit well with a male identity'. And given that women were seen as the main consumers of popular fiction, the male novelist could be in the predicament of either catering to 'feeble feminine taste', or withdrawing from masculine achievement in the market-place altogether. So the male artist, too, could be in a bind: 'neither pure artist nor fully masculine, and unable to alter one side of the pairing without damaging the other'.[74] The power of creativity, the Muse, has not infrequently been presented as feminine; and Virginia Woolf's own work, discussed in connection with the city, can be presented as an exploration of feminine creativity, opening up the whole issue of the gendered dynamics of the imagination.

The trouble is that to argue either that 'women's novels' are indeed necessarily *women's* novels – that they are 'feminine writing' as well as 'written by women' – or, conversely, that they necessarily *disguise* an underlying femininity, an essential identity and continuity, is, in both cases, to subscribe to the modern notion that gender distinctions possess a 'natural' underlying unity; yet it is precisely this assumption that is in need of examination.[75] In the second case, it is as misleading to think that women's identities have been totally dominated by their role as 'other' to men as to think that the only alternative is to 'pretend' to be 'women' (for men) while preserving a 'real' femininity underneath. It is also, of course, misleading to think that women's identities and roles can be understood in complete independence of these constraints. It is more useful to see gender identities as ongoing, tentative, relational constructs, products rather than origins, always traversed by tensions and paradoxes.

Let us now turn to reading. This, too, was seen as a challenge and a danger, when it became an established part of middle-class life in the late eighteenth century. In particular, it was conventionally thought to be a danger to women; it was widely thought that it was mainly women who used the new circulating libraries.[76] Reading, after all, is an individual and private act; as Cora Kaplan puts it, the activity can be seen as 'defiantly announcing the mental autonomy of individual subjects' since it 'sets up, or enables, a space for reflective thought'. The problems that this might pose for social control and moral propriety were much debated: was there not a danger, if the imagination could wander freely, of disruption or corruption? Educated, middle-class men, it was conventionally thought, were less likely to succumb to these temptations. Kaplan writes that such men were presented as 'the origin of their own identities, as developing individual subjects, the makers and controllers of narrative rather than its enthralled and captive audience'; hence 'They understood the difference between fiction and fact, between imagination and reason.'[77]

Not so with women. Their imagination was more prey to the emotions, less likely to be disciplined by reason. Women faced inwards, were introspective rather than active; and this is dangerous. Those who become obsessed with the inner world get lost in it, and that way lies madness or transgression. Authors of the time wrote of how the woman's mind is 'secretly corrupted' by all this reading,[78] of how such reading can produce nymphomania, or uterine disease;[79] romances were particularly bad, since the woman would be 'seduced and ravished by her very reading of the text', as de Bolla puts it.[80] Romance was already on its way to its status as 'a primary category of the female imagination',[81] and a particularly problematical one at that. With less access to public life, women could use novels as a source of identities, roles to try on in the interior world of the imagination; and herein lie what could be seen as both the temptations and the excitements of the novel. Outram suggests that 'The breakdown of distinctions between the self and the characters of the novel rapidly turns into the converse process of turning the real self into a heroic fiction.'[82]

And today? How does all this stand up in the twentieth-century world of mass popular fiction? In her book based on extensive interviews with readers of romantic fiction, Janice Radway comments that these readers consider the *act* of reading, rather than the particulars of plot or character, as being central to their pleasure. Through reading, they can get drawn into the story; it becomes a self-contained activity leading into a self-contained world, a world in which the self can both explore itself, relaxing from the everyday world, and lose itself. And this autonomous, fictional world is experienced as 'real' in quite a strong sense. For a start, such romances, especially when in a historical setting, are often quite strong on accuracy of detail, which helps reinforce the sense of reality of this 'other' world. And the fact that the reading is experienced as 'pleasure' also helps this effect. As Radway writes, the simplicity of the language 'minimizes the labor the reader contributes to the production of the story', which ensures that reading will 'be marked not as 'work' but as 'pleasure' by the women who indulge in it so frequently'. Hence readers do not have to think of this 'congruent world' as a product of language, just as they are 'not aware that the world they inhabit is in part a creation of the codes used to articulate it'; hence they can 'freely assimilate the fictional world to their own, assuming, in effect, that all imaginary worlds 'naturally' resemble the world with which they are familiar'.[83] The result is that the fictional world can be experienced as congruent to the 'real' one, and it becomes possible to translate from one to the other; what is learnt in the 'other' world can be relevant to daily life, and vice versa. Events that occur in one world can be seen as similar in kind to those that occur in the other; the fictional world can become as real as the real world can become fictional. Thus the nature and power of fiction can be further illuminated, together with the dangers it can be seen to pose, now and in the past, to a world dominated by masculine ideas of rationality, project and self-control.

And the pleasures themselves? Barthes has suggested that it is possible to distinguish a 'text of pleasure', which 'contents, fills, grants euphoria', that 'is linked to a *comfortable* practice of reading', and a 'text of bliss' (*jouissance*), that 'imposes a state of loss', that discomforts and unsettles the reader's historical, cultural and psychological assumptions.[84] One celebrates or confirms the consistency of selfhood and the pleasures promised by its conventional social moorings, the other stimulates the pleasures of evading or disrupting this identity. On the face of it, romantic fiction would count as the former, though actually it is not so clear, suggesting that it may be difficult to distinguish these categories so decisively; perhaps they are best seen as aspects of pleasure that may indeed be present together.

Certainly this fiction celebrates the modern way of love, the promise that 'falling in love' is consistent with staying in love, that romantic passion can or should lead smoothly to conjugal love. In effect, suggests Radway, 'romance reading provides a vicarious experience of emotional nurturance *and* erotic anticipation and excitation'.[85] The hero, after all, is masculine and strong, yet caring, too. Miles, indeed, suggests that 'true love' – unconditional, unearned and unsought – is like a 'dream of mother-love', so that the reading re-enacts the ambivalent relationship with the tender, yet unpredictable and threatening mother.[86] But if the hero can possess elements of both lover and mother, then the notion of 'identification' is becoming quite problematical. Kaplan indeed argues that many romances invite the female reader 'to identify across sexual difference and to engage with narrative fantasy from a variety of subject positions',[87] providing an element of release from the conventions of bounded identity.

These processes of identification, like those of reading itself, are active as well as passive; if reading fiction is a way of 'learning the scripts', this is exploration, not mere absorption. Pykett argues that the romance reader's

> presumed surrender to the narrative pleasures of the formulaic text does not necessarily involve her surrender to, or acceptance of, its (usually) conservative ideology. Women romance readers ... do not merely passively consume their chosen texts but commonly read against the grain, negotiating a variety of positions of spectatorship, and appropriating the text and its messages to their own purposes.

Thus there is a 'complex narrative pleasure' for the reader, of spectating, participating, identifying and judging.[88]

In short, the reader can 'let herself go', enjoy a *jouissance* in the reading itself, made possible by this context of security. And if the light cast by this experience of the 'congruent world' can make the 'real' one seem unsatisfying, this very dissatisfaction can fuel the return to the fantasy in another form. Since the novel cannot resolve the tensions of life itself, it can become like any other object of consumption; read, used up, replaced by another, however similar. But it need not *only* be dissatisfaction that does this; Lynn Pearce suggests that 'in so much as none of us can be expected to live without aspirations, such desires cannot be dismissed as the simple wish-fulfilment of frustrated lives'.[89] We are reminded of Campbell's observation that

> The cultural logic of modernity is not merely that of rationality as expressed in the activities of calculation and experiment; it is also that of passion, and the creative

dreaming born of longing . . . modern individuals inhabit not just an 'iron cage' of economic necessity, but a castle of romantic dreams, striving through their conduct to turn the one into the other.[90]

Everyday Narratives and the Moral Life

A growing sense that there was indeed an 'everyday life' of choice-making individuals, negotiating their way towards their own shifting and fluid goals, interacting with others on a reciprocal basis, and that love, too, had become a central value that could be seen in these terms, embedded in this distinctive culture, is encountered increasingly through the eighteenth century, and is reflected in the novels that also served to encourage it. Thus the works of Defoe, Richardson and Fielding manifest what Taylor calls 'an egalitarian affirmation of ordinary life', and it is through the very form of narrative itself that this occurs. A 'basic condition of making sense of ourselves', argues Taylor, is 'that we grasp our lives in a *narrative*'.[91] But of course we are only part-authors of ourselves, just as we also feature in the narrative of others: 'It is because we all live out narratives in our lives and because we understand our own lives in terms of the narratives that we live out that the form of narrative is appropriate for understanding the actions of others', as MacIntyre argues.[92] The importance of narrative is summed up by the philosopher Ricoeur in these terms:

> Our own existence cannot be separated from the account we can give of ourselves. It is in telling our own stories that we give ourselves an identity. We recognize ourselves in the stories that we tell about ourselves. It makes very little difference whether these stories are true or false; fiction as well as verifiable history provides us with an identity.[93]

The narrative emphasis on continuity and development over time lends itself to this unity of self as project, based on a world presented as relatively stable and knowable. 'What better way to avoid contradiction than narrative?', asks Heath. Narrative 'joins and aligns, smooths reading into the forward flow of its progress'; hence narrative becomes 'the transformation of representation into 'Reality', the demonstrating of its truth, the discovery of its meaning', resulting in 'an inevitable coherence of the real'.[94]

Memory is important here; and since memory has gaps, reconstituted through the imagination, memory and imagination can become difficult to separate. Again we see that the 'congruent world' of fiction can be continuous in form and type with the narrative of our lives; hence reality, representation and fiction can all be resources for narrative construction. And history as narrative entails past and future, a linear relationship through which the past can be seen as leading meaningfully towards a future, and one available for reflexive reconstruction in the light of ongoing projects. Narratives are thus simultaneously unpredictable and teleological; and MacIntyre suggests that 'like characters in a fictional narrative we do not know what will happen next, but nonetheless our lives have a certain form which projects itself towards our future'. And we cannot escape our embeddedness in the past, for traditions are co-authors of our present and future, and our lives are only intelligible in these broader terms.

These narratives of everyday life also possess an irreducible moral dimension. The openness to the future entails choices that are moral as well as practical; one is, after all, accountable for one's actions, and the moral resonance of one's actions is always significant. Morality characteristically becomes a matter of the nuances of everyday decisions, problems of action in contexts where guidelines may be unclear or contradictory, rather than a matter of adherence to doctrines or religious visions of perfection.

It seems appropriate to return to Jane Austen in this connection, both because her central concern is with how to be moral though modern, and because, in this concern, her 'moral point of view and the narrative form of her novels coincide', as MacIntyre puts it.[95] Morality is here embedded in the everyday context of a myriad of small decisions, and a few large ones; with her, suggests Peter Conrad, English novels have become 'works of morality in which obscure virtues and destinies can find grounds for exaltation and create a kind of heroism for themselves'.[96] For Trilling, it was Austen who first represented 'the specifically modern personality and the culture in which it had its being', showing how this social context played a key part in the moral life.[97] And it is surely Fanny Price, of *Mansfield Park*, who is closest to Austen's own position.

Although Fanny has been much criticized by commentators, then and since – as 'obsequious' and 'disastrously indoctrinated',[98] for example, or for her 'invalid deathliness, her immobility, her pale purity'[99] – Mary Evans is surely right to suggest that 'In an entirely radical way, she offers to us a woman who is complete in herself.'[100] In a dependent position, she nevertheless becomes, suggests Claudia Johnson, 'what no modest woman ought to be: erotically independent'.[101] Hers is a reactive morality, struggling to achieve independent selfhood through the snares of her status inferiority and the temptations of theatrical indulgence. She attains the ability to manifest 'constancy', the ability to exhibit an essential consistency in her moral stance, as embodied in her everyday sayings and doings, and such constancy is a central virtue in Austen's heroines. She joins a library, enjoying the autonomy this gives her, as she can choose books for the education of Susan; thereby illustrating, of course, the reasons why many male critics so disliked these libraries. In a context where 'boredom is a moral challenge', she can embrace the 'solitary consolations'[102] of reading and thinking, which, far from being corrupting, are here presented as routes to moral integrity and independence.

Perhaps her crucial statement comes in her assertion that 'we have all a better guide in ourselves, if we would attend to it, than any other person can be'; here speaks the true heroine of interiority, confident in her appeal to the developed voice of conscience. In the situations that contrast her with others, Fanny is in effect exploring, testing, notions of propriety. Good conduct has to be more than refined manners, but neither are strong feelings sufficient; the two have to be aligned, and conscience provides both the source and the language of this alignment. And while conscience develops in a distinctive way in each of us, it does so under social tutelage; there is such a thing as 'moral education'. And its absence is a moral cataclysm. Blaming himself for the disastrous behaviour of his daughters, Sir Thomas bemoans the fact that they had never been taught a sense of duty; he had meant them to be good, 'but his cares had been directed to the understanding and manners, not the disposition'.[103] And Darcy, in *Pride and Prejudice*, admits that 'As a child, I was taught what was *right*, but I was not taught to correct my temper. I was given good principles, but left to follow them in pride and conceit.'[104] Neither principles nor manners are adequate to ensure moral behaviour, as they can be adhered to for the wrong reasons; only conscience, guided by self-knowledge and experience, can permit the development of what, for Austen, seems to be the essential moral virtue of everyday life, 'amiability'. This virtue, suggests MacIntyre, requires 'a genuine loving regard for other people as such, and not only the impression of such a regard embodied in manners', and morality for her is 'never the mere inhibition and regulation of the passions'; rather, morality should *educate* the passions.[105]

Neither passion nor propriety, feelings or manners, are enough on their own; each must infuse the other. And this, while feasible, is not straightforward; conventionally, after all, they are in opposition. (And the claim that Austen underestimates the incommensurability of individual desire and social convention has been a central theme of her critics from Charlotte Brontë onwards.) Mary Poovey argues that Austen has both to tame and legitimize romance, control its 'imaginative excesses' while simultaneously utilizing this moralised romance, based on mature feeling, to correct the selfishness and self-indulgence of individualism. She is, therefore, intent on showing 'how individual feeling can become moral and how it can – and must – make room for itself within the very social institutions that threaten to destroy it', those of bourgeois propriety and individualism; 'For only by making romance speak to and answer propriety can she hope to fuse individual desire with social responsibility.'[106] And if Rousseau complains that propriety entails hypocrisy and dishonesty, then Austen's reply is that this merely shows propriety alone to be insufficient; only when fused with passion, under the aegis of the conscience, can it render possible the society where propriety becomes a framework for the small acts of caring and consideration that can make life moral as well as modern. Without this, it is empty: 'I am worn out with civility', complains Edmund, in *Mansfield Park*, after a tiresome social engagement; 'I have been talking incessantly all night, and with nothing to say.'[107]

Self-knowledge is clearly fundamental here. It is acquired gradually, reflexively; through learning about one's mistakes, one develops a reliable language of self-understanding, whereby selfhood is simultaneously grasped and produced, revealed and regulated. Through language, one strives to represent, and know, one's feelings and those of others. Desire is, as it were, written into the self, and it can be read; knowledge becomes both literary and literacy, and to acquire this literacy is to acquire both selfhood and membership of a community of similar selves. Through self-knowledge, one knows one's own desire; through conscience, one knows its limits in a world where one must care also for the desires of others.

Thus Armstrong argues that we should see Austen's novels as 'striving to empower a new class of people – not powerful people, but normal people – whose
ability to interpret human behaviour qualifies them to regulate the conduct of
daily life and reproduce their form of individuality in and through writing'. A
common language for the self is also a language for a distinctive type of community, based on the relative autonomy of personal relationships and the domestic
sphere. Austen wrote, then, for an audience who could grant fiction the status of
a kind of truth, one that served both as description and as model.[108]

And history itself? In typically precise, pointed Austen prose, Catherine
Morland, in *Northanger Abbey*, mounts a critique of history that anticipates
Woolf's denunciation of it as male-dominated posturing, adding the suggestion
that it may anyway be just as fictional as a romance:

> I read it a little as a duty, but it tells me nothing that does not either vex or weary me.
> The quarrels of popes and kings, with wars or pestilences, in every page; the men all
> so good for nothing, and hardly any women at all – it is very tiresome: and yet I often
> think it odd that it should be so dull, for a great deal of it must be invention.

Conversely, the novel as such is a work 'in which the greatest powers of the mind
are displayed', along with 'the most thorough knowledge of human nature'.[109] And
if we explore this, we will find that the novel, as an institution, does imply a
certain, modest kind of history, which can at least make possible what is perhaps
– and not for Austen alone – the only kind of improvement of which we may be
capable.

Austen's novels, suggests Susan Morgan, liberate the idea of character from
any fixed, given moorings, so that choice and change, history itself, become
possible; and history as something other than the repetition of destructive masculine patterns, so effectively ridiculed by Catherine Morland. Morgan sees the
exploration of this possibility of a new, limited, but positive conception of history
as a central theme in nineteenth-century fiction, especially women's fiction
(though not exclusively, as she argues that Scott's novels, too, manifest a critique
of male ideals of heroism). She asserts that these novels contain, by implication, a
view of how the future could conceivably avoid repeating the mistakes of the past,
since

> to continue traditional definitions of gender does mean to be trapped in a cycle of
> repetition, and, therefore, to remain outside history. To change must mean to
> change what we mean by masculine and feminine, male and female. . . . We can all
> escape determination without simply denying the past, we can all hope to make
> better history, if we become the right kind of hero. And that is a heroine.

So Elizabeth Gaskell, for example, 'warns us to step out of that repetitive cycle, to
relinquish the self-assertive victory that is its own defeat' and hence 'make a new
kind of history with new definitions of what progress means', a prospect that is in
some sense feminine.[110] In *Cranford*, the town of Drumble stands for the self-

appointed 'real world', of masculine competition, trade and business, while Cranford is a kind of never-never land where women live; but we never see or visit Drumble; in the end, relative to Cranford, it is both masculine *and* unreal. More accurately, the one time it *is* experienced as real is when the Bank collapses, as though the male world is only real when it's a disaster. The message is that the values dismissed by businessmen and heroes as trivial or naive, values like 'amiability', caring and forgiveness, rather than revenge, triumph or justice, are far from being out of touch with reality; they are a powerful force in creating and shaping reality, and need to be recognized as such, and diffused more widely. These values celebrate moral community rather than historical determinism, or self-seeking individualism; they imply an ability to confront problems of choice, rather than just repeat tired patterns, while all the time believing that one is 'progressing'. Not that this is easy; Austen's novels illustrate the problems, and again return to the issue of self-knowledge. Only gradually does the heroine of *Emma* disentangle her right to make moral choices from her power to interfere in the lives of others, thus showing that 'true creative power, the power to create one's own life, not somebody else's, neither dominates nor excludes. It is not masculine but feminine.'

This is the crux of the matter. We must, writes Morgan,

> free ourselves from those alluring masculine definitions of modernity that focus on scientific and rational principles of control over our environments and ourselves while turning away from the visions of feeling, definitions that cherish a buried understanding that control is a form of authority and an aggression against the past.[111]

And MacIntyre adds that 'to think of a human life as a narrative unity is to think in a way alien to the dominant individualist and bureaucratic modes of modern culture',[112] based as they are on the intersection of competition and control alien to any vision of connectedness. In effect, we find here a notion of narrative being elaborated in distinction to a male-based ethos of project, an attempt to articulate a latent ethos of modernity, one that does not trumpet itself so loudly but is, in its way, quite as fundamental.

It is crucial to realize that the heroines of novels that imply this perspective represent 'not women's values but human values', as Morgan puts it,[113] even though these values are often, and rightly, called 'feminine'. In effect, these values and qualities are not *inherently* or *necessarily* feminine – which would contradict the whole drift of the argument that gender is a *historical* product – but it is significant that they are indeed *contingently* feminine, that they are values that have been coded as such and reproduced as such within the gender politics of modernity, in which male-centred dualism has presented such values as trivial or outdated, and certainly as 'other'. The gender dynamics of this are consistent with Nancy Chodorow's claim that women have a less separate, more fluid, more relationally defined sense of self than men; the male sense of self is more exclusive, bounded, based on the logic of either/or.[114] And the ground for seeing this alternative ethic as having a broad humanistic potential is precisely that it rejects such rigidity and dualism, instead being incorporative, inclusive, emphasizing connections. It suggests an openness to experience, rather than a fear of it, a determination to control it. Morgan thus claims that these novels strive to 'unite qualities that culture has traditionally considered separate: the power to reach out with feeling for others and the power to be strong and firm within ourselves'.[115] And we have seen that such a vision is, in practice, difficult both to articulate and to realize, menaced as it is by theatricality and romantic excess on the one hand, and male-dominated notions of project on the other, and traversed by the tensions of both.

This ethic of civility, passion and self-knowledge may tentatively express an aspiration to community, therefore, but there is no guarantee of success. And what does it offer the individual? Clearly a certain kind of happiness is posited here, as a reasonable goal for the virtuous life. Elizabeth, in *Pride and Prejudice*, makes it quite clear to the interfering Lady Catherine that so long as legitimate claims are recognized, and the norms of duty, honour and gratitude are respected, then one is entitled to pursue one's happiness, and one's hopes for love.[116] And for George Eliot, suggests Morgan, experience is redemptive: 'To become a better person is to live a better life because it is to make life better.'[117] Yet there are no guarantees here, either. Elizabeth herself observes that 'without scheming to do wrong, or to make others unhappy, there may be error, and there may be misery. Thoughtlessness, want of attention to other people's feelings, and want of resolution, will do the business.'[118] Being good may not be good enough; history can as easily frustrate as gratify our aspirations. Dorothea, in *Middlemarch*, fails in her reform projects, because of the times she lives in. But at least there was a quality to her existence, and perhaps it is this quality alone that can infuse life with such small significance as it can hope to manifest in our perplexing, modern world. 'Narratives' are not just 'grand', the bold rhetorics of History and Progress that modernity has told itself about itself, trumpeted as its rationale for a privileged position; they are also humble, embedded in the everyday, in relationships, and generally recounted by women: the stories of our tiny lives. George Eliot concludes her novel by describing Dorothea thus:

> Her full nature . . . spent itself in channels which had no great name on the earth. But the effect of her being on those around her was incalculably diffusive: for the growing good of the world is partly dependent on unhistoric acts; and that things are not so ill with you and me as they might have been, is half owing to the number who lived faithfully a hidden life, and rest in unvisited tombs.[119]

Notes

1 K. Kingston, *Wild Champagne* (Mills and Boon, 1990), pp. 56, 128–9.
2 Almost certainly a pseudonym. (Not that this is necessarily so unusual: Charlotte Brontë and Mary Ann Evans published as Currer Bell and George Eliot, respectively.)

3 A. Miles, 'Confessions of a Harlequin Reader', *Canadian Journal of Political and Social Theory* (1988), XII: 1–2.

4 B. Fowler, *The Alienated Reader: Women and Popular Romantic Literature in the 20th Century* (Harvester, 1991), chs 4, 5; A. Lewallen, '*Lace*: Pornography for Women?', in L. Gamman and M. Marshment (eds.) *The Female Gaze* (Women's Press, 1988).

5 J. Radway, *Reading the Romance: Women, Patriarchy and Popular Literature* (Verso, 1987), p. 40; Miles, 'Confessions', pp. 1, 31; M. Ricci, in *Everywoman* (February 1991); R. Coward, *Female Desire* (Paladin, 1984), p. 189.

6 Kingston, *Wild Champagne*, pp. 6, 8, 92, 26.

7 J. Austen, *Pride and Prejudice* (Dent, 1993), pp. 7, 68.

8 C. Brontë, *Jane Eyre* (Oxford University Press, 1980), pp. 131, 130, 133, 147.

9 T. Modleski, *Loving with a Vengeance: Mass-Produced Fantasies for Women* (Routledge, 1988), pp. 48, 49, 49, and ch. 2 passim.

10 Austen, *Pride*, pp. 181, 280, 280.

11 M. Evans, *Jane Austen and the State* (Tavistock, 1987), pp. 79, 40.

12 R. Polhemus, *Erotic Faith* (University of Chicago Press, 1990), p. 53.

13 T. Tanner, *Adultery in the Novel: Contract and Transgression* (Johns Hopkins University Press, 1979), p. 15.

14 Brontë, *Eyre*, pp. 265, 451.

15 Austen, *Pride*, pp. 16, 285.

16 Brontë, *Eyre*, p. 276.

17 M. Evans, 'Henry Crawford and the "Sphere of Love" in Mansfield Park', in N. Wood (ed.) *Mansfield Park* (Open University Press, 1993), p. 46.

18 A. R. Jones, 'Mills and Boon Meets Feminism', in J. Radford (ed.) *The Progress of Romance: The Politics of Popular Fiction* (Routledge, 1986), p. 213.

19 Polhemus, *Erotic Faith*, pp. 31, 45.

20 N. Armstrong, *Desire and Domestic Fiction* (Oxford University Press, 1987), p. 252.

21 J. Sarsby, *Romantic Love and Society* (Penguin, 1983), chs 1, 2; A. Macfarlane, *Origins of English Individualism* (Blackwell, 1978).

22 C. Taylor, *Sources of the Self* (Cambridge University Press, 1992), p. 226.

23 Sarsby, *Romantic Love*, p. 73.

24 Taylor, *Sources*, p. 291.

25 C. Campbell, *The Romantic Ethic and the Spirit of Modern Consumerism* (Blackwell, 1989), p. 27.

26 J. Habermas, *The Structural Transformation of the Public Sphere* (Polity, 1989), pp. 43–51.

27 A. Giddens, *The Transformation of Intimacy* (Polity, 1992), pp. 130, 44. See also my *Transgressing the Modern* (Blackwell, 1999), ch. 5 (and ch. 2, on selfhood and the civilizing process, is also relevant at points in this chapter).

28 S. Jackson, 'Even Sociologists Fall in Love: An Exploration in the Sociology of Emotions', *Sociology* (1993), 27:2, p. 214.

29 F. Cancian, *Love in America* (Cambridge University Press, 1987), pp. 5, 69.

30 Cited in S. de Beauvoir, *Marquis de Sade* (Calder, 1962), p. 58.

31 J. Mitchell, 'Romantic Love', in her *Women: The Longest Revolution* (Virago, 1984), p. 106.

32 Jackson, 'Even Sociologists', p. 213.

33 Cited in Polhemus, *Erotic Faith*, p. 1.

34 Giddens, *Transformation*, p. 40.

35 P. Conrad, Introduction to J. Austen, *Mansfield Park* (Dent, 1993), p. xvi.

36 Armstrong, *Desire*, passim; and Campbell, *Romantic Ethic*, chs 4, 5, 7, 9.

37 Brontë, *Eyre*, pp. 110, 162, 164.

38 Armstrong, *Desire*, p. 194.

39 I. Ang, 'Melodramatic Identifications: Television Fiction and Women's Fantasy', in M. E. Brown (ed.) *Television and Women's Culture* (Sage, 1990), p. 83.

40 N. Auerbach, *Private Theatricals: The Lives of the Victorians* (Harvard University Press, 1990), p. 17.

41 T. McKeon, *The Origins of the English Novel, 1600–1740* (Johns Hopkins University Press, 1987), p. 27.

42 R. Williams, *Keywords* (Fontana, 1976), pp. 111–12.

43 I. Watt, *The Rise of the Novel* (Hogarth, 1987), p. 32.

44 Tanner, *Adultery*, pp. 3, 12.

45 Williams, *Keywords*, p. 230.

46 L. Langbauer, *Women and Romance: The Consolations of Gender in the English Novel* (Cornell University Press, 1990), pp. 63, 64, 73, 66, 78.

47 See, for example, S. Gilbert and S. Gubar, *The Madwoman in the Attic: The Woman Writer and the Nineteenth-Century Literary Imagination* (Yale University Press, 1979), pp. 44, 68.

48 L. Pykett, *The 'Improper' Feminine: The Women's Sensation Novel and the New Women Writing* (Routledge, 1992). See also R. Jackson, *Fantasy: The Literature of Subversion* (Methuen, 1981), and Modleski, *Loving*, ch. 3 (on Gothic).

49 To G. H. Lewes, 1847, cited in E. Gaskell, *Life of Charlotte Brontë* (Dent, 1992), p. 240.

50 Cited in Jackson, 'Even Sociologists', p. 135.

51 Conrad, Introduction to *Mansfield Park*, p. xxi.

52 T. Tanner, *Jane Austen* (Macmillan, 1986), p. 162.

53 L. Trilling, *The Opposing Self* (Secker and Warburg, 1955), p. 220.

54 Conrad, Introduction to *Mansfield Park*, pp. xxviii, xxix, xxxv.

55 Gilbert and Gubar, *Madwoman*, p. 168.

56 T. Docherty, 'Postmodern Characterization: The Ethics of Alterity', in E. Smyth (ed.) *Postmodernism and Contemporary Fiction* (Batsford, 1991), p. 171.

57 Armstrong, *Desire*, pp. 63, 164.

58 Conrad, Introduction to *Mansfield Park*, p. xix.

59 Cited in ibid., p. xviii.

60 T. Lovell, *Consuming Fiction* (Verso, 1987), p. 9.

61 V. Woolf, *A Room of One's Own* (Penguin, 1993), p. 59.

62 E. Showalter, *Sexual Anarchy* (Virago, 1992), pp. 76–7.

63 Watt, *Rise of the Novel*, pp. 188, 189, 196.

64 P. Gay, *The Bourgeois Experience, Vol. 1: Education of the Senses* (Oxford University Press, 1984), p. 450.

65 P. de Bolla, *The Discourse of the Sublime: Readings in History, Aesthetics and the Subject* (Blackwell, 1989), p. 269. See also M. Favret, *Romantic Correspondence* (Cambridge, 1993).

66 C. Smith-Rosenberg, 'The Female World of Love and Ritual: Relations Between Women in Nineteenth-Century America', in her *Disorderly Conduct* (Oxford University Press, 1986), p. 55. And see, for a later period, G. Hanscombe and V. Smyers, *Writing for their Lives: The Modernist Women 1910–1940* (Women's Press, 1987).

67 Woolf, *Room*, p. 67.

68 Gilbert and Gubar, *Madwoman*, ch. 1.

69 Showalter, *Sexual Anarchy*, ch. 5, especially p. 78; and see J. Tompkins, 'West of Everything', in D. Longhurst (ed.) *Gender, Genre and Narrative Pleasure* (Unwin Hyman, 1989), on the Western as a more recent variant.

70 S. Morgan, *Sisters in Time: Imagining Gender in Nineteenth-Century British Fiction* (Oxford University Press, 1989), pp. 12, 72, 106.

71 Pykett, *'Improper' Feminine*, p. 202.

72 Gilbert and Gubar, *Madwoman*, p. 51.

73 Woolf, *Room*, pp. 67, 70.

74 R. Bowlby, *Just Looking: Consumer Culture in Dreiser, Gissing and Zola* (Methuen, 1985), p. 11.

75 See T. Moi, *Sexual/Textual Politics* (Methuen, 1985), pp. 57–69, for a critique of Gilbert and Gubar, *Madwoman*, along these lines.

76 de Bolla, *Discourse*, ch. 10, especially p. 235, adding that it may actually have been men who did a lot of this reading; and J. Fergus, *Jane Austen: A Literary Life* (Macmillan, 1991), ch. 24.

77 C. Kaplan, '*The Thorn Birds*: Fiction, Fantasy, Femininity', in V. Burgin et al., *Formations of Fantasy* (Methuen, 1986), pp. 147, 147, 148.

78 Cited in M. Poovey, *The Proper Lady and the Woman Writer* (University of Chicago Press, 1984), p. 20.

79 J. Fiske, *Understanding Popular Culture* (Unwin Hyman, 1989), p. 92.

80 de Bolla, *Discourse*, p. 268.

81 A. Snitow, 'Mass Market Romance', in A. Snitow (ed.) *Desire: The Politics of Sexuality* (Virago, 1984), p. 274.

82 D. Outram, *The Body and the French Revolution* (Yale University Press, 1989), p. 151; and de Bolla, *Discourse*, p. 254.

83 Radway, *Reading the Romance*, pp. 86, 196–7, 191.

84 R. Barthes, *The Pleasures of the Text* (Hill and Wang, 1975), p. 14.

85 Radway, *Reading the Romance*, p. 105.

86 Miles, 'Confessions', p. 9.

87 Kaplan, '*Thorn Birds*', p. 165.

88 Pykett, *Improper Feminine*, pp. 77–8, 81.

89 L. Pearce, *Woman/Image/Text: Readings in Pre-Raphaelite Art and Literature* (Harvester, 1991), p. 21.

90 Campbell, *Romantic Ethic*, p. 227.

91 Taylor, *Sources*, pp. 286, 47.

92 A. MacIntyre, *After Virtue* (Duckworth, 1985), p. 212.

93 Cited in A. Kerby, *Narrative and the Self* (Indiana University Press, 1991), pp. 40–1.

94 S. Heath, 'Lessons from Brecht', *Screen* (1974), 15:2, p. 121; see also E. Said, *Beginnings* (Basic Books, 1975), p. 162, on patriarchal aspects.

95 MacIntyre, *After Virtue*, pp. 216, 243.

96 Conrad, Introduction to *Mansfield Park*, p. xix.

97 Trilling, *Opposing Self*, p. 228.

98 C. Johnson, 'Gender, Theory and Jane Austen Culture', in Wood, *Mansfield Park*, p. 105.

99 Gilbert and Gubar, *Madwoman*, p. 165.

100 Evans, 'Henry Crawford', p. 52.

101 Johnson, 'Gender, Theory', p. 112.

102   Conrad, Introduction to *Mansfield Park*, p. xviii.
103   J. Austen, *Mansfield Park* (Dent, 1993), pp. 317, 356.
104   Austen, *Pride*, p. 276.
105   MacIntyre, *After Virtue*, p. 241.
106   Poovey, *Proper Lady*, pp. 193, 208, 209.
107   Austen, *Mansfield Park*, pp. 213–14.
108   Armstrong, *Desire*, pp. 136, 135, 158.
109   J. Austen, *Northanger Abbey* (Everyman, 1984), pp. 85, 24.
110   Morgan, *Sisters*, pp. 12, 72, 106.
111   Ibid., pp. 55, 106.
112   MacIntyre, *After Virtue*, p. 227.
113   Morgan, *Sisters*, p. 73.
114   N. Chodorow, *The Reproduction of Mothering* (California University Press, 1978), pp. 166–70.
115   Morgan, *Sisters*, p. 116.
116   Austen, *Pride*, p. 268.
117   Morgan, *Sisters*, p. 134.
118   Austen, *Pride*, p. 103.
119   G. Eliot, *Middlemarch* (Oxford University Press, 1988), p. 682.

Part II
The Modern Age

7 Sacred, Secular, Sublime:

Modernity Performs the Death of God

There is an important sense in which 'religion' is a modern product: only when Christianity was in decline could it be seen as an instance of a category, rather than simply as revealed truth. Thus McGrane writes that 'It was not in the grey dawn of paleolithic man, but in the Enlightenment that "religion" first emerged', so that 'now, for the first time, Christianity became a species of the new genus "religion"'.[1] And since religion was essentially constituted by the experience of the sacred, the declining hold of religion would, it was thought, necessarily entail a loss of the sense of the sacred. A secular world would therefore be a world in which no experience of the sacred would be possible. This looks even more plausible when one considers the influential Durkheimian assimilation of society and the sacred: since the rise of individualism appears to be associated with a decline in the hold of society, a similar fate would necessarily befall the sacred. However, Durkheim himself, of course, declined to draw these conclusions, suggesting that individualism itself, and notions associated with it such as liberty, progress, and freedom of enquiry, could become socially cohesive ideologies, and therefore manifestations of the sacred.[2] This, in turn, has inaugurated the game of 'hunt the sacred', in which numerous candidates have emerged, including science itself (a kind of 'civic religion'), the nation state, eroticism, art. . . . What all these seem to have in common is the theme of communion with otherness, the attempt to get beyond the boundaries of selfhood; the sacred emerges as transcendence plus transgression.

Perhaps it is the last two candidates that are most significant. It can be argued that there is a sense in which the fascination with the body boundaries and transgressions involved in sexuality can be seen, in effect, as a search for transcendence in a secular and materialist age. Thus, following Bataille and Nietzsche, Foucault has suggested that eroticism could be defined as 'an experience of sexuality which links, for its own ends, an overcoming of limits to the death of God'.[3] Since early nineteenth-century Romanticism, however, there have always been those who have argued that it is the arts that are best equipped for this search. Susan Sontag points to this link between art and the sacred:

If within the last century art conceived as an autonomous activity has come to be invested with an unprecedented stature – the nearest thing to a sacramental human activity acknowledged by secular society – it is because one of the tasks art has assumed is making forays into and taking up positions on the frontiers of consciousness (often very dangerous to the artist as a person) and reporting back what's there.

She adds that 'The need of human beings to transcend "the personal" is no less profound than the need to be a person', and that this leads to a search for 'total experiences' that can easily include eros as well as art.[4]

All of this nevertheless implies that if the sacred does exist, it is not generally recognized as such. Hence the uncertainties; for what *is* to count as 'sacred', in this situation? It does not seem to correspond to any cohesive or distinctive social experience, with a common language or symbolism through which this experience can be shaped, articulated and expressed. But in order to take this further, it may be useful to consider an area of human experience which has traditionally been seen as raising problems that are central both to religion and to the sacred itself: death, and its fate in modernity.

'Death, Thou Shalt Die'

John Donne's death sentence on death has come to have a different meaning from the one that he and his audience would have understood. His own exploration of this, in his *Devotions Upon Emergent Occasions*, describes an episode of typhus in 1623 which he clearly thought was his own death sentence, but which he survived.

It is clear that, for Donne, illness is above all about one's relationship to God, and it is an opportunity to improve this relationship. The physician has only a very limited role here; he is a sort of sentinel, who watches the patient, waits, and gives support, and has to accept in all humility that his very limited skills are derived from God and can only be useful with God's will. Indeed, death, as a rite of passage, was presided over by the dying, not the physician. The relationship between physician and patient is sacramental, and the illness of the body is conceived by analogy with the illness of the soul. The physical becomes an allegory of the spiritual. In her discussion of this, Anne Hawkins writes:

> The symbolic mode of the *Devotions* is nearest to allegory in that it presents the reader with a consistent linking together of two levels of reality, the physical and the spiritual, where there is a one-to-one relationship between the progress of the illness and the progress of the soul. Thus the sick individual figures as a type of Everyman, the body becomes the soul, the disease is equated with sin, the physician analogous to the priest, healing is compared to divine grace, and recovery to resurrection or salvation.[5]

Hence this sacramentalism endows the world of concrete particulars with significance, and enables the patient both to endure his experience and to use it to prepare for the eternal life of the soul. On this model, illness functions both as judgement and as mercy: it is both punishment for sins and an occasion for repentance and atonement. A plague victim in 1633 is described as embracing her own death willingly, showing the marks of the plague on her body and saying: 'I wear my judgement written upon me.'[6] Symptoms are like a language, and Donne represents his illness as God's commentary on the 'text' of his body, a commentary that is simultaneously an exercise of power whereby the body is transformed.[7]

Finally, for Donne illness represents a shift away from the individual, a recognition of the common mortality of all, death as a universal experience through which isolated selves merge in one another and in rapturous love of God: 'No man is an island, entire of itself . . . any man's death diminishes me, because I am involved in mankind, and therefore never send to know for whom the bell tolls; it tolls for thee.'[8] The great epidemic diseases were indeed experienced as an awful visitation, a collective trauma, and the disease did not mark out the afflicted individual as such; the victim was Everyman, an exemplar of the inherently sinful human condition before God. 'The corruption which lay at the root of plague was not only a physical process but also a moral one', writes Slack; 'Disorder of any kind weakened man's defences against plague, and it also provoked God to despatch it', and it could strike just and unjust alike, since they would be judged later anyway, according to their deserts.[9]

Moving forward in time to 1849, we find that both the cultural construction of the death experience, and its relation to disease, have undergone significant shifts. Only a few months after the death of her sister Emily, and on the point of dying from the same disease – tuberculosis – Anne Brontë visited Scarborough. Following the account given in Elizabeth Gaskell's *Life of Charlotte Brontë*, we are told that at around eleven o'clock in the morning, a change came over her. She believed she had not long to live, and asked to see a doctor. When he saw her, he admitted that 'the angel of death was already arrived, and that life was ebbing fast. She thanked him. . . . She still occupied her easy chair, looking so serene, so reliant . . . all knew the separation was at hand.' And at two o'clock 'she calmly and without a sigh passed from the temporal to the eternal'.[10]

This is still a death presided over by the dying – though the doctor has a more important presence now, as the power who confirms that death is indeed at hand – but it is no longer the death of Everyman. Death has been individualized and sanctified as the culmination of life, the ultimate manifestation of the 'quality', the difference, of a person's identity. By the late eighteenth century, writes Elisabeth Bronfen, death had emerged as 'that moment in a person's life where individuality and absolute rarity could finally be attained', so that an 'otherwise incommunicable secret', that of individuality, could be made visible.'[11] And for the Victorians, argues Nina Auerbach, death was when 'the self reveals itself wonderfully and wholly', so that deathbed scenes become 'crescendos of revelation' for their subjects. In an age when religious hope exceeded religious expectation, death becomes 'a final source of the integration lives promise and deny. If life cannot realize us, dying must, for there is nothing beyond.'[12]

And tuberculosis? 'For over a hundred years TB remained the preferred way of giving death a meaning – an edifying, refined disease', claims Sontag, adding that

'It is with TB that the idea of individual illness was articulated, along with the idea that people are made more conscious as they confront their deaths.' With TB, the body is still a text; but the language is no longer that of God's judgement, rather 'a language for dramatizing the mental: a form of self-expression'.[13] A slow, wasting disease, it seemed to enforce an intensification of experience, expressing the perverse creativity and theatricality of selfhood, and indeed made sickness and sadness into powerful signifiers of artistry. Shelley consoled Keats with the words that 'this consumption is a disease particularly fond of people who write such good verses as you have done.'[14]

Drama, artistry: we seem to be in the presence of an aesthetics of death, of death as a staged production, and indeed, an audience seems to be essential. If death becomes representable in the drama of the deathbed, it becomes accessible only to the spectators, and even then only as narrative. As Bronfen puts it, 'Even though death is the measure and limit of all human knowledge and lends authority to life's meaning, the living can have access to death only through the death of another.'[15] Wittgenstein, after all, reminded us that 'Death is not an event in life: we do not live to experience death';[16] so death as culmination of life entails the paradox that the ultimate expression of one's life is inaccessible save vicariously, as the observed and narrated death of the other. And if these deaths are staged, they are indeed just as surely narrated: it hardly seems to matter whether Anne Brontë was an author or a character in one of the novels, so literary is her death in the form it has come down to us, recorded by its contemporary witnesses. Thus can the troublesome theatricality of the self in its excessively staged death be recuperated culturally by a soothing apotheosis, death as the culmination of the narrative of one's life.

It is not so clear, however, that the dead will necessarily be buried so easily. This vital, alive self goes on troubling the Victorians even in death; this, after all, is the great age of ghosts, as though, claims Auerbach, 'Only death brings the self into its inheritance, one so mighty it cannot be killed.'[17] The ghost is the soul in the age of secular selfhood, an age that clung desperately to the religion it could no longer uncritically believe in. Nor was the corpse immune to this empowerment; the Victorian fetishism of the corpse and of representations of the dead body testify to its continuing hold over the living. In this cult of the dead, we witness nevertheless the cultural denial of death that will become stronger in the following century; a connection, as Bronfen argues, between 'a conceptual exclusion of death and its representational ubiquity, as though the more a culture refuses death the more it imagines and speaks of it'.[18] This twin sense of a frantic disavowal both of death and of the death of God enables us to define Victorian culture as a culture of religiosity, and to see one sense in which 'Modernity and religiosity have cohabited quite comfortably', as Carnes puts it.[19]

Exclusion and ubiquity: the otherness of death can be assimilated all too easily to the otherness of the feminine. We encounter, in this way, the cultural theme of the death of woman and woman-as-death. Woman as embodiment of purity becomes a *memento mori*, 'a messenger of the mystical otherness of death', write Gilbert and Gubar, hence leading 'a posthumous existence in her own lifetime'.[20]

Death can so easily be the culmination of her life because it is already there *in* her life, devouring her as insidiously as the TB that can both carry and symbolize it. And Ariès suggests that the purity option is only one manifestation of an erotics of death that runs through from the early modern to the Victorian periods: 'mystical ecstasies of love and death', in which 'holy virgins dying of love, and the little death of sexual pleasure' become confounded with the death of the body.[21]

The scene changes again. In the late 1970s, Cornelius Ryan, author of war books like *A Bridge Too Far*, wrote a detailed account of his struggle against the cancer that was to kill him. The book was completed by his wife after his death, and published in 1979 as *A Private Battle*. The title itself is significant. A *private* battle: now, illness not only individualizes, it cuts people off by rendering their experiences private, separate, sequestered in hospitals, away from the public gaze. People die, writes Elias, 'noiselessly and hygienically'.[22] And the web of privacy extends into secrecy, as though even the patient should be kept away from a knowledge and experience that could render the situation too difficult to bear. Ariès argues that this 'invisible death' extends 'to protect the dying or the invalid from his own emotions by concealing the seriousness of his condition until the end'.[23] A private *battle*: if Donne's strategy could be called a psychology of accept-ance, Ryan's is a psychology of resistance. Through fighting it, illness can serve as an opportunity for courage, even heroism. The book is indeed full of battles, not only against the disease but against the hospital and the doctors, unwilling to give Ryan the knowledge he believed he needed in order to fight effectively, and endeavouring to keep him within the passivity of the patient role.[24]

For Ryan, then, the governing analogy is that between illness and war. Illness is a battleground for the self, disease is the enemy, Ryan himself is both the battlefield and the commander, and the doctors are generals. This is of course influenced by Ryan's own profession as war historian, but these metaphors are widespread in modern culture. Sontag shows how cancer, in particular, seems to have been linked to these metaphors: cancer cells are 'invasive', they 'colonize', they 'overwhelm defenses'; chemotherapy is chemical warfare, radiotherapy is bombardment with toxic rays. Nor is cancer romanticized, unlike TB: 'Far from revealing anything spiritual, it reveals that the body is, all too woefully, just the body.'[25] The doctor, like the patient, must subscribe to these activist, combative values, and medicine is now conceived as a powerful, independent source of cure. Indeed, it has increasingly been the doctor who has presided over the encounter with death, not the dying person.[26] As Hawkins puts it: 'The sacramental contract implicit in the seventeenth-century medical model has not simply been abandoned but has undergone a kind of reversal' whereby 'the patient often expects his doctor to perform nearly miraculous feats of healing and is deeply angry, even outraged, when things go wrong'.[27]

The doctor, too, can contribute to these inflated expectations of what science and medicine can achieve. One always dies *of* something; in this sense, there can always be the hope of specific cures for specific causes. We have thereby, suggests Bauman, 'deconstructed mortality one cannot overcome into a series of afflictions one can',[28] as though this fragmentation and multiplication of death can indeed kill it. When doctors took over the management of dying, death was effaced in the visibility of disease. For doctor and patient, death is the ultimate 'defeat in battle', hence should not have to be confronted as such; the Victorian staging of death is replaced by staging its absence, its concealment, as hospitals have devised elaborate rituals to keep dying and dead bodies out of sight, and patients, too, have to join in by avoiding tiresome displays of emotion.[29] In this sense, suggests Ariès, death has become 'wild' when it used to be 'tame'.[30]

For Ryan, there is no meaning in illness or in the death that results from it. Far from being a logical consummation and manifestation of an individual life, as it was for the Victorians, death has become an arbitrary termination, an intolerable interference with the project of one's life, eroding dignity and self-respect. Life as project gains meaning from the future, but death cuts this future off. Death, argues Illich, 'ceases to be the end of a whole and becomes an interruption in the sequence',[31] it becomes, adds Sontag, 'the obscene mystery, the ultimate affront, the thing that cannot be controlled. It can only be denied.'[32] In a society which values human culture as a triumph over natural limitations, in which, as Crawford puts it, 'Health substitutes for salvation and becomes a salvation of its own',[33] death presents a challenge which is encapsulated by Baudrillard in these terms:

> There is a paradox of modern bourgeois rationality concerning death. To conceive of it as natural, profane and irreversible constitutes the sign of the 'Enlightenment' and Reason, but enters into sharp contradiction with the principles of bourgeois rationality, with its individual values, the unlimited progress of science, and its mastery of nature in all things. Death, neutralised as a 'natural fact', gradually becomes a *scandal*.[34]

This paradox, in turn, gives a clue to significant continuities in the modern way of death, since last century. Bellah refers to depictions of Lincoln's apotheosis, widespread in American homes after the Civil War period, in which the martyred president is shown ascending to Heaven. He is shown as healthy, in his prime, with no trace of the cause of his death.[35] At the funeral, an observer wrote: 'I saw him in his coffin. The face was the same as in life. Death had not changed the kindly countenance in any line.' He then adds, apparently unaware of the tension with what he had just written: 'It was the look of a worn man suddenly relieved.'[36] And this tension is also present in the widespread contemporary practice of embalming, generally associated, particularly in the US, with the ritual of viewing the body. This viewing, suggest Huntington and Metcalf, can serve the ideal of a gentle, pain-free death: the point is to reveal the dead 'at peace', so that the carefully restored body provides 'a truer image of death'.[37] Death becomes a simulacrum of life, its idealized double: life as passivity, repose; life as the life one never lived, now made possible by death. Medicine's failure can become its triumph: life preserved even in death, a consoling cosmetic answer to modern nihilism, a continuation of Victorianism by other means. And ultimately the very perfection of the restored body testifies to the paradox of the enterprise.

Death, radically excluded, becomes omnipresent, a powerful source of cultural fears, images and metaphors, infecting life itself: life's double, its ghost, the death that cannot die.

Withdrawal Symptoms: God's Absent Presence

The modern performance of death, starring a secular self, is therefore in many ways a testament to the haunting presence of the divinity that used to be central to the play. This is perhaps what Hamilton means when he writes that 'We are not talking about the absence of the experience of God, but about the experience of the absence of God.'[38]

A sense that God was withdrawing from the world can be found even before the seventeenth-century Scientific Revolution; for example, it was widely argued that miracles no longer occurred, implying that God no longer intervened directly in the order that he had created. And if God was withdrawing, so was Satan; the demise of the witch hunts by the 1660s, over most of Europe, meant that the Devil, too, came to be less of a presence in people's lives. Nevertheless, there was no sense of any necessary inconsistency between science and religion; not until the nineteenth century would that really become an issue. Science could be the revelation of God-as-Nature, and this 'natural religion' was a powerful presence in eighteenth-century thought; God had a benign but distant presence, seen more as a pillar of moral virtue than in traditional cosmological terms.[39] Even so, this conception of God as the great clockmaker, winding up the universe and then leaving it alone, so that it ran according to laws that were both immutable and discoverable, had already led Pascal, in the mid-seventeenth century, to fear that God had rendered himself both superfluous and inaccessible. He complained that the role of God in Cartesian philosophy was merely to 'give a little tap to start the world off'.[40] This sense that God was 'always absent and always present' was, argues Goldmann, central to the 'tragic vision' expressed in the works of authors like Pascal and Racine.[41]

By the eighteenth century, we also encounter the emergence of the 'supernatural'; and this category, after all, is a product of modernity, since it only makes sense by contrast with the category of the 'natural', the notion of nature as secular, law-governed, available for scientific investigation. Consequently the supernatural has had a controversial status. From the point of view of science – responsible for its very possibility as a category – it has to remain a necessarily empty category. For science, all that exists, whether as yet understood or not, is 'natural'. In popular discourse, however, the supernatural soon acquired its hold as an arena of mystery, particularly powerful by the late eighteenth century, when the Gothic novel explored the 'uncanny', opening up the possibility of aspects of experience that could not be grasped rationally, but were not clearly spiritual either. The otherness of God becomes the mystery in the heart of the world, the strangeness in the ordinary; the void of God's withdrawal could be filled with ghosts and spectres.[42] Ostensibly, these were products of the imagination, hence 'not real'; yet something of the old role of the imagination as a force in the world, able to mediate between the outside and inside worlds, still hung on, and helped reinforce this sense that being in a dark, empty graveyard at night might give you more than you bargained for.

In some ways, these different aspects of the 'presence of God's absence' testify to problems inherent – if normally latent – within the Christian tradition. How are we to 'know' or 'represent' God? 'In the Beginning was the Word', we are told; but although God's Word is necessarily everywhere, its representation to humans as something they can understand is problematical. Indeed, the word 'representation' plays a distinctive role here: Gadamer points out that until the middle of the seventeenth century, *repraesentatio* signified 'the represented presence of the divinity'.[43] To 'represent' was to 'make the divine present'. Hence, words are powerful, and names themselves are potent; if God created through naming, our ability to 'name' his creation correctly necessarily communicates a degree of power, an intervention in the world. Naming is action, not arbitrary convention; properly manipulated in rites and rituals, names institute a relationship with the divine through which power can flow. Hence the crucial significance of 'correct interpretation' for the Church, attacking unauthorized names and rites as magic and heresy.

This is a vision of the world as sacramental, as standing in a relation to God as transcendent, as other, whereby our experience of his world is simultaneously an experience of his presence, his power. The world is not only itself; it points to something else, it *is* something else. In the traditional interpretation of the Eucharist, the bread symbolically unifies the worshipper with the body of Christ, the body of the Church, and the cosmos. 'The crux of the doctrine', argues Mary Douglas, is that 'a real, invisible transformation has taken place at the priest's saying of the sacred words and that the eating of the consecrated host has saving efficacy for those who take it'.[44]

It is this vision of the world that was upset in decisive fashion at the time of the Reformation. Heller argues that an apparently esoteric debate between the reformers Luther and Zwingli is a key moment in this fundamental shift. Zwingli is 'the spokesman of modernity', he writes: 'To Luther the sacrament of the Last Supper is Christ (the bread and the wine *are* what they represent), while Zwingli reduces it to the status of an allegory (as merely representing what, in itself, it is not).'[45] The term 'symbol' increasingly takes over the connotation of being 'secondary', and, suggests Heller, this makes it more and more difficult to make sense of it: when a symbol becomes 'merely' a symbol, it may mean 'this or that or nothing on earth', and hence 'The symbol was made homeless in the real world, and the real world made itself a stranger to the symbol.'[46] He concludes that religion and art 'lost their unquestioned birthright in the homeland of human reality, and turned into strange messengers from the higher unreality', admitted now and then as 'edifying or entertaining songsters at the positivist banquet'.[47]

There might, however – as suggested at the beginning of this chapter – be a sense in which the death of this experience of the world would also be the birth of 'religion' and 'art' in the modern sense of those terms, as differentiated, special-

Plate 1. Passage Choiseul, Paris, 1825–7. Photo © Monique Hayat, Architectural Association Photo Library, London.

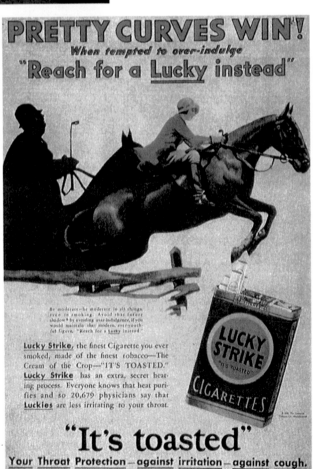

Plate 2. Advertisement for Lucky Strike cigarettes. Source: *American Magazine,* September 1930.

Plate 3. Stiletto. Photo by Chris Bell from *Skin Two, Retro 1: The First Six Issues* (Tim Woodward Publishing Ltd., 1991).

Plate 4. John Galliano, Fallen Angels fashion collection. Photo by Chris Woode.

Plate 6. G. Scott, *La Passagère,* pencil drawing from *L'Aviation* magazine.

Plate 7. The Seagram Building, New York, by Mies van der Rohe and Philip Johnson, 1958. Photo © Joe Kerr, Architectural Association Photo Library, London.

Plate 8. Henri Matisse: *The Red Room,* or *Dessert: Harmony in Red,* 1908. Hermitage, St Petersburg/Bridgeman Art Library, London, © Succession H. Matisse/DACS, 1998.

ized, relatively autonomous sectors of experience, one of which – 'art' – seems to have become significant at the expense of the other. This is perhaps addressed by Heller's claim that 'As reality became more real, so the symbol became more symbolic and art more artistic';[48] the symbol may retreat into art, but it develops a new power in that arena, contrasting with its secondary, indeterminate nature in the wider culture. 'Symbol' is no longer an aspect of the world, but a sign of its absence, an allusion to an otherness that it can express only indirectly, elliptically. Along with this, the world becomes 'reality', amenable to positivist observation and control, and the old theological guarantee gives way to the language of science. In short, concludes Bataille, 'The servants of science have excluded human destiny from the world of truth, and the servants of art have renounced making a true world out of what an anxious destiny has caused them to bring forth.'[49]

It could of course be suggested that reports of God's death have been greatly exaggerated, and that, particularly in the American context, modernity does not seem to have involved any process of remorseless secularization. Indeed, this seems to be graphically confirmed by opinion polls that regularly suggest that some three-quarters of the population believe in miracles, while only around ten per cent believe in Darwinian evolution, and by evidence that belief in God, and church attendance, are higher there than anywhere else in the West.[50] However, in his essay on Protestant sects in the US, Weber long ago argued that religious ritual and belief had taken on important social and economic functions, so that admission to a congregation was a guarantee of 'the moral qualities of a gentleman, especially of those qualities required in business matters'.[51] In effect, writes MacIntyre, 'American religion has survived in industrial society only at the cost of itself becoming secular'.[52] It can be added that there are also strong elements of cultural nationalism in what can clearly be a powerful fusion, so that 'religion celebrates a shared cult of the American way of life', as Gellner puts it.[53]

What does seem to be clear from the American case is that the modern world makes life difficult for religious beliefs if they aspire to be anything more than *beliefs*; if, in short, they make a difference to what believers do in practice. As Carter argues in *The Culture of Disbelief*, someone who wants to 'get ahead' may indeed have some conventional religious affiliation, signifying respectability, but should certainly not let this interfere with daily life: 'whatever you do, do not on any account take your religion seriously'. What this can mean is illustrated by a 1985 case in which the Supreme Court struck down a Connecticut law requiring employers to allow employees who wanted to do so to observe the Sabbath. The reason for this decision, stated one of the justices, was that it would have given all employees 'the right to select the day of the week in which to refrain from labor'. But as Carter points out, Jews do not feel that they have 'selected' the Sabbath; it is God who did that. 'If the sabbath is just another day off, then religious choice is essentially arbitrary and unimportant.'[54] If your ritual happens not to fit in with the exigencies of modern life, then just change it; and if you are unwilling to do so, you are just being irrational. One cannot, in short, both be rational *and* take religion seriously. This is surely the crux of the matter: not that modernity necessarily banishes religion, but that it devalues the significance of religious commitment, making it just another form of consumerism. One can buy it or not buy it, and if one buys it, there are numerous brands on offer; but they're all much the same, and none of it matters much anyway, either way. Liberal claims to religious tolerance are in a very real sense a sham, and anyone who does want to take their religion seriously is, by that very fact, almost bound both to be viewed as an extremist, and indeed to become such. If there is a sense in which God is dead, as Nietzsche suggests, it is perhaps to be found here, in the way in which God's presence can no longer be recognized or seen as significant; though there are also hints, in the wave of cults and revivalist movements, that perhaps this in turn ensures his rebirth. . . .

It is indeed to Nietzsche – and his successor, Max Weber – that we must turn, for further development of these themes. In a celebrated parable in *The Gay Science*, Nietzsche tells of a madman who enters the market-place one bright morning, holding a lantern, and claims to be searching for God. Onlookers gather round and mock him. Is God hiding? Has he emigrated? Then the madman gives his answer:

> Where has God gone? I shall tell you. *We have killed him – you and I.* We are all his murderers. . . . God is dead. . . . How shall we, the murderers of all murderers, console ourselves? That which was holiest and mightiest of all that the world has yet possessed has bled to death under our knives. Who will wipe this blood off us? . . . Is not the greatness of this deed too great for us? Must we not ourselves become gods simply to seem worthy of it?

However, the only response he gets is amazement; so he smashes his lantern on the ground, and walks off, saying that he has come too soon.[55]

If it is Nietzsche himself who thus seeks to illuminate the light of day, his guise as madman is significant. Madness has not, in the modern period, been allowed the role of mediator between the human and the divine. Consequently, 'If God no longer shines through madness, it is because the divine light itself has been extinguished from the world', argues Connolly. 'To laugh at the announcement of the madman is to reveal unwittingly the truth of his proclamation.' Yet there is another side to this. The madman represents unreason, the exclusions of the Enlightenment project. Hence if it is a madman, he who cannot speak sense, who proclaims the death of God, then since his is the voice of the excluded other, who has been rendered voiceless, his very utterances condemn themselves, and his claims can remain unheard by an audience that would find their implications frightening, and that merely wants to carry on as before. For this proclamation of the death of God is, implicitly, that of the Enlightenment project too: if God goes, so does any possibility of justification for the ideal of human emancipation based on the objective certainties of science and morality as revealed by reason. Modernity seeks secure foundations in these areas, but the very project of modernity itself ultimately subverts the possibility of such foundations. The basis for any ultimate claims to scientific and moral knowledge has been destroyed.

Science itself tries to rest its claims on a correspondence or reflection theory of truth; but Nietzsche suggests that once the religious postulates that cement words to the world are removed, the effect is to subvert all such theories of representation. 'In a world without a divine designer knowing is not a correspondence but an imposition of form upon the objects of knowledge', claims Connolly.[56] Instead, then, there is a shift towards pragmatism,[57] knowledge as power, embodied in technology, and an emphasis on the tentative nature of scientific theories, each doomed to be outdated and replaced in turn. Science can answer the technical questions, writes Weber, but not questions about meaning or purpose; it leaves to one side the issue of 'whether we should and do wish to master life technically and whether it ultimately makes sense to do so'.[58] Nor can science itself, as an orientation, be given any value-free foundation, any ultimate justification. Hence 'the unpalatable condition of modernity', writes Whimster, following Weber, is that 'there is no scientific underpinning to scientific presuppositions'.[59] Any resort to 'faith' in order to justify a claim to 'truth' has to be bad faith, in this context, argues Connolly. It amounts to 'a demand for external guarantees inside a culture that has erased the ontological preconditions for them'; faith is unacceptable, yet 'faith is necessary to ground the superiority of modern life'.[60]

The key element that is lost with the collapse of the theological guarantee is the sense of a unified purposefulness, a rational telos governing both universe and self. The value spheres separate out: morality, politics, religion, the arts are governed by their own separate aims and criteria and, for Weber, there is no way of resolving 'the struggle of the gods of the various orders and values'.[61] Beauty, holiness and goodness have no necessary relation to one another; the Kantian equation of the beautiful and the good had already collapsed by the time of Bohemian modernism and Baudelaire.[62] 'Art takes over the function of a this–worldly salvation', suggests Weber, but cannot ultimately succeed.[63] Nor have the great post-religious value systems – humanism, liberalism, socialism – managed to claim any clearly decisive or cohesive rational basis, and the unifying vision of these 'grand narratives' of modernity has proved largely chimerical.[64] Sayer concludes that 'what modernity leaves us with is the unprecedented loneliness of the single individual, in the face, now, of no god at all, and the passing consolation of personal integrity'.[65]

What we encounter, then, is what MacIntyre portrays in *After Virtue* as a kind of moral anarchy, where incommensurable moral beliefs compete and we ultimately choose between them by using what are necessarily non-rational, subjective criteria; moral choices become capricious, intuitive, or guided by self-interest. This is what he calls 'emotivism', the doctrine that evaluative judgements are '*nothing but* expressions of preference, expressions of attitude or feeling', and that appeals to principles can only really be a cover, a mask, for these preferences, however sincere the appeals may be. It also follows that emotivism entails 'the obliteration of any genuine distinction between manipulative and non-manipulative social relations',[66] a state of affairs which has important implications that will be further explored in subsequent chapters. What is important here is that life becomes a matter of endless small-scale projects in which no sense of overall design or purpose, no 'project of projects' is possible. For Pascal, the true end of human life had become unknowable, lost since the Fall; reason can now only be calculative, instrumental, geared to the realization of practical, self-interested aims. This is the world that Durkheim characterized in terms of *anomie*, a world that lacks meaningful structures that can both transcend the imperatives of selfhood yet also render the latter sustainable.[67]

Weber's penetrating reflections on this suggest a close connection between modern ideas of the emancipation of life from natural cycles – seen as central to the meaning of 'culture' itself – and the way resulting ideas of 'progress' and its benefits entail this sense of unease, particularly in the presence of death, that has been seen to be central to modernity. He writes:

> The purely inner-worldly perfection of self of a man of culture, hence the ultimate value to which 'culture' has seemed to be reducible, is meaningless for religious thought. This follows for religious thought from the obvious meaninglessness of death, meaningless precisely when viewed from the inner-worldly standpoint. And under the very conditions of 'culture', senseless death has served only to put the decisive stamp upon the senselessness of life itself. The peasant, like Abraham, could die 'satiated with life'. The feudal landlord and the warrior hero could do likewise. For both fulfilled a cycle of their existence beyond which they did not reach. Each in his own way could attain an inner-worldly perfection as a result of the naive unambiguity of the substance of his life. But the 'cultivated' man who strives for self-perfection, in the sense of acquiring or creating 'cultural values', cannot do this. He can become 'weary of life' but he cannot become 'satiated with life' in the sense of completing a cycle. For the perfectibility of the man of culture in principle progresses indefinitely. . . .

The very fact that progress is conceived as unending entails a sense that what passes becomes outdated, that everything is not only provisional but is doomed to be swept away, that the future offers only the promise of further obsolescence; the ever present, ever growing, weight of a dead past. The exile of 'natural cycles' brings with it an endless repetition of a past that can only be the fulfilment of meaninglessness. Hence 'culture's every step forward seems condemned to lead to an ever more devastating senselessness',[68] since problems are recreated here even as they are removed there, and scientific knowledge can only ever be piecemeal, inconclusive and tentative, however powerful it may seem. Through its own self-constituting limitations, science forces us to ask questions about meaning; but its very existence makes it impossible to answer the questions except in ways that seem obsolete, arbitrary or inconsistent.

Resentment, Transgression and the Sacred

One could say that 'progress' is a secular myth, and in addition, an essay in bad faith, for it implies a telos which is no longer either knowable or possible. There can, no doubt, be progress in specific tasks, relative to specific ends, but the cultural status of 'progress' as a value is that it points beyond that, to the aspiration that these separate projects make some overall, cumulative, cohesive sense, that there is indeed a grand 'project of projects', whether for the individual or the society. And this is where Nietzsche's critique becomes especially powerful, and where its implications can be pursued into the very heart of the secular self of modernity. 'Progress' becomes part of the imperative of selfhood, central to the idea of self-development, the promise that the blemishes and defects can indeed be smoothed out, that one can move towards 'perfecting' oneself. The self must be organized, disciplined, to achieve this state of grace. Self-knowledge is necessary for this; the self must be transparent to itself, just as the world must be made transparent to science. And just as the latter is impossible, so is the former. Nietzsche argues that 'we are necessarily strangers to ourselves, we do not comprehend ourselves, we *have* to misunderstand ourselves . . . we are not "men of knowledge" with respect to ourselves'.[69]

In effect, the subject misrecognizes the dynamics of its own transformation into a subject, its own complicity in the reproduction of the imperfections without which it cannot achieve its status as 'the interiorized and unified self of modernity', as Connolly puts it, following Nietzsche. He adds that 'To be a subject is to be the locus of an internal struggle one strives to suppress; it is to lie to oneself about the origins and bearing of the self one is.' This is the world that Freud, in the generation after Nietzsche, will claim for his own, since 'a world in which the subject prevails is a world where therapy abounds'.[70] Blame and resentment have their sources here, and become powerful influences in culture and politics, powerful social forces. For Nietzsche, systems of morality are essentially products of this resentment directed against life and the other in the name of some transcendent god or principle that can thereby punitively exorcize the corruption and guilt of human imperfection and suffering.[71]

The 'death of God' can be re-examined in this light. It is not widely known that there is a second major treatment of the theme in Nietzsche's work. This occurs in *Thus Spake Zarathustra*, in a chapter significantly entitled 'The Ugliest Man'. Travelling through a 'kingdom of death', a valley where there was 'no grass, no tree, no cry of birds', Zarathustra saw something sitting on the path, 'shaped like a man and yet hardly like a man, something unutterable'. This figure challenges Zarathustra with a riddle: 'what is the *revenge on the witness*?' But Zarathustra knows this 'ugliest man' for who he is: the murderer of God, who took revenge upon the one being who could see through him.[72] The figure admits as much:

'But he – *had* to die: he looked with eyes that saw *everything* – he saw the depths and abysses of man, all man's hidden disgrace and ugliness.

'His pity knew no shame: he crept into my dirtiest corners. This most curious, most over-importunate, over-compassionate god had to die. . . .

'The god who saw everything, *even man*: this god had to die! Man could not *endure* that such a witness should live.'[73]

This is no noble act of liberation, no humanist slaying of a tyrant; this is a squalid act of jealous revenge on he who sees our weakness. Instead of accepting the grandeur of our own failure, we slay that grandeur and then unwittingly elaborate our inadequacies, resentments and guilt into 'slave moralities'. These slave moralities become projections of our inadequacy and imperfection that nevertheless reinforce the sense of failure by their typically categorical, absolute character; our power thereby institutes its very powerlessness and reinforces the sense of resentment,[74] and 'progress' becomes a cover for the revenge of the weak. Selfhood is constructed through punitive self-denial, a self-sacrifice in a culture of self-interest that no longer recognizes the sacrificial. 'The enmity of the self to sacrifice therefore entails a "sacrifice" of part of the self', suggests Connerton,[75] following Horkheimer and Adorno, who add, even more strongly, that 'The history of civilisation is the history of the introversion of the sacrifice. In other words: the history of renunciation.'[76]

Remember the concluding sentence of Nietzsche's first parable of the death of God: 'Must we not ourselves become gods simply to seem worthy of it?' This suggests that God's death itself should be seen as essentially sacrificial. We become God through sacrificing him; we sacrifice to ourselves, rather like the Hindu god who cyclically dismembers himself in a sacrificial act of self-creation. But the logic of sacrifice is a logic of symbolic exchange that makes no sense in modern times, so we attempt to escape its implications by minimizing its effects, hanging on to values and choices that no longer offer consolation. Ultimately, God is killed out of fear of the sacred, inability to confront what it means.

The killing of God should be the ultimate transgressive act; but the implication of the argument so far is that it can hardly be recognized in those terms, terms that would imply our elevation to God's level, our participation in the sacred through the very act of transgression itself. And it is a common theme linking both the Christian tradition and its secular alternatives or successors that transgression and taboo are not part of the sacred. Instead, the transgression is subtly denied and devalued in that God would conventionally be said not to have been killed, but to have been exposed as non-existent, as never having existed, as having been Error, *the* great error of pre-modern humankind. Christ's great self-sacrifice is answered by a merely 'metaphorical' sacrifice, in which we sacrifice only the knowledge of God's existence.

If we are therefore unable to participate in the cycle of death and rebirth through an acceptance of our part in God's death, it is our own deaths, instead, that move centre stage, symbolizing the futility of our godlike pretensions to omnipotence. Death becomes the ultimate horror, the unsanctified transgression, that which gives life its meaning through the very exile, the disavowal, of its power. Death as the ultimate 'end of desire' is basic to Freud's theory of the death instinct, so that the very imperfections of life, the unsatisfiability of desire, gives us this sense of the drive to oblivion as the paradoxical meaning of life itself.[77] This is also central to Bataille's theme of the sacred as a search for continuity through the dissolution and transcendence of the boundaries of the self in transgression, death signifying the ultimate continuity that transcends experience itself.

Bataille takes the dualism of the sacred – the dialectic of holy and unholy, taboo and transgression – and presents its fate as a key to the fate of modernity itself. The sacred is, literally, something 'set apart' as different, and powerful; but so is the word 'taboo', in its original meaning. The word comes from the Polynesian 'tapu', by which something is 'marked out' as sacred, warning people that these are places or objects of power and danger. In this context, transgression and taboo exist in tense but fruitful juxtaposition; the sacred requires the transgression of the everyday boundaries that separate us, through festival, orgiastic carnival and communion, ecstasy, licence, laughter and violence. What normally disgusts or appals us now serves to unite us. Bataille thus suggests that 'The profane world is the world of taboos. The sacred world depends on limited acts of transgression.' To obey the law is human; to break it, divine. A religion that incorporates excess and transgression makes possible the sacred sense of community, though encouraging a creative dis-order.

Within the Christian tradition, however, all this seems strange. 'Christian religious feeling has by and large opposed the spirit of transgression', claims Bataille. The duality of the sacred has been moralized and reduced by *expelling* the unholy and identifying the holy with a transcendental notion of divinity and goodness. 'The sacred' thus becomes fractured. No longer is it true that the impure is as divine as the pure; transgression is no longer the cause of the Devil's divinity, but of his fall, his expulsion from the sacred. 'The realm of religion is reduced to that of the God of Good, whose limits are those of light.'[78] The effect, writes Bataille, is that

> the divine becomes rational and moral and relegates the malefic sacred to the sphere of the profane. . . .
>
> In granting the operative power of the divine over the real, man had in practice subordinated the divine to the real. He slowly reduced its violence to the sanction of the real order that morality constitutes, provided that the real order conforms, precisely in morality, to the universal order of reason . . . morality and reason are divinized.[79]

Paradoxically, then, Christianity prepares the way for its own demise through this splitting of the sacred, but at the same time contributes to shaping the world of modernity. The splitting of the sacred entails its disavowal and misrecognition. On the one hand, we have the remains of the beneficent sacred, located for example in the civilizing process and the control of 'dirt', so that Bernice Martin can argue that 'the sacred quality inherent in the creation and maintenance of domestic order has not disappeared as a *fact* but has simply been expunged from the *language* in which we customarily describe the activity'. Hence, 'Like so many other modern manifestations of the sacred, its ritual nature has become invisible to us.'[80] Yet it is not *simply* a matter of language; the experience itself is affected by this missing dimension of meaning. Discussing the converse situation of the transgressive side of the sacred, Angela Carter makes a related point: observing that 'the very act of defilement reinforces the holiness of the temple', she adds that 'In a secular world, the notion of the impure is meaningless. Only a true believer can see the pure glamour of the blasphemy.'[81] Again, one must be careful: the modern world has not been without the temptations of breaking powerful taboos, even if the religious dimension of meaning is less strong. There may be a sense in which sexuality is very significant here, exemplifying powerful possibilities for transgressive experiences beyond the conventional boundaries of self and body that are normally so strictly adhered to in a self-consciously civilized and rationalized culture: 'all eroticism has a sacramental character', as Bataille puts it.

'Sacredness misunderstood is readily identified with Evil';[82] these transgressive acts are readily denounced by conventional moralists. Yet the real evil may reside elsewhere. 'The flatness to which a dualism without transcendence is limited opens up the mind to the sovereignty of evil which is the unleashing of violence',[83] argues Bataille; in preventing or devaluing the sacred acts of transgression, the domination of secular rationalism may result not just in civilization but in violence and oppression. As Conrad realized, in the figure of Kurtz,[84] and as will be seen in a later chapter, discussing the Holocaust, a civilization that claims to have overcome evil may only end up reproducing it.

Awe, Otherness and Representation: the Subject of the Sublime

God's shadow is of major significance in another area, too. The emergence of the aesthetic of the sublime in the eighteenth century testifies to this sense of a lost yet powerful transcendence, a sense crucial to the forging of a link between art and nature. Weiskel writes that

> The emotions traditionally religious were displaced from the Deity and became associated first with the immensity of space and secondarily with the natural phenomena (oceans, mountains) which seemed to approach that immensity. Soon a sense of the numinous was diffused through all the grander aspects of nature. The mental result was enormously to enhance the prestige of the sensible imagination as the faculty which mediated the divine presence felt to be immanent in nature. . . . Indeed, the imagination became the surest guide and recourse for the moral sense.[85]

Artists and poets increasingly attempted to depict and transmit a sense of the sublime, and 'the sublime' became *the* central category of aesthetic theory. In contrast to the beautiful, the sublime seemed to point 'beyond', communicating the majesty and power of a natural order to which the mystery of the divine still clung.

This 'nature' is not conventional Enlightenment nature, however, nature as lawful and rational; rather, it is spontaneous, uncontrollable, awesome. Hence Kant can argue that 'nature excites the ideas of the sublime in its chaos or in its wildest and most irregular disorder and desolation'.[86] The sublime began where conventional readings of landscape or text broke down; it 'found in that very collapse the foundation for another order of meaning', claims Weiskel, and thus 'dramatized the rhythm of transcendence'.[87] It promised access to transcendence in an era when God's own transcendence had become problematical. Roberts adds that 'when the gods withdraw from the world, then the world itself starts to appear as other, to reveal an imaginary depth which becomes meaningful in itself',[88] posing a challenge and a potential that must be explored.

Part of the significance of this is that it represents a further impetus to the development of selfhood. The emphasis was individualistic, on the self and its experiences. The attempt to transcend the self was the attempt to lose oneself in the grandeur of nature, or its artistic depiction; it pointed away from the social dimensions of community. If 'nature' acquires 'depth' through the notion of appearances that hide deeper truths, so does the self. Taylor sees in this the emergence of what he calls 'expressivism', the idea that we need to 'express' an 'inner voice'. 'It is no longer some impersonal "form" or "nature" which comes to actuality, but a being capable of self-articulation', he writes, adding that 'Depth lies in there being always, inescapably, something beyond our articulative power', yet something that nevertheless *has* to be articulated, as it expresses our inner selfhood. This expressivism has become a basic feature of modern culture, and suggests a sense in which 'We are all called to live up to our originality.'[89]

Thus it is on the terrain of this asocial sacred that we encounter that powerful fusion of elements that constitutes the modern myth of the artist. For the Romantics, reacting against the Enlightenment disenchantment of the world, the work of art is 'a presence which opens onto the infinite', as Roberts puts it, adding that 'Modern art is the continuation of the sacred by other means.'[90] The imagination, now firmly linked to the subject, becomes a powerful source of artistic creativity, even though there is a cost: the constant threat that celebrating its very creativity may detract from the claims to insight into, and representation of, the challenge of transcendence and otherness. Thus there is always a tension in this art, through this very emphasis on the intensely personal experience of the sublime. In a sense, the sublime is unrepresentable, inexpressible, and therefore incommunicable; the attempt to depict it necessarily draws on established images and strategies of representation, but these can never wholly capture it, whereas totally novel strategies necessarily become as incommunicable as the experience they strive to replicate. From here, through Romanticism and Bohemianism to the revolutions of modernism, we encounter the whole paradoxical story of modern art.

Negotiating these tensions required what came to be seen as 'genius'. 'The artist is become a creator God', proclaimed Herder,[91] and Coleridge saw the exercise of the imagination as 'a repetition in the finite mind of the eternal act of creation'.[92] Campbell suggests that God had increasingly become 'a supernatural force, which, whilst present throughout the natural world, also existed within each individual in the form of a unique and personalized spirit; that of his "genius"'.[93] In a development of this theme, Gouldner argues that Romanticism thus becomes crucial to our sense of the 'modern', which begins to emerge 'when man is seen, not merely as a creature that can *discover* the world, but also as one who can *create* new meanings and values, and can thus change himself and fundamentally transform his world', not just unearth or reflect an unchanging order.[94]

While this creativity is a latent power in all of us, it is not easy to realize this power; to do so requires stepping outside the taken-for-granted constraints – and temptations – of everyday life. Here we encounter another sense in which the artist is heir to the sacred, through incorporating its transgressive dimension. The artist necessarily breaks the rules, in the search for insight and transcendence. Bourgeois conventions should be overthrown in the pursuit of the truths of experience and art, and this Romantic myth of the artist as rebel becomes central to the cultural role of art in modernity. And this returns us to the sublime, for Romanticism attacked the precedence given to the beautiful, to 'good taste' and decorum, instead prizing the contingent, the exotic, the grotesque, the incongruous, the dissolution of boundaries; the brightness and clarity of the sun are valued less than the nuances of twilight and moonlight, with their hint of mystery – and possible danger.

It is striking that in his *Philosophical Enquiry into the Origin of our Ideas of the Sublime and the Beautiful* of 1757 – the most influential pre-Kantian treatment of these issues – Edmund Burke frequently reiterates the significance of terror as an element in our feelings of the sublime. Infinity, he suggests, fills the mind with 'delightful horror'; and objects 'are delightful when we have an idea of pain and danger, without being actually in such circumstances. . . . Whatever excites this delight, I call *sublime*.' This idea of proximity plus distance is important: the sublime has a powerful presence in its separateness, an aura. If it produces astonishment, even horror, it can also have milder effects, of admiration, reverence and respect.[95] Much of this is echoed in an early essay by Kant, where he writes that a raging storm can 'arouse enjoyment but with horror', feelings that can also include dread, wonder or melancholy; and whereas 'The sublime *moves*, the beautiful *charms*.'[96]

In both Burke and Kant, suggests Lyotard, 'the sublime emerges when there is no longer a beautiful form', so that the feeling of the sublime is 'the feeling of something monstrous. *Das Unform*. Formless. The retreat of regulation and rules is the cause of the feeling of the sublime.' Hence the contradictory combination of pleasure and displeasure, even terror, and the way the sublime points to 'the importance of death in life, because terror . . . is a feeling of the imminence of death'.[97] The grandeur and power of the other threatens the extinction of self. The sublime – 'sub-limen', underneath or between the boundaries – suggests the limitlessness, the power, of what confronts us. 'I know of nothing sublime which is not some modification of power', writes Burke.[98] It presents us, suggests Hebdige, with 'the threat of the absolute other – the limitations of our language and our capacity to think and judge, the fact of our mortality.'[99] The condition of sublimity is one of unease, restlessness and dissonance, the threat of chaos and collapse, but a threat that can be transformative, bracing, self-constituting through the very threat to self-destruction.[100] Rules, traditions, conventions: all are momentarily suspended in this influx of power that holds the subject in its identity as proximity and distance to the other, since the latter is thus simultaneously present and absent, internal yet separate. The subject is constituted in anxiety, a state that becomes central to individuation itself; and it is also an anxiety that becomes desire for the absent, unease that the present is also a lack. And Weiskel suggests that the sublime is also a kind of homeopathic therapy resolving uneasiness 'by means of the stronger, more concentrated – but momentary – anxiety involved in astonish-ment and terror'.[101] The cause of the disease becomes its vicarious cure.

The ramifications of this are widespread and important. The discourse on alienation seems to have its source in this suggestion that the sublime institutes a dissonance in the heart of modern selfhood, and the Freudian concept of the *Umheimlich*, the 'unhomely' or 'uncanny' captures this sense in which the experi-ence of modernity has entailed an inherent dimension of 'homelessness'. Hence Turner's suggestion that there is a sense in which 'the origins of the modern and modernism may be derived less from the male principles of universalism, ration-ality and coherence than from the uncanny, weird principles of otherness, contra-diction, ambivalence and catastrophe'.[102] Thus the otherness of the sublime may be constitutive of the modern structure of the social as well as of the self; the dialectic of proximity and distance is, after all, a reminder of one of the key figures in modernity, that of the stranger, already encountered in discussing the city, and theatricality. Tester suggests that the milieu of strangers is 'apprehended as content without form', and 'able to overflow the societal ability to understand it'; hence 'the milieu of strangers is formless; we cannot perceive it. It is sublime.'[103] There can be delight in the terrors this can produce, so long as a certain 'distance' is maintained; and, one might add, it is 'civility' that maintains and routinizes the distance, as the mask through which self can be other and other can be another one of us.

Beyond civility, though, lies a more troublesome theatricality, the fantasy incorporation of the otherness of the sublime, and, more particularly, melodrama itself. As has been seen,[104] Brooks argues that melodrama as a cultural form has its source in the late eighteenth century, and is a sacred form for secular times. With melodrama, he argues, there is 'a recognition of the diabolical forces which inhabit our world and our inner being. Since these forces achieve no sacred status as wholly other, they appear, rather, to abide within nature and, particularly, within nature's creature, man.' Thus does melodrama both replicate, and attempt to recuperate, the deep structure of the sublime, glossing the terror of the encounter in moralistic terms, as a battle of good and evil. It thereby keeps open, suggests Brooks, 'the possibility of acceding to the latent through the signs of the world'.[105]

Another dimension to come to the fore is gender. To experience the sublime is to be ravished by a powerful force; for Burke, suggests Eagleton, the sublime is 'the lawless masculine force which violates yet perpetually renews the feminine enclosure of beauty'.[106] The sublime may terrify us, but we enjoy being 'forced to submit'. This is a gendered discourse, then, and as de Bolla argues, it operates the distinction between 'the masculine experience of power, authority and sublimity, and the feminine experience of subjection, obedience and beauty'.[107] Kant's own essay explicitly maps the sublime/beauty contrast on to the masculine/feminine, and he adds that 'sublime attitudes stimulate esteem, but beautiful ones, love'.[108] But this is not the 'esteem' that might be felt for law or morality, rather it is awe at unbridled potency, together with desire for it; if beauty is reassuring, the sublime is the opposite, yet both can be sought after. The yearning for the sublime is a craving for the charisma of origin, the aura of the sacred, the moment that founds law, morality or tradition yet exceeds and denies it, the violence of creation that cannot be tamed and restrained. Turner hints at this when he points to Derrida's suggestion that *Gewalt*, in German, means violence, force, power, might, but is also associated with the concept of valuation, the sacred, and has connotations of strength and immensity; and he adds that, in the Judaeo-Christian tradition, 'God is simultaneously the male, the almighty and the source of all values, but also the origin of violence, retribution and jealousy.'[109] Eagleton develops these themes as follows:

> The Kantian sublime is in effect a kind of unconscious process of infinite desire. . . . The subject of the sublime is accordingly decentred, plunged into loss and pain, undergoes a crisis and fading of identity; yet without this unwelcome violence we would never be stirred out of ourselves, never prodded into enterprise and achievement. We would lapse back into the feminine enclosure of the imaginary, where desire is captivated and suspended.[110]

So all this is powerfully suggestive of an illicit subtext, a disruption of orthodox gender-coding; the 'masculine' sublime hints at the attractions of passivity and feminisation. De Bolla cites a 1781 text in which the sublime 'transports', 'ravishes', 'commands', and the person at its mercy is 'unable to resist', since 'his passions are no longer his own'.[111] To submit to the masculine sublime is to be 'unmanned', even as one thereby attains creative potency.

Finally, we can return to the problems of representation posed by the sublime. The experience of the sublime clearly entails as much emphasis on the subject as on the object of experience. It is crucial to Kant's argument that it is not natural phenomena in themselves that are sublime, but human responses: sublimity, he writes, is 'found in the mind, for no sensible form can contain the sublime properly so-called', and what is sublime is 'not so much the object, as our own state of mind in the estimation of it'.[112] We cannot experience or represent 'the infinite' or 'awesome grandeur' in themselves; it is rather that natural phenomena precipitate a response in us that we characterize in these terms. 'No object of Sense is sublime in itself; but only as far as I make it a symbol of some Idea', wrote Coleridge; for example, a circle can become sublime 'when I contemplate eternity under that figure'.[113] Through the symbol what is beyond reach can, in a sense, be attainable. However, it must be remembered that just as natural phenomena are not 'really' sublime, so the concepts of reason themselves (infinity, totality, and so on) cannot 'really' be imaged, presented in concrete form. Mary Warnock argues that the sublime

> excites in us ideas which we realize *cannot* be represented by any visible or otherwise sensible forms – ideas which cannot be restricted or brought down to earth by any image-making power of the imagination. . . .
> The idea somehow embodied in the sublime object is beyond representation or explanation, but *yet* can be apprehended by the human mind. *We* are grand, in that we can touch such grandeur and be touched by it, though we shall always struggle and fail to say what it means.

Thus can an object become 'a symbol of something which is forever beyond it'.[114] Presented with images of objects, nature, the mind cannot wholly grasp these through ideas; and confronted with ideas, it cannot wholly realize them by embedding them in images of the object. The symbol is constituted as a relation between two incommensurables, present to each other through absence.

If, as de Bolla has argued, this 'discourse of the sublime' was crucial in the emergence of the modern, autonomous subject, then this subject is constituted with a structure of absence within.[115] 'Mind' is an inner space that cannot wholly be filled: trying to grasp the sublime, the subject grasps this inexpressible, interior dimension; trying to express itself, it finds itself forever unable to do so adequately. The influx of the sublime brings with it both excess and emptiness. It presents us with the excess in experience as an experience of excess, the recalcitrance of experience to concept; it also presents us with the inadequacy of concept to experience, the gap, the inner discontinuity.[116] The sublime points to the inability to attain what is beyond yet also within, constituted as a subjectivity with depth, mind as a creativity that is inaccessible to its own reflexive grasp. The sublime is the failure of representation, the attempt to represent the unrepresentable. As Roberts puts it, 'At the heart of the modern is the irruption of the sublime, the unbridgeable chasm between our capacity to imagine and our capacity to think the world.'[117] Lyotard goes further, suggesting that 'modernity takes place in the withdrawal of the real and according to the sublime relation between the presentable and the conceivable'.[118] The death of God institutes a discontinuity in the heart of the world. The sublime, one can conclude, is the alienated presence of the mystery of representation; it thereby performs the presence of the absence of God.

Notes

1   B. McGrane, *Beyond Anthropology* (California University Press, 1989), p. 57.
2   E. Durkheim, *Elementary Forms of the Religious Life* (Allen and Unwin, 1915), p. 213; see also his 'Individualism and the Intellectuals', in W. Pickering (ed.) *Durkheim on Religion* (Routledge, 1975).
3   M. Foucault, 'Preface to Transgression', in his *Language, Counter-Memory, Practice* (Cornell University Press, 1977), p. 33. See also my *Transgressing the Modern* (Blackwell, 1999), ch. 7.
4   S. Sontag, *A Susan Sontag Reader* (Penguin, 1983), pp. 212, 231.
5   A. Hawkins, 'Two Pathographies: A Study in Illness and Literature', *Journal of Medicine and Philosophy* (1984), 9:3.
6   Cited in C. Herzlich and J. Pierret, *Illness and Self in Society* (Johns Hopkins University Press, 1987), p. 146.
7   Hawkins, 'Two Pathographies', p. 243.
8   Cited in ibid., p. 245.
9   P. Slack, *The Impact of Plague in Tudor and Stuart England* (Routledge, 1985), pp. 29, 29, 39.
10 E. Gaskell, *The Life of Charlotte Brontë* (Everyman, 1992), p. 281.

11   E. Bronfen, *Over Her Dead Body: Death, Femininity and the Aesthetic* (Manchester University Press, 1992), p. 77.

12   N. Auerbach, *Private Theatricals: The Lives of the Victorians* (Harvard University Press, 1990), pp. 87, 87, 89–90.

13   S. Sontag, *Illness as Metaphor* (Penguin, 1983), pp. 20, 35, 48.

14   Cited in ibid., pp. 36–7.

15   Bronfen, *Over Her Dead Body*, p. 84.

16   L. Wittgenstein, *Tractatus Logico-Philosophicus* (Routledge, 1963), 6.4311.

17   Auerbach, *Private Theatricals*, p. 109.

18   Bronfen, *Over Her Dead Body*, p. 88.

19   M. Carnes, *Secret Ritual and Manhood in Victorian America* (Yale University Press, 1989), p. 152.

20   S. Gilbert and S. Gubar, *The Madwoman in the Attic* (Yale University Press, 1979), pp. 24, 25. See also my *Transgressing the Modern*, ch. 5.

21   P. Ariès, *The Hour of Our Death* (Vintage, 1982), p. 373.

22   N. Elias, *The Loneliness of the Dying* (Blackwell, 1985), p. 85.

23   Ariès, *Hour of Our Death*, p. 612.

24   See discussion in Hawkins, 'Two Pathographies', passim.

25   Sontag, *Illness*, pp. 68–9, 22–3.

26   Herzlich and Pierret, *Illness and Self*, ch. 3; and I. Illich, *Medical Nemesis* (Calder and Boyars, 1975), p. 143.

27   Hawkins, 'Two Pathographies', pp. 237–8.

28   Z. Bauman, *Mortality, Immortality, and Other Life Strategies* (Polity, 1992), p. 163

29   D. Sudnow, *Passing On: The Social Organization of Dying* (Prentice-Hall, 1967), ch. 3. See also L. Prior, *The Social Organisation of Death* (Macmillan, 1989), and, for an overview of recent trends, P. Mellor and C. Shilling, 'Modernity, self-identity and the sequestration of death', *Sociology* (1993), 27:3.

30   Ariès, *Hour of Our Death*, p. 28.

31   Illich, *Medical Nemesis*, p. 128.

32   Sontag, *Illness*, p. 59.

33   R. Crawford, 'A cultural account of "health": control, release, and the social body', in J. B. McKinlay (ed.) *Issues in the Political Economy of Health Care* (Tavistock, 1984), p. 63.

34   J. Baudrillard, *Symbolic Exchange and Death* (Sage, 1993), p. 160.

35   R. N. Bellah, 'Civil Religion in America', in *Daedalus* (1967), 96:1; and R. Huntington and P. Metcalf, *Celebrations of Death: The Anthropology of Mortuary Ritual* (Cambridge University Press, 1979), p. 207.

36   Cited in Huntington and Metcalf, *Celebrations*, p. 207.

37   Huntington and Metcalf, *Celebrations*, p. 205.

38   W. Hamilton, 'Death of God Theologies Today', in T. Altizer and W. Hamilton (eds.) *Radical Theology and the Death of God* (Bobbs-Merrill, 1966), p. 28.

39   See A. Funkenstein, *Theology and the Scientific Imagination* (Princeton University Press, 1986), and D. Zaret, 'Religion, Science and Printing in the Public Spheres in Seventeenth-Century England', in C. Calhoun (ed.) *Habermas and the Public Sphere* (MIT Press, 1992).

40   Cited in L. Goldmann, *The Hidden God* (Routledge, 1964), p. 29.

41   Goldmann, *Hidden God*, p. 37 and passim.

42   R. Jackson, *Fantasy: The Literature of Subversion* (Methuen, 1981), p. 19 and ch. 8.

43   H.-G. Gadamer, *Truth and Method* (Seabury, 1975), p. 514.

44 M. Douglas, *Natural Symbols* (Penguin, 1973), p. 70.

45 E. Heller, *Kafka* (Fontana, 1974), p. 119.

46 E. Heller, *The Disinherited Mind* (Penguin, 1961), pp. 231, 232.

47 Heller, *Kafka*, p. 120.

48 Heller, *Disinherited Mind*, p. 231.

49 G. Bataille, 'The Sorcerer's Apprentice', in his *Visions of Excess* (Minnesota University Press, 1985), p. 225.

50 S. L. Carter, *The Culture of Disbelief* (Basic Books, 1993), p. 4. See also J. Butler, *Awash in a Sea of Faith* (Harvard University Press, 1990).

51 M. Weber, 'The Protestant Sects and the Spirit of Capitalism', in *From Max Weber* (Routledge, 1970), p. 305.

52 A. MacIntyre, *Secularization and Moral Change* (Oxford University Press, 1967), p. 32.

53 E. Gellner, *Postmodernism, Reason and Religion* (Routledge, 1992), p. 5. See also J. McLeod, 'The Cult of Divine America', *International Journal of Moral and Social Sciences* (1991), 6:2.

54 Carter, *Culture of Disbelief*, pp. 15, 5, 6.

55 F. Nietzsche, *The Gay Science* (Vintage, 1974), Aphorism 125.

56 W. Connolly, *Political Theory and Modernity* (Blackwell, 1989), pp. 9, 10.

57 R. Rorty, *Philosophy and The Mirror of Nature* (Princeton University Press, 1980).

58 M. Weber, 'Science as a Vocation', in *From Max Weber*, p. 144.

59 S. Whimster, 'The Secular Ethic and the Culture of Modernism', in S. Lash and S. Whimster (eds.) *Max Weber, Rationality and Modernity* (Allen and Unwin, 1987), p. 265.

60 Connolly, *Political Theory*, p. 11.

61 Weber, 'Science' in *From Max Weber*, p. 148.

62 Whimster, 'The Secular Ethic', p. 281.

63 M. Weber, 'Religious Rejections of the World and their Directions', in *From Max Weber*, p. 342.

64 See J.-F. Lyotard, *The Postmodern Condition* (Minnesota University Press, 1984).

65 D. Sayer, *Capitalism and Modernity: An Excursus on Marx and Weber* (Routledge, 1991), p. 152.

66 A. MacIntyre, *After Virtue* (Duckworth, 1985), pp. 12, 23, and ch. 2.

67 E. Durkheim, *Selected Writings* (Cambridge University Press, 1972), ch. 8, brings together the most relevant pieces.

68 Weber, 'Religious Rejections', in *From Max Weber*, pp. 356, 357; and see also p. 140.

69 F. Nietzsche, *On the Genealogy of Morals* (Random House, 1969), section I, p. 15.

70 Connolly, *Political Theory*, pp. 150, 157, 157.

71 G. Stauth and B. Turner, *Nietzsche's Dance: Resentment, Reciprocity and Resistance in Social Life* (Blackwell, 1988), and B. Turner, *For Weber* (Routledge, 1981), ch. 5, include relevant discussion.

72 F. Nietzsche, *Thus Spake Zarathustra* (Penguin, 1961), pp. 275–6.

73 Ibid., pp. 278, 279.

74 Nietzsche, *Genealogy*, section I.

75 P. Connerton, *The Tragedy of Enlightenment* (Cambridge University Press, 1980), p. 70.

76 M. Horkheimer and T. Adorno, *The Dialectic of Enlightenment* (Seabury, 1972), p. 55; and Stauth and Turner, *Nietzsche's Dance*, p. 227.

77 S. Freud, *Civilization and its Discontents* (Hogarth, 1930).

78 G. Bataille, *Eroticism* (Marion Boyars, 1987), pp. 68, 118, 123; see also pp. 120–3. See also the account in M. Richardson, *Georges Bataille* (Routledge, 1994), ch. 6.

79 G. Bataille, *Theory of Religion* (Zone Books, 1989), pp. 72, 71.

80 B. Martin, '"Mother Wouldn't Like It!": Housework as Magic', in *Theory, Culture and Society* (1984), 2:2, pp. 24–5.

81 A. Carter, *The Sadeian Woman* (Virago, 1979), p. 72. See also my *Transgressing the Modern*, ch. 7, for a discussion of sexuality in this context.

82 Bataille, *Eroticism*, pp. 15–16, 124.

83 Bataille, *Theory of Religion*, p. 79.

84 See my *Transgressing the Modern*, ch. 3.

85 T. Weiskel, *The Romantic Sublime: Studies in the Structure and Psychology of Transcendence* (Johns Hopkins University Press, 1986), p. 14.

86 I. Kant, *Critique of Judgement* (Hafner, 1951), section 23.

87 Weiskel, *Romantic Sublime*, p. 22.

88 D. Roberts, 'Sublime Theories: Reason and Imagination in Modernity', in G. Robinson and J. Rundell (eds.) *Rethinking Imagination: Culture and Creativity* (Routledge, 1994), p. 173.

89 C. Taylor, *Sources of the Self* (Cambridge University Press, 1992), pp. 375, 390, 376.

90 Roberts, 'Sublime Theories', p. 173.

91 Cited in Taylor, *Sources*, p. 378.

92 S. T. Coleridge, *Biographia Literaria* (Dent, 1975), p. 167.

93 C. Campbell, *The Romantic Ethic and the Spirit of Modern Consumerism* (Blackwell, 1989), p. 182.

94 A. Gouldner, *For Sociology* (Penguin, 1975), p. 330, and ch. 11.

95 E. Burke, *A Philosophical Enquiry into the Origin of our Ideas of the Sublime and Beautiful* (Blackwell, 1987), pp. 73, 51, 57.

96 I. Kant, *Observations on the Feeling of the Beautiful and Sublime* (California University Press, 1991), p. 47; and see section 28.

97 J.-F. Lyotard, 'Complexity and the Sublime', in L. Appignanesi (ed.) *Postmodernism* (Free Association Books, 1989), pp. 24, 22.

98 Burke, *Philosophical Enquiry*, p. 64.

99 D. Hebdige, 'The Impossible Object: Towards a Sociology of the Sublime', *New Formations* (1987), 1, p. 51.

100 J. Rundell, 'Creativity and Judgement: Kant on Reason and Imagination', in Robinson and Rundell, *Rethinking Imagination*, p. 103.

101 Weiskel, *Romantic Sublime*, p. 18.

102 B. Turner, Introduction to C. Buci-Glucksmann, *Baroque Reason: The Aesthetics of Modernity* (Sage, 1994), p. 33.

103 K. Tester, *Civil Society* (Routledge, 1992), pp. 159, 154.

104 See ch. 1.

105 P. Brooks, *The Melodramatic Imagination* (Yale University Press, 1976), pp. 205, 18–19, 202.

106 T. Eagleton, *The Ideology of the Aesthetic* (Blackwell, 1990), p. 54.

107 P. de Bolla, *The Discourse of the Sublime: Readings in History, Aesthetics and the Subject* (Blackwell, 1989), p. 58.

108 Kant, *Observations*, p. 51, and section 3.

109 Turner, Introduction to Buci-Glucksmann, *Baroque Reason*, p. 33.

110 Eagleton, *Ideology*, p. 90.

111 Cited in de Bolla, *Discourse of Sublime*, p. 57.

112 Kant, *Critique*, sections 23, 26.
113 Cited in de Bolla, *Discourse of Sublime*, p. 46.
114 M. Warnock, *Imagination* (Faber, 1976), pp. 56, 61, 63.
115 de Bolla, *Discourse of Sublime*, p. 6.
116 Ibid., p. 12; and Weiskel, *Romantic Sublime*, p. 17.
117 Roberts, 'Sublime theories', p. 174.
118 J.-F. Lyotard, 'Answering the Question: What is Postmodernism?', in *Postmodern Condition*, p. 79.

8 Machines and Skyscrapers:

Technology as Experience, Hope and Fear

The Railway Machine

'The modern world began with the coming of the railways. They turned the known universe upside down. They made a greater and more immediate impact than any other mechanical or industrial innovation before or since.'[1] Faith expands this bold claim by pointing out that in the UK, it took only a quarter of a century after the first passenger service began in 1830 for the essentials of the present-day rail network to be put in place, and by the end of the century the railway revolution had transformed, redefined and expanded the limits of the 'civilized world' throughout Europe, Russia, North America, and beyond. Nor was this just a matter of economics, politics and geography. It was surely the railways that provided the most graphic embodiment of the new power of technology as a force that was shaping and reshaping people's lives, bringing new experiences of space and time, of self and other (whether fellow passengers or hitherto unknown towns and peoples), of travel and landscape, of individualism yet also a sense of being one of a new 'mass public'. In opening up new experiences and new possibilities of experience, the railways simultaneously provided a language and a symbolism with which to report them, and contributed to the constitution of the passengers as modern subjects capable of having – and knowing – such experiences. The railway thus becomes both a precipitant of modernity and an allegory of it: cause and experience, story and representation, all in one. 'In their railway journeys', writes Trachtenberg, 'nineteenth-century people encountered the new conditions of their lives; they encountered themselves as moderns, as dwellers within new structures of regulation and need.'[2]

It is hardly surprising that the railway, in this multiple role as agent, experience and symbol, should feature strongly in the novel, since the latter is well suited to exploiting this multiplicity and allowing the railway to feature as a powerful presence in its own right. Railway journeys themselves provide an engine to move the plot along in *Anna Karenina*, and the train itself constitutes a dynamic force that Tolstoy draws on for both its metaphorical and its literal potential. In the second of the three major episodes featuring train journeys, Anna returns to St Petersburg, knowing that she is powerfully attracted to Vronsky, and the journey becomes so strongly linked to her own shifting emotions that it is difficult to separate the two.

Anna entered the carriage and soon 'took out a paper knife and an English novel and settled down to read'. Initially, though, she found it difficult to concentrate, being distracted by a snowstorm outside. But afterwards, 'it grew monotonous; there was the same jolting and jarring, the same snow . . . the same voices, and little by little her attention became absorbed in the book'.[3] The regular pulse of the train's motion, together with its capacity for sudden acceleration, and the views outside, do indeed seem generally to have stimulated this mixture of excitement and lethargy in the passengers. For Dickens, writes Gay, such travel was 'at once exciting and soporific',[4] and the author himself commented that the railway carriage was 'always a wonderfully suggestive place to me when I am alone'.[5] Nor was Anna the only rail traveller to take up reading. The tendency for the middle classes to read on trains was remarked on from very early on, and a certain W. H. Smith got his big break in the late 1840s by gaining the exclusive right to sell books at several major railway stations. Newspaper reading was given a big fillip, and Routledge founded a Railway Library with novels by Hawthorne and Cooper.[6] Schivelbusch suggests that 'The travelers in the train compartment did not know what to do with each other, and reading became a surrogate for the communication that no longer took place.'

Such reading individualizes; and this gives a clue to the major alternative attraction, as exemplified by Anna's initial interest in the snowstorm, namely the contemplation of the view outside. In the compartment, the traveller was separated from the landscape, which passed by as a fleeting, evanescent picture; the view is without depth, like a constantly shifting painted surface, an essay in impressionism. Velocity blurred the foreground objects, so effectively the foreground was obliterated.[7] 'The flowers by the side of the road are no longer flowers but flecks, or rather streaks, of red or white', wrote Victor Hugo; 'there are no longer any points, everything becomes a streak . . . the towns, the steeples, and the trees perform a crazy mingling dance on the horizon'.[8] Later, Simmel referred to 'the rapid crowding of changing images, the sharp discontinuity in the grasp of a single glance and the unexpectedness of onrushing impressions'.[9] The traveller was now decisively separated from the landscape, rather than part of it. Michel de Certeau comments on this spectatorial distance: 'You shall not touch; the more you see, the less you hold – a dispossession of the land in favour of a greater trajectory for the eye.'[10] In effect, we encounter the transformation of landscape into panorama; the railroad 'choreographed the landscape', as Schivelbusch puts it. This experience of landscape as panorama could be alienating, monotonous, or aesthetically pleasing, but both responses depend on this initial experience of detachment, of passing *by* even as one is passing *through*. In contrast to traditional perception, argues Schivelbusch, such panoramic perception 'no longer belonged to the same space as the perceived objects: the traveller saw the objects, etc. *through* the apparatus which moved him through the world',[11] and this 'apparatus', of glass and iron, incarcerates and separates the subject of experience even as it convinces that subject of its wholeness, its invincible unity.

In a sense, though, that conviction never fully convinces, and the train journey also serves both to reveal and produce the experiences that threaten the constructed unity of this subject of the panoramic vision. The impressionism of vision can easily become an impressionism of selfhood. When Anna became absorbed in the book, she entered into the lives of the characters, but kept returning to her own situation, the jolts of the train corresponding to the jolts of her own consciousness, sliding in and out of recognition of her quandary and the conflicts of pleasure and shame that her emerging feelings about Vronsky provoked. Suddenly she saw her reflection in the carriage window: 'And what am I doing here? Am I myself or someone else? . . . She was terrified at her own reflections, but could not draw herself away from them.' Then, further confused, she realized they had come to a station, and she got out for a few minutes, to try to regain her bearings. This was the point at which she saw Vronsky again, and realized that he had followed her on to the train. When they finally reached St Petersburg, to be met by her husband, the disorientation, the changes of perception, continued. He seemed different; she noticed things she had never noticed before. 'Heavens! Why are his ears so large?' At the same time, she had hoped or expected him to look different – in some unspecific way – as though in recognition of her own sense of instability and change. And she realized that the stability of the two selves was a kind of hypocrisy, that 'A sort of pretence characterized her relations with her husband.'[12] One is reminded of Faith's claim that railways and stations were 'the ideal setting for farewells and greetings, redolent of first ventures into new worlds, memorable punctuation marks in people's lives'.[13]

It is another novelist, Proust, who can take us further here. For Proust, railway travel was like a metaphor in that it 'united two distinct individualities of the world, took us from one name to another name'.[14] One is reminded of de Certeau's observation that in modern Athens, vehicles of mass transportation are *metaphorai*; to go to work, or to get home again, you take a metaphor.[15] Anna's journey transposed her between identities, her confusion worse confounded by the shifts in and out of the identities provided by the novel she was attempting to read. The jolts of the train bring her back to her 'self', but in ways that confuse her, and constantly provoke those memories of the past – whether distant, or, as in her case, very recent – that are key moments in the ongoing construction of self-identity as an imaginative linkage between past and present, unity and difference. Memory, for Proust, is itself a metaphor that links these shifting images, of present and past, makes them metaphors of a self that is always contingent, in process. 'Nothing exists until it is corrected by memory to a former existence; the connection between two nonrealities gives them an existence',[16] as Moss puts it. And it is through art that these metaphorical linkages can be crystallized most vividly, so that rail travel could serve not only to provide novel experiences to challenge conventions of artistic representation, but could also stimulate theoretical reflection, thus contributing to the aesthetics of the modernist movement.

The railway journey, then, is also a journey of the self, and it is through metaphor that this can be revealed, given this powerful capacity of metaphor to bridge the inner and outer worlds. This comes out vividly in another great railway novel, *Dombey & Son*. Cutting ruthlessly through communities, destroying all in its path, the railroad symbolizes the indifference and greed of Dombey and Carker, and Dombey's railway journey, after the death of his son Paul, becomes as one with the death of feeling inside him: 'he carried monotony with him, through the rushing landscape', and 'hurried headlong, not through a rich and varied country, but a wilderness of blighted plans and gnawing jealousies'.[17] When Kern concludes that for Proust, as for Joyce, 'travel took place in the mind as much as in the world, and distances depended on the effect of memory, the force of emotions, and the passage of time', this is clearly true of Dickens also.[18]

Ironically, the passenger may simultaneously hang on to the security of the railway compartment and what it represents, while also being frightened of it, in its implicit negation of the change and fluidity through which the self develops. The early compartments were locked and isolated, with no side corridor, and these created a degree of fear and dislike, as if the ability to 'circulate' was vital and its denial was in contradiction to the very nature of travel itself. By the 1860s, indeed, we see the emergence of a medical literature on railway fears and neuroses; distressed dreams could both repeat or anticipate accidents, and a doctor in *The Lancet*, in 1866, reported a female patient 'complaining that she saw the engine coming in at the window', in a violation of the inner/outer boundary that neatly anticipates Freud.[19] However, the train also anticipates, in dreams, the early experience of the cinema, described by Faith as 'an art form seemingly devised with the railways in mind';[20] the train simultaneously links and questions not only the inner/outer boundary, but the reality/representation one as well. The first real motion picture, by Lumière, featured a train arriving at a station, and early audiences reacted with horror to the moving image of the train coming towards them, out of the screen.

The experience of the train journey, then, was significant both because it required boundaries and because it challenged them; it both enforced the dichotomies of identity and precipitated the hopes and fears of their subversion. Through 'circulation' – which became a key concept in nineteenth-century science – both people and commodities could cross the boundaries, embody the metaphorical resolution of the paradox of being two things, in two places, at once.[21] And in the convergence of the panoramic gaze and the experience of circulation, the railways 'created and defined mass tourism', as Faith claims.[22] Passenger and consumer became one. Schivelbusch concludes:

> Henceforth, the localities were no longer spatially individual or autonomous: they were points in the circulation of traffic that made them accessible. From that time on, the places visited by the traveler became increasingly similar to the commodities that were part of the same circulation system. For the twentieth-century tourist, the world has become one huge department store of countrysides and cities.[23]

Thus we see how, as de Certeau suggests, railway travel 'combines dreams with technology'.[24]

And Anna? Her end is foreshadowed at the beginning. At her initial meeting with Vronsky, the guard was run over by the train, and killed; and towards the end of the book, and at the end of the doomed affair, her final train journey to nowhere becomes a journey to her own death, under the wheels of the train itself, the final spur to her suicide being the memory of that earlier death.[25] Indeed, the novel seems to proceed as remorselessly as one of those driverless trains that feature strongly in the late nineteenth-century imagination, and which remind us that dreams can easily be nightmares. Thus, in Zola's *La Bête Humaine*, Lantier and his fireman fall to the rails in their death struggle, and are severed by the wheels, as the train, full of soldiers, accelerates to destruction: 'it roared on and on, a blind and deaf beast let loose amid death and destruction, laden with cannon-fodder.'[26]

A prescient symbol of Europe rushing helplessly to war, this can also be seen, however, to have resonance at other levels. Here, as in Dickens, the train can symbolize the 'self-destructive energy of technological power uncontrolled by ethics', as Sussman puts it, and the closely related link between economic power and moral indifference.[27] In *Dombey & Son*, Carker's death, like Anna's, seems to engage with this fear of powerful technology that is, simultaneously, an attraction to it. Just before the episode – half-accident, half-suicide – in which he is killed by a train, Carker observes an engine, a 'fiery devil', going by. He reflected on 'what a cruel power and might it had. Ugh! To see the great wheels slowly turning, and to think of being run down and crushed!'[28] Many observers wrote of the spectacle of a great train rushing through the night, the mixed emotions at its awesome splendour, this striking visitation of the technological sublime.[29] The train journey, embodying this, could easily induce an excitement that would be tinged with apprehension and fear, an awareness of the violence and destruction latent in the machine. The 'expression of terror' on Anna's face as she embarked on her last journey was not motivated solely by her emotional turmoil.[30]

Encountering ourselves as moderns, then, entails encountering the paradoxes of control in our lives, the way technology, symbol of our triumphs, always has its dark side. Machinery is never only machinery: a means to enable humans to manipulate the environment more effectively, it is therefore also an 'extension' of the human, the organic; and the possibility that it might be the other way round, that the human might be 'only' an organic machine, has been implicit in the dreams and nightmares of the modern imagination of technology since the beginning. We might be an extension of the machine, rather than vice versa, and the machine, ostensibly our servant, might become our master. The machine, exploiting the otherness of nature for our benefit, could become a vengeful other in itself. This is a nightmare of modernity as project, the control that gets out of hand, returning to dominate us and thereby symbolizing our enslavement by our very efforts at domination, the embodiment of our own hubris.

Space and Time

If the whole experience of travel was transformed by the railways, this was most obvious in relation to the fact of speed itself. Although the English 'transport revolution' began before the railways, so that travelling times between cities had halved between 1770 and 1830, even the earliest trains then proceeded to cut these times by two-thirds.[31] With the increased importance of precise timetabling and timekeeping, the sense of time was transformed. Marx referred to the 'annihilation of time and space',[32] echoing these contemporary changes, and, more recently, Harvey has described the 'time–space compression' that he sees as central to the experience of modernity.[33] There is a kind of contraction of the world itself: the reduction in travel time is imaged as a shrinkage of space. However, Schivelbusch points out that this could also be seen as an *expansion* of space, and was often so characterized; new areas were incorporated into the transport network, and the metropolis expanded to include the outlying parts of the nation (or the Empire, as with the British in India). By destroying distance, the railway opened up space. And whereas pre-industrial travel was embedded in the landscape, rather than striking purposefully through it, so that overland motion followed the irregularities of the land and depended on the physical powers of the animals, and ships moved with wind and water currents, the new steam power seemed essentially independent of these constraints, essentially autonomous, a form of artificial energy.[34] The railways – along with the telegraph – therefore helped produce the modern sense of space, time and travel.

In pre-modern periods, micro-time – the time of everyday life – is essentially dependent on the daily tasks, rather than being used to organize such tasks; it reverses the characteristic modern arrangement. Time is embedded in life, rather than life being embedded in time.[35] And macro-time depends not so much on a sense of history but of cycles, the rhythms of nature and the cultural rituals that embody a similar sense of prefigurement and repetition. Time – as fate – becomes internal to the person or object, not merely contingent, external. Similarly with space; writing of objects in the medieval period, McGrane claims that 'The place they occupied was internal to them; it had an intrinsic, immanent, formative influence upon their being', so that bodies and places have an 'expressive' relation.[36] Place itself can be seen in terms of the idea of rootedness, the ideological notion of an organic connection between person, community and locality. The aggregate of such places defined a pre-given order, Lefebvre's 'absolute space',[37] and this was manifest in the maps used to represent such space, which subordinated representation, in the modern sense, to expressiveness, so that places would be shown not by abstract symbols but by analogies of themselves: a hill by a picture of a hill, for example. The map itself becomes an emanation of the order it depicts.[38]

All this was radically transformed by the post-Renaissance development of abstract space and time, conceived as formal, geometrical, homogeneous and quantitative, a framework within which objects pass in ways that are essentially contingent, in a relation of 'indifferent exteriority',[39] hence unaffected by the frame itself. The diffusion of clocks both illustrates this process and contributes significantly to it. Mechanical clocks go back to the fourteenth century or earlier, and by the sixteenth century most towns and parishes had church clocks, although the pocket watch did not become widespread till the eighteenth century.[40] Although the hour hand had been there since medieval times, the minute hand did not become widespread until the late seventeenth century, an intriguing illustration of the 'speeding up' in the sense of time, and the increasing rationalization of its measurement.[41] By 1900, Simmel could comment on the 'universal diffusion of pocket watches', and the impact of this in accelerating modern life and in instilling a sense of punctuality, calculability and exactness. This diffusion of a modern time sense actually served to reproduce a significant feature of pre-modern time, namely its specificity to particular places, though now with a greater awareness of this as a problem. London time was four minutes ahead of Reading, and if a traveller from Washington to San Francisco in 1870 set his watch in every town he passed through, he would have had to set it over two hundred times.[42] Railway companies, too, operated their own times; in Pittsburgh, using six different lines, clocks showed six different times.[43] By the 1880s, this was everywhere being standardized, and by 1890 von Moltke, a young German officer, was calling for this process to be internationalized. In 1912, the dramatic news of the sinking of the *Titanic* went round the world, by wireless and cable, by the next morning: the world had become a unified time system.[44]

Along with this, the modern sense of space has increasingly dominated older senses of place, and one's relation to where one lives becomes essentially contingent, a matter of convenience, even of sentiment, but not of what Heidegger calls 'dwelling', embeddedness.[45] Particular places become mere 'positions', defined by coordinates on a map, whatever their particular differences. Politically, this has meant that hierarchical notions of place have been largely swept away by the abstract universality of space, implying a social levelling, but the modern politics of space cannot be left there; the liberation of space from hierarchy has nevertheless meant its availability for appropriation as private property, and for control through modern strategies of surveillance.[46] Time and space become commodities. Time can be both a measurement of productivity, and something that can itself be hired or saved, bought and sold. Control over time becomes a crucial dimension of power in the workplace. 'Time is now currency', writes Thompson; 'it is not passed but spent'.[47] Time must be used, purposefully; it is not good enough merely to 'pass the time'. Charlie Chaplin's 1936 film *Modern Times* shows time as a remorseless, consuming machine, requiring the humans who 'control' it to become machines too ('clockwork'), its mere appendages.

We can see that there is a deep structure to these modern notions of space and time. The very idea of 'project' has certain connotations. It implies future-oriented action, and action as the rational realization of a coherently formulated plan. It implies a temporal direction, with the future growing logically out of the past, and a stable context with standardized and consistent notions of space and time; time itself becomes linear. And it implies the emancipation of time from natural cycles: time can become history, the arena in which individual and collective projects can be realized. In this sense, time takes priority over space; the latter essentially becomes a resource and a context for the former, with time entering into the very core of an orientation to the world governed by project. 'Since space is a "fact" of nature, this meant that the conquest and rational ordering of space became an integral part of the modernizing project', as Harvey puts it.[48] Something of this experience of time is captured by Carey's claim that the telegraph 'invented the future as a new zone of uncertainty and a new region of practical action',[49] the uncertainty being a dynamic impetus to the envisaged action, with the measurability of time providing a reliable framework for the technical innovations needed to bring about the desired results.

The time and space of project, then, have two related dimensions: time and space as abstract, homogeneous, subject to calculation; and time and space as appropriation, with history as linear, future-oriented, and irreversible, and space as the environment within which such a process occurs, and the environment that is acted on by such a process, so that objects become products, related to externally, in terms of human plans, shaped by human design. Modernity has therefore entailed the construction of the self as abstract subject, able to experience the diversity and heterogeneity of the world but only through the imposition of this abstract, functional, spatio-temporal framework, thereby rendering these experiences both varied and multiple yet in a sense one-dimensional. In this experience of selfhood, time seems somehow more basic, entering into the very subjecthood of the active, evolving self, with space as the externality within which this self-development occurs, the 'outside' that is to be appropriated, penetrated and controlled.

It is hardly surprising that this emerges as strongly gender-coded; the links between project and masculinity have already been mentioned,[50] and Doreen Massey spells out the implications for space and time:

> It is, moreover, time which is typically coded masculine and space, being absence or lack, as feminine. Moreover, the same gendering operates through the series of dualisms which are linked to time and space. It is time which is aligned with history, progress, civilization, politics and transcendence and coded masculine. And it is the opposites of these things which have, in the traditions of western thought, been coded feminine.[51]

She points also to the association between 'penetrability and vulnerability' in conceptions of space and place, with space as subject to mastery and conquest.[52] One can add that if the self is constituted through time, the body occupies space, again constituting a matrix some implications of which have been explored in connection with the 'civilizing process'.[53] Kristin Ross adds that time 'excludes and subordinates where space tolerates and coordinates'.[54]

The cultural ramifications of this are complex. Space, in relation to place, can after all be coded as masculine; in its abstraction and universality it represents the freeplay of a masculinity that can never reach its goal, never attain release. 'Over abstract space reigns phallic solitude and the self-destruction of desire', writes Lefebvre.[55] This is the infinite universe that so frightened Pascal, and that, extended in time, can imply a neurotic structure of never-ending quest at the heart of masculine selfhood. Linear time can become an empty ritual of meaningless repetition. Hence, argues Massey, we see 'the need for the security of boundaries, the requirement for . . . a defensive and counter-positional definition of identity', which she describes as 'culturally masculine'.[56] Kristeva extends this, arguing that this linear time of masculinity stumbles over the facts of finitude and death and becomes 'at once both civilizational and obsessional', so that we can recognize 'in the mastery of time the true structure of the slave'.[57] *Modern Times* indeed.

What is coded as relatively feminine may, in turn, not simply be devalued, or seen as suppressed; it can derive an attraction, commensurate with its usefulness as a resource for nostalgia. Time as cycles becomes simultaneously 'woman' and 'nature' – problematical, but no longer such a challenge to project; indeed, a component of the 'green nostalgia' so common in late modernity. In turn, 'place' can easily be seen as feminine – cosy and local, in contrast to 'space' – so that if the private/public distinction is mapped on to this, and 'space' becomes open, broad, public, then we find, writes Massey, 'a view of place as bounded, as in various ways a site of an authenticity, as singular, fixed and unproblematic in its identity'.[58] Place is where one's roots are, where home is, where Mother is (or should be).

This nostalgic and ideological recuperation of place should not, however, blind us to an important truth: that the experience of place in modernity is irreducible to the spatial politics of project. Michel de Certeau has explored this, in the context of the spatial practices of everyday city life, in ways that complement our earlier discussion of the city.[59] Pointing out that 'To walk is to lack a place', so that the moving about that the city invites and requires 'makes the city itself an immense social experience of lacking a place', he is concerned to show that this is liberating rather than merely nostalgic. This use of space is never reducible to the functional, the imposed, the 'rational', and the walker doesn't just realize the planned, pre-given possibilities, but 'moves them about and invents others', since the improvization of walking both transforms and abandons spatial elements.[60] Place-names themselves imply and embody an experiential residue – they become 'liberated spaces that can be occupied' – hence city planners and bureaucrats always prefer to replace them by numbers. If experience itself is fluid, irreducible to the coherence of project, then this is true particularly of the experience of place; places are not isolated, well-bounded, but relational, linked through processes of experience and imagination.[61] 'Stories about places are makeshift things. They are composed with the world's debris', as de Certeau puts it. And places always *do* have stories; graphically, he explains that 'There is no place that is not haunted by many different spirits hidden there in silence, spirits one can "invoke" or not. Haunted places are the only ones people can live in.' Hence 'The memorable is that which can be dreamed about a place.'[62] Places – like the journeys between them – become the memories and metaphors of identity. And it is this dimension which, as will be seen, is systematically violated or neglected by the spatial dynamics of modern architecture. Above all, it serves to remind us that the space and time of modernity raise issues of experience, imagination and representation that are not reducible to project, issues that will be explored in later discussions of modernism.

Phones, Planes and Robots: Living with the Machine

'The call of the telephone is incessant and unremitting', Avital Ronell reminds us. 'When you hang up, it does not disappear but goes into remission.' In short, 'you are always on call'. The phone is unpredictable, and may shatter your privacy at any time. Moreover, it demands to be answered, and takes priority over most other demands. This tyranny of the telephone nevertheless goes hand in hand with its perceived benefits; and this, together with its role as exemplifier of the 'space–time compression' already discussed, means it can usefully serve to introduce wider issues raised by the ubiquitous presence of the modern machine.

'Maintaining and joining, the telephone line holds together what it separates', continues Ronell. It 'connects where there has been little or no relation, it globalizes and unifies, suturing a country like a wound'.[63] At the most general level, then, the significance of the phone is that it lets you be in two places at once; temporal and spatial distance is abolished in a radical simultaneity and immediacy. Letter-writing, embodying the possibility of a deeper narrative out of the past, a gradual evolution of the story of one's life, becomes less significant than the phone call, with the greater priority it attaches to the present and the near future, in both the active and the expectant modes.

The telephone can be said both to break through barriers, and to subtly maintain them; it reminds us that breaking through barriers is not the same as breaking them down. It breaks through the public/private divide, violating our sense of privacy, of home as a separate sphere; yet what are experienced as its virtues and vices, its pleasures and the attendant fears, rest on the very fact of that powerful division and its maintenance. There are other social aspects, too. If, initially, phone ads of the 1880s and 1890s seemed to suggest that its major use was domestic, permitting the more efficient organization and control of the servants,[64] this was accompanied by, and largely replaced by, a view of the phone as a democratic instrument. Thus Kern suggests that telephones 'break down barriers of distance – horizontally across the face of the land and vertically across social strata. They make all places equidistant from the seat of power and hence of equal value.'[65] However, while this may reflect both the fears and the aspirations of early commentators, it is perhaps more accurate to suggest that the phone has contradictory effects. Thus de Solla Pool argues that 'The phone invades our privacy with its ring, but it protects our privacy by allowing us to transact affairs from the fastness of our homes'; and it 'allows dispersal of centres of authority, but it also allows tight continuous supervision of field offices from the center'.[66] Anyone who has ever faced the need for a difficult call to a powerful bureaucrat will sympathize with the predicament of Kafka's hero in *The Castle*, trying to use the phone to penetrate the Byzantine ways of his alleged employer: 'K. hesitated to announce himself, for he was at the mercy of the telephone, the other could shout him down or hang up the receiver, and that might mean the blocking of a not unimportant way of access.'[67]

The telephone – both in itself and in the cultural meanings it collects around itself – can be seen as a typical product of the 'Second Industrial Revolution', that remarkable couple of decades, around the 1880s and 1890s or thereabouts, when electric lighting, X-rays, radio, film, the gramophone record, the box camera, synthetic fibres, plastics, canned food, modern medicine, cars, planes, bicycles, machine guns, typewriters and skyscrapers, were invented. With the partial exception of the car, these could all be said to be typical products of what Mumford has called the 'neotechnic' age, in contrast with the 'paleotechnic' age of the 'First Industrial Revolution'.[68] These developments are manifested in a certain shift from 'dirty' coal and smoking chimneys, to 'clean' electricity, and from production-centred artefacts (for metalworking and textiles) to consumption goods, as sources of the imagery and stereotypes whereby the impact of technology was captured and explored in the culture of the age.[69] In the post-railway age, it is neotechnic imagery, of the machine as ordered, clean, efficient, yet remorseless and soulless, that has provided the key to the popular imagination of technology, supplanting the previous imaginative power held by images of fire, smoke and destruction, drawn from mining and laying railways.

By the 1920s, neotechnic utopianism had become a central strand in modernist culture. It was revealed especially in the enthusiasm for speed, for change, for sweeping away the old and the obsolete. The car, seen as embodying these ideals, was already an icon of the modern. 'Cars, cars! Speed, speed! One is carried away, seized by enthusiasm, by joy . . . enthusiasm over the joy of power', proclaimed Le Corbusier, embarking on his career as architectural revolutionary.[70] But perhaps it is really the plane that brings this out most effectively, along with the contentious political undercurrents. For Le Corbusier, writing in 1935, the plane was 'the vanguard of the conquering armies of the New Age',[71] a formulation which combines the celebration of the new with a quasi-fascist glorification of brute power. Although, as Wohl remarks, the plane contrasted with the other new technologies in having little or no effect on most people's lives, its invention 'inspired an extraordinary outpouring of feeling and gave rise to utopian hopes and gnawing fears'. There was a close relationship between aviation and the modernist avant-garde; Marinetti's first Futurist manifesto was published within a year of Wilbur Wright's first flight, in August 1908, and he was attracted particularly by the potential of the plane for 'liberating humanity from its two great enemies, time and space'.[72] Flying at speed over distance meant the obliteration of space and the transcendence of time. Mussolini, too, wrote an article on flying, in 1909, praising the aviators, who embodied the heroism of the age, and endorsing 'movement' as the key to the new century: 'Movement everywhere, and acceleration in the rhythm of our lives.'[73]

These new gods nevertheless had to pay for transcending human limitation; their immortality was not bought cheaply (plate 6). As Wohl puts it:

> The urge to dominate, to master, to conquer, was the motivation that drove men to fly. Speed was the divinity of the new century, to be worshipped at any cost. The cult of movement required victims. In its service, no sacrifice was too great. . . . Death was the price that men would have to pay in order to live like gods in a world of fast machines.[74]

Yeats's Irish airman of 1916, foreseeing his death 'Somewhere among the clouds above', driven on by 'A lonely impulse of delight',[75] was in effect one of the first 'flying aces', a notable creation of the mass media in the inter-war years. The ace was thus an embodiment of Marinetti's pre-war fantasies, as 'the aviator fused with his machine and transformed into an engine of death'.[76] On the general significance of this, Judy Davies claims that

> As his creation, machinery was logically man's subordinate. Yet from the outset the machine was felt to be more than this: it was a kind of fetish endowed with magical powers that took man beyond the human, into a mystical meeting with himself where he was perceived both as a creature of infinite possibilities and as subject to a frail mortality.[77]

In this fusion of man and machine we encounter both a central strand in proto-fascist aesthetics and a key component of the reaction to the machine that makes modernism possible. Marinetti called for a 'mechanical man with replaceable parts', adding that 'in the flesh of man wings lie sleeping'.[78] 'Think of the pilot as a machine!', wrote an aviator. 'The system of levers which runs from the ailerons does not stop until it reaches his shoulder socket', and hence 'They are not two machines, they are one.'[79] As a machine, the man's will would become steel. Thus the aviator – very definitely male, of course – becomes as hard as his machine, wedded to it; and with such machines characteristically coded as masculine, one begins to sense the latent homoerotic fears and possibilities. Perhaps, as Judy Davies argues, beneath the aggressive surface of futurist writing there is 'a subtext which suggests the exorcism of a fear, or a lurking ambiguity of response held in check by an energy of violation'.[80] And speed itself – a frenzied pursuit of movement over goal – emerges as a manic self-celebration of progress in an age when confidence in its direction can no longer be so easily sustained.

This promise of technology, then, is a promise to abolish the restraints of nature by transcending the organic, and this can only be done through the man-machine. In the light of this, we can even return to the humble telephone, since this, too, can be seen as a fusion of the organic and the technological – and one that reveals, in its origins, the deeply disturbing and problematic nature of this ambition. The telephone is an extension of the human ear and, one can add, it requires the simultaneous presence of the invisible mouth and ear of the other, an 'other' who, it turns out, can veer from the all-too-physical to the spectral. A real human ear, from a corpse, was used in Alexander Graham Bell's original experiments; and Thomas Watson, his assistant, attended *séances* where he tells us that he made contact with the dead, and in addition used a medium to help with one of the technical problems.

It is hardly surprising, then, that Ronell refers to 'the ghostly origins of these technologies', adding that the phone was 'hardly a beloved or universally celebrated little monster'; indeed, it inspired fear, 'playing on fresh forms of anxiety which were to be part of a new package deal of the invisible'.[81] For a culture concerned with 'hidden depths', with the notion of a 'deeper reality' behind appearance, the telephone was both fascinating and fearful. In *The Trial*, Kafka observes that people on the phone appeared to be 'mumbling to themselves and observing some process unfold within the receiver';[82] person, voice, mouth, ear and apparatus all seemed to be held together in new ways that simultaneously fragmented them, confusing the identity of self and other, subject and object. 'Hearing voices' is not, after all, so unproblematic an activity. Ronell remarks that, from early on, it became clear that 'schizophrenia recognizes the telephone as its own, appropriating it as a microphone for the singular emission of its pain'; schizophrenics were drawn to Bell as neurotics were to Freud, several contacting his laboratory in its first year or two. If we also remember that Kafka wrote of how 'Sometimes I absolutely dance with apprehension around the telephone, the receiver at my ear, and yet can't help divulging secrets',[83] a picture emerges of the telephone as a power that not only permits, but also enforces communication, and not just about externals but about the self also, and the self in its relation to other selves, wherever they may be, in whatever world of the normal or abnormal. The telephone, a fusion of the human and the technological, fragments even as it unifies, and operates across registers of being – organic, physical, psychic – all in one.

These undercurrents of anxiety already suggest that technology could be thought likely to take its revenge for the grandiose hopes placed in it, but it is with the man-machine *stricto sensu* that this becomes more evident. The term 'robot', from a Slavic root meaning 'work', was invented by the Czech dramatist Karel Capek in 1917, and came into widespread prominence after robots featured in a play of his in 1920. The ambiguity about their status has always been present, revealed in the twin meanings given by the dictionary: 'a living being that acts automatically' and 'a machine devised to function in place of a living agent'. A robot is the logical outcome of the project of modernity: the point where machine and human may no longer be intrinsically distinguishable, given that both are subsumed under the notion of 'efficiency'. In this transcendence of natural limitations, we again find a revenge of nature, since robots become as programmed as worker ants, effectively slaves, totally harnessed to the efficient performance of their functions. However, the creativity implicit in the human ability to produce the robots in the first place adds to robotic drudgery a significant element of danger: the possibility that the robots could master this creativity itself, that their intelligence could become self-fuelling, growing exponentially to exceed that of their erstwhile masters. Or, conversely, much the same potentially destructive effect could be achieved by an accidental malfunction, so that the robots run amok, out of (human) control. Both extreme efficiency and its opposite are, in effect, rendered all the more likely, and simultaneously all the more potentially trouble-some, by the modern attitude of world mastery. The dream of modernity slides easily into nightmare.

We find, then, that this man-machine can be a potent source of cultural symbolism, and can be used to represent 'the relation of the body to the social, the relation of the sexes to each other, the structure of the psyche, or the workings of history', as Constance Penley writes.[84] This is revealed vividly in the celebrated Fritz Lang film of 1926, *Metropolis*. The workers are portrayed as a mass, devoid of individuality, and enslaved by time, and within these human robots lurks the potential for revolt, triggered indeed by a 'real' robot, in the likeness of a human; yet, in the end, order is restored, and the promise of a 'humane' technology reaffirmed. 'The film drew on a naive faith in technology and simultaneously expressed a primitive fear of machines', claims Jordanova, hence 'the double character of machines in their capacity to both liberate and enslave'.[85] The fear comes out particularly strongly in a visionary scene in which the machines are transformed into monsters – named after pagan gods – that consume a stream of workers, thus portraying technology, in Huyssen's words, as 'an autono-mous deified force demanding worship, surrender, and ritual sacrifice'.[86] Indeed, Rotwang, the evil scientist who creates the robot, is himself portrayed as a strange mixture of the modern and the primitive, as much magician as scientist, a tech-nologist with his roots in the black arts. In going beyond the limits, he becomes as one with the strange forces he seeks to harness and control, a Kurtz for the machine age.

In producing an android, Rotwang transcends the nature–culture split, but in a way that spells disaster, since the project of mastery thereby turns to consume itself. Wollen writes that the robot 'urges the workers to destroy the machines in a frenzy of auto-castration and infanticide',[87] a formulation that draws to our attention an important gender dimension emphasized in the analyses of both Jordanova and Huyssen; for the robot is female, and the workers being urged to destroy their creativity and their 'offspring' are of course male. Indeed, since the late nineteenth century, the machine-woman seems to have become a common repository of the fears produced by rationalization and automation; women and machines were both viewed as potential challenges to male authority in an era of acute gender tension. We encounter, once again, the dualistic separation of 'woman' into the good, the pure, and the independent, the wicked, and the wilful, a dualism projected on to a technology that can thereby be experienced as passive and obedient or threatening and 'out of control'.[88]

The issue of creativity is also important here. Huyssen refers to the desire 'to create that other, woman, thus depriving it of its otherness', and adds:

By creating a female android, Rotwang fulfills the male phantasm of a creation without mother; but more than that, he produces not just any natural life, but woman herself, the epitome of nature. The nature/culture split seems healed. The most complete technologization of nature appears as re-naturalization, as a progress back to nature. Man is at long last alone and at one with himself.[89]

But Rotwang's robot is an enchantress, hence unnatural; she falls outside masculine reason and feminine 'natural' procreation. Only when she – and her creator – are destroyed can class and gender order be restored, and technology given back its rightful, more limited place. Male technological 'fecundity' is at one with sterility, an endless reproduction of the same, a perpetual self-identity and self-sufficiency. In these 'bachelor machines', argues Penley, we always find embedded the fantasy of 'closure, perfectibility and mastery',[90] a fantasy doomed to disappointment through the ultimate irreducibility of experience and history to project.

As has been seen from these examples, technology frequently seems to question its own status, casting doubt on the clarity of distinctions between nature and culture, the organic and the psychic. If, as Rosalind Williams suggests, 'the vocabulary of sublimity was gradually but persistently transferred from nature to industry'[91] during the nineteenth century, then this can offer further insight, since the sublime, as a category, necessarily refuses clear boundaries.[92] For example, when President Grant opened the Philadelphia Centennial Exposition of 1876 by starting up the gigantic Corliss steam engine – 39 feet tall, weighing 680 tons – which supplied all the power, Kasson comments that the descriptions of it given by visitors seemed to endow it with life. The machine emerged as 'a kind of fabulous automaton – part animal, part machine, part god'; and 'In the melodrama which various visitors projected, the engine played the part of a legendary giant, whose stupendous brute force, they congratulated and titillated themselves, was harnessed and controlled by man.' A contemporary journalist described the machine as 'slave' to the engineer, adding that it could nevertheless 'crush' him with its 'lightest touch', so the 'control' was not, perhaps, so absolute as to prevent all fear.[93] Indeed, Williams suggests that if a sense of helplessness and awe before the power of the other is indeed frequent in these accounts of the machine, then there are clear hints of technological determinism in this aesthetic of sublimity: 'Sublime technology is autonomous technology, technology-out-of-control.' The spectator submits to the power of the technological spectacle. One can add that if this technological sublime can be 'part animal, part machine, part god', it can also be 'part society', since a sense of 'the social' as 'out of control' is strong in middle-class commentators of the period, in their vivid descriptions of the dangers of the 'mass',[94] a theme that is also clearly present in *Metropolis*.

Technology, then, calls for submission. If its promise is to be realized, it must be granted power; but if it then betrays us, it may be too late to take back the power. The fact that technological triumph has tended to be inseparable from technological blight, the destruction or corruption of nature, has long been re-marked on. Williams points out that appealing to nature, against technology, has always been an option, since, as she suggests, 'were nature hidden or destroyed, people would have no independent source of value by which to judge the dominant order'.[95] Nevertheless, although this has appealed to some,[96] it has been more usual to present technology as a paradoxical solution to the very problems it causes, with self-contained technological utopias promising escape from the destructiveness of technology itself. Williams claims that

> The two basic types of technological environment – one invading the natural environment, the other sealed off from nature – are dialectically related. The more human-made structures degrade the natural environment, the more alluring becomes the self-enclosed, self-constructed paradise. Technological blight promotes technological fantasy . . . a retreat from technology into technology.

But this solution, too, has seemed dangerous; if humankind is too insulated from nature's hazards, it could ossify.[97] Writing in 1937, Orwell claimed that 'what is usually called progress also entails what is usually called degeneracy'.[98] Hence, both progress realized and progress unrealized are powerful sources of fear: 'The technological trap snaps shut. Either by conquering nature or by not conquering it, humanity will degenerate.'[99] This characteristic nineteenth-century language of 'degeneracy' should not obscure the fact that this is basically still the dilemma articulated above: a nature/technology opposition generates a melodramatic structure of conflict in which neither side can win, or rather, victory becomes its own defeat. A self-contained technological utopia becomes a perpetual bachelor machine, a land of endlessly self-cloning lotus-eaters, no longer capable of memory – for what would there be to remember? – and hence, the ultimate triumph of repetition over reproduction.

In practice, it is modern architecture and city design that have most obviously embodied visions of technological utopia, and it is these that must now be considered.

Building the Modern: Machines For Living In

Let us take the Seagram Building, New York, 1956–8, by Mies van der Rohe, an outstanding example of 'International Style' modernism, dominant from the 1930s till the 1970s (plate 7). It is very tall, rectangular, basically simple in design, using the nineteenth-century technological innovation whereby steel and reinforced concrete can enable girders, rather than walls, to carry the weight of the structure, making large expanses of glass windows possible. Its appearance is dark, sleek, uniform, manifesting an aggressive simplicity and purity of design; it represents, suggests Hughes, 'an architecture of ineloquence and absolute renunciation'.[100] In short, it is unquestionably not only 'modern', but 'modernist', too.

What is normally referred to as 'modern' architecture is a modernist celebration of the project of modernity. As such, modernist architecture – as it might more accurately be labelled – is distinguishable both from other forms of architecture that may be in some way 'modern' but do not reflect this programme, and from other forms of modernism, in the arts more generally, which characteristically embody a more problematic, even critical response to the modernity from which they spring. Of course, architecture necessarily has a practical, functional dimension, but modernism has involved a distinctive response to this. If, as Habermas suggests, architecture in the late nineteenth century was facing a threefold challenge – how to meet a massive new demand for industry and housing, with newly available materials and construction techniques, and with a greater importance attached to strictly functional and economic criteria[101] – then the challenge was met by an architecture that was as much visionary as practical. As Barthes claims, 'architecture is always dream and function, expression of a utopia and instrument of a convenience'.[102] The relation between technology and function is not straightforward; there is never just one way in which a specific need has to be met. Control of light, for example, can be achieved in a variety of ways – window shades, awnings, size of window, tinted glass, and so on – so, in general, decisions of this kind are more likely to be a reflection of the modernist programme and the modernist aesthetic, rather than simple response to need.

When Mies van der Rohe claimed, in the grandiose way typical of architectural modernists, that 'Architecture is the will of the age conceived in spatial terms',[103] this certainly captures the ambition of the modernist elite, its confidence that the architect could not merely reflect but also shape the destiny of the time. Architecture and town planning could be a key to human emancipation, a carrier of the Enlightenment ideal. 'The machinery of Society' was 'out of gear', wrote Le Corbusier, and it was a choice of 'architecture or revolution'.[104] For the Bauhaus – that great stimulus to architecture and design in the 1920s – the machine was not only an embodiment of a new aesthetic but a force for democratization, an attack on the old order, a vision held in common with the populist aspirations of manufacturers like Ford, Morris, Renault and Porsche, opening up the mass motor-car market.[105] But by the 1930s, with the development of the International Style, based on the sleek, standardized design of mass-production skyscrapers, a greater conservatism was apparent, and it has become clear that the political dimensions of architectural modernism were always ambiguous. In the influential Charter of Athens, produced by the International Congress of Modern Architects in 1933, politics was to be reduced to the 'rational' organization of space by the bureaucrat and the expert; town planning was certainly not a matter for the general public. Urban experience was to become a specialized, administered spectacle.[106] These ideas are deeply 'political', if not in any orthodox left/right sense of the term: Henry Ford was widely read, and his ideas copied, in both the USSR and Germany, with both Stalin and Hitler trying to model their factories on his; and these ideas could as easily influence Hitler's engineers, designing concentration camps, as they could influence Robert Moses, tearing out the heart of old New York in the decades from the 1930s to the 1950s to build expressways,[107] or the architects of the first tower blocks for housing former slum dwellers in Labour's New Britain of the late 1940s (and of course subsequent decades). And when Burnham proclaimed that 'Good citizenship is the prime object of good city planning'[108] one is reminded of the sense in which the citizen is also the subject, of panoptic control strategies.[109]

Le Corbusier's famous pronouncement that a house is 'a machine for living in'[110] encapsulates this ethos of technology, this desire that buildings should proclaim their own rationality and functionality. A building should simply manifest what it is: appearance and reality should coincide. While later modernists took their distance from the determinism implicit in Sullivan's slogan 'Form follows function', the idea that the two can and should 'express' themselves through each other, that function could in itself have artistic value, is central to the modernist aesthetic. The form of a building should be as simple and pure as possible, in line with its function. Since functions are always in varying degrees specific, separate functions either had to be met by separate parts of a building, by separate buildings, and, on a city planning level, by separate zones; or, in the case of the individual building, walls had to be mere movable partitions, incorporating flexibility. This no doubt accounts for Le Corbusier's hostility to the old boulevards ('We must kill the street!'),[111] with their 'inefficient' mixture of vehicles and pedestrians. Whether in a building or in a whole city, the architect should strive to realize the purity of aesthetic form through the streamlined practicality of his design; it should be a perfect embodiment of the modern sense of space. This is what Jencks calls the 'univalence' of the modernist building, the aspiration to a consistency of appearance, form and function.[112] This always pushes towards abstraction, the ideal of geometrical perfection; it is pure materiality but also pure form. Le Corbusier claimed that 'Architectural emotion exists when the work rings within us in tune with a universe whose laws we obey, recognize and respect. When certain harmonies have been attained, the work captures us.'[113] Through this notion of 'natural laws', form and mechanism can coincide; here we encounter the belief that, as Banham puts it, 'the perennial laws of geometry were about to drive accident and variability from the visual world, that the equipment of daily life was about to achieve final and typical form'.[114]

That there are tensions and problems in this aesthetic has long been apparent. Machines are not necessarily or normally symmetrical, with flat or uniform surfaces; a machine aesthetic cannot easily embody platonic ideals. Formal purity in the geometrical sense, and a full use of technological innovation, can only seem to fit naturally together by a sleight of hand. In effect, the skyscraper provides us with a smooth exterior shell around a concealed mechanism, and 'functional design' becomes an ideological catchphrase, the abstraction of the style well suited to the impersonality of the market; thus the maverick American modernist Frank Lloyd Wright could denounce the result as 'only the prostitute semblance of the architecture it professes to be'.[115] This is also a clue to a related paradox in modernist architecture: the celebration of functionality, of technology, would on the face of it be a celebration of change, since constant innovation is a feature of technology, whereas actually the buildings exhibit a monumentality, a defiance of change. Banham argues that this reveals a tension between the institutionalized 'academicism' of professional architecture since the 1930s, and the 'futurism' of the original modernist impulse, suggesting that the conflict may be irreconcilable; the architect who accepts the need for rapid change may have to discard 'the professional garments by which he is recognised as an architect', while the refusal to do so may mean that 'a technological culture has decided to go on without him'.[116]

Theoretical tensions have practical implications. Solutions chosen can often be dysfunctional. Large, flat roofs are difficult to maintain; and as Blake observes, the world treats puritan plainness with disdain, cracking it, buckling, staining and rotting it.[117] One can, indeed, always ask 'functional for whom?' In his critique, Brolin quotes an architectural journal from 1950, denouncing the addition of a roof to a footbridge for betraying the simplicity of the original design; but presumably the users, able to keep dry in the rain, did not complain.[118] One is reminded of the attempts by Le Corbusier to prevent tenants from 'personalizing' the austere apartments in his *Unité d'Habitation* block at Marseilles. While cost-cutting and economic constraints have doubtless also played a role, as well as the problems inherent in the modernist programme itself,[119] the result has been the unpopular, frequently vandalized tower blocks and deserted walkways, the 'dead public space', the 'isolation in the midst of public visibility', attacked by Sennett and other critics.[120] 'These are the new landscapes of urban despair', writes Hughes; 'bright, brutish, crime-wracked, and scarred by the vandalism they invite'.[121] Berman concludes that 'The tragic irony of modernist urbanism is that its triumph has helped to destroy the very urban life it helped to set free.'[122]

Let us return, once more, to the Seagram Building. What, in the end, is this building trying to tell us? What statement does it make? In a sense, these questions seem strange; this is not, on the face of it, a building that seeks to communicate. There is no elaborate language of ornamentation to decode, no intricacy of form to interpret. It is a positivist building, one that seeks to exclude questions of meaning and interpretation altogether; ornamentation in building is like metaphor in language, a source of disruptive irrelevance, interfering with the possibility of pure, unmediated representation whereby the world can simply appear as it is, its own self-sufficient representation of itself. Connor aptly points to the resulting tension:

> At one and the same time, such buildings assert and deny their form. If they proclaim their simplicity and integrity, saying, this square, this concrete box, is what I am and nothing else – then they also claim a kind of otherworldliness in their approximation to geometrical perfection. The univalence of the modernist building seems to establish its absolute self-sufficiency, as an ideal principle made solid and visible. . . . The modernist building is simultaneously pure materiality, and pure sign, which does not refer to anything outside itself by quotation or allusion.[123]

Such a building is a product of abstract form, related to others in a system of abstractions; it aspires to a self-referential transparency, as an architectural window on the infinite, embodied in the paradoxical materiality of pure, realized abstraction: a space of pure representation. These are self-contained buildings that are nevertheless linked with each other in a reciprocal non-relationship, windowless monads with windows, silently reflecting each other's hermetic self-sufficiency: technology's dream of utopia, independent of the unpredictable incursions of nature as the uncontrollable other, seemingly self-reproducing – the ultimate bachelor machines.

So, despite the disavowals, these buildings inevitably do carry meanings. In its self-sufficiency, with the air-conditioning, central heating and artificial lighting that make it independent of weather and season, the modern building inevitably makes a statement about its ability to emancipate itself from its environment; its self-contained separation asserts its disciplined purposefulness, its independence of the chaotic diversity of street and square, its aspiration to re-place 'place' with 'position';[124] the expanses of clear glass proclaim the dissolution of solid mass in vision, the invisible but ubiquitous workings of the panoptic gaze. It signifies, in its boldness and defiance, the assertiveness, simultaneously abstract and concrete, that has no point beyond that very assertiveness: the fact of power itself. And like the modern world it has often been used to symbolize, it aspires to a godlike ability to construct, and simultaneously know, itself, to be a fusion of power and knowledge in absolute self-identity; and its inability to achieve this has a resonance at many levels.

Technology Goes to War

In 1912 World Standard Time had been proclaimed; in 1914 Europe went to war. The Chief of the German General Staff was now von Moltke, and it was his railway timetables that governed mobilization. It was commented on as a wonder of the age, the way millions of men were shifted smoothly across Europe, by rail, to the fronts; and the process was experienced as remorseless. Once mobilization was ordered there was no going back; synchronizing the mass movements of men, trains and armaments permitted no interference. Kern observes that war itself was a further impetus to the standardization of time. Before the war, wristwatches were thought to be unmanly; during the war they became standard issue. Before the battles, wristwatches were synchronized carefully, so that everyone went over the top at the appointed time.

At this level, the war was a further exercise in the rationalization of time and work. The battle plan for one British army corps, for just the first day of the Battle of the Somme, ran to 31 pages.[125] If it became quite common to describe the war as a 'slaughterhouse', this figure of speech has an appropriate resonance. Haussmann's La Villette slaughterhouse of the 1860s, remarkable for its planning and scale, had been succeeded by even larger ones in Chicago over the next decade or so, based on sophisticated new production and a complex division of labour, using every part of the animal. Pick writes:

> A new 'humane' order of killing . . . went hand in hand with a new vastness of death, a hitherto inconceivably rationalised and industrialised processing of meat. Not by chance was the metaphor of the slaughterhouse to become so inextricably intertwined with the language of modern war; they emerged so closely together.[126]

At one level, then, the war imposed the rationalized, homogeneous, 'public' time of project; but this is only one aspect. Kern suggests that

The sense of the future depended on rank. The officers attempted to appropriate the future actively with carefully devised battle plans. . . . For the officers, war time was essentially a sum of discrete, sequential units out of which the scenarios for battle were constructed, while for the soldiers in the trenches it was a seemingly endless flux, a composition in time that had neither a beginning nor an end. . . . The strange newness and overwhelming force of experience clamped the soldier in the present as if bracketed from past and future.[127]

A soldier in the trenches had no sense of the past or future; rather, he experienced an intense, everlasting present. This sense of a present both fragmented and endlessly recurrent is a constant theme in letters home, and subsequent memoirs. Neither history nor project could provide moorings; ideas of progress and evolution fractured beneath this weight of experience, this drama of simultaneity in which the overwhelming impact of the timeless moment stands out against any sense of a smooth, linear flow of time. And this becomes very important, as will be seen, in the modernist movement in literature, painting and the arts, which seek to explore this experience of time in the present, in the 'stream of consciousness'.

On the one hand, then, the war exemplified – and intensified – the project of modernity, and *one* effect of it was to produce a feeling that only a further development of the project, using technology, could avert future disasters. As has been seen, this was the idealistic impetus behind modernism in architecture. But, just as significantly, the war stimulated the development of modernism in the arts, and culture more generally, in a contrary way, through emphasizing the irreducibility of experience to project, and intensifying the cultural sense of the former as subjective, heterogeneous, entailing a new consciousness, and calling for new modes of artistic and literary representation. Fussell argues for a direct connection between these war experiences and modernism in the arts: 'To the degree that conscripts become alienated from official culture, with its rationalisation and heroic fictions, they enact one of cultural modernism's main gestures',[128] since 'A disillusion resembling that of soldiers who have fought is one of the most noticeable motifs in modernist culture.'[129] And with modernism, the questionings and uncertainties of the modern West become ever more insistent. . . .

Notes

1   N. Faith, *The World the Railways Made* (Bodley Head, 1990), p. 1.
2   A. Trachtenberg, Foreword to W. Schivelbusch, *The Railway Journey: The Industrialization of Time and Space in the 19th Century* (Berg, 1986), p. xv.
3   N. Tolstoy, *Anna Karenina* (Penguin, 1978), ch. I: xxix.
4   P. Gay, *The Bourgeois Experience, Vol. II: The Tender Passion* (Oxford University Press, 1986), p. 323.
5   C. Dickens, cited in H. L. Sussman, *The Victorians and the Machine* (Harvard University Press, 1968), p. 47.
6   Faith, *World*, pp. 247, 246.
7   Schivelbusch, *Railway Journey*, pp. 67, 61, 63.

8   Cited in ibid., p. 55.
9   Cited in K. Wolff (ed.) *Sociology of Georg Simmel* (Glencoe, 1950), p. 410.
10 M. de Certeau, *The Practice of Everyday Life* (California University Press, 1984), p. 112.
11 Schivelbusch, *Railway Journey*, pp. 60, 64.
12 Tolstoy, *Anna*, ch. I: xxix, xxx.
13 Faith, *World*, p. 36.
14 Cited in S. Kern, *The Culture of Time and Space, 1880–1918* (Harvard University Press, 1983), pp. 217–18.
15 de Certeau, *Practice*, p. 115.
16 H. Moss, *The Magic Lantern of Marcel Proust* (Faber, 1962), p. 110.
17 C. Dickens, *Dombey & Son* (Penguin, 1970), ch. xx.
18 Kern, *Culture*, p. 218.
19 Schivelbusch, *Railway Journey*, pp. 196, 140.
20 Faith, *World*, p. 253.
21 Schivelbusch, *Railway Journey*, pp. 194–6.
22 Faith, *World*, p. 271.
23 Schivelbusch, *Railway Journey*, p. 197.
24 de Certeau, *Practice*, p. 113.
25 Tolstoy, *Anna* chs I: xviii, VII: xxxi.
26 D. Pick, *War Machine: The Rationalisation of Slaughter in the Modern Age* (Yale University Press, 1993), p. 106.
27 Sussman, *Victorians*, pp. 58, 56.
28 Dickens, *Dombey*, ch. LV.
29 See, for example, J. F. Kasson, *Civilizing the Machine: Technology and Republican Values in America, 1776–1900* (Penguin, 1980), p. 172.
30 Tolstoy, *Anna*, ch. VII: xxxi.
31 Schivelbusch, *Railway Journey*, p. 34.
32 K. Marx, *Gründrisse* (Penguin, 1973), p. 539.
33 D. Harvey, *The Condition of Postmodernity* (Blackwell, 1989), p. 240.
34 Schivelbusch, *Railway Journey*, pp. 35, 9, 10.
35 E. P. Thompson, 'Time, Work-discipline, and Industrial Capitalism', *Past and Present* (1967), 38, p. 59.
36 B. McGrane, *Beyond Anthropology* (Columbia University Press, 1989), p. 40.
37 H. Lefebvre, *The Production of Space* (Blackwell, 1991), especially ch. 4.
38 Harvey, *Condition*, p. 249.
39 McGrane, *Beyond Anthropology*, p. 40.
40 See C. Cipolla, *Clocks and Culture 1300–1700* (Collins, 1967), and S. Macey, *Clocks and the Cosmos: Time in Western Life and Thought* (Shoe String Press, 1980).
41 Thompson, 'Time, Work-discipline', p. 64.
42 Kern, *Culture*, pp. 111, 12.
43 Schivelbusch, *Railway Journey*, p. 44.
44 Kern, *Culture*, p. 66.
45 M. Heidegger, *The Question Concerning Technology, And Other Essays* (Harper and Row, 1977), passim.
46 Harvey, *Condition*, pp. 257, 228, 246.
47 Thompson, 'Time, Work-discipline', p. 61.
48 Harvey, *Condition*, p. 249.
49 J. Carey, *Communication as Culture* (Tavistock, 1989), p. 218.

50   And see ch. 5 of my *Transgressing the Modern* (Blackwell, 1999).

51   D. Massey, *Space, Place and Gender* (Polity, 1994), p. 6.

52   D. Massey, 'Power-geometry and a Progressive Sense of Place', in J. Bird et al., *Mapping the Futures* (Routledge, 1993), p. 67.

53   See ch. 2 of my *Transgressing the Modern*.

54   K. Ross, *The Emergence of Social Space: Rimbaud and the Paris Commune* (Macmillan, 1988), p. 8.

55   Lefebvre, *Production*, p. 309.

56   Massey, *Space, Place*, p. 7.

57   J. Kristeva, 'Women's Time', *Signs* (1981), 7:1, p. 18.

58   Massey, *Space, Place*, p. 5.

59   See ch. 3.

60   de Certeau, *Practice*, pp. 103, 98.

61   Massey, 'Power-geometry', p. 66.

62   de Certeau, *Practice*, p. 109.

63   A. Ronell, *The Telephone Book* (Nebraska University Press, 1989), pp. xv, xv, 4, 8.

64   A. Briggs, 'The Pleasure Telephone', in I. de Solla Pool (ed.) *The Social Impact of the Telephone* (MIT Press, 1977), p. 120.

65   Kern, *Culture*, p. 316; see also p. 208.

66   I. de Solla Pool, Introduction to *Social Impact*, p. 4.

67   F. Kafka, *The Castle* (Penguin, 1957), p. 26.

68   L. Mumford, *Technics and Civilization* (Harcourt, Brace, 1934), pp. 245–6.

69   R. Williams, *Notes on the Underground: An Essay on Technology, Society, and the Imagination* (MIT Press, 1990), p. 70.

70   Cited in R. Hughes, *The Shock of the New: Art and the Century of Change* (Thames and Hudson, 1991), p. 188.

71   Cited in R. Wohl, *A Passion for Wings: Aviation and the Western Imagination, 1908–1918* (Yale University Press, 1994), p. 2.

72   Wohl, *Passion*, pp. 1, 143.

73   Cited in ibid., p. 287.

74   Wohl, *Passion*, p. 288.

75   W. B. Yeats, 'An Irish Airman Foresees his Death', in *Collected Poems* (Macmillan, 1961), p. 152.

76   Wohl, *Passion*, p. 282.

77   J. Davies, 'Mechanical Millennium: Sant'Elia and the Poetry of Futurism', in E. Timms and D. Kelley (eds.) *Unreal City* (Manchester University Press, 1985), p. 75.

78   Cited in ibid., p. 76.

79   Cited in Wohl, *Passion*, p. 308.

80   Davies, 'Mechanical Millennium', p. 68.

81   Ronell, *Telephone*, p. 264, and see pp. 99, 265, 260.

82   F. Kafka, *The Trial* (Penguin, 1953), p. 39.

83   Ronell, *Telephone*, pp. 264, 410.

84   C. Penley, *The Future of an Illusion: Film, Feminism and Psychoanalysis* (Routledge, 1989), p. 57.

85   L. Jordanova, 'Science, Machines and Gender', in her *Sexual Visions* (Harvester, 1989), pp. 122–3.

86   A. Huyssen, 'The Vamp and the Machine', in his *After the Great Divide: Modernism, Mass Culture and Postmodernism* (Macmillan, 1986), p. 67.

87 P. Wollen, *Raiding the Icebox: Reflections on Twentieth-Century Culture* (Verso, 1993), p. 46, and see pp. 41–7.
88 Huyssen, 'Vamp', pp. 70, 73, and Jordanova, 'Science', pp. 130–2.
89 Huyssen, 'Vamp', p. 71.
90 Penley, *Future*, p. 58.
91 Williams, *Notes on Underground*, p. 88.
92 See ch. 7.
93 Kasson, *Civilizing the Machine*, pp. 162, 162, 165.
94 Williams, *Notes on Underground*, pp. 90, 149–50.
95 Ibid., p. 147.
96 L. Marx, *The Machine in the Garden* (Oxford University Press, 1964), ch. 5.
97 Williams, *Notes on Underground*, pp. 114, 185, 123.
98 G. Orwell, *The Road to Wigan Pier* (Penguin, 1963), p. 172.
99 Williams, *Notes on Underground*, p. 125.
100 Hughes, *Shock*, p. 184.
101 J. Habermas, 'Modern and Postmodern Architecture', in his *The New Conservatism* (Polity, 1989), p. 8.
102 R. Barthes, *The Eiffel Tower and Other Mythologies* (Hill and Wang, 1979), p. 6.
103 Hughes, *Shock*, p. 181.
104 Le Corbusier, *Towards a New Architecture* (Architectural Press, 1974, originally 1923), p. 14.
105 R. Overy, 'Heralds of Modernity: Cars and Planes from Invention to Necessity', in M. Teich and R. Porter (eds.) *Fin de siècle and its legacy* (Cambridge University Press, 1992), p. 62.
106 H. Caygill, 'Architectural Postmodernism', in R. Boyne and A. Rattansi (eds.) *Postmodernism and Society* (Macmillan, 1990), p. 266.
107 M. Berman, *All That Is Solid Melts into Air* (Verso, 1983), ch. V.
108 Cited in S. Ewen, *All Consuming Images* (Basic Books, 1988), p. 206.
109 See ch. 2.
110 Le Corbusier, *New Architecture*, p. 10.
111 Cited in Berman, *All That Is Solid*, p. 168.
112 See C. Jencks, *The Language of Post-Modern Architecture* (Academy Editions, 1978), and *What is Post-Modernism* (Academy Editions, 1989), for further discussion.
113 Le Corbusier, *New Architecture*, p. 23.
114 R. Banham, *Theory and Design in the First Machine Age* (Architectural Press, 1960), p. 213.
115 Cited in Ewen, *All Consuming Images*, pp. 148, 170.
116 Banham, *Theory and Design*, pp. 327, 330.
117 P. Blake, *Form Follows Fiasco: Why Modern Architecture Hasn't Worked* (Atlantic–Little, Brown, 1974), p. 40.
118 B. C. Brolin, *The Failure of Modern Architecture* (Van Nostrand Reinhold, 1976), p. 40.
119 Harvey, *Condition*, p. 70.
120 R. Sennett, *The Fall of Public Man* (Faber, 1986), pp. 12, 15.
121 Hughes, *Shock*, p. 207.
122 Berman, *All That Is Solid*, p. 169.
123 S. Connor, *Postmodernist Culture* (Blackwell, 1989), p. 70.
124 S. Watson, '*In Situ*: Beyond the Architectonics of the Modern', in H. Silverman (ed.) *Postmodernism – Philosophy and the Arts* (Routledge, 1990), pp. 92, 95.

125   Kern, *Culture*, pp. 288, 295.
126   Pick, *War Machine*, p. 185.
127   Kern, *Culture*, pp. 295, 290, 292.
128   P. Fussell, Introduction to P. Fussell (ed.) *The Norton Book of Modern War* (Norton, 1991), p. 23.
129   P. Fussell, *The Great War and Modern Memory* (Oxford University Press, 1979), p. 21.

9 From Enlightenment to Holocaust:

Modernity and the End of Morality

The Marquis de Condorcet, one of the leading Enlightenment *philosophes*, greeted the French Revolution as a further manifestation of 'human reason slowly forming through the natural progress of civilisation'. Such progress was indeed a 'law of nature', and hence applied just as much to 'the intellectual and moral faculties of man' as to anything else.[1] Yet Condorcet wrote this in 1794, while in hiding from the Jacobins; and, since he was then recaptured, it is likely that only his sudden death, in mysterious circumstances, saved him from the guillotine.

The guillotine: a powerful symbol of the Revolution, its story can also be presented as a kind of allegory of Enlightenment. Dr Guillotin had proposed to the Constituent Assembly in 1789 that the existing methods of execution should be replaced, and that 'in all cases of capital punishment it shall be of the same kind – that is, decapitation – and it shall be executed by means of a machine'. It was widely agreed that the diverse existing practices were discriminating and inefficient, indeed barbaric, in that they frequently involved prolonged pain and even torture.[2] In short, execution should be the same for everyone, and should be carried out with scientific efficiency to make it as instantaneous as possible. The introduction of the guillotine in 1792 was, then, presented as a humane act of enlightened public policy; and indeed it *was* more humane than the alternatives (including hanging, still widely used). Decapitation had become democratized, and the guillotine a symbol of civic virtue.

The guillotine was also efficient in another way, however; it can be used to dispose of a large number of victims in a relatively short period of time. And it can be associated with three other developments, as Singer points out.[3] Firstly, the decline of popular violence in the Revolution. With the possible exception of the 'September Massacres', there had anyway been very few victims of popular riots and street violence, and now this element disappeared altogether. And secondly, the appropriation of violence by the state, and its control through a legal institution, that of the revolutionary tribunal. Violence in the people's name is actually placed under the law. And finally, this violence ceased to be a public spectacle. The guillotine was first moved to the suburbs, and then disappeared into the prisons themselves. State violence may be extensive, but it tends to be *concealed*. If Elias is right about the decline in the acceptability of violence in everyday life, then it needs to be remembered that this goes hand in hand with a possible rise in state-sponsored violence; as Freud observed, in a later period, the state forbids wrongdoing and violence, 'not because it desires to abolish it, but because it desires to monopolize it'.[4] And the result is, as Bauman suggests, that 'Pacification of daily life means at the same time its defencelessness.'[5] Overall, we see here the 'rationalization of violence', a process resulting from the politics of Enlightenment and modernity that suggests that the link between these and notions of morality and 'progress' is by no means clear-cut.

Remaining in the same period, we can raise, through the work of Goya, another disturbing theme, namely that the *bringing* of Enlightenment could itself produce evil. Enlightenment, it seems, always comes from elsewhere: there are the unenlightened, and those who do the enlightening. Goya was painting in the Spain that was being 'liberated' by the French troops; as an educated Spaniard, he was drawn to the rationalist ideals of the Enlightenment, yet here were those ideals being realized through the destruction of Spanish independence and culture. Yet the common people, in their struggle for liberty *against* the French, defended what he saw as the most obscurantist and reactionary side of Spanish culture: the Inquisition, royalism, and witchcraft beliefs. Williams suggests that this is a situation in which 'The French of the liberating revolution, of that "Enlighten-ment" to which many of the best spirits among Spaniards have responded, bring the future to Spain and plunge it into barbarism',[6] and the ordinary people fight back in kind; and this generates the creative dynamism behind many of Goya's paintings and etchings. 'The People' emerge as Beast–Hero, portrayed ambigu-ously, sardonically, savagely: mules may be carried on the backs of suffering peasants, or the peasants can *be* mules, carrying grotesque creatures (Church and State) on their shoulders; an educated man is shown being killed, horribly, by the people he wanted to liberate.

A situation like this may generate a deep pessimism about the very content of the Enlightenment programme. What, after all, do the French bring? In practice, little more than the demand for obedience. And Bauman suggests that this is more generally true of the Enlightenment project; that it actually reveals a deep distrust of the people. In the abstract, 'the people' were idealized; in practice, *actual* people were inferior, even disgusting; a rabble, a multitude, 'the mass', from which the notion of a backward, undifferentiated 'mass culture' will be born. Diderot, for example, wrote that 'The people are the most foolish and the most wicked of all men'; and for d'Alembert, the multitude is 'ignorant and stupefied'.[7] And McGrane suggests that the unenlightened were seen as not merely ignorant, but – even more contemptible – as ignorant of their ignorance: 'Not knowing that there are unknown causes of which we are ignorant is the deep nature of Igno-rance, of Unenlightenment, of the Other.'[8] As Bauman puts it, 'The substance of enlightened radicalism is revealed as the drive to legislate, organize and regulate, rather than disseminate knowledge';[9] and the 'civilizing process' could all too easily turn out to be self-discipline and self-improvement for the elite, and 'polic-ing' for the masses.

The goals of the Enlightenment were anyway crucially indeterminate. The problem is that notions like 'progress' and 'civilization' are inherently value-loaded, but in an age where religion no longer provided an agreed language, values and goals, the emancipatory language of Enlightenment became either indetermi-nate or dogmatic. Enlightenment ideas can generate conflicting moral and political programmes.[10] In practice, what has tended to happen is that 'progress' comes to be identified with the means used, rather than the particular goals, with proce-dures rather than outcome. Reason becomes a matter of 'correct procedures', of 'following the rules', whether this is conceived in instrumental terms (means–end rationality), in juridical and bureaucratic terms (subsumption under appropriate categories), or in cognitive and scientific terms ('testing').[11] Each of those aspects of modern rationality emphasizes impersonality, efficiency, consistency and objec-tivity, and attempts to exclude expressive, relational and value dimensions. In other words, a variety of possible goals could be represented as 'progress', so long as the means used to attain them could be taken as consistent with the formal and procedural criteria of modern science, bureaucracy and law. Not only do formal criteria of method and calculation come to the fore, but increasingly the tendency is to pursue only such goals as are consistent with these methods, achievable by their use. And since the problems they can solve are those of the manipulation and control of the world, 'progress' comes to be assimilated to the pre-eminence of this orientation to the world. The project of Enlightenment, the aspiration to a humane social order, slides inexorably into the project of modernity, the aspiration to rational mastery of the world, and 'reason' as a critical faculty of mind becomes 'rationalization' as a world-transforming social process. But to take the relation-ship between modernity, rationalization and Enlightenment further, we will con-sider a more recent and dramatic episode: the Nazi attempt to exterminate the Jews in the Second World War.

The Organization of Extermination

It is not simply a matter of numbers. If the total of Jewish and other victims of the Holocaust exceeded six million, and may have reached seven million, this is still only a third of the total who may have died in the network of Stalin's labour camps, the Gulag.[12] The peculiar hold of the Holocaust on our consciousness comes rather from the combination of its moral challenge – it was an uncompro-mising, deliberate, systematic attempt to eradicate a whole culture – and its challenge to our explanatory understanding, in that while the Gulag, as a conse-quence of communist state power, can be identified as an heir of the Enlighten-ment tradition, this is not so clear with the Holocaust. If in some crucial respects an offspring of modernity, it does not seem easy to see it wholly in such terms; Nazi ideology, for example, seems hard to reconcile with Enlightenment ideas, and the horror of the whole episode has suggested the presence of deeply atavistic forces, even if at times clothed in deceptively modern garb.

The claim that the Holocaust is intelligible as a product of modernity – made most effectively in Bauman's work[13] – is the claim that the characteristic modes of organization of the modern world, and the accompanying attitudes, are entirely consistent with what we know of the Holocaust: in particular, the applied technology of mass production is the same as the applied technology of mass destruction. That modern bureaucracy could well entail danger had been foreseen by Weber, along with the political context in which the dangers would be more likely to be realized: 'the great state and the mass party are the classic soil for bureaucratization',[14] he wrote, and this would lead to a 'dictatorship of the official'.[15] The only hope of a way out would be that '*politicians* must give the counterweight to this domination by officials',[16] but it is clear that for Weber there is not much hope of this, for reasons made clear by his theory of rationalization. Substantive goals are only meaningful when translated into the achievable language of formal rationality: the politician can only 'impose' his goals on the official when the goals are made consistent with the norms of efficiency, procedural rationality and technical skill that define the imperatives of the organization and its *modus operandi*. There cannot be any heterogeneity between means and end; indeed, 'ends' may need to be redefined in the light of the available means, and this may be a continuous process.

Hitler had specified that one of the key goals of Nazi policy was that Germany should be *judenfrei*, 'free of Jews'. As Germany expanded its conquests, so the goal became that of a *judenfrei* Europe. The term is of course vague; it does not in itself necessarily imply extermination. And initially, the officials entrusted with the task of implementing the goal did not plan extermination at all. Himmler initially envisaged a Jewish enclosure in Eastern Europe, and as Russia was conquered the proposed site shifted eastwards. When problems arose, months were spent on a scheme to take over Madagascar and make that into a Jewish colony.[17] Only gradually did the camps develop, as they came to be seen increasingly as the most 'rational' means to attain the goal. The stalemate on the Russian front seems to have been decisive; further enforced emigration of Jews eastwards was proving increasingly difficult. By autumn 1941 the death camps had begun, in a rather unsystematic fashion, and at the Wannsee Conference in January 1942 this was placed on an official, organized footing, and large-scale plans were put into operation: the 'Final Solution' had indeed become death.[18] Hitler now explicitly referred to extermination.[19] 'What had hitherto been tentative, fragmentary and spasmodic was to become formal, comprehensive and efficient', writes Gilbert: 'The technical services such as the railways, the bureaucracy and the diplomats would work in harmony, towards a single goal.'[20] We can begin to see how, as Bauman claims, the choice of physical extermination was '*a product of routine bureaucratic procedures*: means–end calculus, budget balancing, universal rule application',[21] and there is extensive documentation of the 'machinery of destruction',[22] the minutely detailed planning and execution of the scheme, the sense in which it was indeed 'an exercise in social engineering on a grandiose scale'.[23]

In form at least, the solution had nothing in common with the spontaneous or manipulated episodes of large-scale crowd violence against the Jews that have been a feature of anti-Semitic outbreaks in many European countries in both modern and pre-modern times. Such pogroms did, indeed, occur in the early years of Nazi rule. They culminated in the notorious 'Crystal Night' of 9–10 November 1938, when the broken windows of the Jewish shops were accompanied by far worse horrors: a significant number of Jews were butchered, and over 20,000 were detained in camps.[24] But this was indeed, as Mayer suggests, 'more an echo of the pogroms . . . than a prefiguration of the coming Judeocide';[25] if these outbreaks were attempts to intimidate the Jews into flight, then their irrationality and inefficiency, however well they were manipulated, together with the accompanying disruption of social order, and the bad international publicity, led to their cessation. The rationalization of violence in the modern state rendered such episodes increasingly obsolete.

And the officials involved in the Holocaust? Given the extent and necessary complexity of the organizational problems, the number of bureaucrats and soldiers involved was very considerable; and it is significant that they were not selected for being in any way particularly committed to the ideological goal. Rather the contrary: the SS took some trouble to weed out sadists and intense anti-Semites. Strongly committed Jew-haters, it was thought, would be too unbalanced, would not make good 'organization men', which was what was required. They should just be ordinary people; reasonably responsible, efficient and obedient, capable of carrying out their tasks in a detached, objective manner. One is reminded of Weber's requirement for bureaucratic discipline: 'the consistently rationalized, methodically trained and exact execution of the received order, in which all personal criticism is unconditionally suspended'.[26] Hilberg concludes that 'The bureaucrats who were drawn into the destruction process were not different in their moral makeup from the rest of the population.'[27]

One aspect of bureaucratic discipline is the production and reproduction of secrecy. This secrecy was as yet imperfect at Auschwitz, not a purpose-built death camp. 'By contrast', writes Mayer, 'at Treblinka and the other three quintessential killing sites, the torment of the Jews was totally isolated and concealed.'[28] Organizationally, secrecy is always useful in minimizing the risk of outside involvement, and hence maintaining institutional autonomy and control over goals and practices, while at the same time proving difficult to maintain without further refinement of these practices. The division of labour proves crucial here. The Holocaust involved the movement of vast numbers of Jews across Europe, extensive problems of transport co-ordination and resettlement; a person involved at any particular stage of the vast apparatus, arranging train timetables, and so on, would never have to confront the full horrors that resulted. Long means–end chains of action make it more difficult to be aware of the overall logic of the situation, and can leave the end result in convenient obscurity. When death occurs at long range – with the press of a button, for example – killing can become 'morally invisible', just another technical outcome of chains of technical action. Even the official who poured the lethal chemicals into the gas chamber was carefully isolated from ever seeing the physical result. When ignorance becomes increasingly less possible, mechanisms of disavowal take over; people are generally quite good at providing rationalizations for themselves, at not seeing what it is not in their interest to see. Hence secrecy can easily slide into rationalization, a retrospective excuse for those embarrassed by their all-too knowing involvement.

Secrecy is only one aspect of the deeper dynamic that Bauman refers to as 'the production of moral invisibility'. Just as ends and means become assimilated in a technical language of mastery, so the moral and the technical fuse in a neutral language of 'value-free' objectivity. Bauman argues that 'Bureaucracy's double feat is the moralization of technology, coupled with the denial of the moral significance of non-technical issues.'[29] Nothing outside the process itself can be of moral relevance; external values come to be seen as meaningless; and in this moral vacuum, it is the self-sufficient process of bureaucratic rationality that alone retains a ghostly moral presence. The victims, defined simply as manipulable objects, become effectively dehumanized, since the wider moral implications of one's actions lie latent or concealed. End-orientated rational action, geared to goals described in technical, neutral language, takes us away from moral restraints, indeed the whole notion of 'morality' slides into the background. As Sayer puts it, 'Disembodied, the very forms of our sociality turn against us, and within them there is no place for humane values.'[30]

The very language used can powerfully reinforce these effects. Allied bomber pilots, in the war, wreaking havoc on German cities, would not talk of 'killing people'; the talk would be of 'hitting targets'. And since then, the language of war has become more 'neutral' still; in the Gulf War, the talk was of 'taking out installations'. Such care with language is an important feature of military training; technical euphemisms help to shield people from any direct awareness of the moral implications of their actions. Bauman informs us that the SS department for the destruction of the Jews was officially entitled the 'Section of Administration and Economy'; and the aforementioned official who poured the 'disinfecting chemicals' down a hole into the gas chambers was the 'sanitation officer'.[31]

None of this, of course, would suffice to establish that the Holocaust was in any way an inevitable result of modernity, but it does suggest a connection: if modernity was not a sufficient condition for the disaster to occur, it may nevertheless have been a necessary one. This, in effect, is Bauman's conclusion: 'Without modern civilization and its most essential achievements, there would be no Holocaust'; and 'The Holocaust is a by-product of the modern drive to a fully designed, fully controlled world, once the drive is getting out of control.'[32] And if the project of modernity is essentially an embodiment, an application of Enlightenment ideas, then the Enlightenment itself appears once again in a very ambiguous light: if it does not render the Holocaust inevitable, it does nothing to render it impossible or inconceivable.

But this is inevitably controversial. Huyssen, for example, argues that Auschwitz, after all, 'did *not* result from too much enlightened reason – even though it was organized as a perfectly rationalized death factory – but from a violent anti-enlightenment and anti-modernity affect, which exploited modernity ruthlessly for its own purposes'.[33] Analysing Nazi ideas, Mayer claims that their basic thrust 'was to negate reason, science, and progress in favor of irrationalism, intuition, and a return to an idealized past', amounting to a 'wholesale rejection of the Enlightenment'. For Hitler, the Jew represented the 'polymorphous modernity'[34] that he hated, so striking at the Jew enabled him to attack the forces of emancipation and modernization, which were for him 'the ultimate source of pollution'.[35] And in the end, Hitler was quite prepared to use those aspects of modernity that suited his anti-modernist purposes; bureaucracy could readily be adapted as an instrument for extermination. And, once resolved upon, this goal became absolute. 'In principle, no economic consideration whatsoever will be taken into account in the solution of this problem', stated Hitler's minister Rosenberg.[36] In one sense, the goal had been 'rationalized' – rendered achievable according to organizational dynamics – but its very absoluteness defied further rationalization, and this poses a problem.

In this connection, Herf has used the phrase 'reactionary modernism' to characterize the outlook of the Nazis, seeing it as an attempt to combine a cult of technology with romantic irrationalism, thus managing to be both 'modern' and anti-Enlightenment. He summarizes thus:

> They removed technology from the world of Enlightenment reason, that is, of *Zivilisation*, and placed it into the language of German nationalism, that is, of *Kultur*. They claimed that technology could be described with the jargon of authenticity, that is, slogans celebrating immediacy, experience, the self, soul, feeling, blood, permanence, will, instinct, and finally the race, rather than what they viewed as the lifeless abstractions of intellect, analysis, mind, concepts, money, and the Jews.[37]

As Hitler's propaganda chief, Goebbels, put it, the Nazis had understood how to take 'the soulless framework of technology and fill it with the rhythm and hot impulses of our time', thus discovering 'a new romanticism'.[38]

This suggests that an analytical distinction needs to be made between modernity and Enlightenment. The project of modernity entails the appropriation and transformation of the world under the aegis of instrumental reason, through a combination of technical mastery and organizational sophistication, and of the self-disciplined structure of personhood necessary to 'carry' this orientation. In this schema, no ends are absolute, save that of the reproduction of that very orientation itself. Enlightenment, on the other hand, refers to the goal, the possibility of realizing a community of citizenship and the social institutions and values required to maintain it. The problems arise as soon as it is realized that Enlightenment *as a project* must entail a close connection with modernity as project, and that the very attempt to constitute citizens as such will inevitably raise questions about power and its consequences, as we have seen in a previous chapter. The two projects may well overlap in their dynamics and their results. Nevertheless, the distinction is necessary if we are to make sense of the Holocaust debate, since it is clearly not unimportant that Nazi aims were not, on the face of it, consistent with Enlightenment ideals, while their opponents did (and do) draw heavily on these ideals for their struggles against these aims and policies.

However, this cannot, of itself, be sufficient to acquit the Enlightenment. Gellner points out that although Nazi ideology repudiated Enlightenment humanitarianism, 'it took with utmost seriousness the incorporation of man in Nature. . . . It is our *group* that matters, and it happens to be, they claimed, the biological group.'[39] If, as the Blochs argue, nature was, for the Enlightenment, 'the source whereby society, morals, education, even medicine, are to be reformed and purified',[40] then something of this, albeit in perverted form, remains present in Nazi ideology. Burleigh and Wippermann capture an aspect of this ambiguous inheritance when they suggest that the Nazi aim was 'to create a utopian society organised in accordance with the principles of race'.[41] And in their critique of Enlightenment, Horkheimer and Adorno argue that, for the Nazis, race is 'a reduction to the natural', and that their doctrines sought 'to make the rebellion of suppressed nature against domination directly useful to domination'.[42] Race was nature's revenge on culture, a twisting of Enlightenment naturalism to very anti-Enlightenment ends.

One can hardly discuss Nazi ideology without referring to modern nationalism, of which it is an extreme example, and this again reveals the complexity of the Enlightenment inheritance. For modern nationalism hardly makes sense without the universalist aspirations of modern citizenship, and the paradox of the appropriation of this by the modern state: one remembers, again, the French revolutionary armies, spreading *both* the 'rights of man' *and* French imperial power. 'If the *telos* of modern politics is universality', claims Bauman, 'its *practice* is the war declared on difference.'[43] But neither can one make sense of nationalism without drawing on Romanticism and the reaction *against* Enlightenment, especially in Germany, since it is this that provides the distinctive content of modern nationalism. Herder's *Volk* is the people as a cultural entity, with its own pattern of life and thought, so that 'culture' is irreducible to the abstract universality of reason.[44] The Nazi case is unusual here in drawing so heavily on race; for most theorists of the nation, like Barrès, race, as such, is too restrictive as a basis for national identity, reducing the ability of the nation–state to grow and develop.[45]

Yet all this still seems merely to scratch the surface. Perhaps that's all that discussions of the Holocaust ever do; and there has always been a school of thought that calls for an end to all the talk. Thus Steiner's view is that 'The best now, after so much has been set forth, is, perhaps, to be silent; not to add the trivia of literary sociological debate, to the unspeakable.'[46] Yet this very view points us towards fundamental issues of representation and morality that cannot be evaded. . . .

Enigmas of Evil

To suggest that the Holocaust cannot be adequately grasped, cannot be represented, is to raise the stakes. After all, it is only the gap between experience and knowledge that permits issues of representation to arise at all, just as this very gap, this absence, makes the pursuit of 'representational fullness' or 'adequacy' a chimera. So there must be something absolute, and absolutely distinctive, about the Holocaust, if it is to precipitate a crisis of representation that takes us beyond these standard dilemmas.

It is clear that this 'gap' – within which the whole gamut of the figurative power of language resides – does indeed cause great anxiety in these discussions. Jacqueline Rose reminds us of the critical abuse heaped on Sylvia Plath for daring to draw on Holocaust imagery in her powerful poem *Daddy*, in which her father becomes 'A man in black with a Meinkampf look/And a love of the rack and the screw', and she pictures herself in an engine, 'Chuffing me off like a Jew', to Dachau, Auschwitz, Belsen. . . . Rose suggests that, for her critics, it is as though 'The Holocaust can only represent itself, the Holocaust can only fail to be represented. The singularity of the Holocaust is that it is proper only to itself.'[47] The Holocaust represents the unrepresentable experience, and if this is so, any use of it as a resource for image and metaphor becomes both vain and trivializing. To draw on it in this way is to betray its essence – although we are no closer to what this 'essence' may be, with its calamitous consequences for our very ability to grasp it.

If figurative representation is seen as challenged by the Holocaust, this is true also of non-figurative representation and direct knowledge claims. Given the combination of secrecy and thoroughness that characterized the death camps, Lyotard outlines what could be called a 'dilemma of witness'. Of Auschwitz, he writes: 'if death is there, you are not there; if you are there, death is not there. Either way it is impossible to prove that death is there.'[48] The dead alone are the witnesses; and 'since the only witnesses are the victims, and since there are no victims but dead ones, no place can be identified as a gas chamber'. Perhaps, he adds, 'It is in the nature of a victim not to be able to prove that one has been done a wrong.'[49] Well, perhaps. But again, perhaps this is all too clever, offensively so, reinforcing Steiner's objection. After all, a sufficient weight of circumstantial evidence would serve as adequate proof, in a court of law; and of course there were survivors. If only two survived out of 400,000 Jews incarcerated and killed at Chelmno, one of the specialized purpose-built death camps, those two saw enough.

As I write this, it is the fiftieth anniversary of the entry of allied troops into Auschwitz, largest of the death camps, where as many as 20,000 were killed in a day, and a survivor is being interviewed on the television news: she tells of the horrors, the sights, the experiences, and, above all, of the stench of burning flesh; and she says that although she was 'liberated' all those years ago, she has never really left. . . .

Underlying all this, there is perhaps a sense that if the Holocaust defies representation, then it does so on behalf of morality; it is not so much that it *is* unrepresentable, as that it challenges the moral credibility of representation in the context of evil. If evil, in its status *as* evil, is questioned too closely, the questioning becomes obscene, partaking of the evil itself; if one debates it, or tries to represent it, use it as a source of imagery, one betrays and debases the horror of the experience itself. If there is something absolute about the Holocaust, then, it is perhaps this sense that it embodies absolute evil. This experience of evil cannot be known or reproduced in any way that is detached from the experience itself; all subsequent attempts to grasp it come too late, fracturing into soulless representation or empty moralizing. So the Holocaust presents us with the suggestion of an indeterminacy principle at the heart of our capacity to grasp evil, in which knowledge and sensitivity, representation and condemnation, become mutually exclusive and equally inadequate.

At this point it is necessary to consider the work of Hannah Arendt. She attended the trial of Adolf Eichmann – one of the leading officials responsible for the day-to-day organization of the Holocaust – in 1961, and in the book based on this experience[50] she rejected the concept of 'radical evil' used in her earlier work.[51] She retained the idea that evil could be in a sense unpunishable – as no punishment would be commensurate with the crime – and unforgiveable, but not the idea that it was rooted in motives that were so base as to be beyond our comprehension. Indeed, what struck her about Eichmann was that he seemed so mundane, his motives so straightforward as to be uninteresting in themselves; he was an official, doing his job. 'When motives become superfluous', she writes, 'evil is banal.' The 'banality' of evil is that it can spread over the surface of the world, become a feature of everyday life, uninteresting in its very ordinariness; and it is this that defeats our attempts to grasp it, not its impenetrable mystery. Evil 'possesses neither depth nor any demonic dimension'.[52] Evil that is banal is evil that is bureaucratized, rationalized; a product of modern modes of organization, illustrating the points made previously about the ability of these modes of organization to define ends independently of moral questions and to empty practical decisions of moral content, thereby implicitly rendering them all the more morally loaded. But it goes further than this, bringing in the Enlightenment heritage more directly still. Summarizing Arendt's view, Young-Bruehl writes:

> The refusal to connive with evil and the refusal to claim knowledge of the future are of a piece: it is an image of the future good, often linked to a theory of historical inevitability . . . which seduces good men into accepting an evil means. If evil is banal, no faulty nature or original sinfulness is required to become ensnarled in it; indeed, the best, not knowing what they do, are likely to become ensnarled for the sake of a future good.[53]

This is the moral universe that also makes Stalin's Gulag possible. And if Eichmann's evil is banal, that of the cog in the machine, this other dimension reminds us of the fact that the machine is nevertheless set purposefully in motion, and that more needs to be said of those who are directing it, or are involved in it, through conviction.

On joining the elite SS, a young man described his new comrades in these terms: 'I perceived them as strong, generous and pitiless: beings without weakness who would never putrefy.'[54] Generous to each other, they would be pitiless to The Other, gaining eternity through annihilation, a triumph over death through taking death further than it had ever been taken before; it would be a triumph of the embodied will, of the body as flesh and blood become steel, defying the ravages of nature and time. Hence we see what Friedlander calls 'the constant identification of Nazism and death', in which 'a ritualized, stylized and aestheticized death'[55] represents a transcendence of physical death and decay. And this ethos penetrated the whole Nazi elite. Here is Heinrich Himmler, addressing his SS generals in Poland in October 1943:

> Most of you know what it means to look at 100 corpses, 500 corpses, 1,000 corpses. Having borne that and nevertheless . . . having remained decent has hardened us . . . we have not sustained any damage to our inner self, our soul and our character.

He added that nobody had stolen anything from a single corpse; anyone who took so much as a mark or a cigarette would be executed at once, since 'we do not wish to become infected by the germ'.[56] In this purifying ritual of death, we encounter an equation in which the triviality of stealing a cigarette meets the same implacable justice as does the mass of innocent victims, an equation obscene in its monstrous disproportion. This triumph over nature, over putrefaction and pollution, is an exercise of pure domination, a celebration of unflinching masculine brutalism; reduced to mere power, the difference of culture is thereby implicitly denied, rendered one-dimensional. As Eagleton puts it:

> Fascism thus gives us the worst of all possible worlds: the torn, wounded Nature over which an imperious reason has trampled returns with a vengeance as blood, guts and soil, but in the cruellest of ironies is now harnessed to that brutally instrumental reason itself, in an unholy coupling of the atavistic and futuristic, savage irrationalism and technological domination.[57]

All that is left is dominance and submission, a macabre melodrama in which 'evil' is to be destroyed through an apotheosis that serves only to make the evil absolute. And in this celebration of power over otherness that defines absolute evil, it is modernity that is encountered in its own dreams – or nightmares – of omnipotence. On this terrain of fantasy, the sublime returns as obscenity, as absolute evil, a triumph of will which entails absolute destruction. Friedlander comments that

> Modern society and the bourgeois order are perceived both as an accomplishment and as an unbearable yoke. Hence this constant coming and going between the need for submission and the reveries of total destruction, between love of harmony and the phantasms of apocalypse, between the enchantment of Good Friday and the twilight of the gods.[58]

The aspiration for total power is the supreme transgression, the ultimate challenge, resolvable only by Armageddon, a cultural manifestation of the struggle whereby the triumph over nature always collapses back into it. Here the Enlightenment exile of otherness wreaks a terrible revenge in a fusion of modernity and anti-Enlightenment malevolence. And it is on the Jew that this venom is concentrated.

In *Mein Kampf*, Hitler stated: 'With the Jew there can be no coming to terms, but only the implacable "either-or".'[59] He tells of his first encounter with a Jew in traditional attire, and the drama of this 'recognition', suggests Garber, at once codes the Jew as 'the *umheimlich*, the uncanny, the repressed that will always return – the very essence of the Wandering Jew'.[60]

And we can return to Lyotard, for his claim actually points to an important truth. If it is indeed 'in the nature of a victim not to be able to prove that one has been done a wrong', then this entails the victim's complicity – or death. And if the victim's death is also to embody the triumph over death, then that death itself must be effaced. Victims have to be nameless, their bodies destroyed, every trace removed not only of their fate but of their individuality, their very existence; above all, their otherness. In the camps, then, writes Mayer, 'both the executioner and the victim were and remained strictly anonymous. . . . Theirs was an encounter of radical mutual exclusion and enmity.'[61] And Lyotard can state that

> The individual name must be killed (whence the use of serial numbers). . . . This death must therefore be killed, and that is what is worse than death. For if death can be exterminated, that is because there is nothing to kill. Not even the name Jew. . . .
>   Nazism requires nothing from what is not 'Aryan', except for the cessation of its appearing to exist.[62]

Otherness must not only disappear; it must become unthinkable – except that it needs to be constantly recreated, to enforce the necessity for its own cataclysmic destruction.

Ambiguous Legacy: Enlightenment and Otherness

Nazi ideas are sometimes portrayed as heirs to Nietzsche. In most respects, this is seriously misleading; but there are distant echoes of an earlier thinker: the Marquis de Sade. This should not be taken too far: the aristocratic individualist and libertarian would doubtless have detested the mass discipline, the bureaucratically organized brutalism, of the Nazi regime. Yet when Horkheimer and Adorno claim, of the Enlightenment, that it was Sade who 'mercilessly declared its shocking truth',[63] and when Connolly argues that Sade is 'the other of Enlightenment, using its own devices against it, perhaps bringing out implications it had left in the dark',[64] one could develop their claims to suggest that the ideas of Sade and the Nazis do at any rate manifest an analogous relationship to the Enlightenment. The argument, in effect, is that their ideas are, simultaneously, quite fundamentally anti-Enlightenment, while yet being inconceivable without it, and deeply marked by it, so that in this respect they cast a disturbing light on some of its central assumptions, and the practices in which they are embedded. What Bauman and others have claimed of the Nazi regime is, after all, comparable to Angela Carter's claim that Juliette, one of Sade's heroines, 'attacks civilisation with its own weapons', that 'she exercises vigorously rational thought; she creates systems; she exhibits an iron self-control', all the while proclaiming that 'I have no light to guide me but my reason.'[65] To develop this, we need a further consideration of Enlightenment ideas, and of Enlightenment as project.

Evil was not, fundamentally, seen as a problem during the high phase of Enlightenment optimism. Of course, oppression existed and was widespread, but it was essentially irrationalism, prejudice and tradition, and would not be able to withstand the light of reason. But although God was no longer so powerful a force in the world, the old theological problem of theodicy – how to reconcile God's goodness with the existence of evil in his creation – was destined not to disappear, but to be reborn in a more powerful and secular guise. For, as we have seen, the very proclamation of Enlightenment as a programme both called the 'unenlightened' into being and made their very existence a challenge. Not only that, but the recalcitrance of the unenlightened necessarily provoked a crisis in the programme; if Enlightenment was the self-evident truth of benevolent reason, its opponents could easily become not just irrational, but wicked. In effect, we find a sense of this project emerging *as history*; Enlightenment becomes a struggle, for a future that must and will be better, but cannot yet be. And it becomes a psychology, too: the enlightened must struggle not only with forces of reaction that are all around, but are in themselves as well, and the awesome responsibility exacts its toll. It is all too easy to come to need one's failure, one's inadequacy to a task that is so great; Enlightenment constantly requires an alibi, internal or external.

This has been articulated clearly by Connerton. Noting that the Enlightenment necessarily drives towards universality, he argues that 'it must entail the creation of a world for which man himself bears responsibility . . . it is man himself who makes his world'. And the theodicy problem returns with a vengeance; it is those who *have* made history, in the past, who can be blamed, along with those who constitute the present-day others who resist, through ignorance or malevolence. And these others have to be powerful, if they are to provide the alibi, the excuse for failure on the part of those who can see themselves as not *yet* makers of history: 'Only such an opponent can provide those who proclaim their intention of being the subject with the cast-iron alibi which they seek', hence 'Only thus can they guarantee their own impotence.'[66]

There are also significant tensions within the Enlightenment programme that have a bearing on this, so we need to consider these ideas in more depth. For the radical Enlightenment, sweeping away superstition and obsolete customs would make a harmonious, progressive social order possible. Utilitarian, empiricist assumptions, argues Taylor, nevertheless went hand in hand with a belief in 'the beneficent fruits of rational understanding'. We are capable of conceiving impartially of the universal good, 'And from this it was assumed that we would want to encompass it.'[67] Benevolence flows inseparably from the growth of a reason that is nevertheless based on self-interest. This optimistic doctrine was widely seen, however, as a sleight of hand, little more than an act of faith. Thus Diderot, sympathetic to the doctrine, nevertheless proved unable, in his influential *Rameau's Nephew*, to demonstrate the consistency of altruism and egoistic individualism, since it seemed self-evident that in a corrupt society it is self-interest rather than concern for others that is likely to lead to success.[68] One way out of this, favoured by economists, was to view social progress and cohesion as an unintended but inherent feature of self-interested interaction in the market (Adam Smith's 'invisible hand'); an alternative was to advocate a key role for the state as harmonizer of these competing interests. In an era when enlightened absolutism frequently made efforts to co-opt the bourgeoisie, and to plan centrally in the interests of economic growth, these two programmes did not seem necessarily incompatible, though there has more generally been a tension between them. MacIntyre summarizes this inheritance as follows, suggesting that on this model

> there are only two alternative modes of social life open to us, one in which the free and arbitrary choices of individuals are sovereign and one in which the bureaucracy is sovereign, precisely so that it may limit the free and arbitrary choices of individuals. Given this deep cultural agreement, it is unsurprising that the politics of modern societies oscillate between a freedom which is nothing but a lack of regulation of individual behaviour and forms of collectivist control designed only to limit the anarchy of self-interest.[69]

For Kant, neither version was acceptable: neither does justice to the autonomy and universality of human reason, reducing it in one case to the drives and instincts of nature, and in the other to culture conceived merely as power. Only by claiming that reason could, from within itself, provide a self-sufficient basis for a moral order, could this dilemma be avoided; indeed, on this basis, reason could also justify a limited role for self-interest and state power. Individuals are thus seen as embodying a capacity for rational autonomy. Taylor argues that, for Kant,

> if the decision to act morally is the decision to act with the ultimate purpose of conforming my action to universal law, then this amounts to the determination to act according to my true nature as a rational being. And acting according to the demands of what I truly am, of my reason, is freedom. . . . The moral law is what comes from within; it can no longer be defined by any external order. But it is not defined by the impulse of nature in me either, but only by the nature of reasoning.[70]

The 'categorical imperative' of morality thus entails a self-limiting autonomy of the rational self in which the need to obey the universal moral law, binding all free and rational beings equally, must itself entail respecting the autonomy of others, with whom we thereby constitute a universal 'kingdom of ends'. The form of the moral law is universal, and its content is given by this necessity to treat others as ends, never as means.

But this ambitious resolution of the Enlightenment heritage has proved notoriously unstable and indeterminate.[71] As observed earlier, there have always been competing visions of the rational–humane social order, each as apparently justifiable and consistent as any other; hence the risk that in the absence of the self-evident necessity of reason, the only way any one of these in particular could be realized would be through one or another form of authoritarianism. And if, conversely, the moral law retains the purity of the abstract, it purchases this at the price of its own mysterious impenetrability, becoming in turn an unknowable tyranny, a situation described in these terms by Deleuze:

> Clearly THE LAW, as defined by its pure form, without substance or object or any determination whatsoever, is such that no one knows nor can know what it is. It operates without making itself known. It defines a realm of transgression where one is already guilty, and where one oversteps the bounds without knowing what they are. . . . Even guilt and punishment do not tell us what the law is, but leave it in a state of indeterminacy equaled only by the extreme specificity of the punishment.

'This', he adds, 'is the world described by Kafka',[72] a world in which one's efforts to ascertain the law by which one has been tried and judged are always doomed, always too late, a world in which the mysteries of providence are replaced by the equally arbitrary and arcane workings of a 'rational law' that is all the more tyrannical because we have made it ourselves.

And to all this, the Marquis de Sade will reply that if we are indeed in such a world, then why not just relish the guilt? Why not just break the law willingly and knowingly, since one is bound to do so anyway? Sade juxtaposes the Enlightenment traditions, and draws dark conclusions. Yes, reason serves self-interest, he agrees with the utilitarian–empiricist strand, but there is no way any 'natural harmony' can be magically produced out of this. As Connolly suggests, he refuses 'to make optimistic assumptions either about the regulatory power of the market or harmonizing authority of community'.[73] And insofar as the Kantian position is right, that morality is both necessarily present and irreducible to nature, then it is also an imposition, since it necessarily enjoins us to do what we are reluctant to do; and it follows that, far from being a product of reason, it must be subverted by the latter. The problem in the Kantian formulation is pointed to by Dolar:

> it is only moral Law that constitutes me as a subject: for it is the Law that the subject imposes 'from within' that destroys the illusion of an autonomous subject. It is only in this pure autonomy that the subject has the experience of not being master in his/ her house. . . . The very element that was supposed to secure inner autonomy is ultimately what disrupts it; autonomy imposed internal heteronomy as its traumatic core.[74]

Morality becomes tyranny; and in challenging it, reason serves freedom. If reason tells us to pursue happiness even at the expense of others, then why not? The Kantian synthesis is sundered: morality and reason fly apart, and nature takes its revenge on the presumptions of culture. For Sade, writes Bürger, 'the instinctual drive is always in the right when it encounters any sign of resistance on the part of the object of desire'.[75]

In effect, Sade's critique homes in on the central assumptions of the Kantian synthesis: the rationality of virtue, as duty under the moral law; and the autonomy of reason, as it rests on the heteronomy of nature and culture. Reason is not autonomous; it serves the passions, the interests, or virtue. As for the latter, its charms are limited, and, on examination, it collapses into its opposite anyway. It preaches humility, but thereby serves pride; it proclaims honesty, but is deceitful about human motives.[76] Sade's characters, claims Bürger, 'take the stage as convinced partisans of the Enlightenment whose principal intention is to expose virtuous behaviour as a form of unenlightened conduct', one that is determined by 'prejudices and empty imaginings'.[77] Human culture is based on a natural egoism, so it is irrational to be motivated by anything other than self-interest and passion. Reason and nature are here conjoined, as rationalism takes its distance from humanism. 'The domination of the strong over the weak has always been one of the laws of nature', Sade assures us; and the tyrant or wrongdoer can 'abandon himself blindly to the idea of any crime that occurs to him: it is simply the voice of nature which suggests these ideas and this is the only way she can make us into agents of her laws'.[78] This is nature emptied of any cosy residual hopes of 'natural harmony', any implicit telos; as Connolly puts it, 'nature now allows anything and everything'.[79] Reason now serves domination; and if this includes domination over nature, in the interests of humans, it is also a domination by nature, a continuation of the egoistic competitiveness of nature by other means.

We return, then, to Enlightenment as struggle, directed against an enemy who may be inner as well as outer; and the two are connected. The heteronomy of the subject (self-interest versus moral law), central to its very autonomy, both reflects and creates, or recreates, a necessary otherness, constituent of its identity yet feared, rejected, blamed, projected outwards, as other. Hence the resistance to Enlightenment – in any of its forms – that is nevertheless essential to it, that defines it as *project*, in its very struggle for self-realization. We encounter again the knowledge–power dynamic referred to elsewhere in this book, characterized by Habermas as a 'sheer will to cognitive self-mastery',[80] a perspective central to Foucault's explorations of this theme in the project of modernity. Habermas summarizes this perspective as claiming that the modern form of knowledge manifests a tension, insofar as 'the cognitive subject, having become self-referential, rises from the ruins of metaphysics to pledge itself, in full awareness of its finite powers, to a project that would demand infinite power'.[81] The will to knowledge as power is thus driven by this paradox, to close the gap between self-realization and self-knowledge in a closure of identity that is forever unattainable; and this gap constitutes project as history, and history as struggle.

The hope of modernity, originating in the Enlightenment, was that 'evil' could become a category that was thinkable but unfilled, an empty category. We now know that it can be, has been, filled to overflowing, in ways that bear the indelible stamp of the modern, though doubtless not of that alone. And so, the world of project comes to star in its own – misrecognized – theatrical production. It plays the role of hero, of the good, while the excluded and disavowed other can all too easily be cast as evil, and can all too easily be seen as playing out the role, to the full. If this happens, the world of modernity can be a stage for a cosmic melodrama that has become all too real, a struggle of good and evil in which good can never, or never fully, triumph, because it is itself implicated in the evil which constitutes its baleful opponent.

Imagining Enlightenment

Has the dream of Enlightenment, then, turned so totally to nightmare that all we can hope for is to wake up from it? Some might argue that perhaps the real tragedy of modernity is not so much the direct evil that the grandiose schemes of social transformation have produced, but the daily moral squalor of political life in rationalized modern society, in which instrumentality, egoism and bureaucratic domination interact in a practical fusion of the Enlightenment traditions that empties everyday life of any meaningful moral and social content. But does the Enlightenment itself perhaps produce resources with which to combat this? While it is no part of my aim in this book to suggest some rival philosophical or practical alternative to the world of Enlightenment aspirations, discussed above, we can at least ask the question; and in a sense, suggests Habermas, the question has been there from the start:

> the self-critique of the Enlightenment is as old as the Enlightenment itself. Anyone who did not know the limits of the intellect was always considered irrational. If the intellect is inflated to the totality and usurps the place of reason, the mind loses its capacity to reflect on the limits of intellectual activity. Thus it is of the very nature of the Enlightenment to enlighten itself about itself, and about the harm that it does.[82]

This is actually quite close to Foucault's suggestion that what is most valuable about Enlightenment is precisely the attitude of *critique*; not the attempt to construct utopia, but the effort to expose institutions and ideas that frustrate freedom, and, more particularly, the effort to deconstruct the very products of Enlightenment itself, when they, too, have this effect. If modernity can only draw its rationale from itself – that is central to what 'modernity' *means* – then reason, as its characteristic mouthpiece, must make possible its own self-critique. Thus Foucault refers to 'a reason, the autonomy of whose structures carries with it a history of dogmatism and despotism', a reason which can therefore 'only have an effect of emancipation on condition that it manages to liberate itself from itself',[83] and suggests that the thread that connects us to Enlightenment is 'not faithfulness to doctrinal elements, but rather the permanent reactivation of an attitude', an ethos that involves 'a permanent critique of our historical era'. Hence 'the critique of what we are is at one and the same time the historical analysis of the limits that are imposed on us and an experiment with the possibility of going beyond them'.[84] Nevertheless, the debate in the early 1980s between these two authors tended to emphasize their differences: while, for Foucault, this notion of critique was really all that remained of use, for Habermas, a critical defender of the Enlightenment tradition and its emancipatory potential, what mattered most was to 'complete' Enlightenment by developing an intersubjective, communicative notion of reason to replace the subject-centred and narrowly instrumental model of reason found within the modern world.[85]

However, for a sense of what is at stake, let us return to Weber, whose despair at the 'iron cage' of rationalization, the dominance of bureaucracy and 'specialists without spirit',[86] was nevertheless complemented by scattered attempts to elaborate an ethic of how to live in the modern world and even, perhaps, make possible a continuation of piecemeal progress. And the limitations of Weber's model point reasonably clearly at those aspects of modern rationality that stand in need of critique and amendment.

For Weber, the old religious notion of the 'calling' – whereby one serves a God whose intentions are ultimately inscrutable, and does this with unquestioning commitment – can be reworked into a modern notion of 'mission' or 'vocation', whereby the tension alluded to earlier, between values and goals on the one hand, and procedures on the other, can be partially resolved by acting impersonally, conscientiously, and yet with passion. Without this, writes Goldman in his account of Weber's views, we would leave 'politics to bureaucracy without leaders, economics to bureaucracy without entrepreneurs, science to technique without innovators'.[87] The rational organization of the tasks of life, whether in science or the arts – the world of project – must be at the heart of this, for only thus can one acquire real 'personality'. To have 'personality' is not a matter of immersion in the world of experience, which would be mere 'intellectualist romanticism',[88] but requires being 'devoted *solely* to the work at hand'.[89] It is through goal-directed service that true selfhood can be realized, and such service, writes Goldman, 'must exclude all motives of self and orientation to others; one's purposes or goals must be impersonal in the most radical sense'. Once again, the Kantian law that must be obeyed, the awesome sense of universal duty, comes into view; for Weber, it is precisely this 'lack of regard for the "personal" aspects of the task' that 'allows one to become a "person" in the fullest sense'. And Goldman concludes:

> Thus, personality and calling can serve as badges of authenticity within society, a basis for the mutual recognition of the elect and for the reconstruction of society.
> The true source of personality, then, is submission or devotion to the work or object as an ultimate value, coupled with systematic, rational effort in the calling to realize these values in the world.[90]

And this effort, writes Weber, calls for 'qualities of passion, responsibility and proportion'. Passion without self-discipline is dangerous; self-discipline without passion produces the 'cog in the machine'.

In effect, argues Roslyn Bologh, we find here a very specific model of rationality, one that doubles as a model of manliness. Power, claims Weber, should not be an end in itself, or it becomes 'purely personal self-intoxication';[91] it must be subordinated to a cause. And this employment of strength and power in the service of some cause he celebrates as 'manliness', writes Bologh, and this manliness is distinguished by the emphasis on charisma, an element of 'spirit and inspiration': 'masculinity (concern for strength, power, courage) as an end in itself expressed in vanity and boastfulness, he devalues and condemns'. His conception of manliness idealizes 'individualism, independence, power and greatness', so other qualities and values tend to fall by the wayside: 'Reflection and contemplation, responsiveness to that which is other and those who are other, represent distractions that threaten to obstruct decisive action and to disrupt unity of purpose.' In short, Weber is an authentic spokesman for modernity as project and the rationality it embodies, in which we encounter two aspects of the modern masculine ideal: 'the strong, forceful, committed, ethical individual (value rationality) and the calculating, self-interested, aggressive individual (instrumental rationality)'.[92] And this model of identity also reveals the mechanism of dualistic exclusiveness, the emphasis on what Weber calls 'the unbridgeable deadly struggle'[93] between God and Devil, in which the adherence to one value or goal necessarily entails struggle against the others, which thereby tend to congeal into an Other, an embodiment of evil.

Whether one wants to argue that this project-centred notion of rationality, central to the Enlightenment tradition, needs to be complemented by – or incorporated within – a different one, based on situational, communal and intersubjective criteria, the fluidity of experience and relationship rather than the fixity of identity, or whether one wants to say that 'rationality' is itself too narrow a notion anyway, it is clear that any self-critique of reason must raise the issue. And in conclusion, it is appropriate to reflect briefly on the idea of self-reflection itself, and on this 'other' that has to be grasped in, or by, it.

Foucault suggests that the Enlightenment was a cultural process 'which came to self-awareness through the act of naming itself, situating itself in relation to its past and its future, and prescribing the operation which it was itself required to effect upon its own present'.[94] Yet there is something odd about this; Enlightenment as self-consciousness seems to involve a hubris, an arrogance that contradicts the very claim itself. Perhaps those who are enlightened can show it but not say it; those who *say* they are enlightened thereby disqualify themselves; and those who seek to enlighten others are the last people who should be entitled to do so. Perhaps the very idea of a self-conscious *project* of Enlightenment is contradictory, necessarily involving a dualistic projection of an unacceptable otherness which has to be reduced, overcome, assimilated – or destroyed. But can there be Enlightenment without project?

All roads lead back to Kant; and there are hints of this 'other' Enlightenment in his work. In one of his most optimistic texts, he claims that 'Enlightenment is man's emergence from his self-incurred immaturity', that this 'immaturity' is the inability to think for oneself, and that it is 'self-incurred' through a lack of resolution that enables some to set themselves up as 'guardians' and inhibit public debate; but so long as the latter occurs, the 'guardians' can be defeated. So long as this freedom to make public use of reason occurs, the public will enlighten itself. Ultimately, 'men will of their own accord gradually work their way out of barbarism so long as artificial measures are not deliberately adopted to keep them in it'.[95] As Rundell argues, we see Kant developing 'a notion of enlightenment through a strengthened and radicalised idea of the public', and the latter is a fusion of participation and publicity; free, acting subjects can thus emerge, since in the public, 'the actor is *both* spectator and player'.[96] And it is 'enthusiasm' that is the yeast that ferments this.

Here we encounter that apparently obscure and little-known side of Kant: the philosopher as enthusiast, Kant as the enthralled spectator of revolution, excited as the news came in of the latest events in Paris. Those who welcomed the French Revolution showed, by their enthusiasm, he claimed, something of the moral disposition of humanity, for 'genuine enthusiasm always moves only toward what is ideal and, indeed, to what is purely moral', not to self-interest.[97] The implications of this are left largely unexplicated in Kant, but have been taken up by Lyotard. This 'enthusiasm' of the spectators, he writes, is 'a modality of the sublime feeling'. The imagination, which cannot adequately represent this, can nevertheless 'unlimit itself' through these feelings, which serve as a 'sign' of culture itself, as that through which nature attains reflective potential.[98] Hence the imagination can lead us to a feeling for the 'Idea of humanity',[99] for 'spectating mankind must *already* have made progress in culture to be able to feel this feeling. . . . This sign *is* progress in its present state.'[100] In this sense, the sublime points to the fact of community itself, but community as potential, as 'communicability',[101] and a communicability that rests on a sense of the positive and mutually limiting role of the feelings and the imagination, as well as the intellect. In this sense, a 'rational' and 'enlightened' community would not be one that saw itself in those terms. Instead of reflexive self-awareness, separating itself from a 'barbarism' located firmly elsewhere, there would have to be an awareness of barbarism as a possible product of such a conviction itself, in its dangerous complacency. And instead of a subordination of everything to reason, there would be a sensitivity to its limits, through the very fact of the sublime, grasped through the theatre of the imagination that alone makes possible our participation in the play of others.

Notes

1   N. Parker, *Portrayals of Revolution* (Harvester, 1990), p. 107.
2   M. Foucault, *Discipline and Punish* (Peregrine, 1979), Part One.
3   P. Singer, 'Violence in the French Revolution', *Social Research* (1989), 56:1. See also R. Janes, 'Beheadings', *Representations* (1991), 35, which brings out gender symbolism (guillotine as devouring mother, etc.).
4   S. Freud, 'Thoughts for the Times on War and Death' (1915), in S. Freud, *Civilization, Society and Religion* (Penguin, 1985), p. 66.
5   Z. Bauman, *Modernity and the Holocaust* (Polity, 1991), p. 107.
6   G. Williams, *Goya and the Impossible Revolution* (Peregrine, 1984), p. 8.
7   Z. Bauman, *Legislators and Interpreters* (Polity, 1987), p. 78.
8   B. McGrane, *Beyond Anthropology* (Columbia University Press, 1989), p. 72.
9   Bauman, *Legislators*, p. 74.
10   A. MacIntyre, *After Virtue* (Duckworth, 1985), p. 39 and ch. 5.
11   R. Poole, 'Modernity, Rationality and "the Masculine"', in T. Threadgold and A. Cranny-Francis (eds.) *Feminine, Masculine and Representation* (Allen and

Unwin, 1990), especially pp. 50–3. Weber's work is relevant: see notes 14, 86, 91 below.

12 C. S. Maier, *The Unmasterable Past: History, Holocaust and German National Identity* (Harvard University Press, 1988), ch. 3.

13 Bauman, *Modernity and Holocaust*.

14 M. Weber, 'Bureaucracy', in M. Weber, *From Max Weber* (Routledge, 1970), p. 209.

15 M. Weber, cited in H. H. Gerth and C. Wright Mills, Introduction to *From Max Weber*, p. 50.

16 M. Weber, cited in H. Goldman, *Politics, Death and the Devil: Self and Power in Max Weber and Thomas Mann* (California University Press, 1992), p. 169.

17 M. Marrus, *The Holocaust in History* (Weidenfeld and Nicolson, 1988), p. 31.

18 Ibid., pp. 32–3; M. Gilbert, *The Holocaust* (Collins, 1986), ch. 17; A. J. Mayer, *Why Did the Heavens Not Darken?* (Verso, 1990), ch. IX.

19 Mayer, *Heavens*, p. 307.

20 Gilbert, *Holocaust*, p. 283.

21 Bauman, *Modernity and Holocaust*, p. 17 (original emphasis).

22 R. Hilberg, *Destruction of the European Jews* (Holmes and Meier, 1985); Marrus, *Holocaust*, pp. 48–9.

23 Bauman, *Modernity and Holocaust*, p. 66.

24 N. Frei, *National Socialist Rule in Germany: The Führer State 1933–1945* (Blackwell, 1993), p. 135; Mayer, *Heavens*, p. 10.

25 Mayer, *Heavens*, p. 10.

26 M. Weber, *On Charisma and Institution Building* (University of Chicago Press, 1968), p. 28.

27 Cited in Marrus, *Holocaust*, p. 49.

28 Mayer, *Heavens*, p. 15; see also Frei, *National Socialist Rule*, p. 135.

29 Bauman, *Modernity and Holocaust*, pp. 98–102, 160; see also ch. 4, passim.

30 D. Sayer, *Capitalism and Modernity: An Excursus on Marx and Weber* (Routledge, 1991), p. 154.

31 Bauman, *Modernity and Holocaust*, pp. 14, 26.

32 Ibid., pp. 87, 93.

33 A. Huyssen, *After the Great Divide: Modernism, Mass Culture and Postmodernism* (Macmillan, 1986), p. 203.

34 Mayer, *Heavens*, pp. 90, 90–1, 94.

35 Mayer, *Heavens*, p. 107; M. Burleigh and W. Wippermann, *The Racial State: Germany 1933–45* (Cambridge University Press, 1991), p. 4.

36 Cited in S. Friedlander, *Reflections of Nazism: An Essay on Kitsch and Death* (Indiana University Press, 1993), p. 124.

37 J. Herf, *Reactionary Modernism: Technology, Culture, and Politics in Weimar and the Third Reich* (Cambridge University Press, 1984), p. 224; see also pp. 224–7, and ch. 1.

38 Cited in ibid., p. 196.

39 E. Gellner, *Postmodernism, Reason and Religion* (Routledge, 1992), p. 88.

40 M. and J. H. Bloch, 'Women and the Dialectics of Nature in Eighteenth-century French Thought', in C. MacCormack and M. Strathern (eds.) *Nature, Culture and Gender* (Cambridge University Press, 1980), p. 31.

41 Burleigh and Wippermann, *Racial State*, p. 3.

42 M. Horkheimer and T. Adorno, *Dialectic of Enlightenment* (Seabury, 1972), p. 185.

43 Z. Bauman, *Mortality, Immortality and Other Life Strategies* (Polity, 1992), p. 112.

44 C. Taylor, *Sources of the Self* (Cambridge University Press, 1992), p. 376.

45 Bauman, *Mortality*, pp. 106–8.

46 G. Steiner, *Language and Silence* (Faber, 1967), p. 163; see also pp. 123–4.

47 J. Rose, *The Haunting of Sylvia Plath* (Virago, 1991), p. 215, and ch. 6, passim.

48 Cited in M. Krieger (ed.) *The Aims of Representation: Subject, Text, History* (California University Press, 1987), p. 59.

49 J.-F. Lyotard, *The Differend: Phrases in Dispute* (Manchester University Press, 1988), pp. 5, 8.

50 H. Arendt, *Eichmann in Jerusalem: A Report on the Banality of Evil* (Faber, 1963).

51 Notably in her *The Origins of Totalitarianism* (Allen and Unwin, 1967).

52 Cited in E. Young-Bruehl, *Hannah Arendt: For Love of the World* (Yale University Press, 1982), p. 369.

53 Young-Bruehl, *Hannah Arendt*, p. 373.

54 Cited in Friedlander, *Reflections of Nazism*, p. 34.

55 Friedlander, *Reflections of Nazism*, p. 43.

56 Cited in ibid., pp. 102–3.

57 T. Eagleton, *The Ideology of the Aesthetic* (Blackwell, 1990), p. 348.

58 Friedlander, *Reflections of Nazism*, p. 135 (emphasized in the original).

59 Cited in Mayer, *Heavens*, p. 99.

60 M. Garber, *Vested Interests* (Penguin, 1993), p. 232.

61 Mayer, *Heavens*, pp. 376–7.

62 Lyotard, *Differend*, pp. 101, 103.

63 Horkheimer and Adorno, *Dialectic*, p. 118.

64 W. Connolly, *Political Theory and Modernity* (Blackwell, 1989), p. 72.

65 A. Carter, *The Sadeian Woman* (Virago, 1979), pp. 148, 35.

66 P. Connerton, *The Tragedy of Enlightenment* (Cambridge University Press, 1980), pp. 116, 119.

67 C. Taylor, *Sources*, pp. 329–30.

68 P. Bürger, 'Morality and Society in Diderot and de Sade', in his *The Decline of Modernism* (Polity, 1992), p. 84.

69 MacIntyre, *After Virtue*, p. 35.

70 Taylor, *Sources*, pp. 363, 364.

71 MacIntyre, *After Virtue*, ch. 5.

72 G. Deleuze, 'Coldness and Cruelty', from G. Deleuze and L. von Sacher-Masoch, *Masochism* (Zone Books, 1989), pp. 83–4.

73 Connolly, *Political Theory*, p. 77.

74 M. Dolar, 'The Legacy of Enlightenment: Foucault and Lacan', *New Formations* (1991), 14, p. 52.

75 Bürger, 'Morality and Society', p. 86.

76 Ibid., p. 86; Connolly, *Political Theory*, pp. 73–4.

77 Bürger, 'Morality and Society', p. 86.

78 Cited in ibid., pp. 174, 175–6.

79 Connolly, *Political Theory*, p. 78.

80 J. Habermas, *The Philosophical Discourse of Modernity* (Polity, 1990), p. 261.

81 J. Habermas, *The New Conservatism* (Polity, 1989), p. 177; and see M. Foucault, *The Order of Things* (Tavistock, 1970), pp. 308–9.

82 Habermas, *New Conservatism*, p. 201.

83 M. Foucault, 'Georges Canguilhem: Philosopher of Error', *Ideology and Consciousness* (1980), 7, p. 54.

84 M. Foucault, 'What is Enlightenment?', in P. Rabinow (ed.) *The Foucault Reader* (Peregrine, 1986), pp. 42, 42, 50.

85 See P. Osborne, 'Modernity is a Qualitative, Not a Chronological, Category', *New Left Review* (1992), p. 192; and Habermas, *Philosophical Discourse*, Lecture XI.

86 M. Weber, *The Protestant Ethic and the Spirit of Capitalism* (Unwin, 1930), pp. 181, 182.

87 Goldman, *Politics, Death*, p. 83.

88 Cited in ibid., p. 65.

89 Weber, 'Science as a Vocation', in *From Max Weber*, p. 137. See also R. Brubaker, *The Limits of Rationality* (Allen and Unwin, 1984), ch. 4.

90 Goldman, *Politics, Death*, pp. 68, 72, 73.

91 Weber, 'Politics as a Vocation', in *From Max Weber*, p. 116.

92 R. W. Bologh, *Love or Greatness: Max Weber and Masculine Thinking – A Feminist Inquiry* (Unwin Hyman, 1990), pp. 34, 51, 133, 134.

93 Cited in Goldman, *Politics, Death*, p. 75.

94 M. Foucault, 'Kant on Enlightenment and Revolution', *Economy and Society* (1986), p. 90.

95 I. Kant, 'An Answer to the Question: What is Enlightenment?' (1784), in *Kant's Political Writings* (Cambridge University Press, 1970), pp. 54 (emphasized in the original), 55, 59.

96 J. Rundell, *Origins of Modernity: The Origins of Modern Social Theory from Kant to Hegel to Marx* (Polity, 1987), pp. 25, 30.

97 I. Kant, *Kant on History* (Bobbs-Merrill, 1963), pp. 143–5, 145.

98 J.-F. Lyotard, 'The Sign of History', in *The Lyotard Reader* (Blackwell, 1989), pp. 402, 403–4.

99 I. Kant, cited in Lyotard, *Differend*, p. 165.

100 Lyotard, 'Sign of History', p. 407.

101 Lyotard, *Differend*, p. 166; and see Foucault, 'Kant on Enlightenment', p. 94.

10 Modernism, Art and Culture

'Modernism' is a problem: unlike most other topics discussed in the individual chapters of this book, it lacks any relatively clear everyday meaning. Everyone has some experience or knowledge of the city, fashion, or whatever, but to be aware of 'modernism' entails some knowledge of literature, painting or music *and* a particular perspective on them. It is as though to discuss modernism is to become a member of some obscure cult, at some distance from the concerns of most people in their ordinary lives. And to do this with any awareness that this *is* what one is doing is necessarily to angle the discussion, to adopt an ironic, demystifying pose, a reflexive tone, so that one moves more than half-way towards a postmodern stance. Perhaps this is itself to recapitulate the tortuous history of these movements, to participate in the dissemination and emancipation of a modernist consciousness that is, arguably, what the postmodern moment amounts to. At least this may have the effect of reminding us that the arcane aspects of modernism are nevertheless rooted in everyday modern experience, even if not generally seen in these terms; and that while modernism in the arts may still be inherently puzzling for most people – dissonant, tuneless music, opaque paintings that aren't proper pictures, 'difficult' novels without conventional narrative – such 'modernism' in other areas (like advertising) may be 'read', even enjoyed, unproblematically. Certainly modernism, like postmodernism, gives us a sense of a world that is already embedded in its own discussions of itself, its own reflections and images, a world that is inherently – whether puzzlingly, stiflingly or creatively – *representational*.

For a start, there are several historical waves of modernism. There is the mid-nineteenth-century surge associated with Baudelaire, Manet and Flaubert, and further consolidated by movements like Impressionism. Then there is the early twentieth-century surge, from roughly the 1900s to the 1930s, the period often referred to as 'high' modernism, with the successive revolutions in art (Picasso, Matisse, Kandinsky, Mondrian, through to Surrealism), and the experimental literature of the 1920s (Eliot, Joyce, Pound, Woolf, following on from Kafka and Proust). Some would also distinguish a later period, in the case of painting, an

'American modernism' of the Abstract Expressionists of the 1940s, when New York replaced Paris as capital of the art world.

But some further clarifications are clearly called for as well, however tentative. There is 'modernism' as the experience of modernity in everyday life and consciousness; I will refer to this as the 'modern experience' when it is necessary to distinguish it from a second, more specific sense, that of the refinement, appropriation and development of this in the arts themselves, and the transformations these have undergone. But there is a third level, too. We need to remember that 'modernism' in the arts has not, generally, been a unified, self-conscious movement. (There are exceptions to this; for example, Italian Futurism comes close to proclaiming a general ideology of modernism.) So in this sense, 'modernism' is a creation of critics and theorists, from Baudelaire in the 1850s to Greenberg a century later; and, particularly in the more recent cases, this has produced a highly contentious account of modernist art practices, with an emphasis on the autonomy, self-sufficiency and formal characteristics of the modern art work.[1]

This can be clarified if we return to the origins of modernism, in the time of Baudelaire and Manet. Clark suggests that it is during these decades that a decisive change occurred in painting and the other arts, which he characterizes as 'a kind of scepticism, or at least unsureness, as to the nature of representation in art'.[2] In effect, the experience of modernity in the city provoked a crisis of representation, a breakdown of the codes traditionally governing the depiction of reality. Increasingly, it seemed as though 'realism' – itself an earlier, modern innovation – was no longer realistic enough, that the unstable truths of the modern experience necessitated a re-thinking of the links between imagination, emotion and description. This 'modernism' is in the first place, therefore, an exploration of what is new in the modern experience, which in turn becomes a reflexive critique of representation itself. If the modern world is so fluid, so challenging, can it be transfixed in painting, thereby rendered static? Would this not itself be a form of untruth? The shift in the arts towards a focus on everyday, transient experiences, leads on to a focus on the artist's own immersion in this process, a fascination with the means of representation that alone, perhaps, promise a fixed point in the shifting sands, the 'eternal in the transient' sought by Baudelaire and Eliot alike. And if the hope proves illusory, a reflexive awareness is all the more important: the form of artistic representation increasingly becomes its own subject matter. Raymond Williams points to the social dynamics of this: separated from provincial cultures, exposed to new languages and traditions and a novel environment, artists and writers 'found the only community available to them: a community of the medium; of their own practices'. Thus were found 'certain productive kinds of strangeness and distance: a new consciousness of conventions and thus of changeable, because now open, conventions'.[3] And this can in turn result in the paradox of a modernism that is radical in challenging these conventions, yet conservative in guarding its own social autonomy, its institutional and cultural separation, its distance from the corruptions of 'mass culture'.

Situating modernism is difficult, therefore. When Berman claims that 'All forms of modernist art and thought have a dual character: they are at once expressions of and protests against the process of modernization',[4] the earlier discussion of architecture as a celebration of the project of modernity suggests reservations.[5] But as we move into literature, the theatre and painting, so the claim becomes much more apt, for much of 'modernism' in these areas does indeed embody, implicitly or explicitly, a dislike or critique of the results of the modern project. But this, too, is difficult: such distaste can lead either in a conservative direction, towards a yearning for the traditional certainties of gender difference, for example (Eliot, Lawrence), or towards a more radical questioning of these aspects (Woolf, Barnes, the surrealists). Ultimately, modernism is criss-crossed by tensions; yet even conservative modernists convey, in their work, a sense of confrontation with an otherness otherwise disavowed. Indeed, it could be argued that this is crucial to the significance of modernism, that it is here that modernity's repressions, exclusions and disavowals knock most insistently at the door, managing to achieve an explicitness, a presence, denied elsewhere. Modernism is haunted by ghosts, even as it opens up the revolutionary exploration of the new.

It is time for examples. These are deliberately chosen as slightly 'off-centre': rather than Picasso, we encounter Matisse; in place of Eliot or Joyce, Woolf and Barnes. This focus on the ex-centric may help illuminate the modernist canon, rather than merely reproduce its constitutive assumptions, its own self-evaluation.

Visions and Revisions: Modernist Vignettes

Harmony in Red

In Matisse's picture (reproduced in plate 8), we see a woman laying the table for a meal. Behind her, to the left, we can see a view of spring flowers and trees in bloom, through a window. This, so far, is to say little enough; but even that may be a little too much. Take the 'window'. The flatness of the view 'beyond' may not be beyond at all; the 'world outside' may be just a picture, hanging on the wall. The 'frame' is systematically ambiguous between these possibilities, and indeed lacks any of the obvious clues that would mark it out as a *window* frame: it is not apparent how it would be opened, nor does the 'window' function as a source of light. Perhaps it is 'just' a picture. Perhaps that is the fate of the 'world outside', in modern art: to be present only in its absence, as a picture of itself, as though the world is no longer something 'there', to be pictured, depicted, but is already pictorial, always already part of the frame, as real or unreal as the picture itself. Hence Flam suggests that 'The window view therefore functions primarily as a picture within the picture, a framed rectangle that exists in an ambiguous realm somewhere between the real and the imagined',[6] as though that, perhaps, is where everything has to exist. Hughes adds that 'This sense of slippage between image and object is one of the sources of modernist disquiet.'[7]

The painting dates from 1908, a significant year in the revolutionary changes that characterized artistic modernism; while Matisse was pushing his own art dramatically forward with this canvas, Braque, at L'Estaque, was painting the canvases that inaugurated Cubism. And clearly this painting plays its full part in the representational crisis that is central to modernism. It is clearly in some sense representational, but it does not depict; it makes no effort at naturalistic description. Matisse himself claimed that 'I cannot copy nature in a servile way; I must interpret nature and submit it to the spirit of the picture.'[8] In particular, this picture – along with the contemporary canvases of Braque and Picasso – challenges classical perspectivism at its core. Perspectivism had long been the dominant visual regime of modernity, one that was so successful as 'to convince an entire civilization that it possessed an infallible method of representation', writes Mitchell, adding that its hegemony can be seen in 'the way it denies its own artificiality and lays claim to being a "natural" representation of "the way things look"'.[9] If perspectivism has been described as presenting a painting as a view through a window, as if it were a recess in a wall through which the viewer could observe the world beyond, then Matisse's 'window' emerges as a parody of perspectivism: there is no illusion of recess, but a manifestly flat surface, with no way of looking through it, and no confidence as to a 'world beyond' at all. In its play of illusions, it exposes the illusions of perspectivism itself, its inherent artifice.

After all, perspectivism has always carried its own problems. Whose is this eye, this monocular unblinking fixed eye of the perspectival subject? Jay points to a tension between the assumption of 'a transcendental subjectivity characteristic of universalist humanism', with the eye as somehow 'outside' the world it perceives, and an inherently relativistic contingency, 'solely dependent on the particular, individual vision of distinct beholders',[10] a version of the observer–participant, self-body duality that can be related to the civilizing process.[11] Matisse's painting can be said both to reflect and resolve this tension: there is no privileged transcendental viewer, but neither is there a specific one, tied to a particular time or place, embedded in the atmosphere of a particular moment. Indeed, no assumption of a unitary viewing subject is made.

Instead, attention shifts to 'the tensions between two- and three-dimensionality which gives the picture so much of its force', as Flam puts it.[12] Here, we can recall an observation made by the art critic Denis in 1900, that 'a picture – before being a war horse, a nude woman, or an anecdote – is essentially a flat surface covered with colors assembled in a certain order'.[13] This is central to the modernist programme, pointing to a self-consciousness about method, an awareness that the properties of the medium necessarily affect the result and must therefore be made central to the artistic process itself; and this affects the viewer, too, in rupturing the taken-for-granted, communal framework of shared perception in a violent reflexive act that demands that the viewer consider *how* the painting represents, before considering *what* it represents. The picture must achieve its goals, hold its interest, through its own qualities, rather than because of 'external' criteria, like verisimilitude: art must accept and display its artifice. In the Matisse painting, the sense of flatness encourages an awareness that everything that is needed is in the picture – there is no need to go 'beyond' or 'behind'. The painting constitutes itself as self-sufficient; it is the relations, the patterns, that are central.

This is a very full painting; there is an overflowing abundance of space, a sense of space as a plenum, in which gaps between objects become as real – or unreal – as objects themselves, and certainly just as vividly present, through the dramatic use of colour and line. Kern argues that this corresponds to profound shifts in the sense of space and form in the period when Matisse was painting. Space was no longer inert, a void between objects, but active and full. He refers to 'a breakdown of absolute distinctiveness between the plenum of matter and the void of space in physics, between subject and background in painting, between figure and ground in perception', so that 'what was formerly regarded as a void now has a constituent function', and draws the conclusion that 'If figure and ground, print and blanks . . . are of equal value, or at least essential to the creating of meaning, then the traditional hierarchies are also open to revaluation.'[14] Matisse himself comments that 'For me, the subject of a picture and its background have the same value . . . there is no principal feature, only the pattern is important.'[15]

This, so far, would be common ground to Matisse and the cubists, and one specific feature of Matisse's painting may be used to illustrate this. The distinction between table and wall is marked in a very inconspicuous way, by a faint line running left–right across the canvas, rather like a hinge that 'opens out' the contents of the room, as though they are all displayed for us on a two-dimensional surface (as indeed they are, of course). This tactic also features in cubist still-life paintings, many of which include a similar scene of table and objects. Again, this reminds us of challenges posed by contemporary visual experience. The millions who had ascended the Eiffel Tower had seen the earth as a flat pattern, a map of itself, in which perspective and depth become less significant,[16] an experience also commented on by the early aviators. The development of military camouflage in this period, too, 'broke up the conventional visual borders between object and background', as Kern puts it,[17] and this may be a case of art, in turn, reacting back on life. We have the testimony of one of the first camouflage experts, that 'In order to totally deform objects, I employed the means Cubists used to represent them.'[18]

There are, however, important differences. In the Matisse, the brash red of wall and table obliterates any clear distinction between them, while the objects situated by this framing retain their identities. With a cubist work, on the other hand, colour and line are less significant than the sculptural moulding of space in geometrical forms, separated by shading, with objects and spaces treated similarly. This produces a solid materiality, whereas in the Matisse space and objects take on an ethereal quality, as though the separate objects – the rolls, carafes and fruit – are only as real as the decorative yet dynamic arabesques that snake across the table-cloth and up the table–wall continuum. . . .

It is here that the contrast with Cubism comes into sharper focus. The vine-like creepers, the arabesques, seem to have a living energy, carrying a sense of exuberant profusion, as though menacing the calm order of the picture, yet also a central part of it. Flam suggests that the forces within the room thereby 'become an overt symbolic translation of the forces that underlie the predominantly green spring landscape outside'. And over all this presides the woman: 'energy flows from her hand to the fruit and sets the forces of growing things in motion',[19] and the painting becomes a meditation on fecundity, conveying a sense of pleasure that is perhaps inseparable from the artist's feeling that he, too, participates in this universe of creativity.

This offers clues to the subsequent history of the reputations of these paintings. Matisse himself seems to have been impatient with Braque's innovations in 1908, and rejected some of his paintings for an exhibition later that year. Yet Braque, and, above all, Picasso, have had their revenge: in modernism's 'myth of origin' it is always Cubism that is seen as *the* central movement in modern art,[20] and although Matisse's status is recognized, his contribution has tended to be sidelined, his sensuous curves and luscious colours seen as somehow secondary, tangential. Thus, claims Butler, 'The Matissean "decorative" tradition in art could be made to seem trivial . . . contaminated by hedonist and "bourgeois" habits of perception.'[21] Again, the crucial importance of colour in Matisse poses problems. Tamar Garb argues that by the late nineteenth century,

> drawing (*dessin*) with its connotations of linearity and reason, and the closely associated design (*dessein*), with its connotations of rational planning and the cerebral organization of the elements on the surface, were firmly gendered in the masculine. . . . Colour, on the other hand, with its associations with contingency, flux, change and surface appearance was firmly grounded in the sphere of the feminine.[22]

She adds that when, by the 1890s, Impressionism had fallen out of fashion in France, it was denounced precisely for what were seen as its excessively feminine features. Conversely, the straight line, sanctified by modern architecture and Cubism, duly became an 'emblem of modernity'.[23] In this scale of values, Matisse can hardly seem central.

The Waves

Virginia Woolf's development of key themes in literary modernism – the use of multiple perspectives, experience as plenitude, the fascination with 'the trivial', and the relation of time, reflexivity and selfhood – can be examined in *The Waves*, where the world of events and experiences is refracted through the consciousness of the various characters, each of whom emerges not only as a distinct individual but as a distinctive perspective on the world.

Take Louis, for example. One response to the challenges of contemporary experiences is to take refuge in the certainties of the public, masculine world of project, and this is the strategy he embodies. This is the world whose strengths Woolf recognized while yet taking her distance from it, struggling with it, through her whole career. Louis finds even his name reassuring, reassuringly solid: 'Clear, firm, unequivocal, there it stands, my name. Clear-cut and unequivocal am I, too.' Louis is important; one of those running the Empire. He loves to hear 'the heavy male tread of responsible feet down the corridors'. It is important to stay 'buttoned up', control meandering thoughts, stay well-organized and punctual. Such unity and purpose of self is vital: 'if I do not nail these impressions to the board and out of the many men in me make one . . . then I shall fall like snow and be wasted'.[24] So Louis is frightened of the multiplicity within, has a sense of the precariousness of this conscious, governing self, as though it might at any time be overrun by the horde of unruly others.

Bernard, however, is struggling towards a different conception, one he feels is truer to experience, one that does not involve narrative imposition. For Bernard, as for modernists in general, 'The world is no longer story-shaped', as Eagleton puts it;[25] and while some may bemoan this fact, Bernard does not seem unduly worried:

> I have made up thousands of stories; I have filled innumerable notebooks with phrases to be used when I have found the true story, the one story to which all these phrases refer. But I have never yet found that story. And I begin to ask, 'Are there stories? . . . to give you my life, I must tell you a story – and there are so many, and so many . . . and none of them are true. . . . How tired I am of stories, how tired I am of phrases that come down beautifully with all their feet on the ground! Also, how I distrust neat designs of life that are drawn upon half-sheets of note-paper.

For Bernard, the world, whether of clouds crossing the sky, or people crossing one's path, does not provide evidence of 'design', whether human or divine, save as an artefact of one's rationalizations, one's story-telling propensities. If each moment is a stage in life, there is no end to these, nor is there a process culminating in revelation, a point at which all becomes clear. If anyone proclaims 'this is the truth', claims Bernard, then 'instantly I perceive a sandy cat filching a piece of fish in the background. Look, you have forgotten the cat, I say.'[26] *The* truth escapes one's reflexive grasp; but truths are possible, perspectival truths, insights in a community of others. The confidence in History and Truth may have evaporated; but someone may always notice the cat. . . .

Dreams, street cries, and sandy cats filching fish: this is life as the everyday, the commonplace, the trivial, and a focus on this is common to modernists generally, in literature and painting alike. And if it is what is conventionally coded as trivial that becomes important, under the writer's gaze – just as, in practice, it is important to the texture, the quality of our everyday lives – so this implies a critique of the traditional, particularly masculine, novel, with its focus on 'important doings' and events, its creation of contrived plots and narrative flow. Turning the tables, Woolf attacks such authors for making 'the trivial and the transitory appear the true and the enduring'; they are 'materialists', who concentrate on unimportant externals,[27] and these priorities unwittingly reinforce prejudicial gender stereotypes, devaluing the contributions of women, especially in the domestic sphere. The feminine and the trivial are simultaneously assimilated and devalued. And conversely, for Woolf, there is nothing more important than the trivial. . . .

This stream of everyday life, 'alive and deep',[28] seems to have a paradoxical quality, in that its 'depth' lies all too close to the surface, so close that we tend not to notice it. For Woolf, and other modernists, a focus on this 'stream' necessitates an 'inward turn', an attempt to retrieve and display the world of experience, experience that is in some sense 'interior' yet firmly embedded in the tissue, the flow of everyday life: it can open us to what Taylor calls 'the usually hidden appearances of things'. And as we have seen, these 'appearances' may be 'hidden' by a framework of preconceptions about gender and selfhood that may be difficult to perceive and question. What can seem like a mere change in subject matter therefore has a more profound significance, and this can be deeply threatening, as we found with Louis (and is also the case with male modernists like Eliot). When Taylor adds that 'The recognition that we live on many levels has to be won against the presumptions of the unified self, controlling or expressive', this reminds us that the 'inward turn' is not necessarily subjectivist, committed to the idea of an integrated subject 'expressing' itself in some pure way, through the art form, even though this clearly has an influence in some strands of modernism (notably Expressionism). Rather, it is a 'decentring of the subject',[29] displacing the centre of interest on to language, imagery, the framing of experience, so that the subject loses its unity and control in the very act of trying to grasp it through the experience and consciousness whereby it is constituted.

This, then, is the 'reflexive turn', so central to modernism,[30] indicating the way the 'inward focus' displaces the self into its products, which thereby become allegories of selfhood, making possible a fascination with *how* this occurs. Woolf here participates in a shift of emphasis – found, in different ways, in Henry James, Proust, Joyce, and Dorothy Richardson – towards the novel as a manifestation of that very consciousness it strives to portray, participating in a flow of life that yet has to be its subject matter, hence raising acute problems of reflexivity and representation. The world the artist reflects on and strives to represent is already a product of similar strategies we all use in everyday life, so the attempt to portray this world can only be an attempt to portray the strategies of representation whereby that world is constituted as such for us. Meisel thus argues that the prose of authors like Woolf and Joyce can be found to be 'identifying by means of its reflexive realism the structures of the world it represents with the structures that represent it'.[31] Art becomes an imaginative transformation of the world that is nonetheless true to the modes whereby the world is incorporated and transformed in everyday consciousness. It is relations, processes and patterns that become central, and 'depth' is between, among, not 'beneath'; thus Woolf describes her aim as being to 'trace the pattern, however disconnected and incoherent in appearance, which each sight or incident scores upon the consciousness'.[32] Traditional realism now seems naive; words cannot simply depict the world. 'Words fluttered sideways and struck the object inches too low', writes Woolf in *To the Lighthouse*;[33] and this isn't a tragedy, rather it permits a reinvigoration of language, which can intensify our awareness of experience even as it problematizes our representation of it. In exploring language, modernist fiction can become playful, imaginative, ironic, just as it can also become nostalgic, yearning for an imagined unity of word and world (as in Eliot). Either way, it is allegorical, carrying resonances of the 'reality' it cannot capture.

For Jinny, this world of experience is one of constant flux, endlessly busy, full to overflowing, so one just has to plunge in. 'People are so soon gone; let us catch them. . . . One must be quick and add facts deftly, like toys to a tree, fixing them with a twist of the fingers.' This experiential empiricism involves a fusion of mind and body, an unreflective immediacy of impact: 'we who live in the body see with the body's imagination things in outline. I see rocks in bright sunshine. I cannot take these facts into some cave and, shading my eyes, grade their yellows, blues, umbers into one substance'; hence, 'I cannot tell you if life is this or that.' Jinny cannot remain seated for long, detached from the flow, but must 'push out into the heterogeneous crowd', so that things happen:

> Someone moves. Did I raise my arm? Did I look? Did my yellow scarf with the strawberry spots float and signal? He has broken from the wall. He follows. I am pursued through the forest. All is rapt, all is nocturnal, and the parrots go screaming through the branches. All my senses stand erect.[34]

Jinny therefore has an acute sense of the present, of life experienced in the present, life as presence. The present, experienced intensely, expands to encompass everything. Something of this is captured by Neville, observing that 'to sit with you, alone with you, in this firelit room, you there, I here, is all'. There is nothing beyond. The moment of presence is both eternal and fleeting, hewn out of the flow of time, a reflexive act of awareness, the moment when time 'lets fall its drop', a discontinuity rupturing the clear flow of 'before' into 'after'.[35] And if Neville's room expands to fill the world, it is also true that the world overflows to fill the room. Kern points to the enlarged sense of simultaneity made possible by telephone, telegraph and wireless, so that the present becomes 'a simultaneity of multiple distant events', so that '"now" became an extended interval of time that could, indeed must, include events around the world'.[36] For Joyce in *Ulysses*, one day in Dublin expands to encompass history and the world. . . .

There are really two differing experiences of time emphasized in modernist texts: time as fractured, discontinuous, and time as flow, duration.[37] These may, however, coexist. 'Stream of consciousness' writing, as in Dorothy Richardson's novels, attempts to grasp the experience of time as duration but inevitably conveys, just as strongly, the impossibility of capturing the 'smooth flow' in language, which fragments even as it describes. What these have in common is an exploration of time as experience, which is not clock time. There is, writes Woolf, an 'extraordinary discrepancy between time on the clock and time in the mind', so that 'The true length of a person's life . . . is always a matter of dispute.'[38] In effect, this is Kern's distinction between public, standardized, measurable time and the private, heterogeneous, subjective time of consciousness and experience, the latter becoming a key focus of interest for novelists and philosophers by the turn of the century, as the standardization of time produced a reactive awareness of these other dimensions of time. We could say, then, that the self operates in these two worlds, of linear, homogeneous, irreversible time – and is thus constructed as subject of, and to, time – but also lives these 'other' times, fluid and discontinuous, mingling daydreams, hopes and memories in an encompassing present. Kern points out the radical implications of this affirmation of these other dimensions of time, arguing that this 'eroded conventional views about the stability and objectivity of the material world and of the mind's ability to comprehend it. Man cannot know the world "as it really is", if he cannot know what time it really is.'[39] By the 1920s and 1930s, then, with Einstein's theories being widely (if misleadingly) seen as overthrowing the Newtonian programme of a science that would give us absolute, objective knowledge of the world – 'relativity' entailing 'relativism' – and with Freud's theories of the self as multi-levelled and densely opaque to itself, defying self-understanding, modernism emerges as an aspect of a profound sense of cultural crisis.

Nightwood

In 1936, after the high tide of literary modernism had receded, Djuna Barnes published *Nightwood*, a story based on Paris in the 1920s, and drawing, no doubt, on her own experiences as an American exile in this marginal world of avant-garde writers, of gender experiment and reaction, of the 'third sex' and the 'New Woman'. The book carried a laudatory preface by an acknowledged master of the modernist canon, Eliot himself, but does not seem to have been particularly successful at the time, being rediscovered in the feminist revival of the 1970s and later. The book can be used as a gateway to an 'other' modernism, of the margins and exclusions, existing in an intriguing relationship to better-known male modernist texts, notably James Joyce's *Ulysses*.

'Nightwood': the title itself resonates with the novel's themes. A wood at night is a mysterious, potentially dangerous place: shapes loom up, unrecognizable; every sound, every crack of a twig, challenges the senses and the imagination; a wood at night, writes Carroll Smith-Rosenberg, is 'a world without structure, a haunted place, invested with primitive magic'.[40] The 'hero' of the novel, the seriously weird Doctor Matthew O'Connor, much given to oracular pronouncements, profound and meaningless, has this to say on the subject of the night:

> Let a man lay himself down in the Great Bed and his 'identity' is no longer his own, his 'trust' is not with him. . . . His distress is wild and anonymous. He sleeps in a Town of Darkness, member of a secret brotherhood. . . .
>
> We wake from our doings in a deep sweat for that they happened in a house without an address, in a street in no town, citizened with people with no names with which to deny them. Their very lack of identity makes them ourselves. For by a street number, by a house, by a name, we cease to accuse ourselves. Sleep demands of us a guilty immunity. There is not one of us who, given an eternal incognito, a thumbprint nowhere set against our souls, would not commit rape, murder and all abominations.

Hence 'The sleeper is the proprietor of an unknown land', a land in which identity becomes an exploration of the undifferentiated, the primal, an engagement with the others that haunt the modernist imagination even as they are repressed or devalued. O'Connor adds that 'the reason the doctor knows everything is because he's been everywhere at the wrong time and has now become anonymous'.[41] A denizen of the night, he is left with a non-identity; a nowhere man.

With O'Connor, the modern link between knowledge and power appears to be broken. Like Tiresias, in *The Waste Land*, he can see everything and change nothing. He would seem, therefore, to join the Pantheon listed by Gilbert and Gubar: Eliot's wounded, sterile Fisher King, Hemingway's emasculated Jake Barnes, Lawrence's paralysed Clifford Chatterley. They write that these 'gloomily bruised modernist antiheroes churned out by the war' have been rendered impotent, as though 'having traveled literally or figuratively through no man's land, all have become not just no-men, nobodies, but *not* men, *un*men'. O'Connor has indeed seen war service, and he indeed seems like one of those young men in the trenches whose despair troubled the age, who felt exiled from their own culture, as though now 'their only land was no man's land, a land that was *not*, a country of the impossible'. Yet this land was 'real in its bizarre unreality'.[42] The night wood is after all a world of real fears, strange doings, the day's uncanny double; a world of exiles, of exile from place, from identity, from fixity; the modern world itself, of people as strangers not only to others but to themselves. 'Not one can claim a certain identity, few a clear gender', writes Smith-Rosenberg of the characters in the book, and their world. 'Their existence denies the inevitability of all structure and categories. They are liminal.'[43]

Nevertheless, in his introduction Eliot refers to O'Connor's 'helpless power among the helpless', and this formulation shows that his affinity with the wounded should not be pushed too far. O'Connor's pronouncements about the night occur in a key scene in which he is being visited by Nora, who needs to consult him (as we all do); 'consult' in a sense that is close to that of a patient consulting an analyst. Yet this is a parody of a consultation, a topsy-turvy reversal in which it is the patient who seems well and the doctor mad, and that serves both to ridicule the pretensions of analysis while also hinting at strange powers 'beyond'. Nora finds him in bed 'in a wig with long pendant curls that touched his shoulders . . . heavily rouged and his lashes painted'. The room, dirty and untidy, was a veritable wonder-cabinet of objects, 'a rusty pair of forceps, a broken scalpel . . . pomades, creams, rouges, powder boxes and puffs . . . laces, ribands, stockings, ladies' underclothing', and 'A swill-pail stood at the head of the bed, brimming with abominations.' Nor do we know whether this doctor is 'really' a doctor, as this is a world of 'splendid reeking falsification'; and O'Connor himself remarks that 'I tuck myself in at night, well content because I am my own charlatan', and content, perhaps, in thus embodying the truth of the profession. And his clothes, his make-up? Nora asks:

> Is not the gown the natural raiment of extremity? What nation, what religion, what ghost, what dream has not worn it – infants, angels, priests, the dead; why should not the doctor, in the grave dilemma of his alchemy, wear his dress?[44]

In short, the doctor is a shaman, in a culture that no longer believes in shamans, but nevertheless has a place for them, if only in its bad faith, its twilight zones, its nightmares, so that O'Connor has to be a living contradiction, male and female, real and unreal; 'a divine idiot and a wise man', as he says of himself, adding that 'A man is whole only when he takes into account his shadow as well as himself.' Still, this is not the whole story; there is another identity here:

> The wise men say that the remembrance of things past is all that we have for a future, and am I to blame if I've turned up this time as I shouldn't have been, when it was a high soprano I wanted, and deep corn curls to my bum, with a womb as big as the king's kettle, and a bosom as high as the bowspit of a fishing schooner? . . . No, I'm a fart in a gale of wind, a humble violet, under a cow pad.[45]

He is now the bawdy fool, Carnival reincarnate; thus does Barnes encompass, in this manic, exuberant language, what Jane Marcus calls an 'aesthetic of the Modernist Grotesque' which also 'marks the return of the repressed savage and unconscious desire'. Barnes is thus the 'female Rabelais'.[46] Clearly the elements are all there: the inversions, transgressions, earthy humour, above all the interest in the low, the base, which also reminds us of Surrealism, particularly Dalí's excremental visions. But in the end this return of Carnival is no Bakhtinian celebration. If, as Shari Benstock suggests, 'the oppositions that inhabit the moral structure of the novel are artificially produced in society by the very effort to suppress one component in the series of doubles', then *Nightwood* displays the results of this curse, but cannot lift it.[47] This carnivalesque pageant no longer has such affirmative power in its own culture.

We must return to a feature of this novel, one shared with other, more central, modernist texts: the endless allusions to other authors, other texts, others. The doctor, commenting on 'the remembrance of things past',[48] is clearly aware that he is in a modernist novel, dropping in a covert reference to Proust, to test his readers, let them show themselves to be worthy of the honour of inclusion in the charmed circle (as I show myself to be, of course, in pointing it out). The text is indeed littered with literary references and allusions. If this book is, to an extent, a New Woman's commentary on a tradition that is alien to her, yet inevitably one that has also shaped her, does it ultimately become trapped, recycling the past within a sealed, hermetic tradition? This perspective on literary modernism has been widely advocated, after all: the emphasis on the new, the experimental, seems inseparable from a sense of *déjà vu*; the tradition is played out, yet there is nowhere else to go. Thus Meisel suggests that modernist texts 'both thematize and dramatize the reality of coming too late in a tradition',[49] and Smith comments that in Eliot's poetry we encounter 'the totally new because self-conscious experience of stale recurrence itself';[50] language is constantly returning on itself, the narratives repeat themselves endlessly through a subject who can do little but rearrange the fragments. Woolf herself remarked that all the time 'some phrase which does not fit insists upon coming to the rescue – the penalty of living in an old civilization with a notebook'.[51] Modernism is in this sense trapped in the past it reflects on and parodies, particularly in that it continues the social exclusiveness of art as its own self-sufficient community and tradition. Inevitably this affects Barnes, too, despite her efforts to break out. Her modernist carnivalesque is arty, self-conscious and exclusive. It is not so much the people's second life as the novel's second life, or modernism's own parody of itself, displaying its own repressions and inhibitions in a language of textual excess; not a solution to its own separation from life, as literature, but a continuation of it.

However, it is surely Joyce's *Ulysses* that is the key point of reference, the nearest we have to a male modernist carnival text, in its sprawling vastness, its elephantine chapters, each exploring a different language, pushing them to their limits – already a grotesque body of a text, parodying the styles of everything from official institutions to the language of literature and the everyday. Certainly this polyphony of voices and experiences, seeming to escape the unifying power of any subject, exemplifies Bakhtin's claim that 'one language can . . . see itself only in the light of another language',[52] conveying a sense of the animating power of juxtaposed, interpenetrating languages and cultures, shifting and blurring the boundaries. In one area, though, *Nightwood* – which can be read, in part, as a response to *Ulysses* – goes further. Bloom's exploration of 'baseness' occurs in one episode, a sadomasochistic sexual scenario, a 'parodic Feast of Misrule', as Sandra Gilbert puts it,[53] whereas O'Connor lives his ambiguity and marginality on a daily basis, thereby questioning more subtly and radically the taken-for-granted assumptions about the coherence of identity, the modern ontology of the real and the unreal.

Perhaps, then, there *is* a sense in which the most powerful modernist works point to the 'second life', life lived in its 'other' aspects, even though their very status as novels (or paintings), hence problematically 'autonomous', can blunt the power of this. Makiko Minow-Pinkney writes:

> In order to put the category of the 'real' into question, the fantastic needs realistic forms, at least initially. Through such forms it speaks all that is unsaid and unsayable in the positivist narrative. Fantasy exists in the shifting of the 'real' and the 'imaginary'.

Indeed, *Nightwood* is realist in this initial sense, just as it is also fantastic. The juxtaposition of the two serves to relativize both, suggesting both as aspects of life and consciousness. And it could be that a key point of articulation between the two realms is that of the 'splendid and reeking falsification', the prevalence of disguise, the sense that things both are, and aren't, as they seem. Minow-Pinkney comments that '"Disguise" is a play with the boundary between seeming and being, blurring their sharp distinction and opening up a space of heterogeneity within unitary being.'[54] So in the case of *Ulysses*, argues Lane, we find that 'The conception of a realistic world, a present, concrete, and apprehensible actuality is conjoined with that of an ideal world, absent, essential, mediated through allusion and symbol'; and 'Neither is permitted hegemony, since each is understood to depend upon the other.' The upshot is a book which says everything and nothing, and its claims rest entirely on itself, 'upon its own paradoxical actuality as fiction, a reality which is not true, a truth which is not reality'.[55] As fiction, these works reveal the juxtaposed worlds as themselves fictions; they have truth as 'perspectives', but cannot be 'true' by being validated against the world they 'represent', for this world only exists, for us, through them. In their very separation, their triviality as 'mere' texts, their exploration of their otherness to themselves questions the status of the constituent categories of modern 'reality' itself.

Summary: experience, consciousness, representation

These explorations of modernism illustrate what Stevenson refers to as the trend away from 'the rational, logical and deductive, towards the intuitive, the unconscious, and the emotional',[56] from project to experience and representation. There is a focus on experience as plenitude, and the challenge posed by this to representational strategies in the arts, together with the way this enforces a concern with the ordinary, everyday world; there is an increasing self-consciousness in the arts, a 'reflexive turn', in the twin senses of an interest in which techniques to use, and the medium itself (words, paint, surface), along with what this in turn suggests about our capacity to grasp our experiences of space, time and the present, and the sense of self embedded therein; and there is a kind of 'return of the other', an interest in the way experience and its presuppositions necessarily open up 'other' dimensions, of gender, culture and the unconscious. The implications of these shifts are profound:[57] multiple perspectives become necessary in a world that is multidimensional or fractured, ever-shifting in our experience of it; indeed, the whole notion of representational adequacy becomes questionable, representation being, after all, a 'spatialization' which 'freezes the flow of experience and in so doing distorts what it strives to represent',[58] as Harvey puts it; and art, turning inward to explore its own possibilities, properties and problems, becomes introverted, emphasizing its social autonomy and attempting to ground its own authority on itself. Sass therefore concludes that there are two aspects of reflexivity in modernism: the rejection of naturalistic representation, leading to pure self-sufficiency, formalism; and a more 'deconstructive' focus on the narrative and representational conventions themselves.[59]

Let us take experience itself, and its relation to consciousness and representation. It is not easy for consciousness to grasp experience when experience is already inseparable from it, continuous with it; in effect, the attempt to do so enforces the sense of a gap between them, due to the very act of reflection itself. If, argues Connor, modernism involves a 'discovery of experience', it is also

the moment when self-consciousness invaded experience. If a modern sensibility is characterized by a sense of the urgent, painful gap between experience and consciousness and the desire to replenish rational consciousness with the intensities of experience, then this itself marks an awareness of the necessary and inescapable dependence of experience upon consciousness and vice versa. Every kind of split between experience and self-understanding is itself produced from forms of knowledge, or self-understanding.

In Woolf's efforts to represent inner experience, for example, we encounter 'an apparently irrevocable tension between the way human beings felt they lived and the forms used to render that sensation'.[60] It is as though representation becomes the perpetual quest for the unrepresentable.

The subject is in a sense separated from its own experiences, even as it seeks to grasp them; and since 'experience' thereby becomes something one has to examine from the outside, its 'integrity', both as the subject's *own* experience, and as a unified, taken-for-granted whole, becomes threatened. When, in turn, the self becomes itself an object to this reflexive gaze, it disintegrates, fragments: the self examined is the self in pieces, or else the very fact of absence itself. Similarly with 'consciousness': the aspiration to represent it inevitably comes up against the fact that consciousness is inevitably consciousness *of*, and that to reflect on this is inevitably to enter into a regress in which it is really the aspiration to severance itself that becomes the object. Modernism thus recoils on the subject. Trying to represent the unrepresentable, whether the 'outer' or 'inner' worlds – and the convergence of the two in experience and consciousness – results in relativism, fragmentation, and an uncertainty over boundaries, as though this is a culture that encourages schizophrenia by being already half-way down that road.[61] Modernist novels reveal the self as multiple or split, expressionist or cubist art shows the human form to be distorted, decomposed or recomposed.

This has widespread cultural ramifications. In modernist linguistics and sociology, the gap opens up: words, concepts, meanings, and the world, signifier and signified, are sundered, become matters of convention, with no possible guarantee of any 'real' or 'natural' basis of representation. Steiner regards this as the deepest significance of modernism, the end of 'language as Logos', the 'saying of being': 'It is this break of the covenant between word and world which constitutes one of the very few genuine revolutions of spirit in Western history', and this indeed serves to define modernism itself.[62] When the French symbolist poet Mallarmé declared that the word 'rose' has, as its sole life force, 'l'absence de toute rose', he announces the end of 'presence': 'The truth of the word is the absence of the world.'[63] Meisel suggests that this absence, this decentring, is present throughout a work like *Heart of Darkness*, and that the 'horror' at which Kurtz exclaims, at his death, is his sense of this, the impossibility of a grounding, a meaning, and this is precisely the meaning of the book, one that 'makes of absence the ground of presence itself'.[64] Gaps, absences, discontinuities: these have an impact throughout the culture of modernism, becoming a source of anguish to those who yearn for the alleged certainties of tradition, and a challenge to the innovators who see them as a stimulus, a spur to concentrate on the relations, the interspaces, the transverse links between appearances that constitute the real 'depths' when depth has become absence. Relations, gaps, become real; again, we can see that ground becomes as important as figure, background as important as subject. So 'what was formally regarded as a void now has a constituent function', as Kern puts it, and 'constituent negativities' appear everywhere (cubist interspaces, Mallarmé's blanks, Conrad's darkness . . .).[65] Steiner concludes that when Logos, with God as its ultimate guarantor, ceases to hold sway, then this 'break with the postulate of the sacred' becomes 'the break with any stable, potentially ascertainable meaning of meaning'.[66]

Hence the unease apparent in many versions of modernism. Butler detects a tension between 'an introspective alienation and a celebration of the sheer energy and collective diversity of life'.[67] Thus the conservative strand draws on the plethora of experience not to celebrate it but to order it, discipline it, in a kind of paranoid reaction formation that reveals both fascination and fear. The disorder of experience is taken as a mirror of the disorder of social and gender relations more widely, and art becomes both an escape and a corrective. Thus the paradox of Eliot is the paradox of the dominant, conservative strand in modernism: unsparing in analysis, innovatory in form, yet geared to traditional values, embodied in 'an assault on unconstrained personal expression and an insistence on order, intelligence and form', as Levenson argues.[68] Art becomes a form of authority; and it can only exercise this if it retains an autonomy from the corrupt temptation of the world around it. This modernism thus raises fundamental questions about the nature, status and possibility of art in the modern period, and like art itself, emerges as paradoxically both culturally revolutionary and socially conservative: its themes and methods radical, its social role highbrow, elitist.

Charisma, Creativity, Autonomy: Art and the Social Order

If, as Smith suggests, *The Waste Land* is 'full of deposed powers . . . where all the icons of authority have been toppled',[69] then this does not seem to affect the status of the work itself. Eliot's poem is Art, laying claim to insight and originality and the creative autonomy on which these must rest; and it is canonical, one of an approved list of 'great works', a revolutionary piece that nonetheless seems happy to join the Great Tradition. Its creator inherits the mantle of Genius, along with a position as 'artist' that dates essentially from the eighteenth century, the period of the institutional foundation of 'art' as an aspect of the convoluted birth of the modern.

Within that period, a threefold distinction became established, in which the 'fine arts' – which alone are truly 'art' – are distinguished both from the sciences, seen as fundamentally empirical strategies for understanding and mastering nature, and the crafts, practised by artisans, skilled in making things that may have decorative aspects but are basically governed by utility. More generally, art becomes modern when it becomes separate from the cognitive, ethical, political and practical spheres in the modern division of labour. The term 'creative', previously referring specifically to God's creation, moved across to characterize the godlike powers of the artist, acquiring connotations of 'originality' on the way; and the latter term no longer referred merely to origins but also to the sense of novelty.

The new aesthetics, developing from mid-century, crowned these developments by sanctifying the arts as the selective reproduction and representation of 'nature' under the canons of 'beauty'.[70] Through insight, art can give us a sense of the whole, thus subsuming the more partial and piecemeal approach of science and the formalism of morality. Its very separation can give it a vital role, therefore. The work of art thus comes to be an 'epiphany', argues Taylor: 'the locus of a manifestation which brings us into the presence of something which is otherwise inaccessible, and which is of the highest moral and spiritual significance'. The art work thus 'makes something manifest while at the same time realizing it, completing it';[71] it has an allegorical dimension.

This high status is not achieved without cost. Eagleton reminds us that 'Aesthetics is born as a discourse of the body', one which relates to the whole arena of perception and sensation. Yet, from the start, its potential for celebrating the body's experiences and pleasures is denied. Appropriated by philosophy, promulgated as a specialism, it extends 'a reified Enlightenment rationality into vital regions which are otherwise beyond its reach'.[72] This develops into a key distinction between the 'taste of sense' and the 'taste of reflection', fundamental to 'high' aesthetics since Kant, and characterized by Bourdieu in these terms: '"Pure" taste and the aesthetics which provides its theory are founded on a refusal of "impure" taste and of *aisthesis* (sensation), the simple primitive form of pleasure reduced to a pleasure of the senses.' 'Pure' pleasure, then, is reflective, distanced, sublimated, contemplative, refined, 'pleasure purified of pleasure', in contrast to 'facile' pleasure, which is coarse, vulgar, 'natural', shallow, exhibitionist, body-centred, participatory: going to the opera rather than going to a rave. From this point of view, argues Bourdieu, the object of pleasure, of enjoyment, 'annihilates the distancing power of representation, the essentially human power of suspending immediate, animal attachment to the sensible and refusing submission to the pure affect'.[73] And it becomes clear how art and cultural consumption can become centrally implicated in the politics of status and social distinctions: 'culture' in this sense becomes a mark of refinement, of 'civilization', of the educated bourgeois. Here, in essence, is the whole split between 'high' art and 'mass' culture, the latter condemned for providing cheap, easy, undemanding, uncritical pleasures through valueless genres like melodrama, soap opera and romance fiction.

This problematical social position of the arts – simultaneously autonomous, a specialized product of the modern division of labour, while conservatively embedded in the social order through dependence on canons of 'good taste' – understandably creates difficulties for the artist. The tension will not necessarily be too great for an artist committed to a more conventional aesthetic of the beautiful; but the aesthetics of the sublime cannot so easily be assimilated, as we have seen earlier, in discussing 'genius'.[74] The genius is necessarily inspirational, spontaneous, in no way bound by convention. And here we encounter the two central myths of modern art: that of the artist as autonomous, heroically exploring the truth of his insight and experience whatever the resulting social ostracism or condemnation to which he or she is subjected; and that of the work of art itself as a product of the individual consciousness, independent of social influences and constraints.

In effect, the genius becomes charismatic creator, the fount of originality, the transmitter of powerful, transformative new insights. Yet such charisma always carries with it the problem of recognition. If, on the one side, the artist is threatened by the banal, the collapse into mere reproduction of ossified 'truths', on the other the risk is of utter incomprehensibility, the total originality of madness. Even in just recognizing his or her own work *as* art, as meaningful, the artist necessarily appeals, at least implicitly, to a possible community of those with a similar perception, hence implicitly accepting that the original cannot be totally novel. It must, in some degree, be a repetition. Charismatic innovation rests on an implicit appeal to the very tradition it disavows. For the beholder, writes Rosalind Krauss, 'singularity depends on being recognized as such, a re-cognition made possible only by a prior example'; there is a sense in which we encounter 'the ever-present reality of the copy as *the underlying condition of the original*'.[75] It is as though the work of genius can only be recognized through an implicit denial of its originality; the artist, responding to this paradox, may thus be threatened by the very recognition he or she craves.

These tensions become ever more evident with the rise of modernism itself, with its cult of new forms to capture the ever-changing experience of the modern, and its accompanying sense that the distinctively modern artist is condemned to an ever-repeated originality, the very repetitiveness of which serves as a constant reminder of the unoriginality at its heart. And this sense that 'To be *original* is to reproduce, or re-produce, that which is there already', as Smith puts it,[76] can break into the awareness of the artist, become an overt dimension of the art work itself, so that in Eliot, for example, we have a sense that culture has indeed become a wasteland in which nothing new is left to be said. More generally, when artists from Baudelaire to Eliot tell us to capture both the permanent and the transient, they are in effect pointing not only to this tension in the world but in the approach of the artist, too. It is as though 'the present' cannot be represented in itself, or else that it can be represented only as repetition, implicitly denying its own status as original and originating. And this in turn implies a crisis of authority for the artist: any appeal to 'the new' is an appeal to what necessarily lacks authority, in its transience. Only the uniquely present, the new, the now, can claim authority; but the claim's validity slips away even as it is made, reminding us of the already-existing in the new, the reproducible in the unique, the copy in the original, and charismatic authority therefore again emerges as constantly self-subverting.

The tendency, then, is for modernism to repress this unoriginal condition of originality, the referent itself, the signified, whether as world or subject, so as to emphasize the self-sufficiency of the art object in its own distinctiveness, embodiment of its own mysterious charisma. This both produces and helps reproduce the myth of the autonomy of art. Owens summarizes what this implies:

> Modernist theory presupposes that mimesis, the adequation of an image to a referent, can be bracketed or suspended, and that the art object itself can be substituted

(metaphorically) for its referent. This is the rhetorical strategy of self-reference upon which modernism is based, and from Kant onwards it is identified as the source of aesthetic pleasure.[77]

In this 'high modernist' phase, the art object comes to express its own truth, rather than a truth from elsewhere. Thus, earlier this century, the Russian artist Malevich proclaimed that art 'wants to have nothing to do with the object as such, and believes that it can exist, in and for itself, without things'.[78] When beauty is derived from an inner finality of form, locked within the art work's self-sufficiency, a Greenbergian formalist aesthetic results; when the emphasis is rather on the work's failure to attain pure reflexive self-sufficiency, the way it still bears the marks of the struggle that locate it in the world in its very inability to escape, then it becomes sublime, unknowable to itself save through its own otherness. This is what Eagleton refers to as the 'internal slippage' in the art work, 'this impossibility of ever coinciding exactly with itself, which provides the very source of its critical power'.

Notions of originality in art have problematical implications, therefore; and the problems become even more marked when the implications of 'autonomy' are further considered. If, since the Enlightenment, art has embodied within itself the vision, the promise of totality, the integration of the rational and moral in the harmony of the beautiful, then this has socially ambiguous implications, manifest in a tension between the conservative and the radical or emancipatory potential of art. After all, the moment of art is the moment of dissolution: it promises unity, totality, in the very act of separation by which it is constituted as art. On the one hand, as Eagleton points out, both art and the bourgeois subject celebrate 'autonomy'; there is a certain homology between the two.[79] Consequently, sensibility, refined and purified into beauty, could provide a unifying consciousness, help bind together the existing social order. The work of art may thus purchase its status, its autonomy, at the cost of blunting its critical edge. On the other hand, its separation gives it an emancipatory potential, pointing to a possible future harmony, a utopia, transcending the tensions and divisions in the present alienating, unjust social order. Hence Shelley's vision of the poet as the 'unacknowledged legislator for mankind'.[80]

There is a trap here, though. The very separation of art can be both a condition for its capacity to criticize, to offer an 'alternative vision', yet also threatens to plunge it into a permanent state of 'bad faith'. Art requires the very separation it aspires to heal, hence posits the very object it seeks to destroy; it negates by its very existence the critique it offers. If it is this guilty complicity in the social order that 'spurs art into protest', suggests Eagleton, then this also condemns the protest to being 'agonized and ineffectual'.[81] Summarizing this perspective on art, and pointing to another implication, Schulte-Sasse writes:

> Individual works may have criticized negative aspects of society, but the anticipation of social harmony as psychic harmony, which is part of the aesthetic enjoyment for the individual, risks degenerating into a mere cerebral compensation for society's

shortcomings, and thus of affirming precisely what is criticized by the contents of the work.

In other words, 'The mode of reception undermines the critical content of the work',[82] and 'the very images of harmony threaten to hijack the radical impulses they hope to promote', as Eagleton adds.[83] And this returns us to the issue of art and its audience, suggesting how this abstract tension, this existential paradox in the whole position of art, may actually provide a central dynamic for its evolution, as a social institution, in the modern period.

The concept of the avant-garde is fundamental here: the avant-garde becomes agent of a 'civilizing process' of culture, precisely through being alienated from the bourgeois order. This pattern was already clear by the 1830s, in bohemian Paris,[84] and by the 1870s the avant-garde had become a widely recognized phenomenon, existing not just as a critical movement in the arts but taking on a radical political tinge. These artists and critics believed, writes Calinescu, that 'to revolutionize art was the same as to revolutionize life'; art could then overthrow the whole bourgeois system of values.[85] But the trap remained, the paradoxes of charisma and recognition, critique and separation. Public taste had to be changed; but public acceptability, for the artist, was always a threat. How could one be sure that such acceptance was not a betrayal of one's values, one's radical vocation as artist? It was as though the artist needed rejection as much as acceptance; rejection became a signifier of one's creative purity. Bauman argues that the avant-garde therefore needs 'to be *in*, but most emphatically *not of* this world; to declare that defeat is the ultimate sign of victory'; and to find in the very rejection by the mortal world the proof of one's immortality.[86] Thus we find Baudelaire exclaiming 'I should like to stir up the whole human race against me; in universal hostility I see a kind of satisfaction that would console me for everything else.'[87] It is as though bohemian and bourgeois need each other to pillory and denounce, tied together in a strange collusion.

Not surprisingly, then, the avant-garde is fragile. Acceptance, institutionalization, mean destruction. As Levenson observes, 'Avant-garde movements always threaten to disappear, either shattering into a collection of individualities or ossifying into an old guard', because of this permanent tension.[88] With modernism itself, Bürger and Eagleton point to a greater emphasis on autonomy as self-absorption, a withdrawal from wider involvement, and signs of this are evident in the vignettes discussed above. With Surrealism, however, we find an art which denounces the aesthetic; this is the avant-garde that turns against the institutional identity of art itself, its complicity in the order it attacks, its formalism, the way modernist art could be said to have sublimated its own evasiveness in a self-indulgent reflexivity. In the end, we are left with the empty gestures of art as anti-art, the shock for its own sake, producing an outrage that validates the gesture while confirming its impotence.[89] When Duchamp's urinal becomes an art-gallery object, the provocation is appropriated, turned into its opposite. As Bürger argues, when 'the protest of the historical avant-garde against art as institution is accepted as *art*, the gesture of protest of the neo-avant-garde becomes inauthentic'.[90] Shock rapidly becomes unshocking, and the once-revolutionary works become appropriated into the canon, the 'Great Tradition'.

The upshot is a crisis in the whole status of art. The exuberant waves of revolution that constituted the successive phases of modernism in the arts leave a sense of exhaustion. With each revolution implicitly or explicitly questioning the criteria used to assess art, and asserting its own quality controls as part of its revolutionary apparatus, the whole idea of 'standards' in art becomes increasingly unclear. If there can be no appeal to 'public taste' – if there is such a thing – and if the artistic revolutions leave a cumulative sense of uncertainty over criteria and values, how can standards be other than mere subjective preference? Modernism in the arts shatters older conventions, but necessarily subverts any claims it may itself make to timeless or absolute values. Art either collapses into the popular culture it has long feared, ironically becoming subject to the fashion it particularly affects to despise, or else retreats into ever more arcane, self-justifying and self-parodying acts of defiance: the twin possibilities that define the postmodern moment.

Other Modernisms, Modernism's Others

'High' modernism, especially as appropriated, or constructed, by critics and historians – 'modernism' in the third sense distinguished at the beginning of this chapter – has in effect been 'official' modernism; and modernism, in this aspect, repeats modernity itself, with its own exclusions, repressions, and disavowals of unacceptable presences, of others that will nevertheless not go away, as they are crucially constitutive of its own identity. Mass culture, and the pervasive sense of gender insecurity, are prominent here; but so also are the fear of the theatrical and the ornamental or decorative, apparently trivial dimensions that nonetheless take us to the core of these issues. But first, it is necessary to consider the ordering principles of modernism itself.

In the accommodation with science and technology, the arts were left free to explore their sovereign domains of representation and meaning, on condition they excluded themselves from the empirically descriptive and the practical. The old pre-modern fusions of 'knowledge', 'art' and 'design' (or craft), beloved of Ruskin and Morris in the generation or two before the main impact of modernism, would be no more; though a version of this, transformed into a radically modern guise as a utopian programme for the future, based on the hope that there could be an *aesthetic* renewal of design, fed into the Russian experiments in the revolutionary years of the 1920s. The arts are therefore menaced by utilitarianism and naturalistic depiction on the one hand (whether in the form of technological design, novelistic 'realism', or photography), and by the seductive temptations of mass culture on the other. Thus Harrison comments on how developments in modernity itself have served to give the arts a distinctive place, and 'to impel distinctions between art and design, and between high and low forms of art'.[91] Hence the coexistence of positivism and functionalism in science and technology, and modernism in the arts.

For modernists, then, the central task appeared to be the necessity to explore the conditions of possibility of their art, their own methods, and thereby, through this reflexive turn, theorize and safeguard their own art form. Greenberg, most influential advocate of this perspective, argues that the 'essence' of modernism lies precisely 'in the use of the characteristic methods of a discipline to criticize the discipline itself – not in order to subvert it, but to entrench it more firmly in its area of competence'; hence, the task of self-criticism is 'to eliminate from the effects of each art any and every effect that might conceivably be borrowed from or by the medium of any other art'.[92] Each art form becomes self-defining, each instance of it becoming 'civilized' through purification. Autonomy thereby ensures internal quality and external closure, exclusiveness.

When Huyssen claims that modernism 'constitutes itself through a conscious strategy of exclusion, an anxiety of contamination by its other', he points out that it is above all the ever-engulfing 'mass culture' that plays this latter role.[93] Greenberg sees a struggle between art and the forces of 'cultural decline', proclaiming that 'cultivated taste' is not within the reach of ordinary people or people without some 'comfortable leisure';[94] nor are the fundamental attitudes of Marxist critics like Adorno so different. Carey, in turn, exposes the elitism of literary modernists, seeing 'the exclusion of the masses' as the central principle of modernist culture.[95] And Huyssen points to another dimension of this. It was already taken as commonplace, by Flaubert's time, that women read romantic fiction, and Emma Bovary reads it too, even as her creator becomes 'one of the fathers of modernism, one of the paradigmatic master voices of an aesthetic based on the uncompromising repudiation of what Emma Bovary loved to read'. By the late nineteenth century the idea that 'mass culture is somehow associated with women while real, authentic culture remains the prerogative of men' had gained ground.[96] By the 1890s, with the rise of the New Woman and the controversies over homosexuality, a pervasive sense of gender crisis produced a male takeover of the 'high culture' novel,[97] and Lyn Pykett identifies a growing concern by male modernist authors with 'the negotiation and/or reestablishment of the boundaries between a feminized mass culture and a masculinized high art'.[98] And while women modernists like Woolf, Barnes, Richardson, Stein, et al. sought to articulate a distinctively female voice in modernism, they too remained, by and large, trapped within the divide, not wishing to be aligned with 'mass culture', thus intensifying the paradoxes of their position.

Nietzsche reflects these attitudes when he laments the decline of 'genuine culture' in the age of the masses and 'feminization', and denounces Wagner for succumbing to the 'adoring women' by 'transforming music into mere spectacle, theater, delusion'.[99] The theatre was indeed widely denounced as imitative and corrupted by pandering to the masses. But there is more to it than this. The issue, again, is autonomy. Theatricality, as Connor suggests, is seen as compromising the 'concentrated self-identity' of a work of art; it refers to 'the contamination of any artefact that is dependent upon conditions outside, or other than, its own',[100] whether this 'other' is some other art form, or mass culture itself. The critic and historian Fried, influenced by Greenberg, endorses this anti-theatricality, claiming that theatricality compromises the self-absorption that is the essential principle of modernism, protecting the art work from the two temptations of representation and spectator involvement. Theatricality also compromises autonomy through its tolerance of intermixing between the arts, contradicting the principle that each art must be governed by its own distinctive aesthetic: 'What lies *between* the arts is theatre', and 'Art degenerates as it approaches the condition of theatre.'[101]

Modernism draws here on a long tradition. Already, in the eighteenth century, argues Fried, some art was trying to escape what Diderot denounced as 'the theatrical', with its coy falsity, pandering to the spectator; painting should project its own self-absorption, not be self-conscious, as if aware of being looked at, full of rhetorical effects.[102] Similar points could be made about the novel. While both thematically and in its narrative form, the novel could be said to embody anti-theatricality, there was often a covert theatricality in practice, as in the rhetorical tactics by which Victorian authors self-consciously distanced themselves from their story, even appealing to the reader directly. As with the equivalent in painting, it is as though the novelist can be so confident of a taken-for-granted author–reader relationship that an explicit awareness of the novel's unreality can be permitted, and comments on the characters can become a kind of in-joke.[103] There is, in short, a sense of community between artist and spectator or reader, albeit a socially exclusive one, and it provides a framework in which the novel or painting can address an audience. In this sense, something extrinsic to the art form itself is always in play.

With modernism, this changes. The author breaks the links with the reader; the art work becomes its own self-sufficient reality. In the novel, it tends to be the consciousness of a protagonist *in* the novel that defines reality as a perspective on experience, providing a 'point of view' that frames reality while sacrificing community, since all points of view are different. In this sense, the anti-theatricality of modernism attacks community not just in the relationship between the work and its consumer, but in what it implies for the idea of community in the very content of the work. Here we do have a certain convergence between authors like Eliot and Woolf, and Einstein: the objective world is knowable through perspectives, and these perspectives are necessarily different, corresponding to different spectator positions. The author, like the reader, is on the sidelines, watching the depiction of the consciousness of the central character. Authorial licence grows, though in a way that can be seen as the 'death of the author', for it is the work itself that commands attention; author, like reader, becomes in a sense marginalized. Hence the frequent mixture of expressivism and detachment here: the artist must 'dig deep', but in the end, what matters is the product, and its qualities as art.

The other major dimension of modernist exclusion, the ornamental or decorative, has in common with theatricality the fact that although both risk the dangerous encounter with the temptations of mass culture, they can become attractive as a way of avoiding the domination of science and technology, and naturalistic representation. The Symbolists in the 1880s – important precursors of modernism – praised the decorative for embodying aesthetic values that went beyond the 'merely' descriptive and imitative. It could even be seen as embodying the distinctively 'modern'.[104] But by the 1900s, writes Gill Perry, the term 'decorative' had become unstable, and was used '*both* as a marker of the work's modernity, and in a more pejorative sense to signify the *ornamentation* of the applied arts'.[105] On the other hand, then, we see how the decorative also came to be rejected as kitsch, trivial, unnecessary, a symptom of mass culture – and the feminine. A worried Kandinsky, moving towards abstraction, asked in 1913: 'What should replace the missing object? The danger of ornamentation was clear.'[106] Hence what Fer refers to as the 'aversion to individual subjectivity, to decoration, ornament and luxury', and to 'backwardness, ostentation and vulgarity'.[107] This could easily lead to a machine aesthetic, and reminds us again of the distinctive position of modernist architecture: for architecture necessarily possesses a functional dimension, and may well embrace the first horn of the dilemma – science and technology – quite happily. Even here, though, most modernist architects prefer, like Mies, to proclaim a *fusion* of the functional and the aesthetic, rather than a reduction of the latter to the former.[108]

The contrast with Art Nouveau and its variants (*Jugendstil* in Germany, *style moderne* in France, *modernismo* in Spain) is instructive. Art Nouveau – the main rival to emergent modernism in the 1890s and 1900s – used the new industrial techniques and materials, yet was fluid, extravagant, languid, sensual, celebrating the non-rational, the pre-civilized. Ewen suggests that it was neither masculine nor straightforwardly feminine; it 'delved, instead, into the polymorphous sensuality of some imagined, primordial life'. He summarizes the contrast as follows:

> On the one side, the rise of mechanical production led to a visual idealization of the machine and its principles: rationalized order, geometric progression, and a methodically controlled social and material environment. On the other hand, Art Nouveau explored the churning reservoirs of an awakened and restless subjectivity: disordered, instinctive, driven by primordial nature. . . . Together these two tendencies of style may be said to constitute an aestheticization of the modern psyche: the concurrent tensions between conscience and desire, standardization and individual autonomy, mass society and human freedom.[109]

And although Art Nouveau continued to have an (often unremarked) influence, by the 1920s it was clear that the future belonged to modernism.

Modernist architecture, then, was born of a dramatic rejection of ornament. Gropius, director of the Bauhaus, denounced the architecture of 'florid aestheticism . . . in which the art of building became synonymous with the meticulous concealment of the verities of structure under a welter of heterogeneous ornament'.[110] Adolf Loos, in his 1908 manifesto revealingly entitled *Ornament and Crime*, proclaimed that 'The evolution of culture is synonymous with the removal of ornament from utilitarian objects', and he added that ornament was 'wasted labour power and hence wasted health'. Decoration was excremental, and its abolition as necessary as toilet-training, a perspective also seemingly implicit in Le Corbusier's preference for the 'White World' of rational order against the 'Brown World' of muddle, clutter and compromise.[111] In the context of the novel, this is reminiscent of Henry James's advocacy of 'a deep-breathing economy', since 'waste is only life sacrificed and thereby prevented from "counting"', and should be excluded.[112] For Loos, art itself represented an irrational, unbridled eroticism, and must be channelled and disciplined. Thus the extremism of these attacks reveals a characteristic obsession with order, cleanliness and control, a fear of excess, of the swamping of rational defences, the overwhelming of categories by the powerful energy of desire. Ewen points out that this was often posed as an opposition between male and female styles, so that modernists 'saw themselves as champions of an orderly masculinity, as cultural saviours from the feminized depravity marked by ornamentation',[113] a reflection in architecture of the gender politics of modernism more generally.

However, leaving ornamentality behind is not so easy, after all. A form of exterior patterned geometrical ornamentation is quite common in modernist architecture, as if the architect is trying, through mathematical form, to develop a non-ornamental ornament, one that 'expresses' the basic formal geometry of the buildings themselves. Another possibility, present in 'late modern' constructions like the Pompidou Centre and the Lloyd's Building, is that their modernity can be exhibited through pipes, ducts and girders featuring prominently on the outside, so that the buildings become, as Connor puts it, a revelation of 'the ornamentality at the heart of modernism, in their decorative display of the self-conscious signs of functionality'.[114] Neither version appeals to the purists: the former because it is 'mere' design, superficial, uninvolving, and the latter because of its exhibitionism, its baroque theatricality. Nevertheless, in painting, too, Greenberg accepts that the decorative is ineliminable, so he attempts to discipline it, incorporate it as an element in the unity of 'the pictorial', distinguishing an 'acceptable' decorative from an unacceptable ('ornamental') one.[115]

The irony of all this is that if art is divorced from practical social functions, it must in some sense be inherently 'decorative': the picture on the wall, the novel, celebrating the non-necessary, occupying 'free time', appealing to the varieties of pleasure. Even in the case of architecture, we can remember that 'the functional' is never *merely* functional. And if ornament can be seen as the manifest embodiment of the decorative, its overflow on to and into the surface of the art form, it reminds us that art cannot avoid the decorative; indeed, it must call on it, depend on it, to achieve its own independence, yet it also fears it and must disavow it, as the principle of the uncontrollable, the possibility of excess or dis-order that threatens art's ability to realize its own visions of order, of harmony. If 'decoration' is the appropriation in art of the excess of experience over project, it is acceptable only when 'disciplined', yet such discipline threatens its integrity, its difference. Ultimately, ornamentation is the excess that grounds and overflows the possibility of realized form in the first place, the 'something other in' the construction of the art work that makes it a relation of form and substance, abstract and concrete, the predictable and the unpredictable, showing how experience and representation always escape project even as they are realized in it. As Wollen suggests, in his wide-ranging discussion, this dimension constituted modernism's 'symptomatic shadow' from the beginning.[116]

There is, however, one movement in the arts that has been simultaneously an outgrowth of modernism and yet its baroque excess, aspiring almost self-consciously to the status of modernism's other: Surrealism. It is, appropriately, denounced by Fried as inherently theatrical, inherently polluting of modernist purity, transgressing boundaries.[117] It is hardly surprising that the surrealists were intrigued by Art Nouveau, caught as it was between the modern and the dated, the contemporary and the obsolete. Dalí called these buildings 'a dream world so pure and so disturbing . . . a true realization in themselves of desires grown solid'.[118] In relation to modern architecture, Foster suggests that 'The surrealists associated old architecture with its unconscious in part because they understood its outmoding to be its repressing', and adds:

> Surrealism is about *desire*; in order to allow it back into architecture it fixes on the outmoded and the ornamental, the very forms tabooed in such functionalism, associated as they became not only with the historical and the fantastic, but with the infantile and the feminine . . . the forces repressed in modernism often return in surrealism as demonically feminine.[119]

There is certainly a strong case for Fer's contention that 'the "feminine" was Surrealism's central organizing metaphor of difference'.[120] Not only was this a fundamental concern thematically, with Breton loudly proclaiming the failure of the masculine perspective on the world, but Surrealism (even more than Impressionism before it) was one of the few movements in art with a significant participation by women. The implications of this in practice, however, are not so clear. The famous 1927 issue of *La Révolution Surréaliste* contains a photo of a young woman dressed as a schoolgirl, seated awkwardly at a child's desk, pen poised, eyes open but vacant; the title is *L'Ecriture Automatique*, the young woman supposedly awaiting the stream of automatic images that will empower her creativity. But as Whitney Chadwick observes, this image of the naive, innocent yet sexualized woman–child, fount of inspiration, hardly serves as more than a projection of a masculine fantasy of the unconscious.[121] In many ways, Surrealism indulges, brings to the surface, this association of the feminine and the unconscious, rather than questioning it, or going beyond it; nevertheless, this 'aestheticization of hysteria', as Foster calls it, can be as destabilizing for the masculine subject as it is a problematic objectification of the feminine.[122]

Describing the qualities of Surrealism, along with those of Art Nouveau – and indeed, *Nightwood* – as 'baroque' is no mere figure of speech. Christine Buci-Glucksmann argues that our age is haunted by the baroque. With its 'theatricization of existence and its logic of ambivalence', baroque reason is 'not merely another reason within modernity. Above all, it is the *Reason of the Other*, of its overbrimming excess.'[123] It is as though just as modernity itself both grew out of, and suppressed, the extravagance and artifice of the baroque imagination, its rhetoric and theatricality, so the latter returns to haunt modernism and provide both its antithesis and its hidden dynamic. The Eiffel Tower suggests something of the complexity of interpretation here. It was hoped by Eiffel that it would be practical, used for aerodynamic measurements, radio-electric research, meteorology; but as Barthes argues, 'although Eiffel saw his Tower in the form of a serious object, rational, useful', nevertheless 'men return it to him in the form of a great baroque dream which quite naturally touches on the borders of the irrational', as 'an utterly *useless* monument',[124] extravagant, absurd: an appropriate icon of modernism – and of modernity itself?

Notes

1   See N. Blake and F. Frascina, 'Modern Practices of Art and Modernity', in F. Frascina et al., *Modernity and Modernism: French Painting in the Nineteenth Century* (Yale University Press, 1993), p. 127. See also S. Lash, *Sociology of Postmodernism* (Routledge, 1990), ch. 8, on varieties of modernism.

2   T. J. Clark, *The Painting of Modern Life: Paris in the Art of Manet and his Followers* (Thames and Hudson, 1985), p. 10. See also J. Crary, *Techniques of the Observer: On Vision and Modernity in the Nineteenth Century* (MIT Press, 1990), on changing regimes of the visual that preceded high modernism.

3   R. Williams, 'The Metropolis and the Emergence of Modernism', in E. Timms and D. Kelley (eds.) *Unreal City: Urban Experience in Modern European Literature and Art* (Manchester University Press, 1985), pp. 21, 22.

4   M. Berman, *All That Is Solid Melts into Air* (Verso, 1983), p. 235.

5   See ch. 8.

6   J. D. Flam, *Matisse: The Man and His Art, 1869–1918* (Thames and Hudson, 1986), p. 230.

7   R. Hughes, *The Shock of the New* (Thames and Hudson, 1991), p. 247.

8   Cited in C. Butler, *Early Modernism* (Oxford University Press, 1994), p. 36.

9   W. J. T. Mitchell, *Iconology: Image, Text, Ideology* (University of Chicago Press, 1987), p. 37.

10 M. Jay, 'Scopic Regimes of Modernity', in S. Lash and J. Friedman (eds.) *Modernity and Identity* (Blackwell, 1992), p. 183.

11 See ch. 2 of my *Transgressing the Modern* (Blackwell, 1999); and M. Foucault, *The Order of Things* (Tavistock, 1970), pp. 318–19, 322.

12 Flam, *Matisse*, pp. 230, 232.

13 Cited in S. Kern, *The Culture of Time and Space, 1880–1918* (Harvard University Press, 1983), p. 145.

14 Kern, *Culture*, pp. 153, 177, 179–80.

15 Cited in J. D. Flam (ed.) *Matisse on Art* (Phaidon, 1978), p. 72.

16 Hughes, *Shock*, p. 14.

17 Kern, *Culture*, p. 304.

18 Cited in ibid., p. 303.

19 Flam, *Matisse*, p. 230.

20 P. Wollen, *Raiding the Icebox: Reflections on Twentieth-Century Culture* (Verso, 1993), p. 17.

21 Butler, *Early Modernism*, p. 254.

22 T. Garb, 'Gender and Representation', in Frascina, *Modernity*, p. 285.

23 B. Fer, 'The Language of Construction', in B. Fer et al., *Realism, Rationalism, Surrealism* (Yale University Press, 1993), p. 157.

24 V. Woolf, *The Waves* (Grafton, 1977, originally 1931), pp. 112, 114, 114, 115.

25 T. Eagleton, *The Ideology of the Aesthetic* (Blackwell, 1990), p. 140.

26 Woolf, *Waves*, pp. 161, 126.

27 V. Woolf, 'Modern Fiction', in her *The Crowded Dance of Modern Life* (Penguin, 1993), p. 7.

28 Woolf, *Waves*, p. 173.

29 C. Taylor, *Sources of the Self* (Cambridge University Press, 1992), pp. 461, 468, 480, 456.

30 Ibid., pp. 467, 480.

31 P. Meisel, *The Myth of the Modern: A Study in British Literature and Criticism after 1850* (Yale University Press, 1987), pp. 162, 161.

32 Woolf, 'Modern Fiction', p. 9.

33 V. Woolf, *To the Lighthouse* (Penguin, 1992, originally 1927), p. 193.

34 Woolf, *Waves*, pp. 117, 119, 119.

35 Ibid., pp. 119–20, 124.

36 Kern, *Culture*, pp. 68, 314.

37 R. Stevenson, *Modernist Fiction* (Harvester, 1992), p. 136.

38 V. Woolf, *Orlando* (Grafton, 1977, originally 1928), pp. 61, 191.

39 Kern, *Culture*, pp. 11, 33–4, 314.

40 C. Smith-Rosenberg, 'The New Woman as Androgyne', in her *Disorderly Conduct* (Oxford University Press, 1985), p. 290.

41 D. Barnes, *Nightwood* (Faber, 1985), pp. 119, 128, 127, 121.

42 S. Gilbert and S. Gubar, *No Man's Land, Vol. 2: Sexchanges* (Yale University Press, 1989), pp. 260, 267, 268.

43 Smith-Rosenberg, 'New Woman', p. 290.

44 Barnes, *Nightwood*, pp. 117, 116, 25, 139, 118.

45 Ibid., pp. 65, 171, 132, 139.

46 J. Marcus, 'Laughing at Leviticus: *Nightwood* as Woman's Circus Epic', in M. L. Broe (ed.) *Silence and Power: A Reevaluation of Djuna Barnes* (Southern Illinois University Press, 1991), pp. 227, 227, 226. See also ch. 1 of my *Transgressing the Modern*, on carnival.

47 S. Benstock, *Women of the Left Bank: Paris, 1900–1940* (Virago, 1987), p. 265; and see S. Stevenson, 'Writing the Grotesque Body: Djuna Barnes' Carnival Parody', in Broe, *Silence and Power*, p. 86.

48 Barnes, *Nightwood*, p. 132.

49 Meisel, *Myth of the Modern*, p. 8.

50 S. Smith, *The Origins of Modernism: Eliot, Pound, Yeats and the Rhetorics of Renewal* (Harvester, 1994), p. 44.

51 Woolf, *Waves*, p. 124.

52 M. Bakhtin, *The Dialogic Imagination* (University of Texas Press, 1981), p. 12.

53 S. Gilbert, 'Costumes of the Mind: Transvestism as Metaphor in Modern Literature', in E. Abel (ed.) *Writing and Sexual Difference* (Harvester, 1982), p. 201; see also p. 199.

54   M. Minow-Pinkney, *Virginia Woolf and the Problem of the Subject* (Harvester, 1987), pp. 131, 132.

55   J. Lane, 'Ulysses', in P. Faulkner, *Modernism* (Methuen, 1977), pp. 56, 56, 51.

56   Stevenson, *Modernist Fiction*, p. 105.

57   For summaries, see E. Lunn, *Marxism and Modernism* (California University Press, 1982), ch. 2, and A. Huyssen, *After the Great Divide: Modernism, Mass Culture, and Postmodernism* (Macmillan, 1986), pp. 53–4.

58   D. Harvey, *The Condition of Postmodernity* (Blackwell, 1989), p. 206.

59   L. Sass, *Madness and Modernism* (Basic Books, 1992), p. 35.

60   S. Connor, *Postmodernist Culture* (Blackwell, 1989), p. 4.

61   See ch. 4 of my *Transgressing the Modern*.

62   G. Steiner, *Real Presences* (Faber, 1989), pp. 93, 93 (emphasized in the original).

63   Cited in ibid., p. 96.

64   Meisel, *Myth of the Modern*, pp. 240, 243.

65   Kern, *Culture*, pp. 177, 179; and see Taylor, *Sources*, p. 477.

66   Steiner, *Real Presences*, p. 132.

67   Butler, *Early Modernism*, p. 137.

68   M. H. Levenson, *A Genealogy of Modernism: A Study of English Literary Doctrine 1908–1922* (Cambridge University Press, 1984), p. 159.

69   Smith, *Origins*, p. 126.

70   R. Williams, *Keywords* (Fontana, 1976), pp. 32–4, 73, 192–3.

71   Taylor, *Sources*, pp. 420, 377.

72   Eagleton, *Ideology*, pp. 13, 16.

73   P. Bourdieu, *Distinction* (Routledge, 1984), pp. 486, 487, 489; and see also pp. 6, 7.

74   See ch. 7, and P. Bürger, *The Decline of Modernism* (Polity, 1992).

75   R. Krauss, 'The Originality of the Avant-Garde: A Postmodernist Repetition', in B. Wallis (ed.) *Art After Modernism: Rethinking Representation* (Godine, 1984), pp. 23, 22.

76   Smith, *Origins*, p. 5.

77   C. Owens, 'The Allegorical Impulse: Toward a Theory of Postmodernism', in Wallis, *Art After Modernism*, p. 235.

78   Cited in S. Gablik, *Has Modernism Failed?* (Thames and Hudson, 1984), p. 21.

79   Eagleton, *Ideology*, pp. 349, 20, 23.

80   Cited in R. Williams, *Culture and Society, 1780–1950* (Chatto and Windus, 1960), p. 43.

81   Eagleton, *Ideology*, p. 348.

82   J. Schulte-Sasse, 'Foreword: Theory of Modernism versus Theory of the Avant-Garde', in P. Bürger, *Theory of the Avant-Garde* (Minnesota University Press, 1984), p. xi.

83   Eagleton, *Ideology*, p. 371.

84   See J. Seigel, *Bohemian Paris* (Penguin, 1986).

85   M. Calinescu, *Five Faces of Modernity* (Duke University Press, 1987), pp. 112, 119.

86   Z. Bauman, *Mortality, Immortality and Other Life Strategies* (Polity, 1992), p. 73.

87   Letter, cited in G. Bataille, *Manet* (Skira, 1955), p. 30.

88   Levenson, *Genealogy*, p. 218; and Calinescu, *Five Faces*, p. 124.

89   Eagleton, *Ideology*, pp. 370, 372.

90   Bürger, *Theory*, pp. 52, 53.

91   C. Harrison, 'Abstraction', in C. Harrison et al., *Primitivism, Cubism, Abstraction* (Yale University Press, 1993), p. 204.

92 C. Greenberg, 'Modernist Painting', in F. Frascina and C. Harrison (eds.) *Modern Art and Modernism* (Harper and Row, 1982), pp. 5, 5–6.
93 Huyssen, *After the Great Divide*, p. vii.
94 Cited in D. Kuspit, *Clement Greenberg: Art Critic* (Wisconsin University Press, 1979), pp. 58, 146.
95 J. Carey, *The Intellectuals and the Masses: Pride and Prejudice among the Literary Intelligentsia, 1880–1939* (Faber, 1992), p. 21.
96 Huyssen, *After the Great Divide*, pp. 45, 47.
97 See G. Tuchman, *Edging Women Out: Victorian Novelists, Publishers and Social Change* (Routledge, 1989).
98 L. Pykett, *Engendering Fictions* (Edward Arnold, 1995), p. 34; and see S. Gilbert and S. Gubar, *No Man's Land, Vol. 1: The War of the Words* (Yale University Press, 1988), p. 156.
99 Cited in Huyssen, *After the Great Divide*, p. 51.
100 Connor, *Postmodernist Culture*, pp. 133, 134.
101 M. Fried, 'Art and Objecthood', in G. Bantock (ed.) *Minimal Art* (Dutton, 1968), pp. 142, 141.
102 See M. Fried, *Absorption and Theatricality: Painting and Beholder in the Age of Diderot* (California University Press, 1980).
103 Faulkner, *Modernism*, pp. 1–5; and see ch. 13.
104 Harrison, 'Abstraction', p. 204.
105 G. Perry, 'Primitivism and the "Modern"', in Harrison, *Primitivism*, p. 53.
106 Cited in Harrison, 'Abstraction', p. 204.
107 Fer, 'Language of Construction', pp. 154, 155.
108 See ch. 8 for modernism in architecture.
109 S. Ewen, *All Consuming Images* (Basic Books, 1988), pp. 130, 133.
110 W. Gropius, *The New Architecture and the Bauhaus* (MIT Press, 1965), p. 81.
111 Cited in Hughes, *Shock*, pp. 168 (emphasized in the original), 170, 191.
112 Cited in Faulkner, *Modernism*, p. 8.
113 Ewen, *All Consuming Images*, p. 130.
114 Connor, *Postmodernist Culture*, p. 77.
115 Kuspit, *Greenberg*, pp. 59, 70–1.
116 Wollen, *Raiding the Icebox*, p. 29.
117 Fried, 'Art and Objecthood', p. 145.
118 Cited in H. Foster, *Compulsive Beauty* (MIT Press, 1993), p. 182.
119 Foster, *Compulsive Beauty*, pp. 189, 190.
120 B. Fer, 'Surrealism, Myth and Psychoanalysis', in Fer, *Realism, Rationalism*, p. 171.
121 W. Chadwick, *Women Artists and the Surrealist Movement* (Thames and Hudson, 1985), pp. 65, 33. On the gender dimension, see also M. A. Caws, 'Ladies Shot and Painted: Female Embodiment in Surrealist Art', in S. R. Suleiman (ed.) *The Female Body in Western Culture* (Harvard University Press, 1985).
122 Foster, *Compulsive Beauty*, p. 191.
123 C. Buci-Glucksmann, *Baroque Reason: The Aesthetics of Modernity* (Sage, 1994), p. 39.
124 R. Barthes, *The Eiffel Tower and Other Mythologies* (Hill and Wang, 1979), pp. 6, 5.

11 The Image, the Spectral and the Spectacle:

Technologies of the Visual

'The image exists somewhere between imagination and reality', writes Flam; it inhabits 'a symbolic space where the past merges with the present, the visible with the invisible'.[1] This usefully encapsulates central features of the image, while hinting at the challenges it poses: the 'somewhere' of the image is certainly a troublesome place.

Images are everywhere, and appear to have an intimate relation to our sense of ourselves as 'modern'. Susan Sontag claims that 'A society becomes "modern" when one of its chief activities is producing and consuming images',[2] and Barthes refers to our 'civilization of the image'. Nor is this perception new. In 1859, Baudelaire was proclaiming that the whole visible world had become 'nothing but a storehouse of images and signs',[3] and his near-contemporary Feuerbach complained that the age 'prefers the image to the thing, the copy to the original, the representation to the reality'. This implies a sense in which the image can even substitute for the reality it points to, and that direct perception becomes subordinate to perception mediated through the image; thus Zola could suggest that 'you cannot claim to have really seen something until you have photographed it'.[4] Only through the image does reality become real, a consequence that could also be said to follow from the sheer diffusion of images. What we manage to represent, argues Mitchell, is 'not any sort of naked reality but a world already clothed in our systems of representation',[5] so that increasingly it is representations themselves that become objects of perception. This again confirms the vertigo of the image, its mysterious 'somewhere' status; for the image, as itself an object of perception, is already clothed in the abstraction of the subject's own categories, as well as referring us to the concrete materiality of the real.

Recent research into 'regimes of the visual' suggests, in Jay's words, that vision can be understood to be 'the master sense of the modern era', an era that is itself frequently characterized in essentially visual terms, as the heyday of Cartesian perspectivalism, the society of the spectacle, or the age of surveillance and the panoptic gaze.[6] This priority of vision is also hinted at by Elias, who observes that in the civilizing process 'the sense of smell . . . comes to be restricted as something animal-like', and the eye becomes increasingly significant as a 'mediator of pleasure'.[7] Another aspect of this is described by Jay as 'the secular autonomization of the visual as a realm unto itself',[8] the process whereby the visual and the image became freed from the trappings of the 'cosmic text' – the interlocking network of 'similitudes' that held the pre-modern world together as a manifestation of the sacred[9] – and thereby became available for the new explorations of the visual in science and art.

The nineteenth century – aptly described as living in a 'frenzy of the visible'[10] – saw an explosion of technologies of the visual, many becoming crucial to the emerging industries of mass entertainment. From the 1790s, panoramas were being displayed in Paris and London, culminating in the London Colosseum in the 1820s, where the public would enter the darkened space below, rise in the newly invented lift to the viewing-point, and contemplate the painted scenic panorama all around them. By now dioramas, in which a series of screens and special lighting effects could be manipulated to give the illusion of day changing into night, or summer into winter, had also come into fashion, followed by phenakistiscopes, kaleidoscopes and stereoscopes, smaller instruments which enabled these pleasures of the visual to be imported into the home itself.[11] Crary characterizes the decades of the 1820s and 1830s as a period when these optical devices embodied a radical reorganization of the visual field, implicitly challenging notions of perspective and the detached observer and preparing the ground for modernism in the arts. From this point of view, the *flâneur* emerges as 'a mobile consumer of a ceaseless succession of illusory commodity-like images', an active participant in the emerging spectacle of the visual.[12]

The culminating invention of the period was of course the camera: from the late 1820s and through the 1830s Nièpce, Daguerre and Fox Talbot all developed methods to record images permanently, and from 1839 the camera burst into the public domain, at once capturing the popular imagination. From very early on, the photograph was a powerful component of popular culture, and this was reinforced by the arrival of Eastman's Kodak and mass-produced postcards in the last decades of the century (followed by the instant camera, the Polaroid, after 1948).[13] The camera represented a democratization of the gaze, a potential for recording and intensifying the significance of everyday occasions through encapsulating the little ceremonies that constitute the framework of family memories, linking public drama and personal experience. Chaney suggests that the domain of pleasurable leisure activities, too, is 'constituted to a greater or lesser extent through the possibility of their being photographed'.[14] But there is another side to this. After the revolutionary events of the Paris Commune in 1871, the police made extensive use of photographs to track down and trap the participants, and Tagg has explored the implications of the camera for the culture of surveillance to which it makes a crucial contribution.[15] Similarly, Virilio has detailed the intimate links between developments in camera and war technologies.[16] Chaney concludes that, overall, 'the camera provides a resource for bestowing dignity on popular life while simultaneously facilitating the creation and operation of bureaucratic apparatuses'.[17]

The great appeal of the photograph is its 'realism'; it ostensibly captures what is 'really there' in a way that can make a painting seem both jaded and fanciful. This has certainly been central to its role in popular culture.[18] The photo was a 'mirror with a memory'.[19] Yet, right from the start, this 'realism' has been problematical. The ability to retouch photos had been developed by the late 1840s, and combination of images was possible by the 1850s; with these skills came the fashion for the charlatan photos of 'spirits' in the 1860s. Yet the problems go deeper. While the photo shows everything in sharp focus from edge to edge, with all details clearly delineated, this is not how we actually see the world; and the eye, with no shutters or exposure time, can register movement in a way the camera cannot. If, as Ewen suggests, the photographic image 'offered a representation of reality more compelling than reality itself, and – perhaps – even threw the very definition of *reality* into question',[20] this is not because it can be taken as simply 'more accurate' but because of this very *difference*. This could be illustrated from the development of chronophotography in the 1870s and 1880s. Muybridge's photos of a galloping horse demonstrated the movements but not the motion, not what you actually see;[21] the difference between the two dramatically illustrates the dependence of visual representation on codes, on frameworks that constitute the real *as* real. Indeed, this enabled the sculptor Rodin to make a pitch for the representational potential of art. He pointed out that while instantaneous photos of men in motion make them look frozen, a painting can condense several successive movements into a single image, so that 'if the representation as a whole is false in showing these movements as simultaneous, it is true when the parts are observed in sequence', and it is this truth that counts since 'it is what we see and what impresses us'.[22]

The power of the photo, then, is the power and promise of realism, but the power betrays the promise. Insofar as realism is possible, the real becomes reproducible in its image, a part of the world which, lifted off the surface of the world, becomes totally translucent, having no properties of its own, implicitly denying its own materiality, its independence *qua* image: a ghostlike, uncanny presence, captured appropriately enough by those Victorian spirit photographs, exemplars of this potent unreality at the heart of realist representations of the real. Conversely, if the materiality of the image is conceded, it becomes the double that endangers the original, threatening its status *as* original, embodying a problematical otherness, even as its materiality subjects it to the market, making it into the image as commodity. Thus, representing the original yet freed from it, image becomes simulacrum: from Daguerre to Baudrillard is but a short step. But of course the possibility of realism can be disputed anyway. Thus Maltby observes that the 'real' is here defined as being 'that which is unmediated by representation', and that 'Since it is outside representation, it cannot be represented: representations can be only more or less inadequate imitations or substitutes for it.'[23] If the latter part of this is true, it cannot be known to be true, since we necessarily cannot have access to the 'real' against which a representation is measured as 'inadequate'. Hence Freedberg formulates the 'epiphanic problem of representation' in these terms: 'The image declares and makes present that which is absent, hidden, and which we cannot possibly know – but then do'. Hence 'The real, apparently graspable image pictures the inconceivable. What cannot be conceived is – inconceivably – grasped in the painting or sculpture' (or photograph).[24]

Ultimately, the image can be dangerous because it fails to fulfil the promise of representation, it is deception, illusion; but it can also be dangerous because it succeeds too well, becomes simulacrum, a replacement or substitute. The triumph of 'realism' in the photo oscillates between these poles, and ultimately the photographic image, too, becomes subject to the distrust of the image that has been fundamental to the Western tradition. The general issue is stated well by Brantlinger:

> The domination of visual imagery in any cultural medium will perhaps always evoke questions about what is not shown, about the reality behind the apparitions on the surface. . . . The visible is only surface and present, never so vast as the invisible or as the past and future, which are infinite. . . .
>
> Because the invisible surrounds and in some sense transcends the visible, the reduction of experience to visual imagery by any cultural medium will seem to liquidate essence, leaving only the hollow forms of an idolatrous liturgy or of a narcissistic self-worship behind.[25]

Images are concrete, specific, material; in their immediacy, they refer to the 'here and now', and their relation to the 'beyond' or 'beneath' is always unclear. The Christian tradition has been obsessed with the threat of 'graven images', the risk that the transcendence of God will be corrupted by over-identification with the images or icons that are nevertheless venerated as evidence of his presence to, or in, the world. Iconoclasm and iconolatry feed off each other in endless conflict. The early modern reassertion of the transcendent otherness of God, withdrawing from a world that was increasingly to become subject to scientific investigation, was accompanied by dramatic episodes of iconoclastic destruction in the churches.[26] The Enlightenment hope for pure transparency, so that the world could be apprehended through a kind of immediate self-disclosure, was coupled, particularly in the Rousseauian tradition, culminating in the Jacobins, with a virulent attack on the image as a distortion and deception of reason, a carrier of ideological mystification.[27]

That this distrust has remained basic in the modern period, and has taken on wider implications, linking it with other topics, is clear in this summary by Mitchell:

> The condemnation of luxury, of theatricality, shows, and 'sensationalism', of ornaments, trinkets, cosmetics, and figurative language, of printed 'visible' language, and of the visual arts (especially photography) routinely employs an iconoclastic rhetoric that depicts the idolater as infantile, feminine, and narcissistic – in a word, as 'unmanly'.[28]

Denunciations of the image always return us to its prevalence in popular culture, its alleged role as a seducer of the masses. And this, too, rests on a real feature of the image in its modern guise. Its very realism means that 'we see both it and what it represents as a piece of reality', as Freedberg puts it;[29] as representation *and* substitute, it becomes a powerful resource for fantasy and fetishism. If the image can be real, be a part of the reality it also points to, it can be arousing; sacred iconolatry can become secular fetishism, in a way that will be explored later. Both the stereoscope and the camera became involved in the production of pornographic images from very early on. Teresa de Lauretis thus reminds us that images can articulate meaning and desire more powerfully or immediately than words: 'not only semantic and social values but affect and fantasy as well, are bound to images'.[30]

It remains true that, as Mitchell puts it, 'an image cannot be seen *as such* without a paradoxical trick of consciousness, an ability to see something as "there" and "not there" at the same time'.[31] We have to see *through* the image (to what is represented), while seeing it *as* ('mere') image. The inseparability of the image from these 'tricks of consciousness' must now be examined.

Phantasmagoria

In London, in 1801–2, the fashionable public flocked to see the new magic spectre show. Ushered into a suitably dark, mysterious, enclosed space, such as a crypt, they would be subjected to the pleasure of being scared out of their wits by the production of ghostlike spectres that would appear before them – even over or among them – and which could increase or decrease in size, or dissolve into one another. So realistic were they, that members of the audience would cry out or scream, and men would strike at them with their canes, in self-defence. Thus did the 'phantasmagoria' arrive, repeating its 1798 triumph in Paris; over the next decade or so, it retained its popularity, and it was still being adapted and improved as late as the 1860s. The technology was a development of the magic lantern, the ancestor of slide and cinematic projectors, which had already been around for several centuries: a candle and mirror in a box were employed to project a painted image on to a screen, and further refinements made the image appear free-floating. Later, gaslight and photographic transparencies were used.

Appropriating the concept in its wider cultural resonance, Adorno defines phantasmagoria as the 'illusion of the absolute reality of the unreal'.[32] This is actually very close to Orr's definition of the image as 'an unreal object which negates the real':[33] it is 'not there', but in so far as it *is* there, it questions the status and boundaries of the real. In her fascinating exploration of these themes, Terry Castle points out that the early magic-lantern shows were presented as educational, as scientific demystification; yet since the illusionists did not, of course, reveal their own tricks, the results could be real enough terrors. One really *saw* the spectres: 'They floated before the eye just like real ghosts. And in a crazy way they *were* real ghosts . . . not mere effects of imagination.' Hence 'One knew ghosts did not exist, yet one saw them anyway.'

In effect, we witness here one consequence of the profound epistemological revolutions of modernity, which by the second half of the eighteenth century had instituted a firm barrier between the imagination, reconstructed as a faculty of mind, and the 'real' world outside. This in turn led to deep uncertainties over the status of the mental image, and Castle's argument is that ordinary thought becomes in a sense 'phantasmagorical' as a result. Even before the phantasmagoria, Goethe had used the idea of the mind as a magic lantern to suggest that desire could produce 'phantoms' in the 'mind's eye',[34] and by the 1820s the idea of the mind as itself a phantasmagoria, a magic lantern whereby image-traces could be projected on to an internal screen, capable of producing illusion, delirium and madness, but also new insight, had become a cultural commonplace, and particularly influenced Romantic theories of artistic creativity.

Indeed, reflected in Kant's philosophy, the attempt to safeguard the boundary between the knowable world and the knowing subject had precisely the opposite result. By splitting reality into the world of all possible experience, necessarily conforming to our categories, and the unknowable world lurking behind, Kant implied, argues Sass, that 'the mind experiences objects that can feel like its own phantoms (the "phenomena") and that seem *un*real in comparison with the unseen, but somehow imagined, realm of the "noumenal" or true world'.[35] This left us, complained Schelling, 'lonely and forsaken amidst the world, surrounded everywhere by spectres'.[36]

This revolution both made the ghost impossible, *and* created it, in its modern form. Illicitly posited, in its 'reality', in some unclear mediating zone between self and world, a residue of sacred notions of 'spirit', the ghost had to be firmly relocated on the subjective side, as a 'mere' illusion of mind, while constantly threatening to escape this imprisonment. The term 'hallucination' had come into popular use around the beginning of the nineteenth century, and a mass of anti-ghost texts, 'explaining' ghost beliefs in a Lockean empiricist framework, poured off the presses. Yet this reflexive turn results in a paradoxical 'spectralization' of mental space. Objects of mental contemplation can easily appear object-like: between an idea, an image and a phantom there are only differences of degree, and the everyday processes of remembering and imagining necessarily involve 'seeing things', just as we can be 'haunted' by thoughts. Rationalism thus 'depends on this primal internalization of the spectral' whereby ghosts are not so much exorcised as reproduced internally, becoming 'hallucinatory thoughts'. Ghosts are thoughts, condensed into images, but thoughts thereby become ghostlike. Hence, 'In the very act of denying the spirit-world of our ancestors, we have been forced to relocate it in our theory of the imagination', resulting in 'the spectral nature of our own thoughts', so that 'Through a strange process of rhetorical displacement, thought itself had become phantasmagorical.'[37] The attempts to stabilize the boundaries between inside and outside, mind and world, illusion and reality, can easily break down, so that one experiences one's thoughts as uncanny, embodied, 'a kind of bizarre, alienating spectacle imposed from without', a reminder of the schizophrenic potential of the modern project. And we can return to those

Victorian ghost photos, which can be seen both as a commentary on 'the luminous figure of thought itself', and on 'the uncanny nature of photography, the ultimate ghost-producing technology of the nineteenth century'.[38]

This photographic ghost production works at several levels. Discussing his response to being photographed, Barthes tells us that he becomes 'a subject who feels he is becoming an object', in a scaled-down version of dying itself: 'I am truly becoming a specter.' The photograph freezes its subject eternally, at a point in time: in this sense, the photo is always a photo of the dead. But the 'eternally' is real enough, too: the photograph grants an after-life. Anyone who has felt the power of an old, yellowing photograph will have experienced this vivid presence of the dead, alive to us in the immediacy of the gaze, and will understand how Barthes can claim that in the photo we encounter 'the return of the dead', so that photography becomes a form of resurrection. He adds, with a Victorian flourish, that the photographic object is 'like the ectoplasm of "what-had-been": neither image nor reality, a new being, really: a reality one can no longer touch'.[39] This is, indeed, not so far from Balzac, who tells us, according to the photographer Nadar, writing in 1900, that his 'vague dread' of being photographed was due to his view that a body was made up of 'a series of ghostly images superimposed in layers', and that each photo was bound to 'lay hold of, detach, and use up one of the layers of the body'.[40]

Here we encounter the idea that a photo is not *just* an image, it is a trace, a residue or stencil of the real, like a footprint or a death mask; 'it is not only like its subject. . . . It is part of, an extension of that subject', as Sontag puts it.[41] For Barthes, too, the photograph is 'an emanation of *past reality*: a *magic*, not an art'.[42] This again gives the photograph a paradoxical status. As a 'mere' image, it is supposed to be safely on the representational side of the representation/reality divide; but as we have seen, that boundary is anything but secure. Freeing the image from the sacred does not deprive it of its fetishistic power: it merely opens it to a new form of this, hence our sense of 'something magical' about it.[43] Rosalind Krauss points out that the idea of the trace does, after all, have a physical basis in the very nature of the transmission and fixing of the photographic image. It was seen as having a 'revelatory power' due to 'the power of light to transmit the invisible and imprint it on phenomena'. Light was indeed 'the conduit between the world of sense impressions and the world of the spirit';[44] it was itself a material force, and could contribute to constituting the image in all its powerful insubstantiality. After all, Daguerre, one of the inventors of the camera, had previously made his name as an inventor of the diorama, and was a pioneer in the trickery of the visual spectacle. Photography is born in the theatre of illusion, strange offspring of a marriage between science and spiritualism; an inheritance it has tried, with limited success, to throw off or cover up ever since.

In 1896, Maxim Gorky made his first visit to the *Cinématographe Lumière*, the moving picture show, newly arrived in Russia. He wrote afterwards of how 'Last night I was in the Kingdom of Shadows.' In the improvised, darkened cinema auditorium, the silent, ghostly figures in their shades of grey flickered past: 'It is not life but its shadows, it is not motion but its soundless spectre.'[45] Seated in the dark, among strangers, in front of the big screen, the 'cinema experience' can indeed carry a powerful resonance. 'Cinema began in wonder', writes Sontag; 'the wonder that reality can be transcribed with such magical immediacy',[46] so that reality can be 'there' even while it is 'not there'. When the Lumière brothers' train pulled into the station at La Ciotat (1895), members of the audience cried out and ducked as it appeared to approach them; confronted with the roller-coaster ride at the beginning of *This is Cinerama* (1952), viewers swayed or felt sick.[47] Orr suggests that

> When film is at its most alluring, audiences view a spectacle which masquerades as magical. It is easy to forget that one sees a composite of images changing rapidly on a huge screen. Since film involves frames changing faster than the human eye can register, the continuity of the image is an illusion. Such 'continuous' images are part of an elaborate magic-show which seems to have a life of its own.

And the image to which we are powerfully attracted remains 'out there', yet strangely insubstantial; in a remark that reminds us of the men with canes stabbing at the spectres, Orr adds that 'If spectators hurl bottles at actors on screen, they can break the screen, but not the image.'[48]

The cinema, in its all-encompassing visuality, does after all face a challenge: how to capture what is absent, either because it is beyond the perceptual horizon at any given moment – existing as memory, for example – or because it is in some sense 'unreal', fantasy or imagination. If the triumph of the photograph is to capture what is there, the challenge for the cinematic image is to capture what is not there. And the success of the cinematic project requires a kind of ontological levelling: if the absent, imaginary or illusory can be depicted, it becomes as 'real' *qua* image, as an image of the real. . . . Thus Maltby argues that, in this respect, 'The audience trusts the images it sees, because the camera cannot show something that is not, in some sense, there.' Consequently, movie images 'cannot be unreliable in the ways that a verbal narrator can be . . . we cannot choose to believe half of an image and not the other half'.[49] There is thus what Orr calls an 'equality of images, of real and unreal objects alike', which makes the perceptual itself seem imaginary, through these instabilities of the visual. The imaginary can become as real as the real appears imaginary; there can be no absolute boundary between them. Presence and absence, the real and the imaginary, coexist in the cinematic image, and modern film, which knows that the real is 'haunted by the imaginary',[50] uses these ambiguities, plays with them endlessly.

This haunting image is, in effect, a form of doubling, and, as such, refers to a dimension of the naturalistic representation so central to the appeal of photograph and film. On this model, reality can somehow be posited as reproducible, in its fantasy wholeness and integrity, by a simulacrum, a double of itself, thereby both itself and other to itself. It is, of course, the reality of selfhood that is particularly in play here. In a world in which the self is projected, and only becomes knowable, through self-image, in which moderns 'feel that they are images, and are made real by photographs', as Sontag puts it,[51] the image becomes both self and other, something to be simultaneously identified with and distanced from, both real and unreal. The Romantic ideal of wholeness and integrity hence encourages this problematic of projection and introjection, of an intimate relation with the image that figures the real even as it exists in troublesome independence of it. Film, suggests Orr, 'proclaims itself as a fruition of the nineteenth-century romantic longing for wholeness' but simultaneously 'presents us with the image that got away'; its mimesis of the human figure 'echoes the romantic imaging of an alienated Other, a shadowing phantom'.[52]

This implies that the unity, the integrity, is indeed imaginary. Just as this model of representation in effect splits reality, by positing part of it as a double of the rest, so the self becomes split; the image, as a projection of self, is also its broken other, representing the impossibility of the fantasy of integrity and wholeness, the inevitable presence of dissolution and death. This duality is captured by Elisabeth Bronfen, who suggests that representation thus 'serves as a triumph over and against material decomposition in the realm or system of the real', while this double is also 'a figure signifying that something that was whole and unique has been split'. Not surprisingly, she also cites Freud's theory of the uncanny, and this returns us quite directly to the world of phantasmagoria; for she suggests that *das Umheimliche* refers to 'A situation of undecidability', one where 'the question whether something is animate (alive) or inanimate (dead), whether something is real or imagined, unique, original or a repetition, a copy, can not be decided'. The spectral presence is the familiar in the unfamiliar, the unreality of the real, the image alienated in the other. Bronfen adds that 'the uncanny always entails anxieties about fragmentation, about the disruption or destruction of any narcissistically informed sense of personal stability'.[53]

When it is the dimension of wholeness that is emphasized, in the doubling, it is issues of narcissistic identification that are foregrounded; when it is the fragmentation and splitting that are explored, a concern with fetishistic identification becomes more likely.[54] Both can be explored in the context of film, where doubling is not only a feature of the spectator–hero relationship, but is encountered in the possibilities of 'doubling' relationships between heroes, heroines and villains. The 'true' and the 'false' Maria in Fritz Lang's *Metropolis* (1926) can be recalled here, as can the relation between Harry Lime and Holly Martens in Carol Reed's *The Third Man* (1949). Orr concludes that the doubles of these heroes or heroines 'seem to mirror in their separation from each other the estrangement of the screen figure's image from its audience in a darkened auditorium';[55] one form of doubling reflexively mirrors another. The potential for the play of spectator identification and desire in this cinematic phantasmagoria is thus all the greater.

Finally, one can observe that the figure of phantasmagoria has been drawn on quite widely in other areas. Best known, probably, is Marx's use of it to uncover the contradictions in the commodity as the key to understanding the dynamics of capitalism. In the commodity, he writes, 'It is only the particular social relation between people that here takes on the phantasmagoric form of a relation between things';[56] the commodity emerges as a spectral deception, both real and unreal, natural and social, available to be 'fetishized'. And Paris as described by Benjamin, following on from Baudelaire, was a phantasmagoria, a 'magic-lantern show of optical illusions, rapidly changing size and blending into one another',[57] and it is in the fetishism of fashion that this phantasmagoria of commodities becomes most vivid. On the one hand, this points forward to the link between phantasmagoria and spectacle; but first, aspects of fragmentation and fetishism will be explored further, in the context of allegory.

The Photograph and the Allegorical Imagination

'For me, everything becomes allegory', wrote Baudelaire,[58] and this sense that the modern world is appropriated through an imagination that is essentially allegorical links the first wave of modernism to the later work of Benjamin, writing in the era of high modernism; and as this is also, after all, the period when the photograph made its appearance and its impact – it was, indeed, commented on by both writers – examining the possible links between a world of allegory and a world of photography may serve to illuminate both. Given the role of the photographic image in popular culture, this will also remind us that 'modernism', before also being a specialist perspective in the arts, is central to the everyday experience of the modern.

Conventionally, an allegory is a story in which the surface events and characters embody or convey a deeper meaning, moral or spiritual. The allegory, like the photograph, raises the spectre of the double: allegory is one text doubling another. Commentary and critique are allegorical, as is psychoanalysis; and modernism, constructed in Baudelaire's terms as the reading of the eternal in the transient, the past in the present, becomes allegorical. For Baudelaire and other modernists, modernity is not something 'out there', to be 'copied', but an exercise of the imagination, which for Baudelaire himself meant penetrating 'beyond the banality of observable appearances into a world of "correspondences", where ephemerality and eternity are one', as Calinescu puts it.[59] Such an imagination is always 'thinking beyond', inherently comparative, metaphorical.

However, the idea of a 'deeper meaning' needs clarification; in a sense, modernity read allegorically is read in such a way that the 'depth' that is sought is ever-elusive, and only ever returns us to surfaces. It is as though the 'other' dimension is elsewhere, rather than hidden. Indeed, 'allegory' derives from the Greek, meaning 'speaking figuratively' or 'other-discourse', the assimilation of the two being significant here. Buci-Glucksmann characterizes allegory as 'a vocalization and staging of an otherness which eludes direct speech and presents itself as an elsewhere'.[60] Nor can this otherness be definitively located. Allegory is not hermeneutics: the meaning it finds is inseparable from the meaning it constructs; a supplement, an addition. In this sense, what the world 'means' can only be what we put there.

This gives a clue to the distinctiveness of the term in the Baudelaire–Benjamin tradition. It is as though the modern becomes allegorical in a context where there can be no rational ground for assuming that there is some uniform, objective,

underlying meaning, and consequently no clear guidelines for attributing significance to the swirling fragments of experience that we encounter all around. And
yet they *are* read allegorically, as puzzling mementoes of a history that now seems
opaque, and this can engender a sense of nostalgia or pathos, or – less frequently
– an exuberance, at the awesome imperative that forces us to create even as we
hope to understand.

These reactions correspond to the two poles of allegory, the destructive and the
creative. As Benjamin puts it, 'That which is touched by the allegorical intention
is torn from the context of life's interconnections: it is simultaneously shattered
and conserved. Allegory attaches itself to the rubble.'[61] And thus 'the false illusion
of totality is extinguished'.[62] But the allegorist also draws together fragments, to
create a new meaning, necessarily artificial and precarious. In this sense, the
fragments both lose meaning and become potentially full of it, overflowing,
depending as they do on the allegorist. Hence allegory, suggests Owens, is extravagant, 'an expenditure of surplus value; it is always *in excess*'.[63] Eagleton concludes
that 'any phenomenon can come by the wily resourcefulness of the allegorist to
signify absolutely anything else, in a kind of profane parody of the creative naming
of God'.[64] Meaningfulness is everywhere, and meaning nowhere. Consequently, if
this is a world in which the *flâneur* and the artist can gain inspiration, it is also a
world in which indifference, *ennui*, even despair, are equally possible, from
Baudelaire's 'spleen' to Benjamin's melancholy. Modern life, no longer conceivable as a pre-given or teleological unity of project, becomes an elusive allegory of
itself, attaching arbitrary meanings to the fragments, its own reflexive musings; in
the allegorical imagination of the modern, life exists only in fragments, always
present to itself yet always inaccessible.

Inaccessible – yet collectable. In the modern period, argues Benjamin, the
souvenir, the material carrier of past meanings, becomes an allegorical object *par
excellence*: 'The *souvenir* is the relic secularized', deriving as it does from 'deceased
experience'.[65] Fragments of memory cling to it, existing only as embedded in it,
hence it can stimulate reflection in the present. So if allegory is, in a sense, always
backward-looking, it also draws on the past to intensify the present. Benjamin's
own work shows a fascination with old debris, bric-à-brac, and quotations from
other authors, thus 'redeeming' these items by juxtaposing them with others in the
vividness of the now. And it is the photograph that is the ultimate souvenir:
representation and reality, past and present, convenient consumer commodity, all
in one.

The essence of the photo, writes Barthes, is 'to ratify what it represents'; it is a
'certificate of presence'.[66] The photographic object is a powerful presence since it
bears the trace of the experience it represents, and thereby becomes itself a
fragment of the world it purports to picture. For Benjamin, this is crucial to the
observer's engagement with the photograph: we look for 'the tiny spark of chance,
of the here and now, with which reality has, as it were, seared the character in the
picture'.[67] And if 'the image is that in which, what has been, enters into a constel-
lation with the "Now" in a sudden flash',[68] then this is most vividly true of the
photograph itself.

Photographs both collect experiences, and are themselves collectable. 'To collect photographs is to collect the world', as Sontag puts it, and the effect is to reinforce an attitude of 'aesthetic consumerism'. The photographer, like the collector, approaches this bric-à-brac world in an unsystematic fashion. The photo is a fragment; as allegory, it is anti-Romantic; there is no symbolism of unified wholeness here. The camera conveys reality as piecemeal, denying continuity and connectedness. For Sontag, 'The contingency of photographs confirms that everything is perishable; the arbitrariness of photographic evidence indicates that reality is fundamentally unclassifiable.' Hence the proliferation of photos 'contributes to the erosion of the very notion of meaning'.[69]

On the face of it, however, the souvenir photo *can* have meaning for the individual, through its linking of memory and narrative. It is obviously true that the range of memory can be increased through the use of the camera. At the same time, we need to recall Proust's disparagement of photos as mere 'voluntary memory',[70] and the claim by Barthes that the photo 'actually blocks memory, quickly becomes a counter-memory'. The power of involuntary recall can be stifled, restrained; arbitrary images can impose a distortion. Experience becomes subject to the photographic, rather than a determinant of it, and the resulting narrative can distance the experience, rather than grasp it. Susan Stewart suggests that 'Through narrative the souvenir substitutes a context of perpetual consumption for its context of origin.' Above all, though, the narrative of the photo is a language of loss and yearning, of mourning for the irreplaceable and desire for a substitute. 'The souvenir speaks to a context of origin through a language of longing', adds Stewart.[71] There is a poignancy, a pathos about these photos, graphically captured by Sontag's observation that 'Photographs state the innocence, the vulnerability of lives heading toward their own destruction.'[72] Ultimately, then, the photo conveys both distance and presence, and shows how experience as representation becomes both fragmented and irrecoverable: the bits and pieces of life out of which our myths are made. Through its photos, the self becomes an allegory of itself.

Supplement to the world, object *in* the world, as much as picture of it, the photo embodies the materiality of the sign. Allegory comes into its own in a world where everything can be considered sign or referent, image or object, so there is never any shortage of material for the play of allegorical representation. And it is a world in which signs can be commodities, commodities can be signs. Eagleton adds that if allegory 'thus mimes the levelling, equivalencing operations of the commodity', the sense in which everything becomes interchangeable, then 'Like the commodity, the meaning of the allegorical object is always elsewhere, eccentric to its material being', added by the allegorist. So it is not just words or images that become allegorical fragments, but objects, even the body, perform the role of signs. As language and image reveal their materiality, so the body becomes a resource for representation. 'If the body is constructed out of images, images are in their turn forms of material practice', as Eagleton reminds us.[73] Since the self, after all, has to be embodied in material signifiers, so the efforts to read the distinctive peculiarities of the particular person return us from 'inner' to 'outer', to the world of clothes, body parts, into which the self is doomed to disappear even as it is revealed. The photo is, first and foremost, a photo of the body, through which we construct our allegories of self-identity.

In addition, as explored elsewhere,[74] the reflexive attempt to grasp selfhood splits the self: self-awareness constitutes the self as other to itself, a fantasy double that can also be read in the broken fragments of the gaze, allegory of a totality that is lost or impossible. The fantasy double, and the all-too real material remains of selfhood, are all that is left, linked through the yearnings of nostalgic projection. The dissolution of history in the now, and the dissolution of the now in reflexive appropriation, constitute modern consciousness as both allegorical and fetishistic.

In this world of objects and fragments, then, there lurks always the urge to blend with or possess, lose oneself in or dominate, be dispersed into or collect. This is a world in which clothes, bodies, artefacts generally, become strange objects of desire, a world of fetishism.[75] Desire itself fragments, no longer recognizes itself, hides in the objects through which it is constituted and which challenge the reflexive gaze even as they fascinate it and are simultaneously fragmented and reified under its decadent power. Baudrillard has pointed out that a 'fetish' was originally 'a *fabrication*, an artefact, a labour of appearances and signs',[76] a labour that involves an 'investment', a projection, but one that is disavowed and misrecognized, so that the object itself seems to possess power. The reflexive gaze, the Medusa's head of modernity, reduces the organic to the inert and the image, while empowering them as objects of desire. When fragments of desire gel with their own objects through the image, the modern world of fetishism is born: details replace a whole (real or imagined) and thereby supplement it, and a displaced authority is read into these objects and their images, clings to them even when other sources of authority disintegrate.

A fetish is a snapshot of congealed desire, frozen in time, a material artefact of the imagination, an obscure allegory of the self, a theatre in which self displays itself as object, indeed as 'a story masquerading as an object', as Stoller puts it.[77] And a snapshot can be a fetish: the role of the photo in consolidating modern fetishism is as obvious as it is relatively undiscussed. The collector 'always retains some traces of the fetishist', observes Benjamin.[78] If identity becomes dependent on objects and images in this way, these can become 'fetishised icons' that simultaneously reassure us, give us something to cling to, yet also keep us apart, by inscribing such icons in the very content of our desires, mediating our relationships through them. If the body and its attributes, and its clothes, can become part of the language of identity, they also become partially constitutive of desire itself, resulting in a 'consumer fetishism of the erotic'.[79] Out of this matrix of bodies, organs, clothes and other fragments, the fetishistic consciousness thus becomes a central mode of modernism, spilling over into fashion and culture generally: the celebration – often desperate – of reminders and metaphors, bits and pieces, embodying a nostalgia for a unity and presence forever unattainable, but also a potential for imaginative recombination and juxtaposition (as in Surrealism).[80]

Summarizing Benjamin's perspective, Featherstone writes of the way

> a stable hierarchically ordered meaning is dissolved and the allegory points only to kaleidoscopic fragments which resist any coherent notion of what it stands for. In this aestheticised commodity world the department stores, arcades, trams, trains, streets and fabric of buildings and the goods on display, as well as the people who stroll through these spaces, summon up half-forgotten dreams, as the curiosity and memory of the stroller is fed by the ever-changing landscape in which objects appear divorced from their context and subject to mysterious connections which are read on the surface of things.[81]

One can add that this promiscuity of allegory has not made it popular with theorists of high modernism and others affected by the anti-allegorical tendency of Romantic art theory, its dismissal of allegory as secondary, trivial and unoriginal. Owens reminds us that 'The allegorical work is synthetic; it crosses aesthetic boundaries', and suggests that film, a genre in alliance with 'popular art forms', has become the 'primary vehicle' for modern allegory.[82]

Dream Machine and Spectacle

The cinema, the dominant form of mass entertainment this century, is also unique to the century, and contemporary with it. Its hold on the popular imagination would be hard to exaggerate. By 1912, after little more than a decade, London already had 500 cinemas, and other major European and North American cities could boast equivalent figures. By 1946, when cinema attendance peaked, one-third of the adult population in the UK and the US went to the movies every week. In the early 1950s, cinema attendance was several times greater than attendance at all other places of entertainment combined (including sports). Admissions then fell steadily, so that by 1983 under a quarter of the US population went once a month;[83] this decline was contemporary with the rise of television and, later, of video, though of course both retain a high film content.

But such figures only tell part of the story. The wider cultural significance of film was being debated from very early on. A 1913 article was already suggesting that the dominance of imagery in the medium was replacing meaningful social experience by passive, anaesthetized spectatorship and subjection to illusion and manipulation,[84] and a 1914 study of motion-picture audiences suggested that women responded more readily than men to the synaesthetic and kinetic aspects of film, and were more interested in social melodramas and romantic situations[85] – all themes that return to prominence later as staples of film theory and media sociology. While its own status as art has been contested, there is little doubt that it influenced the other arts: silent cinema, for example, being refracted in the writings of the literary modernists, with consciousness projected as a screen on which flickering images play.[86] And film was a form that could inspire devotion among its followers. Sontag points to the 'cinephilia' that was 'born of the sense that cinema was an art unlike any other: quintessentially modern; distinctively accessible; poetic and mysterious and erotic and moral – all at the same time', so that 'lovers of cinema could think there was only cinema. That the movies encapsulated everything – and they did.'[87] And hence Denzin could postulate a pervasive 'cinematic imagination', so that America increasingly became 'a cinematic culture, a culture which came to know itself, collectively and individually, through the images and stories that Hollywood produced'.[88]

But the 'cinema experience' encompasses more than the film itself: there is also the impact of sitting in the darkened auditorium, in the company of strangers. All contribute to the possibilities for fantasy fulfilment, the sense that film has a dreamlike quality, however naturalistic the images or story may be. Benjamin remarks on this capacity of film to 'burst this prison-world' of everyday life so that we 'calmly and adventurously go travelling'; hence film both 'extends our comprehension of the necessities which rule our lives' and manages to assure us of 'an immense and unexpected field of action'.[89] And in *Star Gazing*, Jackie Stacey has explored the significance of the Hollywood dream machine for women growing up in the 1940s and 1950s, its rich potential for fantasy identification, a theme also touched on in the discussion of theatricality and melodrama in an earlier chapter.[90]

For its critics, film has always been open to the double charge of being either a mechanical copy or merely a diverting spectacle;[91] and these possibilities are already present in the first films, in 1895, with the Lumière brothers' emphasis on realism, the transmission of 'unstaged' reality, contrasting with the fantasy, artifice and illusion celebrated in the Méliès films. However, the exigencies of plot and role-play soon ensured that the 'realism' became itself illusionary, a simulation, hence swinging towards the other pole. The difference of emphasis, of intention, nonetheless remains, and in general it is useful to see a triangulation of film styles in play here. Classic realist cinema, drawing on the more 'respectable' strands of the nineteenth-century novel and theatre, explores and defends the validity of the image as a vehicle for naturalistic representation, linked to conventional notions of narrative; the cinema of spectacle, in turn developing genres within it (melodrama, the musical), draws on other antecedents to explore the possibilities of fantasy and excess; and modernist cinema – influential in the 1920s, followed by the 'New Wave' neo-modernism of Godard, Truffaut et al. in the 1960s – self-exploratory, seeks to dislocate conventional notions of image and narrative, problematizing their mimetic pretensions and their aspirations to convey a harmonious, unified sense of reality.[92] Modernism, in particular, tended to adopt a critical attitude towards conventions of bourgeois modernity more generally, an anti-heroic stance, transmitting 'profane images of the bourgeoisie',[93] but this can also be found elsewhere, even as a subtext in apparently more conventional Hollywood narratives. And while to some extent all this can stand as a typology of film, it is more useful to see these categories as dimensions, aspects of film, often present in the same film, in a state of tension that is crucial to the dynamic of the film.

The vicissitudes of colour in the history of film can throw light on this. Neale points out that part of the appeal of colour has always been its greater realism, yet there was controversy and uncertainty over the general value of colour. He points to a contradiction between 'colour as an index of realism and colour as a mark of fantasy'; in the balance between narrative and spectacle, colour always tended to emphasize the latter, since however tightly controlled, 'colour as a spectacle was . . . to some extent incompatible with narrative and drama'. Yet colour, along with spectacle, became important in the battle with television,[94] to the extent that by the 1980s Teresa de Lauretis could argue that 'what matters is once again spectacle, as in the earliest days of cinema', and it is this that provides the 'no longer simple but excessive, "perverse" pleasure of current cinema'.[95] The gender issue is also important here. Neale argues that in classic Hollywood cinema, the role of the female body was one 'both of focusing and motivating a set of colour effects within a system dependent on plot and narrative', thus providing a sense of *controlled* spectacle, and 'of marking and containing the erotic component involved in the desire to look at the coloured image'.[96]

There is a sense in which film always provides spectacle, always embodies, in its visual sumptuousness and its use of colour, an excess of meaning that is difficult to contain within the storyline; hence any coherence has to be provided, claims Andrew, 'by way of calculated or ideological limitation of this excess'.[97] More generally, Maltby is surely right to argue that 'narrative functions as part of the provision of pleasure in cinema entertainment, not as the point of it', and hence storytelling 'helps ensure that the movie can be consumed as a coherent event, but it holds no privileged place among the pleasures a movie offers'.[98] Film as spectacle, concludes Chaney, can combine 'breathtaking pictorialism with the logic of melodramatic narrative' to produce a particularly powerful transfiguration of reality. In short, any differentiation between aspects of film itself takes place on a terrain that is *already* that of spectacle, even if the more conventionally realist films have to treat this as problematical, seek to disavow or control it. If, as Chaney argues, 'The essence of spectacle is to provide a way in which to dramatise communal vision through displays which lift themes or values out of the ordinary',[99] then spectacle would indeed seem to be inherent in cinematography.

Emphasizing film as spectacle helps to highlight links with other aspects of mass entertainment and popular culture. There is the irreducible connection with consumerism, for example. Not only is the female star a major source of spectacle in film, she also embodies, in her artifice and glamour, her display of fashionable accessories, the power of the consumer spectacle itself. Films have deliberately targeted the female consumer (and, increasingly, the youth market), cinema chains were built in close proximity to shopping areas, and the cinema screen itself became a shop window. Debord's suggestion that the 'society of the spectacle' dates from the 1920s would reinforce this sense of the affinity between the spread of cinema culture and the rise of mass consumerism. In her analysis of this in the context of classic Hollywood cinema, Jane Gaines points out that 'Costume extravagance came to be associated with consumerism', which made it a threat both to 'narrative coherence' and to 'a notion of art that stands apart from the vicissitudes of commerce'.[100] Later, the unabashed triumph of consumerism, sweeping away the 'high art' pretensions of Hollywood cinema, would destroy this specific aspect of the resistance to spectacle.

This gives us clues to ways in which spectacle had emerged as a key feature of nineteenth-century culture, so that spectacle in cinema – and cinema as spectacle – both grew out of, and were modelled on, an experience of modern life that already manifested elements of the spectacular in its mode of self-presentation. It is the development of modern lighting, above all, that is central to this. Gas lamps spread rapidly in the early years of the century, and incandescent quicklime was introduced into theatres from the 1850s, producing the 'limelight' that enabled entertainment to be extended well into the night; but the most dramatic innovations came with Edison's electrical lighting, in the 1890s.[101] The 1900 Paris exposition used it on a massive scale, to keep open late at night, creating what an observer at the time called a 'fairyland spectacle',[102] one which served as a distraction from architectural and other deficiencies. Thus Virilio can suggest that artificial light 'helped turn reality into illusion', adding that street lighting, the 'democratisation of lighting', was 'a spectacle soon to be made available to all'.[103] Williams concludes that 'the advent of electrical power invested everyday life with fabulous qualities', hence embodying a 'material realization of fantasies' hitherto only possible in the imagination.[104] Spectacle emerges as a kind of democratization of the sublime in the age of consumerism.

The previously dominant form of modern lighting, gaslight, had been important in the emergence of Paris as a city of visual challenge and fascination, in earlier decades. Haussmann's Paris, suggests Clark, had involved constructing 'a set of forms in which the city appeared to be visible, even intelligible: 'Paris . . . was becoming a spectacle.'[105] Paris as spectacle was a self-referring world of artifice, of experience mediated by image in a world transformed by technology and the commodity. For Baudelaire, Paris had become surreal, allegorical, imagistic, a hermetic world of magical correspondences in which nature only existed in its absence, so that it could only be recaptured by artifice, which is itself a kind of doubling of nature. Hence 'artifice and nature coincide when the former becomes totally sealed and self-enclosed', as Clark puts it.[106] The spectacle becomes its own self-contained world, existing in problematic relation to the reality it both represents, replaces and disavows; a fantasy of an enclosed world of drama and pleasure, the artificial paradise of the consumer, but a fantasy in which even fantasy itself might be constructed in advance, given its prescribed place. For Richards, the great nineteenth-century exhibitions 'succeeded in making commodity culture virtually coterminous with the symbolic apparatus of spectacle'.[107]

And cinema? Here too we encounter a self-contained world of artifice, which by that very fact must exclude reality even as it reproduces it. The cinematic apparatus can only grasp part of the visible. 'It is what resists cinematic representation, limiting it on all sides and from within, which constitutes equally its force', writes Comolli; 'what makes it falter makes it go'.[108] The relationship between what is grasped and what is excluded in the very process of representation is a dynamic one: the subject of film is both the filmed and the unfilmed, and the reproduction of the difference between them. And Benjamin draws attention to the artificiality of 'reality' in the film, commenting on the clutter of the film studio and the importance of cutting in film technology: 'The equipment-free aspect of reality here has become the height of artifice; the sight of immediate reality has become an orchid in the land of technology.'[109]

And the spectators at this cinematic spectacle? Bazin suggests that 'There is nothing to prevent us from identifying ourselves in imagination with the moving world before us, which becomes *the* world.'[110] This is of course true, and at one level what is involved is straightforward enough; the filmgoer does not have to be duped, the 'illusion' is there on the surface. At the same time, there are complex processes of fiction-making and disavowal involved. Comolli thus argues that

> There is no uncertainty, no mistake, no misunderstanding or manipulation. There is ambivalence, play. The spectacle is always a game, requiring the spectators' partici-pation not as 'passive', 'alienated' consumers, but as players, accomplices, masters of the game even if they are also what is at stake. . . . Different in this to ideological and political representations, spectatorial representations declare their existence as simulacrum and, on that contractual basis, invite the spectator to *use* the simulacrum to fool him or herself.[111]

The viewer can hence believe in the reality of what is on screen while 'knowing' it as simulacrum, as an unreality that is real in its autonomy from the absent real. Modernity emerges as a world of images that simultaneously incorporates and excludes participation, that renders us both active and passive, 'together' in our distance from one another and from the others on the screen, 'separate' and 'unified' as selves but only through images of otherness: subjects of entertainment and the media.

When Maltby claims that 'Hollywood's cinematic apparatus simultaneously proffers us attractive illusions of ourselves as unified and autonomous identities and positions us as its ideological subjects',[112] it is important, in consequence, to add that spectatorship in some respects subverts this. There is a sense in which the spectator, like the film itself, is constituted as a dialectic of difference and continu-ity, presence and absence, illusion and reality; and there can be no essential unity, no simple resting place. The position of the spectatorial subject, triangulated between camera, viewer, and the actors and action on screen, is inherently unsta-ble. 'In the cinema', writes Orr, 'all human subjects, film-makers, actors and spectators alike, are both subject and object, viewed and viewing, looked upon and looking. There are no fixed points of experience, no absolute certainties in percep-tion.'[113] This is accentuated in modernist film, with its heightened interest in the paradoxes of reflexivity.

When Debord, theorist of the spectacle, writes that 'The images which de-tached themselves from every aspect of life fuse in a common stream . . . as a pseudo-world apart', and that 'In the spectacle, one part of the world *represents itself* before the world. . . . The spectacle is nothing more than a common language of this separation', he is not directly referring to the cinema, but might as well be. It is as though the cinema is a crystallization of the issues of image and representation that are produced by the world that makes spectacle possible. Spectacle is not the product of the mass dissemination of images; it *is* this world, 'become actual, materially translated. It is a vision of the world which has become objectified.' Lived reality itself comes to take on elements of spectacle: 'reality rises up within the spectacle, and the spectacle is real'.[114] Reality becomes doubled by its own representations, becomes spectacle. But if spectacle is about the power of the image in its separation, its self-sufficiency, its alienation from – and in – experience, then, as has been seen, this rests on, and reproduces, characteristic distinctions between the included and the excluded, illusion and reality, even as it questions these. The world of simulation, however, threatens to move beyond these distinctions. . . .

Image and Simulacrum: Towards the Postmodern?

Long before I had ever heard of Baudrillard, I can remember my own first acquaintance with the idea of simulation. Some problem had occurred on an American space flight, and I heard the commentator at NASA saying 'We don't know what the malfunction is. We're trying to simulate it on the computer.' That intrigued me. It seemed to suggest that only when we can simulate something do we really know what it is; to reproduce the unknown is to bestow identity on it, as though 'reality' results from superimposing the unreal on the unknowable. In this sense, it is the simulation that makes it real; to be real is to be capable of simulation.

But there is paradox here, bound up with the very origins of the word 'simu-late', meaning 'copy' or 'imitate'. On the one hand, we can talk of 'simulating illness', pretending to be ill, with the implication of dishonesty; on the other hand, to use another example from space exploration, scientists talk of 'simulating weightlessness', referring to the experimental reproduction of the conditions of its occurrence, that is, making a working model to understand or learn how to cope with it. And this duality, this sense that simulation both is, and isn't, what it purports to be, is central to it – as we saw earlier with the simulacrum, the image in its material embodiment. At the same time, one must be more precise about what is involved here. In Baudrillard's sense, *simulating* illness is not the same as merely *pretending* to be ill: simulation is not dissimulation. To simulate illness is to produce some of the symptoms in oneself, to *make* oneself in some sense 'ill'; as a result, one is not clearly either 'ill' or 'not-ill'. Consequently, argues Baudrillard, while mere pretence leaves the 'reality principle' intact, 'simulation threatens the difference between "true" and "false", between "real" and "imaginary"'.[115] One could take the example of hysteria, anorexia and similar conditions: traditionally distrusted by medicine because of the suspicion of patient involvement through fakery or wilfulness, these become the conditions that actually serve to question the ontological categories of medical orthodoxy itself.[116]

Discussing the early development of simulation techniques in modern technol-ogy, Woolley too suggests that this is not a matter of mere mimicry. Early aircraft trainers from the 1930s could not really represent the way a plane actually flew, the precise relation between the aircraft controls and the changes in position, speed and altitude that resulted from their use. Such a trainer could imitate flying, but not simulate it. By 1948–9, it was found that instructions issued to computers could produce specific patterns on a screen, even a 'ball game', animating a 'ball' that had no physical existence outside the screen, and Woolley sees this as the decisive move into simulation. By the 1960s, it was clear that any shape that could be described mathematically could exist in computer-generated space, and that humans could 'interact' with such simulations.[117] And now, technological simulacra have become part of war itself: 'the images and information which furnish the material for exercises and war games become indistinguishable from what would be encountered in a real conflict', as Patton puts it.[118] And, as seen in the case of illness, all this leaves the status of such simulations unclear: are they real, or imaginary? 'They partake in a new mode of existence', suggests Woolley, 'a mode that is not actual nor yet imaginary – the mode that has been called virtual.'[119]

Doubtless it is in relation to the media, particularly 'media events', that these issues have been explored most thoroughly. Woolley tells of a day in 1988 when an unusual degree of noise in the vicinity of his office led him to investigate; he found crowds of people milling around what he took to be the site of some railway accident, and then went back to work. What had happened only became clear later that evening, on television. Indeed, the whole site had itself become a television set, and that contributed to its clarity; for he now knew it to be the 'Clapham rail disaster', the worst of its kind for 20 years. He concluded that 'What I had witnessed that day "for real" at the end of the road was something quite different from what I had seen on television – and it was on television that, ultimately, the event happened, for me as much as for anyone else.' At one level, the event as experienced and the event as represented were not the same events; yet it was the latter that 'became' the event, constituted it *as* the event in question. Much the same could be said to be true of the 1991 Gulf War, which existed first and foremost as a media event: 'the entire war, at least at the level where anyone could make sense of it, was just a pattern on a screen'.[120]

It is indeed the Gulf War that has become central to these debates on media events, ever since Baudrillard wrote a provocative series of articles as the events themselves unfolded, later published as a booklet under the equally provocative title *The Gulf War Did Not Take Place*. And certainly one had a strong sense, at the time, of the war's 'unreal' quality, as if it was a composite of computer game and cinematic projection. The war began in true Hollywood fashion with a spectacular 'firework display' over Baghdad, and then continued in similar vein, so that a pilot could be quoted as saying 'It was exactly like the movies!'[121] Citing the case of a pilot who had to return to bomb a target again – even though he knew it had been destroyed the first time – because it didn't look good on film, Virilio comments: 'People used to die for a coat of arms, an image on a pennant or flag; now they died to improve the sharpness of a film.' War had finally become a dimension of cinema.[122] The war was presented on our screens as 'live'; but it was as carefully edited, cut, pasted, as any film. Nor was it necessarily so different for many of the participants: missile targets and troop movements were map coordinates and computer-enhanced images on a screen. The 'live' war, there before our eyes, was all a matter of images, pictures, screens, representations, simulations. . . .

Summarizing the implications of Baudrillard's perspective, Patton claims that

> while televisual information claims to provide immediate access to real events, in fact what it does is produce informational events which stand in for the real. . . . The result is a new kind of entity, qualitatively different to 'real' or 'imaginary' events as these were understood prior to the advent of modern communications technology: virtual media events. These are informational entities and one of their defining characteristics is to be always open to interpretation.[123]

Or, as Baudrillard himself puts it, 'everything which is turned into information becomes the object of endless speculation, the site of total uncertainty',[124] as instanced in the way the Gulf War has itself become subject to unresolved and unresolvable controversies, and appeals to rival conspiracy theories.[125] Appeal to the 'real world' offers no solution: either it is already simulacral, or is too fragmented and incoherent to do the job, as with Woolley's presence at the crash, or the reporter at a scene in the Gulf War, describing how a fighter-bomber attacked a distant target: it was as though 'sound and vision no longer marry up . . . reality is broken apart like a film whose soundtrack has wobbled out of sync. Shells burst in silence; explosions have no source.'[126] It is as though reality cannot compete with the simulacra that purport to reflect it but actually precede it, and thereby constitute it for us. This is Baudrillard's ' precession of simulacra',[127] whereby 'As simulacra, images precede the real to the extent that they invert the causal and logical order of the real and its reproduction', so that 'reality is the effect of the sign'.[128] Thus Heim can write that when flying an F–16 at supersonic speeds, 'the less you see of the real world, the more control you can have over your aircraft'; a cockpit can make the virtual more real than the real. . . .[129]

The consequence of the fact that simulacra are both reality-defining and multiple, full of information yet lacking in clear meaning, is that 'reality' itself necessarily becomes *contestable*. There can be no *one* reality, no master version against which to test the others and find them lacking, 'mere' simulacra. The representational crisis of modernity ultimately threatens to sweep away the very possibility of 'representation' itself. This 'lack of differentiation between image and reality', writes Baudrillard, 'no longer leaves room for representation as such';[130] hence 'simulation envelops the whole edifice of representation as itself a simulacrum'.[131] If the development of modernity could be said to have increasingly undermined the plausibility of the 'grand narratives' of history through which it has tried, reflexively, to make sense of itself, so it undermines the plausibility of 'grand representations', definitive pictures or images of the real, as well. 'Reality' emerges as an increasingly loaded, disputable concept. The project of modernity has to rely on an imposition of 'reality', when it can no longer plausibly be said to be known as such; 'order always opts for the real', as Baudrillard puts it sardonically, so power tries to 'reinject realness and referentiality everywhere'. It is in this context of increasingly desperate attempts to defend, or reinstate, traditional notions of the real that history is increasingly reconstructed as nostalgia: 'When the real is no longer what it used to be, nostalgia assumes its full meaning.'[132] If reality exists in the set of different simulacra through which it is constituted, the different viewpoints from which it can be experienced, then this threatens a spiral to infinity and indeterminacy; and authority always perceives that as troublesome.

Something of the feel of this is powerfully portrayed in Ridley Scott's film *Blade Runner* (1982). Set in Los Angeles in 2019, it confronts us with a streetworld of chaotic, dangerous and transient interactions between assorted beings – humans, simulacra, replicants – incoherent or conflicting signs and messages, fragmentation and uncertainty, a kind of recycling of the nineteenth-century city of the modernist imagination, in a form both nightmarish and vibrant. Simulacra are everywhere, signs are endlessly read and decoded, 'scrutinised and contested as the very foundation of our existence and self-knowledge', as Wakefield puts it in his analysis; to control these signs and their interpretations is to control life.[133] And above street level is indeed the high-tech world of corporate power, intervening when necessary to impose a privileged definition of reality, restrain the plethora of invention when it threatens to get 'out of control'.[134]

Above all, it is the replicants that must be controlled. Simulated humans, created in laboratories as slave labour for developing space colonies, they are programmed to self-destruct in four years so that if they do escape, there will be a limit to the damage they can do. Replicants are near-perfect simulacra, virtually indistinguishable from humans save in one respect: the circumstances of their creation mean that they have no history. They are condemned to a life in the present; they can have no real sense of past, or memory, and no hope of a future. Hence their sense of personal identity can at best be fragmentary. The replicants are serial, not copies, imitations or clones of a specific human person (unlike the 'false Maria' in *Metropolis*). They are hence ideal exemplifications of simulacra; they are all *different*, both from each other and from individual humans. This is the sense in which Giuliana Bruno can write of them that 'No original is thus invoked as point of comparison, and no distinction between real and copy remains.'[135] This is the real source of their challenge, then, of the danger they pose: their very existence questions the notions of 'reality' and 'authenticity' of humans themselves. Another theorist of the simulacrum, Deleuze, reminds us that 'The simulacrum is not degraded copy, rather it contains a positive power which negates both original and copy, both model and reproduction'; and this, he adds, is a 'phantasmatic power'.[136] The simulacrum is the doubling of the real, but the double that embodies a powerful otherness, that boundary between identity and difference that threatens the self-sufficiency and integrity of the real: it is the double that posits the real itself as phantasm.

When Baudrillard writes that 'The unreal is no longer that of dream or of fantasy, of a beyond or a within, it is that of a *hallucinatory resemblance of the real with itself*',[137] Bruno adds that 'The replicant performs such hallucinatory resemblance.'[138] Deckard himself, the 'blade runner', licensed to kill escaped replicants, muses on the resemblances between replicants and blade runners; his faith in his own authenticity wobbles, especially as he finds himself falling in love with

Rachel, a suspected replicant. And this, for Harvey, is the most 'depressing' side of the film: the fact that, in the end, 'the difference between the replicant and the human becomes so unrecognizable that they can indeed fall in love'.[139] Here, revealingly, speaks the true voice of modernist nostalgia for the real. One might, after all, reply that in an era when notions of a human 'essence' and 'human nature' become ever more unclear, so that definitions of human identity become fundamentally questionable, a definition of a human being as 'someone you can fall in love with' might serve as well as any other. Does it matter if your lover is a replicant? We all have our little quirks, after all. . . .

It is indeed in Rachel that the system has reached perfection, for she is the 'replicant' whose status as replicant is unclear. She, unlike the others, does not know whether she is a replicant or not; Deckard initially assumes she is, learns she is 'different' in some way, and becomes unsure. Bruno suggests that 'To say that she simulates her symptoms, her sexuality, her memory, is to say that she realizes, experiences them.'[140] She becomes what she appears to be; as with the hysteric, her very existence questions the ontology of depth and surface, essence and appearance, and the categories of medical and scientific epistemology that rest on these (health/illness; human/replicant), along with the power relations they embody.

Rachel does, however, have a photo. It purports to be of her and her mother. 'Photography and the mother', observes Bruno, 'are the missing link between past, present, and future'. As with Barthes in *Camera Lucida*, the photo of Mother is ultimately the only one that counts. This is the guarantee, the proof of identity, the link with irreducible history, at its most personal. Except that we know that history becomes allegory, that history is 'the trace of the dream of unity, of its impossibility'. The Mother of memory is also the Mother of fantasy; and as for the photo, it is 'proof', yes – proof that there *was* someone there, that there was *someone* there. 'In a world of fragmented temporality', concludes Bruno, 'the research of history finds its image, its photographic simulacrum, while history itself remains out of reach.'[141] Reality itself recedes, prowling ghostlike in the world of bright lights and flickering screens, summoned by allegorical interventions that always reproduce its loss; or, in Burgin's words, 'Through the "media", objective reality has become a membrane of simulacra stretched over the real; in it we glimpse our reflected, media-inflected, desires and fears.'[142]

Replicants are reproductions that in a sense replace the real, even though they may be modelled on it. Hence they give clues to Baudrillard's generalized model of simulation as hyperreality, which elaborates the idea that reality becomes reproducible even as it becomes no longer self-identical. As for the latter, 'What has happened', he argues, 'is that the negation of reality has now been incorporated into "reality" itself', so that 'what we have now is a principle of non-reality based on "reality" – a principle of "hyperreality"'.[143] As for the former aspect, 'The very definition of the real becomes: *that of which it is possible to give an equivalent reproduction*', so that the real is 'not only what can be produced, but *that which is always already produced*. The hyperreal.' In short, the hyperreal is 'the generation by models of a real without origin or reality', the reproducible world of simulations.[144] A hyperreal world of simulation is one where the representation and the reproduction of reality are no longer distinguishable.

Baudrillard mentions the fate of the prehistoric paintings in the caves at Lascaux. Menaced by deterioration, endangered by their visitors, the caves have been closed and a replica constructed nearby. The simulation may even be better than the original, since doubtless the opportunity to remove minor blemishes will have been seized. Thus is the real 'ceaselessly manufactured as an intensified version of itself, as hyperreality', as Connor puts it.[145] And the effect, for Baudrillard, is that both real and simulacrum become homogeneous: 'the duplication is sufficient to render both artificial'.[146] Many similar instances are documented by Eco, who argues that history, art and nature all suffer the same fate; all are reborn as simulacra. As for nature, 'it is erased by artifice precisely so that it can be presented as uncontaminated'; 'nature' in 'nature reserves' is a carefully structured product of human intervention. In the case of art, he instances waxwork and other reproductions of the Leonardo painting of the Last Supper that are presented as 'more real' than the original, flaking away as it is into self-destruction; and history is reconstructed as heritage, preserved as 'authentic' copy, hence embodying 'a philosophy of immortality as duplication'. In the end, 'The "completely real" becomes identified with the "completely fake". Absolute unreality is offered as real presence.'[147]

The world of modern experience, then, becomes increasingly dominated by images, signs and simulacra; reality becomes inseparable from the codes of representation through which it is constituted. As a conclusion, it may be worth adapting and developing some ideas of Hebdige to set up a speculative contrast, so as to clarify the issues by polarizing them.[148] In effect, one can draw a distinction between a 'culture of narrative', or a 'depth culture', on the one hand, and a 'culture of the image', or 'surface culture', on the other. In the first, priority is given to written and spoken language – 'discourse' – and sets of experts police the boundaries between these discourses, which become elaborated into separate occupations and disciplines. Word counts for more than image, narrative is superior to the visual. The latter remains important, of course, notably as the framework through which the self can be rendered subject to, disciplined by, panoptic control; but this, too, entails subordinating the self to norms of narrative coherence. As embedded in the various discourses, narrative is developed and protected by the appropriate experts, since this is taken to ensure access to the truth; truth is therefore always in some sense *hidden*, the secret revealed at the end of the story. Francis Bacon, proclaiming that 'truth is to be sought in the deepest mines of nature',[149] articulates this clearly. Since narrative has a temporal structure, it is linked to the priority of linear time; indeed, narrative becomes a model for history, history becomes a story. Narrative is also linked to the unified self; the self, too, unfolds in linear time, constructing its life as a story.

Let us now contrast this 'first world' with the 'second world', of images and appearances. Now, picture has priority over text. The task of language is to service the image, not control or explain it. Time is no longer linear, but is rather the time of the present; time loses its depth, and fragments into images that can be endlessly recycled in an eternal present. Nor does one have to dig deep for truth; as Hebdige puts it, 'There is nothing underneath or behind the image and hence there is no hidden truth to be revealed.'[150] In the world of image, media and simulacra, everything is as real as it pretends to be. As images are multiple, so is truth. It is the 'place' of images that matters, in relation to context and other images, this is their 'meaning'; there is no secret sense to be decoded. Nor are images guarded by experts in carefully bounded disciplines; the whole point of the image is to circulate. Flexibility takes priority over stable roles; expertise becomes horizontal rather than hierarchical, more a matter of adaptability than specialization, making connections rather than analysing. Crossing boundaries becomes more important than maintaining them.

With the self, unification and exclusion become less important than diffusion and incorporation, and self-identity is increasingly defined in terms of self-image. Problems of authenticity and alienation, so central to debates over theatricality, no longer seem so meaningful. Self-presentation cannot betray any deeper integrity of self, for the self simply *is* how it presents itself at any given moment, with no deep coherence linking these successive presentations. Problems are posed for concepts like 'ideology' and 'false consciousness'; appearances cannot be 'misleading' if there is no depth that they can 'misrepresent'. So Wakefield argues that hyperreality, in 'refusing to distinguish between manufactured (degraded) and natural (authentic) experience, therefore denies us the luxury of the old-fashioned ideological critique, couched as it was between the terms of misrepresentation and falsification'.[151] Instead, other issues come to the fore: how 'truth' is produced as an *effect* of surfaces and appearances, how content and context are constituted through the image and its transformations, how 'multiple realities' are constructed, reproduced – and contested.

The 'first world', then, the culture of narrative, both rests on, and reproduces, certain essential distinctions: between reality and appearance, truth and ideology or mystification, world and representation, authenticity and artifice or alienation. The narratives we construct enable us to learn the secret, get to the truth, control the world. In the 'second world', however, these distinctions become relativized, or collapse altogether. But to say that there are 'only surfaces, not depths', would be paradoxical: 'surface' only makes sense relative to 'depth', after all. But this paradox could embody a significant truth. Wakefield concludes his discussion of *Blade Runner* by arguing that the film

> accommodates tensions – tensions between the second world understanding that the simulacrum conceals nothing, and the desire to invest the empty form of the simulacra with at least the vestiges of first world meaning. The success of *Blade Runner* lies in its ability to invoke the 'first world' as a difference component of the second, without becoming in the process an equally empty, nostalgic referential.

In this perspective, the second world does not replace the first; it is superimposed, so that the first world is refracted through it, in an allegorical relation of 'double-coding'.[152] And if we use this as a perspective on modernity itself, we could say that the postmodern emerges as its uncanny double (or vice versa?). When the second world is superimposed on the first world, with the generalized doubling of reality by its representations, phantasmagoria become simulacra, and modern becomes postmodern.

Notes

1 J. Flam, *Matisse: The Man and His Art, 1869–1918* (Thames and Hudson, 1986), p. 230.
2 S. Sontag, *On Photography* (Penguin, 1987), p. 53.
3 C. Baudelaire, 'The Salon of 1859', in his *Selected Writings on Art and Literature* (Penguin, 1992), p. 306.
4 Cited in Sontag, *Photography*, pp. 53, 87.
5 W. J. T. Mitchell, *Iconology: Image, Text, Ideology* (University of Chicago Press, 1986), p. 38.
6 M. Jay, *Downcast Eyes: The Denigration of Vision in Twentieth-Century French Thought* (California University Press, 1993), p. 543. See also J. Crary, *Techniques of the Observer: On Vision and Modernity in the Nineteenth Century* (MIT Press, 1990).
7 N. Elias, *The Civilizing Process, Vol. I: The History of Manners* (Blackwell, 1978), p. 203.
8 Jay, *Downcast Eyes*, p. 44.
9 M. Foucault, *The Order of Things* (Tavistock, 1970), ch. 2.
10 J.-L. Comolli, 'Machines of the Visible', in T. de Lauretis and S. Heath (eds.) *The Cinematic Apparatus* (Macmillan, 1980), p. 122.
11 Crary, *Techniques*, ch. 4; S. Neale, *Cinema and Technology* (Macmillan, 1985), pp. 26–8; and T. Markus, *Buildings and Power* (Routledge, 1993), ch. 8.
12 Crary, *Techniques*, ch. 1, and p. 21.
13 Jay, *Downcast Eyes*, ch. 2.
14 D. Chaney, *Fictions of Collective Life: Public Drama in Late Modern Culture* (Routledge, 1993), p. 84.
15 J. Tagg, *The Burden of Representation: Essays on Photographies and Histories* (Macmillan, 1988).
16 P. Virilio, *War and Cinema* (Verso, 1989).
17 Chaney, *Fictions*, p. 99.
18 Explored in N. Abercrombie et al., 'Popular Representation: Recasting Realism', in S. Lash and J. Friedman (eds.) *Modernity and Identity* (Blackwell, 1992).
19 Oliver Wendell Holmes, 1859, cited in S. Ewen, *All Consuming Images* (Basic Books, 1988), p. 24.
20 Ewen, *All Consuming Images*, p. 25.
21 Jay, *Downcast Eyes*, p. 135.
22 Cited in P. Virilio, *The Vision Machine* (Indiana University Press, 1994), p. 2 (emphasized in the original).
23 R. Maltby, *Hollywood Cinema* (Blackwell, 1995), p. 150.
24 D. Freedberg, *The Power of Images* (University of Chicago Press, 1989), p. 404.
25 P. Brantlinger, *Bread and Circuses: Theories of Mass Culture as Social Decay* (Cornell University Press, 1983), pp. 260, 261.
26 See Jay, *Downcast Eyes*, pp. 34–47; Freedberg, *Power of Images*, ch. 14.

27   See Mitchell, *Iconology*, p. 8; Jay, *Downcast Eyes*, pp. 93–5; and M. Iversen, 'Imagining the Republic: The Sign and Sexual Politics in France', in P. Hulme and L. Jordanova (eds.) *The Enlightenment and Its Shadows* (Routledge, 1990).

28   Mitchell, *Iconology*, p. 194.

29   Freedberg, *Power of Images*, p. 438.

30   T. de Lauretis, *Alice Doesn't* (Macmillan, 1984), p. 38.

31   Mitchell, *Iconology*, p. 17.

32   T. Adorno, *In Search of Wagner* (New Left Books, 1981), p. 90.

33   J. Orr, *Cinema and Modernity* (Polity, 1993), p. 87.

34   T. Castle, 'Phantasmagoria: Spectral Technology and the Metaphorics of Modern Reverie', *Critical Inquiry* (1988), 15:1, pp. 49, 30, 45.

35   L. A. Sass, *Madness and Modernism* (Harvard University Press, 1992), p. 92.

36   Cited in ibid., p. 92.

37   Castle, 'Phantasmagoria', pp. 56, 29, 52, 30, 29, 31.

38   Ibid., p. 61.

39   R. Barthes, *Camera Lucida* (Vintage, 1993), pp. 14, 14, 9, 87.

40   Cited in R. Krauss, 'Tracing Nadar', *October* (1978), 5, pp. 31–2.

41   Sontag, *Photography*, p. 155.

42   Barthes, *Camera*, p. 42.

43   Sontag, *Photography*, p. 155.

44   Krauss, 'Tracing Nadar', pp. 42, 37.

45   Cited in N. Burch, *Life to those Shadows* (British Film Institute, 1990), p. 23.

46   S. Sontag, *Guardian* (2 March 1996), p. 27.

47   Maltby, *Hollywood*, p. 199.

48   Orr, *Cinema*, p. 36.

49   Maltby, *Hollywood*, p. 330.

50   Orr, *Cinema*, p. 87; and see pp. 85–6.

51   Sontag, *Photography*, p. 161.

52   Orr, *Cinema*, pp. 36–7, 37.

53   E. Bronfen, *Over Her Dead Body: Death, Femininity and the Aesthetic* (Manchester University Press, 1992), pp. 114, 114, 113, 113, 113.

54   See J. Gaines and C. Herzog (eds.) *Fabrications* (Routledge, 1991), especially chapters by J. Gaines and G. Studlar.

55   Orr, *Cinema*, pp. 40–1, 43.

56   The analysis is developed in K. Marx, *Capital*, Vol. I, Part 1, ch. 1, section 4, on the 'Fetishism of Commodities'.

57   S. Buck-Morss, *The Dialectics of Seeing* (MIT Press, 1991), p. 81.

58   C. Baudelaire, 'Le Cygne', in *Les Fleurs du Mal*, my translation; and see W. Benjamin, *Charles Baudelaire* (Verso, 1983), p. 170.

59   M. Calinescu, *Five Faces of Modernity* (Duke University Press, 1987), p. 54.

60   C. Buci-Glucksmann, *Baroque Reason: The Aesthetics of Modernity* (Sage, 1994), p. 138.

61   W. Benjamin, 'Central Park', in *New German Critique* (1985), 34, p. 38.

62   Cited in H. Geyer-Ryan, 'Counterfactual Artefacts: Walter Benjamin's Philosophy of History', in E. Timms and P. Collier (eds.) *Visions and Blueprints* (Manchester University Press, 1988), p. 76.

63   C. Owens, 'The Allegorical Impulse: Toward a Theory of Postmodernism', in B. Wallis (ed.) *Art After Modernism: Rethinking Representation* (Godine, 1984), p. 215.

64   T. Eagleton, *The Ideology of the Aesthetic* (Blackwell, 1990), p. 326.

65 Benjamin, 'Central Park', p. 48.

66 Barthes, *Camera*, pp. 85, 87.

67 W. Benjamin, 'A Short History of Photography', *Screen* (1972), 13:1, p. 7.

68 Cited in Geyer-Ryan, 'Counterfactual Artefacts', p. 68.

69 Sontag, *Photography*, pp. 3, 24, 80, 106.

70 Barthes, *Camera*, p. 91.

71 S. Stewart, *On Longing: Narratives of the Miniature, the Gigantic, the Souvenir, the Collection* (Duke UP, 1993), p. 135.

72 Sontag, *Photography*, p. 70.

73 Eagleton, *Ideology*, pp. 326, 327, 336.

74 See my *Transgressing the Modern* (Blackwell, 1999), especially chs. 2, 4.

75 See L. Gamman and M. Makinen, *Female Fetishism* (Lawrence and Wishart, 1994).

76 J. Baudrillard, *For a Critique of the Political Economy of the Sign* (Telos, 1981), p. 91.

77 R. Stoller, *Observing the Erotic Imagination* (Yale University Press, 1985), p. 155.

78 W. Benjamin, 'The Work of Art in the Age of Mechanical Reproduction', in his *Illuminations* (Fontana, 1992), Note 6, p. 237.

79 Gamman and Makinen, *Female Fetishism*, p. 182, and see ch. 2.

80 See, for example, P. Bürger, *Theory of the Avant-Garde* (Minnesota University Press, 1984), pp. 70–3; and A. Shelton (ed.) *Fetishism: Visualising Power and Desire* (Lund Humphries, 1995), passim.

81 M. Featherstone, *Consumer Culture and Postmodernism* (Sage, 1991), p. 16.

82 Owens, 'Allegorical Impulse', pp. 209, 229, 230.

83 See P. Brantlinger, 'Mass Media and Culture in *Fin-de-Siècle* Europe', in M. Teich and R. Porter (eds.) *Fin de Siècle and its Legacy* (Cambridge University Press, 1990), p. 99; J. Stacey, *Star Gazing: Hollywood Cinema and Female Spectatorship* (Routledge, 1994), ch. 4; and Maltby, *Hollywood*, p. 10.

84 R. Williams, *Dream Worlds* (California University Press, 1982), pp. 78–84.

85 M. Hansen, 'Benjamin, Cinema and Experience', *New German Critique* (1987), 40, p. 218.

86 Orr, *Cinema*, p. 15.

87 Sontag, *Guardian*, p. 27.

88 N. Denzin, *The Cinematic Society: The Voyeur's Gaze* (Sage, 1995), pp. 34, 24.

89 Benjamin, 'Work of Art', pp. xiii, 229.

90 See ch. 1; and, for Stacey reference, note 83.

91 P. Wollen, *Raiding the Icebox: Reflections on Twentieth-Century Culture* (Verso, 1993), p. 47.

92 See discussions in Orr, *Cinema*, pp. 1–9; Neale, *Cinema*, pp. 139–58; and S. Connor, *Postmodernist Culture* (Blackwell, 1989), p. 175.

93 Orr, *Cinema*, p. 8.

94 Neale, *Cinema*, pp. 147, 150, 143.

95 T. de Lauretis, *Alice Doesn't*, p. 46.

96 Neale, *Cinema*, p. 155.

97 D. Andrew, *Concepts in Film Theory* (Oxford University Press, 1984), pp. 75–6.

98 Maltby, *Hollywood*, p. 324; and see J. Gaines (ed.) *Classical Hollywood Narrative* (Duke University Press, 1992), p. 1.

99 Chaney, *Fictions*, pp. 79, 21.

100 J. Gaines, 'Costume and Narrative: How Dress Tells the Woman's Story', in Gaines and Herzog, *Fabrications*, p. 198.

101   Jay, *Downcast Eyes*, pp. 123–4; W. Schivelbusch, *Disenchanted Night: The Industri-alisation of Light in the 19th Century* (Berg, 1988), passim; and see also ch. 1, on theatre and spectacle.

102   Cited in Williams, *Dream Worlds*, p. 87.

103   Virilio, *Vision Machine*, p. 9.

104   Williams, *Dream Worlds*, p. 84.

105   T. J. Clark, *The Painting of Modern Life: Paris in the Art of Manet and His Followers* (Thames and Hudson, 1985), p. 66.

106   T. J. Clark, *The Absolute Bourgeois: Artists and Politics in France 1848–51* (Thames and Hudson, 1973), p. 175.

107   T. Richards, *The Commodity Culture of Victorian England: Advertising and Spectacle, 1851–1914* (Verso, 1991), p. 58, and see ch. 1.

108   Comolli, 'Machines', p. 141.

109   Benjamin, 'Work of Art', pp. xi, 226.

110   Cited in Jay, *Downcast Eyes*, p. 460.

111   Comolli, 'Machines', p. 140.

112   Maltby, *Hollywood*, p. 432.

113   Orr, *Cinema*, p. 10.

114   G. Debord, *Society of the Spectacle* (Black & Red, Detroit, 1970), pp. 2, 29, 5, 8.

115   J. Baudrillard, *Simulations* (Semiotext(e), 1983), p. 5.

116   See, for example, S. Heath, *The Sexual Fix* (Macmillan, 1982), pp. 25–49, on hysteria; and M. Lawrence (ed.) *Fed Up and Hungry* (Women's Press, 1987), pp. 62, 220, and passim, on anorexia.

117   B. Woolley, *Virtual Worlds* (Penguin, 1993), ch. 2.

118   P. Patton, Introduction to J. Baudrillard, *The Gulf War Did Not Take Place* (Power Institute Publications, Sydney, 1995), p. 4.

119   Woolley, *Virtual Worlds*, p. 55.

120   Ibid., pp. 196, 193.

121   Cited in ibid., p. 191.

122   Virilio, *War and Cinema*, p. 85.

123   Patton, Introduction, p. 10.

124   Baudrillard, *Gulf War*, p. 41.

125   See, for example, D. Kellner, *The Persian Gulf TV War* (Westview Press, 1992), pp. 7, 15.

126   Cited in Woolley, *Virtual Worlds*, p. 195.

127   Baudrillard, *Simulations*, chapter heading.

128   J. Baudrillard, *The Evil Demon of Images* (Power Institute Publications, Sydney, 1987), p. 47 (second quote emphasized in the original). Note that most of this, and the first half of *Simulations*, are now available as *Simulacra and Simulation* (Michigan University Press, 1994).

129   M. Heim, *The Metaphysics of Virtual Reality* (Oxford University Press, 1993), p. 113.

130   Baudrillard, *Evil Demon*, p. 27.

131   Baudrillard, *Simulations*, p. 11.

132   Ibid., pp. 42, 42, 12.

133   N. Wakefield, *Postmodernism: The Twilight of the Real* (Pluto, 1990), p. 117, and ch. 8.

134   D. Harvey, *The Condition of Postmodernity* (Blackwell, 1989), p. 311, and see ch. 18.

135   G. Bruno, 'Postmodernism and *Blade Runner*', October (1987), 41, p. 68.

136 G. Deleuze, 'Plato and the Simulacrum', *October* (1983), 27, p. 53 (in the original, emphasized from 'both'), and p. 51.
137 Baudrillard, *Simulations*, p. 142.
138 Bruno, 'Postmodernism', p. 68.
139 Harvey, *Condition*, p. 313.
140 Bruno, 'Postmodernism', p. 68.
141 Ibid., pp. 71, 72, 74.
142 V. Burgin, *The End of Art Theory* (Macmillan, 1986), p. 170.
143 Baudrillard, *Demon*, p. 51.
144 Baudrillard, *Simulations*, pp. 146, 2 (original emphasis).
145 Connor, *Postmodernist Culture*, p. 151.
146 Baudrillard, *Simulations*, p. 18.
147 U. Eco, 'Travels in Hyperreality', in his *Faith in Fakes* (Secker and Warburg, 1986), pp. 52, 18, 6, 7.
148 D. Hebdige, *Hiding in the Light* (Routledge, 1988), ch. 7. See also Wakefield, *Postmodernism*, ch. 7, and S. Lash, *Sociology of Postmodernism* (Routledge, 1990), ch. 7.
149 Cited in R. Williams, *Notes on the Underground* (MIT Press, 1990), p. 46.
150 Hebdige, *Hiding*, p. 159.
151 Wakefield, *Postmodernism*, pp. 100–1.
152 Ibid., pp. 130, 128. On double-coding, see also, in the context of architecture, C. Jencks, *What is Post-Modernism* (Academy Editions, 1989), p. 14.

12 Postmodern Times?

The Modern Project and its Fate

'Project' includes notions of control, rationality and reflexivity. The project of modernity has entailed the attempt to reconstruct the world – the world of nature and the world of the social – on rational principles, and this process has an element of self-awareness about it, both at the personal and the institutional levels, so that the process itself becomes something to be reflected on, learnt from, and thereby furthered. And it has become increasingly clear, over time, that this world-transforming orientation is fraught with paradox and unforeseen results.

It is not just the unpredictable consequences of actions or events, but the possible disproportion between cause and consequence, that is significant here. A world in which components in refrigerators can cause a hole in the ozone layer, and an accident in a power plant in Russia can poison sheep as far away as the Lake District, has indeed become a world of complex interconnections where minor changes can have devastating ramifications through the system.[1] And this is a world which constantly reminds us of its modernity, for the impact of the latter has in effect made it increasingly difficult to separate 'nature' and 'culture'. The natural world increasingly becomes a created environment, a historical product, 'inside' modernity, an aspect of it, rather than existing in a relation of exteriority. And this, of course, is just as true of the body itself.[2]

Pointing out that in the eighteenth century, 'accident' was still more or less synonymous with 'coincidence', Schivelbusch argues that the nineteenth-century experience of mining and the railways transformed it into a function of technology; no longer a product of a purely external 'natural world', an accident is now seen as cultural. This is because there is 'an exact ratio between the level of the technology with which nature is controlled, and the degree of severity of its accidents. The pre-industrial era did not know any technological accidents in that sense.'[3] Rosalind Williams adds that this reveals 'the breakdown of the age-old distinction between nature as a source of hazard and technology as a source of safety'.[4] For example, we know that in various ways human intervention to combat disease itself produces disease; the use of modern drugs becomes self-defeating, as the viruses and bacteria become resistant, or new strains develop. It is perfectly possible that modern medicine will itself contribute to a return of the age of plague and pestilence.[5] In such a 'risk society', the distribution of risks and hazards becomes material for political conflict. It is not that, for the individual, 'risk' is necessarily any greater in the modern world – in some respects, this would seem highly implausible – but that the massive scale of human impact on the world has produced a change in our sense and awareness of risk, and that attempts to minimize risk can in turn unwittingly add to it, while generating a vast superstructure of risk calculation, risk management and insurance.[6]

In short, our world is experienced as a world of risk, in which the incalculable and unaccountable consequences of our actions both stimulate the imperative to greater order and control, yet also, subtly, subvert it, since as Beck argues, 'risks tell us what should not be done but not what should be done', and hence, 'Someone who depicts the world as risk will ultimately become incapable of action.'[7] The former strand, the imperative to control, doubtless remains dominant; the project of modernity generates its own momentum. Confronted with disasters that may have been caused partly by their own previous actions, modern bureaucrats and politicians are adept at using this as *further* evidence for the need for yet *more* 'rational' intervention and control; a more refined and careful use of 'improved' technology, for example. If modernity produces disasters, it is nonetheless easy to be persuaded that these can hardly be remedied by anything other than a further dose of modernity: the poison is also the cure. Progress fails because of the very attempt to attain it, but the very failure rekindles the attempt. Yet the second strand is also present, as is revealed in the language of recycling, whereby the modern world is encouraged towards a kind of stasis based on an eternal return of its own waste. Either way, the consequences of modernity itself become the problems that the modern world has to cope with. 'All that remains', suggests Baudrillard, 'is to play with the pieces.'[8] Pieces, faeces: 'progress' thus progresses from the emancipatory to the excremental. It is as though all that is left is to clear up our own mess. . . .

The effects of all this on our general outlook are profound. There is a sense in which the more we know about the world, the more uncontrollable and unpredictable it seems to become. Control means predictability and power, but also uncertainty, in that whatever is *not* subject to control is all the more threatening, and the awareness of its recalcitrance becomes all the more acute. In the age of AIDS, it is again doubtless disease that provides the most graphic examples. Studying the impact of childhood leukaemia on the families coping with it, attempting to make sense of the mysteries of why it strikes and its erratic development, Comaroff and Maguire conclude that medicine is ambiguous in a double sense: 'the more it appears to control, the more threatening appear the domains where its knowledge is still lacking; and the more it controls, the more alienated is the layman himself from control over its effects'.[9] There are two tensions here, then – between the known and the unknown, the chaotic, the threatening, and between the lay and the professional worlds of knowledge and experience – and both reinforce this sense of a world of nature and culture that remains defiant and impenetrable in its otherness. 'Our quest to build an ever-safer technological shelter from natural hazards has paradoxically led to a profound and pervasive sense of insecurity', concludes Williams.[10]

The growth of knowledge and control thus intensify the gap between project and experience, and in this gap intriguing sense-making strategies develop. If there is a belief that 'one can, in principle, master all things by calculation', as Weber put it,[11] so that there must *be* intelligible answers, along with a sense of the pervasive all-encompassing impact of human culture and technology in the world, then a search for understanding slides easily into a search for blame. Schivelbusch claims that the notion of negligence is modern, and comes into legal prominence with the age of the railway and railway accidents, as indeed does accident insurance;[12] and Sontag points to the variety of powerful folk notions that have clustered around diseases – notably cancer and TB – in the 'secular' modern age, usually involving elements of victim-blaming.[13] It is increasingly as though anything that goes wrong in a world that is seen as irredeemably transformed by human intervention must have a human cause; someone, somewhere, must be to blame; and thus does the state of the world of late modernity rejoin the early modern or pre-modern universe of interlocking and mysterious determinisms, recreating the experiential and conceptual space out of which witchcraft beliefs once grew. While Weber, in the early years of the century, could claim that now 'there are no mysterious, incalculable forces that come into play', and hence that 'the world is disenchanted',[14] Beck, writing today, gives a notably different emphasis:

> Threats from civilization are bringing about a kind of new 'shadow kingdom', comparable to the realm of the gods and demons in antiquity, which is hidden behind the visible world and threatens human life on this Earth. . . . Dangerous, hostile substances lie concealed behind the harmless façades. Everything must be viewed with a double gaze, and can only be correctly understood and judged through this doubling. The world of the visible must be investigated, relativized, evaluated with respect to a second reality, only existent in thought and yet concealed in the world. . . .
>
> Everywhere, pollutants and toxins laugh and play their tricks like devils in the Middle Ages. . . . Their invisibility is no proof of their non-existence; instead, since their reality takes place in the realm of the invisible anyway, it gives their suspected mischief almost unlimited space.[15]

It is as though the modern regime of the visible, converting the world into surfaces and appearances, brings with it its own doubling, its own spectral other in the invisible itself. And this link between risk and visibility reminds us that questions of representation are central here.

It is a commonplace that we live in a media-inflected age, that our very experience of the world is shaped and influenced by the images and narratives of the mass media. Take 'news' itself: the fact that we read about it, and watch it, on a daily basis, is one of the more distinctive peculiarities of the modern world. 'News' is a conjunction of the 'new' and the 'newsworthy': it has to have qualities of challenge, suddenness, difference, something that is brought to a head. And the newsworthy is also the personalized: news is about specific persons or small groups, producing a focus through vicarious identification and difference, along with attributions of blame, ridicule or praise. Subtleties of social context, complexities of motivation, become lost in the simple tabloid and televisual melodramas of good and evil. Overall, news has to be instantly believable; it has to be a possible experience in life, continuous with the range of modern experiences, however geographically or socially distant the specific item may be.

Above all, then, news tells us of a world of challenge, of risk; it all helps to reproduce a picture of a world that is constantly troubled and troublesome, a world that may be fascinating but is also dangerous. Sociologists and historians may protest that muggings are not a recent invention, and that the groups and individuals who most fear violence are not those most likely to suffer from it, but none of this alters the perception that we live in a world of risk. Once we perceive risk and danger as being potentially ever-present, they become real for us: the representation and the reality blend subtly together. This is indeed reinforced by the recurrence of these kinds of news items. News is always new, and, through recurrence, always the same. Wars, terrorism, murders, disasters of all kinds, all seep into each other in an endlessly recycled sense of the 'now' that is also the eternal, an unchanging ever-changing world of risk and violence, supercharged melodramas of the 'human condition'. It is not primarily a matter of 'media manipulation' or 'ideological distortion' (though those may be around in plenty, too); rather is it that the media world operates as a 'spectacular' reinforcement of tendencies already there in late modernity, in which the world we transformed returns to trouble us, and to play with our reflexive sense of who we are and where we are going.

Weber pointed out that people who drive cars do not generally have much idea of how they work; in everyday life, it is assumed that there are experts who will know the answers when something breaks down.[16] Referring to present-day environmental risks, Beck suggests that 'The harmful, threatening, inimical lies in wait everywhere, but whether it is inimical or friendly is beyond one's own power of judgement'; thus we depend on experts, and our 'cognitive sovereignty' is threatened.[17] But it follows from the inevitable imponderables of environmental risk that there has to be a strong sense in which the experts can't know either, whatever their pretensions. The power of experts and managers over our lives may be real enough, but it rests on collective mystification as much as real expertise. In his critique of modern bureaucracy, MacIntyre argues that 'The fetishism of commodities has been supplemented by another just as important fetishism, that of bureaucratic skills'; so-called 'managerial expertise' is a 'moral fiction, because the kind of knowledge which would be required to sustain it does not exist'. He concludes that

> all too often, when imputed organizational skill and power are deployed and the desired effect follows, all that we have witnessed is the same kind of sequence to be

observed when a clergyman is fortunate enough to pray for rain just before the unpredicted end of a drought.[18]

Hence the levers of power produce effects unsystematically and often only coincidentally related to their purported aims. When Weber concluded that 'One need no longer have recourse to magical means in order to master or implore the spirits', since 'Technical means and calculations perform the service',[19] he may have been more right than he realized. . . .

It is in this context that we can return to the issue of reflexivity. Since the urge to control is so strong, and yet constantly encounters the gap, our experience of the limits and dysfunctions of this in practice, the recalcitrance of a world that always partly escapes, modern organizations have to develop strategies to cope with the resulting strains. Two in particular merit attention: first, to treat the world *as if* knowable, calculable, and second, to engage in a reflexive re-examination of the methods used and their premises, so as to improve the rationality of the enterprise. Thus we increasingly live in a world of 'performance indicators', 'accounting procedures', 'quality controls' and the other bizarre means whereby we try to persuade ourselves and the wider public of the rationality and efficiency of our organizational practices. And these two strategies become mutually self-reinforcing. Reflexive examination comes to constitute and define the organization in terms of the set of 'rational', accountable procedures that it itself uses to define and solve its problems; and this implicitly constitutes the world with which it deals in terms of these same procedures and problems. 'Reality' comes to be defined reflexively, in terms that render it suitable to the methods whereby it is to be known. And the whole project becomes threatened by circularity: knowledge claims become self-validating, assessed against the world they have themselves constituted. Self-validating, but ultimately productive of uncertainty and unease.

After all, the gap remains, and will always remain. If the reflexive enterprise transforms its object in the very act of 'knowing' it, or redefines the problem in the very act of 'solving' it, any deductions or predictions will necessarily be affected, and may be vitiated. After all, none of these elaborate self-referential systems of internal monitoring can achieve final success. The dialectic of self-reflection and self-constitution, reflexivity and reconstruction, consciousness and action, is driven on by the very impossibility of a self-knowledge that is totally adequate to itself. Its own presuppositions become opaque in the very search for them, the very process of self-examination itself. Trying to know, or control, a totality of which one is necessarily a part, a system in which one's own assumptions and decisions will have obscure consequences, is bound to be paradoxical and self-defeating – not that this seems to inhibit the attempt.

Those who have had the dubious pleasure of working in the universities in recent years – and doubtless this goes for numerous other organizational environments, too – may well experience a sense of weary familiarity with all this. With more and more time spent on accounting procedures, reviews of what we are doing, or would – or might – be doing, if we weren't reviewing it, 'reality' becomes both the product of these reflexive activities, which thereby constitute what they purport to measure or review, and a latent, haunting shadow that coexists uneasily, invisibly, within it, in our sense that 'real' reality has little to do with all this, its 'official', hyperreal version. The effect is a kind of 'doubling' in the world of experience, whereby reality remains, dimly discernible, as an uneasy presence, the ghost at the hyperreal banquet.

The project of modernity thus prepares both the triumphs and the ultimate limitations of our experience of the modern world. If experience becomes increasingly the experience of the consequences of project itself, it is above all the experience of life as shadow-play, a phantasmagoria, a puzzle, life as unending irresolution, a sense of the world as recalcitrant and mysterious even as we ostensibly dominate it. Project thereby produces the experience of a world that escapes it; agency enacted becomes agency fragmented, incomprehensible in its effects. Panopticism, as a will to transparency and total control, can all too easily produce its opposite, reflected in the cultural resonance of images and metaphors of the labyrinth and the uncanny.

Thrills, Spills and *Ennui*: Dimensions of Modern Experience

A sense of risk seems inherent in novelty, uncertainty and change, all central features of the modern age and its consciousness; and risk as realized becomes refracted in experience as *shock*. In this sense, an awareness of shock as a dimension of the modern experience – something to be coped with, defended against, but also, in some ways, something to seek out, a source of excitement – has been central to theories and commentaries on the modern.

For Baudelaire, shock was inseparable from the experience of modernity in city life, in the need to negotiate the challenge of the masses, the world of strangers, the traffic. Alertness becomes a strategy of survival while, conversely, immersion, an opposite quality, becomes an aesthetic imperative, permitting a 'depth experience' of modernity, in its very transience and superficiality, that can be transmuted into art, and can contribute to a certain aestheticization of everyday life. Later, Freud and Elias present consciousness itself as a mode of defence, a way of blocking out, or controlling, the rush of sensations, almost a kind of 'armour' that the modern body has to acquire around itself. And the reference to Elias reminds us that this has its sources in the civilizing process, with the pressure towards being self-aware, and to concern oneself with presentation in public. Any violation or neglect of the appropriate social rules was commonly described as 'shocking'.[20] But the very mechanisms for dealing with these challenges in turn bred another characteristic modernist response: that of *ennui*, or spleen, a world-weariness or frustration frequently embedded in narratives of nostalgia, of loss.

A defence against shock, if successful, largely denudes the experience of its power and merely registers it as an event, as a point in time.[21] Consciousness thereby operates as a snapshot or filing mechanism, insulating against the experience of shock while recording it, and thereby ensuring that important sources and forms of experience are never really absorbed as such, never really 'lived'. The sense of embeddedness – in a past, a community, an environment – is lost, and this is true not only of experience but of the self also, for the impetus to reflexive awareness constitutes one's self-identity as separate, cut off from others.

In the modern period, then, consciousness is very much in the service of project, and it is not just that the unpredictable must be controlled, but that experience as such should be shaped, to fit in with the exigencies of one's life narrative. The possibility that experience might be relished as such, even celebrated for its very challenge to the reflexive consciousness, therefore becomes problematical; there is a sense in which what is excluded by and in consciousness is the very fact of experience itself in its fullness, as plenitude. This always exceeds the ability of consciousness to register it as such, and hence it can only be drawn on allusively, elusively, in the imagination and the arts, or lived out, vicariously, through the forms of popular culture.

The tensions here are explored most insightfully, perhaps, in the reflections of Walter Benjamin, focusing as they do on the transformations of experience in the late modern world of media, mass culture and photographic reproduction, in which images and simulacra become increasingly central to the context and content of experience itself. In effect, Benjamin draws a distinction between 'depth' and 'surface' in the world of experience, and in order to do this he invokes Proust's distinction between 'voluntary' and 'involuntary' memory. For Proust, 'only what has not been experienced explicitly and consciously, what has not happened to the subject as an experience, can become a component of the *mémoire involontaire*',[22] and it is the latter that Crowther, following Benjamin, calls 'the depth factor in human experience', possessing, as it does, 'sensory richness and affective plenitude'.[23] For Freud, too, the psychic energy of conscious events leaves no trace, and the more people are exposed to shocks, the less material is laid down in the involuntary memory, and the more impoverished becomes the reserve of emotional and sensuous experience. Voluntary and involuntary memory can no longer become fused, mutually self-reinforcing, as they can in communities with a live sense of collective ritual and tradition.[24]

Hence there is a cleavage in experience itself, as though experience comes to incorporate a sense of its own loss. The depth experience becomes the presence of the absence of depth, parallel to the absence of God. It can only return through involuntary memory, which by definition is not under our control. Thus does the aspiration to control bring about its own defeat in creating the experience that is only possible when uncontrolled, unsupervised, when the reflexive consciousness withdraws, daydreams or sleeps. In this sense, modernity produces and reproduces its own unconsciousness, along with the inability to gain access to it, save through routes both indirect and unpredictable.

What becomes problematical, then, is auratic experience: experience as experience of aura, of fullness; of the relationship, in its immediacy, of the experiencing subject and the object of experience, as present in its irreducible, irreplaceable distinctiveness, located in its own place and time, with its own history. Aura, claims Benjamin, is 'the unique phenomenon of a distance, however close it may be';[25] one could say that it corresponds to a sense of something as other but recognizable, unique but of cultural significance. And there is a relation between aura and memory; in particular, 'aura is at home in the *mémoire involontaire*', and images that arise from it have a powerful aura.[26] Experience as auratic cannot be assimilated by voluntary memory; it rests on an element of recognition that is intuitive, based on an implicit, non-reflexive depth memory that defies ready recall. In short, the object of auratic experience becomes both sacred and difficult to access, and 'aura', like 'nature', becomes a possible concept only when the reality it purports to describe is threatened or lost. These are terms that are pregnant with their potential as allegories of nostalgia.

The claim, then, is that defence against shock inhibits the capacity to experience aura. Benjamin refers to 'the disintegration of the aura in the experience of shock', suggesting that 'the eye of the city dweller is over-burdened with protective functions' and that 'There is no daydreaming surrender to faraway things in the protective eye.'[27] From this angle, shock is the experience of novelty that cannot be grasped as auratic because it requires conscious defence mechanisms, an assertion of control, and hence is recorded in the 'voluntary' memory. Indeed, and conversely, there is a powerful sense in which modernity extends the power and scope of our voluntary recall, through technological innovation, notably the reproduction of image material, even as it renders auratic experience problematical. Through photos, fragments of the past become immediately and permanently retrievable. Making remoteness accessible by tourism is analogous to making art available through posters: both destroy uniqueness and distance in the interest of reproduction and convenience. So 'that which withers in the age of mechanical reproduction is the aura of the work of art', argues Benjamin, since 'the technique of reproduction . . . substitutes a plurality of copies for a unique existence'.[28] The overall effect, then, is that these techniques of mechanical reproduction facilitate the containment of shocks through extending the scope of appropriative selection and voluntary recall.

There is, however, considerable ambivalence in our attitudes to risk and shock. Benjamin observes that reading the newspaper does not enable the reader to assimilate information as 'part of his own experience'; rather, it serves 'to isolate what happens from the realm in which it could affect the experience of the reader'.[29] It is a shock defence, via a kind of vaccination principle. But elsewhere, Benjamin is aware that shock can come to hold an attraction for the reader or observer: from shock defence, through vicarious enjoyment of the *threat* of shock, to enjoyment of *actually experienced* shock, is a slide that can easily be made. Film, with its dramatic changes of place and pace, its thrills and surprises, involves a kind of rehearsal of the shock experience, a cultivated receptivity to shocks,[30] and this would seem to be true of 'media events' generally. Crowther therefore suggests that 'the decay of aura is compensated for by the development of a sensibility orientated towards shocks'.[31]

Defence against shock can, after all, induce a sense of boredom, as can the routine, repetitive aspects of life generally. When culture is mediated into consumable differences, choice can easily become afflicted by *ennui*. The erosion of integrated narratives of experience and selfhood in the consumer flow can thus produce the Baudelairean experience of 'spleen', of 'the world's deadly mimicry of our own lassitude and despair', as Clark puts it.[32] By contrast, instancing the attractions of the Ferris wheel and the roller-coaster, which present the 'synergetic' delights of total bodily involvement in the shock experience, de Cauthen argues that '"modern amusement" is often the creation of pleasure from shock itself';[33] hence the search for 'kicks', which can be physical as well as psychological and visual. But all this occurs in a context where 'experience' itself has been transformed, where the 'shocks' exist on the knife-edge between control and uncontrol, real and hyperreal, and where the 'letting go' is, generally, a *simulation* of risk rather than the genuinely unexpected exposure to the 'real thing'. Of course, this in turn can be 'real enough'; when Benjamin writes that 'man's need to expose himself to shock effects is his adjustment to the dangers threatening him',[34] one can observe that the 'adjustment' can be as dangerous as the dangers – and as addictive.

The fate of taboo and transgression in our time is also relevant here. In a culture of consumable differences, the differences come to seem minor, unimportant; all differences become the same, as it were. If everything is interchangeable, why this rather than that? With consumerism, taboos may be reduced to raw material for new consumer choices, mere fashion items: closet S/M mutates into bondage chic. The element of *risk*, inherent in the attraction of breaking a taboo, is thereby lost. In a hyperreal world, there is no 'outside' to which the other can be expelled as the illicit, and from whence it returns, in obscure ways, as a powerfully dynamic focus and language of our craving: no taboo, no desire? Indeed, in such a world 'Desire' would become 'desires', as flexible, transient and superficial as the objects that satisfy them, and both modern sexuality and consumerism would meet an uncertain fate.[35] We could well encounter a consumer panic zone, as bored shoppers and voyeurs have to be inveigled into consuming by ever more desperate expedients. But there could be other influences here, too.

After all, a culture of visibility and the 'panoptic gaze' subtly contributes to the production of the transgressions that it ostensibly seeks to minimize and control. Intensified panopticism, whether through street video cameras or neighbourhood watch, produces an increased awareness of crime, a greater sense of its ubiquity, and a greater awareness of risk, and this becomes a self-reinforcing cycle. In a general sense, after all, transgression exists through the mechanisms that distinguish and identify it, and modern panopticism becomes a machine for the manufacture of the abnormal and the deviant. When everything can be captured on video, when sophisticated surveillance possibilities increasingly destroy the alleged privacy of the 'private sphere', as a 'free zone' in which to retreat, the resulting apparent overabundance of transgressive acts – even if most may be minor – reminds us not only of the threat, but also of the temptations of transgression, of how it can be attracted to visibility: part of the appeal of deviance is that it be known as such. At the same time, to be known is to be tamed, controlled, risks decline into the ordinary, the living death of the unfashionable; so further transgression must be tried, to avoid this trap of the commonplace. Between transgression and conformity, then, lies 'subculture', the zone of fluid, transient groups on the margin, exploring the gap between the permitted and the proscribed, playing with the 'boundary between surveillance and the evasion of surveillance', as Hebdige puts it.[36]

And always there is an excess: the panoptic machine produces too much transgression and, even in the form of what clearly counts as crime, the police always have to choose. Transgression is tolerated here even as it is persecuted there; and in this arena of the random, fashion and the media again become crucial. Media panics are central to definitions of transgression, creating the victims necessary for the panic to run its course, ostensibly reinforcing the boundaries of the normal, but actually revealing the caprice, the irrationality, at its heart, and reinforcing the risk consciousness of everyday life. The media event, then, can easily become the media moral panic, the frantic construction of a victim or victims: those who may not seek a transgressive identity can nevertheless find it foisted on to them.[37] Fears of disorder and breakdown can thereby be magnified.

Ultimately, these dimensions even enter the structure of selfhood itself: we anticipate or fear risk, we also take risk, we break rules, we risk detection; the self comes to be partially defined through its violations. In a culture of individualism, transgression, however vicarious, becomes part of one's self-definition, a badge of membership, signifying one's reflexive awareness, one's existence as a distinctive, separate individual. If consumerism threatens to 'tame' transgression, panopticism and the pressure towards self-realization in some ways encourage it.

We have seen that the media are crucial in the process whereby meaning is appropriated, defined and concentrated. In a consumer culture, a culture of circulation, without purpose or end, it is as though meaning tends to pile up at particular points, overflowing at awkward junctions on the circuit: points of risk, points of uncertainty, points of challenge. This excess of meaning, which can induce a sense of meaninglessness, can also, therefore, provide a potent resource for the opposite. Dramatization becomes the exuberance of the ordinary, the mode of its self-presentation, the guarantee that experience of the mundane need not be mundane experience. Through dramatization, experience draws attention to itself, negates its own inconsequentiality through display. And this dramatization of experience becomes a simulation of risk, a vicarious indulgence that can also be protective, and that reminds us of the significance of melodrama; for melodrama is particularly attuned to risk, danger and excess, condensing the flood of meaning into the absolutes of good and evil. Melodrama exteriorizes, even creates, conflict, shapes and displays emotion in powerful ways, explores the active and the passive in experience, and articulates the unspeakable.[38] In short, it is charged with meaning, yet it is a meaning that always bears the hallmarks of its own artifice; a meaning that resists being pinned down too specifically, yet has to be. In the case of transgression, theatricality can be drawn on to act out the illicit, and images or stereotypes of the transgressive can be powerfully emphasized by media witch hunts.

In short, modernity confronts us with a situation in which the expectations and the experience of change, coupled with the emphasis on project as control, intensify a sense of risk, of lack of control. The coping mechanism, regulating or preventing shock, can in turn contribute to the 'stress' that is then subjected to the 'stress discourse' of the therapy industries; and, conversely, both shock itself and shock prevention mechanisms can become addictive, paradoxical sources of pleasure. Stress and shock can be sought after, producing 'highs', the thrills and spills to counter *ennui*; and hence the possibility of a fixation on media events and life as a media event, life as a spectacular distraction from life itself, or its melodramatic intensification. This is not so much escapism as an experience of the *vicarious*, life as hyperreal. And we see a suggestion that this occurs in the context of a shift towards a post-auratic – postmodern? – culture, in which mechanical reproduction, transience, imminence, consumption, personality, image and surface become ever more central, while the auratic qualities of uniqueness, authenticity, originality, transcendence, character, narrative and depth retain a fascination as resources for nostalgia even while their meaning becomes ever more contestable.

Culture, Consumption and Identity

All this is symptomatic of a culture in which the auratic experience is in crisis. In becoming marketable, everything becomes reproducible. The media, too, reinforce this effect. Sontag writes that where the 'traditional fine arts' rely on 'the distinction between authentic and fake, between original and copy, between good taste and bad taste', the media 'blur, if they do not abolish outright, these distinctions'.[39] It becomes increasingly clear that auratic concepts like 'originality' and 'authenticity' are debatable and contentious. We are told that the number of Rembrandts in museums and general circulation has declined steeply in recent years – not because they have disintegrated or been stolen, but because art historians have decided they are not 'Rembrandts' at all. If a 'Rembrandt' is mainly painted by a pupil, but signed by the master, is it 'really' a Rembrandt? We know that Handel and other musicians lifted their tunes from each other and from popular music of the time, that there is frequently no agreed 'final version' of works like *Messiah*, that artists like Picasso are frequently unable to recognize their own works or able to tell them from fakes. Notions like 'originality' seem increasingly to be meaningless residues of the Romantic myth of the artist, and a crucial support of aura is thus knocked away. If Handel recycled his own tunes, why shouldn't we? What can be wrong, in principle, with CDs of 'Mozart's greatest hits'? As for 'authenticity', tourists who seek it generally end up with folk dances recreated for the tourist market or 'handmade' local products that are mass-produced. Both originality and authenticity are auratic qualities that reveal their own artifice all the more clearly in the era of hyperreality and mass reproduction.

Simultaneously, however, managing to sustain an apparently *successful* claim to aura is a source both of status and of wealth. The 'real' Rembrandts increase in value, 'untouched' nature becomes an object of veneration and preservation, the Mona Lisa becomes all the more priceless as the posters and postcards of it multiply. Aura becomes like an ancestral power, a spirit presence that sustains the world of simulation precisely by asserting its difference, its essential incompatibility. And aura has a paradoxical relationship with the market: marketability destroys aura, yet aura is eminently marketable. The market imposes the uniformity of commodity status, hence undermining aura; at the same time, the *really* valuable item is valuable because of its aura and, indeed, at the extreme, aura takes the commodity beyond the market altogether: it becomes 'priceless'.[40] The ultimate 'consumer object' is the one that can be neither exchanged nor consumed.

Something of these tensions can be seen in the relationship between the 'live' and the recorded in popular music. Even in this area, there is still a nostalgia for the 'real' experience, for 'being there', with the live performance being seen as the really authentic form. If you went to Bob Dylan concerts in the 1970s, for example, you would see a tiny figure on a distant stage and, occasionally, when the wind was in the right direction, you could even hear snatches of music; you got aura and not much else, as it were, but at least you were *there*. Then, with the Bruce Springsteen or Madonna concerts of the mid- to late 1980s, many of the technical problems were solved, with all-round stereo sound-systems and large video screens, so that the magnified superstar would be within easy reach wherever you might be. Nevertheless, the distance remained, or even, paradoxically, seemed to increase; the effect of the technology was at one level to abolish, but at another level, to re-emphasize, the distance between star and fan. Connor concludes from this that there is a strong sense in which originals actually become dependent on copies:

> The intense 'reality' of the performance is not something that lies behind the particulars of the setting, the technology and the audience; its reality consists in all of that apparatus of representation. . . . The live is always in a sense the quotation of itself – never the live, always the 'live'.[41]

So the alleged 'reality' of a live performance is itself a product of the processes of reproduction and representation, not a guarantee or foundation of their 'truth'.

More generally, it is as though voluntary recall increasingly presents us with the world as an image bank or sound archive, with images invested with all the power of the real. A world of images and surfaces is a world of visual consumption, a world in which the uneasy tension in the *flâneur*, between active appropriation and passive spectatorship, is reflected in his latter-day descendant, the tourist. The cosmopolitan experience, central to modernity, is an experience of images and of movement, a vicarious experience of otherness; thus Lash and Urry point to the emergence of an 'aesthetic cosmopolitanism', involving 'the proliferation of images and symbols operating at the level of feeling and consolidated around judgements of taste and distinction about different natures and different societies',[42] and central to the modern tourist experience. Applied to history itself, this tourist gaze in the era of consumerism produces and reproduces history as heritage, simultaneously a consumer spectacle and an exercise in cultural fabrication.[43]

This area, where consumerism meets with popular culture, raises important issues of cultural politics, which in turn have implications for cultural and personal identity. At a time when pessimists proclaim a 'collapse of standards', and optimists a 'democratization of culture', it is clear that this whole question of standards, of criteria of quality, of mechanisms of inclusion and exclusion, remains hotly debated. Any indie or rock bands that define themselves as close to 'street' culture differentiate themselves from what they see as commercially-oriented 'pop music', pumped into supposedly passive consumers, much as the carriers of 'high art' have tended to contrast themselves with 'the masses'. And if rival cultural forms and groupings multiply and fragment endlessly, they do so while defining their own values and criteria just as confidently and dogmatically. But the *effect* of all this is to reemphasize the sense of a 'collapse of values', for if values and possibilities multiply, without any clear, agreed criteria for evaluating them, then indeed the whole notion of a rational basis for choice and judgement enters into crisis, and relativism or pluralism become the order of the day. This would link up with the alleged 'collapse of grand narratives',[44] for these powerful narratives of political emancipation or self-development indeed serve to provide moral and aesthetic guidelines which, in principle, aim at universalizability, and a pluralization of these systems may have many of the same consequences as a 'collapse'.

In short, we live in a world of consumer choice in which it is no longer clear how the consumer is supposed to choose; indeed, since it is assumed that consumer choice is non-rational anyway, the spread of consumerism throughout the culture inevitably carries with it a crisis of rationality in decision-making, resulting in a tendency towards making choices by 'mere' subjective preference or arbitrary whim.[45] Along with this, there is a sense in which choice is politicized; when it becomes difficult to appeal to 'reason' as anything more than a rationalization of the fact of choice itself, it is natural to fall back on the enforcement of the choice, through psychological mechanisms (in personal relations), for example, or media manipulation (in politics). The fact of choice is trivialized, while the making of a choice is not necessarily any easier, since so much can be at stake: it doesn't really matter what I wear, or buy, yet it is also true that it does, as it frames the self-presentation whereby I exist in the world, the surface on which I write my script, the image that becomes the public self. Action, too, becomes problematical in a world of choice, since action excludes – it is this *or* that – and the existence of multiple possibilities means they can't all be realized together. And, as has been seen in the case of religion,[46] the resulting *lack* of tolerance at the level of real life choices embedded in *action* helps to prepare the return of *non*-modern 'grand narratives', promising an end to these strains and confusions of choice. A pick-'n' mix culture is not necessarily easy to live in, when choices are simultaneously unimportant and bursting with significance, and the absence of clear social or rational criteria leaves the self dangerously exposed. As we know, a self that consumes is also one that destroys, devours, and is at risk of meeting the same fate.

Indeed, when we think of leisure, or of 'popular culture' more generally, there *is* a sense in which there is a void at its centre. Exploring the outlook and behaviour of visitors to Liverpool's redeveloped Albert Dock, Mellor observes that what is most significant is what these visitors are *not* doing, and that 'the most important thing that visitors to the Dock are not doing, is anything in particular'. That is, they wander around in relatively aimless fashion. 'What most of these people are doing is "nothing". It is rather like the nothing that they used to do when they were kids.' And, he adds, 'doing nothing is an important activity when there's nothing very much to do'. But of course adults are generally loath to accept that this is what they are doing; most visitors prefaced their accounts with the half-apologetic 'just'. ('Just wanted to have a look round.') After all, work and responsibility are crucial to the adult self-image; especially, perhaps, to those busy middle-class individuals most afflicted by the importance of project, 'purposeful people intent on improving the shining hour'.[47] But this self-image serves as a mask, a form of ideological complacency; and the significance of popular culture is surely that it unmasks these pretensions. In its own pointlessness, its sense of killing time that is inseparable from spending or making time, it questions the world of project, of purposeful activity, especially work. How much of this is really as rational as it purports to be – or is it filling up time so that the threat of emptiness can be kept at bay? After all, much 'work' appears to be pointless routine or manic hyperactivity, 'keeping busy'. Popular culture can never be the transcendence of the world of project, but surely embodies its nemesis, the void at its heart.

This strange, symbiotic relation of mutual incomprehension between the 'official' world of project and the world of 'popular culture' can indeed be observed more generally.[48] A feature of the behaviour just referred to can give a clue: the way 'doing nothing' not only offends against the sense that time is precious, so we should do 'something' with it, but against the sense that time is linear, so that 'doing nothing' becomes a form of repetition, and all the more 'wasteful' for that. And repetition is significant, for both the form and fact of repetition tell us that repetition is always the return of the excluded other; and this in turn reminds us of links with tradition and ritual, both of which embody a sense of time as repetition.

A culture that privileges linear temporality, constant change, and 'progress' will have problems with repetition, which can easily be presented as irrational, maladaptive and backward-looking, hence *addictive*, in the rather loaded terms offered by Giddens: 'An addiction is an inability to colonise the future and as such transgresses one of the prime concerns with which individuals now reflexively have to cope', and it therefore 'casts a shadow over the competence of the self'.[49] To take one example, romance reading can certainly be seen to exhibit some features of addiction: the 'high' itself, the sense of 'time out' from everyday life, of being in 'another world', and the abdication of self. As for the shame that can accompany dependence on the 'habit', this could reflect the wider cultural censure previously discussed.[50]

Radway, though, suggests an alternative way of looking at it, namely that the repetitiveness of the stories, and the reading, mean that romances can function as myth. The act of reading a romance, like the act of recounting a myth, permits the self both to experience 'novelty' and to repeat patterns, in a context coded as fictional and yet also, subtly, 'real'; it therefore manifests elements of ritual, albeit both disavowed and distorted in its modern cultural context.[51] And Ros Ballaster suggests that 'Cyclical temporalities are disparaged and devalued in masculinist cultures', and 'only in popular culture are feminised patterns of temporality and narrative indulged'.[52]

We must, however, return to the sense of 'compulsiveness', which is surely significant, whether or not it takes the more specific form of 'addiction'; for what this reveals is that repetition replaces tradition. In Freud's patients, we can see how the decaying fragments of collective folk rituals and traditions had become the raw material of compulsive repetition in the individual,[53] and we can remember that, for Freud, there was a powerful sense in which normality is only a form of manageable neurosis. Indeed, Giddens goes further, to argue that Weber's discussion of the Protestant work ethic is, in effect, an analysis of 'the obsessional nature of modernity'. Work becomes compulsive, neurotic, work for work's sake, a driven asceticism, an endless treadmill; in effect, a 'tradition without traditionalism'.[54] The world of rational, reflexive modernity again confronts its own neuroses in its denunciation of the irrationalities of popular culture, and its disparagement of other activities – like 'housework' – that actually resemble 'work' in precisely the 'irrationalities' so disparaged, namely, the routine, the fetishism, the excess of point and purpose that makes the whole project self-defeating.[55]

Our sense of identity cannot be unaffected by all this. Identity emerges as a theatrical construct, with elements of the desperate about it: a panic construct, a search for solidity, unity and continuity in a world with no fixed moorings. The modern idea of the productive, autonomous self, moving purposefully towards its goals in life, continues to be affirmed, all the more frantically, while increasingly it has to coexist with a more fluid, decentred model,[56] with more emphasis on image, mood and feeling, more sensitivity to the transient. 'Aura' becomes 'personality': the self is recycled out of the fragments, reconstructed as we go along, dependent on situations; continuity and integrity are challenged by responsiveness and adaptability; and the linearity of narrative has to coexist with the repetitive and the cyclical.

In a media age, names, labels and images are central to identity, yet are always precarious and contested: we encounter what Weeks calls 'identity politics'.[57] Clichés of cultural identity have become advertising slogans, and images of national, cultural or gender identity are part of the commercial logic of popular culture, so that identity itself becomes an increasingly arbitrary, pick-'n' mix construct, and one that is inevitably affected by fashion. Maffesoli refers to 'neo-tribalism': these new 'tribes' are no longer tightly structured, but are constituted through individual acts of self-identification, and membership is flexible, fluid, not involving long-term obligations. It is all a matter of aesthetic role-play in a theatre without point, in which the 'audience' is other role-players. Self-definition as fixity or coherent narrative gives way to role-play in cosmopolitan contexts and communities of contingency. Since fashion and display are important, such 'tribes' cannot have long lives; the visible is also the impermanent.[58] Hence the 1980s explosion of 'street culture', with groups defined by differences in music, clothes and lifestyle, transient but also manifesting intense commitment at any given moment. So the increased uncertainty over the boundaries of identity does *not* imply that the distinctions themselves disappear: groups and individuals remain concerned, even obsessed, with the signs and marks of identity and status, but these are difficult to cement, always liable to subversion by the dynamics of boredom and novelty so central to consumerism and fashion.

Hence the paradox that is central to any 'politics of identity': in the end, the artifice of such identity always threatens to result in yet further fragmentation, and can only precariously be held at bay by an equally artificial intensity of commitment. The very assertion of such identity thus contributes to undermining it. Attacking the fixity of a stereotypical, oppressive and essentialist 'homosexual identity' in the 1970s, the gay liberation movement was necessarily unable to offer any clear alternative, and fragmented even as it became prominent, with numerous gay identities consolidating into ever-shifting and precarious groupings, then dissolving again; and an acceptance of the artifice at the heart of identity was central to the mutation of 'gay' into 'queer' in the 1990s.[59]

As for 'intensity of commitment', this comes out particularly clearly in the more overtly political aspects of this, for example the 'new tribes' that developed out of the disintegration of the communist monolith in Eastern Europe. Here the phrase 'imagined communities' has been much used of late,[60] referring to the sense in which these tribes, ostensibly recovering a submerged identity, are actually engaged in an enterprise that is as much creation as recovery or revival. These new tribes do not have a secure sense of tradition to fall back on; rather, they have to create an imaginary tradition, out of the debris of history, in the very act of asserting their communal identity; and they have to perform this contortion while asserting, and believing, that they are doing the precise opposite. Such identities are therefore brittle, fragile and shifting, while held to all the more obsessively and tenaciously. But this only really reveals the instability at the heart of modern identity, the increasingly persistent attempts to define identity out of, and against, the givens of nature or history, and finding that these attempts are constantly threatened by the artifice at the heart of the project; identity is revealed as a channelling of the excess of meaning into a relatively structured form, the melodrama of an existence perpetually menaced by incoherence.

Taken together with the implications of consumerism, this can also provide a perspective on other topics of current debate. Names, labels, images, are also entities, commodities, resources to squabble over, items that can in some sense be 'owned', a dimension of arguments over property. For example, if people of a certain skin colour and cultural background want to call themselves 'blacks', have they the right to do this, have they the power to exert control over this label and how it is used, and are they entitled to insist on respect for how they want it to be used? What emerges is that debates over 'political correctness'[61] are precisely debates over identity, how it can be asserted, who controls the names and images that are central to identity claims, and what the real-life consequences are. Again, if words and images are not just representations of reality, but are part of it, if we are increasingly uncertain about the boundaries between representation and reality in a 'hyperreal' world, then such words and images can exercise real power, have real causal significance in our lives – an issue that comes to the fore in controversies over pornography and television violence.

Popular, Public, Mass: Debating Culture

Is there any longer a 'public sphere', in the era of the mass media and 'popular culture'? A tangled skein of issues is in play here. It is clear that trends that have been widely commented on – the prominence and influence of the populist/sensationalist mass media, the shift from a culture of narrative to a culture of the image, the commodification and globalization of culture in the age of mass consumerism – must have implications for established notions of public debate and the possibilities of emancipatory politics. Generally, the implications of these shifts have been seen as negative, as contributing to the alleged demise of the Enlightenment project and the atrophy of any meaningful political culture: the public sphere of rational, open and democratic discussion declines, and politics becomes merely the administration of the spectacle. Running across these debates, but inseparably connected, are the controversies over 'popular culture' itself: is it really just a gloss for 'mass culture', the passive, lumpen result of the levelling, homogenizing effects of the media and the consumption industries, or does it represent a vibrant, independent source of renewal and opposition in the very heart of late modernity itself? One can hardly hope to resolve these issues; but – building on earlier chapters – it is worth trying to undermine some of the more simplistic alternatives. In order to do this, it is necessary to re-examine the notion of the 'public sphere' itself, and its relation to 'culture' in its wider aspect, particularly 'popular' culture.[62]

Part of the problem here is that any distinction between the public sphere and the Enlightenment project is frequently elided in the literature: the former is presented as simply the social dimension of the latter. But if we return to what is conventionally taken as the institutional origin of the public sphere – the coffee house, as it developed from the late seventeenth through to the mid-eighteenth century, initially in England and the German states – the picture becomes more cloudy. For a penny, in London, *any* man could drink and join in the conversation, and hence that has been taken to be the fundamental significance of the institution: the fact that the possibility of debate and discussion rested on a suspension of interest in a person's social status *outside* the coffee house. Reference to a person's origins became 'bad form', an offence against civility.[63] Civility is indeed crucial here: 'the public' is constituted as a zone of good manners, based on notions of refinement, decorum and politeness which encouraged the exercise of judgement, discrimination and rational debate.[64]

The public sphere comes into being as a work of fiction: it presupposes that issues of class and gender identity can be 'left outside', with one's coat, at the entrance. Habermas himself – a defender of the public sphere as carrier of the Enlightenment project – has to echo Marx in seeing the bourgeois public sphere, in this sense, as a 'fictitious identity' of the two roles of the 'private' individual:

property owner and 'human being pure and simple'.[65] Inside the coffee house, one could simply *be* the latter, in abstraction from the particularities and interests of the former. Similarly with gender, though here it is posed more explicitly: only men could enter the coffee house, but they supposedly entered not *as* men, but as citizens.

This tension is central to the way in which one can see the Enlightenment project as latent in the emergence of a public sphere. The latter can easily be hijacked by the universalizing pretensions of abstract reason, geared to the formal, the impersonal, and the urge to control, intolerant of the local and the contextual, operating through dichotomy and exclusion rather than through continuum and inclusion. When the universal is set up against the particular, the 'general' against the 'local', the abstract against the concrete, the resulting ideology can mask what may all too easily be highly specific interests, even as, through the link with 'progress', it can become a driving force for generating and imposing a standardization and homogenization of social life. The notion of 'citizenship' can be linked to those of 'welfare' and 'progress' to make possible the world-transforming ideologies of the Enlightenment project, so that what Habermas describes as 'The system-exploding consequences of a philosophy of history that implied its own political intent' come to the fore.[66] And of course the consequences of this are still very much with us, leaving, for example, a difficult legacy for contemporary feminism. Should women use the language of Enlightenment rationality in defending and extending their rights, at the risk of implicitly endorsing what may be masculinist notions of politics and the public sphere? Or should they use the postmodern language of 'difference', arguing that universalizing norms have been insensitive to women's aspirations and rights to their own identities, even though it is clear that, historically, 'difference' can easily slide into 'inequality' and 'inferiority', and that anyway such a strategy could fall victim to the dilemmas of 'identity politics' discussed above?[67]

In the light of this, we must return to the relation between Enlightenment and the public sphere in the earlier phase. 'Public' can be linked to notions of citizenship: the 'citizen' participates in public debate on issues of general concern, and is kept informed on such issues by 'publicity'. But 'issues of general concern', as a formulation, is deliberately vague: 'general' need not mean 'universal', nor need it necessarily be opposed to 'particular' or 'local'. There is, in principle, a continuum here, not a dichotomy. In her critique of the notion of the 'public sphere', Nancy Fraser points to the various meanings of 'public' that are relevant here – accessible to everyone; pertaining to the common good; non-domestic, non-private – and argues that public deliberation need not *only* be about the common good, it can also be about clarifying the needs and aspirations of particular groups and their relations with other groups, and the whole fluid process whereby issues can shift between the private and the public, the individual, the group-centred and the universal.[68] What constitutes 'the public' can itself be a topic of debate, and 'the public' itself evolves through such debate, becoming an emergent product of the discursive practices through which it is itself constructed. In this sense, the 'public sphere' emerges as intensely precarious: caught between the exclusions constitutive of its very existence, as a realm of civility, and the tempting imperialism and dynamism of the Enlightenment project, promising a resolution of the dichotomous tensions that run through it. And *if* the coffee house can be taken as exemplifying this, one could say of it that it was (relatively) enlightened but not (yet) Enlightenment. It could be seen as pointing towards two possible futures, not just one: that of the 'grand narratives' of Enlightenment, but also that of the 'humble narratives' of everyday life. Both, after all, can lay claims, in their contrasting ways, to a status as 'public'. And both have been fundamental to the modern experience.

To explore this further, one can point to other aspects of gender relations in the period of the coffee house. Clery has argued that men in coffee houses had to act *as if* women were present: 'gentle' manners were required, and a certain 'feminization' of public culture in the age of civility and the cult of 'sensibility' was evident more generally.[69] If the public sphere was a work of fiction, it was not the only such; this was the age of the emergence of the novel, after all, and women were very active in the developing culture of literacy, both as producers and consumers. And Habermas points out that the German '*Publikum*' was a 'world of readers', adding that the word 'publicity' emerged at about the same time, in both France and England.[70] So it is not just politics and the high arts, but the zone of 'everyday life', that increasingly emerges both as a topic for conversation and debate, and an implicit context within which such discussion could be situated. And we can say that if the *later* development of the public sphere saw a narrowing to a masculine-oriented form of politics, which in turn rendered these wider dimensions of public life relatively invisible, then that is not inherent in the notion of a 'public'.[71]

After all, to call the public sphere a work of fiction is not to say that it is necessarily, or primarily, a form of ideological mystification. Rather, it serves to remind us of the significance of civility, and of the continued presence of theatricality in the world of the modern project and the drive to rationalization. We can recall that civility involves donning the mask of otherness, a 'taking on' and 'acting out' of identity as a public construct: 'the public' exists through this drama of mutual interaction, involving an emancipation from the constraints (or privileges) of the private and the personal. And 'public debate', after all, is not a philosophical disputation, nor a kind of calculus, nor the imposition of a blueprint for the future; it is an arena in which reason and feeling both play a role, through the masking whereby selfhood exists as a public construct only in relation to others. But we must now consider the implications for all this of the rise of the mass media.

That the mass media have had a major impact can hardly be in doubt. By the last decades of the nineteenth century mass-circulation newspapers had arrived, the new mass market being made possible by the combination of advertising and sensationalist journalism; and, with national systems of education in place, illiteracy rates had tumbled.[72] At the very least, this clearly represents a widening of the constituency of public debate, together with a transformation of its form. And while the critics, then as now, seem frequently to be afflicted with an elitist nostalgia for a mythical state of lost political innocence, they could rightly point out that consumerism and rational debate indeed make uneasy bedfellows, and that the problems of choice and its rationale, discussed above, can hardly fail to affect politics itself. Sennett, for example, argues that the prevalence of the language of authenticity, which we can see as a logical outgrowth of the purifying, disciplinary dimension of project, entails an inability to play, to explore the beneficial artifice of civility.[73] For such critics, writes Brantlinger, 'a central paradox is that the highly public mass media erode the public sphere by subjectivizing or privatizing it', hence producing the passive subjects of media manipulation, along with forms of entertainment, notably television, that 'stimulate narcissism rather than true self-reflection and public involvement'.[74] The media may increase our knowledge of each other, but decrease our real contact with each other, and involvement in politics; debate and participation decline into spectacle and simulation.[75] In this context, Baudrillard's suggestion that we encounter not so much manipulation as sullen resistance, that 'the masses' are 'neither misled nor mystified', and that 'this indifference of the masses is their true, their only practice . . . a refusal to participate in the recommended ideals, however enlightened',[76] has much to commend it; what we increasingly witness, perhaps, is a withdrawal from a hyperreal politics that has become all show, and, as such, less entertaining than other shows in town. But clearly we are now embroiled in the debates over 'mass' and 'popular' culture.

What indeed is 'popular' culture? The term has a powerful resonance: 'popular' meaning 'of the people', hence democratic, open access, participatory, not the specialized preserve of some social or artistic elite; and 'popular' meaning a source of pleasure, of approval. This conjunction gives a clue to its controversial status, for the 'pleasure' of the popular is not dependent on elite definitions of artistic quality or political desirability; it is an emergent property of popular involvement in, and appropriation of, whatever that involvement and appropriation themselves constitute as 'culture'. As is argued elsewhere, the Enlightenment and the civilizing process had destroyed much of the earlier 'popular culture'; later, these influences joined the dominant strains of the emerging modernist elite in the arts to sentimentalize what remained of it, as 'folk culture',[77] while denouncing its contemporary successors, the new mass cultural products like spectator sport and music hall, as 'mass culture'.

This tension between the terms 'popular' and 'mass' corresponds to real problems in the object of analysis. After all, who are 'the people'? This could refer to an idealization, an aspiration, a project, corresponding to the Enlightenment drive to overcome the split between the abstract and the concrete, the ideal and the real. In this sense, 'the people' are a would-be product of social and political intervention. Ironically, this is not so different from 'the people' as a product of the mass media and the culture industries, which is also a bizarre fusion of abstraction and object of policy, even though the latter is now commercial rather than political policy. So when advocates of the former denounce the latter, they denounce something that is *also* a result of the modern project, also an abstraction, the unity of people-as-mass. Both approaches imply a degree of homogeneity, levelling and uniformity, in the very positing of the object of analysis. Both tend to imply a conception of 'culture' as a product of administration and imposition; Shields, for example, reminds us that 'leisure' derives from 'lex' (law), so that leisure is what is *licensed*, as 'legitimate pleasure'.[78]

Conversely, to see 'the people' as producers *and* as products of 'popular culture' is to change the terms of debate; 'the people' then becomes the set of differences between relatively fluid groups, constituting and reconstituting themselves in the shifting balances and contrasts that make up the relatively precarious sense of identity that is possible among such groups. And this gives a sense that 'the popular' is more a matter of interacting cultures, or culture as transculture, than of a unified, shared culture. One might say that 'mass' and 'popular' correspond to different aspects of culture – and the tension between them is real enough. In short, if 'mass culture' refers to the homogenizing aspect of culture, with its twin sources in the Enlightenment culture of project and the media culture of the constructed subject of media representations, then 'popular culture' refers to the mutations whereby individuals and groups appropriate, incorporate and transform these – and other – resources into the lived experience that constitutes the culture of our everyday lives. 'Popular' culture is culture as a celebration – or indulgence – of its own plenitude, constituting itself reflexively through its own artifice: the revenge of experience on project in an age of mass media and simulation.

If we view culture as popular culture, then, we get a different perspective on the criticisms mentioned above. The other side of the narcissism coin, for example, is that 'personality' comes into focus as a theatrical construct whereby identities can be rehearsed or developed in a world in which images have become a key part of the language in which relations with others are transacted; culture is given dramatic, public shape through personification.[79] Identity becomes a matter of active appropriation and participation, not passive indoctrination; mass-media products, such as television soaps, can provide material for reflection and discussion by their audiences, who use them as a critical resource for negotiating the public and private traumas and temptations of everyday life.[80] Willis has shown how young people actively make sense of, and transform, received popular forms, and construct a sense of self through the culture of consumerism. He argues that they 'always transform the meaning of bought goods, appropriating or recontextualizing mass-market styles', altering the categories and matches – including the gender categories – promoted by shops.[81]

Overall, both the form and the content of popular culture can pose problems for the cultures of narrative, whether the 'grand' narratives of the Enlightenment tradition, or the 'humble' narratives of everyday life. Raymond Williams has pointed out that those versed in literacy and the novel can have particular difficulties with the televisual aesthetic of mobility, juxtaposition, superimposition and fragmentation,[82] an aesthetic that is also a feature of musical forms like techno and house. Again, much popular culture explores the margins, the inversions, the not or barely respectable, the out-of-bounds. In short, much of this is carnivalesque, challenging the harshness of fate and history. The grotesque body returns, for example, in forms of popular humour, in wrestling, in advertising.[83] When

Goethe, discussing the Roman Carnival of 1788, claimed that one participated as 'both actor and spectator',[84] he was perhaps witnessing the fate of Carnival in our own time, the transformation of Carnival into carnivalesque, into spectacle, but nevertheless still a resource for popular appropriation; not so much the people's second life, but still a distinctive aspect of culture, embodying a distinctive 'form of critical reason', as Docker puts it. This 'carnivalesque reason' has its place, in that

> the flow of mass culture may possess its own forms of reason, not reason in a rationalist sense, of attention to discrete ordered sequences of information and interpretation, but of sudden juxtapositions, swift contrasts, heterogeneity ... carnivalesque remains an always dangerous supplement, challenging, destabilising, relativising, pluralising single notions of true culture, true reason, true broadcasting, true art.[85]

Hence carnivalesque parody, inversion and grotesque humour retain an ability to unsettle both the defenders of the rational, disciplined zone of project, and the modernist avant-garde, revealing the truth in Shiach's observation that 'Basically "the popular" has always been "the other".'[86] This may be even more true, though, of those elements lying on the far boundaries of popular culture itself, or beyond: the hippies, crusties, travellers, ravers, eco-warriors, and other denizens of the nightmare world of the respectable middle classes, embodying Carnival's message of the primacy and potency of the undifferentiated.[87]

Let us move towards a conclusion. Deconstructing notions of the 'public sphere', we can perhaps say that there are three modes of being modern. First, there is the modernity of project and the civilizing process, of purposeful, 'rational' transformation of self and world, legitimated through the ideas and ideals of 'high' modernism, in the emancipatory 'grand narratives' of progress, and embedded in the self-anointed 'public sphere' of enlightened Reason. Second, there is modernity as an experience, of change and continuity, of ever-shifting, ever-altering frameworks and episodes of everyday life, manifested in 'humble' narratives, the stories of fortune and misfortune, drama and triviality, the love and pain of ordinary relationships, among ordinary people, in a secular and individualist age. And third, there is a modernity of the excluded, the repressed, the barely tolerated, modernity as other, embodied above all in carnivalesque dissolution and inversion, and in other aspects of 'popular culture'. Perhaps these latter two could be referred to as 'low' modernism,[88] in the sense that they are both relatively disparaged – and less discussed – compared to the first; and they, too, possess 'public' dimensions. The civilization of the modern West has rested on the ever-uncertain, ever-tense, relations between these modes, relations that exist in an overall context defined by the attempted dominance of the first, its inherent imperialism. And as the representational dynamics of these modes alter – with the heightened emphasis on reflexivity, self-consciousness, questions of style and image, the rise of the mass media – so we see a shift towards the hyperreal that inevitably questions some of the boundaries and assumptions that have sustained modern reality and the world of project.

If these correspond to three modes of identity, such that we inevitably have to move between them, we can again see the centrality of theatricality to the modern construction of selfhood and social interaction in everyday situations, which thereby become 'scenarios'. And we again see the inevitability of a positive engagement with otherness, theatricality being *one* form this engagement can take, an engagement that is increasingly played out in the world of consumer spectacle and the management of risk, and an engagement that necessarily reminds us of popular culture's investment of energy in the non-rational, the world of images and bodies, where the body is inseparable from the immateriality of its image, and where the image, in its material embodiment, becomes all the more real.

This all coexists uneasily with the universalizing pretensions of the first mode, modernity as project. Modern culture, after all, involves an *ethos*, an ongoing, ever-evolving framework of everyday life in which our choices and experiences occur, and are made sense of in ways that are emergent – and frequently unexplicated – properties of those frameworks themselves. Our choices involve issues of decision, of judgement, which in turn involve reflection and, in principle, a willingness to discuss, to offer reasons, even though these reasons can never be decisive, and are not necessarily an appeal to the universal. If rationality is to be defined in terms of the latter, one could say that its absence does not prevent one's choices from being 'reasonable', indeed it may be a *condition* for this. Perhaps we have been so concerned with being 'rational' that the more humdrum, but perhaps more important, task of being 'reasonable' has not come sufficiently into focus. This is the domain of the humble narrative; and this, too, is modernity.

Furthermore, an ethos implies *limits*; there is a sense in which one cannot do, or know, everything. This is a truism, but its implications are nonetheless important. It throws into question the idea that a 'reflexive project of the self' should be the central focus of our lives. If Taylor is right to suggest that moral agency 'requires some kind of reflexive awareness of standards one is living by',[89] so too is Steiner, in pointing out that 'there is always, there always will be, a sense in which we do not know what it is we are experiencing and talk about when we experience and talk about that which is', and that 'no human discourse . . . can make final sense of sense itself'.[90] Even Habermas has to admit that self-awareness 'can never completely illuminate the implicit, the prepredicative, the not focally present background of the lifeworld'.[91] And this *embeddedness* is something that is never reflexively graspable *in toto*, because reflexivity is fundamentally an act of consciousness, whereas embeddedness refers us to the tissue of the unexamined life in its local context – and this also reminds us of the sense in which context is *always* local, and always threatened by the universalizing, globalizing dynamic of project.

In short, an important part of self-awareness is the understanding of its inevitable inconclusiveness, its limits in particular times and contexts,.the way wisdom is not about knowledge but about an attitude and an ethos that take over where knowledge ends, a recognition that much has to be shown, manifested, that cannot be said. In the end, one exists in relationships; one's relation to oneself is a relationship, just as much as one's relation to others; and we cannot simultaneously reflect *on* this and *be* it, or *in* it. One cannot grasp this with reflexive adequacy, on pain of schizophrenic fragmentation or infinite regress. And it is this 'embeddedness', what is 'left behind' in the reflexive grasp, that gives life such 'meaning' as it may possess for us – not the meaning of project, not a purpose or point, but meaning as the meaningless immersion in a totality that goes beyond, that is within yet also outside – sacred, sublime, other. These are dimensions that modernity itself draws our attention to, even theorizes, but simultaneously closes off, making access difficult or impossible: the reality that is exiled even as it is mastered. And if, influenced by Kant, we have tended to see this relation as ultimately a hymn to the splendour of Reason, a Reason that can after all theorize intellectually what cannot be pictured or grasped reflexively, we need to remember that this is ultimately just part of modernist self-delusion. The sublime is that which affirms our sense of simultaneous distance and belonging, the grandeur and pain of our membership of what Bateson calls the 'ecological tautology',[92] the world that is other before it is self.

'Postmodern'?

Is this word helpful for understanding any of the trends outlined here, and in the previous chapter? I have indeed used it a few times already, in this book, when it seemed appropriate. (*Why* it might have seemed appropriate is, of course, part of what now needs investigating.) The last chapter of a book on modernity is hardly the right place to attempt to develop any theory of the postmodern, but one can hardly avoid saying something about it, troublesome though it is.

Part of the trouble is the word itself. Taking 'postmodern' literally, as 'after-modern', gets us quickly into contradictions. If the postmodern is the next stage of history, and justifies itself as representing 'progress' beyond the modern, then this all seems to remain characteristically modern, since this evolutionary conception of history has been fundamental to modernity itself. Or, if we make the other move in the modernity game, assimilating the modern to the contemporary, then the opposite happens: since the modern is the here and now, the present as it moves beyond the past, which was therefore just as modern in its own time, its own present, it follows that the modern is always already postmodern. 'A work can become modern only if it is first postmodern', writes Lyotard;[93] and an intriguing history of ideas vignette is revealed by Smith, namely that the first use of the term he could locate, in a book entitled *Postmodernism and Other Essays*, published in America in 1926, preceded by a year the first comparable use of 'modernist', in the Graves and Riding *Survey of Modernist Poetry*.[94] The fact remains that this way of posing the issue seems to lead to a dead end – though not wholly so, perhaps, since this sense of a necessary relation between the modern and the postmodern may be important for grasping features of modernity itself and what is at stake in thinking about its limits and possibilities.

Let us therefore return to more substantive issues, via a consideration of the context in which the term came into use. Here, it is appropriate to begin, more specifically, with postmodern*ism*, a term that had become widespread by the 1970s, in both architecture and literature. Both of these were art forms where 'modernism' had previously acquired a relatively clear identity as a movement or trend so that, in principle, the idea of being 'post-' modernist did not seem intrinsically unreasonable. Indeed, architecture remains perhaps the only area where a relatively clear sense of the term can be distinguished. Thus, Jencks uses the term 'double-coding' to refer to the way postmodernist architecture uses the techniques and technology of modernism, but at the same time marks its difference by the addition of decorative and non-functional ornamentation, historical allusion and pastiche, playful or ironic commentary, and elements of the vernacular. The postmodern hence presupposes the modern, while conveying a very different aesthetic, a different 'feel'.[95]

Then, from the late 1970s, the term spread rapidly through the arts and into the social sciences and fashionable dinner-party discourse generally, a key moment, perhaps, being the English-language publication of Lyotard's *The Postmodern Condition* in 1984, with its proclamation of the end of the 'grand narratives' through which we had made sense of the world of modernity. Along the way, attempts have been made to distinguish 'postmodernism' and 'postmodernity', the former referring to the convulsions in the arts and culture generally, the latter to the socioeconomic changes allegedly accompanying this; but this distinction, in turn, generates problems, and has not been applied consistently. This may be because the postmodern itself seems to render any such distinction questionable, as in Connor's suggestion that the term may refer to 'those plural conditions in which the social and the cultural become indistinguishable',[96] or Lash's idea that, more generally, the postmodern involves 'de-differentiation',[97] a breakdown of the modern division of labour between separate spheres. I shall therefore use 'postmodern' as a general, inclusive term, reserving 'postmodernism' for occasions when it is necessary to refer more specifically to movements in the arts.[98]

Postmodernism itself certainly seems to have developed out of a reaction against the seriousness and elitism of the 'high' modernism of the 1920s and 1930s. In the age of consumerism, advertising and fashion, it attacked the exclusiveness, the cultural pretensions of modernism; and in an age of mass production and reproduction of images, it attacked the auratic pretensions of the artist, the claims to originality and uniqueness. Art and life, culture and commerce, were distinctions that came increasingly under fire; life becomes aestheticized as culture becomes commercialized, and 'popular culture' becomes the arena in which these traditionally separate areas, these distinctions – both within and between the arts, and between the arts and the wider world – have increasingly broken down. The case of ads is interesting: previously regarded as an embarrassment, expelled from the category 'art' in a ritual of purification, they have come to be seen as art forms themselves, reminding art of its inherent materiality and its inevitable compromises with a culture of commercialism.[99] In effect, postmodernism is necessarily *not* restricted to the arts; it must necessarily both entail, and grow out of, 'postmodern culture' more generally. In this context, it functions as an ideology of popular culture, culture in the age of mass consumerism; it proclaims the revenge of popular culture on the elitism of modernism, but it is a revenge that, ironically, generalizes the insights and implications of the latter, the questioning of established forms and canons of representation. And, of course, it is a revenge that can betray its own impulses: postmodernists, too, are capable of cliquishness and obscurantism.

One might say that if the modern way is to have relatively stable notions of group and personal identity, then the postmodern way is to multiply the margins and transitions: we all become betwixt and between, flows and circuits rather than fixed points in a moving world. If we become tourists of the postmodern spectacle, it is because we, like the rest of the spectacle, become precarious composites of the real and the fake, the same and the different, the stable and the fluid. Again, take the city: if the modern city has been taken to be well-defined, well-bounded, centred, clearly contrasting with nature, the postmodern city has become the conurbation, the urban sprawl, with no centre and no boundary. Newman suggests that, for the postmodern, 'nature is already culture and culture is a second nature: the city and the mass media are forests of signs'.[100] This formulation, simultaneously Baudelaire and Baudrillard, also reminds us of the context in which all this occurs, frequently characterized as the 'aestheticization' of life; and Baudrillard himself summarizes this forcefully:

> We live everywhere already in an 'aesthetic' hallucination of reality. . . . And so art is everywhere, since artifice is at the very heart of reality. And so art is dead, not only because its critical transcendence is gone, but because reality itself, entirely impregnated by an aesthetic which is inseparable from its own structure, has been confused with its own image.[101]

Various points seem implied here: that the boundary between 'life' and 'art' is subverted; that life indeed becomes artifice, a matter of style and surface, manufactured rather than 'natural'; that everyday life has become saturated with signs and images, as the essential language of consumerism itself; and that experience itself has become simulacral, post-auratic, dissolving distance and depth into presence and flow, emphasizing repetition and pattern over development and uniqueness.[102] In this sense, the postmodern looks primarily like a generalization and intensification of the experience of modernity itself, the subordination of project and history to the eternal contemporary, rather than anything radically new.

And is there any place for otherness in such a world? The possibility that the postmodern might in some sense entail a return or revenge of the other has been floated, and a plausible version of this is implicit in Bauman's suggestion that although modernity offered us a narrative about itself in terms of attributes like rationality and universality, actually we find that it has embodied the opposite qualities, as often as not; and that, in consequence, modernity 'lived in and through self-deception'.[103] The hollowness of the claim to universality is inseparable from the repression of particular others. Presumably, then, the postmodern would expose this bad faith, and live the truth of what had been thus submerged.

Nevertheless, strictly speaking, any simple reversal would leave us trapped in the same structure, merely inverting the terms. Perhaps what would really need to be at stake would be the dissolution of the boundaries whereby modernity constructed itself through contrast with 'the other', a contrast that is constitutive of its self-identity.

Controversies over gender serve to illustrate some of these points. If the project of modernity is in some sense coded masculine, and both rests on, and reproduces, a certain fixity in gender positions, then the postmodern could be seen either as the revenge of the feminine or, more plausibly, as a de-differentiation or questioning of the gender boundary itself, an exploration of its artifice. Suzanne Moore points to a more conservative version of these possibilities when she writes that much postmodern theory 'seems to be about a shifting in the position of masculinity, an uncertainty about manhood, a loss of faith in patriarchal authority'; and this may serve not so much to threaten the boundaries as to attempt to reconstitute them – the panic reaction. But she also points to the links with theories of the hyperreal:

> For who are already experts in simulation if not women? Femininity itself has come to be understood as existing only in and through representation, as constructed discursively rather than being a reflection of some inner state of being. Femininity is the perfect simulacrum – the exact copy of something that never really existed in the first place.[104]

Women have been postmodern already, so to speak; and once again, we encounter the suggestion that the postmodern is not necessarily so new. It is indeed an implication of this book that much that is conventionally regarded as 'postmodern' not only has its roots deep within the modern, but may even be an aspect of the latter, inseparable from it. It is as though the choice of this particular term implies a kind of forgetfulness, a historical amnesia, even if what the term points to can be important.

However, these references to the simulacral and the 'hyperreal' need to be pursued, since if there were to be a substantive theory of the postmodern, it would probably have this at its core. From the arguments of this chapter, one can say that there are two sources of the hyperreal. First, the drive of modernity towards mastery results increasingly in a world that is itself a product of modernity, along with systems of science and technology that both know and constitute this world; and the whole circle of 'reality', knowledge and transformation aspires to closure, to becoming self-constituting and self-validating. In trying to attain the impossible goal of absolute self-knowledge and self-identity, modernity shifts towards the hyperreal. And since modernity cannot know and control everything – it cannot, for example, capture itself reflexively without remainder – it follows that reality still prowls around, ghostlike, in its effects. This disjunction between project and its claims and results is experienced as *risk*, the recalcitrance of the world to our strategies for grasping and ordering it. Second, there is the expansion of image and communication technology whereby 'representation' becomes both increasingly autonomous and increasingly 'realistic' in its forms and consequences, again generating a powerful sense of a self-sufficient, 'hyperreal' world, coexisting uneasily with its shadow. These dimensions come together in reproduction, whether of nature or culture, and, in particular, in cloning: if the ultimate form of control is the control of reproduction, as suggested in the chapter on technology, then cloning is the apotheosis of reproduction that subverts the 'original' even as it represents/reproduces it. And this, in turn, can be experienced in the feelings of 'unreality' that are captured by Marcus in writing that 'When everything that was directly lived had moved away into a representation, there was no real life, yet no other life seemed real.'[105]

Internet culture encapsulates many of these problems. On the one hand, the Internet is heir to the universalizing imperative of the modern project, and the dream of technological utopia to which it can be yoked: hence the way it can be seen as a liberating force, promoting public access to the information superhighway, bringing closer the ideal of push-button democracy. But it also reminds us that when reality becomes virtual, when life becomes a vicarious exploration of the unbounded, and freedom becomes freedom from the constraints of real situations and real environments, then life becomes an escape from life itself, from the complexities and limitations of the local, the contextual, and the embodied – the finitude of the merely mortal.[106] Nor does any of this technology imply any absence of conflict and controversy: questions of power remain central, as individuals and groups dispute control over the means and outcomes of communication and simulation.

It is hardly surprising, then, if all this leaves our concepts broken-backed, offering at best a confusing guide to a world they participate in, rather than just refer to; a world in which we must nevertheless find our way around, between reality and simulacrum, modern and postmodern. But this reminds us that if there have been substantive theories of the postmodern, the term has also been used in an exploratory, questioning way.

In this perspective, the postmodern would not be something that could succeed the modern, replace it; nor would it be the negation of modernity, since it is inseparable from it. Rather, it emerges as the reflexive, critical mode of modernity itself; that move *in* the modernity game that raises questions *about* the game. It is a perspective *on* modernity that cannot ultimately escape being part *of* it. It could be said to be a supplement to modernity, or something other in it. As such, the term necessarily reflects the paradoxes of reflexivity. It is, after all, difficult to 'stand outside', to attempt to grasp the significance of changes in our own time. If we *really* understood, we probably wouldn't use the term; we would use something more specific. But at least we can say that if discussions of the postmodern turn out to have encouraged new modes of analysis, a new agenda for emergent problems, with new scenarios for what may often be old themes, then they will have been worthwhile, whatever the fate of the term itself.

Whether or not there could be an end to modernity, there can certainly be an end to 'modernity', in the terminal exhaustion of its own interminable discourse about itself. It is perfectly possible to conceive of not viewing and experiencing the world in terms of 'modernity' or its opposite(s). In this sense, the 'postmodern' could refer to the end of a 'discourse on modernity', an emerging focus on themes and issues that develop out of an experience of the world that has to be grasped in different ways. As modernity becomes global, so it mutates. There is Western modernity; but there are, after all, other ways of being modern, other cultures and civilizations of modernity, other ways of incorporating or destroying the non-modern; and all of these are now interrelated. Perhaps, indeed, these mutations have been there from the start; perhaps modernity has always existed primarily as a story that exaggerates its own unity and distinctiveness. So the postmodern move is the move that questions the story, and cannot be answered from within it. At the end of this book, we can no longer be entirely sure what it was about.

Notes

1   J. Gleick, *Chaos* (Cardinal, 1988), ch. 1.
2   A. Giddens, *Modernity and Self-Identity* (Polity, 1991), pp. 144, 165, 218; U. Beck, *The Risk Society* (Sage, 1992), pp. 80–1; B. McKibben, *The End of Nature* (Penguin, 1990).
3   W. Schivelbusch, *The Railway Journey* (Berg, 1986), p. 131.
4   R. Williams, *Notes on the Underground* (MIT Press, 1990), p. 189.
5   See A. Karlen, *Plague's Progress* (Indigo, 1995), passim.
6   R. Castel, 'From Dangerousness to Risk', in G. Burchell et al., *The Foucault Effect* (Harvester, 1991); Beck, *Risk Society*.
7   U. Beck, 'The Reinvention of Politics: Towards a Theory of Reflexive Modernization', in U. Beck et al., *Reflexive Modernization* (Polity, 1994), p. 9.
8   J. Baudrillard, cited in D. Kellner, *Jean Baudrillard* (Polity, 1989), p. 116.
9   J. Comaroff and P. Maguire, 'Ambiguity and the Search for Meaning: Childhood Leukaemia in the Modern Clinical Context', *Social Science and Medicine* (1981), 15B, p. 116.
10   Williams, *Notes on Underground*, p. 191.
11   M. Weber, 'Science as a Vocation', in *From Max Weber* (Routledge, 1970), p. 139.
12   Schivelbusch, *Railway Journey*, p. 135.
13   S. Sontag, *Illness as Metaphor* (Penguin, 1983).
14   Weber, 'Science', p. 139.
15   Beck, *Risk Society*, pp. 72, 73.
16   Weber, 'Science', p. 139.
17   Beck, *Risk Society*, p. 53.
18   A. MacIntyre, *After Virtue* (Duckworth, 1985), pp. 107, 75, 75.
19   Weber, 'Science', p. 139.
20   Schivelbusch, *Railway Journey*, p. 168.
21   W. Benjamin, 'Some Motifs in Baudelaire', in his *Charles Baudelaire: A Lyric Poet in the Era of High Capitalism* (Verso, 1983), section III, p. 117.
22   Ibid., II–IV, and p. 114.
23   P. Crowther, *Critical Aesthetics and Postmodernism* (Clarendon, 1993), p. 5. The whole chapter ('Experience and Mechanical Reproduction') is useful.
24   Benjamin, 'Some Motifs', II, p. 113.

25 W. Benjamin, 'The Work of Art in the Age of Mechanical Reproduction', in his *Illuminations* (Fontana, 1992), III, p. 216.

26 Benjamin, 'Some Motifs', XI, p. 147.

27 Ibid., XII, p. 154, and XI, pp. 151, 151.

28 Benjamin, 'Work of Art', II, p. 215.

29 Benjamin, 'Some Motifs', II, p. 112.

30 Benjamin, 'Work of Art', XIII–XV, pp. 229–32.

31 Crowther, *Critical Aesthetics*, p. 2, and see pp. 18–20.

32 T. J. Clark, *The Absolute Bourgeois: Artists and Politics in France 1848–1851* (Thames and Hudson, 1973), p. 176.

33 L. de Cauthen, 'The Panoramic Ecstasy: On World Exhibitions and the Disintegration of Experience', *Theory, Culture and Society* (1993), 10:4, p. 19.

34 Benjamin, 'Work of Art', footnote 19, p. 243.

35 Bataille argues that 'real' transgression becomes impossible, with the death of God: see *Eroticism* (Marion Boyars, 1987), chs XII, XIII. See also the discussion in ch. 7 of my *Transgressing the Modern* (Blackwell, 1999).

36 D. Hebdige, *Hiding in the Light* (Routledge, 1988), p. 35.

37 See A. McRobbie, *Postmodernism and Popular Culture* (Routledge, 1994), ch. 11, for a brief discussion.

38 P. Brooks, *The Melodramatic Imagination* (Yale University Press, 1976); J. Docker, *Postmodernism and Popular Culture* (Cambridge University Press, 1994), ch. 18; and see the discussion of theatricality, melodrama and personality in chapter 1.

39 S. Sontag, *On Photography* (Penguin, 1987), p. 49.

40 M. Featherstone, *Consumer Culture and Postmodernism* (Sage, 1991), p. 9.

41 S. Connor, *Postmodernist Culture* (Blackwell, 1989), p. 153.

42 S. Lash and J. Urry, *Economies of Signs and Space* (Sage, 1994), p. 256. See also J. Urry, *The Tourist Gaze* (Sage, 1990).

43 U. Eco, 'Travels in Hyperreality', in his *Faith in Fakes* (Secker and Warburg, 1986); Featherstone, *Consumer Culture*, ch. 7.

44 J.-F. Lyotard, *The Postmodern Condition* (Minnesota University Press, 1984).

45 See MacIntyre, *After Virtue*, chs 2, 3, on 'emotivism'.

46 See ch. 7.

47 A. Mellor, 'Enterprise and Heritage in the Dock', in J. Corner and S. Harvey (eds.) *Enterprise and Heritage* (Routledge, 1991), pp. 107, 108, 108, 108, 107.

48 See also ch. 10, where it is pointed out that this is also central to the relationship between 'art' and popular culture.

49 A. Giddens, *The Transformation of Intimacy* (Polity, 1992), p. 76.

50 See ch. 6.

51 J. Radway, *Reading the Romance* (Verso, 1987), pp. 198, 212.

52 R. Ballaster et al., *Women's Worlds* (Macmillan, 1991), p. 30.

53 P. Stallybrass and A. White, *The Politics and Poetics of Transgression* (Methuen, 1986), ch. 5.

54 Giddens, *Transformation*, pp. 68, 70 (emphasized in the original).

55 B. Martin, '"Mother Wouldn't Like It!": Housework as Magic', *Theory, Culture and Society* (1984), 2:2.

56 D. Harvey, *The Condition of Postmodernity* (Blackwell, 1989), p. 53.

57 J. Weeks, *Sexuality and its Discontents* (Routledge, 1985), ch. 8.

58 M. Maffesoli, *The Time of the Tribes* (Sage, 1996), and '*Jeux de Masques*: Postmodern Tribalism', *Design Issues* (1988), IV: 1, 2. See also T. Polhemus, *Streetstyle* (Thames and Hudson, 1994), pp. 13–16.

59 M. Meyer, Introduction to M. Meyer (ed.) *The Politics and Poetics of Camp* (Routledge, 1994), pp. 1–5. See also Weeks, *Sexuality*, ch. 8.

60 B. Anderson, *Imagined Communities* (Verso, 1983).

61 See S. Dunant (ed.) *The War of the Words* (Virago, 1994).

62 See N. Stevenson, *Understanding Media Cultures* (Sage, 1995), for a recent overview of these debates.

63 J. Habermas, *The Structural Transformation of the Public Sphere* (Polity, 1989), p. 36; R. Sennett, *The Fall of Public Man* (Faber, 1986), pp. 81–2.

64 On the exclusions implicit in this, see Stallybrass and White, *Politics and Poetics*, p. 89 and passim; and Docker, *Postmodernism*, p. 281.

65 Habermas, *Structural Transformation*, p. 56.

66 Ibid., p. 116.

67 For an overview of feminist debates on this, see H. Bertens, *The Idea of the Postmodern* (Routledge, 1995), pp. 199–205.

68 N. Fraser, 'Rethinking the Public Sphere', in C. Calhoun (ed.) *Habermas and the Public Sphere* (MIT Press, 1992).

69 E. J. Clery, 'Women, Publicity and the Coffee-House Myth', in *Women: A Cultural Review* (1991), 2:2.

70 Habermas, *Structural Transformation*, p. 26; and D. Outram, *The Body in the French Revolution* (Yale University Press, 1989), p. 17.

71 For an example of this 'invisibility', see M. Ryan, *Women in Public: Between Banners and Ballots, 1825–1880* (Johns Hopkins University Press, 1990), on women's philanthropic and reform organizations in America.

72 P. Brantlinger, 'Mass Media and Culture in *Fin-de-Siècle* Europe', in M. Teich and R. Porter (eds.) *Fin de Siècle and its Legacy* (Cambridge University Press, 1990).

73 Sennett, *Fall*, ch. 1 and p. 336.

74 P. Brantlinger, *Bread and Circuses: Theories of Mass Culture as Social Decay* (Cornell University Press, 1983), pp. 259, 276.

75 Sennett, *Fall*, pp. 282–3; J. Baudrillard, *Simulations* (Semiotext(e), 1983), p. 130.

76 J. Baudrillard, *In the Shadow of the Silent Majorities* (Semiotext(e), 1983), p. 14.

77 P. Burke, *Popular Culture in Early Modern Europe* (Temple Smith, 1978), ch. 9. See also my *Transgressing the Modern*, ch. 2.

78 R. Shields, *Places on the Margin: Alternative geographies of modernity* (Routledge, 1991), p. 96.

79 See ch. 1, and D. Chaney, *Fictions of Collective Life* (Routledge, 1993), p. 141 and passim.

80 See, for example, Radway, *Reading the Romance*; C. Geraghty, *Women and Soap Opera* (Polity, 1991); D. Hobson, *Crossroads* (Methuen, 1982).

81 P. Willis, *Common Culture* (Open University Press, 1990), p. 85. See also McRobbie, *Postmodernism*, chs 8, 9.

82 R. Williams, *Television: Technology and Cultural Form* (Fontana, 1974); and see the discussion in Docker, *Postmodernism*, pp. 147–50.

83 See, for example, Shields, *Places*, ch. 2, and J. Fiske, *Understanding Popular Culture* (Unwin Hyman, 1989), ch. 4. See also ch. 1 of my *Transgressing the Modern*.

84 J. W. Goethe, *Italian Journey* (Penguin, 1982), p. 469.

85 Docker, *Postmodernism*, pp. 281, 284, 284.

86   M. Shiach, *Discourses on Popular Culture* (Polity, 1989), p. 31.

87   See R. Lowe and W. Shaw, *Travellers* (Fourth Estate, 1993), and N. Saunders, *Ecstasy and the Dance Culture* (London, 1995).

88   See S. Lash and J. Friedman, Introduction to S. Lash and J. Friedman (eds.) *Modernity and Identity* (Blackwell, 1992), p. 5, for a related use of the term 'low' modernism.

89   C. Taylor, *Human Agency and Language* (Cambridge University Press, 1985), p. 103.

90   G. Steiner, *Real Presences* (Faber, 1989), p. 215.

91   J. Habermas, *The Philosophical Discourse of Modernity* (Polity, 1990), p. 300. For a useful account of philosophical aspects of reflexivity, see H. Lawson, *Reflexivity* (Hutchinson, 1985).

92   G. Bateson, *Man and Nature* (Fontana, 1980), p. 225. Among social theorists, it is surely Durkheim who has the best grasp of all this: see his *Elementary Forms of the Religious Life* (Allen and Unwin, 1915), passim.

93   Lyotard, *Postmodern Condition*, p. 79.

94   S. Smith, *Origins of Modernism* (Harvester, 1994), p. 14.

95   C. Jencks, *What is Post-Modernism* (Academy Editions, 1989), p. 14; H. Caygill, 'Architectural Postmodernism', in R. Boyne and A. Rattansi (eds.) *Postmodernism and Society* (Macmillan, 1990); and Urry, *Tourist Gaze*, pp. 120–8.

96   Connor, *Postmodernist Culture*, p. 61.

97   S. Lash, *The Sociology of Postmodernism* (Routledge, 1990), p. 11.

98   The best account of postmodernism in the arts is Connor, *Postmodernist Culture*; the most thorough treatment of 'postmodern' and its variants is Bertens, *Idea of the Postmodern*. See also F. Jameson, *Postmodernism* (Verso, 1991), ch. 1.

99   M. Nava, *Changing Cultures* (Sage, 1992), pp. 174–8; S. Frith and H. Horne, *Art into Pop* (Methuen, 1987), chs 1, 4, 5.

100 M. Newman, 'Postmodernism', in L. Appignanesi (ed.) *Postmodernism* (Free Association Books, 1989), p. 133.

101 Baudrillard, *Simulations*, pp. 147–8, 151–2.

102 Featherstone, *Consumer Culture*, ch. 5.

103 Z. Bauman, *Modernity and Ambivalence* (Polity, 1993), p. 232.

104 S. Moore, 'Getting a Bit of the Other: the Pimps of Postmodernism', in R. Chapman and J. Rutherford (eds.) *Male Order* (Lawrence and Wishart, 1988), pp. 179, 181. See also discussions in L. Nicholson (ed.) *Feminism/Postmodernism* (Routledge, 1990), and S. Bordo, *Unbearable Weight: Feminism, Western Culture and the Body* (California University Press, 1993), especially Introduction and Part III.

105 G. Marcus, *Lipstick Traces* (Secker and Warburg, 1990), p. 104.

106 For discussion, see D. Heim, *The Metaphysics of Virtual Reality* (Oxford University Press, 1993); J. Brook and I. Boal, *Resisting the Virtual Life* (City Lights, 1995); and M. Slouka, *War of the Worlds* (Abacus, 1995).

Key Terms

Some terms – generally in everyday use – have acquired a semi-technical meaning in recent academic discourse, and may in turn have developed a distinctive slant in this book. The following notes – inevitably rather brief and abstract – may be of some help here, as a summary or initial orientation. They are not a substitute for a dictionary, nor are terms included here when they have a relatively established and conventional meaning – whether in academic or non-academic discourse – that the book does not significantly depart from (sublime, melodrama, image), or when they are terms that are sufficiently discussed in the chapters where they occur most centrally (masquerade, allegory, postmodernism – see chapters 5, 11 and 12 respectively). For 'modernity' and 'modernism', see the Introduction (second section); and, for modernism, the first page or two of chapter 10.

Subject   In effect, a fusion of two everyday senses of the term: 'subject' as grammatical subject, a position in language; and 'subject' as subject of power, subject as entailing 'subjection'. The subject is constituted as active, but this capacity for agency depends on networks of discursive and political practices, as embedded in everyday life. Mapped on to the self, such 'subjecthood' gives us a model of the self as subject to self-control: the modern, reflexive self, disciplined yet autonomous.

Transgression   The exploration of the exclusions and disavowals, the taboos, that both surround and contribute to defining the modern identity; the experience of the crossing, the violation, of these boundaries. Central to this is the reality/fantasy boundary, given the essential role that it plays in constituting the modern self and its desires. Fantasy is an important mode through which those possibilities that are disavowed and excluded in the modern project can nevertheless remain important as sources of meaning and experience, and it is transgression that permits the vicarious exploration of this otherness.

Narrative   Identity as a story we tell ourselves about ourselves; a story viewed as a reflexively organized property of its own unfolding in linear time. *Grand narratives* are the ideological elaborations of these stories into theories of history, politics, evolution and 'progress' based on increasing emancipation from the constraints of nature and tradition; conversely, *humble narratives* organize the stories of our everyday lives in terms that emphasize the moral embeddedness of our choices, situations and relationships, and can include an exploration of aspects of the repetitive and the cyclical. Grand narratives have an intimate relationship to the project of modernity; humble narratives are crucially linked to the emergence and development of the novel.

Project Purposeful future-oriented activity, geared to the achievement of practical, secular goals, and capable of elaboration into life-governing values and priorities that can make sense of – and in – individual life narratives. This in turn entails the subjection of self and other to norms of instrumental activity; and, when this is expanded into the scientific and technological orientation to the world, treating the latter as a manipulable and divisible resource, organized according to the technical–bureaucratic division of labour, we have the *project of modernity*. Where the emphasis is on the sociopolitical dimensions, the aspiration to realize a rational, emancipated social order, independent of tradition, religion and imposed hierarchies, this becomes the *Enlightenment project*. The overlap between this and the project of modernity is particularly clear in the shared orientation towards an ethos of control, and in the association with the grand narratives of progress, notably socialism and capitalism, with their divergent implications for patterns of social organization that nevertheless reveal some features in common.

Reflexivity The basic sense is that of self-consciousness and self-reference, fundamental to the modern attitude that self-understanding and self-control are essential in organizing life according to project. This involves bringing into explicit focus what is otherwise only implicit or presupposed, but inevitably this generates elements of paradox: when the drive of the subject to know itself results in positing itself as its own object, a process of alienation or splitting occurs. In practice, then, this reflexive attitude is inseparable from reconstructing the object; self-reflection becomes self-constitution, and is inseparable from it. Reflexivity involves a sense of 'making it up as we go along'; it involves the organization of the self, or the social world, through these very attempts at self-analysis and self-regulation.

Theatricality Presents identity as a play of masks; through fantasy identifications, projections and roles, the self emerges as multiple, always other to itself. Social interaction becomes an 'acting out' of identity, an exploration of the artifice at the heart of modern culture. These aspects of selfhood suggest that the self is multidimensional, open to the variety of experiences made possible by modernity, and not necessarily disciplining this in the interests of project. Indeed, theatricality is always, in principle, in tension with the world of narrative and project; but, when harnessed to the latter, permits a degree of controlled flexibility and adaptability in relation to the world of others. In the age of spectacle and mass media, theatricality becomes an essential component of self-identity through 'personality', the rehearsal of individuality as a distinctive attribute of each person.

Representation When we ask how notions of personal and cultural identity come to be constructed, we necessarily raise questions about how imagery serves as a basis for recognition, how cultural forms come to be representations, both of self and world. Images, metaphors and descriptions have their own autonomy, their own distinctive attributes; yet they also serve to 'represent' something else, standing in for it, displacing it, while yet referring to it, or even embodying it. This dualism in representation, whereby the representation is both itself and something else, becomes particularly problematical in modernity; the positivist distrust of symbolism reduces it to 'mere' representation while simultaneously making possible the troublesome independence of such signifying systems. This has implications across the whole field of the cultural politics of representation – including the dynamics of political representation itself.

Spectacle   Takes up the everyday sense of the word, referring to a rather extravagant 'visual entertainment'; hence spectacle dramatizes the excess of representation, its ability to replace the world it represents and, in so doing, to position the self as subject to it – simultaneously incorporated in this panorama, yet excluded from real participation. Spectacle thereby also dramatizes and projects the passivity of experience, its dependence on canons of representation through which its meaning is shaped and defined.

Hyperreality   One of a group of words (virtual reality, simulation, cyberspace) introduced in an attempt to grapple with the perceived implications of computing and multimedia technology for our ways of representing, experiencing and manipulating the world of late (or post-) modernity. When the world of representations is sufficiently autonomous and powerful to be independent of reality, so that operations can be carried out on/in this world that have real-enough consequences for our lives, then this can be characterized as 'hyperreality'. But these consequences can also be said to follow from other developments of project in late modernity, such that the world increasingly becomes a world that is a function of our own systems of knowledge and control.

Biographical Notes

I have found some theorists, critics and essayists particularly useful for thinking about the issues raised in this book; here are a few comments on each, to indicate their central interests and help 'situate' them.

Bakhtin, Mikhail (1895–1975) Russian literary theorist, authority on carnival, the novel, and popular culture, believing that the latter embodied possibilities of dynamic, creative communication absent from 'official' culture; not surprisingly, fell foul of Stalinism, and his *Rabelais and His World*, put together in the 1930s, was not published till 1965.

Bataille, Georges (1897–1962) Sometime anthropologist, surrealist, Marxist, literary critic and pornographer; the most shadowy and subversive of these authors, an influence on better-known successors (e.g. Foucault), now being more widely read in his own right. Interested in the interplay between taboo and transgression, restraint and excess, order and disorder, and seeking in these polarities a creative principle that underlies areas as apparently separate as the sacred, the erotic and the economic.

Baudelaire, Charles (1821–67) French poet, essayist, major influence on the aesthetics of modernity. The title of his most famous collection of poems – *The Flowers of Evil* – reveals his view that the artist had to capture the beauty in evil; this, and the necessity to search for the permanent in the transient and fragmentary, had to be at the core of the artistic response to the experience of 'the modern'.

Baudrillard, Jean (1929–) Currently influential French theorist of consumerism, sign systems, the media and postmodernity, fascinated by the way 'simulacra' obliterate traditional distinctions between the real and the unreal, depth and surface, essence and appearance.

Benjamin, Walter (1892–1940) German cultural critic and essayist, influenced by surrealism and Marxism, and one whose own influence is as diffuse as his writings, but continues to grow. An insightful, if impressionistic guide to the melancholy of the modernist dream, the impact of commodity fetishism on culture, and the prevalence of nostalgia and fragmentation in the modern experience.

Debord, Guy (1931–95) Politically active on the French anarchist fringe in the 1950s and 1960s as leading theorist of the situationists, advocating creative disruption of the 'society of the spectacle'; developed the latter concept through applying Marx's analysis of commodity fetishism to the age of the media and 'mass culture'. Influential both on cultural outbursts like punk and on theorists like Baudrillard.

Elias, Norbert (1897–1990)   German historical sociologist, exiled during the Nazi period; studied the way Western civilization has involved the regulation of the body through complex codes of manners, seen as related to the development of the modern state, and has explored this theme in areas as diverse as sport, science, ageing and death.

Foucault, Michel (1926–84)   French social theorist, very influential over the last decade or so; author of books on madness, medicine, science, the penal system and sexuality, trying to show in each case how a 'discourse' elaborates an object of knowledge that simultaneously involves the exercise of power, thereby emphasizing the relativity of knowledge-claims and their inherently political dimension.

Habermas, Jürgen (1929–)   The most influential German social theorist since Weber. Has his roots in the 'Frankfurt School' of critical theory, and is indeed a critic of the distortions of the Enlightenment tradition that result from the subordination of rational discussion to technological and bureaucratic control. Nevertheless, he is basically a defender of this tradition against its latter-day detractors (e.g. Foucault, Lyotard).

Nietzsche, Friedrich (1844–1900)   German philosopher who seems to have become *the* philosopher of the postmodern; a major influence on later authors from Weber to Baudrillard. Explored the implications of the collapse of the self-confidence of the Enlightenment project, and of what he saw as the impossibility of absolute moral and epistemological values after the 'death of God'.

Rousseau, Jean-Jacques (1712–88)   French social and political theorist; a complex figure, standing at the source of the divergent French and German traditions in social thought. A contemporary of the Enlightenment, but took his distance from it; anticipated many later criticisms of modernity, exploring the artificiality of the modern self as a social product, and the problems of social and political representation that result from this.

Sade, Marquis de (1740–1814)   Generally dismissed in Anglo-American culture as a 'mere pornographer'; taken seriously in France and Germany as a philosophical critic of the Enlightenment, arguing against the assumption that virtue, reason and freedom could be reconciled in a harmonious social order, or that 'nature' could provide a foundation for such an order.

Sontag, Susan (1933–)   American critic, essayist, novelist and insightful commentator on the paradoxical power of the image and metaphor in post-religious culture, a power that can both intensify and endanger our experience of reality; raised these issues in ways that would later be seen as harbingers of the 'postmodern' approach.

Weber, Max (1858–1920)   Major German social theorist, still the most influential of all; grasped the fact that the major achievements of modernity, in the technical mastery and 'disenchantment' of the world, are also the clue to its major limitations, the development of the 'iron cage' of bureaucracy and specialism and the resulting impotence of value-choices and political ideals.

Wilde, Oscar (1854–1900)   Dramatist, essayist, wit and gay icon, his works shed an intriguing light on manners, the civilizing process, the artifice of gender identity and the place of theatricality in modernity.

Woolf, Virginia (1882–1941)   Major English novelist and essayist, a subtle explorer of the nuances, artificialities and implications of gendered identity in the modern city, attempting to develop an aesthetic that would be both feminist and modernist.

Guide to Further Reading

The titles I regard as the best sources for each topic will generally be apparent from the endnotes to each chapter. In addition, the works of key theorists – whose names are listed elsewhere – are worth pursuing. Here, I just wish to indicate some books that are particularly useful in that they range over several areas and bring out underlying themes; I found the four titles in bold to be particularly thought-provoking.

Z. Bauman, *Legislators and Interpreters* (Polity, 1987)

M. Berman, *All That Is Solid Melts into Air: The Experience of Modernity* (Verso, 1983)

P. Brooks, *The Melodramatic Imagination* (Yale University Press, 1976)

C. Campbell, *The Romantic Ethic and the Spirit of Modern Consumerism* (Blackwell, 1987)

D. Chaney, *Fictions of Collective Life: Public Drama in a Late Modern Culture* (Routledge, 1993)

T. J. Clark, *The Painting of Modern Life; Paris in the Art of Manet and His Followers* (Thames and Hudson, 1985)

W. Connolly, *Political Theory and Modernity* (Blackwell, 1987)

T. Eagleton, *The Ideology of the Aesthetic* (Blackwell, 1990)

S. Ewen, *All Consuming Images* (Basic Books, 1984)

A. Giddens, *Modernity and Self-Identity* (Polity, 1991)

S. Kern, *The Culture of Time and Space 1880–1918* (Harvard University Press, 1983)

G. Marcus, *Lipstick Traces: A Secret History of the Twentieth Century* (Secker and Warburg, 1989)

L. Sass, *Madness and Modernism* (Basic Books, 1992)

R. Sennett, *The Fall of Public Man* (Faber, 1986)

C. Taylor, *Sources of the Self* (Cambridge University Press, 1989)

B. Turner, *The Body and Society* (Blackwell, 1984)

These pursue gender-related themes in more depth:

N. Armstrong, *Desire and Domestic Fiction* (Oxford University Press, 1987)

S. Bordo, *Unbearable Weight: Feminism, Western Culture, and the Body* (California University Press, 1993)

E. Bronfen, *Over Her Dead Body: Death, Femininity and the Aesthetic* (Manchester University Press, 1992)

J. Butler, *Gender Trouble: Feminism and the Subversion of Identity* (Routledge, 1990)

M. Garber, *Vested Interests: Cross-Dressing and Cultural Anxiety* (Penguin, 1993)

D. Outram, *The Body and the French Revolution* (Yale University Press, 1989)

C. Smith-Rosenberg, *Disorderly Conduct: Visions of Gender in Victorian America* (Oxford University Press, 1986)

J. Walkowitz, *City of Dreadful Delight: Narratives of Sexual Danger in Late-Victorian London* (Virago, 1992)

These emphasize contemporary developments:

W. Bogard, *The Simulation of Surveillance* (Cambridge University Press, 1996)

S. Connor, *Postmodernist Culture* (Blackwell, 1997)

J. Docker, *Postmodernism and Popular Culture* (Cambridge University Press, 1994)

M. Featherstone, *Consumer Culture and Postmodernism* (Sage, 1991)

D. Harvey, *The Condition of Postmodernity* (Blackwell, 1989)

A. Huyssen, *After the Great Divide; Modernism, Mass Culture and Postmodernism* (Macmillan, 1986)

B. Woolley, *Virtual Worlds* (Penguin, 1993)

Index

References to Key Terms and Biographical Notes are in bold type

actors 24, 25, 30
addiction 323–4
Adorno, Theodor 190, 234, 238, 271, 284
advertisements 86, 91–3, 97–101, 107, 334
aesthetics 266, 270
Agnew, J.-C. 20–1, 27–8, 37
alienation 9, 67, 195
allegory 289–93
ambivalence 4–5, 9–10
Ang, Ien 33, 34–5, 37, 156
Anna Karenina (Tolstoy) 202–4, 206
anorexia 103–4
Aragon, Louis 66, 68–9, 83, 84–5
architecture 217–21, 251–2, 273–4, 275, 334
Arendt, Hannah 44, 236
Ariès, P. 181, 182
Armstrong, D. 47, 53
Armstrong, Nancy 48, 151, 155, 159, 168
Arney, W. R. 50–1
art 100–1, 184–5, 187, 192, 303
  and the sacred 177–8, 193
Art Nouveau 273, 275
artifice 16, 22, 27, 33–4, 141, *see also* excess
artists 10, 265, 266, 267
  and the city 68, 72, 79
arts
  modernism 250–2, 270–6;

postmodernism 334–5; and the social order 265–70; *see also* architecture; cinema; novels
aspiration 93, 94
audience 19, 20, 24, 25, 27–8
  and art 269–70; and cinema 297; and French Revolution 42; and soap opera 37
Auerbach, Nina 17, 18, 156, 179, 180
aura 316–17, 320–1, 324
Austen, Jane 155, 159, 161, 168, 169
  Mansfield Park 158, 166–7; *Pride and Prejudice* 148–50, 151, 160, 167, 170
authenticity 29, 30, 31, 32, 77, 320, 329
authorship 24–5, 272
autonomy 265, 267–8, 269, 271
avant-garde 269–70
aviation 212–13

Bakhtin, Mikhail 262, **345**
Ballaster, Ros 323–4
Balzac, Honoré de 30, 66, 75–6
Barber, B. 26, 28
Barish, J. 26
Barnes, Djuna 137, 259–63, 275
baroque 275–6
Barth, G. 94, 95
Barthes, Roland 140, 163, 218, 276, 280
  fashion 119, 124; photographs 286, 290, 291, 302

Bartlett, Neil 15, 17
Bataille, Georges 111–12, 185, 190–1, 192, **345**
Baudelaire, Charles 4, 5, 251, **345**
  allegory 289; artists 10, 68, 72; as dandy 129; dreams 85; *flâneur* 78–9; hostility 269; images 280; novelty 66; Paris 66, 296; prostitution 83, 84; shock 315; spleen 290, 317–18
Baudrillard, Jean 110, 292, 311, 335, **345**
  death 182; Gulf War 299–300; seduction 141; simulacra 298, 301, 302–3
Bauhaus 218, 273
Bauman, Z. 7, 228, 234, 335
  avant-garde 269; conformity 108; death 181–2; Holocaust 230, 232, 238
beauty 132, 187, 266
Beck, U. 311, 312, 313
Belsey, Catherine 20, 77
Benjamin, Walter **345**
  allegory 289–90; cinema 294, 296–7; detective fiction 77; experience 316, 317; fashion 124–5, 127; fetishism 292; *flâneur* 78, 79; Paris 70, 75, 76, 85, 288–9; photography 290; prostitution 83, 84; shock 318
Bentham, Jeremy 46, 55–6, 58
Bergen, B. J. 51
Berger, J. 132, 133
Berger, P. 29–30
Berlin 66, 78, 84
Berman, M. 66, 74, 75, 220, 251–2
Bernheimer, C. 82, 84
biography 17–18
Blade Runner 301–2, 304
Blake, William 67
body
  and consumerism 103–4; courtesans 82; and fashion 119–20, 131; and fetishism 292; and photographs 291–2; *see also* embodiment
Bon Marché 94–5, 96
boundaries 81, 105, 136
Bourdieu, P. 120, 266

Bowlby, Rachel 73, 96, 162
Brand, Dana 76–7
brands 100–1
Brantlinger, P. 283, 329
Braque, Georges 252–3, 255
Bristol, M. 24, 25
Bronfen, Elisabeth 179, 180, 288
Brontë, Anne 179, 180
Brontë, Charlotte 148, 149, 150–2, 155, 156, 158
Brontë, Emily 152, 155
Brooks, P. 32, 33–4, 195
Brummell, Beau 129, 130
Bruno, Giuliana 301, 302
Brunsdon, C. 36–7
Buci-Glucksmann, Christine 275, 289
Buck-Morss, Susan 85, 86
bureaucracy 231, 233, 244, 313–14
Bürger, P. 241, 242, 269
Burke, Edmund 194, 195
Burns, E. 19
Butler, C. 255, 265
Butler, Josephine 18
Butler, Judith 136, 137, 138
Byars, J. 33, 34

Calinescu, M. 269, 289
Campbell, C. 120–1, 164–5, 193
  consumerism 108, 109–10, 112, 130; desire 104, 105, 106; love 152, 164–5, 193
cancer 181
Cancian, Francesca 153
capitalism 59, 94, 110, 111
Carey, J. 209, 271
Carnival 261, 262, 331
Carter, Angela 130, 137, 140, 191, 238–9
Carter, S. L. 185
Castel, R. 50, 51
Castle, T. 21, 120, 284, 285
censorship 24–5
Chanel, Gabrielle 'Coco' 123, 125, 131, 132, 140
Chaney, D. 28, 35, 101, 281, 295
change 7, 68, 124
Charles, RuPaul 135
Charles-Roux, E. 131
childbirth 49–51
choice 322

Christianity 177, 190, 191, 283
cigarettes 91–3, 102
cinema 35, 37, 286–8, 293–8, 317
    and railways 205; stardom 31, 32; and
        war 299
citizenship 58, 59, 60, 218, 234, 327
city 65–9, 210, 315, 335
    crowd, class and prostitution 79–84;
        death and transfiguration 84–6;
        flâneur 75–9; Woolf 69–75
civility 22–3, 66, 93, 195, 326, 328, 329
civilization 66, 229, 266
civilizing process 6–7, 93–4, 228–9
    and avant-garde 269; and fashion 128;
        and novels 159; and popular
        culture 329; taste 120; and
        vision 280–1
Clark, T. J. 82–3, 251, 296, 318
class
    and the city 79–81; and fashion 122–3,
        127; and taste 120
cloning 337
clothes 21–2, 67, 76, 117, 119–23, 140–1;
    see also fashion; transvestism
coffee houses 326–7, 328
Coleridge, S. T. 193, 196
colour 294–5
Comolli, J.-L. 296, 297
compulsiveness 324
Conan Doyle, Sir Arthur 77
Condorcet, Marquis de 227
confession 52–4, 148
conformity 108–9, 110, 111, 122, 142,
    318–19
Connerton, P. 190, 239
Connolly, W. 186, 187, 189, 238, 241, 242
Connor, S. 220, 263–4, 271–2, 274, 303,
    321, 334
Conrad, Peter 154, 158, 159, 166
consciousness 255–9, 263–4, 315–16
conspicuous consumption 130
consumerism 91, 93–6, 322
    advertising 97–101; cinema 295; and
        the city 68, 75; dandies 129–30;
        daydreams and desires 104–8;
        fashion 128; production and
        excess 108–12; and religion 185–6;
        taboos 318; and transgression 319
consumption 93, 102, 110, 111–12

contemporary 5–6, 66
control 38, 75, 78, 105, 310, 311–12, 319,
    327
    and consumerism 103; and the
        family 48, 49–51
corsets 118–19
courtesans 82
courtly consumption 93–4
Craik, Jennifer 117, 128
Crawford, R. 103, 182
creativity 193, 265
    the city 71, 72, 74, 79; fashion 141,
        142; literary 161, 162; robots 214,
        215–16
critique 243
cross-dressing 134–7, 135
crowds 67, 76, 79–81
Crowther, P. 316, 317
Cubism 253, 254, 255
culture 70, 110, 141, 148, 162, 188, 266;
    see also mass culture; popular culture

Dalí, Salvador 275
dandies 129–30, 131
Davidson, M. 93, 97, 100, 101, 102–3
Davies, Judy 213
daydreams 106–7, 142
de Beauvoir, Simone 132, 133
de Bolla, P. 163, 195, 196, 197
de Certeau, Michel 203, 204, 206, 210
de Lauretis, Teresa 284, 295
de Staël, Madame 159
death 71, 178–83, 188, 190
    and the city 84–6; of God 184–6, 189–
        90, 197; and Nazism 236–7
Debord, Guy 295, 297, **345–6**
deception 283
decoration 272–4
Deleuze, G. 241, 301
democracy 58–9, 91, 95
Demoiselles d'Avignon (Picasso) 84
department stores 94–5, 96
Derrida, J. 141, 196
design 98–9
desire 53, 54, 167, 292, 318
    and consumerism 93, 103, 104–5, 106–
        7, 111, 112
despair 83–4
diaries 160

Dickens, Charles 47, 68, 96, 203, 205, 206
dictatorship 59–60
Diderot, Denis 25, 107, 228, 239–40, 272
Dijkstra, B. 104, 132
Dior, C. 117, 123
discipline 46–48, 49–51, 53, 54, 55, 58,
    see also Foucault
disease 47–8, 102, 179–80, 181–2, 310–
    11, 312
Docherty, T. 7, 159
Docker, J. 331
'Docks of London, The' (Woolf) 72
Dolar, M. 241
Dollimore, J. 16, 26
Dombey & Son (Dickens) 205, 206
domination 59–60, 237, 242
Donald, J. 46, 57
Donne, John 178, 179, 181
Donzelot, J. 48, 49
doubling 288, 289, 315
drag 134–7
dreams 85, 95–6, 205, 294, *see also*
    daydreams
dress 140, *see also* clothes
drugs 97, 102–3
du Camp, Maxime 82
Durkheim, E. 48, 177, 188
Dyer, R. 32

Eagleton, T. 195, 196, 237, 256, 266, 268,
    269, 290, 291
Eco, U. 303
education 45–6
effeminacy 135–6
Eichmann, Adolf 236
Eiffel Tower 276
Einstein, Albert 259, 272
Elias, Norbert 137, 181, 228, 280–1, 315,
    346
Eliot, George 170
Eliot, T. S. 71, 127, 138, 259, 260, 261,
    265, 267, 272
embeddedness 332–3
embodiment 6–7
Emma (Austen) 169
emotion 22, 105
emotivism 187
Enlightenment 7–8, 45, 159, 228–9, 243–
    6, 283

and Holocaust 232–4; and
    otherness 237, 238–42; and popular
    culture 329; and public sphere 326–
    8
Enlightenment project 233, 239, 242, 245,
    343
ennui 78, 290, 315, 317–18, 320, *see also*
    Baudelaire
enthusiasm 246
equality 150–1
eroticism 177, 274
Evans, C. 119, 125, 126, 130, 134, 139
Evans, Linda 132
Evans, Mary 150, 151, 166
evil 192, 235–7, 239, 242, 245
Ewen, S. 67, 94, 98, 99, 101, 273, 274, 282
excess 30, 32–3, 38, 86, 101, 111–12, 295,
    see also meaninglessness; ornament
experience 9, 11, 78, 170, 183, 319
    and the city 65, 67, 68–70, 74; and
    consciousness and representation
    263–4, 265; and project 312–13, 315;
    shock 315–18; *see also* modernity
expressivism 193

Faith, N. 202, 204, 205
family 46, 48–9
fantasy 11, 53, 71, 142, 155
    advertising 99; and cinema 294; and
    consumerism 95, 98; and fiction 156
fashion 5, 17, 53, 117–20, 141–2
    and anorexia 104; and beauty 132–4;
    and change 124–7; and clothes 120–
    3; and consumerism 108, 109; and
    courtesans 82; and gaze 134; and
    gender 127–32; and waste 101
Faurschou, G. 107–8, 127
Featherstone, M. 108, 293
fecundity 71, 85, 255
Felski, Rita 8
femininity 136, 169
    and culture 162; and fashion 129, 131–
    2; masquerade 138–41; space and
    time 210; and Surrealism 275; and
    transvestism 135, 137; *see also*
    women
feminism 4, 327
Fer, B. 273, 275
fetishism 118, 119, 139, 292

fiction, *see* novels
Fielding, Henry 21
film, *see* cinema
Fiske, J. 109, 122, 123
Flam, J. D. 252, 253, 254, 280
flâneur 74, 83, 86, 281, 290, 321; *see also* Baudelaire
Flaubert, Gustave 271
foetal monitoring 50
folk culture 329
Ford, Henry 218
forgery 16
Foster, H. 275
Foucault, Michel 45, 48, 137, 177, **346**
   confession 52; critique 243;
      domination 59, 60; Enlightenment
      245; panopticism 57; power 46, 47,
      57–8, 60, 61, 242; prisons 55;
      sexuality 49, 54
Freedberg, D. 282–3, 284
freedom 59–61, 79
French Revolution 42–5, 58, 124, 227–8,
      234, 246
   melodrama 34, 38
Freud, S. 189, 190, 228, 259, 288, 315,
      316, 324
Fried, M. 272, 275
Friedlander, S. 237
functionality 219, 273, 274
Furedi, F. 7–8
Fussell, P. 222

Gaines, Jane 121, 295
Galliano, John 124
gaps 264–5, 314
Garb, Tamar 255
Garber, Marjorie 135, 137, 238
Garland, Judy 32
Gaskell, Elizabeth 80–1, 154, 158, 168–9,
      179
gaslight 296
Gay, Peter 160, 203
gaze 45, 50, 75, 84, 281
   gendered 133–4, 139; panoptic 54–7
gender 8, 69, 141
   and cigarettes 91, 92, 93; and cinema
      295; the city 69–72, 77–9, 80, 81, 85;
      and clothes 137–8; and coffee
      houses 328; and machines 215–16;

and postmodern 336; and romance
      148, 157–8; and sex 138; and
      shopping 95, 96; space and time
      209–10; and the sublime 195–6; *see
      also* fashion; femininity; masculinity
gender identities 136–7, 162
gender stereotypes 69, 78
genius 193, 265, 266, 267
Geraghty, Christine 36–7
Geremek, Bronislaw 59
ghosts 284–6
Giddens, A. 153, 154, 323, 324
Gilbert, Sandra 138, 159, 161, 180, 260,
      262
Gilligan, Carol 36
Gissing, George 80
Gledhill, Christine 31, 32, 37
God 183–6, 189–90, 197
Goethe, Johann Wolfgang von 285, 331
Goldman, H. 244
Goncourt brothers 82, 84
Gorky, Maxim 286–7
Gouldner, A. 105, 193
Goya, Francisco 228
Greenberg, C. 251, 271, 274
Greenblatt, S. 19, 23, 25–6
Gropius, W. 273
Gubar, Susan 159, 161, 180, 260
guillotine 227–8
Gulf War 299–300

Habermas, Jürgen 218, 242, 243, 326–7,
      328, 332, **346**
happiness 58, 241
Harvey, D. 207, 209, 263
haute couture 123, 125
Havel, Václav 24, 59–60, 61
Hawkins, Anne 178, 181
health 48, 51, 92, 102–3
Heath, S. 138–9, 140, 165
Hebdige, D. 57, 126, 127, 194, 303, 304,
      319
Heller, E. 184, 185
Herf, J. 233
heroes 43–4
heroism of the modern 68, 78
Himmler, Heinrich 237
history 7, 165, 168, 239, 300, 302, 303,
      321

Hitler, Adolf 230, 233, 238
Hobbes, Thomas 21, 25
holidays 95, 100
Hollywood 31, 37, 121, 295
Holocaust 229–38
home 74, 77
homelessness 9, 195
homosexuality 135–6, 271, 325
Horkheimer, M. 190, 234, 238
Hudson, Rock 136
Hughes, R. 217, 220, 252
Hugo, Victor 66, 203
Hunt, L. 43–4
Hutton, P. 54
Huyssen, A. 80, 215–16, 232–3, 271
hygiene 48
hyperreality 304, 320, 331, 336–7, **344**
hypocrites 44–5

identity 17, 21, 68, 74, 112, 324–5, 330
    and fashion 121–2, 127–8, 141; *see also*
    gender
illness 178–9, 181, 299
illusion 23–4, 283, 286
images 280, 283, 326
    phantasmagoria 284–9; popular
    culture 283–4; and simulacra
    298–305; *see also* cinema;
    photographs
imagination 23, 105, 106, 107, 155, 193,
    289
    and supernatural 183–4
immigration 66–7
impersonation 19–20
individualism 15, 60, 77, 152, 177
individuality 22, 30, 60
individuation 60
insincerity 16
interiority 152–3
International Style 217, 218
Internet 337
irrationality 110, 111

Jacobsen, B. 92–3
James, Henry 257, 274
Jane Eyre (Brontë) 148, 149, 150–2, 155,
    156, 158
Jay, Martin 57, 253, 280, 281
Jews 230–1, 237–8

Joyce, James 138, 257, 258, 259, 262–3

Kafka, F. 212, 214, 241
Kandinsky, Wassily 273
Kant, I. 104, 120, 192, 245–6, 285, 333
    morality 240, 241; sublime 194, 195
Kaplan, Cora 162, 164
Kern, S. 205, 211, 221–2, 254, 258–9,
    264–5
Kingston, K. 147, 148, 150
knowledge 242, 260, 311, 312, 314
Krauss, Rosalind 267, 286

labyrinth 78
Lacan, J. 133, 140
Lane, J. 262–3
Lang, Fritz 215, 216, 288
Langbauer, Laurie 157
Lasch, C. 134
Lash, S. 321, 334
Le Bon, Gustave 80
Le Corbusier 212, 218–19, 220, 274
leisure 330
Lennox, Annie 135
Lennox, Charlotte 157
lesbianism 138
letter-writing 160, 211
Levenson, M. H. 265, 269
liberation 118
lighting 296
London 66, 67, 69–75, 94
longings 106–8
look, the 133, 134
Loos, Adolf 273–4
Lord of the Rings (Tolkien) 56
love 22, 151–4, 164
Lucky Strike 91, 92
Lyotard, J.-F. 194, 197, 235, 238, 246,
    333, 334

McCracken, G. 107
McGrane, B. 177, 207, 228
machines 206, 212, 213, 214–15, 219; *see
    also* technology; telephones
MacIntyre, A. 165–6, 167, 169, 185, 187,
    240, 313
madness 186
Madonna 119
Malevich, Kazimir 268

Mallarmé, Stephane 264
Maltby, R. 282, 287, 295, 297
Man of the Crowd, The (Poe) 76–7
Manchester 80–1, 94
mannequins 84
manners 93
Mansfield Park (Austen) 158–9, 166–7
Marcus, Jane 72, 261
Marcus, T. 135
Marinetti, Filippo Tommaso 212, 213
market 20, 21, 83, 240, 321
marriage 150, 152
Marshall, D. 27, 28, 53
Marx, Karl 124, 207, 288
Mary Barton (Gaskell) 158
masculinity 135, 244–5, 274
    and fashion 128–9, 130, 136, 137, 140;
    and homosexuality 135; and space
    209–10
masks 29, 78
masochism 134
masquerade 26, 138–40
mass culture 148, 270, 271, 272–3, 326,
    329–30; *see also* popular culture
mass media 319, 328–9
masses 79
Massey, Doreen 209, 210
masturbation 49
Matisse, Henri 252–5
Mayer, A. J. 231, 233, 235, 238
meaning 126, 290, 295, 319, 333
meaninglessness 141, 319
media 319, 328–9
medicine 48, 49–51, 102–3
Meisel, P. 257, 261, 264
melancholia 78, 79
Mellor, A. 322–3
melodrama 18, 19, 29, 30–8, 158, 195, 319
memory 165, 204, 291, 316, 317
men 149
    and cigarettes 92; and fashion
    128–30, 140, 141; as *flâneurs* 77;
    gender stereotypes 8; and love
    153; reading 162; transvestism
    134–7; writing 161; *see also*
    masculinity
mental illness 47–8
Metropolis 215, 216, 288
Middlemarch (Eliot) 170

Mies van der Rohe, Ludwig 217, 218, 273
Miles, Angela 148, 164
Miller, D. 46, 47, 93
Miller, M. 94–5
Mills and Boon 147–8
Minow-Pinkney, Makiko 262
mirrors 132–3, 134
Mitchell, W. J. T. 253, 280, 283, 284
modern
    definition 5–6; design 99; and
    postmodern 333; typology of the
    331
Modern Times 208
modernism 10, 66, 250–2, 267
    architecture 217–18; arts 270–6;
    Chanel 140; cinema 294; fashion
    141–2; official 270; and prostitution
    84
modernity 10–11, 243
    ambivalence and reflexivity 4–5, 9–10;
    and artists 10; and city 65, 66; as the
    contemporary 5–6; and
    Enlightenment 233; existential 68;
    as experience 9, 251, 331; gender
    stereotypes 78; and ill health 92;
    and modernism 270; and popular
    culture 331; and postmodern 337–8;
    as project 6–9, 331, 332, **343**; as
    representation 5, 11
Modleski, Tania 36, 149
money 83, 149–50
Moore, Suzanne 30, 336
moral occult 33, 35
morality 189, 228, 235
    in novels 166–7; and reason 186, 240,
    241; soap opera 36
Morgan, Susan 161, 168, 169, 170
Mort, F. 107, 126, 128
motivation 52, 149–50
Muir, Jean 125
Mulvey, Laura 37, 139
music 321
Mussolini, Benito 212

narcissism 96, 133, 134, 139
narrative 180, 295, 303, 304, 326, **342–3**
    everyday life 165–6, 169; and love
    153–4
nationalism 234

nature 8, 70
    and advertising 101; and art 192, 266;
    and consumerism 111; and fashion
    124; and reason 242; and religion
    183; and simulacra 303; and
    technology 216–17
Nava, Mica 108, 109, 110
Nazis 229–34, 238
Nead, Lynda 49, 79, 81
Neale, S. 294–5
neurosis 47, 78
New Look 117, 122
New Wave 294
New Woman 131–2, 137–8, 140, 259,
    261, 271
New York 66, 94, 218
news 312–13
Nietzsche, Friedrich 140, 141, 238, 271,
    346
    death of God 186, 187, 189
Nightwood (Barnes) 259–63, 275
Nineteen Eighty-Four (Orwell) 56
Nixon, Richard 31, 32
non-rationality 111
North and South (Gaskell) 80–1
Northanger Abbey (Austen) 168
novels 154–9, 257, 271
    and the decorative 274; and love 153–
    4; modernism 250, 255–63;
    narratives 165–70; and railways
    202–6; romance 147–52;
    theatricality 21, 272; *see also* reading;
    writing
novelty 66, 125, 126; *see also* creativity

Oliver Twist (Dickens) 47
Olsen, D. J. 75
originality 267–8, 320
Orlando (Woolf) 71, 138
ornament 272–4
Orr, J. 284, 287, 288, 297
Orwell, George 56, 217
otherness 4, 7, 9, 154, 157–8, 177, 180,
    238, 242, 259, 263, 270, 292
Outram, D. 42, 163
Owens, C. 267–8, 290, 293
'Oxford Street Tide' (Woolf) 70

painting 250–1, 272, 274

panopticism 55–7, 315, 318; *see also*
    Foucault
panopticon 58
paranoia 56, 57
Paris 66, 70, 75–9, 94, 288–9, 296
parody 125, 126
Partington, Angela 122–3, 139
Pascal, Blaise 183, 187–8, 210
passion 167, 244
passivity 108, 109, 141
past 85, 124–5, 261–2
patterns 3
Patton, P. 299, 300
Penley, Constance 215, 216
people, the 42, 45, 228, 329–30
personality 121, 244, 324
    and the city 68, 76, 77; and
    theatricality 29–30, 38, 330
personification 19
perspectivism 253
pessimism 85–6
phantasmagoria 284–9
philanthropy 49
photographs 281–3, 286, 302
    and allegory 289, 290–2;
    phantasmagoria 284–9
Picasso, P. 84, 253, 255
Pick, D. 221
place 208, 210
Plath, Sylvia 235
pleasure 100, 105, 106, 111, 266
Poe, Edgar Allan 76–7
Polhemus, R. 150, 151
police 46, 47
politics 31, 34, 61, 159, 218
politics of everyday life 42, 45
Pollock, Griselda 75, 77
popular culture 142, 283–4, 321–3, 326,
    329–31, 334–5; *see also* mass culture
positivism 271
post-totalitarianism 59–60
postmodern 305, 333, 334–8
postmodernism 333–5
postmodernity 334
power 45–7, 57–8, 60, 221, 244, 337
    disciplinary 47, 54, 55; and knowledge
    242, 260
Prague 61
present 222, 267

Pride and Prejudice (Austen) 148–9, 149–50, 151, 160, 167, 170
Pringle, Rosemary 109
prisons 55
privacy 181
production 108, 110–11
progress 91, 188–9, 190, 217, 228, 229, 311, 327
project 61, 78, **343**
　and the city 65, 67, 69, 75; and consciousness 316; as control 319; and desire 106; and Enlightenment 233, 239, 242, 245; and fashion 141; and machine 206; modernist arts 263; of modernity 6–9, 10, 11, 310–15; and popular culture 323; and production 110; space and time 208–9; and war 221–2
propriety 167
prostitution 81–4
Proust, Marcel 204, 205, 257, 261, 291, 316
psychoanalysis 53–4
public life 21–2, 30–1
public sphere 326–8
punk 126, 127
Puritanism 152
Pykett, Lyn 158, 161, 164, 271

Raban, J. 66, 67–8, 68, 73, 77
race 234
Radway, Janice 163, 164, 323
railways 202–6, 221
rationality 229, 310, 332, 335
　and advertising 98; of the city 67, 68; and consumerism 109–10; and Holocaust 230, 231; project-centred 244–5; *see also* reason
reading 109, 162–5, 203
reality 304, 321
　cinema 294, 296–7, 298; fiction 155–6, 163, 165; images 280, 287; photographs 282–3, 284; and reflexivity 314–15; and simulacra 300–3; and symbol 185; theatre 23, 26; *see also* hyperreality
reason 275–6, 322
　Enlightenment 229, 243, 327; Kant 240, 241–2, 333; *see also* rationality

recognition 82, 149
Red Room, The (Matisse) 252–5
reflexivity 5, 10, 310, 314, **343**
　and fiction 154, 257; *see also* self-awareness; self-knowledge
release 103, 105
religion 177–8, 183–6
repetition 85, 323
representation 5, 11, 336–7, **343**
　God 184; and Holocaust 234–5; images 280, 282–3, 288, 296; and modernism 250, 251, 253, 263–4; prostitution 82; romance 149; and the sublime 196–7; and theatricality 20, 21, 43
reproduction 48–9, 71, 337
resistance 108–9, 110, 111
Richards, T. 95, 101, 102, 103, 296
Richardson, Dorothy 158, 257
risk 83, 311, 312, 313, 318, 336
Rivière, Joan 138
Roberts, D. 192–3, 197
Robespierre 45, 58
robots 214–15
Rodin, Auguste 282
role-playing 20–1, 23, 25, 37
　courtesans 82; French Revolution 42; and selfhood 29–30; *see also* theatricality
romance 147–52, 157–8, 163, 164, 271, 323; *see also* novels
Romanticism 105, 193, 194, 234, 285
Ronell, Avital 211, 214
Room of One's Own, A (Woolf) 160, 161
Rose, Jacqueline 235
Rose, N. 46, 48, 49, 52–3
Rousseau, Jean-Jacques 42, 44, 153, 167, **346**
　Confessions 52–3; consumption 94, 108; theatre 26–7, 28
Ryan, Cornelius 181, 182

sacred 177–8, 190–2, 286
sacrifice 190
Sade, Marquis de 238–9, 241–2, **346**
Sass, L. A. 263, 285
Sayer, D. 187, 232
Schiaparelli, Elsa 139
Schivelbusch, W. 203, 205, 207, 310, 312

Schudson, M. 91, 92, 97
Schulte-Sasse, J. 268–9
science 183, 186–7, 270–1
Seagram Building 217, 220
secrecy 181, 231–2
self
  as abstract subject 209; and
    authenticity 32–3; and confession
    52–4; and expressivism 193;
    fragmentation 84, 264; interiority
    105, 137, 152–3; and melodrama 38;
    and role-playing 20–1; and
    theatricality 17–18, 27, 29, 37; *see
    also* reflexivity
self-awareness 10, 54, 57, 292, 332
self-discipline 46, 53, 60–1
self-empowerment 60–1
self-identity 27–8, 74, 105–6
self-image 133, 287, 304
  and consumerism 93, 96; and
    possessions 107
self-knowledge 27, 158, 167–8, 169, 189
self-sacrifice 190
Sennett, R. 54, 66, 75, 134, 329
  audience 19, 20; personality 30, 31,
    76, 121; theatricality 21, 22–3, 24,
    26–7
sexuality 48–9, 54
  and clothes 125; and homosexuality
    135; and prostitution 83; and
    shopping 96; and stilettos 118;
    transgression 177, 192
Shelley, Percy Bysshe 180, 268
Sherman, Cindy 139
Shields, R. 108–9, 330
shock 269–70, 315–18, 320; *see also*
    Benjamin
shopping 94–6, 107
Showalter, Elaine 140, 161
Silverman, Kaja 129, 134
Simpson, Mark 137, 140
simulacra 283, 298–305, 336
Skin Two 118
slaughterhouses 221
Smith, Adam 27, 28
Smith, S. 261, 265, 267, 333
Smith-Rosenberg, Carroll 137, 138, 160,
    259, 260
soap opera 36–7

Sontag, Susan 182, 320, **346**
  art and the sacred 177–8; disease 179–
    80, 181, 312; images 280, 286, 287–
    8, 291, 293–4
space 207–11, 254
spectacle 27, 29, 75, **344**
  cinema 294, 295–8; clothes 139;
    consumerism 93–5; media 101;
    melodrama 35–6; and punishment
    55
spectators, *see* audience
spleen 78, 290, 315, 317–18, 320; *see also*
    Baudelaire
Squier, Susan 73, 74
Stacey, Jackie 134, 294
Stallybrass, P. 67, 81
Star is Born, A 32
stardom 29, 30–3
status 120, 121, 123, 141
Stead, William 18
Steele, Valerie 118, 128, 129, 130–1
Steiner, G. 234, 235, 264, 265, 332
stilettos 117–18
stranger, strangers 21, 72–3
street culture 324–5
'Street Haunting' (Woolf) 69–70
stress 320
stroller 74, 83, 86, 281, 290, 321
style 98–9, 120, 125, 130
subculture 318–19
subject 49–51, 52, 109, 209, **342**
subjection 59–60
sublime 192–7, 216, 246, 333
subordination, *see* conformity
supernatural 183–4
Surrealism 261, 269, 275–6, 292
surveillance 54–7, 75, 281, 318; *see also*
    panopticism
Symbolists 273
symbols 43, 184–5, 197
sympathy 27–8

taboo 190–2, 318
Tanner, T. 150, 156, 158
taste 120–1, 122, 126, 266, 271
Taylor, C. 239, 240, 257, 266, 332
  companionate marriage 152;
    expressivism 105–6, 193;
    interiority 137; narrative 165

technology 202, 215, 216–17, 270–1
    architecture 218; and Holocaust 230,
        232; and simulation 298–9; visual
        281; *see also* machines
telephones 211–12, 213–14
television 36–7
theatricality 9, 15–19, 37–8, 328, 332,
        343
    baroque 275–6; the city 65, 67–8;
        consumerism 95; exclusion from
        modernism 271–2; fashion 141;
        fiction 158–9; French Revolution
        42; heroism of the modern 78;
        melodrama 33–7; and panopticism
        57; personality 29–30; and public
        life 19–23; and self-discipline 53;
        and spectacle 23–8; stardom 30–3;
        and Surrealism 275; Velvet
        Revolution 61
Third Man, The 288
Thornton, M. 119, 125, 126, 130, 134,
        139
time 207–11, 221, 258–9, 303–4, 323
timelessness 125, 127
Tolkien, J. R. R. 56
Tolstoy, N. 202–4, 206
Tootsie 135
totalitarianism 58–60
tourism 321–2
transcendence 177–8, 192
transgression 96, 177, 188–92, 318–19,
        342
transparency 43–4
transvestism 134–7, 135
Trilling, L. 29, 45, 158, 166
triviality 4, 141, 256
tuberculosis 179–80
Turner, B. 26, 60, 103, 118–19, 195, 196
    social health 48, 49

ugliness 68
Ulysses (Joyce) 258, 259, 262–3
uncanny 195, 238, 288
undress 140
Unheimlich 195, 238, 288
United States, religion 185
universality 335
unreality 23, 26, 337; *see also* reality
Urry, J. 321

Velvet Revolution 61
victims 235, 238
    of consumerism 109, 110; fashion 123,
        127
Victorians
    consumer culture 95–6; death 179,
        180; fashion 130–1; theatricality 17–
        18
violence 227–8
Virilio, P. 281, 296, 299
virtue 29, 42–5, 58, 241–2
virtuosi 30
visibility 54, 57
visual 280–1, 303
vogueing 134
Voltaire 94
voyeurism 139

Wakefield, N. 302, 304
Walkowitz, Judith 18, 77, 81–2
war 181, 221–2, 260
    language 232; and railways 206; and
        simulacra 299–300
Warnock, Mary 196
waste 101–2
Waste Land, The (Eliot) 260, 265
Watt, Ian 156, 160
Weber, Max 244–5, 312, 313, 314, **346**
    bureaucracy 230, 231; culture 188;
        religion 185; science and morality
        186, 187
Weeks, J. 54, 324
Weiskel, T. 192, 194–5
Westerns 31–2, 134
Westwood, Vivienne 119, 125–6, 139
White, A. 67, 81
Wild Champagne (Kingston) 147, 148, 150
Wilde, Oscar 15–17, 18, 38, 130, **346**
Williams, Raymond 19, 67, 74, 77, 251,
        330
Williams, Rosalind 100, 102, 129, 296
    civilizing process 93, 94; dream
        worlds 95, 106, 108; nature and
        technology 216–17, 310, 312
Williamson, Judith 86, 100, 139
Willis, P. 110, 330
Wilson, Elizabeth 68, 83, 86, 94, 130
    fashion 118, 122, 125; *flâneur* 78, 79;
        women and the city 69, 70, 77, 80

Wittgenstein, L. 180
Wohl, R. 212, 213
Wollen, P. 215, 274
women
  and advertising 99; and the body 104;
    and childbirth 50, 51; and cigarettes
    91, 92; and cinema 293, 294; and the
    city 69, 72, 74, 77; and clothes 118–
    19, 130–2, 135, 140, 141; and
    consumerism 96, 109, 111; and death
    180–1; gaze 134; gender stereotypes
    8; image 91, 139; and love 153–4;
    and machines 215–16; and mass
    culture 271; and melodrama 36–7;
    and mirrors 132–3; and punk 126;
    and romance 148, 157–8; social
    control 49; and stilettos 117, 118;
    and Surrealism 275; as writers and
    readers 159, 160–5; *see also*
    femininity
Woolf, Virginia 137, 138, 168, 261–2,
  264, 272, **346**

and the city 66, 69–75, 77, 79, 85;
  A Room of One's Own 160, 161;
  To the Lighthouse 257; *The Waves*
  255–9
Woolley, B. 298–9, 300
Wordsworth, William 67
world
  as consumer spectacle 93; in fiction
    155–6; and melodrama 38; as
    sacramental 184; as spectacle 35–6;
    as theatre 19, 24
world-weariness 78, 290, 315, 317–18,
  320
Wright, Frank Lloyd 219
Wright, Lee 117, 118
writing 160–2

Yeats, W. B. 213
Young-Bruehl, E. 236

Zola, Emile 96, 206, 280